D0984108

THE
EXPOSITOR'S
BIBLE
COMMENTARY

General Editor:

FRANK E. GAEBELEIN
Former Headmaster, Stony Brook School;
Former Coeditor, *Christianity Today*

Associate Editor:

J. D. DOUGLAS
Editor, *The New International
Dictionary of the Christian Church*

Consulting Editors, Old Testament:

WALTER C. KAISER, JR.
Professor of Semitic Languages
and Old Testament,
Trinity Evangelical Divinity School

BRUCE K. WALTKE
(Consulting Editor, 1972–1984)
Professor of Old Testament,
Regent College

RALPH H. ALEXANDER
(Consulting Editor, 1984—)
Professor of Hebrew Scripture
Western Seminary, Portland, Oregon

Consulting Editors, New Testament:

JAMES MONTGOMERY BOICE
Pastor, Tenth Presbyterian Church,
Philadelphia, Pennsylvania

MERRILL C. TENNEY
Professor of Bible and Theology, Emeritus,
Wheaton College

Manuscript Editor:
RICHARD P. POLCYN
Zondervan Publishing House

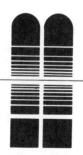

THE
EXPOSITOR'S BIBLE COMMENTARY

with
The New International Version
of
The Holy Bible

IN TWELVE VOLUMES

VOLUME 11

(EPHESIANS - PHILEMON)

Regency
Reference Library
Zondervan Publishing House
Grand Rapids, Michigan

THE EXPOSITOR'S BIBLE COMMENTARY, VOLUME 11
Copyright © 1978 by The Zondervan Corporation
Grand Rapids, Michigan

Requests for information should be addressed to:
Zondervan Publishing House
Academic and Professional Books
Grand Rapids, Michigan 49530

Library of Congress Cataloging in Publication Data (Revised)

Main entry under title:
The Expositor's Bible commentary

  Includes bibliographies.
  CONTENTS: v. 1. Articles.
v. 10. Romans—Galatians. — v. 11. Ephesians—Philemon.
  1. Bible—Commentaries. I. Gaebelein, Frank Ely,
1899-   II. Douglas, James Dixon. III. Bible
English. New international. 1978.
BS491.2E96   220.7   76-41334
ISBN 0-310-36530-9 (v. 11)

All rights reserved. No part of this publication may be reproduced, stored in a
retrieval system, or transmitted in any form or by any means—electronic,
mechanical, photocopy, recording, or any other—except for brief quotations in
printed reviews, without the prior permission of the publisher.

All scripture quotations, unless otherwise noted, are taken from the HOLY
BIBLE: NEW INTERNATIONAL VERSION (North American Edition).
Copyright © 1973, 1978, 1984, by The International Bible Society. Used by
permission of Zondervan Bible Publishers.

Printed in the United States of America

  92 93 94 95 / DH / 23 22 21

This edition is printed on acid-free paper and meets the American National
Standards Institute Z39.48 standard.

CONTENTS

Contributors to Volume 11.............................. vi

Preface vii

Abbreviations... ix

Transliterations.. xv

Ephesians 1

Philippians 93

Colossians 161

1 Thessalonians 227

2 Thessalonians 299

1 Timothy 339

2 Timothy 391

Titus 419

Philemon 451

CONTRIBUTORS TO VOLUME 11

Ephesians: A. Skevington Wood
B.A., University of London; Ph.D., University of Edinburgh
Principal, Cliff College, Derbyshire, England

Philippians: Homer A. Kent, Jr.
B.A., Bob Jones University; B.D., Th.M., Th.D., Grace Theological Seminary
President, Grace Theological Seminary

Colossians: Curtis Vaughan
A.B., Union University; B.D., Th.D., Southwestern Baptist Theological Seminary
Professor of New Testament, Southwestern Baptist Theological Seminary

1, 2 Thessalonians: Robert L. Thomas
B.M.E., Georgia Institute of Technology; Th.M., Th.D., Dallas Theological Seminary
Professor of New Testament Language and Literature, Talbot Theological Seminary

1, 2 Timothy: Ralph Earle
A.B., Eastern Nazarene College; M.A., Boston University; B.D., Th.D., Gordon Divinity School; D.D., Eastern Nazarene College
Distinguished Professor Emeritus of New Testament, Nazarene Theological Seminary, 1945-1977

Titus: D. Edmond Hiebert
A.B., John Fletcher College; Th.M., Th.D., Southern Baptist Theological Seminary
Professor Emeritus of New Testament, Mennonite Brethren Biblical Seminary

Philemon: Arthur A. Rupprecht
B.A., Houghton College; A.M., University of Illinois; B.D., Faith Theological Seminary; Ph.D., University of Pennsylvania
Professor of Classical Languages, Wheaton College

PREFACE

The title of this work defines its purpose. Written primarily by expositors for expositors, it aims to provide preachers, teachers, and students of the Bible with a new and comprehensive commentary on the books of the Old and New Testaments. Its stance is that of a scholarly evangelicalism committed to the divine inspiration, complete trustworthiness, and full authority of the Bible. Its seventy-eight contributors come from the United States, Canada, England, Scotland, Australia, New Zealand, and Switzerland, and from various religious groups, including Anglican, Baptist, Brethren, Free, Independent, Methodist, Nazarene, Presbyterian, and Reformed churches. Most of them teach at colleges, universities, or theological seminaries.

No book has been more closely studied over a longer period of time than the Bible. From the Midrashic commentaries going back to the period of Ezra, through parts of the Dead Sea Scrolls and the Patristic literature, and on to the present, the Scriptures have been expounded. Indeed, there have been times when, as in the Reformation and on occasions since then, exposition has been at the cutting edge of Christian advance. Luther was a powerful exegete, and Calvin is still called "the prince of expositors."

Their successors have been many. And now, when the outburst of new translations and their unparalleled circulation have expanded the readership of the Bible, the need for exposition takes on fresh urgency.

Not that God's Word can ever become captive to its expositors. Among all other books, it stands first in its combination of perspicuity and profundity. Though a child can be made "wise for salvation" by believing its witness to Christ, the greatest mind cannot plumb the depths of its truth (2 Tim. 3:15; Rom. 11:33). As Gregory the Great said, "Holy Scripture is a stream of running water, where alike the elephant may swim, and the lamb walk." So, because of the inexhaustible nature of Scripture, the task of opening up its meaning is still a perennial obligation of biblical scholarship.

How that task is done inevitably reflects the outlook of those engaged in it. Every biblical scholar has presuppositions. To this neither the editors of these volumes nor the contributors to them are exceptions. They share a common commitment to the supernatural Christianity set forth in the inspired Word. Their purpose is not to supplant the many valuable commentaries that have preceded this work and from which both the editors and contributors have learned. It is rather to draw on the resources of contemporary evangelical scholarship in producing a new reference work for understanding the Scriptures.

A commentary that will continue to be useful through the years should handle contemporary trends in biblical studies in such a way as to avoid becoming outdated when critical fashions change. Biblical criticism is not in itself inadmissible, as some have mistakenly thought. When scholars investigate the authorship, date, literary characteristics, and purpose of a biblical document, they are practicing biblical criticism. So also when, in order to ascertain as nearly as possible the original form of the text, they deal with variant readings, scribal errors, emendations, and other phenomena in the manuscripts. To do these things is essential to responsible exegesis and exposition. And always there is the need to distinguish hypothesis from fact, conjecture from truth.

The chief principle of interpretation followed in this commentary is the grammatico-historical one—namely, that the primary aim of the exegete is to make clear the meaning of the text at the time and in the circumstances of its writing. This endeavor to understand what in the first instance the inspired writers actually said must not be confused with an inflexible literalism. Scripture makes lavish use of symbols and figures of speech; great portions of it are poetical. Yet when it speaks in this way, it speaks no less truly than it does in its historical and doctrinal portions. To understand its message requires attention to matters of grammar and syntax, word meanings, idioms, and literary forms—all in relation to the historical and cultural setting of the text.

The contributors to this work necessarily reflect varying convictions. In certain controversial matters the policy is that of clear statement of the contributors' own views followed by fair presentation of other ones. The treatment of eschatology, though it reflects differences of interpretation, is consistent with a general premillennial position. (Not all contributors, however, are premillennial.) But prophecy is more than prediction, and so this commentary gives due recognition to the major lode of godly social concern in the prophetic writings.

THE EXPOSITOR'S BIBLE COMMENTARY is presented as a scholarly work, though not primarily one of technical criticism. In its main portion, the Exposition, and in Volume 1 (General and Special Articles), all Semitic and Greek words are transliterated and the English equivalents given. As for the Notes, here Semitic and Greek characters are used but always with transliterations and English meanings, so that this portion of the commentary will be as accessible as possible to readers unacquainted with the original languages.

It is the conviction of the general editor, shared by his colleagues in the Zondervan editorial department, that in writing about the Bible, lucidity is not incompatible with scholarship. They are therefore endeavoring to make this a clear and understandable work.

The translation used in it is the New International Version (North American Edition). To the International Bible Society thanks are due for permission to use this most recent of the major Bible translations. The editors and publisher have chosen it because of the clarity and beauty of its style and its faithfulness to the original texts.

To the associate editor, Dr. J. D. Douglas, and to the contributing editors—Dr. Walter C. Kaiser, Jr. and Dr. Bruce K. Waltke for the Old Testament, and Dr. James Montgomery Boice and Dr. Merrill C. Tenney for the New Testament—the general editor expresses his gratitude for their unfailing cooperation and their generosity in advising him out of their expert scholarship. And to the many other contributors he is indebted for their invaluable part in this work. Finally, he owes a special debt of gratitude to Dr. Robert K. DeVries, executive vice-president of the Zondervan Publishing House; Rev. Gerard Terpstra, manuscript editor; and Miss Elizabeth Brown, secretary to Dr. DeVries, for their continual assistance and encouragement.

Whatever else it is—the greatest and most beautiful of books, the primary source of law and morality, the fountain of wisdom, and the infallible guide to life—the Bible is above all the inspired witness to Jesus Christ. May this work fulfill its function of expounding the Scriptures with grace and clarity, so that its users may find that both Old and New Testaments do indeed lead to our Lord Jesus Christ, who alone could say, "I have come that they may have life, and have it to the full" (John 10:10).

FRANK E. GAEBELEIN

ABBREVIATIONS

A. General Abbreviations

A	Codex Alexandrinus	MT	Masoretic text
Akkad.	Akkadian	n.	note
ℵ	Codex Sinaiticus	n.d.	no date
Ap. Lit.	Apocalyptic Literature	Nestle	Nestle (ed.) *Novum*
Apoc.	Apocrypha		*Testamentum Graece*
Aq.	Aquila's Greek Translation	no.	number
	of the Old Testament	NT	New Testament
Arab.	Arabic	obs.	obsolete
Aram.	Aramaic	OL	Old Latin
b	Babylonian Gemara	OS	Old Syriac
B	Codex Vaticanus	OT	Old Testament
C	Codex Ephraemi Syri	p., pp.	page, pages
c.	*circa,* about	par.	paragraph
cf.	*confer,* compare	‖	parallel passage(s)
ch., chs.	chapter, chapters	Pers.	Persian
cod., codd.	codex, codices	Pesh.	Peshitta
contra	in contrast to	Phoen.	Phoenician
D	Codex Bezae	pl.	plural
DSS	Dead Sea Scrolls (see E.)	Pseudep.	Pseudepigrapha
ed., edd.	edited, edition, editor; editions	Q	Quelle ("Sayings" source
e.g.	*exempli gratia,* for example		in the Gospels)
Egyp.	Egyptian	qt.	quoted by
et al.	*et alii,* and others	q.v.	*quod vide,* which see
EV	English Versions of the Bible	R	Rabbah
fem.	feminine	rev.	revised, reviser, revision
ff.	following (verses, pages, etc.)	Rom.	Roman
fl.	flourished	RVm	Revised Version margin
ft.	foot, feet	Samar.	Samaritan recension
gen.	genitive	SCM	Student Christian Movement Press
Gr.	Greek	Sem.	Semitic
Heb.	Hebrew	sing.	singular
Hitt.	Hittite	SPCK	Society for the Promotion
ibid.	*ibidem,* in the same place		of Christian Knowledge
id.	*idem,* the same	Sumer.	Sumerian
i.e.	*id est,* that is	s.v.	*sub verbo,* under the word
impf.	imperfect	Syr.	Syriac
infra.	below	Symm.	Symmachus
in loc.	*in loco,* in the place cited	T	Talmud
j	Jerusalem or	Targ.	Targum
	Palestinian Gemara	Theod.	Theodotion
Lat.	Latin	TR	Textus Receptus
LL.	Late Latin	tr.	translation, translator,
LXX	Septuagint		translated
M	Mishnah	UBS	The United Bible Societies'
masc.	masculine		Greek Text
mg.	margin	Ugar.	Ugaritic
Mid	Midrash	u.s.	*ut supra,* as above
MS(S)	Manuscript(s)	viz.	*videlicet,* namely

vol.	volume	Vul.	Vulgate
v., vv.	verse, verses	WH	Westcott and Hort, *The*
vs.	versus		*New Testament in Greek*

B. Abbreviations for Modern Translations and Paraphrases

AmT	Smith and Goodspeed, *The Complete Bible, An American Translation*	LB	The Living Bible
		Mof	J. Moffatt, *A New Translation of the Bible*
ASV	American Standard Version, American Revised Version (1901)	NAB	The New American Bible
		NASB	New American Standard Bible
		NEB	The New English Bible
Beck	Beck, *The New Testament in the Language of Today*	NIV	The New International Version
		Ph	J. B. Phillips *The New Testament in Modern English*
BV	Berkeley Version (The Modern Language Bible)		
		RSV	Revised Standard Version
JB	The Jerusalem Bible	RV	Revised Version — 1881–1885
JPS	*Jewish Publication Society Version of the Old Testament*	TCNT	Twentieth Century New Testament
KJV	King James Version	TEV	Today's English Version
Knox	R.G. Knox, *The Holy Bible: A Translation from the Latin Vulgate in the Light of the Hebrew and Greek Original*	Wey	*Weymouth's New Testament in Modern Speech*
		Wms	C. B. Williams, *The New Testament: A Translation in the Language of the People*

C. Abbreviations for Periodicals and Reference Works

AASOR	*Annual of the American Schools of Oriental Research*	BAG	Bauer, Arndt, and Gingrich: *Greek-English Lexicon of the New Testament*
AB	*Anchor Bible*		
AIs	de Vaux: *Ancient Israel*	BC	Foakes-Jackson and Lake: *The Beginnings of Christianity*
AJA	*American Journal of Archaeology*		
AJSL	*American Journal of Semitic Languages and Literatures*	BDB	Brown, Driver, and Briggs: *Hebrew-English Lexicon of the Old Testament*
AJT	*American Journal of Theology*	BDF	Blass, Debrunner, and Funk: *A Greek Grammar of the New Testament and Other Early Christian Literature*
Alf	Alford: *Greek Testament Commentary*		
ANEA	*Ancient Near Eastern Archaeology*	BDT	Harrison: *Baker's Dictionary of Theology*
ANET	Pritchard: *Ancient Near Eastern Texts*	Beng.	Bengel's *Gnomon*
		BETS	*Bulletin of the Evangelical Theological Society*
ANF	Roberts and Donaldson: *The Ante-Nicene Fathers*	BJRL	*Bulletin of the John Rylands Library*
ANT	M. R. James: *The Apocryphal New Testament*	BS	*Bibliotheca Sacra*
A-S	Abbot-Smith: *Manual Greek Lexicon of the New Testament*	BT	*Babylonian Talmud*
		BTh	*Biblical Theology*
AThR	*Anglican Theological Review*	BW	*Biblical World*
BA	*Biblical Archaeologist*	CAH	*Cambridge Ancient History*
BASOR	*Bulletin of the American Schools of Oriental Research*	CanJTh	*Canadian Journal of Theology*
		CBQ	*Catholic Biblical Quarterly*

CBSC	Cambridge Bible for Schools and Colleges	HUCA	Hebrew Union College Annual
CE	Catholic Encyclopedia	IB	The Interpreter's Bible
CGT	Cambridge Greek Testament	ICC	International Critical Commentary
CHS	Lange: Commentary on the Holy Scriptures	IDB	The Interpreter's Dictionary of the Bible
ChT	Christianity Today	IEJ	Israel Exploration Journal
Crem	Cremer: Biblico-Theological Lexicon of the New Testament Greek	Int	Interpretation
		INT	E. Harrison: Introduction to the New Testament
DDB	Davis' Dictionary of the Bible	IOT	R. K. Harrison: Introduction to the Old Testament
Deiss BS	Deissmann: Bible Studies	ISBE	The International Standard Bible Encyclopedia
Deiss LAE	Deissmann: Light From the Ancient East	ITQ	Irish Theological Quarterly
DNTT	Dictionary of New Testament Theology	JAAR	Journal of American Academy of Religion
EBC	The Expositor's Bible Commentary	JAOS	Journal of American Oriental Society
EBi	Encyclopaedia Biblica	JBL	Journal of Biblical Literature
EBr	Encyclopaedia Britannica	JE	Jewish Encyclopedia
EDB	Encyclopedic Dictionary of the Bible	JETS	Journal of Evangelical Theological Society
EGT	Nicoll: Expositor's Greek Testament	JFB	Jamieson, Fausset, and Brown: Commentary on the Old and New Testament
EQ	Evangelical Quarterly		
ET	Evangelische Theologie		
ExB	The Expositor's Bible	JNES	Journal of Near Eastern Studies
Exp	The Expositor		
ExpT	The Expository Times	Jos. Antiq.	Josephus: The Antiquities of the Jews
FLAP	Finegan: Light From the Ancient Past		
		Jos. War	Josephus: The Jewish War
GR	Gordon Review	JQR	Jewish Quarterly Review
HBD	Harper's Bible Dictionary	JR	Journal of Religion
HDAC	Hastings: Dictionary of the Apostolic Church	JSJ	Journal for the Study of Judaism in the Persian, Hellenistic and Roman Periods
HDB	Hastings: Dictionary of the Bible		
		JSOR	Journal of the Society of Oriental Research
HDBrev.	Hastings: Dictionary of the Bible, one-vol. rev. by Grant and Rowley		
		JSS	Journal of Semitic Studies
HDCG	Hastings: Dictionary of Christ and the Gospels	JT	Jerusalem Talmud
		JTS	Journal of Theological Studies
HERE	Hastings: Encyclopedia of Religion and Ethics	KAHL	Kenyon: Archaeology in the Holy Land
HGEOTP	Heidel: The Gilgamesh Epic and Old Testament Parallels	KB	Koehler-Baumgartner: Lexicon in Veteris Testament Libros
HJP	Schurer: A History of the Jewish People in the Time of Christ	KD	Keil and Delitzsch: Commentary on the Old Testament
		LSJ	Liddell, Scott, Jones: Greek-English Lexicon
HR	Hatch and Redpath: Concordance to the Septuagint	LTJM	Edersheim: The Life and Times of Jesus the Messiah
HTR	Harvard Theological Review		

MM	Moulton and Milligan: *The Vocabulary of the Greek Testament*		*Testament aus Talmud und Midrash*
MNT	Moffatt: *New Testament Commentary*	SHERK	*The New Schaff-Herzog Encyclopedia of Religious Knowledge*
MST	McClintock and Strong: *Cyclopedia of Biblical, Theological, and Ecclesiastical Literature*	SJT	*Scottish Journal of Theology*
NBC	Davidson, Kevan, and Stibbs: *The New Bible Commentary*, 1st ed.	SOT	Girdlestone: *Synonyms of Old Testament*
		SOTI	Archer: *A Survey of Old Testament Introduction*
NBCrev.	Guthrie and Motyer: *The New Bible Commentary*, rev. ed.	ST	*Studia Theologica*
		TCERK	Loetscher: *The Twentieth Century Encyclopedia of Religious Knowledge*
NBD	J. D. Douglas: *The New Bible Dictionary*	TDNT	Kittel: *Theological Dictionary of the New Testament*
NCB	*New Century Bible*		
NCE	*New Catholic Encyclopedia*	TDOT	*Theological Dictionary of the Old Testament*
NIC	*New International Commentary*	Theol	*Theology*
NIDCC	Douglas: *The New International Dictionary of the Christian Church*	ThT	*Theology Today*
		TNTC	*Tyndale New Testament Commentaries*
NovTest	*Novum Testamentum*	Trench	Trench: *Synonyms of the New Testament*
NSI	Cooke: *Handbook of North Semitic Inscriptions*		
NTS	*New Testament Studies*	UBD	*Unger's Bible Dictionary*
ODCC	*The Oxford Dictionary of the Christian Church*, rev. ed.	UT	Gordon: *Ugaritic Textbook*
		VB	Allmen: *Vocabulary of the Bible*
Peake	Black and Rowley: *Peake's Commentary on the Bible*	VetTest	*Vetus Testamentum*
PEQ	*Palestine Exploration Quarterly*	Vincent	Vincent: *Word-Pictures in the New Testament*
PNFl	P. Schaff: *The Nicene and Post-Nicene Fathers* (1st series)	WBC	*Wycliffe Bible Commentary*
		WBE	*Wycliffe Bible Encyclopedia*
		WC	*Westminster Commentaries*
PNF2	P. Schaff and H. Wace: *The Nicene and Post-Nicene Fathers* (2nd series)	WesBC	*Wesleyan Bible Commentaries*
		WTJ	*Westminster Theological Journal*
PTR	*Princeton Theological Review*	ZAW	*Zeitschrift für die alttestamentliche Wissenschaft*
RB	*Revue Biblique*		
RHG	Robertson's *Grammar of the Greek New Testament in the Light of Historical Research*	ZNW	*Zeitschrift für die neutestamentliche Wissenschaft*
		ZPBD	*The Zondervan Pictorial Bible Dictionary*
RTWB	Richardson: *A Theological Wordbook of the Bible*	ZPEB	*The Zondervan Pictorial Encyclopedia of the Bible*
SBK	Strack and Billerbeck: *Kommentar zum Neuen*	ZWT	*Zeitschrift für wissenschaftliche Theologie*

D. Abbreviations for Books of the Bible, the Apocrypha, and the Pseudepigrapha

OLD TESTAMENT

Gen	2 Chron	Dan
Exod	Ezra	Hos
Lev	Neh	Joel
Num	Esth	Amos
Deut	Job	Obad
Josh	Ps(Pss)	Jonah
Judg	Prov	Mic
Ruth	Eccl	Nah
1 Sam	S of Songs	Hab
2 Sam	Isa	Zeph
1 Kings	Jer	Hag
2 Kings	Lam	Zech
1 Chron	Ezek	Mal

NEW TESTAMENT

Matt	1 Tim
Mark	2 Tim
Luke	Titus
John	Philem
Acts	Heb
Rom	James
1 Cor	1 Peter
2 Cor	2 Peter
Gal	1 John
Eph	2 John
Phil	3 John
Col	Jude
1 Thess	Rev
2 Thess	

APOCRYPHA

1 Esd	1 Esdras
2 Esd	2 Esdras
Tobit	Tobit
Jud	Judith
Add Esth	Additions to Esther
Wisd Sol	Wisdom of Solomon
Ecclus	Ecclesiasticus (Wisdom of Jesus the Son of Sirach)
Baruch	Baruch
Ep Jer	Epistle of Jeremy
S Th Ch	Song of the Three Children (or Young Men)
Sus	Susanna
Bel	Bel and the Dragon
Pr Man	Prayer of Manasseh
1 Macc	1 Maccabees
2 Macc	2 Maccabees

PSEUDEPIGRAPHA

As Moses	Assumption of Moses
2 Baruch	Syriac Apocalypse of Baruch
3 Baruch	Greek Apocalypse of Baruch
1 Enoch	Ethiopic Book of Enoch
2 Enoch	Slavonic Book of Enoch
3 Enoch	Hebrew Book of Enoch
4 Ezra	4 Ezra
JA	Joseph and Asenath
Jub	Book of Jubilees
L Aristeas	Letter of Aristeas
Life AE	Life of Adam and Eve
Liv Proph	Lives of the Prophets
MA Isa	Martyrdom and Ascension of Isaiah
3 Macc	3 Maccabees
4 Macc	4 Maccabees
Odes Sol	Odes of Solomon
P Jer	Paralipomena of Jeremiah
Pirke Aboth	Pirke Aboth
Ps 151	Psalm 151
Pss Sol	Psalms of Solomon
Sib Oracles	Sibylline Oracles
Story Ah	Story of Ahikar
T Abram	Testament of Abraham
T Adam	Testament of Adam
T Benjamin	Testament of Benjamin
T Dan	Testament of Dan
T Gad	Testament of Gad
T Job	Testament of Job
T Jos	Testament of Joseph
T Levi	Testament of Levi
T Naph	Testament of Naphtali
T 12 Pat	Testaments of the Twelve Patriarchs
Zad Frag	Zadokite Fragments

E. Abbreviations of Names of Dead Sea Scrolls and Related Texts

CD	Cairo (Genizah text of the) Damascus (Document)	1QSa	Appendix A (Rule of the Congregation) to 1QS
DSS	Dead Sea Scrolls	1QSb	Appendix B (Blessings) to 1QS
Hev	Nahal Hever texts	3Q15	Copper Scroll from Qumran Cave 3
Mas	Masada Texts		
Mird	Khirbet mird texts	4QFlor	Florilegium (or Eschatological Midrashim) from Qumran Cave 4
Mur	Wadi Murabba'at texts		
P	Pesher (commentary)		
Q	Qumran	4Qmess ar	Aramaic "Messianic" text from Qumran Cave 4
1Q,2Q,etc.	Numbered caves of Qumran, yielding written material; followed by abbreviation of biblical or apocryphal book.	4QPrNab	Prayer of Nabonidus from Qumran Cave 4
		4QTest	Testimonia text from Qumran Cave 4
QL	Qumran Literature		
1QapGen	Genesis Apocryphon of Qumran Cave 1	4QTLevi	Testament of Levi from Qumran Cave 4
1QH	*Hodayot* (Thanksgiving Hymns) from Qumran Cave 1	4QPhyl	Phylacteries from Qumran Cave 4
1QIsa[a, b]	First or second copy of Isaiah from Qumran Cave 1	11QMelch	Melchizedek text from Qumran Cave 11
1QpHab	Pesher on Habakkuk from Qumran Cave 1	11QtgJob	Targum of Job from Qumran Cave 11
1QM	*Milhamah* (War Scroll)		
1QS	*Serek Hayyahad* (Rule of the Community, Manual of Discipline)		

TRANSLITERATIONS

Hebrew

א = '	ד = $\underline{d}$	י = y	ס = s	ר = r
ב = b	ה = h	כ = k	ע = $‘$	שׁ = $ś$
ב = $\underline{b}$	ו = w	כ = $\underline{k}$	פ = p	שׁ = $š$
ג = g	ז = z	ל = l	פ = $\underline{p}$	ת = t
ג = $\underline{g}$	ח = $ḥ$	מ = m	צ = $ṣ$	ת = $\underline{t}$
ד = d	ט = $ṭ$	נ = n	ק = q	

(ה)ָ = $\hat{a}$ (h)	ָ = $\bar{a}$	ַ = a	ֳ = ^{a}
ֵי = $\hat{e}$		ֲ = e	ֱ = ^{e}
ִי = $\hat{i}$	ֵ = $\bar{e}$	ִ = i	ְ = ^{e} (if vocal)
וֹ = $\hat{o}$	ֹ = $\bar{o}$	ָ = o	ֳ = ^{o}
וּ = $\hat{u}$		ֻ = u	

Aramaic

ʾ b g d h w z $ḥ$ $ṭ$ y k l m n s $‘$ p $ṣ$ q r $ś$ $š$ t

Arabic

ʾ b t $\underline{t}$ $ǧ$ $ḥ$ $ḫ$ d $\underline{d}$ r z s $š$ $ṣ$ $ḍ$ $ṭ$ $ẓ$ $‘$ $ġ$ f q k l m n h w y

Ugaritic

ʾ b g d $\underline{d}$ h w z $ḥ$ $ḫ$ $ṭ$ $ẓ$ y k l m n s $ś$ $‘$ $ġ$ $ṗ$ $ṣ$ q r $š$ t $ṱ$

Greek

α	—	a	π	—	p	αι	—	ai
β	—	b	ρ	—	r	αὐ	—	au
γ	—	g	σ,ς	—	s	ει	—	ei
δ	—	d	τ	—	t	εὐ	—	eu
ε	—	e	υ	—	y	ηὐ	—	ēu
ζ	—	z	φ	—	ph	οι	—	oi
η	—	ē	χ	—	ch	οὐ	—	ou
θ	—	th	ψ	—	ps	υι	—	hui
ι	—	i	ω	—	ō			
κ	—	k				ῥ	—	rh
λ	—	l	γγ	—	ng	‘	—	h
μ	—	m	γκ	—	nk			
ν	—	n	γξ	—	nx	ᾳ	—	ā
ξ	—	x	γχ	—	nch	ῃ	—	ē
ο	—	o				ῳ	—	ō

EPHESIANS

A. Skevington Wood

EPHESIANS

Introduction

1. Authorship
2. Destination
3. Background
4. Place of Origin
5. Date
6. Occasion
7. Purpose
8. Literary Form
9. Theological Values
10. Canonicity
11. Text
12. Bibliography
13. Outline

1. Authorship

The letter to the Ephesians was generally regarded as the work of the apostle Paul until the rise of rationalistic criticism at the turn of the eighteenth century. Unable to reconcile the title with the contents, Evanson pronounced it a forgery in 1792.[1] Schleiermacher suggested that Ephesians may have been commissioned by Paul but composed by Tychicus.[2] In 1826 de Wette came to the conclusion that the Epistle is a verbose expansion of Colossians and not to be attributed even indirectly to Paul.[3] Such denials of Pauline authorship have persisted to the present day among a considerable body of scholars. We must therefore begin by setting out the positive grounds on which the traditional view is based.

a. The Case for Pauline Authorship

1) *Internal evidence.* Ephesians clearly claims to have been written by Paul. In the introduction the writer identifies himself and then proceeds in typically Pauline fashion to ascribe his apostolic authority to the will of God (Eph 1:1; cf. 2 Cor 1:1; Gal 1:1; Col 1:1). Paul's actual name reappears later (3:1) as in his undisputed letters (2 Cor 10:1; Gal 5:2; Col 1:23; 1 Thess 2:18). The writer often uses the first person singular and the

---

[1] Edward Evanson, *A New Testament: or the New Covenant According to Luke, Paul, and John*, ed. T. Brown (London: Richard Phillips, 1807); cf. Joachim Gnilka, *Der Epheserbrief* (Freiburg: Herder, 1971), p. 13.

[2] Friedrich D. E. Schleiermacher, *Einleitung in das Neue Testament*, in *Sämmtliche Werke*, ed. G. Wolde (Berlin: G. Reimer, 1845), 1:165, 166.

[3] W.M.L. de Wette, *Einleitung in das Neue Testament* (Leipzig: Messner und Lünemann, 1826).

self-portrait that emerges from these passages corresponds with what we know about Paul from other sources. There is nothing in the letter itself that is demonstrably incompatible with Pauline authorship, though some have argued to the contrary.

2) *External attestation.* As Kümmel recognizes, "without question Ephesians was extraordinarily well attested in the early Church."[4] By the middle of the second century it was widely circulated. It was listed in the earliest canon of the NT—that of the heresiarch Marcion (c. A.D. 140)—though under the title of "Laodiceans." Marcion approved only what he considered to be the genuine writings of Paul. Ephesians was included in the Muratorian Canon (c. A.D. 180) among the Pauline Epistles. The earliest evidence for Latin and Syriac versions includes it in the same category. According to Hippolytus, Ephesians was known to some of the Gnostic sects. There are also distinct echoes of Ephesians in Clement of Rome, Hermas, Barnabas, Ignatius, and Polycarp and more obvious references in Tertullian, Clement of Alexandria, and Origen.

Ephesians, then, was unhesitatingly assigned to Paul from the time when the NT corpus began to be recognized as such in the mid-second century. Since Clement of Rome reflected its language when he wrote to Corinth in A.D. 95, it is likely that this attestation runs back to the first century.

3) *Literary affinities.* The structure of Ephesians is in line with the rest of Paul's correspondence. We can trace the same sequence of salutation, thanksgiving, doctrinal exposition, moral appeal, final courtesies, and benediction. This outline, of course, represents the usual practice in letter writing in Paul's day, but a comparison with the non-Pauline documents underlines his distinctive approach, particularly in his treatment of ethics as an extension of theology.

The language of Ephesians, while suited to its theme and drawing on resources of vocabulary not represented in other Epistles, is nevertheless sufficiently similar to that of the other Epistles to substantiate the traditional view of its authorship. Many words not found elsewhere in the NT occur both in Ephesians and in the rest of Paul's letters. As has been pointed out by several scholars, the vocabulary approximates more closely to that of the earlier Pauline correspondence than does that of Colossians, the authenticity of which is scarcely questioned.

The literary parallels between Ephesians and Colossians, which have led some to wonder whether Paul could have been responsible for the former as well as the latter, may even more convincingly corroborate the common authorship of both Epistles.

4) *Theological consistency.* A strong argument for the accepted authorship of Ephesians is that its doctrinal stance is so characteristically Pauline. Indeed, Dodd regarded the Epistle as representing the crown of Paulinism![5] While it is true that fresh emphases appear (particularly in the doctrine of the church), the reader gains the overall impression of continuity with Pauline thought. The familiar themes recur: God's gracious sovereignty (1:3, 9, 11, 12; 2:4–7); the centrality of Christ's work of reconciliation on the cross (1:7; 2:13–18); the resurrection and exaltation of Christ (1:20–22); and the distinctive ministry of the Holy Spirit (2:18, 22; 3:5, 16; 4:1–4, 30; 5:18; 6:18).

---

[4]W.G. Kümmel, *Introduction to the New Testament* Eng. T. (London: S.C.M., 1966), p. 251.

[5]C.H. Dodd, "Colossians and Philemon," in *The Abingdon Bible Commentary*, ed. F.C. Eiselen, E. Lewis, and D.G. Downey (New York: Abingdon, n.d.), pp. 1224, 1225.

There is, however, a significant difference in the treatment of these themes; but it is a difference by no means inconsistent with Pauline authorship. In the earlier Epistles they are dealt with in the context of the problems that have arisen in the life of the churches the apostle is writing to in the midst of his travels. In Ephesians, he displays a measure of detachment and seeks to relate the great evangelical doctrines he has previously handled to the concept of the church as the body of Christ through which the purpose of God is fulfilled.

It is on such an impressive basis that the case for authenticity rests. When unanimous external attestation is supported by sufficiently convincing internal evidence, we are surely justified in insisting that the burden of proof lies with those who wish to repudiate the Pauline authorship of Ephesians. Even Mitton, who rejects the traditional view, begins by conceding that "Pauline authorship can rightly be assumed until it is disproved."[6] It is essential that the foregoing positive testimony should be kept in mind as we go on to review the thesis of those who deny that Paul wrote Ephesians.

b. The Arguments Against Pauline Authorship

Evanson, Schleiermacher, and de Wette were soon followed by Baur[7] and later by Holtzmann[8] in setting aside the hitherto unchallenged acceptance of Paul's responsibility for the Epistle. Today variations of this theme are explored under the influence especially of Mitton and Goodspeed.[9] The argument has to be developed exclusively in terms of internal evidence, because the external attestation is unassailable.

1) *Vocabulary and style.* Almost a hundred words and phrases in Ephesians are not found elsewhere in Paul. They do, however, recur in other NT writings and in those of the apostolic fathers. Instances cited are "in the heavenly realms" (1:3, 20; 2:6; 3:10; 6:12), "the One he loves" (1:6), and "flesh and blood" (6:12). Certain prepositions (like ἐν [in] and κατά [according to]) crop up more frequently than is usual in Paul's writings. Synonyms and genitival constructions are more common even than in Colossians (1:19; 2:2; 6:18). Goodspeed contended that most of these features can be paralleled in Luke–Acts, 1 Peter, and Hebrews (dated by him as late first century), as well as in 1 Clement (A.D. 95).

The style of Ephesians is thought to be much more complex and cumbersome than Paul's usual lively presentation. There are several long, involved, and virtually unclassifiable sentences, as in 1:15–23 and 4:11–16. Kuhn recognizes more reminiscences of the Qumran scrolls in Ephesians than in the rest of the Pauline collection.[10]

2) *Dependence.* The alleged dependence of Ephesians on the other Pauline letters, and on Colossians in particular, is taken as an indication that the writer was not Paul himself but one who freely appropriated his material.

---

[6]C.L. Mitton, *The Epistle to the Ephesians* (Oxford: Clarendon Press, 1951), p. 7.

[7]F.C. Baur, *Paul the Apostle of Jesus Christ,* Eng. T. (London: Williams and Norgate), 1873–5, 2 vols.

[8]H.J. Holtzmann, *Kritik der Epheser- und Kolosserbriefe* (Leipsig: W. Engelmann, 1872), pp. 46–55; cf. *Lehrbuch der historisch-kritischen Einleitung in das Neue Testament* (Freiburg: J.C.B. Mohr, 1885).

[9]Edgar J. Goodspeed, *The Meaning of Ephesians* (Chicago: University Press, 1933); *The Key to Ephesians* (Chicago: University Press, 1956).

[10]K.G. Kuhn, "Der Epheserbrief im Lichte der Qumrantexte," in *New Testament Studies* (1960–1961), 7:334–346.

a) *Colossians.* Moffatt regarded Ephesians as a catholicized version of Colossians.[11] The overlapping is considerably greater than that between any other two Pauline writings. Approximately one-third of the words in Colossians are repeated in Ephesians; Goguel claimed that seventy-three verses in Ephesians contain similarities with Colossians.[12] These parallels are spread fairly evenly throughout Ephesians. Only a few brief paragraphs lack them (2:6–19; 4:5–13; 5:29–33). Some scholars therefore ask the question whether Paul would have thus borrowed from himself. Is it not more probable that another hand was at work?

The situation is complicated still further in that words and phrases are not only reproduced from Colossians but also seem to bear a different meaning on occasion. Assuming that Ephesians was composed shortly after Colossians, is it probable that Paul would have so quickly revised the application of such pivotal terms as οἰκονομία (*oiko-nomia*) (Col 1:25; Eph 1:10; 3:2, 8, 9), μυστήριον (*mystērion*) (Col 1:25–27; 2:2; Eph 3:4–6), and πλήρωμα (*plērōma*) (Col 1:19; 2:9; Eph 3:19; 4:13)?

b) *Other Pauline letters.* No other letter attributed to Paul displays so many resemblances with the rest of the Pauline correspondence as Ephesians. Goodspeed went so far as to claim that out of 618 short phrases into which Ephesians may be divided, no fewer than 550 could be matched in the undisputed Epistles.[13] Yet what might more obviously be accepted as evidence of authenticity is regarded with suspicion by those who reject Pauline authorship on the ground that a genius like Paul would not have needed to depend so fully on what he had previously written. Resemblances between Ephesians and other NT writings are also thought to indicate a late date for the Epistle and therefore to exclude the possibility that Paul was its author.

3) *Personal references.* The allusions to Paul in Ephesians are held to be artificial. In 3:2 the apostle appears to be uncertain as to whether his readers are informed about the particular ministry he has been called to exercise. In 3:4 Paul is said to be unduly boastful about his insight into the mystery of Christ and the reference to "holy apostles" in the following verse is regarded as somewhat pretentious since he himself was one. And how can that be reconciled with his confession in v.8 that he is less than the least of all God's people? The absence of personal salutations at the close of the Epistle is taken to be un-Pauline.

4) *Theological discrepancies.* It is argued that the doctrinal differences between Ephesians and the known Pauline writings are so wide as to render common authorship unlikely. The theology of Ephesians is thought to be much more advanced than that of the apostle and even at times to contradict it.

Developments beyond Paul are held to include the concept of the church as universal, an emphasis on apostolic authority, and a refined Christology that sees our Lord as the agent of cosmic reconciliation. Items that might seem to conflict with Pauline theology are the use of the formula "in Christ," which in Ephesians is instrumental rather than mystical; a direct address to God as "Father" in supplication (1:17; 3:14); an enhanced

---

[11]J. Moffatt, *An Introduction to the Literature of the New Testament* (Edinburgh: T. & T. Clark, 1911), p. 393.

[12]M. Goguel, "Esquisse d'une solution nouvelle du problème de l'epître aux Ephésiens" in *Revue de l'histoire des Religions* (1935), 111:254–284; (1936), 112:73–99.

[13]*Meaning of Ephesians; Key to Ephesians.*

interpretation of marriage as compared with 1 Corinthians 7 (5:25–33); and an absence of references either to the preexistence of Christ or the Parousia.

5) *An alternative theory.* The cumulative effect of these arguments has led a number of modern critics to seek another answer to the question of authorship. They usually declare that Ephesians was the work of some admirer of Paul who reproduced much of the apostle's language in a pseudonymous letter, adapting it to his own purpose as he presented a more mature theology.

Some wonder whether this was Onesimus, Philemon's slave, who is tentatively equated with a Bishop of Ephesus bearing the same name and mentioned by Ignatius (*Ad Eph* 1.3). But Ephesians is recognized as the product of a distinctly Semitic mind while, so far as we can gather, Onesimus was a Gentile. Tychicus is another candidate, as we have seen.

The most influential theory today is that proposed by Goodspeed (and Knox[14]) and supported by Mitton. It regards Ephesians as an introduction to the first published collection of Paul's letters, dated about A.D. 90. The compiler was also the composer of Ephesians. No specific data can be adduced and Mitton admits that this attempt at identification is speculative in the extreme.

c. The Vindication of Pauline Authorship

The case for the Pauline authorship of Ephesians has already been presented. Its strength lies in the incontestability of the external attestation corroborated by impressive internal testimony. Only an overwhelmingly conclusive counterargument could disturb the traditional interpretation. Those who reject Pauline authorship appeal to internal data. Even if objections of this kind were to be sustained, the consistent historical authentication of Ephesians would remain as an insurmountable barrier. Any alternative theory must satisfactorily explain why an inaccurate tradition prevailed.

We must now subject the arguments against Pauline authorship to critical examination.

1) *Vocabulary and style.* The fact that Paul resorts to a number of new words and expressions in this Epistle is not without precedent. Nor is it surprising, since he is dealing with themes not previously covered. Even Houlden, whose approach is notably radical, acknowledges that this criterion is a tool of the most uncertain accuracy, especially in view of the distinctive nature of Ephesians.[15] It would be valid only if it could be demonstrated that it was quite impossible for Paul to have employed such language.

Obviously the style of Ephesians does differ from that of Paul's other letters. But then the circumstances were different too. He was not facing the problems of a particular church, as we shall see. He could afford to be more reflective. The style of Ephesians matches Paul's mood. Could an imitator have given birth to anything at once so authentic and yet so original? If he rivaled Paul himself as a spiritual genius, it is strange that the primitive church knew nothing of him.

---

[14]J. Knox, *Chapters in a Life of Paul* (New York: Abingdon-Cokesbury, 1950), pp. 19, 20; cf. *Philemon Among the Letters of Paul* (Chicago: University Press, 1935).

[15]J.L. Houlden, *Paul's Letters from Prison: Philippians, Colossians, Philemon, and Ephesians* (London: Penguin, 1970), p. 249.

2) Dependence.

a) *Colossians.* Much of the argument against Pauline authorship revolves around the similarities between Ephesians and Colossians. Not all the resemblances are equally striking and some are virtually nonexistent. Scholars find it hard to agree on a catena of parallels. There are also conspicuous differences between Ephesians and Colossians. The evidence is insufficient to demonstrate that the same writer could not have been responsible for each. Indeed, it can be maintained that the result is precisely what we might expect of Paul had he treated the same themes in successive letters. On the other hand, would an imitator have dealt so freely with the text of Colossians? Is it not probable that he would have adhered more slavishly to the script? It is when an author borrows from himself that he can take liberties with what is after all his own material.

Such an author may even modify or elaborate on the sense of terms he has used before. It was not unusual for Paul to do this. In the instances cited, the area of variation is not so wide as some have imagined. The repetition of a word with an extended connotation does not in itself constitute a reason for positing a different author. It would take other grounds than this to show that Paul could not possibly have given the word in question that interpretation.

b) *Other Pauline letters.* The hypothesis identifying the pseudonymous author of Ephesians with the collector of the Pauline corpus assumes that Ephesians is dependent on the other Pauline letters (excluding the Pastorals, which are assigned to a second-century Paulinist). This is the nub of the argument and it is hard to sustain. There are resemblances between Ephesians and the rest of Paul's letters, but these in themselves do not require a theory of direct dependence to account for them. Indeed, they are more convincingly compatible with the acceptance of Pauline authorship.

There is, however, some divergence of opinion among investigators about the precise extent of such resemblances. Most scholars today would recognize the factor without making so much of it as Goodspeed or even Mitton did. Ephesians represents the quintessence of Pauline theology. It supplies a reinterpreted summary of the apostle's previous teaching. Therefore it should not be surprising to discover in it more reminiscences of the other Epistles than elsewhere in Paul's writings.

The similarities between Ephesians and the rest of the NT literature are not such as to establish literary dependence or to invalidate the Pauline authorship of the Epistle.

3) *Personal references.* These are not so conclusive as some would insist. Certainly they are capable of an exegesis that does not require the supposition of pseudonymity.

In 3:2 it is not altogether clear whether the Greek justifies a conditional rendering of the clause. So NEB has "surely you have heard," which obviates the difficulty. In v.4 Paul is not bragging about his insight into the mystery of Christ as if it were due to his own perceptive powers, for he has just emphasized that it was made known to him by revelation (v.3). "Holy apostles" (v.5) is not as pretentious as it sounds, since all believers are described as ἅγιοι (*hagioi*, "saints") (1:1). If some regard the confession of v.8 as theatrical, others see in it a most moving recognition of human unworthiness when contrasted with divine grace. Would an ardent Paulinist ever have permitted Paul to indulge in such self-deprecation?

None of these instances is irreconcilable with Pauline authorship, and the last of them is particularly difficult to reconcile with non-Pauline authorship. The lack of personal greetings at the close of the letter is understandable if, as we shall find, Ephesians was probably composed as an encyclical.

4) *Theological discrepancies.* It was Hort who insisted that mere differences of doctrine cannot be accepted as evidence of dissimilar authorship unless a genuine lack of harmony is proved.[16] Such a lack would be hard to sustain in the case of Ephesians. That the theology of the Epistle is more fully developed than in any of its predecessors is so far from being inimical to the presupposition of a Pauline origin that it actually befriends it. Only if it were established that the mature doctrine of Ephesians moved in the opposite direction to that of Paul, or further than he could conceivably have taken it, could this argument be effectively pressed. This cannot be proved by any of the items cited.

Our conclusion must be that the cumulative internal arguments said to militate against the unexceptionable external attestation to Ephesians fail to carry sufficient weight to overthrow the tradition of its Pauline authorship. Such arguments are often deployed as if Ephesians were an anonymous Epistle, like Hebrews. But, as Sanders correctly insists, Ephesians is Pauline until proved non-Pauline.[17]

2. Destination

To whom was this letter addressed? The title "To the Ephesians" was supplied at least as early as the middle of the second century and appears on all subsequent Greek MSS. The Epistle was almost everywhere received as directed to the Christians in Ephesus. The sole exception is Marcion, who referred to it as the Epistle to the Laodiceans.

a. *Textual Difficulties*

Uncertainty as to the destination of Ephesians and the originality of the title arises from a textual problem relating to the opening verse. The definitive place name "in Ephesus" is omitted from some of the oldest and most reliable MSS. It is not found in the Chester Beatty papyrus P[46] dating from about A.D. 200 (the earliest extant MS of the Pauline Epistles), nor in the major fourth-century codd. Sinaiticus (ℵ) and Vaticanus (B) in their unrevised form. In 67[2], a reputable twelfth century minuscule, it is expunged by a corrector. Lightfoot believed that wherever ℵ B and 67[2] concurred in supporting a Pauline reading, the original text was invariably reflected.[18]

Basil the Great testified that the words "in Ephesus" were not to be discovered in any of the ancient MSS (*Adv. Eunom.* 2.19). Origen's commentary presupposes the omission, as Jerome confirmed. Tertullian accused Marcion of prefixing a spurious title but not of altering the text. On the other hand, "in Ephesus" occurs in commentaries from the time of John Chrysostom onwards. Considering all the evidence, however, the majority of recent textual critics are persuaded that the original reading did not contain the words.

If "in Ephesus" did in fact appear in the original text, then reasons have to be sought to explain its subsequent omission in the important MSS mentioned above. This may simply be due to faulty transmission. Or perhaps at some stage copies were sent to other

---

[16]F.J.A. Hort, *Prolegomena to St. Paul's Epistles to the Romans and the Ephesians* (London: Macmillan, 1895), p. 123.

[17]J.N. Sanders, in *Studies in Ephesians,* ed. Frank L. Cross (London: Mowbray, 1956), p. 16.

[18]J.B. Lightfoot, *Biblical Essays* (London: Macmillan, 1893), p. 380.

churches with the destination erased. A few MSS omit "in Rome" from Romans 1:7, giving rise to the conjecture that this letter too was used for more general distribution. Some wonder whether the words "in Ephesus" were left out for liturgical purposes.

b. Internal Problems

An examination of the letter itself serves to deepen the suspicions aroused by the textual dilemma. Paul does not appear to be acquainted with his readers personally or at least not with all of them. He has only heard of their faith and love (1:15). They have only heard of the stewardship of God's grace entrusted to him (3:2). Paul can only assume that they have been taught the truth about Jesus (4:21). Yet Paul had remained in Ephesus for no less than three years. Could he have written like this to the Christians there?

There is little trace of local coloring in the letter, unless we accept the suggestion that chapter 2 has Diana's temple in mind rather than that in Jerusalem. Timothy was with Paul as he wrote. He was well known in Ephesus (Acts 19:22), yet he is not so much as mentioned in Ephesians, though his name occurs in the other captivity Epistles. There are no personal greetings, which is strange if an Ephesian readership is envisaged. Not a single word of familiarity or affection is to be found. Even the benediction is in the third person and not the second as in every other instance in Paul's letters (6:23, 24). These considerations compel us to subscribe to the general consensus today, which considers it most unlikely that the Ephesian church was exclusively or immediately addressed.

c. Possible Solutions

If Ephesians was not composed specifically for the Christians in Ephesus, or not for them alone, who were the intended recipients and what kind of a letter was it?

1) *A letter with another name.* Was Ephesians addressed to some other church? If "in Ephesus" is missing from the archetypal text, is it conceivable that another location was included in some copies before "in Ephesus" eventually appeared? Laodicea is the only possibility, on the basis of Marcion's canon. But no MS has been discovered that carries such a superscription or that reads "in Laodicea" in Ephesians 1:1. Colossians 4:16 may indicate that Paul did write to the Laodiceans, though "the letter from Laodicea" is not actually attributed to Paul.

If Ephesians is in fact the lost letter to Laodicea, why was the name detached from it? Was it, as von Harnack imagined, because the church there fell into disrepute (Rev 3:14–19)?[19] Or did the recipients release a copy from which their own address was omitted (so McNeile[20])? Again, if Ephesians is really the letter to the Laodiceans and is referred to in Colossians 4:16, why should Paul encourage an exchange when the contents are so similar? Too many unanswered questions surround the solution that Ephesians was a letter with another name.

2) *A letter without a name.* On this assumption the words "in Ephesus" in 1:1 do not

---

[19] Adolf von Harnack, "Die Adresse des Epheserbriefes des Paulus," in *Sitzungberichte der königlich Preussische Akademie der Wissenschaften zu Berlin* (1910), pp. 704, 705.

[20] A.H. McNeile, *Introduction to the Study of the New Testament* 2nd ed. C.S.C. Williams (Oxford: Clarendon, 1953), p. 177.

require replacement, nor should a blank space be left to denote the omission or to allow an insertion. Paul did not intend to indicate the precise destination of Ephesians because in his mind it was addressed to Christians in general. This solution is presented in two ways:

1. Following Origen, some have held that Paul directed his message to the saints "who are" in the special ontological sense that Christians alone achieve true being by virtue of their union with Christ. Yet though such existential subtleties were familiar to Origen, it is most unlikely that Paul intended anything so abstruse in a simple salutation. Elsewhere in his letters the same or a similar expression always prefaces a specific location (Rom 1:7; 1 Cor 1:2; 2 Cor 1:1; Phil 1:1). Why should Ephesians 1:1 be an exception to this?

2. According to the RSV translation, Paul is merely writing "to the saints who are also faithful in Christ Jesus." This is doubtless the most satisfactory way of construing the participle in the absence of "in Ephesus" or some other designation. Nevertheless, it presents considerable grammatical difficulties. It gives undue emphasis to "faithful" and this upsets the balance of the sentence. For Paul, there were no saints who were not also faithful.

If this solution is adopted, some explanation has to be found for the ultimate inclusion of "in Ephesus." It is surmised that the letter was distributed from Ephesus and that the phrase was added in one copy and then eventually repeated in most. This would tie in with Marcion's title associating Ephesians with Laodicea, which may well have been another of the churches to receive it. Others wonder whether the name of Ephesus was written in when the letters of Paul were gathered and circulated toward the end of the century. The editor may have operated from Ephesus, which would be a natural center from which the correspondence could be distributed. It might have been felt that such an important Christian community ought to be accorded a letter from the apostle.

3) *A letter with a blank space.* On this supposition, no place name appeared in the archetypal text because a space was deliberately left to be filled in as circumstances demanded. Ephesians was designed as a circular letter to be dispatched to a group of churches. This solution to the problem of destination was proposed by de Bèze[21] and Grotius,[22] and elaborated by Ussher.[23]

Paul informed the readers of Ephesians about his plans to send Tychicus to visit them (6:21, 22). He had written to the Colossians in virtually identical terms (Col 4:7, 8). On the basis of this evidence, some scholars are inclined to the view that Tychicus was instructed to carry a circular letter to the churches situated on his route to Colosse. If there was only one such letter to be read out in each place, the name may have been interpolated verbally. But perhaps Tychicus took a copy to each church and left it there, or each church made its own transcript of the original. The name of the church would then have been added in the blank space either by the bearer or by the addressees. Because the church at Ephesus was the most notable in the group involved, its copy became the standard from which the majority of MSS and versions have been derived.

This solution is open to a series of objections:

1. Although encyclical letters were not unknown in the ancient world, as Zuntz has

---

[21]Theodore de Bèze, *Annotationes in Novum Testamentum* (Paris: H. Stephanus, 1965).

[22]H. Grotius, *Annotationes in Vetus et Novum Testamentum* (Amsterdam: J. et C. Blaeu, 1642); English ed. Samuel Moody (London: J. Smith, 1727), p. 346.

[23]J. Ussher, *The Annals of the World ... Containing the History of the Old and New Testament* (London: E. Tyler, 1658), pp. 896, 897.

shown, there is no historical precedent for the provision of a blank space to be filled in later with the name of the recipient.[24]

2. There are examples in 2 Corinthians 1:1 and Galatians 1:2 of the mode of address that Paul would be more inclined to adopt in a circular letter.

3. The procedure of leaving a blank space is more suitable to the formality of a legal document than to the simplicity of a personal communication.

4. There is a total lack of MS evidence to substantiate the hypothesis. No trace remains of copies with any other name than Ephesus in the text.

5. If the circular letter was intended to be read by a group of churches in the Lycus Valley, we should expect Paul to convey at least some sort of general greeting as in Colossians. Surely he would have distinguished between those readers he had met and those he had never seen, for Paul was known in other churches in the province of Asia (Acts 19:10; 20:25).

6. The blank-space hypothesis would be more convincing if the "in" had remained in 1:1.

Kümmel decides that "nothing points to an actual circular letter."[25] We may prefer to agree with Guthrie that the presupposition of a blank address is indeed vulnerable, but that there may be a case for a modified form of the encyclical solution.[26] Of the objections listed above, only the fifth tells against a circular letter as such.

4) *A circular letter.* On this view Ephesians is a letter intended to be read by Christians living in the Roman province of Asia, of which Ephesus was the capital. It was not addressed to any particular local congregation, but to all. From Ephesus it was circulated throughout the churches of proconsular Asia, no doubt by means of a courier who may have been Tychicus. This attempt to solve the problem of destination, while not without difficulties, appears to be the least exceptionable.

3. Background

The foundation of the Ephesian church was laid by the apostle Paul on his return from the second missionary journey. On his route from Greece to Syria, the apostle paid a visit to Ephesus, accompanied by Priscilla and Aquila, whom he left behind in the city (Acts 18:18–21). It was only a brief stopover, for he was hurrying on to Jerusalem. He found time, however, to engage in dialogue with the Jewish leaders in the local synagogue. He so impressed them that they begged him to remain. He was unable to change his plans, though he promised to return if that was God's will for him.

Clearly this proved to be so, for he included Ephesus in his itinerary on his next missionary tour and actually extended his stay to a period of more than three years, probably from A.D. 54 to 57 (Acts 20:3). Evidently the apostle realized the strategic potential of the metropolis, which had been sited so as to command the main highway between east and west. Ephesus was surrounded by 230 independent communities within the Roman province of Asia. If the Christian faith were firmly established in the capital city, it could be spread from the hub to the rim.

When he got back to Ephesus, Paul found that Apollos had been active in his absence

---

[24]G. Zuntz, *The Text of the Epistles* (Oxford: University Press, 1963), p. 228n.

[25]*Introduction to the New Testament*, p. 251.

[26]D. Guthrie, *New Testament Introduction: The Pauline Epistles* (London: Tyndale, 1961), p. 131.

(Acts 18:27, 28). By now Apollos had moved on to Corinth and Paul was free to consolidate the work. For three months he resumed his previous confrontation with the Jews and soon aroused opposition. He took his converts with him and transferred to the lecture hall of Tyrannus, where he held daily conferences over a period of two years (Acts 19:9). The result is significant for its bearing on the destination of the Ephesian letter. We are told that all the residents of provincial Asia, Jews and Greeks alike, heard the word of the Lord (Acts 19:10).

The impact of Paul's mission was felt far beyond the boundary of Ephesus itself. The entire area was affected and there were converts everywhere. Those who came into the capital on business or for pleasure could not fail to hear of what was happening. Some apparently became Christians and then went back to their own towns to communicate the gospel. It seems that evangelists, like Epaphras, were sent out from Ephesus to the outlying districts. It is important to realize that Paul's Ephesian mission was by no means limited to the city itself but influenced the whole province. The places in proconsular Asia explicitly named in the NT include the seven churches referred to in Revelation 2 and 3, together with Troas, Assos, Adramyttium, Miletus, Trogyllium, and Hierapolis.

This remarkable expansion led to and was temporarily halted by the disturbance described in Acts 19:23–41 when Demetrius the silversmith rallied his fellow tradeunionists. Paul was already on the point of departure, and this was the signal for his withdrawal as he headed for Rome (Acts 19:23, 24). On his last voyage to Syria, he landed at Miletus and there took leave of the Ephesian presbyters, committing the oversight of the flock to them in a solemn and moving charge (Acts 20:18–35). Paul was never to visit Ephesus again. Yet it is altogether credible that he would wish to write, not simply to the church in Ephesus itself, but to all the Christian communities established during the Ephesian mission. Therefore, an understanding of the background of the Ephesian letter has a determinative bearing on the problem of its destination.

4. Place of Origin

Paul wrote Ephesians from prison (3:1; 4:1; 6:20). Since Tychicus was the bearer of this letter (6:21), as well as of Colossians (4:7) and presumably of Philemon also (cf. v.24), it may be deduced that these three documents belong to the same time and place. Philippians was also written in prison and may be one of the group. But where was Paul imprisoned? Three possibilities present themselves and must be tested by the evidence of all four letters.

a. Rome

The traditional view assigns the captivity Epistles to Rome. This view remained unchallenged for eighteen centuries. We know from the narrative of Acts that Paul was in fact placed under house arrest in Rome for two years (Acts 28:30). The conditions of his free confinement allowed him scope to proclaim the gospel (Acts 28:16, 17, 23, 31; Eph 6:18–20; Phil 1:12–18; Col 4:2–4).

A Roman imprisonment accords well with the personal references in each of the letters involved. The mention of the palace guard and the emperor's household in Philippians 1:13 and 4:22 favor it. The fact that Paul is conscious that he might have to face a sentence of death also confirms a location in Rome (Phil 1:19–26; 2:17, 23). Aristarchus is associated with Paul's greetings in Colossians 4:10, and we are told in Acts 27:2 that he accompanied Paul on the journey to Rome. The presence of Luke (Col 4:14) during the Roman imprisonment is attested by Acts 28:14, 16.

It will have been noted that the internal corroboration of Rome as the likeliest place of origin for the captivity Epistles is drawn from Colossians and Philippians rather than from Ephesians. There is, however, nothing in Ephesians to exclude the Roman imprisonment.

b. *Ephesus*

Following Lisco[27] and Deissmann,[28] attempts have been made of late to make out a case for Ephesus as the scene of Paul's imprisonment and therefore the place from which some or all of the Epistles were written. Although it has only been elaborated in comparatively recent years (notably by Michaelis[29] and Duncan [30]), this possibility was mooted as far back as the second century. The Marcionite Prologue to Colossians explains: "Therefore the apostle already in bonds writes to them from Ephesus." The equivalent Prologue to Philemon, however, assigns that letter to Rome, which makes for confusion, since the internal evidence suggests a common origin.

There is, of course, no mention in Acts of any imprisonment in Ephesus, though in 2 Corinthians 6:5 and 11:23 Paul does say that he has often been in prison. Acts records no imprisonment until Philippi (Acts 16:19–40). Where were the others? We do not know, but the most probable places are those where Paul encountered the fiercest opposition. Ephesus would certainly come into the reckoning. In 1 Corinthians 15:32 the apostle speaks about fighting wild beasts at Ephesus. That may be a proverb or merely a metaphor. But if taken literally, it could mean that Paul was actually thrown to the lions in the arena. In 2 Corinthians 1:8–10 Paul alludes to some serious trouble that overtook him in the province of Asia, and in Romans 16:3, 4 he tells us that Priscilla and Aquila risked their lives to save him. We know that the pair were with Paul in Ephesus, and this opens up the possibility that it was here that they protected him. It is further argued that Ephesus is a natural center from which letters could be distributed to the cities in the Lycus Valley. Here Epaphras would have the shortest route to reach Paul from Colosse (Col 4:12; Philem 23) and Epaphroditus from Philippi (Phil 2:25–30). Here the apostle would be most likely to be surrounded by a substantial number of helpers (Col 4:10, 11). Paul asked Philemon to have a guest room ready for him in Colosse (Philem 22) when he was released; does this not suit nearby Ephesus better than Rome? Again, is it not more feasible that Onesimus should abscond on foot to Ephesus—the nearest big city—rather than venture by sea so far as Rome?

Even if it were possible to concede all these debatable points, which is far from being the case, the silence of Acts remains an insuperable obstacle to the acceptance of this hypothesis.

c. *Caesarea*

If Acts knows nothing of an Ephesian imprisonment, the record of Paul's detention in Caesarea is unambiguous. He was held under open arrest for more than two years at

---

[27]H. Lisco, *Vincula Sanctorum* (Berlin, 1900); *Roma Peregrina* (Berlin, 1901).

[28]A. Deissmann, *Light From the Ancient East*, Eng. T. (London: Hodder and Stoughton, 1910), p. 229n.

[29]W. Michaelis, *Die Gefangenschaft des Paulus in Ephesus* (Gutersolöh, Bertelsmann, 1925); cf. "The Trial of St. Paul at Ephesus," in *Journal of Theological Studies* (1928), 29:368–375.

[30]G.S. Duncan, *St. Paul's Ephesian Ministry* (London: Hodder and Stoughton, 1929), pp. 66–161.

the pleasure of Marcus Antonius Felix, the Roman procurator of Judaea. He was housed in Herod's palace (Acts 24:23), and his friends were allowed free access to him. In this respect his conditions were somewhat similar to those later in Rome. This, along with other factors, had led a number of scholars to inquire whether the captivity Epistles, or at least some of them, were written from Caesarea. The theory was first advanced by the rationalist H.E.G. Paulus[31] at the start of the nineteenth century and more recently revived by Lohmeyer[32] and Johnson.[33]

Exponents of this view contend that the runaway slave Onesimus would have been more inclined to escape from Colosse to Caesarea (some five hundred miles) than to undertake a long voyage to Rome. Ephesus would be too near but Rome too far for the fugitive. Again, if the letters were dispatched from Rome, Tychicus and Onesimus would have first reached Ephesus with three of them and we might anticipate some mention of this fact in Ephesians, together with a commendation of Onesimus in his plight (cf. Col 4:8, 9). If Ephesians was written from Caesarea, their route would have brought them to Colosse before Tychicus proceeded alone to Ephesus. But surely it would have been most discourteous had Paul commended Onesimus to the Christians in Ephesus before he had been reinstated by his master and received by the church at Colosse.

Paul's request to Philemon to prepare a lodging immediately implies a nearness to Colosse that suits Caesarea, so it is claimed, rather than Rome. On the other hand, did Paul really expect to be released from Caesarea at any moment? He was aware that his only resort was to appeal to the emperor and to insure that he would fulfill his God-given commission to preach the gospel in Rome (Rom 1:10–15) and even further west (Rom 15:24).

The arguments in favor of either Caesarea or Ephesus as the place from which Paul wrote the imprisonment letters are insufficiently conclusive to supplant the traditional view, which sees Rome as the location. Even an innovationist like Houlden (pp. 42–44) has the candor to confess that the Roman theory still has the best chance of being right, and he proceeds on that assumption. We propose to do the same.

5. Date

The date of Ephesians is tied up with the question of its place of origin, and, of course, its authorship. Those who attribute it to a disciple of Paul late in the first century consider it to have been composed around the year A.D. 90 when the corpus is thought to have been finalized. The terminal date is probably A.D. 95, for Clement of Rome seems to echo Ephesians in his letter to the Corinthians.

Accepting Pauline authorship, the date then depends on the place of origin and the relevant imprisonment. If written from Ephesus, it must have been between A.D. 54 and 57; Michaelis suggests the winter of A.D. 54/55. If written from Caesarea, the date of Ephesians falls between A.D. 59 and 61.

---

[31]Heinrich E.G. Paulus, *Philologische-kritischer und historischer Kommentar über das Neue Testament* (Lubeck, 1800–1804, Bd. I); cf. Wilhelm Michaelis, *Einleitung in das Neue Testament* (Bern: BEG-Verlag, 1946[2]), p. 205.

[32]E.H. Lohmeyer, *Die Briefe an die Philipper, an die Kolosser und an Philemon* (Gottingen: Vandenhöck und Ruprecht, 1964), p. 3; for different views about the place from which the imprisonment letters were written, see Josef Schmid, *Zeit und Ort der paulinischen Gefangenschaftsbriefe*, (Freiburg, 1931).

[33]L. Johnson, "The Pauline Letters from Caesarea," ExpT (1956–1957), 68:24–26.

We see no compelling reason, however, to discard the view that Paul wrote from Rome. According to the chronology of Ogg, Paul's two-year imprisonment extended from early in A.D. 62 until 64.[34] Although three of the captivity Epistles were penned about the same time, it seems clear that Colossians and Philemon preceded Ephesians. Epaphras had brought disturbing news from Colosse. Meanwhile, Paul was anxious to return Onesimus to his master without delay. It was the combination of these circumstances that prompted Paul to write Colossians and Philemon and dispatch them with Tychicus and Onesimus. He seized the opportunity also to write Ephesians, to be delivered along with the other two. A date in the middle period of Paul's imprisonment is therefore to be preferred, and A.D. 63 is probable. Some, adopting a rather different chronological scheme, and allowing for the possibility of two Roman imprisonments, would decide on A.D. 60 or 61.

6. Occasion

While Paul was under house detention in Rome, he enjoyed certain privileges in what was a relaxed form of custody. Among these was the freedom to receive a constant stream of visitors. No doubt the Christians in Rome availed themselves of the opportunity. We know that representatives of the Jewish community also came to inquire about the ostracized Christian sect (Acts 28:22, 23). Intimate friends like Luke, Aristarchus, and presumably Timothy were often at Paul's side. From time to time he would also receive messengers from the churches beyond Rome.

One of these was Epaphras, whom Paul addressed as his companion in the service of Christ and in his captivity (Col 1:7; 4:12; Philem 23). It seems that it was he who was instrumental in evangelizing the Lycus Valley region at Paul's instigation during the Ephesian mission and who founded the churches in Colosse, Hierapolis, and Laodicea. Epaphras came to Rome to bring Paul a progress report about these congregations. There was much to rejoice the apostle's heart, but he was also concerned to learn that a virulent heresy was threatening Christians in Colosse and perhaps infecting others too.

One of Paul's most trustworthy representatives—Tychicus, a native of Ephesus—was with him at this time. He was actually about to leave for the province of Asia, either under Paul's instructions or for other undisclosed reasons. Paul took advantage of the opportunity to use him as a courier and lost no time in preparing what we now know as the Epistle to the Colossians. Meanwhile, Onesimus, a fugitive slave from Colosse, had been befriended by Paul and had confessed Christ. He had defrauded his master Philemon, and Paul was anxious that he should be pardoned and then perhaps released for Christian service. Paul therefore decided to send Onesimus along with Tychicus, and with this in view he wrote a covering letter to Philemon to accompany this unusual convert.

Before Tychicus left, Paul had finished a third letter, which no doubt he had been preparing for some time. It was sent to Ephesus and to all the churches founded as a result of the mission there throughout the Asian province. As befits a letter intended for more general circulation, Paul did not deal with particular issues, as in Colossians and in much of his other correspondence, but with the implications of the gospel. These he had treated in Romans from the angle of the believer's justification. Now he approached

---

[34]G. Ogg, *The Chronology of the Life of Paul* (London: Epworth, 1968), pp. 176, 177.

them more broadly in terms of the fellowship of Christians in Christ's body, the church, and the reconciliation of the entire universe in him.

7. Purpose

Ephesians, unlike Colossians, was not devised to combat error and expose the inconsistencies of false teaching. Paul's aim was more detached and therefore more exalted. He rose above the smoke of battle and captured a vision of God's sovereign plan that transcends the bitterness of controversy and the necessity for the church militant here on earth to fight incessantly for its very existence.

Paul stood aside from the conflict and contemplated God's overall design for his church and for his world. As he did so, he came to realize as never before the breathtaking scope of God's strategy in Christ for the fullness of time (Eph 1:9, 10). J.A. Robinson captured Paul's mood when he explained that his mind was now free "for one supreme exposition, noncontroversial, positive, fundamental of the great doctrine of his life—that doctrine into which he had been advancing year by year under the discipline of his unique circumstances—the doctrine of the unity of mankind in Christ and the purpose of God for the world through the Church" (p. 10). Yet Paul's objective was not purely inspirational. He sought to relate his vision to the practical demands of Christian living in a hostile society.

8. Literary Form

While retaining the framework of a letter, Ephesians differs from the rest of Paul's compositions because of its peculiar cast. In some places it sounds like a sermon, whereas in others it seems to be a prayer. This unusual combination of the homiletical and the liturgical makes it difficult to classify its literary *genre*.

In considering the style of Ephesians we have already noted that it reflects Paul's contemplative mood. Both McNeile and Scott regarded it as a meditation.[35] Schlier characterizes the Epistle not as " 'kerygma' in the strict sense" but as "sophia, sophia of the mystery ... meditation of the wisdom of the mystery of Christ himself "[36] (qt. Kümmel[37]). But it is not simply a sample of the apostle's devotional reverie. Its form is not to be accounted for exclusively by the circumstances under which it was conceived. In any case, though Paul had ample leisure for reflection during his detention in Rome, he did nevertheless complete this letter along with Colossians and Philemon in a fairly short period of time, with Tychicus and Onesimus all set for their journey.

The meditation, moreover, had a practical purpose. Although not addressed to a particular situation in a single church, like Paul's other Epistles except the Pastorals, it was relevant to the condition of the Asian churches at this juncture. Thompson is probably near the mark when he describes the product as a general manifesto (though he thinks it was written by Tychicus after Paul had laid down the guidelines).[38] It seeks

---

[35]Ernest F. Scott, *The Epistles of Paul to the Colossians, to Philemon, and to the Ephesians* (London: Hodder and Stoughton, 1930), p. 123.

[36]Heinrich Schlier, in *Lexikon für Theologie und Kirche* (Freiburg: Herder, 1959), 3:916–919; cf. *Der Brief an die Epheser,* (Dusseldorf: Patmos-Verlag, 1962).

[37]*Introduction to the New Testament,* p. 255.

[38]G.H.P. Thompson, *The Letters of Paul to the Ephesians, to the Colossians, and to Philemon* (Cambridge: University Press, 1967), p. 19.

to show how the Christian faith could meet the hopes and fears of Asian believers and to remind them both of their responsibilities and privileges.

Sanders regards Ephesians as Paul's spiritual testament to the church. The congregation at Ephesus, perhaps because of its rapid missionary expansion, is taken as a type of the universal church, enabling Paul to deliver a parting message. Without treating Ephesians as a catholic Epistle, we can nevertheless recognize that it epitomizes the whole of Paul's teaching and lifts it to a new level of presentation. In 2 Corinthians he speaks autobiographically about a man who was caught up to the third heaven (2 Cor 12:1–4); in Ephesians he attempts to recapture the content of that or a similar vision. This accounts for the markedly doxological strain of the letter. The section from 1:3 to 3:21 is almost entirely in the form of a Jewish *berākāh*, or blessing, and the element of praise interpenetrates the apostle's later plea for worthy Christian behavior.

If Ephesians was the work of a Pauline imitator, then, of course, the literary form of the Epistle is pseudepigraphic. This device is not clearly attested in primitive Christian literature, nor is such deception compatible with the emphasis on truth that runs through the NT writings, not least in Ephesians itself (4:15, 25; 6:14).

9. Theological Values

We have already discussed the theological consistency of Ephesians (1.a.4; cf. c.4.), showing how most of the major themes of Pauline teaching are reflected. At this point we need do no more than specify the most prominent feature of doctrinal development. As von Soden realized, Ephesians is above all a hymn of unity.[39] Paul's conception of oneness in Christ extends beyond the church to include all creation. God's ultimate purpose is "to bring all things in heaven and on earth together under one head, even Christ" (1:10). Yet our Lord has been appointed as "head over everything for the church, which is his body, the fullness of him who fills everything in every way" (1:22, 23). The corporate aspect of Christ's Saviorhood and lordship, adumbrated in other Epistles and particularly in Colossians, is here expounded more thoroughly.

Unity was a topic of general interest in the first century A.D. The Stoic philosophers recognized an orderliness in the universe which they attributed to the cosmic Reason or Logos that correlated all things. The fact that much of the Mediterranean world was politically unified under the imperial government led to the vision of a universal commonwealth. At the same time the mystery cults, which were gaining in popularity as conventional religion declined, offered a certain sense of oneness in the common quest for deliverance from demonic forces and the achievement of personal integration.

In Ephesians Paul was able to demonstrate that this almost obsessive search for unity finds its ultimate goal only in Christ. It is he who represents the coordinating principle of all life. The ideal of world citizenship, cherished by the philosophers, is realized in the universal church. Man can be liberated from bondage to the principalities and powers that threaten his welfare only as he shares the triumph Christ gained over them at the Cross (1:21; 2:2; 3:10, 11; 6:12, 13; cf. Col 2:15). The distinctive theology of

---

[39]H. von Soden, *The History of Early Church Literature: The Writings of the New Testament,* Eng. T. (London: Williams and Norgate, 1906), p. 292.

Ephesians is no academic abstraction. It was tuned to the contemporary mood and in a deeply divided world today it still conveys a relevant word from God.

10. Canonicity

The canonicity of Ephesians has never been in dispute. Its title appears among the accepted books in every known list since Marcion's *Instrumentum* of A.D. 140. There, as we have observed, it is erroneously entitled "The Epistle to the Laodiceans," but it is unquestionably the same document. It is logged as the eighth book of the NT. Thereafter it is included without exception in the authoritative Pauline corpus.

The compiler of the Muratorian fragment explains that Paul followed his predecessor John in writing by name to seven churches—Corinth, Ephesus, Philippi, Colosse, Galatia, Thessalonica, and Rome. In addition, he addressed second Epistles to Corinth and Thessalonica for the purpose of admonition. Then he sent four letters to individuals (Philemon, Titus, 1 and 2 Timothy). The position of Ephesians in this catalog, dating back to the latter part of the second century, bears sufficient testimony to its prestige.

There are indications that Clement of Rome was familiar with Ephesians and assimilated some of its phraseology (1 Clem 2.1 = Eph 5:31; 36.2 = Eph 1:18; 46.6 = Eph 4:4–6). The same can be said about Ignatius (*Ad Eph* 1.1 = Eph 5:1; 9.1 = Eph 2:20–22) and Polycarp (*Ad Phil* 1.3 = Eph 2:8, 9; 12.1 = Eph 4:26). *The 'Shepherd' of Hermas* exhibits correspondences that are probably more than accidental (*Mand* 10.2.2, 4, 5, = Eph 4:30; *Sim* 9.13.5; 9.17.4; 9.18.4 = Eph 4:3–6), while the so-called *Letter of Barnabas* provides more substantial evidence than was formerly supposed (6.11 = Eph 2:10; 4:22; 6.14 = Eph 3:17; 16.8–10 = Eph 2:21,22; 3:17). Apparent coincidences of language in the *Didache* and the *Letter to Diognetus* afford rather less convincing testimony.

It has to be recognized, of course, that even where we can be reasonably certain that these Christian writers are reproducing the language of Ephesians, this is not enough to endorse its canonicity unless it is specifically quoted as Scripture, which is never done. Ironically the only instance of this kind in the period under review is the Gnostic Valentinus, who refers to Ephesians 3:14–18 as ἡ γραφή, *hē graphē* (Clement of Alexandria, *Strom* 6.34). On the other hand, that Ephesians has already been named in extant canonical catalogs strongly suggests that its phraseology is adopted only because it was regarded as scriptural. The first explicit quotation from Ephesians occurs in Irenaeus (*Adv Haer* 1.8.5 = Eph 5:13; 5.2.3 = Eph 5:30; 5.14.3 = Eph 1:7; 2:13, 15) where the letter is ascribed to the apostle Paul and treated as authoritative. There are similar allusions in Tertullian (*Adv Marc* 5.4.17), Clement of Alexandria (*Paed* 1.5), and Origen (De Princ 2.3.5; 2.11.5; 3.5.4; *Contra Cels* 72). Eusebius of Caesarea, the doyen of church historians, claims to have investigated all the sources available to him in order to discover what Christian writers in each period had said about the canonical and acknowledged books. He reports that the "fourteen epistles" of Paul (which must include Ephesians) are "manifest and clear" so far as their genuineness is concerned and he therefore classifies them among "the divine writings" that are unquestionable (H.E. 3.3.4–7). That has been the consistent verdict of orthodoxy.

The undisputed canonicity of Ephesians carries a significant implication for the more controversial question of authorship. It forms part of the exceptionally impressive external attestation of authenticity. Had there been even the slightest hesitation in accepting it as from Paul himself, its status would have been seriously jeopardized.

11. Text

There are few places in Ephesians where any textual uncertainty is to be found. The opening verse is of great historical importance because of its bearing on the destination of the Epistle. One or two instances involve minor theological considerations (3:19; 4:9, 21). Several are interesting in themselves (1:20; 4:16, 19, 29). Others are of little moment. Apart from 1:1, all of them can readily be explained as due to transcribers' errors. We can therefore be reassured that we possess the text virtually as when Paul dictated it and Tychicus took it to Ephesus and the other Asian churches.

12. Bibliography

Abbott, T.K. *A Critical and Exegetical Commentary on the Epistles to the Ephesians and to the Colossians* (ICC). Edinburgh: Clark, 1897.
Allan, John A. *The Epistle to the Ephesians.* London: S.C.M., 1959.
Barth, Markus. *The Broken Wall: A Study of the Epistle to the Ephesians.* Chicago: Judson, 1959.
Beare, F.W. "The Epistle to the Ephesians." Vol. X. *The Interpreter's Bible.* Ed. G.A. Buttrick. New York: Abingdon, 1953.
Beet, J. Agar. *A Commentary on St. Paul's Epistles to the Ephesians, Philippians, Colossians, and to Philemon.* London: Hodder and Stoughton, 1890.
Bruce, F.F. *The Epistle to the Ephesians.* London: Pickering and Inglis, 1961.
Ellicott, Charles J. *St. Paul's Epistle to the Ephesians.* London: Longmans, Green, 1855.
Findlay, G.G. *The Epistle to the Ephesians.* London: Hodder and Stoughton, 1904.
Foulkes, Francis. *The Epistle of Paul to the Ephesians.* London: Tyndale, 1963.
Hanson, Stig. *The Unity of the Church in the New Testament, Colossians and Ephesians.* Uppsala: Almquist and Wiksells, 1946.
Hendriksen, William. *Ephesians.* Grand Rapids: Baker, 1967.
Houlden, J.L. *Paul's Letters From Prison: Philippians, Colossians, Philemon, and Ephesians.* London: Penguin, 1970.
Johnston, George. *Ephesians, Philippians, Colossians and Philemon.* London: Nelson, 1967.
Kirby, J.C. *Ephesians, Baptism and Pentecost.* London: SPCK, 1968.
Lenski, R.C.H. *The Interpretation of St. Paul's Epistles to the Galatians, to the Ephesians and to the Philippians.* Columbus: Wartburg, 1937.
Lock, W. *St. Paul's Epistle to the Ephesians.* London: Methuen, 1929.
Mackay, John A. *God's Order: The Ephesian Letter and This Present Time.* New York: Macmillan, 1953.
Moule, H.C.G. *The Epistle to the Ephesians.* Cambridge: University Press, 1887.
Robinson, J. Armitage. *St. Paul's Epistle to the Ephesians.* London: Macmillan, 1903.
Salmond, S.D.F. *Ephesians* (EGT). London: Hodder and Stoughton, 1917.
Scott, E.F. *The Epistles of Paul to the Colossians, to Philemon and to the Ephesians.* London: Hodder and Stoughton, 1930.
Simpson, E.K. and Bruce, F.F. *Commentary on the Epistles to the Ephesians and the Colossians.* London: Marshall, Morgan and Scott, 1957.
Thompson, G.H.P. *The Letters of Paul to the Ephesians, to the Colossians and to Philemon.* Cambridge: University Press, 1967.
Zerwick, Max. *The Epistle to the Ephesians.* Eng. T. London: Burns and Oates, 1969.

13. Outline

     I. Salutation (1:1, 2)

    II. Doctrine: The Implications of Christian Faith (1:3–3:21)
        1. An Act of Praise (1:3–14)
        2. A Prayer of Intercession (1:15–23)
        3. Life From Death (2:1–10)
        4. Jews and Gentiles Reconciled (2:11–22)
        5. Grace and Apostleship (3:1–13)
        6. Knowledge and Fullness (3:14–21)

    III. Practice: The Application to Christian Life (4:1–6:20)
        1. The Unity of the Church (4:1–16)
        2. The Changed Life (4:17–24)
        3. Christian Behavior Patterns (4:25–5:2)
        4. Light in the Lord (5:3–20)
        5. Christian Relationships: Marriage (5:21–33)
        6. Christian Relationships: Parenthood (6:1–4)
        7. Christian Relationships: Employment (6:5–9)
        8. Into Battle (6:10–20)

    IV. Conclusion (6:21–24)

Text and Exposition

I. Salutation

1:1,2

[1]Paul, an apostle of Christ Jesus by the will of God,

To the saints in Ephesus, the faithful in Christ Jesus:

[2]Grace and peace to you from God our Father and the Lord Jesus Christ.

1 Here as in his other Epistles Paul adopts the conventional form of address used in letters of the period. Usually the writer identified himself, named the prospective recipients, and added some expressions of greeting. Paul freely expanded or contracted these three items as circumstances required; "he embroiders the conventional shape with specifically Christian features" (Houlden, p. 47).

Each phrase of this salutation can be paralleled in other Pauline letters. He often refers to his apostleship and on occasion traces it to its source in the divine will. He regularly addresses "the saints" in the church to which he writes and in Colossians 1:2 also describes them as "faithful . . . in Christ." The context of the greeting in v.2 is also similar to what is found elsewhere in Paul's Epistles.

"Apostle" is a comprehensive term for one who bears the NT message (TDNT, 1:422). It is applied first to the original disciples and then to other Christian missionaries. Paul claimed that, like that of the Twelve, his commission came directly from Christ (Acts 26:16–18; 1 Cor 9:1). The title stresses the authority of the sender and the accountability of the one sent. Paul does not allude to God's will in order to draw attention to his own status but to reflect his awareness that his mission did not arise from any qualifications he himself might possess.

"Saints" (hagioi) is the normal NT designation for Christians. It denotes inward, personal consecration to God. "Faithful" (pistoi) is a parallel designation of believers combining the ideas of trust and fidelity. This exercise of faith with its matching faithfulness is possible only "in Christ Jesus." For a discussion of the destination of Ephesians, see the Introduction. If no place name or blank space is allowed for, it is possible to read straight on without the words "in Ephesus," although unusual emphasis is thrown on "the faithful" by the omission.

2 "Grace" and "peace" reflect the standard greetings in Greek and Hebrew. The wording here is exactly as in Romans 1:7b. Paul prefers to replace the Greek chaire (rejoice) by charis as embodying the essence of the gospel. For "peace" (Heb. šalôm) cf. Ezra 4:17; 5:7; 7:12; Daniel 4:1; 6:25, et al. Notice how Paul associates "the Lord Jesus Christ" with "God our Father" as the originator of these blessings. The name of Christ appears in each of the three clauses in this opening salutation. What follows in the body of Ephesians has to do with the relationship between "the saints," or "the faithful," and their living Lord.

Notes

1 The omission of ἐν Ἐφέσῳ (en Ephesō, "in Ephesus") from early and reliable MSS has been discussed in the Introduction (2.a.).

II. Doctrine: The Implications of Christian Faith (1:3–3:21)

1. An Act of Praise

1:3–14

³Praise be to the God and Father of our Lord Jesus Christ, who has blessed us in the heavenly realms with every spiritual blessing in Christ. ⁴For he chose us in him before the creation of the world to be holy and blameless in his sight. In love ⁵he predestined us to be adopted as sons through Jesus Christ, in accordance with his pleasure and will—⁶to the praise of his glorious grace, which he has freely given us in the One he loves. ⁷In him we have redemption through his blood, the forgiveness of sins, in accordance with the riches of God's grace ⁸that he lavished on us with all wisdom and understanding. ⁹And he made known to us the mystery of his will according to his good pleasure, which he purposed in Christ, ¹⁰to be put into effect when the times will have reached their fulfillment—to bring all things in heaven and on earth together under one head, even Christ.

¹¹In him we were also chosen, having been predestined according to the plan of him who works out everything in conformity with the purpose of his will, ¹²in order that we, who were the first to hope in Christ, might be for the praise of his glory. ¹³And you also were included in Christ when you heard the word of truth, the gospel of your salvation. In him, when you believed, you were marked with a seal, the promised Holy Spirit, ¹⁴who is a deposit guaranteeing our inheritance until the redemption of those who are God's possession—to the praise of his glory.

As in previous Pauline letters, the first part of Ephesians is doctrinal and the second part practical. In this case, however, the whole section, and not merely the beginning of it, is a thanksgiving expressed in the language of worship and prayer (1:3–3:21). Johnston (p. 9) is justified in seeing this as a eucharist (i.e., thanksgiving).

3 The focus of praise in 1:3–14 is what God has done in Christ. This is the key phrase around which the entire passage revolves. Christian faith and life have their center in God's Son and the Epistle therefore opens with an expression of gratitude for all that is found in him. It is cast in the form of a Jewish bᵉrākāh, or blessing (cf. Kirby, pp. 84–94). Its structure is poetical and ruled by parallelism, though scholars are not agreed as to how its stanzas are to be grouped. Kirby finds that the passage was written in "a state of controlled ecstasy" (p. 128).

"Praise be to" (eulogētos) is used exclusively of God (Father or Son) in the NT to indicate the One who alone is worthy of worship. "Blessed be God . . ." was the customary introduction to a Jewish ascription of praise. "Father of our Lord Jesus Christ" is a distinctively Christian addition arising out of a unique relationship. God who is to be blessed has already blessed all his people in Christ through the saving events of his life, death, and resurrection. In the OT bᵉrākāh denotes the bestowal of good. It is often material and invariably quite specific. God's blessings for us in Christ are more exclusively spiritual but nonetheless definite. The Greek verb eulogeō might possibly hint that they are brought to us through the Word (logos) of God. There is a repetition of three

23

different derivations: *eulogētos, eulogēsas,* and *eulogia.* These benefits are spiritual (*pneumatikos*) in nature because they are communicated to us through the Holy Spirit, whose function it is to make over to the believer all that God has achieved in Christ. They have already been secured "in the heavenly realms" (*en tois epouraniois,* cf. Eph 1:20; 2:6; 3:10; 6:12) where Christ now reigns, having triumphed over "the spiritual forces of evil" (Eph 6:12) that threatened to usurp control. Their value is measured by the price that was paid to obtain them when on the cross the Son of God fought satanic opponents and disarmed them (Col 2:15).

4 Paul now traces "every spiritual blessing" (v.3) to its ultimate source in the eternal purpose of God. Christians were selected in Christ prior to the work of creation. The verb "chose" (*exelexato*) is the usual one employed in LXX in connection with God's choice of Israel. It implies the taking of a smaller number out of a larger. Vergil's *Eclogues* are short, selected excerpts from a more considerable collection of poems. The church is the called-out company of those who are incorporated into Christ. Before the foundations of the world were laid, God had determined that all who believed on his Son should be saved. As Allan puts it, the life of Christians depends on "a love that never began as well as a love that will never end" (p. 48).

Election in Christ has a moral aim in view. It is expressed both positively and negatively. To be "holy" (*hagios*) means to be set apart for God in order to reflect his purity. It is a matter not simply of imputed but actual righteousness. "Blameless" (*amōmos*) is "free from blemish," like the sacrificial animals presented on the altar in the old dispensation. It is applied to Christ himself (Heb 9:14; 1 Peter 1:19), to the ideal church (Eph 5:27), and to Christians at the end of the age (2 Peter 3:14; Jude 24) and also now (Phil 2:15).

5 The NIV takes "in love" (v.4) as starting a new sentence. That has the effect of emphasizing the loving nature of predestination. Any interpretation of this mysterious doctrine that detracts from the love of God is rightly suspect. Its positive intention is underlined here. It has to do with those who through Christ are to be received into God's family by adoption. Under Roman law, an adopted son enjoyed the same status and privileges as a real son. Christ is God's Son "by nature." Believers are so only by adoption and grace, yet they are co-heirs with him (Rom 8:17). The ground of this gracious action is to be discovered in the character of God himself. Behind the fulfillment of his perfect will there lies his pleasure (*eudokia*)—that which brings him satisfaction because it represents the expression of his being.

6 The ultimate aim throughout the divine plan of redemption is that the recognition of God's merciful dealings with men, which are his glory, should evoke unlimited praise. The grace that evokes such praise finds its richest outlet in God's love-gift to man—his Son. This is the grace with which he has "begraced" us, as the Greek literally has it (*echaritōsen*). The context may well vindicate the KJV paraphrase with its emphasis on acceptance—"wherein he hath made us accepted in the beloved." It is the objective grace of God that is in view, indicating his favorable regard, rather than the further ethical effect of that grace in making us gracious.

The Son is referred to as the one the Father loves. "Beloved" is a title applied in LXX to Israel in its special role as God's chosen race, along with "Servant" and "Elect." Because of his filial obedience, Jesus gains the Father's approval.

7 Paul proceeds to list some of the blessings that flow from the matchless grace of God. It may be that an early confession of faith underlies the text. These blessings are all "in

Christ" as being not only their source but their sphere (cf. Col 1:14). They are enjoyed by the believer in the present. The tense is continuous—"we have and are still having."

Redemption (*apolytrōsis*) has to do with the emancipation either of slaves or of prisoners. The NEB has "release." By derivation, the term also implies the payment of a ransom price and this factor is frequently reflected in its usage. Here it is specified as being "through his blood" (Col 1:20). The price paid for man's redemption from bondage to sin was costly beyond measure. It was the very lifeblood of Christ himself, poured out in death. As Leon Morris has shown, the Hebrews understood blood in the sense of "violent death" or "bloodshed" (*The Cross in the New Testament* [Exeter: Paternoster Press, 1965], p. 219). In a sacrificial context the likeliest meaning is not simply "life" but "life yielded up in death." Leviticus 17:11 is to be interpreted in these terms. What was foreshadowed in the Levitical system was realized at the Cross when the Son of God laid down his life in death and ransomed men from sin.

Forgiveness (*aphesis*) is loosing someone from what binds him. It stems from a verb meaning to send away (John 20:23). When God deals with our sin, it is dispatched into the wilderness like the scapegoat (Lev 16:20–22). Here, however, the reference is not to sin (*hamartia*) as in Colossians 1:14, but to sins (*paraptōma*) or deviations from the right path. The first term denotes a sinful condition; the second, sinful acts. Forgiveness deals with both. The magnanimity of God displayed in redemption and remission of sins is in proportion to the rich abundance of his grace. This is one of Paul's favorite expressions, occurring six times in Ephesians (also in 1:18; 2:4, 7; 3:8, 16). William Paley called it one of the apostle's "cant" words (*Horae Paulinae* [London: Faulder, 1790], ch. 6, no. 2).

8 These riches of grace have been showered on us in profusion, Paul continues, using another of his pet phrases. God is never niggardly in his giving. He always gives generously. Paul now enumerates further blessings. God's grace not only brings redemption and forgiveness but every kind of wisdom and insight as well (Col 1:9). Wisdom (*sophia*) is "the knowledge which sees into the heart of things, which knows them as they really are" (Robinson, p. 30). Insight (*phronēsis*) is the understanding and discernment that leads to right action. The sentence could mean that it was with his own wisdom and insight that God lavished his grace-gifts upon us, but the context (v.9) supports the interpretation that wisdom and insight are themselves among the *charismata* (cf. NEB "imparting").

9 What God has thus revealed has to do with his own will. It is not the mystery that is his will or originates from his will. It is the mystery concerning his will. "Mystery" is a recurring term in Ephesians (3:3, 4, 9; 5:32; 6:19). Here, as in the rest of the NT, it simply means a truth once hidden but now made known (Rom 11:25; Col 1:26; cf. Matt 13:11, 35). Both in Jewish apocalyptic literature and in the Qumran documents the word denotes the secret plan of God that will become apparent at the end of the age. But in the NT the unlocking of the mystery has now taken place in Christ and there is no need to wait till the last day in order to know what God's strategy is (TDNT, 4:819–822). The extent to which Christian writers recognized Christ as the fulfillment of messianic hopes is indicated by this transference. "Made known" (*gnōrisas*) denotes what has already happened when Christ came in the flesh. This affirmation may be intended to counteract the incipient Gnosticism appearing in Asia Minor as reflected in Colossians. "Us" does not apply exclusively to Paul or to the apostles. It covers all believers, whether Jews or Gentiles (cf. "we" in vv.11, 12).

All this is in accordance with God's "pleasure" (as in v.5), which has been set out (*proetheto*) in Christ (cf. v.11; Rom 1:13; 3:25). From all eternity the Father cherished in his own mind a plan that was to be carried out in Christ. This has now been revealed to the church through Paul. In the rest of Ephesians the content of the plan is more fully elaborated. Here the apostle restricts himself to a brief summary.

10 The word Paul uses is *oikonomia*, which occurs nine times in the NT (TDNT, 5:151–3). Its basic meaning relates to household management (Luke 16:2–4) and is extended to cover general provision or arrangement. Eventually it represents the divine government of the universe (*Epistle to Diognetus*, 4.5). Here Paul uses it to suggest the administration or putting into effect of God's far-reaching redemptive plan (3:9).

This takes place when the messianic age is inaugurated. Salvation history is regarded as unfolding in a series of "times" (NIV) or seasons (*kairoi*) that reach their climax in the advent of Christ (Gal 4:4). The Christian era has still to run its course, however, and not until its close will God's eternal purpose come to full fruition (Acts 1:6). Then universal reconciliation will be achieved. "All things" (*ta panta*) is literally "the all" (Col 1:17; Heb 1:3) and includes the whole creation. Everything in heaven and on earth will be subsumed under Christ (1 Cor 15:24–28; Phil 2:10, 11). The verb *anakephalaioō* ("to bring together") means to sum up together again (Rom 13:9). It is derived not from *kephalē* ("a head") but from *kephalaion* ("a summary, or sum total"). When a column of figures was added up, the total was placed at the top. At the end of the age everything will be seen to add up to Christ. This recognition of his preeminence will ensure that the original harmony of the universe is restored (Rom 8:18–21). The mission of Christ extends beyond the human race and assumes cosmic dimensions.

11 This ultimate reconciliation is brought about in Christ and so Paul passes on to a further consideration—namely, that Christians have been chosen as heirs (*eklērōthēmen*), or given their share in the heritage (NEB). Israel was regarded as the Lord's inheritance (*naḥalāh*) and portion (*ḥeleq*). The church as constituting the new Israel now enters into the same privilege (Rom 8:17; Gal 3:29; Col 1:12). This apportionment is said to stem from the divine foreordination (cf. vv.4, 5). It is no accident that God has allotted to his new people in Christ the inheritance designed for those who recognize the Savior. In no sense are we to think that Christians have somehow usurped Jewish privileges. Before time began, God marked out those in Christ to be co-heirs with his Son. Whatever he decides is put into effect, for he is the one who ensures that everything is worked out in line with his own will (cf. v.5).

12 So far, what Paul has written applies to Jews and Gentiles alike, united in the one body of Christ. Now he refers in turn to one class (v.12) and then to the other (vv.13, 14). The "first to hope in Christ" (literally, the Christ—the definite article is significant) were Jews who recognized their Messiah prior to the conversion of the Gentiles. This expectation of God's coming deliverer was distinctive to the Jews. The Gentiles entertained no such prospect (2:12). This appears to be the most satisfactory interpretation of *proelpizō* ("hope"), though some think that Paul had the apostles in mind as preceding other believers. In v.6 Paul shows that the adoption of Christians as sons furthers the p raise of God's glorious grace. Here he says that their participation in the divine inheritance will have a similar effect. The glory, or revealed character, of God will shine out through them and evoke praise from the whole universe (3:10).

13 "You also," in contrast to "we," clearly identifies the Gentile Christians in Ephesus (cf. 2:19). They are only addressed in this specific manner in order to remind them that they are fully incorporated into the body of Christ. Jews can no longer cling to their former prerogatives. Gentiles are equal partners and in every respect share the inheritance. In the Christian community there are no second class citizens.

It is the hearing of faith that brings salvation. This was how the Ephesians themselves came to be Christians. They embraced "the word of truth"—that is, the teaching that told them the truth because it was derived from the God of truth (Eph 4:21). The truth they needed to know was that as Gentiles they had a place in God's redemptive plan (2 Cor 6:7; Col 1:5; James 1:18). This was good news indeed and through accepting it they were liberated from bondage to sin.

Hearing, faith, and salvation were immediately followed by the sealing of the Holy Spirit. It was at the moment they believed that the Ephesian Christians received the stamp of the Spirit (cf. Acts 19:2). We are not to take this as a reference to circumcision (Rom 4:11) or to the tattooing of devotees at heathen shrines. Nor does Paul have water baptism primarily in mind, but rather what water baptism symbolizes—namely, the effusion of the Holy Spirit himself. He is made available to the believer according to the promises recorded in the OT and confirmed by Jesus. The Holy Spirit is at once the one promised, and the one in whom the promises are fulfilled. In view of v.14, Paul may also be thinking of him as the one who guarantees future promises.

The "seal" (*sphragis*) had various uses (MM, pp. 617, 618), all of which are instructive as applied to the Holy Spirit. It was affixed to a document to guarantee its genuineness. It was attached to goods in transit to indicate ownership and ensure protection. It also represented a designation of office in the state service.

14 Paul adds a further analogy: The Holy Spirit is a "deposit" (NIV) or an earnest—*arrabōn* (cf. 2 Cor 1:22; 5:5). The word is borrowed from the commercial world and means a deposit or first installment in hire purchase. It is a token payment assuring the vendor that the full amount will eventually follow. It can also be applied to an engagement ring (MM, p. 79). Paul regards the Holy Spirit as the first installment of the Christian's inheritance. At the end of the age God will redeem his pledge and open the treasuries of heaven to all who are his in Christ. Meanwhile, the Spirit gives us the assurance that these things will one day be ours.

Notes

3 Some take ἐν πάσῃ εὐλογίᾳ πνευματικῇ (en pasē eulogia pneumatikē) to mean "with every blessing of the Spirit." Had this been the intention, it would have been more naturally expressed by τοῦ πνεύματος (tou pneumatos, "of the Spirit"). What is in view here is not the source of these blessings but their nature, though, of course, the one determines the other.

The phrase ἐν τοῖς ἐπουρανίοις (en tois epouraniois, "in the heavenly realms") is peculiar to this Epistle, though the adjective occurs elsewhere in the NT. As R. Martin Pope has argued, it is used uniformly in Ephesians with reference to the unseen world (ExpT 23 [1912]: 365–368). It describes the sphere where "every spiritual blessing" is found. Syr. and Ethio. simply have "in heaven."

4,5 What does ἐν ἀγάπῃ (en agapē, "in love") qualify? It seems too remote from ἐξελέξατο (exelexato, "he chose"). Salmond (EGT, 3:250) allowed the possibility of retaining the connection with v.4 and yet interpreting it as divine love by relating it to the complete clause that it concludes. If it is attached to ἁγίους καὶ ἀμώμους (hagious kai amōmous, "holy and blameless"), then the reference is to the love Christians are to display (RV, NEB, JB). In the context, however, it is preferable to assume that it qualifies προορίσας (proorisas, "predestinating"), since it was Paul's aim to show that the divine predestination is motivated by love (cf. Hendriksen, p. 78n.).

8 NIV regards the verb ἐπερίσσευσεν (eperisseusen) as transitive, "lavished"; i.e., "made to abound" (so RV, RSV, NEB, JB, as in Gothic and Ethio.). KJV (with RV mg. following Syr., Vul., Armenian) has the intransitive " he hath abounded." While περισσεύω (perisseuō, "to abound") is usually intransitive in NT (as in classical Gr.), there are some instances of the transitive sense (Matt 13:12; Luke 15:17; 2 Cor 4:15; 9:8; 1 Thess 3:12), of which this appears to be one. As in v.6, ἧς (hēs, "that," "which") is attracted to the gen. of the antecedent. KJV assumes that the gen. hēs stands for the dative ἧ (hē, "in which"), but there is no NT precedent for such attraction.

9 By beginning a new sentence at v.9, NIV assumes that ἐν πάσῃ σοφίᾳ καὶ φρονήσει (en pasē sophia kai phronēsei, "with all wisdom and understanding") is connected with ἐπερίσσευσεν (eperisseusen, "he lavished") in v.8 rather than with γνωρίσας (gnōrisas, "making known"; NIV, "he made known") though the alternative in the footnote allows for the latter possibility. Whichever association is preferred, the reference is to the wisdom and understanding bestowed on believers by God, as Col 1:9 confirms. Πάσα σοφία (pasa sophia, "all wisdom") is not applicable to God, since it is an extensive definition suggesting growth from the partial toward the complete.

"In Christ" assumes the reading ἐν αὐτῷ (en autō, "in him") and is adopted by most modern translations, rather than ἐν αὑτῷ (en hautō, "in himself"), as in KJV. It is debatable whether the contract form of the reflexive in the third person is anywhere evidenced in NT (RHG, p. 226).

11 KJV has "in whom also" for ἐν ᾧ καί (en hō kai), but καί (kai) is clearly linked with the verb. The precise form of ἐκληρώθημεν (eklērōthēmen, "we were ... chosen") is uncertain, quite apart from the question as to whether κληρόω (klēroō) means simply "to appoint by lot" or necessarily involves the idea of inheritance (EGT, 3:263). The alternatives are: (a) passive for middle: "we have obtained an inheritance" (KJV); (b) simple passive: "we were chosen by lot" (Vul., Syr., Gothic, Geneva, Rheims); (c) passive with implicit accusative: "we were made partakers of an inheritance"; and (d) passive in a special sense: "we were made a heritage" (RV). If (b) is preferred (so NIV) the emphasis rests on choice rather than on "by lot," since it would be inappropriate to compare divine election with sortilege. If εἰς τὸ εἶναι ... (eis to einai ..., "in order that [we] ... might be") in v.12 is dependent on eklērōthēmen ("we were chosen"), this meaning is substantiated (BAG, p. 436).

12 The article with the participle τοὺς προηλπικότας (tous proēlpikotas, "the [ones] having previously hoped"; NIV, "the first to hope") stands in emphatic apposition with ἡμᾶς (hēmas, "we"). Attempts to construe tous proēlpikotas as the predicate (so Abbott, p. 21) would yield the sense "in order that we should be those who have before hoped in Christ." Usually, however, the article distinguishes subject from predicate. The prefix προ- (pro-, "before," "first") has been variously explained as applying to the time when Paul wrote, or the coming of Christ either in the incarnation or the parousia. It is probably best understood as meaning "before the conversion of the Gentiles."

14 The Chester Beatty Papyrus P[46] and some important uncials like Codex Alexandrinus (A) and Codex Vaticanus (B) read ὅ (ho, "which") for ὅς (hos, "who"). Normally, relative pronouns agree in gender with their antecedent but can be assimilated to the predicate (RHG, pp. 712–713). The personality of the Holy Spirit is not jeopardized by either usage.

2. A Prayer of Intercession

1:15–23

> [15]For this reason, I, since I heard about your faith in the Lord Jesus and your love for all the saints, [16]have never stopped giving thanks for you, remembering you in my prayers. [17]I keep asking that the God of our Lord Jesus Christ, the glorious Father, may give you the Spirit of wisdom and revelation, so that you may know him better. [18]I pray also that the eyes of your heart may be enlightened in order that you may know the hope to which he has called you, the riches of his glorious inheritance in the saints, [19]and his incomparably great power for us who believe. That power is like the working of his mighty strength, [20]which he exerted in Christ when he raised him from the dead and seated him at his right hand in the heavenly realms, [21]far above all rule and authority, power and dominion, and every title that can be given, not only in the present age but also in the one to come. [22]And God placed all things under his feet and appointed him to be head over everything for the church, [23]which is his body, the fullness of him who fills everything in every way.

The Christian *bᵉrākāh* ("blessing") in vv.3–14 has intervened between the opening salutation and the thanksgiving that normally follows it in Paul's letters. A similar pattern has been traced even in nonbiblical correspondence between those sharing a common religious allegiance. Although Paul uses the customary formula of gratitude in v.16, this section becomes a prayer of intercession from v.17 onwards.

15 Paul's thanksgiving for the spiritual progress of the Ephesian Christians arises out of what he has just written in vv.13, 14 ("you also"). "For this reason" (*dia touto*) is often used by Paul as marking a transition to a new paragraph. News had been brought to him in Rome about the continuing faith and love displayed by those whom he now addresses (cf. Philem 5). There is no need to assume that the reference is to their initial experience of Christ and that Paul therefore did not know them personally. On the other hand, if Ephesians is a circular letter, there may well have been some readers of his words who were not actually known to him. Faith finds its focus in Christ and expresses itself in love to others. Such outgoing love is the evidence of genuine faith (Gal 5:6).

16 Paul assures the Ephesians of his unremitting remembrance of them in his prayers by way of both thankfulness and intercession. He had already taken on similar responsibilities in relation to other churches. "Remembering" (*mneian poioumenos*) is "making mention" and implies that those for whom Paul interceded were actually named before God.

17 The apostle addresses his constant prayer on their behalf to the only one who is capable of answering it (v.3). "Glorious Father" is a typically Hebraic expression that points both to God's essential being and to what proceeds from it in mercy (v.7). Comparing Romans 6:4 and 1 Corinthians 6:14, Schlier (ibid.) observes that glory (*doxa*) and power (*dynamis*) are aspects of the same divine activity.

Paul is praying that his readers may be fully endowed with the Holy Spirit. God has already made provision for this. But it was necessary that they themselves should be quickened with the spiritual powers of wisdom and vision (NEB). "Revelation" (*apocalypsis*) seems to refer here to the insight and discernment the Spirit brings into the mysteries of divine truth (1 Cor 2:14, 16). All this is so that they may get to know God more completely. *Epignōsis* is the fullness of knowledge acquired through personal acquaintance (Trench, pp. 268, 269).

18 Paul now employs an unusual and figurative expression to denote an inner awareness. The "heart" in Scripture is the seat of thought and moral judgment as well as of feeling. This deep, interior enlightenment provided by the Holy Spirit leads the believer to realize all that God has made available to him. Three items are selected for particular attention. *Calling* (NIV, "called") is a favorite Pauline word. Here it is regarded as a pledge of hope. This call has already taken place (2 Tim 1:9) and yet represents an ongoing calling (1 Thess 2:12; 5:24). It looks to the future, since it is attached to the "blessed hope" (Titus 2:13) of eternal glory.

Secondly Paul wants his readers to appreciate that they inherit all the wealth of God himself, as he has already reminded them in vv.11, 14. The old Israel was promised an inheritance on earth; the new Israel is given an inheritance in heaven. The everlasting Canaan-rest of glory is assured all the saints, and God's faithfulness will be vindicated in them.

19 The final item Paul wants his readers to recognize is the enormous power of God. It is presented here as "incomparably great." Only Paul among the NT writers employs this term *hyperballon*. Literally, it suggests that the conception it is attached to is thrown over into another sphere altogether. This unimaginable potency is directed toward all who believe. Here is its intended destination.

Paul proceeds to collect all the synonyms he can lay hands on as he describes how the power (*dynamis*) of God functions according to the operation (*energeia*) of the strength (*kratos*) of his might (*ischys*). *Dynamis* is capability or potential; *energeia* is effective or operational power (3:7; 4:16); *kratos* is power exercised in resistance and control (6:10); *ischys*, used of bodily strength and muscular force, is inherent, vital power (6:10).

20 Having piled up the vocabulary of divine power, Paul shows where it was most impressively exerted (*enērgēsen*)—that is, in the resurrection of Christ from the dead and his subsequent exaltation to the place of authority. Paul has no hesitation in ascribing the resurrection of Jesus to the Father in accordance with other Scriptures. Yet Father and Son are so at one in this as in all things that our Lord could claim in John 10:18 that he had authority both to relinquish his life and to resume it again. Paul links with the resurrection the ascension and heavenly session of Christ. God not only raised his Son from the grave but exalted him to the seat of power. There is an allusion here to Psalm 110:1, which Houlden describes (p. 276) as the most universal early Christian proof-text. The exaltation of the king of Israel as the Lord's anointed was seen as finding its ultimate application in Christ. Although spatial imagery is involved, we are not to think of God's right hand as a place but as a symbol of authority. Similarly, the heavenly realms are not to be identified with outer space (cf. v.3).

21 "Far above" (as in 4:10 and Heb 9:5) is not a dimensional expression but simply indicates the superiority of Christ. "Rule" (*archē*), "authority" (*exousia*), "power" (*dynamis*), and "dominion" (*kyriotētos*) are not to be classified in a graded series nor should we ask whether the ranks are arranged in ascending or descending order. The titles no doubt reflect the various degrees of angels in the Jewish hierarchy. Angels were thought to control human destiny, but Paul sees Christ as controlling them with absolute authority because he is infinitely superior. Paul then proceeds to use a comprehensive phrase ("every title that can be given") to include not only those names known now by men living on earth but also those that will be used in the age to come. The familiar apocalyptic contrast between the present era and the messianic age was adopted by writers in the early church who nevertheless recognized that for those in Christ the last time had already begun.

22 The apostle underlines the exaltation of Christ in a further independent sentence that winds up the opening chapter of Ephesians. The verb *hypotassō* refers not only to the supremacy of Christ but also to the subjection of all things to him. Paul has already employed similar terms (cf. 1 Cor 15:27). Psalm 8:6 (LXX) is clearly in his mind (cf. Heb 2:8). The Psalmist affirms man's dominion on earth. Here Paul claims that Christ, as God's new man, has universal dominion. Man largely forfeited his status through sin but through Christ as the ideal man he is restored to his proper dignity. So far from constituting a threat to the realization of true humanity, the Christian gospel provides the only means by which it can be attained. Only at the end of the age will the consummation take place when death itself has been finally overcome, yet even now the Christian becomes a new creation in Christ Jesus (2 Cor 5:17).

We might have expected the apostle to explain as elsewhere that, as head over everything, Christ is head of his body, the company of believers. But that is not how he puts it. Instead, he says that Christ in his exaltation over the universe is God's gift to the church. He is "the head over every power and authority" (Col 2:10) and as such is bestowed on the church. "There is given to the Church, and for the Church's benefit, a head who is also head over all things. The Church has authority and power to overcome all opposition because her leader and head is Lord of all" (Foulkes, p. 65).

23 The church is described as Christ's body (Col 1:18). It is so not only in symbol but in fact. Paul uses the same language later in Ephesians (4:4, 12, 16; 5:30). The church is not an institution but an organism. It exists and functions only by reason of its vital relationship with the risen Lord who is its Head. This picture of the church as a body deriving life and power from its Head is developed only in Colossians and Ephesians. In Paul's earlier letters the church is regarded as a body because its members are coordinated in a common function: the place of Christ as the head is not stressed (Rom 12:4, 5; 1 Cor 10:17; 12:22-27; but cf. 1 Cor 11:3).

The church, which is the body of Christ, is further described as "the fullness of him who fills everything in every way." The precise significance of these enigmatic words has been widely discussed and commentators vary considerably in their interpretations (cf. TDNT, 6:304). *Plērōma* here may mean: (a) that which is filled with Christ. The sense would then be that the church contains the fullness of Christ (so NEB); (b) that which is filled by Christ. The church is filled by Christ not only with his own life and presence but also with the gifts and blessings he bestows; (c) that which fills up Christ. *Plērōma* can refer to a complement. Is Paul saying here that Christ is in some sense made more complete by the church? Robinson paraphrases: "so that Christ may have no part lacking, but may be wholly completed and fulfilled" (p. 250). But is Christ in any sense incomplete? To make the church essential to the full being of Christ is to reverse the true relationship. The NT regards Christ as essential to the full being of the church, not vice versa; (d) he who is the fullness of God. This alternative regards "which is his body" as parenthetical and takes Paul to mean that in Christ the fullness of God is perpetually resident (Col 2:9). This, of course, is true but unlikely to be what Paul is saying here.

Of these possibilities, the first (or perhaps a combination of the first and second) seems preferable. The church is filled with (and by) Christ. As his body, it manifests him to the world, but it can do so only as he fills it with himself (Col 3:19) and with all the grace-gifts he bestows (Eph 4:7, 11; cf. 1 Cor 12:1–11). But the Christ who fills the church also fills the universe, so that the church is "the fullness of him who fills the whole creation" (JB). Christ is at once immanent within the church and transcendent over it, as he is both within and above the cosmos. This carefully balanced statement of Christ's role was designed to encourage the church militant here on earth.

Notes

---

15 Τὴν ἀγάπην (tēn agapēn, "[the] love") is absent from Codex Sinaiticus (ℵ) as from P⁴⁶ A and B. The parallel in Col 1:4 as well as the general sense favors inclusion with the corrected text of ℵ, other uncials, and versions. The omission is readily accounted for by homoeoarcton as the copyist's eye apparently passed from the first to the second τὴν (tēn).

17 The force of ἵνα (hina, "so that") here has been debated. Is it to be regarded as final ("in order that") or does it merely indicate a result? In Col 1:9 the preceding verb is αἰτούμενοι (aitoumenoi, "asking") and what follows is the content of the request. Here the idea of purpose is more prominent. The volitive use of the optative after hina is evidenced in the classics (RHG, p. 983).

   Is πνεῦμα (pneuma, "spirit") to be understood as referring to the Holy Spirit or subjectively to the human spirit? The absence of the article is not decisive, for anarthrous pneuma often designates the Holy Spirit (cf. Gal 5:5, 16). Salmond's arguments for the objective interpretation are impressive (EGT, 3:274). It should be remembered, however, that here as elsewhere in the NT the interaction of the Holy Spirit and the responsive human pneuma is so close as not to be easily distinguishable.

18 TR διανοίας (dianoias; KJV, "understanding") is poorly attested, and καρδίας (kardias, "heart") is to be read on strong authority. The syntax of the sentence presents complex problems. Three constructions are possible: (a) accusative absolute, in which πεφωτισμένους (pephōtismenous, "having been enlightened") agrees with ὀφθαλμοὺς (ophthalmous, "eyes"): "the eyes of your heart being enlightened"; (b) apposition with πνεῦμα (pneuma, "spirit") and dependent on δώῃ (dōē, "may give") in v.17: "may give you the Spirit, i.e., the eyes of your heart enlightened"; c. anacoluthon with πεφωτισμένους (pephōtismenous, "having been enlightened") standing for πεφωτισμένοις (pephōtismenois, "the ones having been enlightened") and referring to ὑμῖν (hymin, "you") in v.17; τοὺς ὀφθαλμοὺς (tous ophthalmous, "the eyes") being the accusative of nearer definition: "so that you may be enlightened as to the eyes of your heart."

20 The reading ἐνήργηκεν (enērgēken, "he has exerted") is to be preferred to ἐνήργησεν (enērgēsen, "he exerted"). The perfect is more appropriate "because the effect continues while the separate acts in which this ἐνεργεῖν realized itself follow in aorists" (Abbott, p. 31). Textually, it is the more difficult to account for (in view of the succeeding aorists) and therefore more probable.

   The reading adopted by UBS on good evidence is καθίσας (kathisas, "having seated"), a causative participle. A few authorities add αὐτον (auton, "him"). TR ἐκάθισεν (ekathisen, "he seated") is found in some uncials and most MSS, with Coptic, Syr., et al. The latter throws more emphasis on ἐγείρας (egeiras, "raising"; NIV, "when he raised") as the supreme instance of the divine power.

23 Πληρουμένου (plēroumenou, "filling"; NIV, "fills") may be either middle or passive. Lenski regarded it as a true middle, retaining its proper reflexive force and conveying the idea that Christ fills all things for himself. Other exegetes interpret it as a middle with an active meaning and this rendering is found in some of the versions (Armenian, Coptic, Gothic, Syr.²). The sense of filling is certainly appropriate to the context (EGT, 3:281) as we have shown. But some question the grammatical grounds for taking plēroumenou as virtually active. When Paul does speak of Christ ascending "in order to fill the whole universe" (4:10), the unambiguously active

32

voice is used. The passive sense is supported by some early versions (Syr.[1], Coptic, Bohairic, and Sahidic). In this case πάντο ἐν πᾶσιν (*panta en pasin*, "all in all"; NIV, "everything in every way") is to be understood adverbially. The body of Christ is "the fullness of him who all in all is being fulfilled" (cf. Robinson, pp. 42–45).

---

3. *Life From Death*

2:1–10

[1]As for you, you were dead in your transgressions and sins, [2]in which you used to live when you followed the ways of this world and of the ruler of the kingdom of the air, the spirit who is now at work in those who are disobedient. [3]All of us also lived among them at one time, gratifying the cravings of our sinful nature and following its desires and thoughts. Like the rest, we were by nature objects of wrath. [4]But because of his great love for us, God, who is rich in mercy, [5]made us alive with Christ even when we were dead in transgressions—it is by grace you have been saved. [6]And God raised us up with Christ and seated us with him in the heavenly realms in Christ Jesus, [7]in order that in the coming ages he might show the incomparable riches of his grace, expressed in his kindness to us in Christ Jesus. [8]For it is by grace you have been saved, through faith—and this not from yourselves, it is the gift of God—[9]not by works, so that no one can boast. [10]For we are God's workmanship, created in Christ Jesus to do good works, which God prepared in advance for us to do.

The second chapter of Ephesians is an extension and elaboration of the first. In vv.1–10 the theme of redemption (1:7) is developed in terms of God's raising of man from the death of sin to the new life in Christ. Zerwick (p. 45) dubs this section the shorter epistle to the Romans, because it condenses the distinctive doctrinal contents of what Paul had already expounded at greater length. From v.11 on, the theme of reconciliation of 1:10, 22, 23 applies to the relationship between Jews and Gentiles in the church. Throughout the chapter Paul is contrasting man prior to the revelation of faith with man under faith, to use Bultmann's captions.

D.M. Stanley (*Catholic Biblical Quarterly*, 23, 1961, pp. 37, 38) has drawn attention to the resemblances between Ephesians 2 and the parable of the two sons in Luke 15:11–32 (cf. Eph 2:4 = Luke 15:20; Eph 2:1 = Luke 15:24, 32; Eph 2:13 = Luke 15:15; Eph 2:19 = Luke 15:22; Eph 2:14–16 = Luke 15:28–32).

1 "As for you" resumes the second person of 1:13, 15–18 and anticipates v.11 ("you who are Gentiles by birth"). However, as v.3 makes clear, the Jews are in no better condition, for man's sinful nature is shared by all alike (cf. Rom 2). Redemption has made it possible for man to be brought from death to life (v.5). The reference is to the spiritual deadness that characterizes man without God (Col 2:13). He is utterly unable to meet the requirements of the divine law (Rom 7:9). Paul is not speaking about physical death nor only about the sinner's ultimate fate in the second death. Nor again is the expression merely figurative. As Calvin insisted (in loc.), what is meant is "a real and present death." The most vital part of man's personality—the spirit—is dead to the most important factor in life—God.

"Transgressions" (*paraptōmata*) are lapses, while "sins" (*hamartiai*) are shortcomings. We need not follow Jerome in finding here a distinction between thoughts and deeds. The repetition simply serves to underscore the multiplicity of ways in which man's spiritual death is evidenced.

2 Verses 2–4 represent a typically Pauline digression. The mention of "transgressions and sins" in v.1 leads the apostle to supply a fuller account than he had intended of the Ephesians' former way of life. As a result, he does not pick up the thread of his original sentence until v.5. KJV promotes the main verb ("made alive") to v.1 to preserve the unity of a lengthy sentence in Greek. Modern translations break up the passage but tend to obscure its overall thrust.

To "live" (*peripateō*) is literally to walk about. It is the customary word in LXX for manner of life, particularly in the Psalms. The usage is carried over into the NT and is prominent in Paul's writings. It recurs in this letter in 2:10; 4:17; 5:2. The Ephesians' former walk-about, Paul adds, was in accordance with the age (*aiōn*) of this world (*kosmos*). He combines two expressions that elsewhere he has used separately. They are found in successive verses in 1 Corinthians 3:18, 19 but only here compositely. The terms represent the same idea from the standpoints of time and space respectively.

Houlden (p. 281) wonders whether *aiōn* is intended to represent the devil, as it might well have done for the Jews (cf. 1 Cor 2:8). Whether this is so or not, the evil one is certainly identified in the two clauses that follow. He is the "ruler" (*archōn*) of a realm said to be "of the air" (*tou aeros*). Taken literally, this would signify the atmosphere around the earth, which, according to ancient cosmology, is the abode of demons. Is Paul here adopting the traditional scheme of the rabbis or employing a figure of speech to suggest the sphere of Satan's dominion? Hendriksen (p. 114) has strongly argued that the literal meaning is basic, without assuming that Paul has accommodated his thinking to current belief.

Satan is the unholy spirit (1 Cor 2:12) who apes the operations of his divine counterpart by being constantly at work. The verb (*energountos*, "operating"; NIV, "at work") is deliberately chosen to imply rivalry with the Holy Spirit (cf. Eph 1:19, 20). "Sons of disobedience" (NIV, "those who are disobedient") is a Hebrew turn of phrase disclosing the fact that rebellion against God and refusal to believe in him is inherent in man (Eph 5:16; cf. Col 3:6 mg.).

3 "Among them" (*en hois*) refers to the disobedient rather than to "transgressions and sins" (v.1). "Lived" (*anestraphēmen*) is a different verb from the one used in v.2, though the meaning is similar. It is to turn to and fro and hence to behave or act in accordance with certain principles (BAG, p. 60). So far Paul has been depicting the former state of the Gentile Christians. Now he admits that the Jewish believers were in no better case, for they too once lived an earth-bound life in the grip of sin. Nor does he exclude himself from this general indictment ("all of us"), despite his claim to have been technically blameless under the law (Phil 3:6; but cf. Rom 7:7–11).

The past life of Jewish Christians, like that of the Gentiles, was dominated by the appeal of fallen nature. The flesh (*sarx*) is not merely the body but "the whole man orientated away from God and towards its own selfish concerns" (Houlden, p. 282). The word translated "cravings" (*epithymiai*) is here used in its bad sense; it can also stand for legitimate desire. The plural suggests the multiplicity of such urges in the un-redeemed personality. "Following" is actually "doing" (*poiountes*), and "desires" (*thelē-mata*) are rather "dictates" or "demands" (literally, "things willed"). "Thoughts" (*dianoiai*) refers not to the mind itself but to the projects it entertains with uncontrolled abandon. The natural man is altogether at the mercy of the tyrant self and its rash impulses.

Because of all this, the Jewish converts were just as much in danger of judgment as anyone else. The phrase "objects [literally, children] of wrath" (*tekna orgēs*) is a Semitism to denote those who deserve God's punishment. "By nature" (*physei*) contrasts with "by grace" in vv.5, 8. If he prefers to stand on his own and refuses to accept what God has done for him in Christ, man is self-condemned.

4 Over against man's churlish rejection of God, Paul sets God's gracious acceptance of man in Christ. Though he cannot approve of sin if he is to remain righteous, God is not hostile toward those he has created. He loves them and has made possible their reconciliation to himself. Had he decided to destroy his refractory children, he would have been entirely justified, and nothing could have averted the catastrophe (Hos 13:9). Instead, love led to "mercy" (*eleos*). That is God's compassion for the helpless, issuing in action for their relief. The same word can be used of men, but in the NT it has a special reference to what God does in Christ. There is an inexhaustible treasury of such mercy in the loving heart of God.

5 As we have seen, the main verb of this extended sentence in the Greek does not emerge until this verse. What Paul wants to say in the opening paragraph of Ephesians 2 is that God "made us alive with Christ" (*synezoōpoiēsen*, cf. Col 2:15). This is the first of three verbs prefixed by *syn-* (with) that describe what God has done in Christ for every Christian. The other two are in v.6. Here Paul declares that when they were spiritually dead in transgressions (cf. v.1), God gave them new life together with Christ. This is not the language of mysticism but of fact. The life Christians now possess is an effect of which Christ's resurrection was the cause.

Christ's revivification was by an act of God's power. The regeneration of believers is by an act of God's grace. Hence Paul is prompted to make a bold, definitive assertion that is reiterated in v.8. As Scott recognized, "the central idea of Paul's whole theology here finds expression" (p. 164). Salvation is viewed retrospectively. The Ephesians are now in the position of having been saved (*sesōsmenoi*).

6 Two more verbs prefixed by *syn-* suggest what else God has done in Christ. He has raised us up with him (*synēgeiren*, cf. Col 2:12). Christ was not only raised; he actually left the tomb and appeared to his disciples. As Paul has already insisted in Ephesians 1:20, this was a work of omnipotence. God has also enthroned us with Christ (*synekathisen*) "in the heavenly realms" (*en tois epouraniois*). Forty days after the resurrection Jesus ascended to the right hand of the Father (Eph 1:20, 21). Both these events have their counterpart in the experience of believers. Not only do they anticipate and assure resurrection and glorification at the end of the age; they are matched by a present realization of the risen life in Christ and of participation with him in his ascended majesty (Col 3:1–4).

7 All this was done by God in Christ with a single end in view. It was to demonstrate in successive ages "the surpassing wealth of his grace" (William Barclay, *The New Testament: A New Translation* [London: Collins, 1969], 2:119). This was God's publicity program for the whole of history—and beyond. He planned a continuing exhibition of his favor toward man to cover all the centuries between the ascension and the return of Christ, and after that through all eternity (cf. Jude 25). This eschatological dimension implies that it will be for the benefit of angels as well as men. Paul repeatedly refers in Ephesians to the divine affluence (1:7, 18; 2:4, 7; 3:8, 16). He has already used the superlative *hyperballon* (1:19) and will do so again (3:19). "Kindness" (*chrēstotēs*) occurs only in Pauline writings. Trench (pp. 219, 220) supports the Rheims version, which translates it as "benignity" (Gal 5:22) and "sweetness" (2 Cor 6:6). It is love in tender action. God showed his kindness to man when it was most needed (Rom 5:8).

8 Yet again Paul reminds his readers (as in v.5) that they owe their salvation entirely to the undeserved favor of God. Grace is at once the objective, operative, and instrumental cause. He expands the previous statement by adding that the subjective medium (or apprehending cause) of salvation is faith, which is also its necessary condition. Faith, however, is not a quality, a virtue, or a faculty. It is not something man can produce. It is simply a trustful response that is itself evoked by the Holy Spirit.

Lest faith should be in any way misinterpreted as man's contribution to his own salvation, Paul immediately adds a rider to explain that nothing is of our own doing but everything is in the gift of God. Does "and this" (kai touto) connect with "faith," with "saved," or with the entire clause? Probably the latter interpretation is preferable. Hence Barclay translates: "The whole process comes from nothing that we have done or could do." The element of "givenness" applies to faith as well as to grace, for faith is a direct outcome of hearing the saving message (Rom 10:17).

9 With typically Pauline firmness, he excludes every possibility of self-achieved salvation. As if it were insufficient that he should have insisted in v.8 "and this not from yourselves," he adds, "not by works." The apostle does not specify these "works" (erga) as related to the law, since he is not thinking only of Jewish Christians. Any kind of human self-effort is comprehensively ruled out by this terse expression. The reason is immediately attached. It is to prevent the slightest self-congratulation. If salvation is by the sheer unmerited favor of God, boasting is altogether out of place.

10 This is by no means a subsidiary postscript to the paragraph. It is the outcome of the whole. It shows what salvation is for: it is intended to produce the good works that attest its reality. Works play no part at all in securing salvation. But afterwards Christians will prove their faith by works. Here Paul shows himself at one with James, despite the attempt of some to drive a wedge between them (James 2:14–26).

We are God's "workmanship," his "poem" (poiēma) or, as JB has it, his "work of art." The reference is to the new creation, as the rest of the verse makes clear. The verb (ktizō, "to create"; Heb. bārāh) is used only of God and denotes the creative energy he alone can exert. "In Christ Jesus" is emphatic as in vv.6, 7. The life of goodness that regeneration produces has been prepared for believers to "do"—Greek, "walk about in" (peripateō)—from all eternity. The road is already built. Here is a further reason why the Christian has nothing left to boast about. Even the good he now does has its source in God, who has made it possible.

Notes

1 "In your transgressions and sins" is a dative without the preposition—τοῖς παραπτώμασιν καὶ ταῖς ἁμαρτίαις ὑμῶν (tois paraptōmasin kai tais hamartiais hymōn). Syntactically, it could be taken as instrumental: "dead by reason of or due to your transgressions and sins." Many favor "through" (RV, RSV, JB, Amplified Bible). TEV has "because of." But if the meaning had been "put to death by" we would have expected a past instead of a present participle (cf. v.5). On the same grounds the sense "dead to your transgressions and sins" (cf. Rom 6:2, 11) is excluded.

Moule has "in respect of" as indicating the conditioning circumstances. NIV (with KJV, BV, Moff.) assumes that the dative is attached to νεκρούς (*nekrous,* "dead") by way of definition, as in Col 2:14. The parallel passage in Col 2:13 makes it clear that uncircumcision is not the cause of death. Robinson concludes, "We cannot render the dative better than by the preposition 'in' " (p. 153).

TR omitted ὑμῶν (*hymōn,* "your"). It is inserted in UBS on good authority (ℵ B D Syr., Vul., et al.). The reading of A is ἑαυτων (*heautōn,* "yourselves").

4 The participial clause πλούσιος ὢν ἐν ἐλέει (*plousios ōn en eleei,* "being rich in mercy") was thought by Abbott (p. 46) to assign a reason (i.e., "because he is"). Ellicott (p. 37) considered it a secondary predicate of time characterizing the general principle under which the divine compassion is exhibited ("since he is"), the more particular motive being stated in what follows. In classical Gr. πλούσιος (*plousios,* "rich") is normally construed with a gen. of the thing but in NT with ἐν (*en,* "in").

5 The perfect ἐστε σεσωσμένοι (*este sesōsmenoi,* "you have been saved"; cf. v.8) connects the past with the present and shows that those addressed are now still in the position of having been saved. The aorist in Rom 8:24 is appropriate in the context of hope as referring to the initial moment of salvation. Here in the context of grace a resultant condition is in view. This is to be distinguished from the present process of preservation (BAG, p. 17; 1 Cor 1:18; 15:2; 2 Cor 2:15). J.H. Moulton, however, endorsed the tr. "by grace have ye been saved" (RV) as suggesting that on the divine side the work of redemption stands fulfilled, although it has yet to be fully realized in the believer (*A Grammar of the Greek New Testament,* vol. 1, *Prolegomena* [Edinburgh: T & T. Clark, 1906²], p. 127).

7 What is the scope of ἐν τοῖς αἰῶσιν τοῖς ἐπερχομένοις (*en tois aiōsin tois eperchomenois,* "in the coming ages")? Is it simply another form of ὁ αἰὼν ὁ μέλλων (*ho aiōn ho mellōn,* "the coming age")? The pl. appears to preclude such an interpretation. Paul distinguished this age from that which was to come (1:21), but it is not certain that he envisaged successive ages after the present. Expressions like εἰς τοὺς αἰῶνας τῶν αἰώνων (*eis tous aiōnas tōn aiōnōn,* "to the ages of ages") simply mean "to all eternity" (BAG, p. 26). H. Sasse (TDNT, 1:206) insists that the pl. here is to be understood in the light of the eternity formulae. Again, the present participle ἐπερχόμενος (*eperchomenos,* "coming [on]") suggests that the coming ages are those that extend from the ascension of Christ (v.6) and thus include the present age as well as that beyond the parousia.

8 To what does τοῦτο (*touto,* "this") refer? The neuter is compatible with διὰ πίστεως (*dia pisteōs,* "through faith") or again it might be related to a verbal notion derived from πίστις (*pistis,* "faith"). Against this, however, is the connection with οὐκ ἐξ ὑμῶν (*ouk ex hymōn,* "not from yourselves") and οὐκ ἐξ ἔργων (*ouk ex ergōn,* "not of works"). To state that faith is neither of ourselves nor of works is to elaborate the obvious. For these reasons most modern commentators refer καὶ τοῦτο (*kai touto,* "and this") either to ἐστε σεσωσμένοι (*este sesōsmenoi,* "you have been saved") or preferably to the complete clause (RHG, p. 1182).

10 The construction of οἷς προητοίμασεν ὁ θεὸς (*hois proētoimasen ho theos,* "which God prepared in advance") has been much discussed. The οἷς (*hois,* "which") relates to ἐπι ἔργοις ἀγαθοῖς (*epi ergois agathois,* "to [do] good works") in the previous verse and cannot be regarded as masc.: "for whom he previously prepared." Nor is the compound verb to be taken as intransitive, with *hois* as the dative of reference: "for which God made previous preparation." The verb is transitive, but a dative of destination is unlikely, since it would demand the insertion of ἡμας (*hēmas,* "us"): "for which God previously prepared us." It is simplest to regard *hois* as a dative by attraction for ἃ (*ha,* "which" [neut.]) with BAG, p. 712: "which God previously prepared."

4. Jews and Gentiles Reconciled

2:11–22

[11]Therefore, remember that formerly you who are Gentiles by birth and called "uncircumcised" by those who call themselves "the circumcision" (that done in the body by the hands of men)— [12]remember that at that time you were separate from Christ, excluded from citizenship in Israel and foreigners to the covenants of the promise, without hope and without God in the world. [13]But now in Christ Jesus you who once were far away have been brought near through the blood of Christ.

[14]For he himself is our peace, who has made the two one and has destroyed the barrier, the dividing wall of hostility, [15]by abolishing in his flesh the law with its commandments and regulations. His purpose was to create in himself one new man out of the two, thus making peace, [16]and in this one body to reconcile both of them to God through the cross, by which he put to death their hostility. [17]He came and preached peace to you who were far away and peace to those who were near. [18]For through him we both have access to the Father by one Spirit.

[19]Consequently, you are no longer foreigners and aliens, but fellow citizens with God's people and members of God's household, [20]built on the foundation of the apostles and prophets, with Christ Jesus himself as the chief cornerstone. [21]In him the whole building is joined together and rises to become a holy temple in the Lord. [22]And in him you too are being built together to become a dwelling in which God lives by his Spirit.

In vv.1–10 Paul has considered the moral condition of the Gentiles before their conversion to Christianity. Now he reminds them of their previous deprivation in terms of their religious status as estimated from a Jewish point of view.

Some see traces of liturgical elements in this section. While accepting Pauline authorship, Gottfried Schille regards vv.14–18 as comprising early Christian hymn (*Liturgisches Gut im Epheserbrief*, unpublished doctoral dissertation [Göttingen, 1952]). Whereas vv.11–13 and 19–22 are addressed to the readers, vv.14–18 are couched in the first person plural and may thus reflect a community confession of faith. Wolfgang Nauck finds a baptismal poem (*tauflied*) in vv.19–22, while Kirby (pp. 156, 157) divides the section into two strophes (11–16; 17–22) with inverted parallelism.

11 "Therefore" refers back not simply to v.10 but to the entire paragraph (vv.1–10), which presents a single sentence in the Greek text. Second-generation Gentile Christians, such as those now emerging in the Ephesian churches, were apt to forget their former disadvantages. They had been and indeed still were "the Gentiles" (*ta ethnē*; Heb., *haggôyîm*): the article specifies the underprivileged group to which they belonged. They were non-Jews or pagans so far as their physical descent was concerned (*en sarki*, "in the flesh"). The rest of the verse elaborates on the distinction by citing the contemptuous nickname attached to them by the Jews: "uncircumcised" (*akrobustia*, "foreskin"). Paul does not himself use it in a derogatory manner: he simply reports its currency. As a Jew, however, he is quick to point out that the self-styled circumcisionists have nothing to boast about, since an external man-made mark in itself holds no spiritual significance. The real circumcision is of the heart (Gal 5:6). Circumcision used to be a token of the covenant, but its function ceased when redemption was finally accomplished in Christ.

12 The suspended sentence is continued as the apostle urges the Ephesians to recollect what they once were in their heathen state. Four successive phrases depict their debits as compared with those of the Jews (cf. Rom 9:4, 5). In the first place, they were without or apart (NIV, "separate") from Christ (*chōris Christou*). They had no expectation of a Messiah to light up their darkness. They knew nothing at all about him. They had no rights of citizenship (*politeia*) in his kingdom. They were cut off from any such privilege by reason of their birth. *Politeia* is used in contrast with the more intimate expression "members of God's household" in v.19. The word can signify a commonwealth or state. It may even mean a constitution, in which case the contents might be regarded as legal enactments establishing Israel as the people of God (cf. Exod 24:1–11).

The Gentiles were not entitled to the benefits accruing to the covenantal community. In this respect, they were in the position of aliens who could not claim the prerogatives of nationals. As a consequence, they lived in a world devoid of hope (1 Thess 4:13). They were, moreover, "without God" (*atheoi*). This does not imply that they were forsaken by God, but that, since they were ignorant of him (Gal 4:8), they did not believe in him. Paul does not reproach the Gentiles by his use of the epithet. He merely records the sad truth of the matter. The pathos of their plight lay here.

13 Quickly and eagerly Paul turns from the tragedy of the Gentiles' former desolation to the joy of their reconciliation in Christ. "But now" stands in sharp antithesis to v.12. They are no longer "separate from Christ" (v.12) but "in Christ Jesus." He is the sphere of their new possibilities. The historical name *Jesus* is added at this point to suggest that he is not only the anticipated Messiah of the Jews but the Savior of all. Those who trust in him possess a present salvation as well as a future hope. "Jesus is the 'meeting point' with God for all mankind" (Thompson, p. 48).

"Far away" (*makran*) and "near" (*engys*) are Hebrew expressions to describe the position of Gentiles and Jews. The original reference related to distance from Jerusalem. Midrashic interpretations applied the terms to Gentiles and Jews (cf. on Esth 3:9—"No nation is near to God except Israel"). God's word of peace to both groups is recorded by Isaiah 57:19 and fulfilled through the sacrifice of Christ on Calvary (cf. Eph 1:7; 2:17). Notice the centrality of the atonement again in v.15 ("in his flesh") and v.16 ("through the cross").

14 "He himself " (*autos*) is emphatic (cf. v.15, "in himself "). Christ and no other "has solved the problem of our relationships with God and man" (Barclay, p. 120). He draws men to God and to each other in his own person. It is not simply the message he proclaimed or even the message proclaimed about him that effects this reconciliation. It is himself. There is an echo here of Micah 5:5. "Peace" is recognized by the Talmud as a name for God. So Paul can announce that Christ is peace as well as life (Col 3:4) and hope (Col 1:27). The "I am" sayings recorded in the Fourth Gospel provided a foundation in the claims of Jesus for such assertions.

Christ is both peace and peacemaker. He actually brought about the reconciliation of Jew and Gentile when he died on the cross. There he made both into one (cf. vv.15, 16). Paul thinks of two parts being united as one whole. Then he personalizes it and speaks of two men being recreated as one new man. As Chrysostom explained, it is not that Christ has brought one up to the level of the other, but that he has produced a greater: "as if one should melt down one statue of silver and another of lead, and the two together should come out gold" (in loc.). Christ has thus removed the hostility (*echthran*) that existed between these deeply divided groups. The battlement created by hatred has been broken down forever.

This Paul describes as a "barrier" (*phragmos*) and as a "dividing wall" (*mesotoichon*).

39

The first word means simply a "fence" or "railing." The second is much rarer and is literally a "middle wall" (KJV). Josephus used each of these terms separately with reference to the balustrade in the Jerusalem temple separating the court of the Gentiles from ·the temple proper. On it was an inscription that read: "No foreigner may enter within the barricade which surrounds the sanctuary and enclosure. Anyone who is caught doing so will have himself to blame for his ensuing death."

When Jerusalem fell in A.D. 70, this partition was demolished along with the temple itself. But Paul saw it as already destroyed by Christ at the cross. Ironically enough, he himself had been wrongfully accused of taking an Asian Gentile, Trophimus, past this checkpoint (Acts 21:29).

Paul's language here also recalls the common rabbinic idea of the law as a fence dividing the Jews by their observance of it from all other races and thus arousing hostility (*Letter of Aristeas*, p. 139). There may be a further cross-reference to Psalm 80:12 where in LXX *phragmos* is used. The breaking down of the protecting wall that surrounded Israel the vine prepares the way for God's strong man equipped for service (Ps 80:17). Some wonder whether there is an allusion to the Gnostic conception of a wall dividing heaven from earth and its counterpart in philosophical Judaism (cf. 1 Enoch 14:9), but this is less probable.

15 The barrier between Jews and Gentiles was overthrown when Christ effectively disposed of the old law with its meticulously defined sanctions enshrined in its innumerable decrees. Paul explains elsewhere that in itself the law is right and good, but that unregenerate man is incapable of complying with its demands (Rom 3:19–31; 7:7–12; 8:2–4). A somewhat cumbersome phrase (literally, "the law of the commandments in decrees") covers the Mosaic ordinances regarded as a statutory legal code. "Regulations" (*dogmata*) was applied to imperial edicts. "Abolishing" (*katargēsas*, "having abolished") is a favorite Pauline verb not easy to translate. Literally it is to make ineffective or powerless. In Luke 13:7 it refers to ground exhausted by a barren tree. There are instances in the papyri where it means to bring to a standstill or to put out of action (MM, p. 331). Eventually it signifies to invalidate, nullify, quash. F. W. Grosheide thinks that Paul has in mind especially the ceremonial law (*Die Brief Van Paulus Aan De Efeziers* [Kampen, 1960], p. 45), but its application would appear to include the totality of the law considered as a moral burden.

It was in his crucified flesh that our Lord accomplished the annulment of the law (cf. v.17), "so that he might bring into existence" (*hina . . . ktisē*) the new humanity of which he himself as the second Adam is the Head. The Christian is no hybrid but a new creation (v.10). Here was how Christ became "the divine atonemaker" as Tyndale put it (cf. v.14). Some commentators find a eucharistic dimension in the reference to Christ's flesh.

16 The uniquely Pauline verb *apokatalassō* ("to reconcile"; cf. Col 1:20, 22) involves the idea of restoration to a primitive unity (Eph 1:10). The purpose of Christ when he died on the cross was not simply that Jews and Gentiles should be reconciled to each other (v.15), but that both of them together should be reconciled to God. "This one body" is neither the crucified nor the glorified body of Christ, which would be "his body" (1 Peter 2:24). Some take it to be the "one new man" (v.15) of redeemed humanity regarded in terms of corporate personality. E.E. Best, however, argues from other Pauline allusions to "the new man" (Eph 4:24; Col 3:10) that the concept is individualistic. In addition to the Jew and the Gentile, a third type of person has now appeared—the Christian (*One Body in Christ* [London: S.P.C.K., 1955], pp. 153, 154). "This one body" therefore refers to the church (as elsewhere in Ephesians 1:23; 3:6), which in Colossians 3:15 is depicted as the place of peace.

This reconciliation has been brought about "through the cross" and it was "by it" (*en autō*) that the death blow was dealt to the longstanding antipathy between Jew and Gentile and between man and God. So Scott can allude to "the destruction of everything that meant disunion" (p. 173).

17 Another factor in the reconciliation is now added as an independent affirmation. When did Christ come to bring the good news of peace, so that Gentiles far away as well as Jews near at hand could hear it? Clearly it was not during his earthly ministry prior to the cross. Was it after the resurrection and before his ascension? Was it not rather by the Spirit and through the apostles, as the missionary program of the infant church was inaugurated in obedience to the Great Commission (Matt 28:20)? Notice that the once-alienated Gentiles are now accorded priority, though in point of historical fact the gospel was taken first to the Jews.

18 It is solely through Christ ("him" is emphatic) that both Jews and Gentiles now (present tense) have their "access" (*prosagōgē*) to God the Father. In the papyri the word sometimes denotes a landing stage (MM, p. 545; TDNT, 1:133). Again, the *prosagōgeis* was the official in an oriental court who conducted visitors into the king's presence. Simpson (p. 63) considered these possibilities too abstract and preferred the translation "footing."

Is this approach to the Father ensured "by one Spirit" (i.e., the Holy Spirit; cf. 1 Cor 12:13), or "in one spirit" (i.e., the unity in the body of Christ created by the Holy Spirit)? Some believe that the sequence of correspondences favors the latter: one part (v.14), one man (v.15), one body (v.16), one spirit (v.18). If, however, we follow the NIV in referring it to the Holy Spirit, then the trinitarian implications of this verse are obvious.

19 Using a formula he is especially fond of ("consequently," *ara oun*), Paul draws a conclusion from the previous paragraph (vv.14–18). Verses 19–22 represent a further expansion of v.13. Two technical terms commonly denoting inferiority of status are contrasted with *sympolitai* ("fellow citizens"). The first (*xenoi*) applies to "foreigners" in general but in particular to short-term transients. The other (*paroikoi*) were the resident "aliens" who had settled in the country of their choice. The *paroikos* was "a licensed sojourner in a town whose protection and status were secured by the payment of a small tax" (MM, p. 496; cf. TDNT, 5:583). He had no intrinsic rights, however. Such had been the position of the Gentiles in relation to the kingdom of God before the coming of Christ.

But now they enjoy all the privileges of God's new people. They are united with the saints of the past (Eph 1:18) as well as with contemporary Christians. This togetherness is stressed again in vv.21, 22. The Gentiles are not only *sympolitai* but *oikeioi tou theou*, "members of God's household." Wycliffe has "household men of God." As Abbott explained, the phrase describes the theocracy in its domestic aspect.

20 "Built" (*epoikodomēthentes*) picks up *oikeioi* and allows Paul to develop a favorite metaphor of his. When they became Christians, the Gentiles were immediately placed on a firm foundation. From 1 Corinthians 3:11 we learn that this is Christ himself as revealer and redeemer. Some would take it that Paul is here referring to Christ as the foundation on which the apostles and prophets themselves built, or on which they themselves were built, or which they themselves laid and on which others are built. The most obvious interpretation, however, is that the apostles and prophets themselves constitute the foundation as being closely associated with Christ in the establishment of the church. They were the witnesses of his resurrection appearances and the preachers of the good news. "The Church rests on the total unique Event of which Christ is the centre, but in which the apostles and prophets, filled and guided by the Spirit, and doing their work in unique closeness to Christ, had an indispensable and untransmissible part" (Allan, p. 88).

Apostles and prophets head the list of leaders in the church set out in Ephesians 4:11 (cf. 1 Cor 12:28-30). The apostles included Paul himself, although he speaks quite objectively. The prophets were those of the new Israel, not the old, who would have been mentioned first. In 1 Corinthians 3:11 (cf. Isa 28:16) Christ is the foundation: here he is the cornerstone of the building. The word *akrogōniaios* ("cornerstone") literally means at the tip of the angle. It refers to the capstone or binding stone that holds the whole structure together (TDNT, 1:792). It covered a right angle joining two walls, as Sir Henry Layard found, for example, when excavating Nineveh. Often the royal name was inscribed on it. In the East it was considered to be even more important than the foundation.

21 In an example of what Trench called biblical allegory, with figure and reality alternating, Paul expounds the significance of the building. The function of the cornerstone (v.20) is precisely defined by the verb "joined together" (*synarmologoumenē*), found only here and in Ephesians 4:16 in the NT. It embraces the complicated process of masonry by which stones are fitted together. JB has "aligned on him."

Paul refers to all building (*pasa oikodomē;* NIV, "the whole building") rather than to each separate building. The absence of the article implies that the work is still in progress, so the phrase really means "all building that is being done." "Rises" (*auxei*), with its present tense, strengthens the insistence on continuing progress and indeed organic growth. The word used for temple is not *hieron,* which includes the entire precincts, but *naos,* the inner shrine. The temple image is applied in the NT both to the individual and the church. For three hundred years Christians had no buildings of their own. The true temple is the whole church.

Without doubt, Paul had the Jewish temple in mind. But was there a collateral reference to the pagan sanctuaries as well, and in particular to the famous temple of Artemis at Ephesus, which was one of the seven wonders of the world? Hendriksen (pp. 144–146) believes that certain facts favor the supposition—especially the way in which Paul's mission in Ephesus had brought him into head-on collision with the cult of the goddess (Acts 19:23–41). Moreover, the *cella* or inner shrine was the most important part of the Ephesian temple, since it housed the statue of Artemis. The same analogy was shared by the Qumran community, but it is unlikely that Paul was indebted to it.

22 "In him" continues the theme of v.21 (cf. Eph 1:11, 12) and "you too" links with v.13. The emphasis on continued building is brought out by the present tense of *synoikodomeisthe* ("being built together"). The aim of the process is that the church should become God's residence (*katoikētērios*). The term occurs only here and in Revelation 18:2 in the NT but is frequent in LXX to denote the divine resting place either on earth or in heaven. Formerly, God's earthly abode was thought to be on Mount Zion and in the Jerusalem temple. Now he makes his abode in the church. All this is achieved not only *by* but *in* the Spirit. He is at once the means and the element.

Notes

14 The gen. τοῦ φραγμοῦ (tou phragmou, "of partition"; NIV, "dividing") is not simply equivalent to an adjective or participle. It has been explained as a gen. of quality—"the dividing wall that has the character of forming a barrier" (this seems superfluous)—or of origin—"the dividing wall made from the barrier." A possessive gen. is possible—"the dividing wall belonging to the barrier." But the most satisfactory solution is to consider it a gen. of apposition or identification —"the dividing wall that is the barrier" (cf. RHG, p. 498).

A further question arises as to whether τὴν ἔχθραν (tēn echthran, "hostility") is to be associated with what precedes or with what follows, and whether ἐν τῇ σαρκὶ αὐτοῦ (en tē sarki autou, "in his flesh") goes with λύσας (lysas, "having destroyed") or with καταργήσας (katargēsas, "having abolished"). NIV connects tēn echthran with lysas and en tē sarki autou with katargēsas as do RSV and the Amplified Bible. NEB and TEV take both with lysas, whereas others take both with katargēsas, including KJV, ASV, RV, JB, BV, PH, and Moff.

16 Ἐν αὐτῷ (en autō, "in him[self]"; NIV, "by which") relates to διὰ τοῦ σταυροῦ (dia tou staurou, "through the cross"). In it or by it (i.e., the cross), Christ killed the enmity that had existed between Jews and Gentiles. Alford has "on it." Some refer it to ἐν ἑνὶ σώματι (en heni sōmati, "in one body") interpreted as the physical body of Christ. An indifferently attested variant reading has ἐν ἑαυτῷ (en heautō, "in himself"). Apart from this, some take en autō to be reflexive on the basis of v.15 (KJV mg.).

17 The repetition of εἰρήνη (eirēnē, "peace"), as in NIV, is supported by good textual authority (P⁴⁶ א A B D, etc., with Vul. and other versions, except Syr.).

20 The nature of the gen. in τῶν ἀποστόλων καὶ προφητῶν (tōn apostolōn kai prophētōn, "of the apostles and prophets") has been variously understood. Both the possessive and reflexive senses appear to confuse the foundation with Christ the cornerstone. If the gen. indicates the agent or originating cause, then the reference is to the message preached by the apostles and prophets (cf. Rom 15:20; 1 Cor 3:10; Heb 6:1). This interpretation has claimed wide support. It hardly seems as relevant to the context as in 1 Corinthians 3:10, where the building itself is doctrinal. Here it is personal; for this reason it is perhaps best to accept the most obvious meaning and to recognize a gen. of apposition; that is, the apostles and prophets being the foundation (Rev 21:14; cf. RHG, p. 131, 498).

21 The reading πᾶσα ἡ οἰκοδομή (pasa hē oikodomē, "the whole building") is attested by the first corrector of א together with A and C plus some minuscules and versions. The article is absent from the original text of א as well as from B and D with many minuscules and church fathers. Erroneous insertion or omission is improbable and, since intentional insertion is more conceivable than intentional deletion, pasa oikodomē stands in UBS.

Πᾶς (pas, "all") without the article signifies "the whole" only before proper names, mostly geographic (BAG, p. 637), and on occasion with nouns that have acquired a fixed meaning. It is far from certain that πᾶσα οἰκοδομὴ (pasa oikodomē, "the whole building") qualifies for inclusion in this category. Commentators connect ἐν κυρίῳ (en kyriō, "in the Lord") with αὔξει (auxei, "grows"; NIV, "rises"), which seems tautologous; with ἅγιον (hagion, "holy [in the Lord]"; or with ναός (naos, "a temple [in the Lord]"). Salmond argued (EGT, 3:301) that it really qualifies the whole statement about joining and growing, but this is already implied by ἐν ᾧ (en ho, "in whom"; NIV, "in him"). It is best to link it with εἰς ναὸν ἅγιον (eis naon hagion, "into a holy temple") as a phrase, especially in view of its verbal juxtaposition.

5. Grace and Apostleship

3:1-13

¹For this reason I, Paul, the prisoner of Christ Jesus for the sake of you Gentiles—

²Surely you have heard about the administration of God's grace that was given to me for you, ³that is, the mystery made known to me by revelation, as I have already written briefly. ⁴In reading this, then, you will be able to understand my insight into the mystery of Christ, ⁵which was not made known to men in other generations as it has now been revealed by the Spirit to God's holy apostles and prophets. ⁶This mystery is that through the gospel the Gentiles are heirs together with Israel, members together of one body, and sharers together in the promise in Christ Jesus.

⁷I became a servant of this gospel by the gift of God's grace given me through the working of his power. ⁸Although I am less than the least of all God's people, this grace was given me: to preach to the Gentiles the unsearchable riches of Christ, ⁹and to make plain to everyone my administration of this mystery, which for ages past was kept hidden in God, who created all things. ¹⁰His intent was that now, through the church, the manifold wisdom of God should be made known to the rulers and authorities in the heavenly realms, ¹¹according to his eternal purpose which he accomplished in Christ Jesus our Lord. ¹²In him and through faith in him we may approach God with freedom and confidence. ¹³I ask you, therefore, not to be discouraged because of my sufferings for you, which are your glory.

Paul continues the prayer that he began in the opening chapter and has never really abandoned, despite asides and digressions. Once again, however, there is an interruption, for no sooner has he announced in v.1 that it is for the sake of the Gentiles that he finds himself under house arrest than he is diverted from his main theme (resumed in v.14) as he explains how his ministry as the apostle to the nations was given to him. What prompts this parenthesis in vv.2–13 is the mention of his imprisonment in v.1. He hastens to assure the Ephesians that his present circumstances are not to be regarded as a hindrance to his apostolate (v.13). The b^erākāh ("blessing") is taken up again from v.14 to the end of the chapter.

1 "For this reason" (*toutou charin*) is repeated in v.14, when the thread of Paul's discourse is picked up once more. The immediate connection is with Ephesians 2:22, but Paul recalls 2:11–22 and perhaps what lies even further back than that. The nominative "I, Paul" is left suspended without a verb until v.14, where it is at last supplied—"I kneel." Having identified himself by name, Paul is reminded of his captivity in Rome. "He hears as it were the clink of his chain, and remembers where he is and why he is there" (Robinson, p. 74). He refuses to regard himself as a victim either of the Jews or of the Roman emperor Nero. He is "the prisoner of Christ Jesus." No doubt his detractors mocked his plight and tried to undermine the faith of those he wrote to. He insists that his imprisonment is a mark of his apostleship.

Furthermore, it was championship of the Gentile cause that had brought about his arrest in Jerusalem (Acts 21:21, 28). It was on account of an Ephesian convert, Trophimus, that he had eventually fallen foul of the Jewish mob. "You Gentiles" follows on from Ephesians 2:11.

2 Paul elaborates on what is involved in his ministry as a preacher to the Gentiles. He assumes that his readers are aware of his special commission. Some have detected an element of doubt in "surely" (*ei ge*) and then wondered whether Paul could have written like this to any who knew him or even knew of him. But the expression is presumptive rather than suppositional. When Paul uses the same formula in Ephesians 4:21 he is not suggesting for a moment that his readers had never heard of Christ! Either from Paul

himself when he was with them or by report from others, the Ephesian Christians were acquainted with the apostle's unique ministry.

Paul refers to it as an "administration" (*oikonomia*) of divine grace. The term is usually equivalent to stewardship or task (Col 1:25). Here and in Ephesians 1:9, however, it is to be interpreted rather as the implementation of a strategy. Paul is not now referring to saving grace as in Ephesians 2:5, 8 but to the equipment that enabled him to fulfill his calling as a missionary to the Gentiles (cf. vv.7, 8; 4:7–13). Despite his personal unworthiness as one who had persecuted the church of God, Paul was God's chosen instrument to carry his name before the Gentiles as well as to Israel (Acts 9:15). Furthermore, Paul recognizes that the extension of gospel privileges to the Gentiles is itself an act of grace (Acts 11:23). Grace implies "givenness" and Paul underlines this factor. But he adds that such grace was given him for their benefit.

3 The nature of this administration of grace now becomes clear. It has to do with the "mystery" or secret plan (Eph 1:9) by which God determined to incorporate the Gentiles into the one body of the church (2:16) as equal partners with Israel (3:6). This was disclosed (*egnōristhē*, "made known") by means of direct revelation or spiritual enlightenment (1:18). No doubt the reference is to Paul's experience on the Damascus road when he was commissioned as the apostle to the Gentiles. He adds that he has already dealt with this subject in passing, presumably in the previous part of his letter. Some have speculated about another now unknown manifesto explaining his position. Others have asked whether Galatians 1 is in mind. But it is much more likely that the apostle is directing his readers to what he has written to them, for example in Ephesians 2:11–22 or even 1:9, 10. "Briefly" (*en oligō*) means in a few words or a short space. More often it is used of time, though hardly so here.

4 As they thus reread the earlier portions of the Epistle, the Ephesians will be able to judge for themselves whether Paul has really grasped the essence of God's secret plan. "In reading this" (*pros ho . . . anaginōskontes*) seems to refer to v.3b rather than to the general reading of the Scriptures before the congregation. Hort took the allusion to be to the OT prophecies (*Prolegomena to . . . Ephesians*, pp. 150, 151). The verb, however, is often used of apostolic writings and suggests that it is what Paul himself has composed. "Understand" (*noēsai*) is to receive into the mind (*nous*) or perceive (RV). An element of intellectual discrimination is implied. "Insight" (*synesis*) results from the revelation (v.3) and represents the profound comprehension God grants his own (BAG, p. 796). In Colossians 1:27, the "mystery" of Christ is his residence in or among believers, giving them an expectation of future glory. Here it has to do with the inclusion of the Gentiles as those who now inherit such promises (cf. v.6). There is thus no incompatibility between these two aspects of what Paul understands by *mystērion*.

5 Although the blessing of the Gentiles through the people of God was revealed in the OT from Genesis 12:3 onward, it was not proclaimed so fully or so extensively as under the new dispensation. In particular, it was not realized that the old theocracy would be superseded by the body of Christ composed of Jews and Gentiles forming "one new man" (Eph 2:15). "Men" is literally "the sons of men," a Hebraism common in LXX but occurring only once elsewhere in the NT (Mark 3:28). It is not intended as a contrast with "holy apostles and prophets" as being men of God, but rather with "sons of Israel"— the normal designation of Jews. Nor is Paul making the point that men whose fathers were only mere men were incapable of appropriating these truths under the old cove-

45

nant. They were in themselves no more capable after Christ came than before. The apostle is stressing the fact that the mystery had not yet been universally revealed.

This further disclosure was made to the whole church of Christ (Eph 1:8-10, 17, 18) through the "apostles and prophets" (2:20), of whom Paul was one. Indeed, he was the first to receive this truth that was not immediately recognized by the rest. Apostles and prophets are designated as "holy" because they were set apart for the special task of proclaiming Christ. Paul is not arrogantly assuming moral superiority (cf. v.8), nor must it be supposed that he himself could not possibly have written like this and that therefore another author must be postulated. On the contrary, he displays here a serene and modest objectivity.

The instrument of revelation, as always, is the Holy Spirit. There may well be a subtly ambiguous allusion here, as elsewhere in the NT (cf. Rom 1:4, NEB) to the interplay between the Holy Spirit and the human spirit (Eph 1:17; cf. 2:22; 5:18). This is particularly relevant in the context of revelation.

6 The content of the mystery is now stated, summarizing Ephesians 2:11-22. It is that, through the proclamation of the gospel, the Gentiles are received into the fellowship of Christ on an equal footing with Hebrew Christians. This is what Findlay called "their investiture into the franchise of faith" (p. 160). Paul declares that the Gentiles now "*are* heirs together with Israel"—not "should be" (KJV).

Three terms are used, each prefixed by *syn-* ("with" or "co-"; NIV, "together"). Paul is partial to such compounds. The first of these is co-heirs (*sygklēronoma*). In Romans 8:17 Paul speaks of believers being co-heirs with Christ. Here, as in Galatians 3:29 and 4:7, he stresses the fact that in Christ Gentiles are co-inheritors of the kingdom along with the Jews. This is how far the new "withness" of Jew and Gentile stretches. But it extends even further. They are co-members of the same body (*syssoma*) and hence enjoy a corporate relationship. The term *syssoma*, which may have been coined by Paul to meet the unique situation created by the gospel, is found only here in the NT and is afterwards exclusive to Christian writers (BAG, p. 802). No other society is comparable with the Christian church, since Christ is its Head (Eph 4:15; 5:23; Col 1:18). Co-partners or "sharers together" (NIV; *symmetocha*) recurs in Ephesians 5:7 in a different context and stands in contrast with 2:12. Because of Christ, Gentiles are fellow partakers (RV) of the covenant promise made originally though never isolationally to the Jews. This union of Jews and Gentiles in one body, which was so astonishing to all who saw it, is a logical consequence of the central doctrine of the gospel that God accepts all who believe.

7 Paul explains how he himself was enlisted in the service of this gospel, not through any ambition or qualification of his own but solely through the gift and calling of God (v.2; cf. Col 1:23, 25). "I became" is preferred by the NIV to "I was made" (KJV, RSV, NEB) as a rendering of *egenēthēn*. Eduard Schweizer has shown that the Greek language was particularly rich in the vocabulary of high office (*Church Order in the New Testament*, Eng. T. [London: S.C.M., 1961], pp. 171, 172). The NT rejects almost all such titles and fixes on a word altogether unassociated with prestige (cf. Eph 6:21). The servant (*diakonos*) is a table waiter who is always at the bidding of his customers (so in Xenophon, Polybius, Lucian, etc.; cf. BAG, p. 183). The term is used in the NT to denote one who lives and works in the service of Christ and the church.

Once again, as in v.2, Paul stresses the givenness of his apostolic function (cf. also v.8) and adds that it came from God "through the working [*energeia*] of his power [*dyna-*

mis]." He recognizes that the dramatic intervention that transformed him from an enemy into a friend of Christ was nothing less than an act of divine omnipotence. Now his apostleship reflects God's power at work in the church (Eph 1:19, 20).

8 "Given me" forms a link with v.7 (cf. v.2). "Less than the least" (*elachistoterō*) is a unique combination of comparative and superlative. Literally it is "leaster" or "more least." Perhaps there is a playful allusion to his own name (v.1) meaning "little" (*paulos*). In 2 Corinthians 12:11 he acknowledges that in himself he is a nobody while at the same time recognizing that God has made him a somebody. Such humility is an essential qualification for effective service. Beare rightly sees here "the most serious hurdle which confronts those who deny the authenticity of the epistle" (IB, 10:669). Is it conceivable that an admirer of Paul, writing in his name to enhance his reputation in the late-first-century church, would ascribe such a self-demoting confession to him?

Paul's God-given commission is to announce the good news of Christ to the Gentiles. It is the business of an apostle to preach (*euangelisasthai*) to others in continuation of Christ's own ministry (Eph 2:17). "Unsearchable" (*anexichniastos*) is that which cannot be traced out. It is a favorite word in Job in relation to the inscrutability of God's ways and recurs in this context in Romans 11:33. Here, however, the accent lies on the boundless treasury of riches in Christ—"a wealth the limit of which no man can ever find" (Barclay, p. 121). The figurative sense of "riches" (*ploutos*) has no biblical parallel outside the Pauline corpus. Of fourteen occurrences, five are in Ephesians (Eph 1:7, 18; 2:7; 3:8, 16).

9 Paul was called to "make plain" (*phōtisai*) to everyone the outworking of this secret plan of God. He was to shed a flood of light on it, so that no one need to be in the dark about it anymore. A derivative meaning of *phōtizō* as the equivalent of to teach is found in LXX, but in the NT the reference is always directly to light. It either means to light up in the physical sense, to enlighten spiritually or, as here, to bring to light what has previously been hidden.

This mystery (v.6), now available to all, was for long ages consciously concealed in the mind of God so as not to be known even to angelic intelligences (Col 1:26). The phrase *apo tōn aiōnōn* (from the ages) could also mean from the eons regarded as personified powers like those mentioned in the next verse. This was no arbitrary or accidental reticence on God's part: it was in accordance with his deliberate policy. His counsel was formed before time began (1 Cor 2:7), but the concealment dated from the inception of the ages (Rom 16:25). It was in his capacity as the universal Creator that God thus determined what his strategy would be, and the inference is that the world was brought into being with the realization of this purpose in view (Eph 1:9, 10). "God, who created all things" may be directed against heretical teachers in Asia who anticipated the Gnostic dichotomy between creation and redemption, ascribing the former to subordinate agencies.

10 The ultimate goal both of creation and redemption is the manifestation of the divine wisdom. In particular, the commission Paul himself has received to proclaim the mystery is designed to promote this objective as the church becomes its instrument. What had been screened from the angelic hierarchy is now to be declared through the body of Christ on earth (Eph 2:6, 7). The ecclesiological implications of such a verse as this are staggering indeed (cf. 1 Peter 1:12). "The Church becomes a mirror through which the bright ones of heaven see the glory of God. And in order to show them this glory, God committed the gospel to Paul" (Beet, p. 319). Hendriksen (pp. 158–160) sets out cogent reasons for assuming that the reference is only to benign and not to malignant powers. For "rulers" (*archai*) and "authorities" (*exousiai*), see on Ephesians 1:21.

"Manifold" (*polypoikilos*) is a poetical adjective meaning "very varied." Euripides used it of multicolored cloth and Eubulus of flowers. Nowadays it is a technical term in geology, specifying unusually assorted crystals. The wisdom of God displayed in creation and embodied in Christ is a many-splendored thing, iridescent with constantly unfolding beauties.

11 Again Paul reverts to the overall "purpose" (*prothesis*) of God recognizable through all his dealings (Eph 1:11). In Aristotle *prothesis* (literally, "presentation") is used in rhetoric for the statement of a case. In other classical writers it frequently denotes a deliberate plan or scheme (BAG, p. 713). The plural *aiōniōn* ("of the ages"; NIV, "eternal") suggests not only the infinite length but also the complexity of God's agelong purpose (Heb 1:1). "Eternal" places the ages prior to time but, as Lenski (p. 483) points out, in v.9 the "ages past" appear to begin in time and end with Christ. This purpose God "accomplished" (*epoiēsen*, literally, "did" or "made") in Christ. Paul has more than its conception and predetermination in mind here. He is concerned with its historical realization (NEB has "achieved"). The addition of "in Christ Jesus our Lord" would appear to confirm this (Eph 2:7).

12 A practical conclusion is drawn from these considerations. The centrality of Christ has a bearing on the devotional life of believers. It is in Christ and on the ground of faith in him that we can enter God's presence (Eph 2:18) without the inhibitions that might arise from any sort of self-reliance and self-consciousness. "Freedom" (*parrhēsia*) is liberty of speech (literally, "telling all"). It is normally used in relation to men (Eph 6:20), but here and elsewhere (though only once again in Paul) in relation to God. Such openness of speech leads to confidence (*pepoithēsis*) before God, because he graciously accepts those who come to him through Christ. *Pepoithēsis* is found six times in the NT, all in Paul. In turn, after enjoying such freedom of access to God, the Christian acquires a new boldness before men (Eph 6:19).

13 Paul rounds off his account (begun in v.2) of the administration of God's grace that has been entrusted to him. He makes a request, arising from what he had said in v.1 about his imprisonment. There he had made it clear that what he endured was for the sake of the Gentiles. Now he repeats the assertion that his sufferings are for them, but he begs them not to lose heart because of his predicament. The verb *enkakein* means "to become good for nothing," "to grow faint," and hence "to be discouraged" (NIV). Paul uses it five times in his letters: it occurs only once elsewhere in the NT (Luke 18:1).

No subject of the infinitive "to be discouraged" is indicated in the Greek and various possibilities have been proposed. It is improbable that he is asking (or praying) that he himself may not be disheartened. He may be reassuring his readers by confiding in them that he is praying for them to be preserved from despair, but this would anticipate v.16. It is more satisfactory to regard this, as NEB and NIV do, as an entreaty addressed to the Ephesians in which he pleads with them on no account to be perturbed about his "sufferings" (literally, "pressures"). He has learned to take his share of Christ's continuing passion (Col 1:24). E.E. Best, following E.H. Lohmeyer, thinks that the cross reference is to the Messiah's birth pangs to be completed before his return and that Paul seeks to hasten the parousia by exhausting them in himself (*One Body in Christ* [London:

S.P.C.K., 1955], pp. 134–136). Whether that is so or not, they represent the price to be paid for the blessing that has come to the Gentiles. Paul saw his trials as their glory and they must learn to look at them like that too.

Notes

1 The construction is difficult and capable of more than one resolution. The simplest is to supply εἰμί (eimi, "am") after ὁ δέσμιος τοῦ Χριστοῦ Ἰησοῦ (ho desmios tou Christou Iēsou, "the prisoner of Christ Jesus"). This, however, accords an undue prominence to Paul's own deprivations and detracts from the force of ὑπὲρ ὑμῶν (hyper hymōn, "for the sake of you"). In any case, we would not expect the article before δέσμιος (desmios, "prisoner"). On the analogy of Ephesians 4:1, ὁ δέσμιος (ho desmios, "the prisoner") may be taken as in apposition with ἐγὼ Παῦλος (egō Paulos, "I Paul"), the construction being resumed at v.14 with a repeated τούτου χάριν (toutou charin, "for this reason"). Some consider the digression in vv.2–13 to be inadvertent, but Lenski (p. 463) claimed that it is intentional. Ἰησοῦ (Iēsou, "Jesus") is dubiously supported. Some texts insert πρεσβεύω (presbeuō, "I am an ambassador").
2 The idiomatic combination of the particles εἰ (ei, "if") and γε (ge, "indeed") implies a definite assumption: "inasmuch as" (BAG, p. 152; NIV, "surely"). Though the protasis is conditional, its effect is to affirm rather than to deny or dispute (2 Cor 5:3; Eph 4:21; Col 1:23).
3 TR has ἐγνώρισε (egnōrise), which underlies KJV "he made known." The superior reading ἐγνωρίσθη (egnōristhē) is attested by ℵ A B C and other uncials.
Ἐν ὀλίγῳ (en oligō) is equivalent to ἐν βραχεῖ (en brachei) in classical Gr. and means "in brief " (BAG, p. 566). Some connect it with the prefix of προέγραψα (proegrapsa, "I have already written") as if it meant "a short time before," which would in fact be πρὸ ὀλίγου (pro oligou).
4 The gen. τοῦ Χριστοῦ (tou Christou, "of Christ") attached to μυστηρίον (mystērion, "mystery") could be taken as originative—the mystery of which Christ is the author; possessive—the mystery belonging to Christ; appositional—the mystery which is Christ; or objective—the mystery relating to Christ. The last is probably to be preferred. Colossians 1:27, which has been invoked to support the third possibility, is hardly a valid parallel, since there the mystery is "Christ in you."
6 The insertion of αὐτοῦ (autou, "his") after τῆς ἐπαγγελίας (tēs epangelias) is not found in the best authorities and is to be discounted. The reading ἐν τῷ Χριστῷ (en tō Christō, "in the Christ") yields to ἐν Χριστῷ Ἰησοῦ (en Christō Iēsou, "in Christ Jesus") on similar evidence.
7 The less usual ἐγενήθην (egenēthēn, "I became") given by ℵ B and the corrected text of D, supersedes ἐγενόμην (egenomēn, "we became") of TR. The sense, however, is unaffected since egenēthēn is simply a Doric equivalent of egenomēn, which passed into LXX and later Gr. The deponent passive form has an active meaning.
The reading τῆς δοθείσης (tēs dotheisēs, "given") qualifying χάριτος (charitos, "grace") is preferable to the accusative τὴν δοθεῖσαν (tēn dotheisan) qualifying δωρεὰν (dōrean, "gift"). The gen. in charitos is one of definition (cf. χάρις, charis, in v.8), i.e., the gift consisting in the grace, or grace-gift (almost equivalent to charisma). The reference is not to the general bestowal of the Holy Spirit but to a particular endowment, namely that which enabled Paul to fulfill his apostolic vocation as a preacher to the Gentiles (vv.2, 8).
9 Πάντας (pantas, "to everyone") is read by P[46] ℵ[c] B with other uncials, minuscules, and versions, though absent from the uncorrected text of ℵ A and some minuscules. The verb φωτίζω (phōtizō, "to make plain") usually has an accusative in NT and, if pantas is not original, its insertion is explicable on syntactical grounds. The argument cuts both ways, however, and could be used to sustain the originality of pantas, though it would be harder to account for its disappearance from some texts. If pantas is excluded, the sense is as RV mg.: "to bring to light what is" the administration of the mystery. As Abbott (p. 87) observed, the general meaning is

much the same with either reading, since the result of bringing the οἰκονομία (*oikonomia*, "administration") to light is that all are enabled to recognize it (cf. Hendriksen, p. 157).

10 "His intent was" translates the conjunction ἵνα (*hina*, "[so] that") and connects it with ἐν τῷ θεῷ (*en tō theō*, "in God") in the previous verse. Others relate it to the whole of the preceding sentence. It could be attached to οἰκονομία (*oikonomia*, "administration") as defining the end in view when Paul was entrusted with his administration of the mystery. Again, γνωρισθῇ (*gnōristhē*, "might be made known") may stand in antithesis to ἀποκεκρυμμένου (*apokekrymmenou*, "which was kept hidden") in v.9 as does νῦν (*nun*, "now") to ἀπὸ τῶν αἰώνων (*apo tōn aiōnōn*, "from the ages"; NIV, "for ages past"), with *hina* indicating that the former concealment of the mystery was designed to pave the way for the manifestation of God's wisdom in its disclosure and realization. If *hina* is linked with its immediate antecedent at the end of v.9 in the reference to creation, we are confronted with the startling concept that when God brought the cosmos into being, his intent was to display his many-sided wisdom through the church to the angelic hosts. As often in the use of *hina*, purpose and result cannot be clearly differentiated and both elements may well be represented here (BAG, p. 378).

6. Knowledge and Fullness

3:14-21

> [14]For this reason I kneel before the Father, [15]from whom the whole family of believers in heaven and on earth derives its name. [16]I pray that out of his glorious riches he may strengthen you with power through his Spirit in your inner being, [17]so that Christ may dwell in your hearts through faith. And I pray that you, being rooted and established in love, [18]may have power, together with all the saints, to grasp how wide and long and high and deep is the love of Christ, [19]and to know this love that surpasses knowledge—that you may be filled to the measure of all the fullness of God.
> [20]Now to him who is able to do immeasurably more than all we ask or imagine, according to his power that is at work within us, [21]to him be glory in the church and in Christ Jesus throughout all generations, for ever and ever! Amen.

This section contains what Simpson calls "Paul's enraptured supplication" (p. 78). After the parenthesis in vv.2-13, the apostle resumes his prayer, comprising three major petitions (vv. 16, 17a; 17b–19a; 19b), the first two of which lead into the next with the last preparing for the closing doxology (vv.20, 21). Kirby (p. 129) notes the trinitarian outline of this prayer, in which the apostle asks that his readers may possess the strength of the Spirit (v.16), the indwelling of Christ (v.17), and the fullness of God (v.19).

14 "For this reason" (*toutou charin*) is repeated from v.1 as Paul proceeds along the line he had digressed from in vv.2-13. It is because the Gentile Christians are now incorporated into the body of Christ that he prays that they may appropriate their spiritual privileges to the full. Paul says he "kneels" (*kamptō ta gonata mou*, "I bend my knees"). Standing was the more normal posture among the Jews but kneeling was not unknown. Eusebius referred to it as the familiar custom of Christians. It symbolizes submissiveness, solemnity, and adoration. Paul turns in prayer to the Father. "Before" (*pros*) is a face-to-face preposition applicable to an intimate relationship. He addresses God as Father because through the redemptive act of Christ access is now made possible to him through the Spirit (Eph 2:18).

15 The Father is the One after whom "the whole family" (*pasa patria*) is named. There

is a deliberate play on the similar sounding words *patera* ("Father") in v.14 and *patria* ("family"). *Patria* is a group united by descent from a common ancestor: a family, a tribe, or even a nation. It appears frequently in LXX genealogies. It could denote any large class or community, but in the only other NT occurrences it has to do with the family.

If *pasa patria* is translated as "the whole family" the assumption is that it is confined to believers (NEB footnote has "his whole family"). This is altogether in keeping with the context and the inference drawn from Ephesians 2:18, 19 (cf. 2:20, 22; 3:6). That it fails to reproduce the wordplay on *patera* and *patria* is not an insuperable objection. More serious is the consideration that in classical Greek such a rendering would demand the definite article—*pasa hē patria* (literally, "all the family"). It is argued, on the other hand, that NT Greek is more flexible. The family of God is not confined to earth but embraces heaven as well. This may simply refer to the church triumphant, but could include the angelic hosts, described in rabbinical literature as "the higher family."

It is less probable that the thrust of Paul's argument would allow the rendering "every family" (RV, ASV, RSV, NEB, JB, BV, TEV). The emphasis throughout is on oneness rather than on plurality. There is more to be said for the possibility that *pasa patria* should be taken as "all fatherhood" (NIV footnote, RV mg., Barclay, Bruce), recognizing the fatherhood of God as the archetype of every other kind of paternity (cf. Athanasius, *Against Arius*, 1.23). Allan (p. 98) takes *patria* to cover local congregations considered as groups within the total family of God. This, he argues, is only an extension of the custom by which members are called brothers (1 Peter 2:17). In the mystery religions, the association of initiates in any area was sometimes headed by a *pater* and may for this reason have been called a *patria*.

16 Paul now sets out the content of his prayer in three items, each introduced by "so that" (*hina*) in vv.16, 18, 19. As in Ephesians 1:17, 18, the prayer is concerned with the appropriation of God's provision in Christ through the Spirit. The divine resources that make this possible are described as "his glorious riches" (cf. Rom 9:23). "Riches" have already been mentioned in Ephesians 2:4, 7 and "glory" in 1:6, 17. Paul asks that God will endow his readers with spiritual blessings on this lavish scale.

In Ephesians 1:19 Paul used three terms—*dynamis, kratos,* and *ischys*—to indicate aspects of God's power. Now he reverts to them in the context of what is made available to the believer. The verbal form "strengthen" (*krataiōthēnai*) is the opposite of "be discouraged" (*enkakein*) in v.13. It is a common expression in LXX and occurs four times in the NT. The agent of this enablement is the Holy Spirit. No repetition of Pentecost is implied but instead a continuous provision through the Spirit (cf. Phil 1:19). "Inner being" (*ho esō anthrōpos*) is perhaps a Pauline invention, modifying Plato's *ho entos anthrōpos* (the man within). It contrasts with the outward man, which is wasting away, whereas the inward man is daily renewed (2 Cor 4:16; Col 3:10). The preposition "in" (*eis*—literally, into) suggests the depth of the Spirit's penetration.

17 The result will be that Christ takes up his residence in the hearts of believers. The progressive character of Christ's indwelling is apparent from the intransitive use of the verb *katoikēsai* in the present continuous tense. It is as the Christian keeps trusting ("through faith") that Christ continues to indwell. No static condition is in view here but a maintained experience. The heart is the focus of mind, feeling, and will; it stands for the whole personality.

"In love" could be attached to the previous clause (NEB). It rounds off a sentence with emphasis elsewhere in Ephesians (4:2, 16; perhaps 1:4). Yet the connection with what follows is sufficently logical. It is not difficult to realize that love will result from Christ's indwelling presence. Paul mixes biological and architectural metaphors as in 1 Corinthians 3:9. Two pictures are conjured up. One is of a tree with deep roots in the soil of love (Col 2:7). The verb *errizomai* is often used with an ethical implication (Herodotus, Plutarch). The other picture is of a building with strong foundations laid on the rock of love (Col 1:23; 1 Peter 5:10). Jesus himself spoke about trees and buildings (Matt 7:15–20; 24–27).

18 What Paul is praying for is not an isolated experience unique to Christians in Ephesus, but something that is shared by all God's people. In a letter so concerned with the church and its unity we would not expect the corporate aspect of spiritual experience to be overlooked. The verb "may have power" (*exischysēte*) is late and found only here and in Ecclesiasticus 7:6 (LXX). The noun is in Ephesians 1:19. It is questionable whether the meaning is as intensive as has been supposed (MM, p. 224). As in 1:17, 18, empowerment and enlightenment are related. "To grasp" is literally to hold as one's own. In the form found here it is "to perceive" or "comprehend."

The four dimensions Paul now presents as the object of such perception are closely linked with the knowledge of Christ's love, though not necessarily to be equated with it. Zerwick (p. 93) takes them as referring to the "mystery" (Eph 3:6, 9). It is unlikely that Paul intended any allusion to the measurements of the Jewish temple or the shape of the cross. The Stoics resorted to these terms to express the totality of the universe and the astrologers utilized them in their calculations. Such applications, however, are not reflected here. The apostle is simply telling us that the love of Christ, exemplified in his magnanimity to the Gentiles, is too large to be confined by any geometrical measurements. It is wide enough to reach the whole world and beyond (1:9, 10, 20). It is long enough to stretch from eternity to eternity (1:4–6, 18; 3:9). It is high enough to raise both Gentiles and Jews to heavenly places in Christ Jesus (1:13; 2:6). It is deep enough to rescue people from sin's degradation and even from the grip of Satan himself (2:1–5; 6:11, 12). The love of Christ is the love he has for the church as a united body (5:25, 29, 30) and for those who trust in him as individuals (3:17).

19 Paul recognizes, however, that he is attempting to measure the immeasurable and so paradoxically prays that the Ephesian Christians may in fact come to know a love that is ultimately unknowable. It "surpasses (*hyperballousan*) knowledge" (Eph 1:19; 2:7; cf. 1 Cor 8:1; Phil 4:7). It is cast into a totally different realm where the normal faculties of rational apprehension are incapable of functioning. "But even though the love of Christ surpasses human knowledge," observed Theophylact, "yet you shall know it if you have Christ dwelling in you."

The final item in Paul's prayer is introduced with "that" (*hina*) in v.19b, though some regard it simply as a consequence of knowing Christ's love. It seems preferable to treat it as the climax of Paul's intercession. He makes the bold request that his readers may be filled up to the measure of the divine fullness. This is not, of course, to be filled as God himself is full nor, it would seem, with the fullness of God himself (NEB, Barclay). It is rather "the fullness which God requires" (NEB footnote). As Hendriksen argues (p. 174), even the communicable attributes of God are not communicable in the measure in which they exist in God. The fulfillment God intends for man is the maturity that is measured by the full stature of Christ (Eph 4:13).

20 The doxology is plainly the climax of the first half of Ephesians; it may be regarded

as the climax of the whole letter, which rises to a spiritual peak at this point and then concentrates on practical outworkings. If chapters 1–3 are couched in the form of a traditional Jewish *bᵉrākāh* ("blessing") and indeed contain echoes of some synagogue prayers, as Kirby (pp. 133, 134) contends, this parallelism extends to the doxology and Amen (cf. Rom 11:33–36).

The apostle has repeatedly insisted that the end of redemption is the glory of God (Eph 1:6, 12, 14, 18; 2:7; 3:10, 16). In the doxology he rehearses themes already touched on—the abundance of God's gift (1:18, 19; 2:7; 3:19), the power made available to the Christian (1:19; 3:7, 16, 18), and the indissoluble link between Christ and the church (1:22, 23; 3:10).

"Immeasurably more" (*hyperekperissou*) appears only here and in 1 Thessalonians 3:10; 5:13. A predilection for *hyper* compounds is a Pauline hallmark. God's capacity to meet his people's spiritual needs far exceeds anything they can either request in prayer or conceive by way of anticipation (Phil 4:7). It is actualized through his power (*dynamis*), which continually operates (*energoumenēn*) within the lives of believers.

21 This liturgical ascription of glory is a recognition rather than an augmentation of what belongs to God alone. Literally, the Greek reads, "To him the glory!" The close juxtaposition of the church and Christ is arresting. For Paul, body and members form a single entity. Textual variants reflect the daring nature of the original order, which refers to the church first. As Thompson puts it, "The honour of Jesus is in the hands of the Church" (p. 60). In the final formula, two common liturgical expressions are combined (cf. Dan 7:18) to produce a stronger phrase than usual to describe eternity. Once again, the fact that the church is included here is remarkable. In Christ, however, the Bride will live forever (1 Thess 4:17; Rev 22:17). To which the response of all God's people must be "Yes indeed, Lord" (Amen).

Notes

14 TR added τοῦ κυρίου ἡμῶν Ἰησοῦ Χριστοῦ (*tou kyriou hēmōn Iēsou Christou*, "of our Lord Jesus Christ") after τὸν πατέρα (*ton patera*, "the Father"), but the words are lacking in important early uncials (ℵ A B C) as well as P⁴⁶ and are not accepted in modern texts. We can easily understand how such a familiar designation (Eph 1:3) might have been inserted, whereas its excision would be inexplicable. Robinson castigates it as "a mischievous gloss" (p. 174) since it obscures the intimate connection between the absolute πάτερ (*pater*, "father") and πᾶσα πατριὰ (*pasa patria*, "every fatherhood"; NIV, "the whole family").

17 Robinson, who attached ἐν ἀγάπῃ (*en agapē*, "in love") to the preceding clause, contended that the subsequent anacoluthon is more easily resolved if the fresh start is made by the participles ἐρριζωμένοι καὶ τεθεμελιωμένοι (*errizōmenoi kai tethemeliōmenoi*, "having been rooted and founded") and not by an adverbial phrase.

NIV repeats "I pray" and follows KJV and RV in associating the participial clause with ἵνα (*hina*). There are instances in NT where part of a sentence precedes *hina*, but invariably it is to add emphasis, which is hardly the case here. For this reason, some take the perfect participles as related to the indwelling of Christ and expressing a condition: "you having been rooted and grounded in love in order that you may be able."

20 NIV regards ἐνεργοουμένην (*energoumenēn*, "operating"; NIV, "that is at work") as middle rather than passive, with the majority of recent exegetes. The standard NT usage seems to be middle with an impersonal subject (BAG, p. 264). For the contrary view, see K.W. Clark, "The Meaning of ἐνεργέω and κατεργέω in the New Testament," (JBL, 54:93–101).

21 The καὶ (*kai*) in the doxology is omitted by some texts, but the evidence of the most ancient and reliable uncial authorities (א A B C) supported by Vul. substantiates its inclusion. Two MSS reverse the sequence, so that "Christ" precedes "the church."

III. Practice: The Application to Christian Life (4:1–6:20)

1. *The Unity of the Church*

4:1–16

> [1] As a prisoner for the Lord, then, I urge you to live a life worthy of the calling you have received. [2] Be completely humble and gentle; be patient, bearing with one another in love. [3] Make every effort to keep the unity of the Spirit through the bond of peace. [4] There is one body and one Spirit—just as you were called to one hope when you were called—[5] one Lord, one faith, one baptism; [6] one God and Father of all, who is over all and through all and in all.
>
> [7] But to each one of us grace has been given as Christ apportioned it. [8] This is why it says:
>
> > "When he ascended on high,
> > he led captives in his train
> > and gave gifts to men."
>
> [9] (What does "he ascended" mean except that he also descended to the lower, earthly regions? [10] He who descended is the very one who ascended higher than all the heavens, in order to fill the whole universe.) [11] It was he who gave some to be apostles, some to be prophets, some to be evangelists, and some to be pastors and teachers, [12] to prepare God's people for works of service, so that the body of Christ may be built up [13] until we all reach unity in the faith and in the knowledge of the Son of God and become mature, attaining the full measure of perfection found in Christ.
>
> [14] Then we will no longer be infants, tossed back and forth by the waves, and blown here and there by every wind of teaching and by the cunning and craftiness of men in their deceitful scheming. [15] Instead, speaking the truth in love, we will in all things grow up into him who is the Head, that is, Christ. [16] From him the whole body, joined and held together by every supporting ligament, grows and builds itself up in love, as each part does its work.

The opening of chapter 4 marks the principal transition of the entire Epistle. As is his method in other writings, Paul turns from the doctrinal to the practical. It must not be imagined, however, that the break is complete. Theology is not left behind but interwoven with the moral exhortations that make up the bulk of chapters 4–6. Nor does the liturgical style, so apparent in chapters 1–3, disappear altogether. The predominant hortatory element may reflect the content and method of Paul's sermons set here in a context of praise and worship. It is highly significant that the first item on the agenda is the need for Christians to live together in love and unity.

1 Does the retrospective "then" (*oun*) connect only with Ephesians 3:20, 21 or with what precedes those verses? Some consider that the whole doctrinal section is under review, but it is more probable that Paul has in mind certain references in chapters 1–3 to spiritual privileges and the Christian's calling (3:6, 12, 14–19; cf. 1:18; 4:4).

It is "as a prisoner for the Lord" (cf. Eph 3:1, 6:20) that Paul makes his appeal. The verb (*parakaleō*; NIV, "urge") can mean either to entreat or to exhort: in this case it is the latter. What the apostle urges is that the Ephesians may lead the sort of life that matches their Christian vocation. "Worthy" (*axios*) is literally "bringing up the other beam of the scales" and hence indicates equivalence (TDNT, 1:379). Paul is insisting that there shall be a balance between profession and practice. So he provides a criterion by which possible courses of action can be weighed. Christians will always seek to do what is most in keeping with their vocation. By definition it is a calling they have received (literally, "with which they were called")—not one they have acquired by self-effort. Those who share such a divine call constitute the church, the called-out company (*ekklēsia*).

2 The apostle now specifies four graces that evidence this essential proportion between calling and character: humility, gentleness, patience, and forbearance. These are all qualities necessary for good relations with others in the Christian community and beyond. The word for humility (*tapeinophrosynē*) occurs five times in Paul and only once elsewhere in the NT. The adjective and verb are found in LXX. In classical Greek, *tapeinos* is a derogatory term suggesting low-mindedness and groveling servility. The adjective was redeemed by the gospel to represent a distinctively Christian virtue, and this euphonious noun was coined to stand over against the admired high-mindedness of the heathen. Linked with humility is gentleness (*praütēs*) or considerateness. The element of restraint is included so that it denotes controlled strength and not supine weakness.

Patience (*makrothymia*) or clemency is a characteristic of God himself. It can mean steadfastness in the endurance of suffering but more often in the NT it describes reluctance to avenge wrongs. It is to be displayed to other Christians and to everyone else (Rom 12:10, 18). Patience finds its expression in loving forbearance (Col 3:18). To bear with another (literally, "hold him up") is to put up with his faults and idiosyncracies, knowing that we have our own. Love is a recurring theme in Ephesians. The four graces Paul recommends here are all aspects of love and exemplified to perfection in Christ (Phil 2:2, 5).

3 The absence of these qualities may jeopardize Christian unity. That is why Paul presses his readers to exert all their powers to maintain the oneness in Christ that binds all believers to each other because they are bound by him and to him. The verb (*spoudazontes*) suggests difficulty and a resolute determination to overcome it. It is assumed that unity between Christians already exists as given in Christ (Eph 2:13–18) by the Spirit. The "one Spirit" (v.4) is the agent of unity. What Paul envisages is not "a vague spiritual identity, but rather a profound oneness made possible by God's Spirit" (Johnston, p. 18).

"Peace" is the clasp that ensures that this God-given unity will not fall apart. The "bond" (*syndesmos*) strengthens rather than hampers. In Colossians 2:19 Paul uses it with reference to the ligaments of the body and in Colossians 3:14 figuratively of the love that holds Christians together.

4 The reasons why those who belong to Christ should be eager to preserve their unity are now supplied in a crescendo of nouns. In three groups of three items each, Paul's thought ascends from the realization of unity in the Spirit to the focus of unity in the Son and thence to the source of unity in the Father.

"One body" depicts the church as a single visible community. It is not simply a mystical concept. Its unity is recognizable in that Jews and Gentiles are now seen to be reconciled in Christ. In the pagan world there were many religious cults to choose from. Christians, on the other hand, were all members of one body.

"One Spirit" indwells the body of Christ. By him the body lives and moves (1 Cor 12:13). The Spirit is its soul; apart from him it cannot exist. The same Spirit fell on the Jews at Pentecost and on the Gentiles in the house of Cornelius. The "one Spirit" who has already spanned this widest of all gulfs will bring together all other diverse groups within the church.

The Holy Spirit is the pledge of our inheritance (Eph 1:14) and so he is the guarantor of the "one hope" to which we are called (Eph 1:18; 2:12). This is not the hope that stems from the calling but the hope that belongs to the call (v.1). It is, of course, the hope of sharing Christ's glory at the end of the age (1 John 3:2). There is no differentiation between Jewish and Gentile Christians. This eschatological expectation is entertained equally by all.

5 The second trio of unities is related to the "one Lord" or master to whom all Christians owe their allegiance. The three expressions may well be intended to convey a single idea, as Scott has surmised, i.e., "one Lord in whom we all believe and in whose name we are baptized" (p. 204). Certainly Christ is central. He is the sole Head of his body the church. Christians are only such through trusting him and acknowledging his name. The pagan world spawned many lords. Christianity has only one whose claim is absolute. That is why believers cannot call anyone else Lord even to escape death.

"One faith" in the one Lord unites all true believers. Faith here is personal commitment to Christ, yet it is not purely subjective. It involves a recognition of who he is as Son of God and Savior of men. It is thus "one allegiance and one *profession* of allegiance" (Lock, p. 46).

"One baptism" is the external seal of incorporation into the body of Christ. Falling as it does in the second triad (related to Christ) and not in the first (related to the Spirit), it appears to indicate water baptism and not primarily the baptism with the Spirit of which water baptism is the sign. Baptism is regarded as the sacrament of unity. In the Christian church baptisms are not multiplied as with the Jews (Heb 6:2). There are not even two baptisms—one of John and one of Jesus. There is "one baptism" symbolizing identification with Christ in his death and resurrection, sealing with the Spirit, and incorporation into the body of Christ, so that all Christians become one person in Christ Jesus (Eph 1:13; 2:5, 6; 3:15). Baptism is one because it makes one. It provides the evidence that all Christians, without discrimination as to color, race, sex, age, or class, share the grace of Christ. If we ask why Paul does not at this point mention the other dominical sacrament, that of the Lord's Supper (cf. "one bread" in 1 Cor 10:17), the answer may be that he regards the eucharist not as a prerequisite of unity but an expression of it.

6 The last in the ascending scale (though the first in terms of cause) is the Father. As Zerwick (p. 104) points out, he is not associated with other unities like the one Spirit and the one Lord. He stands alone. The triple note, which is still to be found, merely divides up his modes of action. There is "one God," not many as in pagan culture (1 Cor 8:5, 6). He is the "Father of all" with particular reference to his redemptive paternity. Yet his creative fatherhood is not entirely ruled out in view of what follows.

If the first "all" is exclusively personal, the rest are not necessarily so. It looks as if Paul now regards the body of Christ in its cosmic aspect (as in Eph 1:23). God reigns "over" (*epi*) all in his transcendent sovereignty. He works "through" (*dia*) all in his creative activity. He dwells "in" (*en*) all by reason of his immanent pervasiveness.

The trinitarian structure of vv.4, 5 bears out the assumption that here we have an incipient creed. It was on the basis of such biblical passages that the historic affirmations of faith were developed. The reiteration of "one" distinguishes Eastern from Western creeds (the Nicene Creed has "I believe in one God the Father Almighty").

7 The apostle has been considering the church as a totality. Now he focuses on the individual ("each one of us"). Within the body of Christ each member enjoys a share of God's grace. As in Ephesians 3:2, it is equipping rather than saving grace that Paul describes. *Charis* (grace) here is not equated with *charisma* (grace-gift), but denotes the grace provided for and manifested in the gift. The distribution of grace, and so the distribution of grace-gifts, is in Christ's own hands and apportioned as he decides.

8 Paul supplies biblical proof of the foregoing by a quotation from Psalm 68:18. "It says" (*legei*) is not the apostle's usual formula, which positively specifies Scripture (*hē graphē*) as the source. Some expositors infer either *hē graphē* or *ho theos*, "God" (see NIV footnote). Which is assumed is immaterial, because for Paul "the word of the Scripture and the word of its Author are convertible terms" (Moule, p. 106). Others take the verb as indefinite: "it says." The same expression recurs in Ephesians 5:14, introducing what appears to be a primitive Christian hymn. "It says" is satisfactory here only if it is realized that Scripture is intended.

The quotation itself, though indubitably biblical, is not without its difficulties, since Paul does not cite either MT or LXX. Three changes are observable. Two of them are only slight: a transfer of person from "you" (sing.) to "he" and a purely stylistic transformation of a finite verb into a participle ("having ascended"; NIV, "when he ascended"). More substantial is the alteration from "received gifts for men" to "gave gifts to men." Attempts have been made to account for the apparent discrepancy by the conjecture that Paul was quoting from memory and that his recollection was imperfect, or that he arbitrarily doctored the text to suit his line of argument. With more plausibility some have claimed that, under the inspiration of the Spirit, Paul felt free to amplify the meaning of the Psalm, since the giving is implicit in the receiving for. But it seems more probable that the apostle was drawing on an ancient oral tradition reflected in the Aramaic Targum on the Psalter and the Syriac Peshitta version, both of which read, "Thou hast given gifts to men." Early rabbinical comments applied the verse to Moses when he received the Law on Sinai so as to bring it to the people.

9 Ascension presupposes a prior descent, and Paul describes this as being made into "the lower, earthly regions." The rendering of the NIV takes *ta katōtera merē tēs gēs* (literally, "the lower parts of the earth," RSV) as referring to the incarnation of our Lord. It was from earth that he ascended and it had been to earth that he came (John 3:13). This is a perfectly legitimate interpretation approved by the NEB (cf. BV, TEV, PH). NEB footnote has "the regions beneath the earth," in which case an allusion to *šeʾôl* is intended. By the time 1 Peter was written, the belief that Christ descended to the underworld during the interval between his death and resurrection may have established itself (1 Peter 3:19, 20; 4:6), though the passages are variously explained. Again, this obscure expression may simply signify death and burial.

Caird's solution is intriguing. He notes that in the Jewish liturgy Psalm 68 was used at Pentecost and surmises that this prescribed reading was taken over into the Christian celebration of the same feast. The descent would then be Christ's coming in the Spirit when gifts were conveyed to the church (G.B. Caird, "The Descent of Christ in Ephesians 4:7-11," *Studia Evangelica* [1964], 2:537, 541). Verse 10 rather tells against such an ingenious hypothesis.

10 The apostle affirms the identity of the incarnate Savior with the ascended Savior. His exaltation is "higher than all the heavens." The Jews calculated seven heavens, but higher than the highest heaven is the rightful throne of Christ to whom all things are one day to be subjugated (Eph 1:10; cf. 1 Cor 15:28). No one else is qualified thus to "fill all things" (KJV). This is more than the fulfillment of prophetic predictions concerning Christ's cosmic role or the accomplishment of every task entrusted to him by the Father. Nor is Paul alluding to the mysterious process by which in his human nature our Lord passed into the full enjoyment of the divine perfections (so Lenski, p. 524). Hendriksen (p. 195) sees the exalted mediator now filling the universe with blessings. But it is sufficient to recognize without further elaboration that it is with "his presence and himself" (Barclay, p. 122) that he fills all things.

11 The apostle now resumes the train of thought inaugurated in v.7, interrupted by his excursus on the ascent and descent of Christ in vv.8–10. But the diversion was necessary in order to stress that none other than this exalted Lord is the one who has endowed his church with gifts-by-grace, so that it may indeed be his body in the world (Eph 1:23; 4:4). Paul does not list the grace-gifts, however, but only those who receive them. After "each one of us" in v.7 we might have expected him to include all the members of Christ's body (as in 1 Cor 12:4–11). Instead, we read only of those who are appointed to leadership. Their ministry, of course, is exercised for the sake of the whole community (vv.12, 13).

"Apostles" and "prophets" have already been paired as providing a foundation for the Christian temple (Eph 2:20; 3:6). "Evangelists" are not primarily Gospel compilers but missionaries who pioneer outreach in areas where the faith has not as yet been proclaimed. The title is bestowed on Philip (Acts 21:8; cf. 8:6–40). Timothy is to "do the work of an evangelist" (2 Tim 4:5). Epaphras no doubt falls into this category.

Paul turns from itinerant to local ministry. "Pastors and teachers" are grouped together in such a way as to suggest that the two roles are regarded as complementary and often coordinated in the same person. Pastors (literally, "shepherds") probably included presbyters and bishops; they were entrusted with the nurture, protection, and supervision of the flock. Teachers are linked with prophets in Acts 13:1 and follow them in the list contained in 1 Corinthians 12:28.

12 The aim of the ministries mentioned in v.11 is now disclosed. It is the equipment of all God's people for service. "To prepare" (*pros ton katartismon*) is "to put right." In surgery *katartismos* is applied to the setting of a broken bone (BAG, p. 419). In the NT the verb *katartizō* is used for the mending of nets (Matt 4:21) and the restoration of the lapsed (Gal 6:1). It may, however, signify the realization of purpose and the completion of what is already good as far as it goes (1 Cor 1:10; 1 Thess 3:10). Such preparation is in order to the work (*ergon*, sing.) of service (*diakonia*). This is what unites all the members of Christ's body from the apostles to the most apparently insignificant disciple (1 Cor 12:22). Christ himself set the example (Mark 10:45; Luke 22:27). It is by this means that the body of Christ will be consolidated (cf. Eph 2:21).

13 The ultimate end in view is the attainment of completeness in Christ. "We all" clearly includes all believers, but not all men (Eph 3:9). Paul elsewhere insists on the togetherness of Christians in an eschatological context (1 Thess 4:15–17). In v.3 "the unity of the Spirit" is a gift to be guarded. Here "unity in the faith" is a goal to be reached. "We are one now: in the end we shall know ourselves to be one" (Robinson, p. 100). Such a realization of unity will arise from an increasing knowledge of Christ as the Son of God in corporate as well as in personal experience.

In this way the church comes of age. It reaches maturity. The phrase is literally "into a perfect, full-grown man" (*eis andra teleion*). The singular is employed because the church as a whole is seen as "one new man" in Christ (Eph 2:15). Individualism is a mark of immaturity. This perfection or completeness is proportionate to the fullness of Christ himself. *Hēlikia*, translated "perfection," can denote age (Matt 6:27; John 9:21) and may well be used here in this sense, since the context has to do with becoming adult. The meaning would be "attain to the measure of mature age" proper for Christians, who have left infancy behind (v.14). But *hēlikios* also indicates stature (Luke 19:3) and appears with *metron* ("measure," cf. v.7 KJV) in classical writers. The reference would then be to spiritual attainment (as perhaps in Luke 2:52).

Fullness (*plērōma*) has already occurred in Ephesians 1:23 in relation to the church. Here it is the fullness of Christ himself. Just as Christians may be "filled to the measure of all the fullness of God" (Eph 3:19), so together they are to aspire to "the full measure of perfection found in Christ."

14 The metaphor of maturity is carried over from v.13. There must be no symptoms of arrested development among believers, who are to abandon childish attitudes and be their age (1 Cor 13:11). Paul switches from one metaphor to another as he depicts the features of spiritual infantilism. Its victims will be tossed to and fro like a cork in a surging sea (James 1:6) and whirled around by every chance gust of fashionable heterodoxy. "Blown here and there" (*peripheromenoi*) is literally "swung around." It is used of spinning tops and feeling dizzy. Such is the confusing effect of false doctrine.

The source of this dangerous teaching is to be traced in "the slick cleverness of men, craftily calculated to lead us astray" (Barclay, p. 123). "Cunning" (*kybeia*) is cheating at dice and so, by extension, trickery of every kind. "Craftiness" (*panourgia*) is the unscrupulousness that stops at nothing. Error is organized with a deliberate policy to undermine the truth of God. Paul may well be tilting at emergent Gnosticism (Col 2:8).

15 Paul contrasts the deception of heresy with the integrity of the gospel. The church cannot allow falsehood to go uncorrected, yet the truth must always be vindicated in the accents of love. "Speaking the truth" (*alētheuontes;* literally, "truthing") is strictly "doing the truth" and may imply more than verbalization ("dealing truly" RV mg.). This fundamental concern for the truth is the secret of maturity in the church. It is into Christ as the Head that the body grows up. R.A. Knox points out that a baby's head is unusually large in comparison with the rest of its body. As it develops, however, the body grows up into a due proportion with the head (*St. Paul's Gospel* [London: Sheed and Ward, 1953], p. 84). Paul may not have had in mind this physiological analogy but it is instructive, nevertheless.

16 Christ is at once the One into whom all Christians grow and out of whom (*ex hou*) the church consolidates itself in love. This process depends on the fact that the various parts of the body are interrelated. The whole is continually being integrated (*synar-*

mologoumenon) and kept firm (*symbibazomenon*) by each separate ligament (*haphēs*)—"joined and held together by every supporting ligament." The precision with which these medical terms are employed makes us wonder whether Paul checked the details with Luke.

It is only "when each part is working properly" (RSV) that the body receives the support it needs. The word is really "furnishing" (*epichorēgia*) or supply (Phil 1:19). The *chorēgos* was the man who met the cost of staging a Greek play with its chorus. "If we want to be considered members of Christ, let no man be anything for himself, but let us all be whatever we are for the benefit of each other" (Calvin, in loc.).

Notes

1 The formula κάλειν κλήσει (*kalein klēsei*, "to call with a calling") is found in 2 Tim 1:9, which might suggest that the relative ἧς (*hēs*, "with which") here stands for ἧ (*hē*, "which"). Attraction from the dative is not well attested, however, and it is therefore more likely that *hēs* is equivalent to the accusative ἥν (*hēn*, "which"), as in Ephesians 1:6 (RHG, p. 478; BAG, p. 400). Arrian employs the phrase κλῆσιν κάλειν (*klēsin kalein*).

4 It is "in one hope" (ἐν μιᾷ ἐλπίδι, *en mia elpidi*) that Christians are called. The NIV takes ἐν (*en*, "in") to be equivalent to εἰς (*eis*, "into") or ἐπί (*epi*, "on") as Chrysostom did. Others regard it as instrumental or as denoting the sphere in which the calling occurs. Further Pauline instances of κάλειν (*kalein*, "to call") with *en* as in 1 Cor 7:13, Gal 1:6, and 1 Thess 4:7, favor Abbott's solution (p. 108) to the effect that the particle singles out hope as an essential accompaniment of the calling (a *conditio* in the strictly Latin sense).

9 Some authorities insert πρῶτον (*prōton*, "first") after κατέβη (*katebē*, "he descended"). However, the omission is sufficiently substantiated. On the other hand, most recent texts and translations retain μέρη (*merē*, "parts") after κατώτερα (*katōtera*, "lower").

Grammatical considerations alone cannot finally determine the significance of εἰς τὰ κατώτερα μέρη τῆς γῆς (*eis ta katōtera merē tēs gēs*, "to the lower earthly regions"). The gen. may be comparative—"the parts lower than the earth"; partitive—"the lower parts of the earth as distinguished from the higher"; possessive—"the lower parts belonging to the earth"; or appositional—"the lower parts that are or constitute the earth."

13 When the conjunction μέχρι (*mechri*, "until") appears, followed by the aorist subjunctive, without the complementary particle ἄν (*an*), as, e.g., in Mark 13:30 and Gal 4:19, it usually stands for the indefinite future, signifying that the contemplated result is expected but not inevitable (RHG, p. 975).

Πλήρωμα (*plērōma*, "fullness"; NIV, "perfection") is not to be treated as if it were a Semitism for πεπληρωμένος (*peplērōmenos*, "perfect," "complete"), agreeing either with Χριστοῦ (*Christou*, "of Christ")—i.e., the measure of the perfect Christ; or with ἡλικίας (*hēlikias*, "of the stature")—i.e., the perfect, or mature Christ. Nor is τοῦ πληρώματος τοῦ Χριστοῦ (*tou plērōmatos tou Christou*, "the fullness of Christ") that which is filled with or by Christ, as if it were analogous to Eph 1:23. The NIV virtually equates *plērōma* with the perfection discovered in Christ. It is equally possible to interpret the possessive gen. as the full appropriation of all that Christ offers.

15 The application of ἀληθεύοντες (*alētheuontes*, "speaking the truth") is not necessarily confined to truthfulness in speech as in v.25 where the verb "to speak" (λαλέω, *laleō*) is specifically employed. As Abbott (p. 123) correctly insisted, the verb cannot be separated from ἀλήθεια (*alētheia*, "truth"). Verbs ending in -εύω (-*euō*) express the actual performance of what is signified by the corresponding noun ending in -εία (-*eia*) (cf. RHG, p. 148). In classical Gr. the compound ἐπαληθεύω (*epalētheuō*) means "to verify" or "confirm" by acts rather than words (Jos. War 7.8.1). In the NT "truth has a strongly practical side, which expresses itself in virtues like righteousness and holiness" (BAG, p. 35). In Gal 4:16 ἀληθεύω (*alētheuō*) means "being

honest" (NEB). "Truthing it in love" involves not only declaring and defending the faith with charitable words but also matching such words with compatible attitudes and actions.

2. The Changed Life

4:17–24

¹⁷So I tell you this, and insist on it in the Lord, that you must no longer live as the Gentiles do, in the futility of their thinking. ¹⁸They are darkened in their understanding and separated from the life of God because of the ignorance that is in them due to the hardening of their hearts. ¹⁹Having lost all sensitivity, they have given themselves over to sensuality so as to indulge in every kind of impurity, with a continual lust for more.
²⁰You, however, did not come to know Christ that way. ²¹Surely you heard of him and were taught in him in accordance with the truth that is in Jesus. ²²You were taught, with regard to your former way of life, to put off your old self, which is being corrupted by its deceitful desires; ²³to be made new in the attitude of your minds; ²⁴and to put on the new self, created to be like God in true righteousness and holiness.

The practical section of the Epistle opened with an appeal to maintain Christian unity. Paul substantiated it by enlarging on the way in which the body of Christ is built up. Now, before dealing with specific moral injunctions, he reminds his readers about the kind of life they once lived and the need for a clean break with the past (cf. 2:1–3, 11–13).

17 "So" (*oun*) resumes the exhortation in v.3. In a solemn declaration the apostle implores (*martyromai*; NIV, "[I] insist") the Ephesians to abandon all their former practices. He does so because both he and they are "in the Lord." Christians constitute a third race that is neither Jewish nor Gentile. In other letters Paul has not been slow to remind Hebrew Christians that they must not cling to the grave clothes of Judaism. Here in similar vein he urges the Gentiles not to fall back into their old self-indulgent habits. Such permissive behavior springs from an aimless attitude to life that cuts the nerve of moral endeavor. In the NT "futility" (*mataiotēs*) is sometimes associated with idolatry, but the primary reference here is to "good-for-nothing notions" (NEB) underlying irresponsible behavior.

18 This reprehensible attitude is traced to its source. Such men are impeded by a mental fog that blots out the divine light. They are cut off from contact with God (Eph 2:12) and the life he alone can impart. Such a condition arises in turn from deep-seated ignorance. Although inborn, it was not irreversible and might have been removed had they followed such light as came to them. Instead, they steeled their hearts against the truth till they grew altogether impervious to its impact. "Hardening" (*pōrōsis*) describes a state of petrifaction. It is used medically to denote the callus formed when a bone has been fractured and reset. Such a callus is even harder than the bone itself. This dreadful *pōrōsis* has affected the very hearts of the pagans. Their whole personality is incapable of appreciating what God offers.

19 Men like these have "lost all sensitivity" (*apēlgēkotes*). They can no longer respond to moral stimuli. Their consciences are so atrophied that sin registers no stab of pain. They have abandoned themselves to every sort of vice. From Romans 1:24–28 we learn

61

that in such circumstances God leaves the sinner to endure the full consequences of his tragic decision. "Sensuality" (*aselgeia*) is license in the sphere of the physical and hence voluptuousness or debauchery (TDNT, 1:490). In the NT it often refers to sexual excesses. This fearful self-abandonment leads to all kinds of filthy practices, which are so absorbing as almost to become a total preoccupation (*ergasian*).

All this is pursued "in greediness" (RV mg.) or "immoderate, inordinate desire" (cf. Trench, p. 77). The term (*en pleonexia*) is not necessarily associated with sexual misconduct, though the context here suggests it. It means the determination to gratify self-interest at all costs, regardless of the rights and susceptibilities of others. NIV combines both possibilities: "with a continual lust for more."

20 "You" stands in contrast to the insensitive, passion-dominated pagans who exist only to satisfy their lower nature. That was not how the Gentile converts in Ephesus came to know Christ for themselves. The expression is "to learn Christ" (*emathete tou Christou*), which implies more than receiving catechetical instruction, though that is included. It is to learn in such a way as to become a devotee or disciple (*mathetēs*). It was *the* Christ they thus came to know—God's anointed Son, no longer the prerogative of the Jews but shared by the Gentiles.

21 So far from introducing doubt, "surely" (*ei ge*) adds certainty, as in Ephesians 3:2. Of course, the recipients have heard of (literally, "heard") Christ. In the preaching of the Word Christ himself is present (2:17) and so those who hear are introduced to him. Paul's readers were also "taught in [Christ]" (not "by him" as in the KJV). It was in Christ that the one who taught them spoke and in Christ too that they appropriated what he said. They first heard the truth of Christ and so accepted him. Then, as disciples remaining in him (John 15:4, 9, 10), they received further instruction. This "truth" (*alētheia*) (there is no article before the noun) is "in Jesus." Paul does not often employ the historical name and when he does, it is invariably in connection with our Lord's death and resurrection. The truth in Jesus, then, has to do with the fact that the man from Nazareth was shown by his rising again to be the Son of God and Savior of the world.

22 Paul now gives the content of the teaching his readers received, though the verb is not actually repeated. Their previous life style was to be discarded completely. They must forsake their old behavioral haunts (*anastrophēn*; NIV, "your former way of life") and indeed lay aside the costume of their unregenerate selves. The metaphor of doffing and donning garments is common in Scripture and in Greek literature generally. There may also be an allusion here to the fact that baptismal candidates changed into white robes.

The old self is subject to an internal process of disintegration. The present tense "is being corrupted" (*phtheiromenon*) reveals that it is continuous. Moral degeneration has set in and the road to perdition lies ahead. "Deceitful desires" translates a phrase in which the treacherous duplicity of sin is almost personified (literally, "the desires of deceit").

23 In a contrasting positive statement, Paul reminds the Ephesians that instead of being subject to progressive deterioration, they were to be perpetually renovated in mind and spirit (literally, "in the spirit of your minds"). "To be made new" (*ananeousthei*) possibly involves an element of restoration, since the image of God, impaired by the fall, is fully reinstated in the new creation. As over against the futile thinking of the unregenerate

Gentiles (v.17), the Christian converts are to undergo a radical reorientation of their mental outlook—so NIV, "to be made new in the attitude of your minds." This can only take place under the influence of the Holy Spirit, acting on the human spirit (*pneuma*) as it affects the realm of thought.

24 The "new self" (cf. Eph 3:16) assumed by the believer is the direct opposite of the worthless "old self" (v.22). It is not the former nature refurbished but a totally new creation (2:10). This is said to be "after God" (*kata theou*). God is both the author and the pattern of this changed life. In Colossians 3:10 the new self is presented as being "renewed in knowledge in the image of its Creator." Here it is simply "to be like God" as man was at first. The characteristics of the divine image are righteousness and holiness. These are qualities in God that are reproduced in his genuine worshipers: his love of right and his aversion to sin. In the NT "righteousness" (*dikaiosyne*) often stands for the uprightness of those who are made right with God. It is not the usual word for holiness that appears here (*hagiosyne*) but another (*hosiotes*) meaning "free from contamination." It occurs only here and in Luke 1:25 (again in conjunction with *dikaiosyne*).

Notes

21 It is not easy to elucidate the clause καθώς ἐστιν ἀλήθεια ἐν τῷ Ἰησοῦ (*kathos estin aletheia en tō Iēsou*, "just as it is truth in Jesus") or to establish its connections, whether with ἀποθέσθαι (*apothesthai*, "to put off" [v.22]) or ἐδιδάχθητε (*edidachthēte*, "you were taught"). The NIV opts for the latter and closes off the sentence, resuming *edidachthēte* at the beginning of the next. Wycliffe recognized the absence of the article and tr. with strict accuracy: "as is truth in Jesus." Some make Christ the subject of ἐστιν (*estin*, "is")—"as he is truth in Jesus," whereas WH conjecture the dative ἀλήθεια (*alētheia*)—"as he (Christ) is in truth in Jesus." Such a distinction between the Messiah and the historical Jesus seems unduly forced. Houlden thinks it is almost "in the authentic Jesus-way" (p. 318). Perhaps the RV is the most satisfactory: "even as truth is in Jesus."

23 The middle of ἀνανεόω (*ananeoō*, "to renew") appears to be devoid of any reflexive force but is virtually active (BAG, p. 57). This being so, ἀνανεοῦσθαι (*ananeousthai*, "to be renewed") is to be regarded as passive. In classical literature the verb means "to restore to an original condition." On the other hand, the prefix ἀνα- (*ana-*) may only express change.

The phrase τῷ πνεύματι τοῦ νοὸς ὑμῶν (*tō pneumati tou noos hymōn*, "in the attitude [spirit] of your minds") is somewhat indefinite. Its elucidation depends on the nature of both the dative and the gen. and whether πνεύματος (*pneumatos*) refers to the Holy Spirit or the human spirit. If νοὸς (*noos*, "mind") represents a possessive gen., then πνεύματι (*pneumati*, "in the spirit") is an instrumental dative and the reference is to the Holy Spirit bestowed on, and thus now belonging to, the mind. A modification of this view holds that the Holy Spirit is not regarded *per se* but as united with the human spirit. Frequently in the NT the interaction is hard to quantify. If πνεῦμα (*pneuma*, "spirit") here refers to the spirit of man, then the gen. is either partitive (the controlling spirit of the mind) or appositional (the spirit closely related to the mind; cf. NEB, TEV). Most exegetes prefer to take *noos* as a subjective gen. with *pneumati* as a dative of reference (EGT, 3:343), yielding the sense "renewed in respect of the spirit by which your mind is regulated." This interpretation underlies KJV, RV and RSV. Barclay translates (p. 123): "You must have a completely new attitude of mind," which is similar to NIV's rendering.

3. Christian Behavior Patterns

4:25–5:2

25Therefore, each of you must put off falsehood and speak truthfully to his neighbor, for we are all members of one body. 26In your anger do not sin: Do not let the sun go down while you are still angry, 27and do not give the devil a foothold. 28He who has been stealing must steal no longer, but must work, doing something useful with his own hands, that he may have something to share with those in need.

29Do not let any unwholesome talk come out of your mouths, but only what is helpful for building others up according to their needs, that it may benefit those who listen. 30And do not grieve the Holy Spirit of God, with whom you were sealed for the day of redemption. 31Get rid of all bitterness, rage and anger, brawling and slander, along with every form of malice. 32Be kind and compassionate to one another, forgiving each other, just as in Christ God forgave you.

5:1Be imitators of God, therefore, as dearly loved children 2and live a life of love, just as Christ loved us and gave himself up for us as a fragrant offering and sacrifice to God.

From v.17 the apostle has been contrasting the old life with the new without descending to particulars. Now he embarks on a series of detailed warnings against what "deceitful desires" (v.22) may produce. "Therefore" (*dio*) in v.25 makes the connection between principle and practice.

25 The first item to be included in the putting off of the "old self " (v.22) is falsehood (cf. Col 3:8, 9). It is not lying in the abstract but "the lying" or "the lie" (*to pseudos*)— falsehood in all its forms as over against "the truth that is in Jesus" (v.21) and "true righteousness and holiness" (v.24). All that belongs to "deceitful scheming" (v.14) and "deceitful desires" (v.22) is to be left behind. It has no place in the community of Christ. Because our Lord is himself the truth, his body must reflect the truth. Because each member belongs to the rest, the fellowship of the church will be marked by a refreshing openness. Any kind of deception is a sin against the Spirit. "Speak truthfully to his neighbor" recalls Zechariah 8:16 (LXX). Paul has *meta* (with) instead of *pros* (to), stressing the need for mutual frankness. The reference to the body makes it clear that fellow Christians are in view but, of course, the injunction has a universal application.

26 Another quotation (from Ps 4:4) introduces the next admonition: "Be angry and sin not" (RSV). The Hebrew verb *rāgaz* is "to tremble with fear or rage" (BDB, p. 919). Paul, however, has "and" for "but," thus softening any antithesis. The two injunctions are not to be regarded as separate. They belong close together as the NIV rendering rightly suggests. As Hendriksen insists, the meaning is simply "Let not your anger be mixed with sin" (p. 218). There is such a thing as righteous indignation. It is ascribed even to God and to Jesus. So it is legitimate for the Christian.

But it can easily degenerate into bitterness. Hence, the appended prohibition. Under the Mosaic law all sureties were to be returned and all wages paid before sunset (Deut 24:13, 15). Paul discusses reconciliation in v.32; but here he is referring to the Christian's own exasperation (*parorgismos*) or provocation, which, however justifiable, must not be allowed even to simmer overnight.

27 If this advice is followed, the devil will be afforded no leeway. He will have no room to move. Instead, we must leave a place for the wrath of God, because vindication is his prerogative (Rom 12:19). Some have queried whether *diabolos* here represents the evil one or simply any slanderer who provokes the Christian (Tyndale has "the backbiter"). In the NT the noun regularly identifies the devil, as in Ephesians 6:11.

28 In his warning against breaking the seventh commandment, Paul is evidently thinking of some convert who had been in the habit of stealing before he became a Christian. The participle (*ho kleptōn*) does not suggest a professional crook (*ho kleptēs*). Stealing, moreover, covers every kind of misappropriation. For the new man in Christ all this must stop. Rather, he should not be afraid to exert himself to the point of exhaustion (*kopiatō*) in manual labour (1 Cor 4:12; 1 Thess 4:11). Hands that used to pilfer the property of others must now be hardened like Paul's in honest toil (Acts 20:34, 35). He will do "something useful" (literally, the good, *to agathon*) and as a result will be in a position to help those worse off than himself. "To share" (*metadidonai*) means to distribute personally rather than by remote control through some agent or official.

29 Not only will Christians do "the good" (v.28): they will speak it too ("what is helpful," *agathos*). No unhealthy language will pass through their lips. "Unwholesome" (*sapros*) is that which is itself rotten and disseminates rottenness. In connection with "talk" (*logos*), it may signify not simply bad language but malicious gossip and slander. Anything that injures others and sparks dissension is covered by the expression. Christians, however, will only say what is calculated to build up the church (Eph 2:21, 22; 4:12, 16) by encouraging its members. This is to be done whenever the need arises, so that those who hear may profit by it. "That it may benefit" (*hina dō charin*) simply means to confer a blessing, whether temporal or spiritual. The ultimate source of all blessing is God himself. The channel may be human and so even the everyday conversation of Christians may become a means of grace to others.

30 "And" indicates that, while there are various ways of bringing sorrow to the Holy Spirit, it is doing so through "unwholesome talk" (v.29) that Paul is rebuking here. "The tacit assumption clearly is that the Spirit dwells within them" (Ellicott, p. 109). This being the case, the experience of his fullness will have its effect, among other things, in speech (Eph 5:18, 19). Any kind of careless, unbecoming talk pains the Spirit, since it is incompatible with the holiness he conveys to those who belong to Christ. The moving anthropomorphism implicit in "grieve," combined with the full-length title "the Holy Spirit of God," serves to underline the gravity of the prohibition.

The relative clause provides the ground on which the prohibition rests. It is in connection with (*en hō*) the Holy Spirit that believers have been sealed (Eph 1:13, 14) for the eschatological day of deliverance. Redemption (*apolytrōsis*) involves the payment of a ransom (see on 1:7):Christ's death on the cross has purchased not only present but final liberation.

31 A condensed series of imperatives winds up the section starting from v.25 about the Christian's attitude to his neighbor. This verse is negative; v.32 is positive and leads into the next chapter.

"Get rid of " (*arthētō*) is "let it be removed" and therefore "have no more to do with it." Every kind or any trace (*pasa*, "all") of these blemishes is to be forsaken. "Bitterness" (*pikria*; cf. Col 3:19) is the opposite not only of sweetness (*gleukētēs*) but of kindness (*chrēstotēs*). It is the spite that harbors resentment and keeps a score of wrongs (1 Cor 13:5). Aristotle defined those who display it as "hard to be reconciled" (*Nicomachean Ethics* 4.11). "Rage" (*thymos*) is what flows from bitterness in an outburst of uncontrolled passion and frustration. "Anger" (*orgē*) describes the wrath of God in v.6 and of men in v.26. It is associated with rage in Colossians 3:8 and there as here signifies an unjustifiable human emotion that manifests itself in noisy assertiveness (*kraugē*; literally, "shouting"; NIV, "brawling") and abuse (*blasphēmia;* NIV, "slander"). The poisonous source of all these regrettable reassertions of the "old self " (v.22) is named as "malice" (*kakia*, "bad feeling").

32 Having done with all these malicious traits, the Christian will display kindness, compassion, and forgiveness. "Be" is really "become" (*ginesthe*), for Paul realizes that his readers have not yet attained "the full measure of perfection found in Christ" (v.13). To be "kind" (*chrēstoi*) is to show a sweet and generous disposition. The adjective is used here only in the Epistles. "Compassionate" (*eusplangchnoi*) is a rare word. It was used by Hippocrates to describe the healthy function of the intestines. The Greeks located the seat of the emotions in the *splangchna* or internal organs—liver, kidneys, and larger viscera. In Euripides the noun means stoutheartedness. *Eusplangchnos* is not found in LXX, though it occurs in the Prayer of Manasses, a canticle added to the Greek Psalter. The nuance of tenderness is not classical but Jewish, according to Lightfoot.

Mutual forgiveness is a further mark of true Christian fellowship (Col 3:13). There is a give and take in this matter. Paul sets forth the strongest possible motive: Christians are to forgive one another because all of them have already been forgiven by God in Christ, when he became "the atoning sacrifice . . . for the sins of the whole world" (1 John 2:2). "As" (*kathōs*) further implies that our forgiveness of others is to be like God's forgiveness of us. It must flow from ungrudging love. The parable of the unmerciful servant is acutely relevant (Matt 18:23–35).

5:1 The apostle carries these injunctions over from the previous chapter and closes this section on Christian behavior patterns at v.2. Some argue that "therefore" (*oun*) marks the introduction of a new theme, as it does more than once in Ephesians (4:1, 17; 5:15). On occasions, however, the same particle winds up an argument (v.7). There is no obvious gap between 4:32 and 5:1 and so *oun* may be regarded as synoptic—"in a word" (NEB).

"Be" or "become" (*ginesthe*) confirms the close relation between this verse and the last where the same expression has been employed. Here it introduces a staggering conception. Paul invites his readers to imitate God. What follows elucidates his meaning. A child will show himself to be a true child by wanting to grow up like his father. In the same way, God's precious children (*tekna*, those born from him) will be eager to copy him, as he enables them. This was the teaching of Jesus himself.

2 God is love and the life that is like the life of God will be a life of love. If love is the essence of God's nature, it is the essential of the Christian character. We have already noted the repeated emphasis on love in this letter. The model of love is Christ himself. It is because he laid down his life for us that we are to love others to the point of sacrifice. The substitutionary element in the atonement may be implied by the particle "for" (*hyper;* cf. v.25), which can be as strongly vicarious in its significance as *anti.*

Paul borrows two technical terms in Jewish sacrificial vocabulary without differentiation. "Offering" (*prosphora*) is derived from the verb "to bring" and is the Hebrew *minḥāh*, a meal or cereal offering. On the cross, Christ presented himself, and Paul adds that it was "for an odour of a sweet smell" (RV). The phrase (*eis osmēn euōdias*) occurs in a sacrificial context over forty times in the Pentateuch. Paul has it in Philippians 4:18

where it is applied to the gift sent him by means of Epaphroditus. The metaphor suggests that our Lord's self-sacrifice was pleasing to his Father and was thus accepted as a means of reconciliation. "Sacrifice" (*thysia*) indicates that the victim was slain and denotes the peace-offering (*zebah*). Already in Ephesians Paul has spoken of Christ's death on the cross (2:16) and the sacrificial shedding of blood (1:7; 2:13). Because it is identified with Christ in his death, the Christian's life will likewise prove an acceptable sacrifice to God.

Notes

25 The NIV (along with NEB, PH, Wms.) uses two imperatives when in fact the first verb is a participle ἀποθέμενοι (*apothemenoi*, "putting off"; NIV, "[you] must put off"). The aorist could justify "having put away" but it may equally suggest simultaneous action. Lenski (p. 573) favored the former interpretation, regarding the participle as causal not modal: "since you have once put away the lie of falsehood." But the majority of recent commentators adopt the second view, because putting off falsehood and telling the truth are simply two sides of the same coin (cf. Hendriksen, p. 217). The fact that the imperative is preceded by a participle is accurately reflected in KJV, RV, and RSV.

26 The imperatives in Paul's quotation from Ps 4:5 (LXX)—ὀργίζεσθε καὶ μὴ ἁμαρτάνετε (*orgizesthe kai mē hamartanete*)—have been variously construed: The first has been taken as interrogative ("Are you angry? Do not sin") or conditional ("If you are angry, do not sin"). The traditional interpretation assumes that the successive imperatives denote condition and result: "Though you are angry, do not let your anger lead you into sin." Others consider the first imperative to be permissive or concessive and the second to be jussive ("Be angry if you must, but make sure you do not sin"). Again, both imperatives may be taken as genuinely jussive with the inclusion of μὴ (*mē*, "not") strengthening the second. In this case, the καὶ (*kai*, "and"), like *atque*, adds a qualification: "It is allowable to be justly angry and yet this is not to involve sin." The NIV appears to reflect this last alternative.

28 The most probable sequence is ταῖς ἰδίαις χερσὶν τὸ ἀγαθόν (*tais idiais chersin to agathon*, "with his own hands the good") although some MSS omit ἰδίαις (*idiais*, "own") and/or reverse the position of χερσὶν (*chersin*, "hands") and ἀγαθόν (*agathon*, "good"; NIV, "something useful").

29 "According to their needs" translates a gen. form τῆς χρείας (*tēs chreias*). The difficulties involved in determining the precise nature of the gen. probably gave rise to the occasional reading πίστεως (*pisteōs*, "of faith"). The article specifies a particular need related to the context. Hence χρείας (*chreias*, "need") is not a gen. of quality ("seasonable edification") nor is it the abstract and impersonal standing for the concrete and personal ("those who have need"). The KJV regards it as representing the accusative by inversion ("to the use of edifying") but this construction is not easy to sustain. It is best to settle either for an objective gen. ("building up applied to the need"), or a gen. of remoter reference or point of view ("building up as regards the need"; i.e., such as meets the need).

32 The dative ὑμῖν (*hymin*, "you") is on balance better attested than ἡμῖν (*hēmin*, "us"). The latter may have been prompted by Eph 5:2.

5:2 The accusative ἡμᾶς (*hēmas*, "us") is probably superior to ὑμᾶς (*hymas*, "us") while ἡμῶν (*hēmōn*, "of us"; NIV, "for us") is preferable to ὑμῶν (*hymōn*, "of you"). Τῷ θεῷ (*tō theō*, "to God") is not to be connected with the verb παρέδωκεν ἑαυτὸν (*paredōken heauton*, "gave himself up") or with εἰς ὀσμὴν εὐωδίας (*eis osmēn euōdias*, "for an odor of a sweet smell"; NIV, "fragrant"), but rather with προσφορὰν καὶ θυσίαν (*prosphoran kai thysian*, "offering"). The dative is ethical or accommodating rather than transmissive or restrictive.

4. *Light in the Lord*

5:3-20

> ³But among you there must not be even a hint of sexual immorality, or of any kind of impurity, or of greed, because these are improper for God's holy people. ⁴Nor should there be obscenity, foolish talk or coarse joking, which are out of place, but rather thanksgiving. ⁵For of this you can be sure: No immoral, impure, or greedy person—such a man is an idolater—has any inheritance in the kingdom of Christ and of God. ⁶Let no one deceive you with empty words, for because of such things God's wrath comes on those who are disobedient. ⁷Therefore do not be partners with them.
>
> ⁸For you were once darkness, but now you are light in the Lord. Live as children of light ⁹(for the fruit of the light consists in all goodness, righteousness and truth) ¹⁰and find out what pleases the Lord. ¹¹Have nothing to do with the fruitless deeds of darkness, but rather expose them. ¹²For it is shameful even to mention what is done in secret. ¹³But everything exposed by the light becomes visible, ¹⁴for it is light that makes everything visible. This is why it is said:
>
> > "Wake up, O sleeper,
> > rise from the dead,
> > and Christ will shine on you."
>
> ¹⁵Be very careful, then, how you live—not as unwise but as wise, ¹⁶making the most of every opportunity, because the days are evil. ¹⁷Therefore do not be foolish, but understand what the Lord's will is. ¹⁸Do not get drunk on wine, which leads to debauchery. Instead, be filled with the Spirit. ¹⁹Speak to one another with psalms, hymns and spiritual songs. Sing and make music in your heart to the Lord, ²⁰always giving thanks to God the Father for everything, in the name of our Lord Jesus Christ.

Paul has epitomized the Christian behavior pattern as "a life of love" (v.2). Now he turns to another theme: "Live as children of light" (v.8). But they can be "light in the Lord" only because Christ is the world's true light (v.14).

3 The apostle begins by speaking about the effect of light in a life of purity. He resumes the prohibitive character of Ephesians 4:26–31, taking it further by declaring that such aberrations should not only be avoided but not so much as mentioned (v.12), since they are altogether unsuitable for those who belong to the consecrated community of God. As Robinson (p. 115) explained, the apostle is appealing for a new Christian decorum.

"Sexual immorality" (*porneia*) was tolerated in the permissive pagan society of Paul's day (Rom 1:24–32). "Impurity" (*akatharsia*) has already been mentioned in Ephesians 4:19 as a characteristic of secularized existence, along with "greed," or "the lust for more" (*pleonexia*). In Colossians 3:5 *pleonexia* is conceived of as idolatry—as here in v.5—because it makes a god of what it seeks to possess.

4 The three terms ("obscenity," "foolish talk," "coarse joking") each occur only here in the NT. Paul has already warned against "unwholesome talk" (Eph 4:29) because of the harm it does to those who are compelled to hear it. Now he attacks it from another angle, because it is unseemly for Christians and usurps the place of praise. "Obscenity" (*aischrotēs*) in this context is broadly equivalent to "filthy language" (*aischrologia*, Col 3:8; BAG, p. 24). Next comes "foolish talk" (*mōrologia*), which is stupid chatter or silly twaddle. This is combined with *eutrapelia* (literally, "an easy turn of speech"), which means versatility and witty repartee. The NEB has "flippant talk." Because of the determinative content of v.3, however, it may refer to "coarse joking" (NIV) and *double-*

entendre. These things must be repudiated, because they "do not come up to the mark" (BV). Instead, the Christian's mouth will be continually filled with thanks to God (Eph 2:7; 5:18; Col 2:7; 3:15).

5 The apostle warns his readers about the serious consequences of immorality. They must surely be aware that there is no room in the kingdom of God for those who blatantly continue in sensual sin. The three categories of v.3 are singled out again, with the rider that the acquisitive make an idol of their possessions. No one of this sort has any place reserved in the eschatological kingdom. The inheritance (*klēronomia*) is a present title to a future position (Eph 1:14, 18). This cannot be acquired by the disobedient (v.6). In Colossians 1:13 Paul refers to "the kingdom of the Son" whom the Father loves (cf. Eph 1:6). But since it is God who "placed all things under his feet" (Eph 1:22), the kingdom is his as well as Christ's.

6 There were those then as there are now who would protest that Christian standards are too demanding and that people must be allowed to live as they like (1 Cor 15:32). In the name of a spurious freedom, an attempt is made to bring converts into bondage to sin once again. The Ephesians are not to be fooled by such futile arguments (Eph 4:17). They are promoted by the arch-deceiver himself (2:2). Paul is not hitting at any particular group either of embryo Gnostic philosophers or pseudo-Christian antinomians. His indictment includes all the propagandists of permissiveness.

It is on account of "such things" (*tauta*)—the sins mentioned above rather than the deceptive teaching that encourages them—that divine retribution is already on its way ("comes," *erchetai*, present tense). It will keep on coming till in the end it deals with the offenders. They are designated by the same Semitism (literally, "sons of disobedience") as in 2:2.

7 An unambiguous admonition rounds off the paragraph begun at v.3. Christians are not to get mixed up with those who have excluded themselves from the kingdom by their impurity. The word "partners" (*symmetochoi*) is the same one Paul used in 3:6 to describe the way in which the Gentiles now share in the messianic promise.

8 Here Paul enlarges on the contrast between darkness and light. As in Ephesians 2:1–3 and 3:17–24, he reminds his readers of what they once were. One word suffices by way of summary—"darkness." Not only did they live in darkness: they *were* darkness (cf. 4:18). But now they have been rescued from the dominion of darkness and inherit the kingdom of light (Col 1:12, 13). They not only live in the light: they *are* light. This is possible only in union with Christ who is himself the light. "Apart from Christ Satan occupies everything" (Calvin, in loc.). Henceforth they "must behave as those who are at home in the light" (Barclay, p. 124). Here another Semitic expression, "children of light" (cf. 1 Thess 5:5), stands over against "sons of disobedience" (RV) in v.6.

9 A parenthesis explains the command at the end of v.8. Light is known by its effects. When the light of Christ shines in the lives of believers it produces benevolence, fairness, and integrity. These three qualities counteract the dark influence of malice (Eph 4:31), injustice and falsehood (4:25). "Goodness" (*agathōsynē*) is the achievement of moral excellence combined with a generous spirit. "Righteousness" (*dikaiosynē*) was understood by the Greeks as giving all their due. Among a wide range of meanings (cf. TDNT, 1:241) "truth" (*alētheia*) stands for genuineness and honesty. It is not only something to be said but something to be done (see on Eph 4:25; cf. 1 John 1:6; 3:18). The harvest of light is found not only in all these qualities held in balance in the rounded Christian life, but in every aspect of each, which those who have received the light of Christ will want to explore.

10 The exhortation in v.8 is further supplemented by a participial clause, literally "finding out [*dokimazontes*] what is well-pleasing to the Lord" (cf. v.17). The verb has to do with the testing of metals and so can mean to discover by examination, verify, or approve. Here and in 1 Timothy 3:10 the first sense seems appropriate (BAG, p. 201). Those who live as "children of light" (v.8) will be continually endeavoring to ascertain what is the will of God in every situation so that all they do may satisfy him.

11 Yet another exhortation is added to that in v.8. Christians are to have no share (*sygkoinōneite*; cf. v.7) in "the barren deeds of darkness" (NEB). They are not to be involved in them. Notice that it is the "deeds" (*ergoi*) that have to be shunned, not the doers. Paul is not advocating pharisaical separatism. The follower of Christ will go where his master went and meet those his master met. But though he does not withdraw from the world, he refuses to adopt its standards or fall in with its ways. He is concerned to produce "the fruit of the light" (v.9), and darkness is sterile.

So far from participating in them, believers should expose these practices. When the object is a person, the verb (*elegchō*) means to convince or reprove. This is the distinctive work of the Spirit. But when the object is impersonal, *elegchō* may signify to bring to light or expose. This exposure is not effected by what is actually said by way of rebuke, because such repulsive deeds are not so much as to be whispered (vv.3, 12), but simply by letting the light of Christ shine through and show them up.

12 Paul reiterates the insistence of v.3 that the things pagan profligates do under cover of secrecy are not to be breathed among Christians. They are unspeakably abominable. Sometimes sin can be publicized by a reaction against it. What has been done in the dark is best kept dark. Paul goes so far as to say that the shamefulness of these ugly vices may rub off on Christians if they are continually talking about them, even if it is to disapprove of them. Lenski's interpretation (p. 609) that the Christian's reproof of evil works makes them appear shameful to those who engage in them is less convincing.

13 Paul appeals to the effect of light in the natural world. It penetrates wherever it shines, so that everything is lit up by it. In the same way, whenever the light of Christ appears, it shows up sin for what it is. Evil can no longer masquerade as anything else. Paul let the light fall on the ungodliness of the pagan world and exposed it for what it really was (Rom 1:18–32). For, he adds, it is the function of light to make visible. Whatever hidden wickedness is revealed by the light of Christ can no longer be obscured by darkness but is shown up in its real nature. Others see here a reference to the transformation brought about by light. "It is even possible (after all, it happened with you!) for light to turn the thing it shines upon into light also" (PH). The following verse could support such an interpretation. The exposure and reproval of sin by the light of Christ may lead to salvation, as it did for the Ephesians themselves (v.8).

14 The same introductory formula as in Ephesians 4:8 (*dio legei*) prefaces a poetical quotation. The lines form a metrical triplet in a rhythm that was specially associated with religious initiation chants. This may well supply a clue in tracing their origin. They are not a direct quotation of OT Scripture, though they contain echoes of Isaiah 60:1 and possibly other passages in the same prophecy (Isa 9:2; 26:19; 51:17; 52:1). Nor can they be found in any apocryphal book. It is unlikely that Paul's memory was at fault, as some have surmised, and that he imagined he was citing Scripture when in fact he was using some unidentified source. It has also been suggested that the poem was Paul's own composition as he enlarged on scriptural themes, or that he was reproducing the content of prophecy in the light of its fulfillment. Others again speculate as to whether the lines are to be attributed to Jesus himself.

The most likely solution seems to be that this is an early baptismal hymn based on Isaiah 60:1. The rhythm may have been borrowed from the mystery religions and consecrated to a Christian use. Paul is soon to mention hymns in the context of worship (v.19). This may well have been a liturgical chant addressed to those about to be baptized (cf. 1 Tim 3:16). C.F.D. Moule is struck by the similarities between this verse and the story of Peter's release from prison in Acts 12:6–11 and inquires whether the hymn is built around it (*The Birth of the New Testament* [London: A. & C. Black, 1962], p. 25).

The exhortations "wake up" (*egeire*) and "rise from the dead" (*anasta ek tōn nekrōn*) place the hymn firmly in the context of resurrection. It might have been designed for use on Easter day. The connection between resurrection and baptism is so close that there is no need to restrict the intention. Moreover, in the primitive church baptism was described as an enlightenment (*phōtismos*), a usage that may underlie Hebrews 6:4 and 10:32. The verb translated "shine" (*epiphainō*) is applied to the rising of a heavenly body and to the dawn of the day (BAG, 304). Christ, as the morning star, has already risen and sheds his light on all who are raised to newness of life in him.

15 Further exhortations follow, after the interjection in vv.12–14 backing up v.11. Because of his illumination, the believer will pay the most scrupulous attention to his personal behavior (v.8b). *Blepete* is a common Pauline expression for "see to it." Here it is combined with *akribōs* ("accurately," "carefully") to underline the need for the utmost concentration on leading an irreproachable life. The verb translated "to live" is *peripateō* and has been used four times previously in Ephesians 4 and 5. The metaphorical contrast between light and darkness is now replaced by that between wisdom and folly. Christians must no longer act like simpletons (NEB), since God's own wisdom is always available to them (1:8, 9; 3:10).

16 They are to make "the most of every opportunity" (*exagorazomenoi tōn kairōn*). The verb "to buy back" or "take off the market" is used in Galatians 3:13 and 4:5 in connection with redemption from the law. Here and in Colossians 4:5 it is of less certain interpretation. It has nothing to do with gaining time, as in Daniel 2:8, LXX (BAG, p. 271). It is not to be treated allegorically, as if time were being snatched from the devil or from evil men. What is meant is simply to make the best possible use of all circumstances like prudent merchants. *Kairos* ("opportunity," NIV) is the right moment, which Paul urges his readers to grasp lest it be wasted. The days are evil (*ponerai*, "wicked") in a moral sense, not necessarily by reason of hardship and distress, though this may be an accompaniment.

17 "Therefore" (*dia touto*) resumes the thought of v.15 with its exhortation to be wise. "Foolish" (*aphrōn*) is a stronger word than *asophoi* in v.15, alluding to stupid imprudence or senseless folly in action. To "understand" (*syniēmi*) is to give the mind to something so as to get hold of it. It implies that an effort has to be made: so it has the sense of "try to grasp." The object of this determined attempt at apprehension is the Lord's will (v.10). Paul recognizes the divine will as the regulative principle of the Christian life (Eph 1:1, 5, 9). Here he refers to the will of the Lord (i.e., Jesus Christ) perhaps, as Lenski (pp. 616, 617) suggested, because Christ left us an example.

18 A specific instance of the foregoing generalization follows. Quoting Proverbs 23:30, Paul warns against the folly of overindulgence in strong drink. Drunkenness was all too common in the pagan world and cautions in the NT show that it presented a serious temptation to Christians. The danger of drunkenness (Gal 5:21) lies not only in itself but in what it may induce. Debauchery (*asōtia*) in the NT means dissoluteness or dissipation. It is the "wild living" of the prodigal son (Luke 15:13, adverb). In classical Greek it signified extravagant squandering both of money and of the physical appetites. If they are wise, Christians will avoid all such excess.

Instead of continuing in drunkenness, they are to go on being filled with the Spirit. That is a surprising alternative. We might have expected the apostle to plead for abstinence as over against intemperance. But he takes a more startling and positive line. He urges his readers to draw on the reinvigorating resources of the Holy Spirit. On the day of Pentecost the effect of such an experience was mistaken for drunkenness. As Bruce (p. 110) makes clear, Paul is not for a moment implying that the Spirit is a substance a man's personality can be filled with as his body may be filled with wine. Yet the Spirit does produce a genuine exhilaration others vainly seek from alcohol.

"With the Spirit" is actually "in spirit" (*en pneumati*). The Greek text does not indicate whether the Holy Spirit is intended. The word *pneuma* can equally well mean the human spirit as affected by the Holy Spirit (RV mg.). We have noted a similar ambiguity in Ephesians 2:22 and 3:5 and will meet it again in 6:18. Lenski (p. 619) contended that Paul would not have attempted the daring comparison between wine and the Holy Spirit, and that we are not told explicitly with what the believer is to be filled but only where he is to be filled, i.e., in spirit. However, it seems much more probable that the Holy Spirit is intended here, in view of the many scriptural references to being filled with the Spirit.

The theological implications of "be filled" (*plērousthe*) are crucial for a biblical doctrine of the Holy Spirit. The imperative makes it clear that this is a command for all Christians. The present tense rules out any once-for-all reception of the Spirit but points to a continuous replenishment (literally, "go on being filled"). Nor does it appear that Paul is urging his readers to enter into a new experience ("up to now you have not been filled with the Spirit, but you must start to be so"). Rather, he is inviting them to go on as they began ("you have, of course, been filled with the Spirit; keep on like that"). Finally, the verb is passive: "Let yourselves be filled with the Spirit." This is not a manufactured experience, though it can be rejected (cf. Gal 3:2, 5). There may, therefore, be successive fillings of the Spirit; indeed, the Christian life should be an uninterrupted filling. What this verse will not substantiate is the claim that after becoming a Christian, a single, additional, definitive filling is essential for completion.

19 The outcome of being filled with the Spirit is described in vv.19, 20 in a series of four participles that virtually amount to imperatives. It is noticeable that each of these expressions of the Spirit's fullness has to do with praise. The verb "to speak" (*laleō*) is not confined to normal conversation but covers utterance of any kind and so is perfectly applicable to the medium of psalms, hymns, and songs. Such communication is with one another (*heautois*) not "to yourselves" (KJV). "Psalms" seems to refer to the OT Psalter, which was integrated with Christian worship from the first. "Hymns" in pagan circles were sung to eulogize some god or cultic hero. Christian hymns exalted the name of Christ (v.19) or God (v.20). Such canticles appear in the NT itself (as at v.14). "Spiritual songs" (*ōdai pneumatikai*) may be so designated either to differentiate them from secular compositions or because they represent spontaneous singing in the Spirit.

The verb "to make music" is *psallō,* from which "psalm" is derived. It can mean playing a stringed instrument (literally, "to pluck") or singing praise to the accompaniment of a harp. Here it describes the heart's inner melody that keeps in tune with audible praise or may be independent of any outward expression. If it is offered "to the Lord," it does not need to be heard by men.

20 The perpetual accompaniment of all these outlets of the Spirit in the Christian life is thanksgiving. The context is not restricted to that of the church's liturgy as is indicated by "always" (*pantote*). Such gratitude to God is to cover every circumstance, "even if it be disease or poverty" (Chrysostom, in loc.), and is to be addressed to God the Father—the Father of our Lord and Savior Jesus Christ (Eph 1:3, 17), who is also "our God and Father" (Gal 1:4)—in the name of the Son as the one who fully reveals him.

Notes

4 O. Casel, following Origen and Jerome, equates εὐχαριστία (*eucharistia,* "thanksgiving") with εὐχαριτία (*eucharitia*)—that gracious or even ingratiating speech that was considered by the Greeks to be "the mark of fine training" (BAG, 329). The context and Eph 4:29 might seem to confirm this. The noun is not known to have carried such a broad connotation, though the corresponding adjective εὐχάριστος (*eucharistos,* "thankful") was certainly so used.
5 The absence of the article before θεοῦ (*theou,* "of God") has led some commentators to infer that only one person of the Godhead is in view and that the phrase means "the kingdom of him who is both Christ and God" (RHG, p. 786; Moulton, *Prolegomena,* p. 84). It is more probable that the reference includes first the Son and then the Father (cf. Eph 4:5, 6). Θεός (*theos,* "God") is often used without an article (1 Cor 6:9, 10; 15:50; Gal 5:21) and the presence of the article here might even have hinted that the kingdom of Christ was not immediately recognizable as equivalent to the kingdom of God. On the other hand, that Christ and God, though distinct, are subsumed under the one definite article provides impressive evidence of our Lord's divinity.
9 The TR reading πνεύματος (*pneumatos,* "of the Spirit") is obviously a gloss from Gal 5:22 and must yield to φωτός (*phōtos,* "of light") which has weightier textual support. The context confirms the emendation.
10 The NIV (with NEB) interprets the participle δοκιμάζοντες (*dokimazontes,* "proving") imperatively, assuming ἐστε (*este,* is) as in Romans 12:9-13; 19, 20. Abbott (p. 153) thought it to be less natural here between two imperatives. It was once assumed that εὐάρεστος (*euarestos,* "well-pleasing") was confined to biblical and ecclesiastical literature, but for its occurrence in inscriptions and papyri cf. Deissmann, BS, p. 215, and MM, p. 259.
13, 14 The adversative force of δὲ (*de*) is upheld by the NIV ("but"). Τὰ πάντα (*ta panta,* "everything") is taken in a general sense rather than as referring to what has been mentioned in vv.11, 12 ("all these things"). The verse is thus regarded simply as a factual statement about the action of natural light (φῶς, *phōs*) with the verb ἐλέγχω (*elenchō*) meaning "to expose" rather than "to rebuke," since no personal object is expressed. Πᾶν (*pan,* "all") is accepted as neuter and linked with *ta panta,* not as abstract for concrete and thus equivalent to "every man." In each

case the voice of the verb φανερόω (*phaneroō*, "to expose") is taken as passive rather than middle, doubtless on the ground that there is no clear instance of the latter in the NT.

The RV treats vv.13, 14 as a general statement without restricting the application to natural light: "but all things when they are reproved are made manifest." Most recent translations, however, follow the same line as the NIV, though not all take φῶς (*phōs*, "light") as the subject of the second clause. It is possible to regard τὸ φανερούμενον (*to phaneroumenon*) as the subject, and to tr.: "everything that is made visible is light" (cf. RSV, NEB, TEV, JB, Barclay) or even "where everything is made visible there is light" (BV; cf. Amplified Bible). But this demands a spiritual application, because it is not scientifically accurate to say that all that is brought to light actually becomes light itself.

Some cursive texts have the middle ἔγειραι (*egeirai*, "rouse yourselves") for the present imperative ἔγειρε (*egeire*, "wake up") read by all uncials. The latter does not represent an ellipsis of σεαυτόν (*seauton*, "yourself") or an active voice performing as a middle, but an exhortatory formula like ἄγε ἔπειγε (*age epeige*)—"Up!" For ἐπιφαύσει (*epiphausei*, "will shine on") some read ἐπιψαύσεις (*epipsauseis*, "will touch"), i.e., to bring to life.

15 The UBS text underlying the NIV has ἀκριβῶς πῶς (*akribōs pōs*, "carefully how") with strong support, but πῶς ἀκριβῶς (*pōs akribōs*, "how carefully") appears in some witnesses; hence, "see that ye walk circumspectly" (KJV) or "warily" (Wycliffe).

17 The imperative συνίετε (*syniete*, "understand") is adopted by UBS on good authority. The TR has συνιέντες (*synientes*, "understanding") while συνίοντες (*syniontes*, "being with") is also found. If *syniete* is not original it may have been inserted to conform with v.18.

18 The verb πληρόω (*plēroō*, "to be full") is passively construed with the gen. (Luke 2:40; Acts 13:52; 2 Tim 1:4), the dative (Rom 1:29; 2 Cor 7:4), or the accusative (Phil 1:11; Col 1:9) of the thing by or with which the filling takes place. The construction with ἐν (*en*, "in," "with") and the dative is unusual when the sense, as here, is "to be filled" rather than "to be made complete" (as in Col 2:10 and probably 4:12). This has led some to reject the instrumental force of *en* and to regard it as indicating the sphere in which the filling occurs, interpreted either as the Holy Spirit or the human spirit.

19, 20 The four participial clauses derive a certain imperative force from πληροῦσθε ἐν πνεύματι (*plērousthe en pneumati*, "be filled with the Spirit") on which they depend. They are to be treated as coordinate rather than subordinate. They modify the subject and thus describe the condition of those who are continually being filled in the sphere of the Spirit. Theodoret took ὑπὲρ πάντων (*hyper pantōn*, "for everything") as masc.; i.e., that we should thank God for all who have received his blessing, but the context demands the neuter.

---

5. *Christian Relationships: Marriage*

5:21–33

21Submit to one another out of reverence for Christ.

22Wives, submit to your husbands as to the Lord. 23For the husband is the head of the wife as Christ is the head of the church, his body, of which he is the Savior. 24Now as the church submits to Christ, so also wives should submit to their husbands in everything.

25Husbands, love your wives, just as Christ loved the church and gave himself up for her 26to make her holy, cleansing her by the washing with water through the word, 27and to present her to himself as a radiant church, without stain or wrinkle or any other blemish, but holy and blameless. 28In this same way, husbands ought to love their wives as their own bodies. He who loves his wife loves himself. 29After all, no one ever hated his own body, but he feeds and cares for it, just as Christ does the church—30for we are members of his body. 31"For this reason a man will leave his father and mother and be united to his wife, and the two will become one flesh." 32This is a profound mystery—but I am talking about Christ and the church. 33However, each one of you also must love his wife as he loves himself, and the wife must respect her husband.

The basic principle of Christian submissiveness that governs the community life of the church applies also to social relationships. Paul selects the most conspicuous of these and shows how they are transformed when controlled by a prior obedience to Christ. In Ephesians 5:21–33 he deals with wives and husbands; in 6:1–4, with children and parents; and in 6:5–9, with slaves and masters (cf. Col 3:18–4:1 for a close parallel).

Such instructions about the regulation of Christian households are often designated by the technical German term *Haustafel* (Table of Household Duties). It is not, however, a Christian invention, for both Jewish and pagan samples are extant (cf. Houlden, pp. 210, 211). The gospel placed these relationships on a revolutionary new footing, since all are subjected to the lordship of Christ. The Mishnah exempted "women, slaves, and minors" from reciting the *Shema* (Deut 6:4) with its recognition of a common Lord (M. *Berakoth* 3.3).

21 Commentators discuss whether this verse represents the conclusion of the previous section or the start of a new one. While grammatically it may be attached to v.20, its content coincides more naturally with what follows. The verb "to submit" (*hypotassō*) occurs twenty-three times in Paul and denotes subordination to those considered worthy of respect, either because of their inherent qualities or more often because of the position they held. Christians are to submit to civil authorities, to church leaders, to parents, and to masters. The whole structure of society as ordered by God depends on the readiness of its members to recognize these sanctions. Without them anarchy prevails. The Christian, however, observes them not merely for their own sake, or even because they are imposed by God, but out of "reverence" (*phobos*) for Christ (cf. v.17). Moreover, within the fellowship of the church (and Paul has this more prominently in mind than the community at large) this submission to others is reciprocal ("to one another," *allēlous*). No one is to coerce another, for all voluntarily accept the discipline. Hence, any delusions of superiority are banished and no one thinks of himself more highly than he ought.

22 "Submit" is assumed here from the previous verse, since no verb appears. The fact that the sentence depends on v.21 confirms the paragraph arrangement adopted in the NIV. It is to their own (*idios*) husbands that wives are to be subject (Col 3:18). The legally binding exclusiveness of the marriage relationship is thus underlined. "As to the Lord" differs slightly from "as is fitting in the Lord" in Colossians 3:18. In obeying her husband, the Christian wife is obeying the Lord who has sanctioned the marriage contract. It should be noted that all Paul says is within the context of a Christian marriage. He is not implying that women are inferior to men or that all women should be subject to men. The subjection, moreover, is voluntary, not forced. The Christian wife who promises to obey does so because her vow is "as to the Lord."

23 The marriage relationship is now set out as being a reflection of the relationship between Christ and his church. This is to raise it to an unimaginably lofty level. In 1 Corinthians 11:12 Paul had already marked out a hierarchy in which God is seen as the head of Christ, Christ as the head of the man, and the man as the head of the woman. Here he looks at it from another angle. If the head of the woman is the man and the head of the church is Christ (Eph 1:22; 4:12, 16), then it is permissible to draw an analogy between the wife's relationship to her husband and the church's relation to Christ. Marriage is thus interpreted in the sublimest terms. It is compared with the marriage of the Lamb to his bride.

Unless we take the next comment as an aside that bears no relation to the analogy Paul is presenting, it must be assumed that there is an intended parallelism. It remains true, of course, that Christ is the Savior of his body, the church, in a unique manner. The word Savior (*sōtēr*) is never used in the NT except of Christ or God. But having recognized and safeguarded that vital truth, we may legitimately pursue the analogy and assume that Paul regards the husband, even if to an infinitely lesser degree, as the protector of his wife (cf. vv.28, 29).

24 "Now" (*alla*) continues the same line of argument rather than reversing it. In other words, Paul is not saying that even though ultimately the relation of Christ to the church is incomparable, nevertheless wives should submit to their husbands. As Hendriksen explains (p. 249), he is pursuing a likeness rather than pointing out a difference: "as . . . so." Here the verb "submit" stands unambiguously in the text and does not have to be supplied, as in v.23. The church as the bride of Christ readily acknowledges his authority and seeks to please him in every respect. When marriage is seen in the light of this higher relationship between Christ and his body, the wife finds no difficulty in submitting to her husband, for he too has obligations to her in the Lord (vv.25-33).

25 Paul turns to the reciprocal duties of the husband. In Greco-Roman society it was recognized that wives had obligations to their husbands, but not vice versa. In this, as in other respects, Christianity introduced a revolutionary approach to marriage that equalized the rights of wives and husbands and established the institution on a much firmer foundation than ever before. One word summed up the role of the wife—"submit" (v.22). One word does the same for the husband—"love" (*agapate*). This is the highest and distinctively Christian word for loving. As over against *eros* ("sexual passion") and *philia* ("family affection") Paul chooses the verb *agapaō* to insist that the love of a Christian man for his wife must be a response to and an expression of the love of God in Christ extended to the church (cf. vv.1, 2). Colossians 3:19 spells out the practical implications of such love: "do not be harsh with them."

Once again the apostle draws a comparison between the marriage relationship and the relationship of Christ and the church (cf. vv.22-24). It was on the cross that our Lord gave himself up for his bride. The analogy is all the more telling, since *ekklēsia* is feminine. This is an aspect of the atonement not given such prominence elsewhere in the NT. Paul himself has already declared that Christ laid down his life "for our sins" (Rom 4:25; Gal 1:4), or "for me" (Gal 2:20), or "for us all" (Rom 8:32). Now he affirms that our Lord's sacrificial death was "for her," i.e., for the church. "For" (*hyper*) may carry substitutionary overtones, as in v.2.

26 In vv.26, 27 Paul explains more fully the aim of Christ's atonement so far as the church is concerned. It was "to make her holy" (*hagiasē*) (v.26) and "to present her to himself as a radiant church" (v.27). To sanctify (*hagiazō*) is to set apart, and when he died on the cross, our Lord's purpose was that he should separate for himself a people for his own possession. From the beginning the church has been called out in this way, but the ethical demands of such privilege require a response in every age. There is an old Jewish wedding custom in which, when the ring is given, the bridegroom says to the bride: "Behold, thou art sanctified to me."

If the church is to attain the actual holiness that alone befits her status as the bride of Christ, then purification is essential. "Cleansing" is literally "having cleansed" (*katharisas*). The fact that the church must be cleansed before she begins to be holy makes it clear that Paul's concept of sanctification involves an immediate need for a subjective change. While purification may assume a logical priority, however, the process is really simultaneous.

This essential cleansing is effected "by the washing of water" (tō loutrō tou hydatos), which is said to be accompanied by a spoken word (en rhēmati). The term loutron means "a bathing"—the action rather than the bath itself, which would be loutēr. The RV mg. is misleading in suggesting "laver," which could also mean "that which washes," i.e., the water itself, in which case hydatos would be superfluous. It is also possible that Paul was alluding to the purification of the bride before the marriage ceremony (Ezek 16:9).

There seems to be little or no doubt that the reference is to baptism. The "washing with water" here is equivalent to "the washing of rebirth" in Titus 3:5. There is, however, no hint of any mechanical view of the sacrament, as if the mere application of water could in itself bring about the purification it symbolizes. Nowhere does the NT countenance baptismal regeneration in an *ex opere operato* sense.

What is "the word" that accompanies baptism? The Greek term rhēma means something spoken—an utterance. It could refer to the preaching of the gospel at a baptismal service (1 Peter 1:23-25). It is more likely, however, to indicate the formula used at the moment of baptism. In principle, this was trinitarian in shape but on occasion it simply invoked the all-sufficient name of Jesus. Others, again, take rhēma to be the word spoken by the candidate for baptism as he confessed his faith in Christ and called on the Savior's name.

27 The ultimate aim in view when Christ gave himself up for the church (v.25) was that at the end of the age he might be able to present her to himself in unsullied splendor as a bride adorned for her husband (Rev 21:2). The verb (paristēmi, "to place beside") is used of the presentation of Christ in the temple (Luke 2:22). Paul himself applies it to the presentation of the church as a pure virgin to Christ her husband (2 Cor 11:2). It was normally the friend of the bridegroom (John 3:29) who thus handed over the bride. But Christ dispenses with all intermediaries and he alone introduces the bride to the bridegroom, who paradoxically is himself. As Zerwick puts it, Christ is his own "matchmaker" (p. 155).

"Present," however, becomes almost equivalent to "make" or "render" and that aspect of its significance is clearly involved (BAG, p. 633). The eschatological church is transformed by Christ so as to be "all glorious" (Ps 45:13). J. Paul Sampley wonders whether paristēmi may not also be regarded as a technical term in the language of sacrifice, as in Romans 12:1 ("*And the Two Shall Become One Flesh*": *A Study of Traditions in Ephesians 5:21-33* [Cambridge: University Press, 1971], p. 135).

No ugly spots or lines of age disfigure the appearance of the bride. The church becomes what it was intended to be—holy and blameless (Eph 1:4). All this is possible only because Christ is the Savior of his body (v.23).

28 Paul returns to his analogy and declares that just as Christ loves the church so husbands ought to love their wives as being one flesh with themselves. Christ loves the church, not simply as if it were his body, but because it is in fact his body. Husbands therefore are to love their wives, not simply as they love their own bodies, but as being one body with themselves, as indeed they are. Lest the staggering implication of what he has affirmed should fail to register with his readers, Paul puts it in another way to avoid ambiguity. So intimate is the relationship between man and wife that they are fused into a single entity. For a man to love his wife is to love himself. She is not to be treated as a piece of property, as was the custom in Paul's day. She is to be regarded as an extension of a man's own personality and so part of himself.

29 The apostle appeals to a self-evident fact. It will hardly be denied that no one ever hates his own body (*sarx*, "flesh"; cf. Gen 2:23; Eph 5:30, 31). He devotes himself to looking after it. He provides for it in every way. He supplies it with food (*ektrephei*) to promote its development and maintain its health. He cares for it and cherishes it (*thalpei*, literally, "keeps [it] warm"). This is how Christ loves his body, the church (v.25), argues Paul. He appeals to the same principle when addressing husbands as he did when addressing wives. Wives are to obey their husbands as the church obeys Christ. Husbands are to love their wives as Christ loves the church.

30 The reason why Christ thus cares for the church is now made clear. It is because Christians are living parts of his body. In Ephesians 4:25 Paul has dealt with the relationship of the members to one another individually. Here he is concerned with their relationship to the whole. Earlier in the letter he has spoken about the church as a body whose head is Christ (1:22, 23; 4:12, 16). Here he stresses the closeness of the Christian's communion with Christ as a part (*melē*) of himself, just as the branches are part of the vine.

31 According to Foulkes, Genesis 2:24 contains "the most profound and fundamental statement in the whole of Scripture concerning God's plan for marriage" (p. 161). Paul introduces the verse at this point to substantiate his argument from Scripture, as did Jesus himself. It had already been shaping his thought in this section.

"For this reason" (*anti toutou*) is not a preface to the quotation but part of it (LXX has *eneken touto*). When Adam recognized that Eve was part of himself ("bone of my bones, and flesh of my flesh," Gen 2:23), Genesis 2:24 adds: "Therefore a man leaves his father and his mother and cleaves to his wife, and they become one flesh" (RSV). The marriage tie takes precedence over every other human relationship and for this reason is to be regarded as inviolable. Nevertheless, what is basically a divine ordinance is graciously designed for mutual satisfaction and delight. "United" means closely joined (*proskollēsthēsetai*, literally, "will be glued") and, taken in conjunction with the reference to "one flesh," can refer only to sexual intercourse, which is thus hallowed by the approval of God himself. It is because of this exalted biblical view of marital relations that the church has taken its stand on the indissolubility of the marital bond and the impermissibility of polygamy, adultery, or divorce.

32 The RV is grammatically correct in translating "this mystery is great." "Great" (*mega*) expresses magnitude rather than intensity. We might say "it is of far-reaching importance" or "has many implications" (JB) or as NIV has it, "This is a profound mystery." But what is meant by "mystery" here and what mystery is meant? Already we have seen that for Paul in this letter *mystērion* means a secret of revelation made known through a special dispensation of grace (Eph 3:2, 3). Usually it embraces the total sweep of God's purposes in Christ (1:9; 3:3, 4, 9; 6:19), but it may also refer to some specific truth within that wider revelation (as in Rom 11:25 and 1 Cor 15:51). As Foulkes suggests, the sense is "The truth that lies here hidden but revealed in Christ, is a wonderful one" (p. 162; cf. NEB: "It is a great truth that is hidden here"). In other words, Genesis 2:24 enunciates a more profound truth than was realized till Christ came to win his bride, the church, by giving himself for her on the cross (v.25).

Paul does not add the words "but I am talking about Christ and the church" as if he had been diverted from his theme. Rather, he is saying that so far as he is concerned he refers the mystery to the relation between Christ and the church—a mystery into which he himself had been given unusual insight because of the revelation entrusted to him. Although this verse enshrines the highest possible view of marriage, it does not support the Roman doctrine of marriage as a sacrament. The misunderstanding has arisen from the fact that *sacramentum* (Vul.) is the Latin equivalent of *mystērion*. The best Roman Catholic scholarship today repudiates any attempt to appeal to this verse.

33 The final word in this section is a practical one. Whether or not Paul's readers have fully understood his allusions to the "profound mystery" (v.32), they should at least get hold of the essential instructions he has been endeavoring to convey. Paul addresses every husband individually (literally, "you each, one by one") without naming him as such. He is to go on loving his wife as his very self (vv.25, 28, 29).

The wife for her part is to give her husband the respect (*phobētai*) that is due him in the Lord (v.22). As v.21 has made plain, such respect is conditioned by and expressive of reverence (*phobos*) for Christ. It also assumes that the husband will so love his wife as to be worthy of such deference.

Those who are puzzled because Paul does not tell wives that they are to love their husbands fail to appreciate the almost rabbinical precision with which the analogy is handled. Christ loves the church; the church's love for Christ is expressed in submission and obedience.

Notes

21 A fourth participial clause ὑποτασσόμενοι (*hypotassomenoi*, "submitting yourselves") is appended to πληροῦσθε (*plērousthe*, "be filled") in v.18. It supports the contention that syntactically this verse should be attached to what precedes (UBS). If he had meant to make a complete break, Paul would have employed an imperative. There is a close link with what follows, however, since αἱ γυναῖκες, κ.τ.λ. (*hai gynaikes*, etc., "wives, ... ") in v.22 is annexed without a verb of its own (assuming that ὑποτάσσεσθε [*hypotassesthe*] or ὑποτασσέσθωσαν [*hypotassesthōsan*] are glosses) as a further elaboration of *hypotassomenoi*.

24 The implications of ἀλλά (*alla*, "but"; NIV, "now") here have been the subject of considerable discussion among exegetes. Some explain it as resumptive (cf. πλήν [*plēn*, "however"] v.33), though the alleged digression in v.23b does not seriously interrupt the main argument. Others find an antithetic reference following a suppressed negative, such as "do not be disobedient." It may be employed syllogistically to introduce a proof or inference drawn from the previous statement, though *alla* is not equivalent to οὖν (*oun*, "then," "now then," "therefore") or ὥστε (*hōste*, "so that," "therefore"). Some insist that the fully adversative force of *alla* must be retained, so that it is tr. "nevertheless" or "notwithstanding" to stress the fact that the husband cannot be treated as the savior of his wife as Christ is the savior of his body. It is perhaps better to regard αὐτὸς σωτὴρ τοῦ σώματος (*autos sōtēr tou sōmatos*, "he [is] Savior of the body," v.23b) as in apposition to v.23a so that *alla* substantiates the analogy. As an ellipsis, it may be expanded in this way: "then just as the Church is subject to Christ, wives should also be subject to their husbands" (BAG, p. 38).

26 Both the verb ἁγιάσῃ (*hagiasē*, "he might make holy") and the participle καθαρίσας (*katharisas*, "having cleansed") are aorists. If the participle is taken to denote an act antecedent to the verb, the meaning is "having cleansed it" (RV). If on the other hand the participle is assimilated to the verb, then the past tenses are simultaneous and express the manner in which the sanctification is effected.

The grammatical connection of ἐν ῥήματι (en rhēmati, "through the word") demands attention. It may be linked with hagiasē, in which case ἐν (en, "in," "with," "through") is taken as an instrumental dative: "to make her holy by means of the word" (cf. John 17:17). The distance of en rhēmati from the verb makes such a construction more difficult to accept. The phrase may qualify τῷ λουτρῷ τοῦ ὕδατος (tō loutrō tou hydatos, "by the washing of water"), but this would require the repetition of the article. It is thus preferable to regard it as dependent on katharisas or the idea contained in the clause thus introduced. The dative is neither strictly instrumental nor modal, but suggests either the accompaniment or the element of the action described by the verb (EGT, 3:368).

30 The addition of ἐκ τῆς σαρκὸς αὐτοῦ καὶ ἐκ τῶν ὀστέων (ek tēs sarkos autou kai ek tōn osteōn, "of his flesh and of his bones") is not impressively supported. The internal evidence favors omission, since a new and not directly relevant item is introduced with the additional reference to the bones of Jesus.

---

6. Christian Relationships: Parenthood

6:1–4

> ¹Children, obey your parents in the Lord, for this is right. ²"Honor your father and mother"—which is the first commandment with a promise—³"that it may go well with you and that you may enjoy long life on the earth."
> ⁴Fathers, do not exasperate your children; instead, bring them up in the training and instruction of the Lord.

After dealing with the husband-wife relationship, Paul goes on to consider the relationship between parents and children. He has the Christian family in mind: it is assumed that both partners together with their offspring recognize the lordship of Christ (vv.1, 4). No clash of loyalties is envisaged in which God has to be obeyed rather than men.

1 It is interesting that Paul addresses children directly. Their presence in the congregations where the letter is to be read is taken for granted. They are part of the total Christian family, the church. As in the previous paragraph, the less-privileged and subordinate group in the society of the time is given priority of treatment: wives (Eph 5:22) and children. It is the same with slaves in vv.5–9 of this chapter. Social distinctions, rigidly observed in the Roman empire and even in Judaism, are transformed by the gospel so that those previously dispossessed acquire new rights.

Obedience on the part of children consists in listening to the advice given by parents (hypakouete). Many passages of Scripture both in the OT and the NT support such an obligation. Colossians 3:20 adds that this unswerving obedience is to be comprehensive in its scope ("everything"). Isaac's willingness to be offered as a sacrifice is a model of such submission. Disobedience to parents is a symptom of a disintegrating social structure, and Christian families have a particular responsibility not to contribute to the collapse of an ordered community. Both parents are mentioned (tois goneusin, cf. v.2), though in v.4 only fathers are given instructions as to reciprocal behavior. Since he is the head of the family, the husband acts representatively for his wife (as mother) as well as on his own behalf.

All this is "in the Lord" as are the other relationships (cf. Eph 5:21, 22; 6:5–9). Children are invited not simply to copy the example of Jesus when he was subject to his parents, but to realize that both they and their parents are under the authority of the living Christ. This is said to be the right thing (*dikaion*) for them to do. It is not merely suitable or fitting (*prepon*) but an actual duty. In Colossians 3:20, Paul says that it "pleases the Lord." Obedience to parents is part of the divine law. Children need to recognize that some things have to be accepted even though at the time they themselves cannot understand them.

2 The fifth commandment is quoted in confirmation of v.6 (Exod 20:12; Deut 5:16). Paul appeals to what the children had already learned, for their Christian education began with the Decalogue. To honor (*tima*) is more than to obey. It is to respect and esteem. It is "the form love assumes towards those who are placed above us by God" (Lenski, p. 647).

This is said to be "the first commandment with a promise." If we connect "first" and "promise," the difficulty arises that the fifth commandment does not appear to be the first of the ten to which a promise is attached. The second commandment contains one also, unless it is interpreted simply as a description. If that alternative is adopted, the fifth commandment is not merely the first with a promise but the only one with such an addition. It is therefore preferable to separate "with a promise" (*en epangelia*) from "first" (*prōtos*) and insert a comma after "commandment."

In what sense can this commandment be regarded as the first? Various explanations have been offered. It has been suggested that it is the first commandment in the so-called second table. The Jews, however, divided the commandments into two groups of five. Or again it may be taken to mean that it was the first to be taught to children, though it might be thought that Paul would spell it out more explicitly if that is what he meant. It is argued by some that this is the first of all the Mosaic regulations including the legislation introduced by the Decalogue.

It is more probable that *prōtos* here means first in importance rather than in sequence. The rabbis regarded this commandment as the weightiest of all. But were they right? Could it not be claimed that the first commandment stands at the head of the list as the most crucial? Perhaps Paul meant to convey the fact that this is the most important commandment for children (so Beare, p. 730), but Hendriksen is conceivably correct in inferring from the absence of the article before *prōtos* that it is "*a* primary commandment, i.e., one of foremost significance" (p. 260).

3 The promise attached to the fifth commandment in Deuteronomy 5:16 is not in itself appropriate to the church, so Paul stops short of the final clause, which speaks about Israel as the land God has given his people. What was originally a specific assurance to the Jews becomes a generalization for Christians. The prospect of longevity is not held out elsewhere in the NT as part of the Christian hope, and commentators have tended to spiritualize the application by linking it with eternal life. "On the earth" (*epi tēs gēs*) rules out such an exegesis. It is more likely that Paul wished to emphasize that in obedience to their parents, children will live to prove that their true welfare ("that it may go well with thee") depends on God (Deut 5:10).

4 The child-parent relationship is not one-sided. It is a feature of Paul's treatment of these domestic categories that the stronger have obligations to the weaker. The gospel introduced a fresh element into parental responsibility by insisting that the feelings of the child must be taken into consideration. In a society where the father's authority (*patria potestas*) was absolute, this represented a revolutionary concept.

81

Paul addresses fathers (*pateres*) as being heads of their families. The term could mean parents in general (Col 3:21). Above all else, he warns fathers against goading their children into a state of perpetual resentment (*parorgizete*, cf. Eph 4:26). He is not thinking of extreme instances like disinheritance, but the everyday tensions of family life. Fathers must not make unreasonable demands. Otherwise children, being overcorrected, may lose heart (Col 3:21).

Children are a heritage from the Lord; they are to be reared for him. The verb translated "bring up" (*ektrephete*) has to do in the first place with bodily nourishment (Eph 5:29) and then with education in its entirety. Children are to be treated with tenderness. "Let them be fondly cherished," Calvin urged (in loc.).

Paul goes on to mention two aspects of such domestic education. "Training" (*paideia*) in the Greco-Roman world meant strict discipline. "Nurture" (KJV) is too weak a word. The cognate verb signifies "to chasten" but can also be used in the wider context of "instruction." What Paul is referring to here is training in righteousness. "Instruction" (*nouthesia*) is correction by word of mouth. Remonstration and reproof are implied, but also advice and encouragement. Goodspeed saw here the beginnings of Christian education in the home.

Notes

1 If the phrase ἐν κυρίῳ (*en kyriō*, "in the Lord") is original (it is not read by some authorities), it is more naturally attached to ὑπακούετε (*hypakouete*, "obey") than to γονεῦσιν (*goneusin*, "parents") or to both. It indicates the sphere in which the Christian's obedience operates and perhaps also the spirit in which it is yielded.

3 The LXX text runs καὶ ἵνα μακρόχρόνιος γένῃ ἐπὶ τῆς γῆς ἧς κύριος ὁ θεός σου δίδωσί σοι (*kai hina makrochronios genē epi tēs gēs hēs kyrios ho theos sou didōsi soi*, "and that you may live long on the earth, which the Lord your God gives you"). The theory that Paul left the quotation unfinished because he assumed his readers were sufficiently familiar with it is unconvincing. It is more feasible to suppose that he omitted the final clause intentionally as inapplicable to those he addressed. His aim was to generalize the promise as well as the commandment. The future ἔσῃ (*esē*, "that you may") has sometimes been accounted for as a change to direct construction (RV mg.). But it may more probably be regarded as dependent on ἵνα (*hina*, "so that"), which is paralleled elsewhere in the NT (1 Cor 9:18; Gal 2:4; Rev 22:14). In this instance *esē* may be used because there was no aorist conjunctive of the verb (Abbott, p. 177).

7. Christian Relationships: Employment

6:5–9

> [5]Slaves, obey your earthly masters with respect and fear, and with sincerity of heart, just as you would obey Christ. [6]Obey them not only to win their favor when their eye is on you, but like slaves of Christ, doing the will of God from your heart. [7]Serve wholeheartedly, as if you were serving the Lord, not men, [8]because you know that the Lord will reward everyone for whatever good he does, whether he is slave or free.
>
> [9]And masters, treat your slaves in the same way. Do not threaten them, since you know that he who is both their Master and yours is in heaven, and there is no favoritism with him.

The apostle deals finally with the relationship between slaves and masters. He is still concerned with the Christian household, for the majority of slaves were employed in the home. It is estimated that there were over sixty million of them in the Roman empire—about one-third of the total population—and more and more were becoming Christians. Most of them would be in pagan employment, but a few may have had Christian masters, as Onesimus, who was a slave of Philemon.

The fact that Paul has more to say to slaves than to masters (as in Col 3:22–4:1) may reflect the social structure of these Asian churches. He addresses them on an equality with their masters and assumes that they have a Christian vocation. In a society that followed Aristotle in regarding slaves as no more than living tools this was a sufficiently radical change of attitude. It did not immediately lead to emancipation but clearly paved the way. It is significant that, whereas marriage and the family are presented in Scripture as divine ordinances, no such claim is made for the institution of slavery.

5 Slaves are to obey their masters whether they are good or bad. They are only "earthly" (*kata sarkou*, "according to the flesh"). The Christian slave has a heavenly Lord to whom he owes supreme allegiance. Because of this overriding relationship he is enabled to bear the burden of his servitude with equanimity. He is only a slave *kata sarka*. In reality, he is the Lord's freeman.

Respect (*phobos*) and fear (*tromos*) are not to be confused with craven servility but represent "a keen sense of one's shortcomings with a consequent anxiety not to fall into any mistake" (Scott, p. 246). "Sincerity" (*haplotēs*, "singleness") is the opposite of duplicity in thought or action. The word occurs seven times in the NT, all in the Pauline Epistles. It implies openness and concentration of purpose, especially in the context of generosity. The Christian slave has one goal before him. He is determined to obey his human master as an expression of his commitment to the divine Lord.

6 Two unusual compounds (perhaps coined by Paul) are found only here and in Colossians 3:22. Christian slaves are not merely to render eyeservice (*ophthalmodoulia*) by working hard only when their master is watching them. Slaves were under more temptation in this respect than paid laborers, since they had nothing to gain materially from diligence. All the more reason, then, for Christians to do their job well for its own sake and as slaves of Christ under their "great Task-Master's eye" (Milton). C.F.D. Moule thinks the word means "with reference to what the eye can see" (i.e., what is external) and that Christian slaves are being urged to do more than what lies immediately before them (ExpT 59[1947/8]:250). By showing some initiative, they would be acting as free agents and so transcend their social status.

Slaves are not to be out simply "to curry favour with men" (NEB). The term *anthrōpareskos* describes one who does not take God into account and therefore makes it his business to satisfy men (TDNT, 1:456). It is the opposite of an incipient *theareskos* ("God-pleaser"). In this passage it stands over against "just as you would obey Christ" (v.5) and "like slaves of Christ" (cf. v.7). The double reference to Christ is all the more relevant in the light of our Lord's own servanthood. He himself took the form of a slave and performed the menial task of washing his disciples' feet. As servants of the one who became the servant of men, Christian slaves will enthusiastically (*ek psychēs*) embrace the known will of God in this respect.

7 Such service must be rendered with genuine goodwill (*met' eunoias*)—an eagerness that "does not wait to be compelled" (Robinson, p. 211). Among the Oxyrhynchus papyri there is a will dated A.D. 157 in which the testator freed five slaves "because of their good-will and affection" (III. No. 494, lines 5, 6). If even pagan slaves could display such qualities, how much more should Christians do so, without expecting manumission as a reward. "As if" (*hōs*) implies no fiction: they actually do serve the Lord rather than men.

8 Even though Christian slaves will not bank on any material reward, they can be assured of eternal gain (Col 3:24). This is something they fully appreciate because of the catechetical instruction they have been given; it is from the Lord himself that each man will "receive back" (*komisetai*) the equivalent of whatever good he has done. The idea of comity is predominant (cf. Col 3:25). The future tense looks forward to the final judgment when this compensation will be awarded. Like Jesus himself, Paul does not shrink from referring to rewards, since they are all of grace. They are undeserved, since the Christian's goodness is simply what God has enabled him to do.

These rewards are in no way adjusted to social status. What is under review is man's use of God's grace whatever his status. The same principle of recompense applies both to the slave and to the freeman. This being the case, what Paul has said about employment relationships in the context of prevalent slavery is equally applicable in free societies today. Meanwhile, the apostle has provided a natural transition from vv.5–8 dealing with the duties of slaves to v.9 dealing with the duties of masters.

9 The church did not include in its membership many people of higher social rank, and presumably the number of slave-owners in a local congregation was not large. But there must have been some who were "masters," or it would have been pointless for Paul to address them. We know that he wrote a personal letter to Philemon at Colosse about reinstating his fugitive slave, Onesimus.

The golden rule is extended to this most controversial of all relationships within the society of the day. Masters are to treat their slaves as they themselves expect to be treated (literally, "do the same things to them"). Though they give the orders, they are to do so as themselves being under the authority of a heavenly Master. The common factor is that both are seeking to do the will of God (v.6). Masters must therefore refrain from browbeating their slaves by the threat of severe reprisals for unsatisfactory work. Vicious cruelty was rife among pagan slave-owners. Since their victims had no legal redress, they could be kicked around at will. Christian masters were to show themselves different by not cracking the whip but treating their slaves kindly and fairly.

Christian masters as well as Christian slaves (v.8) know that they all serve a heavenly Lord to whom they equally belong. With him no "favoritism" exists. The word is *prosolēmpsia*, which is literally "lifting up the face" or looking to see who someone is before deciding how to treat him. It is found only in the NT and ecclesiastical writers. God has no "teacher's pets." "He is not impressed by one person more than another" (JB). Slaves are as precious in his sight as masters and more is expected from those who are entrusted with greater responsibilities.

Notes

8 The final participle εἰδότες (*eidotes*, "knowing"; NIV, "because you know") supplies a reason, as NIV brings out. It is not to be construed as an imperative, nor as if it were οἱ εἰδότες (*hoi eidotes*, "who know"), since a participle with the article cannot be tr. as if it were anarthrous

(RHG, p. 778). A reasonably well-supported reading is ὅτι ἕκαστος ὃ ἐὰν ποιήσῃ (*hoti hekastos ho ean poiēsē*, "that each whatever he has done") making ἐάν (*ean*) the conditional particle. TR had ὅτι ὃ ἐάν τι ἕκαστος (*hoti ho ean ti hekastos*, "that whatsoever each") with *ean* as a potential ἄν (*an*).

---

8. *Into Battle*

6:10–20

[10]Finally, be strong in the Lord and in his mighty power. [11]Put on the full armor of God so that you can take your stand against the devil's schemes. [12]For our struggle is not against flesh and blood, but against the rulers, against the authorities, against the powers of this dark world and against the spiritual forces of evil in the heavenly realms. [13]Therefore put on the full armor of God, so that when the day of evil comes, you may be able to stand your ground, and after you have done everything, to stand. [14]Stand firm then, with the belt of truth buckled around your waist, with the breastplate of righteousness in place, [15]and with your feet fitted with the readiness that comes from the gospel of peace. [16]In addition to all this, take up the shield of faith, with which you can extinguish all the flaming arrows of the evil one. [17]Take the helmet of salvation and the sword of the Spirit, which is the word of God. [18]And pray in the Spirit on all occasions with all kinds of prayers and requests. With this in mind, be alert and always keep on praying for all the saints.

[19]Pray also for me, that whenever I open my mouth, words may be given me so that I will fearlessly make known the mystery of the gospel, [20]for which I am an ambassador in chains. Pray that I may declare it fearlessly, as I should.

This ringing passage sounds a call to arms. What Paul writes here concerning the Christian warfare is the external counterpart of his emphasis on the inward growth and edification of the church (Eph 4:12, 16). The body of Christ must be united and built up so as to be ready for the inevitable encounter with evil. Each believer needs to be prepared for the fight. This passage may represent a kind of baptismal charge. Its text is "Be on your guard; stand firm in the faith; be men of courage; be strong" (1 Cor 16:13). It is taken for granted that the victory is already assured through what Christ accomplished by his death and resurrection (Eph 1:20–23). What Aulén has characterized as the classic or dramatic interpretation of the Cross finds its biblical foundation in such passages as these (Gustav Aulén, *Christus Victor: An Historical Study of the Three Main Types of the Idea of the Atonement*, Eng. T. [London, S.P.C.K., 1931], pp. 20–23). Christ the Lord is the mighty victor who routed all the hosts of wickedness. The Christian is identified with the deliverer in his conquest (Rom 13:14).

10 "Finally" (*tou loipou*) is "for the rest," i.e., as to what remains for them to do. They are to strengthen themselves or let themselves be strengthened (*endynamousthe*) in Christ himself (Phil 4:13). Even though victory is secure, it has to be won through battle. All the resources the Christian soldier needs are drawn from Christ and "his mighty power" (*en tō kratei tēs ischyos autou*). Three of the four synonyms for power noticed in Ephesians 1:19 (cf. 3:16–21) are brought together again here. Paul's readers will recall that this is the same power that raised Jesus from the dead (1:20) and brought them to life when they were dead in trespasses and sins (2:1). Its adequacy cannot possibly be in doubt.

11 The call to "put on" (*endysasthe*) God's armor is an expression of a similar appeal in 1 Thessalonians 5:8. Paul often uses such language. This accoutrement is provided by

God (NEB) and modeled on what he wears himself (Isa 11:5; 59:17; Wisd Sol 5:17–20). It is a complete outfit (*panoplia;* NIV, "full armor," v.13). The soldier must be protected from head to foot and the *panoplia* is made up of all the various *hopla* or pieces of armor, both defensive and offensive. Polybius has left a detailed description of the heavily armed Roman infantryman or hoplite. Paul may have drawn his picture "live" from the soldier he was chained to in his house arrest, though it is not altogether certain that such a custodian would have been in full battle dress.

"Stand" (*stēte*) is a key word in this passage (cf. vv.13, 14). The equipment enables the soldier to ward off the attacks of the enemy and make a stand against him. *Stēte* is a military term for holding on to a position. Before any offensive can be launched, one must first of all maintain his own ground. The fourfold use of "against" (*pros*) stresses the determined hostility confronting the Christian soldier. The commander-in-chief of the opposing forces is the devil himself, the sworn enemy of the church. He is a master of ingenious stratagems (*methodeias;* cf. 4:14) and his tactics must not be allowed to catch us unawares. Paul had his own experience of such ploys. In the second century A.D. the church interpreted these as torture inflicted on the martyrs. But in the context of Ephesians they are more likely to have been deliberate attempts to destroy the unity of Christ's body (3:14–22; 4:1–16, 27) through the invasion of false doctrine and the fomenting of dissension (4:2, 21, 31, 32; 5:6).

12 In military strategy one must never underestimate the strength of the enemy. Paul is certainly not guilty of such fatal misjudgment but gives a realistic report of its potential. The "struggle" (literally, "wrestling," *palē*) is not merely against human foes but a war to the death against supernatural forces. "Flesh and blood" is actually "blood and flesh." The words appear in this order only here. Blood is perhaps mentioned first lest flesh be regarded as inherently evil, as those who anticipated the Gnostic heresy taught.

Four aspects of corporate menace are presented here. The particular terms are in themselves morally neutral, though with Paul they invariably indicate sinister influences (Eph 1:21; 3:11). "Rulers" (*archoi*) are "cosmic powers" (NEB). Until the end of the age these demonic forces, already defeated by Christ on the cross (4:9), exercise a certain limited authority (*exousia;* here in the plural: *exousias,* "authorities") in temporarily opposing the purposes of God. The title *kosmokrator* (power, potentate) occurs frequently in classical and rabbinical literature. It denotes one who aspires to world control. It was attached to savior gods in the ethnic religions and identified with the sun. So Paul may have implied by "powers" (*kosmokratoroi*) that what purported to be a cult of light is in fact the very opposite.

Beare (pp. 738, 739) sees in the expression "the spiritual forces of wickedness" (*ta pneumatika tēs ponerias*) the language of contemporary astrology in which the heavenly bodies were regarded as the abode of demons who held human lives in their grip. Pagans had no option but to resign themselves to an unalterable destiny. But Christians can fight against such malign influences.

If "the heavenly realms" (*hoi epouranioi*) are assumed to be the habitat of these evil spirits, they correspond to the "air" of Ephesians 2:2. But there is no evidence to show that *hoi epouranioi* can mean earth's atmosphere and Paul certainly does not use the word like this elsewhere in Ephesians (1:3, 20; 2:6; 3:18). There may be a reference here to an inferior heaven as in 2 Enoch. Or again, *hoi epouranioi* could simply denote the unseen world in general, including both good and evil forces.

13 Because the warfare in which Christians are engaged is on the scale described in v.12, the command to take advantage of the panoply God has provided is reiterated from v.11. The verb, though translated in NIV "put on," is a different one from that in v.11 where *endysasthe*, literally, "be clothed in," is used. Here it is *elabete*, "take up, assume." So when the battle is at its fiercest, the soldiers of Christ will still be able to hold their line even against the most determined attack. "The day of evil" is neither a particular juncture like approaching death or the last great satanic outbreak at the end of the age nor the whole of the present age (5:16). It is "when things are at their worst" (NEB)—because of "the devil's schemes" (v. 11).

When the emergency is over for the time being, it will be found that not an inch of territory has been yielded. Christians will "have done everything" (*hapanta katergasamenoi*), not only in preparing for the conflict but also in pursuing it. The verb has to do with achievements either in war or in the games. The KJV mg. has "having overcome all," which R.P. Martin considers to be "just possible" (NBC3, p. 1123) though there is no parallel in the NT.

14 The exhortation to stand repeats the emphasis in vv.11, 13 on the need for immovable steadfastness in the face of a ruthless foe. In v.13 Paul talked about standing firm in the midst of battle. Now he writes at greater length about standing ready in anticipation of it.

The several items of the soldier's armor appear in the order in which they would be put on. Together they comprise the *panoplia* worn before taking the field. First of all, the belt tied tightly around the waist indicated that the soldier was prepared for action. To slacken the belt was to go off duty. The "belt" (*zōnē*) was not an ornament but served an essential purpose. It gathered in the short tunic and helped keep the breastplate in place when the latter was fitted on. From it hung the scabbard in which the sword was sheathed (v.17).

In Isaiah 11:5 the Messiah is depicted as wearing the belt of righteousness around his waist and faithfulness as the sash around his body. Here truth (*alētheia*) is said to be the soldier's belt. It is to be interpreted objectively as the truth of the gospel (Eph 1:13; 4:15), or is it what the psalmist describes as "truth in the inward being" (Ps 51:6 RSV)? Something of both elements may be combined, if we regard it as "the truth that is in Jesus" (Eph 4:21) and "the fruit of the light" (5:9). Because the Christian has accepted the truth of revelation and is now indwelt by the risen Lord, who is himself the truth, his life has truth (or reality) as its basis and he displays the consistency of character that springs from it. Certainly *alētheia* in this verse is closely linked with *dikaiosynē* (righteousness) as elsewhere in Ephesians (4:24; 5:9).

The "breastplate" (*thōrax*) covered the body from the neck to the thighs. Polybius tells us that it was known as a heart-protector. Usually it was made of bronze but the more affluent officers wore a coat of chain mail. The front piece was strictly the breastplate, but a back piece was commonly worn as well. In Isaiah 59:17 we are told that Yahweh himself put on righteousness like a breastplate (cf. Wisd Sol 5:18). In this context *dikaiosynē* ("righteousness") stands for uprightness and integrity of character. But this moral rectitude and reputation for fair dealing results directly from the appropriation of Christ's righteousness (see on Eph 5:9). The Christian's protection is not to be sought in any works of his own but only in what Christ has done for him and in him.

15 Once the breastplate has been fitted into position, the soldier puts on his strong army boots or *caligae*. Josephus described them as "shoes thickly studded with sharp nails"

(War VI.1.8) so as to ensure a good grip. The military successes both of Alexander the Great and of Julius Caesar were due in large measure to their armies' being well shod and thus able to undertake long marches at incredible speed over rough terrain.

Verse 15 is not altogether easy to understand. Literally it reads: "and having shod yourselves as to the feet in readiness [*en hetoimasia*] of the gospel of peace." But what is this readiness or preparation? It can mean preparedness, for the term is applied to a ship's tackling. Part of the Christian soldier's equipment is his readiness to go out at any moment to announce the Good News to others. As in Ephesians 2:17, the apostle may be recalling Isaiah 52:7 with its reference to the feet of the herald. *Hetoimasia* can also signify a prepared foundation or base, as frequently in LXX. In that case the sense would be that the gospel of peace with God through which the believer himself has already been reconciled (Eph 2:17) affords him a sure foothold in the campaign in which he is engaged. This second interpretation is more suitable to the context and had been adopted by the NIV in its first edition "with your feet fitted with the gospel of peace as a firm footing."

16 "In addition to all this" (*epi pasin*), or perhaps "to cover all the rest" (Scott, p. 253), the Christian soldier is to "take up [v.13] the shield [*thyreon*] of faith." Barclay (p. 126) may be right in rendering *epi pasin* as "through thick and thin." *Thyreon* is derived from *thyra* (a door) and refers to the large oblong or oval *scutum* the Roman soldier held in front of him for protection. It consisted of two layers of wood glued together, covered with linen and hide, and bound with iron. Soldiers often fought side by side with a solid wall (*testudo*) of shields. But even a single-handed combatant found himself sufficiently protected. After the siege of Dyrachium, Sceva counted no less than 220 darts sticking into his shield.

For the Christian this protective shield is faith (*pistis*). Most commentators regard it as faith in action rather than in its objective content. But believing cannot be divorced from what is believed, and no rigid line should be drawn between these two aspects.

Only in this instance does Paul indicate the effect of a particular piece of armor. With such a shield the believer can extinguish all the incendiary devices flung by the devil (v.11). Herodotus described how cane darts tipped with tow were dipped in pitch and then ignited. Octavius used such arrows against Antony's fleet at Actium and they were not unknown in OT times. The reference is not, as some have surmised, to poisoned darts producing fever. The Christian's shield effectively counteracts the danger of such diabolical missiles not merely by arresting or deflecting them, but by actually quenching the flames to prevent them from spreading.

17 Two more items of the panoply remain. The shield has to be fixed in place before the helmet (*perikephalaia*), since the handle could not pass over it. As its name implies, the *perikephalaia* covered the head (*kephalē*). It was made of bronze with leather attachments. In Isaiah 59:17 Yahweh wears "the helmet of salvation" along with the breastplate of righteousness. The Christian shares the divine equipment. "Take" is really receive or accept (*dexasthe*). The previous items were laid out for the soldier to pick up. The helmet and sword would be handed him by an attendant or by his armorbearer. The verb is appropriate to the "givenness" of salvation. It is "a present deliverance from sin to be consummated in eternity by complete deliverance from every kind of evil" (Beet, p. 373). In 1 Thessalonians 5:8 the helmet is identified with the hope of full salvation. This may well be the inference here (Eph 1:18).

The final weapon is the sword, for there is no mention of the spear or *pilium,* which was the regular offensive armament of the Roman hoplite. Some have conjectured that Paul did not refer to it because he was taking his personal guard as a model and such a weapon would not be needed indoors. For whatever reason, Paul ignores it and concentrates on the *gladius* (Gr., *machaira*) or short two-edged cut-and-thrust sword wielded by the heavily armed legionary, as distinct from the *rhomphaia* or large Thracian broadsword.

The Christian's only weapon of offence is "the sword of the Spirit," either as supplied by the Spirit (like "the full armor of God" in vv.11, 13), or as used by the Spirit, though these may be complementary rather than alternative ideas. "The word of God" (*rhēma theou*) is the divine utterance or speech ("the words that come from God" NEB). This is not the usual expression, which is *ho logos tou theou.* In Isaiah 11:4 the Messiah is portrayed as one who strikes the ruthless with the rod (*šebeṭ,* a sceptre) of his mouth, i.e., by the authoritative impact of what he says. Elsewhere in Scripture, speech is compared to a sword.

But what is this utterance of God? Some identify it with the recorded word of Scripture in the OT. Some take it to be remembered sayings of Jesus or apostolic *dicta* eventually to be incorporated into the NT. Many think it is the gospel (v.15), which is the power of God (Rom 1:16). Others regard it as words given by the Spirit to meet the critical need of the moment, or as prayer in which the Spirit speaks through the Christian (v.18). Allan concludes that the best interpretation is probably the most obvious: "As Jesus used the words of Scripture to repulse the tempter, so must the Christian the words the Spirit has inspired to drive away Satan" (p. 138). It is significant that in Matthew's temptation narrative Jesus himself (quoting Deut 8:3) refers to "every word [*rhēma*] that comes from the mouth of God" (Matt 4:4) and employs relevant Scriptures to defeat the devil's stratagems.

18 Some would attach this verse to vv.19, 20 to constitute a new paragraph. But the command to "be alert" is in keeping with what has gone before and effectively rounds it off. Prayer is not itself included among the weapons wielded by the Christian combatant. "On all occasions" (*en panti kairō*) suggests that the believer will be in constant prayer in preparation for the battle as well as in the engagement itself. But it is in the critical hour of encounter that such support is most required (cf. "the day of evil" in v.13).

The phrase "in the Spirit" (*en pneumati*) is usually taken to mean in communion with the Spirit or "in the power of the Spirit" (NEB). Barclay (p. 126) has: "Let the Spirit be the atmosphere in which you pray." "Prayers" (*proseuchē,* sing.) represents the approach to God in general and "requests" (*deēsis,* sing.) a special form of it, namely supplication. Every avenue of such praying is to be thoroughly explored.

19 In other letters Paul asks his readers to remember him in their prayers. He recognizes his own dependency upon the intercessions of his friends despite his apostolic vocation. He knows that it is only through what God himself supplies that he is enabled to fulfill his role. But he needs to appropriate it continually. So he invites his readers to pray that the gift of ready speech may be bestowed on him. Lenski (pp. 678, 679) thought that the expression "that words may be given me" (*hina moi dothē logos*) reflects the formal language of diplomatic procedure and means that he may have permission to speak (cf. Acts 26:1). Though Paul is "an ambassador in chains" (v.20), he seeks an opportunity to testify before the imperial court. To "open the mouth" is a common phrase for making a public address or a long defense. It suggests solemnity of utterance. The Greek is literally "in the opening of my mouth" (*en anoixei tou stomatos mou*) and could point to what Paul wants God to do for him. The absence of the article may favor this interpretation with its redoubled emphasis on "givenness."

"Fearlessly" (*en parrhēsia*), repeated in a verbal form in v.20 (*parrhēsiasōmai*), could be taken with the preceding clause ("in the opening of my mouth fearlessly"), but is more naturally attached to "make known" (*gnōrisai*). *Parrhēsia* is a favorite word of Paul, meaning frankness and uninhibited openness of speech (TDNT, 5:883). No doubt the apostle is thinking especially of his appearance before the imperial authorities—perhaps even the emperor himself—when he would have the opportunity to reveal the secret of the gospel. He had been chosen to carry the name of Jesus "before the Gentiles and their kings" (Acts 9:15) and this was to be the climax of his distinctive ministry. Meanwhile, as he awaited his trial, he wanted to make the most of every occasion that could be capitalized in the interests of the kingdom (cf. Acts 28:31).

20 It is because of his faithfulness in preaching the Good News that he has been placed under house arrest. He is an ambassador on behalf of Christ and yet paradoxically he is in chains. Ambassadors normally enjoyed diplomatic immunity, but Paul would be compelled to appear in the imperial court as a prisoner. Instead of wearing a golden chain of office he would be shackled to his guard. "In chains" is actually "in a chain" (*en halysei*); this may be intended to imply that he was handcuffed to one soldier in military custody (Acts 28:20; 2 Tim 1:16).

Paul acknowledged that he was counting on the prayers of the church so that in it (*en autō*)—that is, in "the mystery of the gospel," not in his chain—he might speak out boldly (cf. v.19). "As I should" (*hōs dei*, Col 4:4) is not only "as it is incumbent upon me" but "in the way I ought."

Notes

10 The reading τοῦ λοιποῦ (*tou loipou*, "finally") is preferred by UBS. Strictly, the expression is a gen. of time signifying "from now on," "in the future" (Gal 6:17). The alternative τὸ λοιπόν (*to loipon*) is "as for the rest, beyond that, finally" (2 Cor 13:11; Phil 4:8; 1 Thess 4:1). Here apparently *tou loipou* is substantially equivalent to *to loipon* with reference to the conclusion of the matter (BAG, p. 481).

13 BAG (p. 423) allows for the possibility that κατεργασάμενοι (*katergasamenoi*; NIV, "after you have done everything") may mean "after proving victorious over everything" (cf. TDNT, 3:635–637). Oecumenius and Chrysostom adopted the rendering and have been followed by some modern exegetes. Nowhere else in the NT does the verb have this meaning, however, and in any case the masc. would appear to be required instead of the neuter ἅπαντα (*hapanta*, "all things").

14 The first three participles dependent on στῆτε (*stēte*, "stand") are not to be regarded as aorists used for presents. They describe what the Christian soldiers have already done in a series of definite actions before they take up their position. The participles, moreover, are indirect middles indicating what they did for themselves (not as KJV "having your loins girt . . .").

16 The readings fluctuate between ἐπί (*epi*) and ἐν (*en*). The latter would give the sense "in all" or "among all." Assuming the superiority of *epi*, the reference is not comparative ("above all," KJV), but either local ("over all") or supplementary (as in NIV).

17 The gen. τοῦ πνεύματος (*tou pneumatos*, "of the Spirit") is hardly appositional, since the following words identify the sword with ῥῆμα θεοῦ (*rhēma theou*, "word of God"). Nor is it a

gen. of quality (the spiritual sword). Some make ὅ (*ho*, "which") refer to πνεύματος (*pneumatos*), i.e., "the Spirit who is the word of God," but that is not substantiated in any other NT passage. The gen. is either of possession or better still of origin or source.

IV. Conclusion

6:21-24

> [21]Tychicus, the dear brother and faithful servant in the Lord, will tell you everything, so that you also may know how I am and what I am doing. [22]I am sending him to you for this very purpose, that you may know how we are, and that he may encourage you.
> [23]Peace to the brothers, and love with faith from God the Father and the Lord Jesus Christ. [24]Grace to all who love our Lord Jesus Christ with an undying love.

21 This is almost a word-for-word parallel with Colossians 4:7, 8. Nowhere is the connection between the two captivity Epistles closer than here, and those who reject the Pauline authorship of Ephesians ask whether it is conceivable that the apostle would have duplicated his own language in this fashion. It must be remembered, however, that Paul had only just completed Colossians, and Ephesians had been hurriedly concluded so that Tychicus could act as bearer. Since at this point he had exactly the same information to convey as to the Colossians, it is quite understandable that he employed the same terms. An imitator would surely have been at pains to avoid plagiarism and might also have been inclined to mention Onesimus.

Tychicus was the apostle's personal representative to the churches in Colosse (Col 4:7-9), Ephesus, and, assuming Ephesians to be a circular letter, other Asian churches as well. Later we find him with Paul again and named along with Artemas as a possible relief for Titus in Crete (Titus 3:12). Soon afterwards he was dispatched to Ephesus (2 Tim 4:12). The fact that he was entrusted with these important commissions reflects his reliability. Paul describes Tychicus as a loyal Christian servant and a brother dearly loved, not only by Paul but by all who knew him. He will pass on news Paul did not have time to include at the end of his letter, so that the readers may be brought up to date with details about his affairs and what he was doing.

22 Paul had only one aim in view as he commissioned Tychicus to visit the churches in and around Ephesus. It was to let them know what was happening in relation to him and "to put fresh heart into" them (NEB). There was a danger of their being discouraged because of his sufferings on their behalf (Eph 3:13). It would comfort them to learn that Paul was being well treated and was free to preach to those who visited him (Acts 28:17-31).

23 Ephesians finishes with a truly apostolic benediction, but one different in form from others in Paul's writings. Couched in the third person, not in the second, it has two parts instead of one. "Grace," which usually comes first, stands last. Paul himself might have felt free to vary his usual form of benediction in this way, but a pseudonymous writer would have been less likely to arouse suspicion by departing from it.

The three blessings that figure most prominently in Ephesians—peace, love, and faith—occupy the first half of the benediction. This is more than a farewell greeting; it is a prayer for reconciliation. Paul longs to see the whole brotherhood of believers in Ephesus and its environs—Jews and Gentiles alike—at peace with each other in the one body of Christ (Eph 3:15, 19; 4:3). This will only be brought about through mutual love (1:15; 3:17, 18; 4:2, 16). Love is to be combined with faith from which it is derived (1:15; 3:17; Gal 5:6). The ultimate source of these three essential features of Christian community life is in God himself. The name of Christ the Son is associated with that of God the Father in perfect equality.

24 "Grace" is the hallmark of all Paul's benedictions. It is a recurring theme throughout Ephesians (1:2, 7; 2:5, 7, 8; 3:2, 8; 4:7). The use of the article (*hē charis*) may be due to the mention of the Lord Jesus Christ both before and after, and calculated to focus attention on "the grace of the Lord Jesus Christ" (2 Cor 13:13; Gal 6:18; Phil 4:23). On the other hand, Paul may be referring to the grace he has already written so much about in this Epistle.

He identifies Christians as those who love Christ. "All who love" (*pantōn tōn agapōn-tōn*) is parallel to "believers" (Acts 5:14; 1 Tim 4:12), as love is a necessary corollary of belief. Those who fail to love the Lord are anathematized in 1 Corinthians 16:22 as having no place in the church.

Paul invokes grace on all who love our Lord Jesus Christ "with an undying love" (*en aphtharsia*). That is the last and sealing word of the Epistle. It has been variously interpreted. Literally, it means "in uncorruptness" (RV). The noun denotes a quality of the future life. The adjective means "imperishable" or "unfading." It may thus indicate that Christian love will never die. "In sincerity" (KJV) is supported by PH ("sincerely") and "in uncorruptness" is taken to mean "unfeignedly," with no impurity of motive.

But is *en aphtharsia* to be construed with "love"? Some attach it to "our Lord Jesus Christ" and translate "in his immortality." The reference would then be to the glorified Savior. Martin favors this view (NBC3, p. 1124; cf. BAG, p. 125). Others again link *en aphtharsia* with "grace" and assume that it is the grace that leads to or prepares for incorruption (Jerome), or that "grace and immortality" (NEB)—"grace and eternal life" (JB)—are paired in the benediction (Beare, p. 749). The construction of the sentence, however, seems to separate *charis* from *aphtharsia* rather than combine the two.

If *en aphtharsia* is to be construed with "love," as NIV assumes, it may not in fact describe the quality of love as such. It could be related to the whole phrase "all who love our Lord Jesus Christ" and signify that lovers of the Lord are even now guaranteed and indeed enjoy eternal life—i.e., that they love our Lord Jesus Christ as already tasting immortality (Eph 1:13; BAG, p. 125). The "old self " is "being corrupted by its deceitful desires" (4:22), but when the "new self " is put on (4:24), Christians are recreated and assigned a seat in the heavenly realms (2:6).

The Epistle began with an ascription of praise "to the God and Father of our Lord Jesus Christ who has blessed us in the heavenly realms with every spiritual blessing in Christ" (1:3). On this interpretation, it ends with a benediction invoking God's grace on all who love our Lord Jesus Christ in incorruption, because they are sealed with the Holy Spirit for the day of redemption (1:13, 14; 4:30).

PHILIPPIANS

Homer A. Kent, Jr.

PHILIPPIANS

Introduction

1. Background
2. Authorship and Unity
3. Date and Place of Origin
4. Occasion and Purpose
5. Literary Form
6. Canonicity
7. Bibliography
8. Outline

1. Background

Philippi was located in Macedonia about ten miles inland from the Aegean Sea. The original settlement was called Krenides (presumably because of the presence of a good water supply, inasmuch as the name means "springs"), but in 356 B.C. the name was changed by Philip II, king of Macedonia (359–336 B.C.), when he enlarged the city with many new inhabitants and considerable construction.

In 42 B.C. the Battle of Philippi was fought west of the city between the Second Triumvirate (Octavian, Antony, Lepidus) and the Republicans of Rome (Brutus, Cassius). The victory of Octavian resulted in Philippi's being made a military colony. Following the Battle of Actium in 31 B.C., in which Octavian defeated Antony, the status of Philippi was raised; the city was first given the title "Colonia Julia Philippensis," and later, in 27 B.C., "Colonia Augusta Julia Philippensis" (Jack Finegan, IDB, K–Q, p. 786). The change in status provided the inhabitants with numerous advantages, including autonomous government, immunity from tribute, and treatment as if they actually lived in Italy.[1] Luke calls Philippi *prōtē* ("first, chief ") of the district of Macedonia (Acts 16:12). This cannot mean that Philippi was the capital of the province, for Thessalonica held that distinction; nor does it mean that Philippi was the capital of its district, for Amphipolis served that function. Evidence from a later period shows that *prōtē* was an honorary title given certain cities, and perhaps this explains Luke's use of the term.[2] Some have adopted the conjectural *prōtēs* in place of *prōtē*, and so arrive at this meaning: "a city of the first district of Macedonia" (so UBS). But this can claim no Greek manuscript support. More likely, absence of the article with *prōtē* simply implies "a leading city" in that part of Macedonia. In fact, Philippi was the only "colony" in the area. Reflections of the Philippians' pride in their city may appear in Acts 16:20, 21, as well as in some of Paul's terminology (Phil 1:27; 3:20).

---

[1] F.J. Foakes-Jackson and Kirsopp Lake, *The Acts of the Apostles* (Grand Rapids: Baker, reprint 1965), 4:187–190).

[2] Ibid., pp. 187–189.

The Via Egnatia, the main highway from Asia to the west, passed through Philippi and ran alongside the forum of the city. Near the city was the river Gangites (modern Angitis).

The church at Philippi was founded in A.D. 50 in the course of Paul's second missionary journey (Acts 16). While the apostle was in Troas, he was instructed in a vision to proceed into Macedonia, and Philippi became the first European city in which he preached. Apparently the Jewish population in Philippi was small, at least there was no synagogue. The missionary party, consisting of Paul, Silas, Timothy, and Luke, met first with some women at a Jewish place of prayer by the river bank outside the city. The first convert was Lydia, a "God-fearer" (a term denoting a Gentile who had become a partial adherent to Judaism) who responded to Paul by receiving Christian baptism and opening her home to the missionary party. Other significant incidents were the exorcism of the demon from a slave girl and the conversion of the jailer and his family. These early converts were a most diverse and unlikely group with which to found a local church, but the grace of God overcame their differences.

When the apostolic party moved on, Luke may have been left behind to guide the new work (the use of "we" in the narrative of Acts is dropped until 20:5–6 when Paul returns to Philippi). Luke himself is thought by some to have been a Philippian, and was perhaps the "man from Macedonia" Paul saw in his vision.[3] The new church did not forget its founder, however, for gifts were sent to Paul on several occasions (Phil 4:15, 16).

Paul made a second visit to Philippi in A.D. 55–56 on his third missionary journey (Acts 20:1–6). Actually, he must have passed through the city twice: on his outward trip toward Corinth and again on his return at the time when he was on the way to Jerusalem with the collection for the poor there. Luke apparently rejoined the party at this latter visit. This visit to Jerusalem culminated in Paul's arrest and eventual imprisonment in Rome (Acts 21f.), which in turn brought about the occasion for this Epistle.

2. Authorship and Unity

That the apostle Paul wrote the Epistle to the Philippians is virtually unquestioned. Not until the nineteenth century, beginning with F.C. Baur (1792–1860) and the Tübingen school of Germany, were serious questions raised, and these negative views have not been widely accepted. The straightforward claim of the Epistle (1:1) is supported by the reference to Paul's acquaintances, the reflection of known circumstances in his life, and the many indications of Pauline thought. Even those who have questioned the unity of Philippians have usually concluded that Paul was the author of the various parts.

The unity of Philippians has been questioned on several grounds: (1) the use of "finally" at 3:1, (2) the change in subject matter and tone at 3:1 or 3:2, and (3) Polycarp's use of the plural "epistles" in referring to Paul's communications with the Philippians (To the Philippians, 3.2). These observations have led to various reconstructions, some suggesting a combining of two letters and others of three. Beare has proposed a combination of three units: an interpolated fragment (3:2–4:1), the letter of thanks (4:10–20), and the final letter (1:1–3:1; 4:2–9, 21–23). He concludes that all were written by Paul, but on different occasions, and perhaps one of them to a different group of readers (pp.

---

[3]Ramsay, pp. 200–205; E.M. Blaiklock, *The Acts of the Apostles* (Grand Rapids: Eerdmans, 1959), pp. 123–125.

24-29). A slightly different alignment was proposed by Rahtjen (pp. 167-173), a critique of which was given by Mackay (pp. 161-170).

Although the case for a composite document has been skillfully presented, it has not commended itself to the majority of scholars for the reason that the objections to the unity of Philippians can be answered. There is no manuscript evidence that Philippians ever existed as two or three separate letters. The evidence from Polycarp can be understood either as including other canonical letters from Paul to Macedonia (e.g., the Thessalonian Epistles) or other letters to the Philippians not now extant. The use of "finally" (3:1) can be understood in the sense of "in addition" (BAG, p. 481), and is paralleled by Paul's usage elsewhere (1 Thess 4:1). The change in subject matter and tone could have been due to the receiving of new information from Philippi as Paul was writing the letter or to an interval of several hours or even days between the several parts. Such changes in mood in the light of the problems being discussed should not be surprising.

3. Date and Place of Origin

Inasmuch as Paul was a prisoner at the time Philippians was written (1:7, 13, 16), identification of this imprisonment would make possible the fixing of the date and place of origin of the Epistle. Three possibilities must be considered: Caesarea, Rome, and Ephesus.

1. *Caesarea.* Paul was a prisoner in Caesarea for two years (A.D. 57-59) and his friends had access to him (Acts 24:23, 27). The fugitive slave Onesimus could have fled there (this assumes that the Epistles to the Colossians and Philemon came out of the same imprisonment as Philippians). The "praetorium" (1:13; NIV, "palace guard") could be understood of Herod's palace at Caesarea (Acts 23:35). Furthermore, the polemic against Jewish teachers (3:1-16) fits well the period of Jewish-Gentile controversy.

This theory has not been widely adopted, because there is no positive evidence favoring it. Paul expected prompt release (2:24), but there was little reason for optimism while he was at Caesarea, and this prospect was no longer possible after he had appealed to Caesar. Lack of any mention of the prominent Philip, who lived at Caesarea and had been Paul's host (Acts 21:8-10), also makes this view doubtful.

2. *Rome.* The traditional view places the writing of Philippians during Paul's first imprisonment in Rome during A.D. 59-61 (Acts 28:30). This is the most natural understanding of "palace guard" (1:13) and "Caesar's household" (4:22). Paul's trial was evidently going on during the writing, and its outcome could bring either life or death. Apparently there could be no appeal from its verdict (1:19-24). This was not the situation at Caesarea, for there he could appeal to Caesar (Acts 25:10-12). His circumstances reflected in the letter fit the Roman imprisonment better than the one at Caesarea, since he had freedom to arrange itineration for his associates and opportunity to carry on considerable correspondence. He hoped to visit Philippi soon (2:24); at Caesarea, however, his aim was to go to Rome, and his appeal to Caesar made a trip to Philippi out of the question. The Marcionite Prologue (c. A.D. 170) states that Philippians was sent from Rome. This view is the one most widely held. It will be assumed in this commentary.

3. *Ephesus.* The case for the origination of this Epistle at Ephesus has received increasing attention in recent years (Guthrie, pp. 146-154). This view places the writing in A.D. 53-55 during Paul's three-year stay in Ephesus (Acts 19). The problem that Acts mentions no imprisonment of Paul in Ephesus is met by explaining Romans 16:4, 7; 1 Corinthians 15:32; 2 Corinthians 1:8-10; 11:23 as pointing to such an imprisonment.

But this is by no means established, for it demands treating these passages in Corinthians with wooden literalness rather than as the dramatic figures they are. Furthermore, this view requires taking Romans 16 as written to Ephesus rather than to Rome, a conclusion not warranted by the documentary evidence.

Philippians presupposes several time-consuming journeys between Philippi and Paul's location. Consequently, some scholars hold that an Ephesus origin is more likely than one at Rome. As many as six trips may' have occurred (requiring at least one month each between Philippi and Rome, but only one week between Philippi and Ephesus): (1) News of Paul's plight reaches Philippi, (2) Epaphroditus travels to Rome with a gift to Paul, (3) news of Epaphroditus's illness reaches Philippi, (4) the report of the Philippians' concern reaches Epaphroditus, (5) a trip was made by Timothy to Philippi, and (6) a return trip by Timothy to Paul was contemplated. Nevertheless, several factors weaken the force of this argument. Not all of these trips necessarily originated after Paul's arrival in Rome. It is conceivable that the gift to Paul had been timed to reach him shortly after his arrival. Furthermore, Epaphroditus may have become sick while en route to Rome, and someone could have immediately returned to Philippi with the report. So the time span may not have been so long as some have thought. In any event, Paul's two years in Rome provided sufficient time for these trips, even if they all must be included within that period.

Supporters of the case for Ephesus remind us that reference to the palace guard (1:13) and Caesar's household (4:22) are not proof of the letter's having been written at Rome and that Paul's desire to visit Philippi after his release is easier to fit into an Ephesian imprisonment than a Roman one, inasmuch as Paul had expressed his wish to visit Spain after going to Rome (Rom 15:24). They also assert that the Philippians' not giving to Paul before sending a contribution by Epaphroditus (4:10) is easier to explain by the Ephesus theory, since Paul had been in Ephesus only a short time before leaving for Palestine. Yet it is hardly fair to insist that Paul's desire to visit Spain, expressed before nearly five years of continuous imprisonment, did not undergo some modification. As to the lack of opportunity for a gift, Paul was raising money for the collection when he passed through Philippi and Ephesus earlier and may have avoided taking anything for himself at that time lest suspicion be attached to his motives and the collection project be undermined.

In addition to the above factors, the Ephesus theory is weakened by the fact that at Ephesus Paul could have appealed to Caesar as he did at Caesarea (contra 1:20, 23, 24). Philippians also says nothing about the collection—a project Paul was engaged in while at Ephesus. On the whole, therefore, the Ephesus theory does not seem to have sufficient foundation to dislodge the traditional view that Philippians came out of Paul's first imprisonment at Rome. It seems, however, to be separated from the other prison Epistles (Ephesians, Colossians, Philemon), because it was carried by a different messenger and reflects circumstances apparently somewhat later than those relating to the other three Epistles (his case was actually in court). A date of A.D. 61 is suggested.

4. Occasion and Purpose

The Philippian church sent Epaphroditus to Paul with a gift from the congregation (4:18) and with instructions to minister to his needs through personal service (2:25). He also must have brought news of the progress and problems of the church. In the performance of his responsibilities, Epaphroditus became gravely ill, and the Philippians heard about it. For some reason, this latter circumstance greatly distressed Epaphroditus. Was he embarrassed because he felt he had disappointed the church? Or was he aware that his condition had been misinterpreted and criticized? Paul's request that the church receive Epaphroditus with all joy and that they hold him in high regard (2:29) implies that some misunderstanding had occurred.

But Epaphroditus recovered and was ready to return home. This furnished the occasion for writing the Epistle. Paul wanted the church at Philippi to understand clearly that Epaphroditus had been a real fellow soldier in the Lord's work (2:25), that his illness had been extremely serious (2:27–30), and that he was worthy of a hero's welcome (2:29).

The mention of the Philippians' gift (4:10–20) should not be regarded as Paul's first acknowledgment of their help. Too much time had elapsed since Epaphroditus's arrival for this to be a reasonable inference, nor would this mention have been delayed to the end if it had been the occasion for Paul's writing the Epistle. Because of the several contacts between Philippi and Rome before this time, Paul had undoubtedly sent his initial thanks promptly. We may adequately account for the additional mention of the gift in this Epistle as the apostle's grateful recollection of a very generous contribution.

Other factors of a secondary nature may also have prompted the Epistle, such as Timothy's approaching visit (2:19), Paul's own hope of visiting the church (2:24), and the problem of the two women at Philippi (4:2).

Of all the letters Paul wrote to churches, this one to the Philippians stands out as being the most personal. No sharp rebukes of the congregation mar its joyful spirit: no disturbing problems threaten the progress of the church. The warnings are of a cautionary and preventive nature that are always in order. The frequent emphasis on Christ explains the underlying relationship of Paul to his readers. The names Jesus Christ, Christ Jesus, Lord Jesus Christ, Lord Jesus, Jesus, Christ, Lord, and Savior, occur 51 times in the 104 verses of the Epistle.

5. Literary Form

Philippians exhibits all the characteristics of contemporary letters. Its initial mention of the author and addressees is followed by the greeting. After this comes the body of the letter. Concluding words of greeting round it out.

Except for the question of unity (see 2 above), the only problem of literary form in Philippians concerns the nature of 2:5–11. The rhythmical nature of this portion has caused some to describe it as a christological hymn, either borrowed by Paul from an even earlier Christian source[4] or composed by a Christian contemporary of Paul using language borrowed from pagan songs to "divine Heroes" (Beare, pp. 1, 2), or as composed by Paul himself (Scott, IB, 11:46, 47). An excellent review of the arguments for and against Pauline authorship of the hymn is given by Martin in *Carmen Christi* (pp. 42–62).Textual evidence does not support the view that the passage is a later addition.

There is no problem in seeing the passage as the incorporating of an earlier Christian hymn (1 Tim 3:16 may be another Pauline instance of such quotation). However, Paul himself could write highly poetic passages (as Rom 8:35–39 and 1 Cor 13 show), and the exposition will demonstrate that the content is harmonious with Pauline thought, without any need for resorting to pagan concepts. What is clear is that Paul has provided in

---

[4]Ernst Lohmeyer, *Der Brief an die Philipper* . . . , 13th ed. (Gottingen: Vandenhoeck & Ruprecht, 1964), pp. 8, 90, 91.

this concise statement a sublime summary of Christology, from preexistence to exaltation.

6. Canonicity

Evidence for the early acceptance of this Epistle by the leaders of the church is plentiful and raises no questions. Allusions to its contents appear in Clement of Rome (first century) and Ignatius (early second century). More explicit testimony is found in Polycarp (early second century), who refers directly to Paul's communication with the Philippians by letter and utilizes the terminology of the canonical Epistle (*To the Philippians*, chs. 3, 9, 12).

Philippians appears in the extant second-century lists of canonical books. The Muratorian fragment (c. A.D. 170) includes it among Paul's Epistles, as does the list of the heretic Marcion. It is quoted and attributed to Paul by Irenaeus, Tertullian, and Clement of Alexandria (late second and early third centuries). It was included in the "acknowledged books" of Eusebius (fourth century) and in the list of Athanasius (A.D. 367). No suspicion regarding the canonicity of Philippians is to be found in early external testimony.

7. Bibliography

Books:

Alford, Henry. *The Greek Testament.* London: Rivingtons, 1874.

Barth, Karl. *The Epistle to the Philippians.* Richmond: John Knox Press, 1962.

Beare, F.W. *A Commentary on the Epistle to the Philippians.* London: Adam & Charles Black, 1959.

Davidson, F. "The Epistle to the Philippians." NBC1. Edited by F. Davidson, A.M. Stibbs, and E.F. Kevan. Grand Rapids: Eerdmans, 1954.

Guthrie, Donald. *New Testament Introduction: The Pauline Epistles.* Chicago: Inter-Varsity Press, 1961.

Hendriksen, William. *Exposition of Philippians.* Grand Rapids: Baker, 1962.

Johnstone, Robert. *Lectures Exegetical and Practical on the Epistle of Paul to the Philippians.* Grand Rapids: Baker, repr. of 1875 ed.

Kennedy, H.A.A. "The Epistle to the Philippians." *The Expositor's Greek Testament.* Edited by W. Robertson Nicoll. London: Hodder & Stoughton, 1917.

Lenski, R.C.H. *The Interpretation of St. Paul's Epistles to the Galatians, to the Ephesians and to the Philippians.* Columbus: Wartburg Press, 1946.

Lightfoot, J.B. *Saint Paul's Epistle to the Philippians.* Grand Rapids: Zondervan, repr. of 1913 edition.

Martin, Ralph P. *Carmen Christi: Philippians 2:5–11 in Recent Interpretation and in the Setting of Early Christian Worship.* Cambridge: Cambridge University Press, 1967.

_____. *The Epistle of Paul to the Philippians.* Grand Rapids: Eerdmans, 1959.

Motyer, J.A. *Philippian Studies: The Richness of Christ.* Chicago: Inter-Varsity Press, 1966.

Moule, H.C.G. *The Epistle to the Philippians.* Cambridge: Cambridge University Press, 1873.

Mounce, Robert H. "The Epistle to the Philippians." *Wycliffe Bible Commentary.* Edited by C.F. Pfeiffer and E.F. Harrison. Chicago: Moody, 1962.

Muller, Jac. J. *The Epistles of Paul to the Philippians and to Philemon.* Grand Rapids: Eerdmans, 1955.

Ramsay, W.M. *St. Paul the Traveller and the Roman Citizen.* 3rd ed. London: Hodder & Stoughton, 1897. Repr. Grand Rapids: Baker, 1949.

Scott, Ernest F. and Wicks, Robert R. "The Epistle to the Philippians." *The Interpreter's Bible.* vol. 11. Edited by George A. Buttrick. New York: Abingdon Press, 1955.

Vincent, Marvin R. *The Epistles to the Philippians and to Philemon.* Edinburgh: T. & T. Clark, 1897.

Walvoord, John F. *Philippians: Triumph in Christ.* Chicago: Moody, 1971.

Periodicals:

Jewett, Robert. "The Epistolary Thanksgiving and the Integrity of Philippians." *Novum Testamentum.* vol. 12, fac. 1 (January, 1970): 40–53.

Mackay, B.S. "Further Thoughts on Philippians." *New Testament Studies.* vol. 7, no. 2 (January, 1961): 161–170.

Marshall, I. Howard. "The Christ-Hymn in Philippians 2:5–11." *Tyndale Bulletin.* 1968, no. 19: 104–127.

McClain, Alva J. "The Doctrine of the Kenosis in Philippians 2:5–8," *The Biblical Review Quarterly* (October, 1928). Reprinted in *Grace Journal,* vol. 8, no. 2 (Spring, 1967): 3–13.

Rahtjen, B.D. "The Three Letters of Paul to the Philippians." *New Testament Studies.* vol. 6, no. 2 (January, 1960): 167–173.

Walvoord, John F. "The Humiliation of the Son of God." *Bibliotheca Sacra.* vol. 118, no. 470 (April, 1961): 99–106.

8. Outline

Introduction (1:1–11)
    1. Greeting (1:1, 2)
    2. Thanksgiving (1:3–8)
    3. Prayer (1:9–11)
  I. The Situation of Paul in Rome (1:12–26)
    1. Paul's Circumstances Had Advanced the Gospel in Rome (1:12–18)
    2. Paul's Circumstances Would Turn Out for Salvation (1:19–26)
  II. First Series of Exhortations (1:27–2:18)
    1. Exhortation to Unity and Courage in View of External Foes (1:27–30)
    2. Exhortation to Unity and Humility Toward Those in the Church (2:1–11)
    3. Exhortation to Work Out Their Salvation (2:12–18)
  III. Two Messengers of Paul to the Philippians (2:19–30)
    1. Timothy (2:19–24)
    2. Epaphroditus (2:25–30)
  IV. Warning Against Judaizers and Antinomians (3:1–21)
    1. The Judaizing Danger (3:1–16)
    2. The Antinomian Danger (3:17–21)
  V. Second Series of Exhortations (4:1–9)
    1. Exhortation to Stand Firm in Unity (4:1–3)
    2. Exhortation to Maintain Various Christian Virtues (4:4–9)
  VI. The Philippians' Gifts to Paul (4:10–20)
    1. The Recent Gift (4:10–14)
    2. The Previous Gifts (4:15–20)
Closing Salutation (4:21–23)

Text and Exposition

Introduction (1:1–11)

1. Greeting

1:1, 2

¹Paul and Timothy, servants of Christ Jesus,

To all the saints in Christ Jesus at Philippi, together with the overseers and deacons:

²Grace and peace to you from God our Father and the Lord Jesus Christ.

1 "Paul and Timothy" are associated in the greeting, not because they were co-authors of the letter, but because Timothy was a well-known Christian leader, especially at Philippi, and was now with Paul. It is certain that Paul alone was the author, in view of the singular verb and pronouns in 1:3, 4, as well as the discussion in 2:19–23. Timothy had been present at the founding of the church at Philippi (Acts 16:1–12) and on several subsequent occasions (Acts 19:22; 20:3–6). Perhaps he served as Paul's amanuensis for the letter.

Paul does not use his title "apostle," perhaps because he is not stressing his authority but is rather making a personal appeal. The circumstances may be compared to those in the Epistle to Philemon, where Paul also does not mention his apostleship. In marked contrast is the Epistle to the Galatians, where Paul stresses his authority.

Both Paul and Timothy are designated as "servants of Christ Jesus." This description emphasizes submission and dependence on their Lord. It is not a technical reference to a specific office, but characterizes their willing service of Christ, their divine Master. The same designation appears in the Epistles of James, 2 Peter, and Jude.

The addressees are named as "all the saints in Christ Jesus" who resided in the Macedonian city of Philippi. Paul places no special emphasis on "all," as though he were counteracting some viewpoint that would exclude some in the church. Paul frequently employed "all" in addressing the various churches he wrote to (cf. Rom 1:7; 1 Cor 1:2; 2 Cor 1:1; 1 Thess 1:2). All believers are "saints" through their spiritual union with Christ, a fact Paul often expressed by the phrase "in Christ Jesus" (Rom 8:1, 2; Eph 2:6, 10, 13; 3:6) or "in Christ" (Rom 12:5; 2 Cor 5:17). This use of the term emphasizes not personal holiness, though the believer's conduct should correspond increasingly to his standing, but the objective status each believer possesses because the merits of Christ are imputed to him. Nor does it refer to a condition after death, for these "saints" were very much alive at Philippi.

Though "overseers and deacons" were the two orders of officers in the local NT churches (1 Tim 3:1–3), Philippians is the only Epistle to mention them in its greeting. (On "overseers" NIV has a footnote: "Or *bishops.*") Why Paul includes them here is nowhere stated, but several observations suggest themselves. It is clear that the church at Philippi was organized and that Paul was not by-passing its local order. Doubtless his mention of overseers and deacons was an endorsement of their authority. Also, the Epistle would have been delivered first to the church officers for reading to the congregation. Because Epaphroditus had previously been sent with a monetary gift (2:25), the

103

deacons as well as the overseers may have been particularly involved in the project of aiding Paul (4:14–16).

2 The familiar blessing, "grace and peace," combines Greek and Hebrew expressions but transforms them into a thoroughly Christian greeting. Exactly the same wording was used by Paul in six other Epistles (Rom, 1 and 2 Cor, Gal, Eph, Philem). God's "grace" is his favor, needed by men in countless ways and bestowed without regard to merit. "Peace" is here a reference not to the cessation of hostilities between sinners and God (Rom 5:1), but to the inner assurance and tranquility that God ministers to the hearts of believers and that keeps them spiritually confident and content even in the midst of turmoil (4:7). The source of these blessings is "God our Father and the Lord Jesus Christ." Paul understands that Jesus the Messiah is the divine Lord, ascended to the Father's right hand and equal to him in authority and honor. Just as Christ and the Father joined in the sending of the Holy Spirit (John 14:26; 15:26), so they will jointly convey these blessings.

Notes

1 The term δοῦλοι (*douloi*, "servants") is explained by Adolph Deissmann as a Hellenistic usage, based on the practice of a freed slave's becoming a devotee of the deity (Deiss LAE, pp. 323–330). It is more likely, however, that Paul drew his terminology from the OT, where LXX used δοῦλος (*doulos*) of Moses (Ps 105:26) and other prophets (Jer. 25:4; Amos 3:7), as well as of the divine Servant of Jehovah.

The dative πᾶσιν (*pasin*, "to all") is used with an articular substantive ἁγίοις (*hagiois*, "saints") and denotes totality without any particular contrast in view (Eugene Van Ness Goetchius, *The Language of the New Testament* [New York: Scribner's, 1965], pp. 216–218). Thus, "all the saints" denotes each believer in Philippi, but without any particular emphasis that it is *all* and not just *some*.

"Overseers" (ἐπισκόποις, *episkopois*) denoted the chief administrative officers in local churches. Other versions (e.g., KJV, RSV, NEB) translate the term "bishops" (cf. footnote in NIV); JB has "presiding elders." The term seems to have been interchangeable with "elders" (πρεσβύτερος, *presbyteros*) in the NT (Acts 20:17, 28; Titus 1:5, 7). The former term designated the office as to its function, and the latter, as to its dignity, being a title doubtless derived from the synagogue. "Deacons" (διακόνοις, *diakonois*) were the secondary officers in the church (1 Tim 3:1–13). The office was probably derived from that of the seven men referred to in Acts 6:1–7. Although the name διάκονος (*diakonos*, "deacon") was not used of the seven, the cognates διακονία (*diakonia*, "service"; NIV, "distribution of food") and διακονέω (*diakoneō*, "to serve"; NIV, "to wait on [tables]") appear three times in the passage. The deacons were charged with various temporal concerns of the church, such as the dispensing of aid to the needy.

2 The usual Greek salutation in a letter was χαιρεῖν (*chairein*, "greetings"; cf. Acts 23:26; James 1:1). Paul changed this to χάρις (*charis*), and thus adds a spiritual dimension to his greeting to the church. The word meant "grace" or "favor" and in Christian contexts developed the special sense of the favor that God bestowed on sinners, saving them and providing for their every need.

2. Thanksgiving

1:3–8

> [3]I thank my God every time I remember you. [4]In all my prayers for all of you,
> I always pray with joy [5]because of your partnership in the gospel from the first day

until now, [6]being confident of this, that he who began a good work in you will carry
it on to completion until the day of Christ Jesus.
[7]It is right for me to feel this way about all of you, since I have you in my heart;
for whether I am in chains or defending and confirming the gospel, all of you share
in God's grace with me. [8]God can testify how I long for all of you with the affection
of Christ Jesus.

3 Paul begins his letter by thanking God for his readers. He follows this pattern in all
his Epistles except Galatians, where the absence of such sentiment forebodes the serious
discussion to follow. With the Philippians Paul had a warm relationship, and this tone
is established at the outset of the letter. By stating his thanks to "my God," the author
reveals his personal devotion. This was no stereotyped formula, but the natural outflow
from the heart of a deeply spiritual man. The thanksgiving was prompted by the joyous
memory Paul had of his Philippian friends. It was not that every single memory caused
him to thank God, but that his whole remembrance of them was good.

4 These happy memories were reflected in Paul's prayers (root: *deēsis*) for the Philippians. Joy permeated his prayers even while he prayed for their needs.

5 What caused Paul the deepest satisfaction was the Philippians' "partnership in the
gospel." The rich term *koinōnia* denotes participation or fellowship, and expresses a
two-sided relation (Friedrich Hauck, *Koinōnos*, et al., TDNT, 3:798). In its NT uses it
includes the believer's participation in the life of God (1 Cor 1:9; 1 John 1:3) and also
the sharing of a common faith. Thus it assumes the existence of a brotherly relationship
among believers (2 Cor 8:4; Gal 2:9; 1 John 1:7). Although some have seen here a specific
reference to the Philippians' recent gift, it is likely that the apostle's intent was broader.
The gift was one expression of their partnership, but Paul was grateful and filled with
joy over the frequent evidences of the Philippians' sharing in the work of the gospel.
These had been shown to him "from the first day" he had preached the gospel in
Philippi about ten years before. At that time he had experienced the hospitality of Lydia
(Acts 16:15) and the jailer and his family (Acts 16:33, 34). Later he had received gifts
sent him at Thessalonica (Phil 4:16) and at Corinth (2 Cor 11:9), as well as the more
recent one brought by Epaphroditus.

6 Of course, it was God who had produced their transformed lives by the work of
regeneration. So Paul was confident that God would continue this work until Christ's
return. Even though he rejoiced in the Philippians' generous gift and their evidences
of spiritual growth, his confidence did not rest ultimately on the Philippians themselves,
but on God, who would preserve them and enable them to reach the goal. The "good
work" refers to the salvation begun at their conversion. To see it as a direct and limited
reference to their monetary gift is unwarranted. Paul would not have hinted that their
gift was only a beginning, and that more should follow.

God not only initiates salvation, but continues it and guarantees its consummation. The
apostle's thought relates not to the end of life but to the glorious coming of Jesus Christ
that will vindicate both the Lord and his people. So Paul is asserting that God will bring
his work to completion. Nothing in this life or after death will prevent the successful
accomplishment of God's good work in every Christian.

"The day of Christ Jesus" is a phrase occurring with only slight variations six times in
the NT, three of them in Philippians (1 Cor 1:8; 5:5; 2 Cor 1:14; Phil 1:6, 10; 2:16). The

expression is similar to the "day of the Lord" (1 Thess 5:2) and the OT "day of Jehovah" (Amos 5:18–20). However, in contrast to the OT emphasis on judgment, the "day of Christ Jesus" is mentioned in all cases with reference to the NT church. It will be the time when Christ returns for his church, salvation is finally completed, and believers' works are examined and the believer rewarded.

7 Paul was right in regarding the Philippians so highly, because in a sense they had become partners in his imprisonment and his current legal obligations. To say they were in his "heart" was to use a figure denoting not mere emotions or sentiment, but the essence of consciousness and personality. "Heart" among the Greeks and Hebrews included both mind and will, referring to a person's innermost being (Friedrich Baumgärtel and Johannes Behm, *Kardia*, TDNT, 3:605–614).

The reference to Paul's imprisonment ("I am in chains") belongs with the following rather than the preceding words, as giving evidence of the Philippians' partnership in God's grace. Even when it might have been dangerous to identify themselves openly with Paul, they had treated his misfortunes as their own and had come to his assistance with their gifts. "Defending and confirming the gospel" could be understood as negative and positive aspects of Paul's preaching ministry—i.e., defending the gospel from attacks and proclaiming its message with proofs. There are reasons, however, for regarding these words as legal terminology. The use of *te ... kai* ("both ... and") ties the concept of imprisonment (*desmois*) with that of "defending and confirming." Furthermore, "defending" (*apologia*) is used elsewhere in the NT of a legal defense (Acts 22:1; 25:16; 2 Tim 4:16), and "confirming" (*bebaiōsis*) was a legal technical term (Heb 6:16) for guaranteeing or furnishing security (BAG, p. 138). So Paul may be thinking primarily of his approaching hearing in which he must give a defense of the gospel he preached and in which he hoped also to have occasion to offer clear proofs of the truth of the gospel. In Paul's view, all Christians were on trial with him, for the outcome could ultimately affect them all. The Philippians' assistance by their warm fellowship was a clear reminder that they felt the same way, and thus were sharers of the same grace of God (salvation) as was Paul.

8 Only God could truly vouch for Paul's feelings about his Philippian friends, because they ran so deep. This was not an oath but a statement of fact. Paul's yearnings for this church were not merely the human longing to be with friends but were prompted by the very "affection of Christ Jesus," with whom Paul was in vital union. It was the indwelling Christ who was producing the fruit of love in Paul by the Holy Spirit and who thus enabled him to yearn for their welfare with the compassion of his Lord.

Notes

3 Πάσῃ (*pasē*, "all") is used with τῇ μνείᾳ, (*tē mneia*, "remembrance") in the predicate position, and thus stresses totality, as in 1:1.

The pronoun ὑμῶν (*hymōn*, "of you") can be understood either as a subjective genitive or an objective genitive. If the former, Paul's thanks are based on the Philippians' remembrance of him ("your remembrance") and is a direct reference to the gift that had been sent. It is more likely, however, that the genitive is objective here and that Paul is thankful for all the memories he has of his Philippian friends ("remembrance of you"). This would be consistent with his usage elsewhere, for whenever he uses μνεία (*mneia*) with a genitive, the genitive is always objective (Rom 1:8, 9; 1 Thess 3:6; Philem 4). Also, the passage seems to be naming Paul's activity (the verb is εὐχαριστῶ [*eucharistō*, "I thánk"]), rather than the Philippians'.

4 Is 1:4 a parenthesis, as Lightfoot, Hendriksen, and Martin claim? If so, then 1:5 is dependent on εὐχαριστῶ (*eucharistō*, "I thank") of 1:3, and Paul's thanksgiving stems from the Philippians' fellowship in the gospel. But there appears to be no compelling reason why 1:5 cannot be construed with what immediately precedes; "joy because of your fellowship" is a readily understood concept. This makes unnecessary the insertion of parentheses and does not require that 1:5 be related to the somewhat distant *eucharistō*. This is the sense assumed by NIV and NEB. The view that 1:4 is a parenthesis is reflected in RSV. KJV and NASB leave the matter ambiguous.

Verse 4 contains the first of five uses of χαρά (*chara*, "joy") in Philippians (others are 1:25; 2:2, 29; 4:1). In addition, the verb χαίρω (*chairo*, "rejoice") appears seven times (1:18; 2:17, 18, 28; 3:1; 4:4 [twice]), and the compound συγχαίρω (*synchairō*, "rejoice [with]") occurs twice (2:17, 18). Joy is clearly the prevailing atmosphere of the Epistle.

5 The use of ἐπί (*epi*, "because of ") is more naturally attached to the phrase immediately preceding than to εὐχαριστῶ (*eucharistō*, "I thank") of 1:3. Otherwise, awkwardness results from the use of two *epi* phrases dependent on *eucharistō*.

6 Absence of the article with ἔργον ἀγαθόν (*ergon agathon*, "good work") argues for a wider sense than just the recent gift from the Philippians. The same verbs ἐνάρχομαι (*enarchomai*, "begin") and ἐπιτελέω (*epiteleō*, "carry to completion") are used in Galatians 3:3 in reference to the entire Christian life. The "good work," therefore, should be regarded as God's transforming grace in salvation—a grace that provides for continuing manifestations.

7 Most versions have treated με (*me*, "I," "me") as the subject of the infinitive phrase τὸ ἔχειν με ἐν τῇ καρδίας ὑμᾶς (*to echein me en tē kardias hymas*), thus giving the sense: "I have you in my heart." In contrast, NEB regards ὑμᾶς (*hymas*, "you") as the subject: "You hold me in such affection." Word order decidedly favors *me* as the subject, and the sense of this rendering fits the context well.

"Chains" is δεσμοῖς (*desmois*, "bonds," "fetters"). The term can refer to literal shackles, or to imprisonment in general (BAG, p. 175). Βεβαίωσις (*bebaiōsis*, "confirmation") was a technical legal term used of a seller who confirmed a purchase to a buyer and guaranteed it to him in the face of the claims of a third party. It referred to such confirming proof. Thus, Paul regards his proclamation of the gospel even in prison as a legally valid statement. (Deiss BS, pp. 104-109; Heinrich Schlier, *Bebaios*, et al., TDNT, 1:602, 603.)

8 Σπλάγχνοις (*splanchnois*, "affection[s]") originally denoted in early Gr. the inward parts of an animal sacrifice, particularly the heart, liver, lungs, and kidneys, as distinct from the "intestines" (ἔντερα, *entera*). The term seems to have entered Jewish writings during the intertestamental period. In the NT it is used once in the physical sense of entrails (Acts 1:18), and in all other instances with the figurative sense of the seat of emotions or the feeling itself (Helmut Köster, *Splangchnon*, TDNT, 7:548-559).

---

3. Prayer

1:9-11

> 9And this is my prayer: that your love may abound more and more in knowledge and depth of insight, 10so that you may be able to discern what is best and may be pure and blameless until the day of Christ, 11filled with the fruit of righteousness that comes through Jesus Christ—to the glory and praise of God.

9 Paul's genuine thanks for the fellowship of the Philippian saints caused him to pray for their continued spiritual progress. Concern for others should express itself first in prayer, as one recognizes the importance of the divine factor in any lasting spiritual

growth. The basic petition of Paul's prayer is that his readers' love might abound more and more. Love is a fruit of the Spirit (Gal 5:22) that enables all other spiritual virtues to be exercised properly (1 Cor 13:1–3). Without it no Christian is spiritually complete (Col 3:14). No reason appears in the passage to limit this to love for God, for each other, or for Paul. Most likely, it is unrestricted and refers to the continuing demonstration of this spiritual fruit in any and all ways. The Philippians had already displayed their love in generously giving to Paul, but love never reaches the saturation point.

Love must be intelligent and morally discerning, however, if it would be truly *agapē*. What is encouraged here is not a heedless sentiment, but love based on knowledge, the intellectual perception that has recognized principles from the Word of God as illuminated by the Holy Spirit. Spiritual knowledge, gained from an understanding of divine revelation, enables the believer to love what God commands and in the way he reveals. The joining of the expression "depth of insight" to "knowledge" stresses moral perception and the practical application of knowledge to the myriad circumstances of life. Spiritual knowledge is thus no abstraction but is intended to be applied to life. In this instance it will serve to direct the believers' love into avenues both biblically proper and pure.

10 The discerning atmosphere in which their love should operate will require them continually "to discern what is best." Some things are clearly good or bad. In others the demarcation is not so readily visible. In Christian conduct and the exercise of love, such factors as one's influence on others, as well as the effect on oneself, must be considered (1 Cor 10:32). The question should not only be "Is it harmful?" but "Is it helpful?" (1 Cor 10:23).

The goal in view is the day of Christ, in which every believer must stand before his Lord and give an account of his deeds (2 Cor 5:10). This sobering and joyous prospect for the believer should have a purifying effect on his life (1 John 3:3).

11 The conduct that will receive Christ's commendation must be characterized by "the fruit of righteousness." Transformed lives are the demonstration that God works in believers. Paul desires that when his readers stand before Christ, their lives will have been filled with the right kind of fruit. He is not talking about mere human uprightness measured by outward conformity to law (3:9). He is rather speaking of the spiritual fruit that comes from Jesus Christ, produced in them by the Holy Spirit sent by Christ (Gal 5:22). Consequently, all the glory and praise belongs not to believers but to God, for he has redeemed them by the work of his Son and has implanted within them his Spirit to produce the fruit of righteousness. The thought is similar to that in Ephesians 1:6, 12, 14, where Paul says that the entire plan of redemption should result in praise of God's glory.

Notes

9 The compound form ἐπίγνωσις (*epignōsis*, "knowledge") is often used with no discernible difference in meaning from γνῶσις (*gnōsis*) in LXX, the papyri, and the NT. Only when both forms are used in the same context with evident contrast between them is it certain that the slight differences in their connotation are being stressed (cf. Rom 1:21, 28, verb and noun; 1 Cor 13:12, verbs). *Epignōsis* came to be almost a technical term for "the decisive knowledge of God which is implied in conversion to the Christian faith" (Rudolf Bultmann, *Ginōskō*, TDNT, 1:707). In Phil 1:9 the sense involved is that of thorough and genuine knowledge, but without any attempt to contrast it with something less.

Ἄισθησις (*aisthēsis*, "depth of insight") is part of a word group whose meanings range from sensual perception to intellectual understanding. In LXX it is used mostly for the Hebrew דַעַת (*da'at*) and is comparable to "wisdom." There is an element of moral discrimination in the term (Prov 1:7). *Aisthēsis* appears only this once in the NT, but the context clearly points to the idea of moral and ethical discernment (1:10). The cognates that occur in Luke 9:45 and Heb 5:14 likewise convey this sense (Gerhard Delling, *Aisthanomai*, et al., TDNT, 1:187, 188).

10 Δοκιμάζειν (*dokimazein*) may mean either "to test" or "to approve after testing"; διαφέρειν (*diapherein*) means "to differ," or "to excel" (i.e., to differ to one's advantage). Hence Paul's statement can be read, "to test the things that differ" (ASV mg.) or "to approve what is excellent" (KJV, ASV, RSV, NASB). Ultimately, the sense in this passage is the same, for the testing of various matters is with the intention of finding the best and performing it.

Although the derivation of εἰλικρινής (*eilikrinēs*) is a matter of disagreement, the most likely explanation traces it to ἥλιος (*hēlios*, "sun") and κρίνω (*krinō*, "judge," "test"). Hence, the meaning is "tested by the light of the sun, completely pure, spotless" (Friedrich Büchsel, *Eilikrinēs*, TDNT, 2:397, 398). The other term in the phrase, ἀπρόσκοποι (*aproskopoi*), may denote either the passive sense of "undamaged" or "blameless," or the active sense of "giving no offense." Probably the former is in view here, as in Acts 24:16.

The tr. "until the day of Christ" uses εἰς (*eis*) in the sense of time (so KJV, Ph, NASB, NIV). Yet it is possible that the apostle's purpose was not to state how long this conduct was to be maintained, but to name the greatest incentive for Christian discerning. Hence, "for" or "with a view to" the day of Christ would then convey this meaning, and is a legitimate handling of *eis*. RSV, NEB, and JB understand the phrase in this way.

11 "Fruit of righteousness" is an OT expression (Amos 6:12); it occurs in NIV as "harvest of righteousness" also in Heb 12:11 and James 3:18. If the genitive δικαιοσύνης (*dikaiosynēs*) is regarded as indicating source, the reference is to imputed righteousness from which practical righteousness is to flow. More likely, it is a genitive of apposition, identifying this fruit as the righteous acts of believers. This usage is similar to the other NT occurrences of the phrase noted above.

I. The Situation of Paul in Rome (1:12–26)

1. *Paul's Circumstances Had Advanced the Gospel in Rome*

1:12–18

> [12]Now I want you to know, brothers, that what has happened to me has really served to advance the gospel. [13]As a result, it has became clear throughout the whole palace guard and to everyone else that I am in chains for Christ. [14]Because of my chains, most of the brothers in the Lord have been encouraged to speak the word of God more courageously and fearlessly.
> [15]It is true that some preach Christ out of envy and rivalry, but others out of good will. [16]The latter do so in love, knowing that I am put here for the defense of the gospel. [17]The former preach Christ out of selfish ambition, not sincerely, supposing that they can stir up trouble for me while I am in chains. [18]But what does it matter? The important thing is that in every way, whether from false motives or true, Christ is preached. And because of this I rejoice. Yes, and I will continue to rejoice,

12 "I want you to know" is a variation of a common statement in Paul's letters. It invariably introduces an important assertion and may imply that misunderstanding has

arisen over the matter or that inquiry has been made regarding it. In this instance, the significance of Paul's immediate circumstances was the important matter. On the assumption that the Epistle was written from a Roman imprisonment (see Introduction), Paul is saying that his recent circumstances had not been detrimental but advantageous to the gospel. Verse 12 does not seem to be a reference to his imprisonment, about which previous communication with the Philippians had informed them, but to more recent developments. Perhaps Paul had been moved from his hired house (Acts 28:30) to the Praetorian camp or to some place more accessible to the trial scene. This could easily have been interpreted as bad news, but it had "really served to advance the gospel" in ways to be mentioned subsequently. Paul does not imply that his case has been settled, nor that any official action favoring Christianity had been taken. Nevertheless, his immediate circumstances were to be viewed as a plus for the gospel, not a disaster. The term "to advance" (*prokopēn*) originally denoted making headway in spite of blows and so depicted progress amid difficulties (Gustav Stählin, *Prokopē*, TDNT, 6:704).

13 There were at least two ways in which the gospel had been advanced through Paul's circumstances. The first was that it had been made clear throughout the whole palace guard that Paul's imprisonment was "for Christ." During the first century, prisoners who were sent to Rome from the provinces in cases of appeal were entrusted to the care of the *praefectus praetorio* (F.J. Foakes Jackson and Kirsopp Lake, *The Beginnings of Christianity* [Grand Rapids: Baker Book House, reprint 1966], 5:321, 322). As the guards were assigned in succession to Paul, it soon became clear to them that he was no ordinary captive. The words "for Christ" (*en Christō*) are connected with "clear" (*phanerous*) in the Greek text. Thus Paul was not merely describing his imprisonment as being in the service of Christ ("my chains for Christ"), but was claiming that his relationship to Christ had been made clear to his guards.

The term *praitōriō* ("palace guard") admits of several meanings. In addition to this passage, it is used in the Gospels for Pilate's headquarters in Jerusalem, probably to be identified with the Antonia fortress (Matt 27:27; Mark 15:16; John 18:28 [twice], 33; 19:9). In Acts 23:35 it is used of the Roman governor's headquarters at Caesarea. In Lightfoot's extended note (in loc.) four possibilities are suggested: (1) The emperor's palace in Rome. It may be objected, however, that this term, suggestive of a military despotism, would not likely have been used by Roman citizens for their emperor's residence. Furthermore, no contemporary instance of such use can be cited. (2) The barracks of the praetorian guard attached to the imperial palace. (3) The praetorian camp outside the city wall. These suggestions regard *praitōrion* as a place, but this conflicts with the phrase in 1:13, *kai tois loipois pasin*, literally "and to all the rest," which clearly points to persons. (4) The praetorian guards themselves. This remains the most likely meaning, agreeable to both current usage and to context.

Paul's bold testimony to the gospel of Christ had also been borne "to everyone else" who came to his quarters, including members of the Jewish community (Acts 28:17ff.), at least one Gentile (Philem 10), and many Christian co-workers. Paul was able to get the gospel out from inside prison walls. Instead of falling into self-pity, he took every opportunity to make the gospel known.

14 The second way the gospel had been advanced was that Paul's circumstances had emboldened other Christians in Rome. One might suppose that his imprisonment would have dampened any evangelizing efforts and have caused the believers in Rome to "go underground," but exactly the opposite was true. They drew courage from Paul's example and laid their fears aside. A literal rendering of the clause in the latter part of v.14 is "to a much greater degree they are daring to speak the word of God without fear." That it was "daring" indicates no lessening of the danger but a new infusion of courage. The present tense shows it was no momentary enthusiasm that quickly passed but that it was still the situation as Paul wrote his letter. Surely the apostle's own attitude to his chains must have been largely responsible for these results. If he had become depressed by developments, the effect on others would have been far different. It was Paul's use of the change in his circumstances as a fresh opportunity to spread the Word of God that encouraged the Christians in Rome to do likewise.

15 Not all of the "preachers" in Rome, however, were responding with the highest of motives. Some were proclaiming the message of Christ "out of envy and rivalry." In the light of 1:16, 17, it is clear that their wrong spirit was directed against Paul. Who were these disappointing preachers? Some commentators, like Hendriksen (in loc.), insist that Paul has changed the subject and is no longer speaking of those in 1:14. It has been urged that opponents of Paul (1:15) would not have been reticent to speak out as those of 1:14 had been (Mounce, in loc.). Nevertheless, the most natural way to understand these words is by relating them to 1:14, and to interpret Paul as saying that the newly courageous preachers were of two types. It is not difficult to imagine that even those jealous of Paul could well have been intimidated at first by Paul's imprisonment and have kept quiet to protect themselves.

These opposing preachers have been identified as the Judaizers of 3:1–16 (Lightfoot, pp. 88, 89; Walvoord, *Philippians*; pp. 38, 39). But it is difficult to imagine that Paul would commend such people for speaking "the word of God" (1:14) and then denounce them as "dogs," doers of "evil," and "mutilators of the flesh" (3:2). In Paul's view, Judaizers preached another gospel (Gal 1:6–9). It is more likely that he was referring to a part of the group mentioned in 1:14. They were doctrinally orthodox, but at the same time mean and selfish, using the occasion of Paul's confinement to promote themselves. Because they were envious of Paul, they stirred up discord within the Christian community and hoped to gain a larger following for themselves.

Others, to their credit, were moved by feelings of good will for Paul. Their renewed vigor in proclaiming Christ was a true joining with Paul in the great enterprise of the gospel.

16 These nobler preachers recognized the apostle's sincerity and unselfishness. They realized that his present circumstances were part of a larger divine program and that he had never deviated from it. He had been "put here" (*keimai*), not by his own miscalculations, nor by chance, but by the operation of God's sovereignty. God had brought him to this place and time "for the defense of the gospel." By ways that could never have been foreseen by man alone, God had accomplished within the short space of thirty years the spreading of the gospel of Jesus Christ from its humble beginnings in obscure Judea to its defense before Caesar at the center of the Empire. No doubt it was with some sense of awe that Paul evaluated his situation with the comment, "I am put here." Recognition of the nature of Paul's imprisonment caused many stalwart Christians to respond out of love for him and for the cause he represented. They stepped into the breach and took their stand with him, eager to insure that the gospel did not fail to be proclaimed while Paul was in prison.

17 The former group of preachers (1:15a) were guilty of insincerity, particularly toward

Paul. That they "preach Christ" and that Paul found no fault with the content of their message shows that their problem was not primarily doctrinal but personal. They were not unbelievers or perverters of Christian truth. They were self-seeking opportunists, promoting themselves at Paul's expense. Perhaps they had enjoyed some prominence in the church before he arrived, but had been eclipsed since he came to the city. By taking advantage of Paul's imprisonment, they may have hoped to recover their former popularity. They may have supposed that he would bitterly resent their success (just as they did his) and his imprisonment would become all the more galling to him. If so, they failed to reckon with the greatness of the man.

18 Paul's conclusion, "But what does it matter? . . . ," reveals his sense of values. The importance of the gospel and its proclamation so outweighed any personal considerations that he would not cloud the issue by insisting on settling personal grievances. He was convinced that "Christ is preached" even by these preachers whose motives were suspect. They must have been faithful to the basic message of Christ. They could not have been Judaizers, at least not in the usual sense of that designation. With Paul, to preach "Christ" meant to proclaim the good news of salvation provided freely by God's grace through the redemptive work of Christ and received by men through faith without "works of righteousness" of any kind. It is inconceivable that any Judaizing message with its insistence on performance of Jewish rites would be characterized by Paul as preaching "Christ."

As long as the antagonism was only personal, Paul could rejoice that the greater purpose of disseminating the gospel was being served. Even when some of the preaching was actually a pretext (*prophasei*), utilized to camouflage attacks on Paul, the apostle took the magnanimous view that affronts to himself could be ignored, provided that the truth of the gospel of Christ was proclaimed. He rejoiced in this and intended to maintain this wholesome magnanimity, which rose above all personal feelings.

Although *prophasei* has the sense of pretext, pretense, or "false motives" (NIV), it does not necessarily imply that the antagonistic preachers did not believe what they were preaching, but that their preaching was a pretext to cover other, less-worthy purposes.

Notes

12 The precise formula γινώσκειν δὲ ὑμᾶς βούλομαι (*ginōskein de hymas boulomai*, "Now I want you to know") does not occur again in the NT, but a similar Pauline clause θέλω δὲ ὑμᾶς εἰδέναι (*thelō de hymas eidenai*) appears in 1 Cor 11:3 and Col 2:1, and the negative statement οὐ θέλω δὲ ὑμᾶς ἀγνοεῖν (*ou thelō de hymas agnoein*, "I do not want you to be ignorant") occurs in Rom 1:13; 11:25; 1 Cor 10:1; 12:1; 2 Cor 1:8; and 1 Thess 4:13.

14 The words ἐν κυρίῳ (*en kyriō*, "in the Lord") may be understood either with the preceding phrase τῶν ἀδελφῶν (*tōn adelphōn*, "of the brothers") or the following πεποιθότας (*pepoithotas*, "being confident"). Construing it with the former has led to the objection that "the brethren in the Lord" is a redundancy and has no parallel in the NT (Lightfoot, p. 88). However, there is no more incongruity with this expression than with the reference to ἀδελφοῖς ἐν Χριστῷ (*adelphois en Christō*, "brothers in Christ") in Col 1:2. It is true that "being confident in the Lord" is common Pauline terminology (Rom 14:14; Gal 5:10; Phil 2:24; 2 Thess 3:4), but in every instance *en kyriō* follows rather than precedes the form of πείθω (*peithō*, "to be confident") on which it depends. It is best, therefore, to treat the expression as referring to "the brethren in the Lord," that is, fellow Christians.

Textual variation occurs at 1:14—λόγον τοῦ θεοῦ λαλεῖν (*logon tou theou lalein*, "to speak the word of God"). The Byzantine text-type, supported in this instance by P[46], omits τοῦ θεοῦ (*tou theou*, "of God"). The longer reading is supported by ℵ A B P, as well as by early witnesses among the ancient versions. The sense is not materially affected, for with either reading the reference is to the Word of God.

15–17 NIV accords with RV, ASV, RSV, NEB, and NASB, along with the Gr. texts of WH, Nestle, and UBS, in preserving the chiasma of 1:15–17. KJV, however, follows the TR and transposes vv.16 and 17, presumably to keep the sequence parallel with v.15. But the literary structure of chiasma (in which in a series of four items, item one is paired with item four, and two is paired with three) appears elsewhere in the NT (e.g., Philem 5). Of course, the ultimate sense of the passage is the same, regardless of the sequence:

The word ἐριθείας (*eritheias*) in v.17 was apparently thought to be derived from ἔρις (*eris*, "strife") by the translators of KJV, and thus rendered "contention." However, the term is distinguished from *eris* in 2 Cor 12:20 and Gal 5:20. It is more likely, therefore, that it is related to ἐριθεύω (*eritheuō*, "to work as a day-laborer") and ἔριθος (*erithos*, "a day-laborer"). The development of its meaning as "self-seeking" or "selfish ambition" reflects aristocratic disdain for one who had to earn his daily living instead of being free to donate his services as one of the nobility (Friedrich Büchsel, *Eritheia*, TDNT, 2:660, 661). The meaning "selfish ambition" fits well the six other NT uses of ἐριθεία (Rom 2:8; 2 Cor 12:20; Gal 5:20; Phil 2:3; James 3:14, 16).

18 The expression τί γάρ (*ti gar*) is elliptical and conveys such ideas as "what, then [is the situation]?" or "what does it matter?" (NIV) or "what business is it of mine?" See Rom 3:3; 1 Cor 5:12. (BAG, p. 827.) The elliptical statement continues with πλὴν ... ὅτι (*plēn ... hoti*), which grammatically introduces the clause beginning with Χριστὸς (*Christos*) and indicates the important issue in response to the rhetorical question posed by *ti gar*.

The employment of ἀλλὰ (*alla*; NIV, "yes") to join the two clauses stating Paul's rejoicing illustrates the emphatic use of ἀλλά with the sense of "certainly," "indeed," or "in fact" (H.E. Dana and J.R. Mantey, *A Manual Grammar of the Greek New Testament* [New York: Macmillan, 1946], pp. 240, 241). Whether the clauses should be separated by a full stop, with the second clause regarded as introductory to v.19 (RSV, NEB, NIV), or treated as part of the same statement and both as properly a part of v.18 (KJV, ASV, NASB) is of minor consequence. All will agree that a transition is being made at this point, and the transitional statement at the close of v.18 serves so well to tie both parts together that the exact point of the division is open to debate.

---

2. Paul's Circumstances Would Turn Out for Salvation

1:19–26

[19]for I know that through your prayers and the help given by the Spirit of Jesus Christ, what has happened to me will turn out for my deliverance. [20]I eagerly expect and hope that I will in no way be ashamed, but will have sufficient courage so that now as always Christ will be exalted in my body, whether by life or by death. [21]For to me, to live is Christ and to die is gain. [22]If I am to go on living in the body, this will mean fruitful labor for me. Yet, what shall I choose? I do not know! [23]I am torn between the two: I desire to depart and be with Christ, which is better by far; [24]but it is more necessary for you that I remain in the body. [25]Convinced of this, I know that I will remain, and I will continue with all of you for your progress and joy in the faith, [26]so that through my being with you again your joy in Christ Jesus will overflow on account of me.

19 Paul moves to the second encouraging aspect of his present situation in Rome, which was the prospect it held for his "deliverance" (*sōtērian*). Is this a reference to deliverance from his present imprisonment? It is true that Paul expressed confidence of release in 1:25 and 2:24, but the immediate context puts the "deliverance" as somewhat apart from either life or death (1:21), and the inner struggle described in 1:22-24 makes it questionable whether he would have stated the anticipated result of his Roman trial with this sort of certainty. The other possibility is to treat "deliverance" in the sense of spiritual salvation. Paul viewed salvation as having several aspects—past (Eph 2:8), present (Phil 2:12), and future (Rom 13:11). Here the present and future aspects may be fused into one as the apostle looks to the unfolding of his Christian life and his ultimate hope of standing unashamed both before human judges and before his Lord (cf. v.20).

Paul viewed his deliverance as being accomplished by two means. The first was the effective prayers of the Philippians on his behalf. The second was the support furnished by the Holy Spirit, who is here called "the Spirit of Jesus Christ." These two means were not necessarily unrelated, inasmuch as Paul may have regarded the Philippians' prayers as being answered by the Spirit's increased activity on his behalf.

20 If we interpret "deliverance" in the broadest sense, we understand Paul to say that regardless of the outcome of his immediate physical circumstances, he has every reason to expect spiritual victory to be his. In the Greek text "eagerly expect" and "hope" are nouns, not verbs, and are grammatically joined so as to indicate that they are aspects of a single concept. The noun *apokaradokia* is made up of *kara* ("head") and *dechomai* ("to take," or perhaps originally, "to stretch"). The term denotes "stretching the head forward" (Gerhard Delling, *Apokaradokia*, TDNT, 1:393). The prefix *apo* may suggest looking away with concentration, ignoring other interests (Kennedy, in loc.). Only in Christian literature is the term found, and not earlier than Paul. The only other NT use is in Romans 8:19. The term is linked with *elpis* ("hope") by the use of one article and *kai* ("and"), thus implying an inner connection. Delling states that *elpis* denotes "well-founded hope" and *apokaradokia* means "unreserved waiting" (TDNT, 3:393).

In this time of waiting for the settlement of his case, Paul had a well-founded hope that he would "in no way be ashamed." This is a broad statement referring first to his appearance before the authorities for the final disposition of his case. There may also be overtones of his ultimate appearance before Christ, because he speaks of the possibility of death and of the advantage of being with Christ. He has the confident hope that he will continue to maintain the sort of courage characteristic of his ministry in the past.

The expression *en pasē parrēsia* ("sufficient courage," NIV) conveys the thought of openness, courage, boldness, or confidence, whether toward God or people. Prominent are instances in which this quality is viewed in relation to speech. In 1:20 Paul may be thinking in terms of his coming testimony before his imperial judges. It would not be as easy to give a courageous witness in those circumstances, apart from the help of the Holy Spirit.

Paul wants Christ "to be exalted," regardless of whether "life" (physical) or "death" would be the verdict on his "body." The passive voice of the verb "to be exalted" (*megalunthēsetai*) should be noted. Paul did not say, "I will exalt Christ," but "Christ will be exalted in my body." The apostle was not relying on his own courage, but on the action of the Holy Spirit who would produce this result in response to the prayers of Paul and the Philippians (1:19).

21 "For to me" is placed in the emphatic position, stressing the fact that Paul's own faith was unshaken, regardless of the circumstances. No adverse decision from the court nor the alarm of his friends could alter his firm belief about his present or his future. "To live is Christ." The very essence of Paul's present life was Christ and all that this entailed. From the theological fact that Paul was identified with Christ in a vital spiritual union (Gal 2:20) issued far-reaching practical implications. Christ had become for him the motive of his actions, the goal of his life and ministry, the source of his strength. "To die" after such a life could only mean "gain." Not only would Paul's state after death bring gain, inasmuch as he would be with Christ (1:23), but the act itself of dying at the hands of Rome was no tragedy in Paul's eyes. Such a death would bear added witness to the gospel; it would confirm that Paul's faith was steadfast to the end and it would serve as the gateway to Christ's presence.

22 Nevertheless, if he should continue to live as a result of a favorable disposition of his case in Rome, this would provide continued opportunity for him to labor fruitfully in the cause of Christ. For Paul this never meant an easy life. His labors in establishing churches and nurturing them toward maturity were characterized by frequent opposition, physical hardships, and much spiritual anguish. Yet he looked on his apostolic ministry as a challenge to be grasped and as fruit to be harvested. (The same metaphor appears in Rom 1:13.)

"To go on living in the body" employs *sarki* ("flesh") rather than *sōmati* ("body"). Although this may be merely a synonym employed for literary variety inasmuch as *sōmati* was used in 1:20, it may also have been adopted to convey the thought of the earthly, physical sphere with its limitations and weaknesses.

When the verb *haireomai* occurs in the NT, it is used exclusively in the middle voice with the sense of "choose" or "prefer." The term is used of the election of believers by God (2 Thess 2:13) and of the choice by Moses in aligning himself with his own people (Heb 11:25). In Philippians 1:22 it does not mean that Paul literally had the prerogative of choosing his fate, but it is a reference to his personal preference.

The verb *gnōrizō* ("know," NIV) means "to make known" in each of its other twenty-four NT occurrences (including seventeen other uses by Paul), and the presumption is strong in favor of its having this sense here. Thus, the meaning would be "I cannot tell" or "I cannot declare [to you]." The meaning "to know" does occur in the papyri and LXX, however, and so is a possibility for 1:22 (Rudolf Bultmann, *Gnōrizō*, TDNT, 1:718).

Paul was so positively committed to the will of God that both life and death held certain attractions. If the choice were left to him, he would not know what to decide. How fortunate that God does not force us to make such choices!

23 As Paul thought of his prospects, he felt himself in a dilemma, though in his case either alternative was a good one. The two possibilities were continued life or sudden death inflicted by Rome. "I am torn" suggests the divided nature of his thinking about this matter. The Greek word (*sunechomai*) depicts a person or object held under pressure from two sides so that movement in either direction is difficult or impossible ("I am hard pressed," NASB; "I am in a strait," KJV).

The basic sense of *sunechō* is "to hold something together" (Helmut Köster, *Sunechō*, TDNT, 7:877). Of its twelve NT uses, two are by Paul, nine are by Luke (including Acts), and one is in Matthew. The term is sometimes used of diseases that are viewed as seizing, gripping, or controlling their victims. It also depicts someone occupied with or absorbed in something (Acts 18:5). In the present instance, the idea of distress may be present, as in the cases where the word is used in reference to diseases (cf. Luke 4:38).

From the standpoint of what would be an advantage for him, he had the desire to leave this life and be with Christ. Death for him would be a departure (*analusai*) from his

115

present state, like the release of a prisoner from his bonds (Acts 16:26, *analuthē* [‭א‬ D]) or the departure of a guest from a wedding feast (Luke 12:36, *analusē*). It would be no catastrophe, since it would cause Paul to "be with Christ." He foresaw no soul-sleep while awaiting the resurrection, nor any purgatory. As he had already explained to the Corinthians, absence from the body means for the believer immediate presence with the Lord (2 Cor 5:8). There was no question in Paul's mind as to the ultimate superiority of this. It was "better by far" (*pollō mallon kreisson*), because it would bring him to the goal of his Christian life (3:8–14). It would bring rest from his labors (Rev 14:13) and the joy of eternal fellowship in the very presence of the Lord whom he loved.

24 Yet the apostle also recognized another standpoint from which his future might be viewed. His remaining alive would offer a certain advantage to his Philippian readers. He does not state specifically what this advantage was but the obvious reference is to the ministry he might still perform for them.

25 Paul was confident that his situation was in the Lord's hands (1:19–24) and that what occurred would bring glory to God, regardless of the specific turn it might take. Furthermore, his confidence now prompted him to say, "I know that I will remain." What was the basis of this confidence? Was it the result of a favorable development in the legal proceedings, or of a special revelation from God? Against the idea of a new legal development is the necessity of supposing some sort of break between this verse and those immediately preceding, during which fresh information came to Paul. Yet no hint appears of such a momentous happening. The word "know" (*oida*) cannot be pressed to mean infallible knowledge and it is doubtful whether Paul would have spoken as he did in 1:20–24 if he knew by prophetic inspiration that he would be set free. It is far more likely that the statement represents his personal conviction based on what seemed to be probable in the light of all the factors. The need of many for his apostolic ministry outweighed his own need to be with Christ immediately. Furthermore, he must have known that the case against him was not strong (Acts 23:29; 25:25; 26:31, 32), and thus his hope of release was well-founded. Nevertheless, because likelihood of release was only personal conviction, he makes allowance in his previous explanation for the possibility that things might turn out adversely. Evidence from the pastoral Epistles, confirmed by considerable early historical testimony, indicates that Paul was released from this first Roman imprisonment and had opportunity for travel, including a trip through Macedonia (and presumably Philippi), before being reimprisoned and suffering a martyr's death.

That "know" (*oida*) does not mean infallible knowledge is well indicated by comparison with another Pauline use of it in Acts 20:25, as Lightfoot has pointed out. If both instances demand certainty of knowledge, one of them failed of fulfillment, for Acts 20:25 says Paul "knew" he would not see the Ephesian elders again because of his approaching capture. Yet Philippians 1:25 indicates that he "knew" he would be released from that imprisonment (p. 94). The hypothesis of two Roman imprisonments with a period of freedom between them in which he visited both Ephesus and Macedonia is supported by 1 Timothy 1:3 and other passages in the pastoral Epistles. Among the early Fathers, considerable testimony is found for Paul's release from the first Roman imprisonment (Clement of Rome, *First Epistle to the Corinthians*, ch. 5; Muratorian Canon; Eusebius, *Ecclesiastical History*, II.22).

Paul's continued ministry among the Philippians would be aimed at advancing their spiritual growth and deepening their joy in the Christian faith. The believers' experience should not be static but characterized by a growing understanding of spiritual truth. This in turn would increase their joy as they entered more fully into the understanding of their privileges and prospects in Christ.

26 The "joy" in Paul's thought here was their "ground for boasting or glorying" (*kauchēma*). The emphasis is not on the action itself, but on the basis for it. As the Philippians would experience the progress and joy that Paul's labors among them would produce, they would have new and greater reasons for overflowing (*perisseuē*) with joy. This reason for glorying would be found "in Christ Jesus," of course, but its immediate occasion would be "on account of me" (*en emoi*), said Paul. His ministry among them would enable them to see more clearly the riches of their salvation in Christ.

Notes

19 The wording τοῦτό μοι ἀποβήσεται εἰς σωτηρίαν (*touto moi apobēsetai eis sōtērian*, "this will result in my salvation") is exactly the same as Job 13:16 (LXX). There Job was responding to his accusers by stating that he would be vindicated when he would ultimately stand before God. Paul may have used this language not only because the wording was appropriate for his purposes, but also because the context of ultimate vindication before God was also relevant.

The genitive τοῦ πνεύματος (*tou pneumatos*, "of the Spirit") is probably subjective here, though in this instance both subjective and objective aspects are intertwined and indistinguishable from a practical standpoint. The Spirit would help Paul successfully face these unpleasant experiences and accomplish God's will in his life. By referring to the Spirit as τοῦ πνεύματος Ἰησοῦ Χριστοῦ (*tou pneumatos Iēsou Christou*, "the Spirit of Jesus Christ"), Paul reflects the fact that the Holy Spirit has been bestowed on men by Christ as well as by the Father (John 15:26).

21 The two infinitive phrases are in the present tense: τὸ ζῆν (*to zēn*, "to live"), and the aorist: τὸ ἀποθανεῖν (*to apothanein*, "to die"). The former understandably stresses the progressive nature of living. The aorist looks simply at the fact of dying. It is difficult to see Lightfoot's grammatical justification for stating (p. 92), "The tense denotes not the act of dying but the consequence of dying, the state after death." Such an idea would have been better conveyed by the perfect tense. The aorist names the act in the simplest possible way. Anything more must be drawn from the context. It is best to regard the expression as Paul's reference to his possible death at the hands of Rome. Any connotation of the state after death must be inferred from the mention of "gain," not the tense of ἀποθανεῖν (*apothanein*, "to die").

23 "Better by far" utilizes a triple comparative πολλῷ μᾶλλον κρεῖσσον (*pollō mallon kreisson*), found nowhere else in the NT in this precise form. It employs the comparative form of the adjective κρατύς (*kratys*, "more excellent"), which is commonly used as the comparative of ἀγαθός (*agathos*, "good"), the comparative adverb μᾶλλον (*mallon*, "to a greater extent"), and the dative adjective πολλῷ (*pollō*, "much") used adverbially.

24 The use of τῇ σαρκί (*tē sarki*, "in the flesh") is in the physical sense and as such is virtually synonymous with σῶμα (*sōma*, "body"), as in 1:22. The ethical sense in which this term is sometimes used by Paul to denote the sinful nature of man is not involved here.

25 The verbs μενῶ (*menō*) and παραμενῶ (*paramenō*) convey the idea of remaining, the former in the general sense of "remain alive," and the latter more specifically "to remain with you." Hauck suggests that παραμενῶ (*paramenō*) means "to stay with someone ... with a hint of service" (F. Hauck, *Menō*, et al., TDNT, 4:578).

26 The noun καύχημα (*kauchēma*, "joy") is found in the NT only in the Pauline Epistles and Hebrews. In all cases it denotes either the grounds or cause for boasting (i.e., the thing of which

one is proud), or the content of one's boasting. A cognate καύχησις (*kauchēsis*) depicts the action of boasting. (Rudolf Bultmann, *Kauchaomai*, TDNT, 3:648, 649.)

II. First Series of Exhortations (1:27–2:18)

1. *Exhortation to Unity and Courage in View of External Foes*

1:27–30

> [27]Whatever happens, conduct yourselves in a manner worthy of the gospel of Christ. Then, whether I come and see you or only hear about you in my absence, I wilł know that you stand firm in one spirit, contending as one man for the faith of the gospel [28]without being frightened in any way by those who oppose you. This is a sign to them that they will be destroyed, but that you will be saved—and that by God. [29]For it has been granted to you on behalf of Christ not only to believe on him, but also to suffer for him, [30]since you are going through the same struggle you saw I had, and now hear that I still have.

27 As citizens of a spiritual realm, the Philippians should stand firm in one spirit. This should be true "whatever happens" to Paul, for the responsibility for their spiritual growth rested ultimately with them and their appropriation of the riches in Christ. Whether Paul would be released and thus enabled to visit them in person, or be forced to remain away from them and learn of their progress through the reports of others, his exhortation was the same. They must conduct their lives in a manner appropriate to the gospel of Christ.

In this connection, Paul used a verb that meant literally "to live as a citizen" (*politeues-the*). Although none of its NT uses relate to the political side of life in society as such, it was an apt term for a letter written to a church in a city whose inhabitants were proud of their status as Roman citizens (Acts 16:12, 20, 21). The earliest members of the Philippian church would have known that Paul had used his Roman citizenship to bring about a speedy and dignified release from imprisonment there (Acts 16:36–40). Out of this cultural background the readers were challenged to live as those who had a higher and vastly more significant citizenship (Phil 3:20).

The readers are urged to "stand firm in one spirit." It is possible to regard "spirit" as a reference to the Holy Spirit (Eph 4:3), but the explanatory phrase "as one man" (*miā psychē*, "with one soul") strongly suggests that both are descriptions of Christian unity of thought and action, similar to the expression in Acts 4:32, "of one heart and of one soul." Of course, true unity must be produced by the Holy Spirit; however, the source is not what is stressed here, but the result. It is doubtful whether Paul was trying to draw sharp psychological distinctions between these terms. If such are to be sought to any degree, the former term (*pneumati*) probably denotes man's highest center of motivation, and for the Christian this would be quickened by the Holy Spirit. The latter term (*psychē*) would denote the area of sensory experience.

This exhortation to unified thought and action has in view the goal of contending "for the faith of the gospel." The reference is to the objective faith (i.e., the body of truth) embodied in the gospel message. They are to be "contending" for it, a positive statement of their need to promote and protect the message of Christ, while at the same time implying that adversaries must be faced. The use of the compound form *synathlountes*

118

("contending together") conveys the need for joint effort. The athletic metaphor of teamwork reinforces the previous references to "one spirit" and "one soul," and is a reminder that a unified effort is needed if they are to be victorious in the contest.

28 Paul does not want the Philippians to be terrified in any respect by their opponents. The noble character of their cause and the recognition that Christ is on their side should cause believers to avoid the unreasoning terror that prevents intelligent effort. Who were these opponents? Some have insisted that the reference could not have been to Jews because the Jewish population of Philippi was too small (Lenski, p. 755). This ignores the fact that hostile Jews often dogged Paul's steps and caused trouble in the churches he founded. Such was the case in other Macedonian churches (Thessalonica: Acts 17:5; Berea: Acts 17:13). In the light of Paul's discussion in 3:2-6, it seems clear that Jewish hostility was present. But there is nothing in 1:28 that restricts the reference to Jewish opponents. What is virtually certain is that these were external foes, not false teachers within the church. It is most likely that Paul was speaking generally of adversaries of the church of whatever kind. Whether Jewish or pagan, they usually employed the same tactics, and the need for unity and courage among the believers was crucial.

Failure of the church to be intimidated by enemies was a token of the ultimate failure of the enemies of God. The adversaries may not have recognized this, but it was nonetheless a sign that their attacks were futile and that the church would prevail. This sign or token was intended for the adversaries (not to the adversaries *and* the believers, as the rendering in KJV based on an inferior textual reading suggests), but it was a sign to them of two things: their ultimate destruction and the salvation of the believers. "And that by God" refers grammatically neither to "salvation" nor to "sign" (both of which are feminine nouns, for which the feminine form of "that" would be required, rather than the neuter, which was used), but to the entire fact that believers have been granted courage from God to stand firm in their struggles and so are demonstrating their salvation.

29 The whole situation was part of God's gracious provision for those enlisted in the cause of Christ. The privileges enjoyed by Christians included the ability not only to believe in Christ initially at regeneration and subsequently throughout the Christian life, but also to suffer for him. If we question the propriety of referring to suffering as a privilege and a "gracious gift" (*echaristhē*), we must remember that the NT regards suffering as God's means of achieving his gracious purposes both in his own Son (Heb 2:10) and in all believers (James 1:3, 4; 1 Peter 1:6, 7).

30 In this matter of suffering, the Philippians were experiencing the same sort of struggle Paul had endured throughout his ministry. They had seen some of Paul's sufferings when he had been in Philippi (Acts 16:19-24). They had heard of others he had undergone more recently in Rome (perhaps from reports of travelers or other messengers, including those who conveyed the information about Epaphroditus, 2:26).

In Hellenistic usage *agōn* ("struggle," NIV) originally meant a place of assembly, then a place where athletic contests were held, and later the contest itself. The term also developed a metaphorical use for any kind of conflict. Ethelbert Stauffer has shown the various motifs in which the term appears in the NT. In Philippians 1:28 the thought of "antagonists" appears, and this is consistent with the idea expressed elsewhere of the obstacles, dangers, and even catastrophes that the Christian may face (E. Stauffer, *Agōn*, TDNT, 1:134-140).

Notes

27 The verb πολιτεύομαι (politeuomai, "to conduct oneself") occurs twice in the NT (Acts 23:1; Phil 1:27). Strathmann shows how the term had been influenced by Hellenistic Judaism and denotes a life shaped by religion (Hermann Strathmann, Polis, et al., TDNT, 6:534, 535). The cognate πολίτευμα (politeuma, "citizenship") in 3:20 makes it clear that the citizenship Paul had in mind was not Roman but heavenly.

The εἴτε ... εἴτε (eite ... eite, "whether ... or") construction is somewhat irregular. One would have expected ἀκούων (akouōn, "hearing") or ἀκούσας (akousas, "having heard") following ἀπὼν (apōn, "being absent"), and then a finite verb such as μανθάνω (manthanō, "I understand"). Yet Paul's meaning is not obscured. Whether he comes and sees for himself or is absent and only hears reports, the results, he hopes, will be the same—viz., that his readers are standing firm.

28 The passive participle πτυρόμενοι (ptyromenoi) is from πτύρω (ptyrō), which occurs only here in the NT. It means "to frighten" or "terrify" and was used in referring to the terror of a startled horse (M.R. Vincent, Word Studies in the New Testament [Grand Rapids: Eerdmans, reprinted 1946], 3:427). Diodorus Siculus used it when he wrote about the frightened chariot-horses of Darius at the battle of Issus (17:34).

Various forms of ἀντίκειμαι (antikeimai, "to oppose") are used in the NT to denote opposers of the Christian faith, including opponents of Jesus (Luke 13:17), as well as adversaries of the church, both Jewish and Gentile (1 Cor 16:9; 2 Thess 2:4; 1 Tim 5:14).

The words ἀπωλείας (apōleias, "of destruction") and σωτηρίας (sōtērias, "of salvation") are used in obvious contrast. Ἀπώλεια (apōleia) is the regular NT term for eternal destruction and is so used in the Synoptics (Matt 7:13), Paul (Rom 9:22), Peter (2 Peter 2:1, 3), and John (John 17:12). "What is meant is not a simple extinction of existence ... but an everlasting state of torment and death" (Albrecht Oepke, Apōleia, TDNT, 1:397). This sense is made all the more certain by the contrasting parallel in the verse with σωτηρία (sōtēria), which surely refers here to the spiritual state of believers.

29 The article τὸ (to) with ὑπὲρ Χριστοῦ (hyper Christou) makes a substantive of the phrase, thus: "this matter for the sake of Christ." The two occurrences of ὑπέρ (hyper) in this verse are with the sense of "on behalf of," "for the sake of," or "because of," denoting the moving cause or reason (BAG, p. 846. 1.d).

30 The nominative participle ἔχοντες (echontes, "having") is apparently dependent on πολιτεύεσθε (politeuesthe, "conduct yourselves") or στήκετε (stēkete, "you stand") in 1:27. The only objection to this explanation is the rather considerable distance involved. However, the thought of contending in the struggle resumes the concept of conducting their lives, and the grammar is regular. The alternative is to treat echontes as an anacoluthon or as an independent nominative.

---

2. *Exhortation to Unity and Humility Toward Those in the Church*

2:1–11

[1]If you have any encouragement from being united with Christ, if any comfort from his love, if any fellowship with the Spirit, if any tenderness and compassion, [2]then make my joy complete by being like-minded, having the same love, being one in spirit and purpose. [3]Do nothing out of selfish ambition or vain conceit, but in humility consider others better than yourselves. [4]Each of you should look not only to your own interests, but also to the interests of others.

[5]Your attitude should be the same as that of Christ Jesus:

6Who, being in very nature God,
did not consider equality with God
something to be grasped,
7but made himself nothing,
taking the very nature of a servant,
being made in human likeness.
8And being found in appearance as a man,
he humbled himself
and became obedient to death—
even death on a cross!
9Therefore God exalted him to the highest place
and gave him the name that is above every name,
10that at the name of Jesus every knee should bow,
in heaven and on earth and under the earth,
11and every tongue confess that Jesus Christ is Lord,
to the glory of God the Father.

1 The following exhortation also concerns unity, but this time the focus is turned on problems within the church. To encourage the fulfillment of this injunction, Paul listed four incentives. All are stated as "if " clauses (with the verb understood), but the condition is assumed to be true. Thus, the sense of the first clause is "If there are any grounds for exhortation because you are in Christ, as indeed there are . . . ." As Christians, they were in a vital union with Christ and this placed obvious obligations on them. They were responsible to heed the orders of Christ as issued by him either directly during his ministry or through his apostles. Second, the comfort and encouragement provided by love should prompt the Philippians to join hands in common action. Their love for Christ and for their fellow believers (including Paul) ought to impel them to desist from divisiveness in any form. Third, the fellowship produced by the Holy Spirit should stimulate the practical exercise of unity. They have been made one by the Spirit (cf. 1 Cor 12:13) and thus are partners with him and with each other. Recognition of this theological truth would find expression in their lives. Fourth, the existence of tenderness and compassion among them would make the unity that was being called for the normal and expected thing.

Paraklēsis ("encouragement," NIV) may be translated as either "exhortation" or "consolation." To understand the term in this context as implying more than just comfort is consistent with other Pauline statements on unity. In Ephesians 4:1–3 the unity of the believers is made the subject of an exhortation. The translation "encouragement" can convey both ideas.

In the third of the conditional statements in this verse, *pneumatos* ("Spirit") can be either objective or subjective. If objective, the sense is "fellowship with the Spirit," as reflected in RSV and NIV and supported by scholars such as Martin (*Epistle of Paul to the Philippians*, pp. 48, 49, 91). Others, such as Beare and Hendriksen, understand the expression more broadly to include both aspects—the participation in the Spirit and the common life produced by the Spirit to form the Christian community (Beare, in loc.; Hendriksen, p. 98 n.). That the subjective aspect ("fellowship produced by the Spirit") should be included in the concept is strongly suggested by two of the other clauses, in which the exhortation comes *from* their being in Christ, and their comfort comes *from* love.

2 The exhortation itself is first stated and then elaborated on. Paul exhorted the Philip-

pians to make his joy full by minding the same thing. He was already experiencing joy because of his associations with this church (1:3, 4; 4:10), but one thing was yet needed to make his joy "complete" (*plērōsate*). They needed to be "like-minded" (literally, "mind the same thing"). Of course, this was not a command for unity at the expense of truth. It assumes that "the same thing" is also "the right thing."

The enjoinder to maintain unity in their thought and action is elaborated on in four participial phrases. By complying with these instructions, the readers would create a climate where true unity would flourish. First, they should be possessing a mutual love. Inasmuch as it is assumed that all were believers indwelt by the same Spirit (2:1), the love that is the fruit of the Spirit (Gal 5:22) ought to be demonstrated in every life. Second, they should be setting their minds on unity with oneness of soul. This phrase repeats the thought appearing earlier in the verse and reinforces the conclusion that there was a problem of disharmony within the congregation. It may be unfair to center the problem on Euodia and Syntyche (4:2), but they were at least involved.

3 Third, they should avoid selfish ambition and conceit and consider others above themselves. Paul had experienced adverse effects from this sort of selfish ambition among some unworthy preachers at Rome (1:17). Persons who seek to advance themselves usually enjoy glorying in their success, but all such glory is "vain conceit" (*kenodoxian*). The Christian attitude should reveal itself in "humility" (*tē tapeinophrosunē*). This concept was not highly regarded in Greek literature. Grundmann observes that the Greek concept of a free man led to contempt for any sort of subjection, whereas the Bible proposes that we should be controlled by God and thus assumes that to subject ourselves to God is praiseworthy (Walter Grundmann, *Tapeinos*, et al., TDNT, 8:11, 12). This paved the way for the Christian ethic that calls for believers to be humble toward one another, mindful of their spiritual brotherhood and their ultimate subjection to Christ. In the exercise of humility, Paul instructed his readers to "consider others better than yourselves." This does not mean that we must have false or unrealistic views of our own gifts as compared with those of others. Moral superiority is not in view. What Paul means is that our consideration for others must precede concern for ourselves (Rom 12:10). This will go far toward removing disharmony.

4 Fourth, they should be looking not only to their own interests but also to those of others. The self-centeredness that considers only one's own rights, plans, and interests must be replaced by a broader outlook that includes the interests of one's fellows. "But also" indicates that our own affairs need not be totally ignored, but that the interests of others must also form a part of our concern. The believer should not neglect the welfare of himself and his family (1 Tim 5:8) in order to involve himself in the good of others. What Paul is calling for is a Christian concern that is wide enough to include others in its scope. When each member of the Christian community exercises this mutual concern, problems of disunity quickly disappear.

5 The great example of humility is Christ Jesus. Although verses 5 to 11 contain one of the outstanding Christologies in the NT, they were written to illustrate the point of humility and selflessness. Another instance where Paul makes a sublime statement about Christ almost incidentally in illustrating a practical point is Ephesians 5:25–27.

The literary form of the beautiful passage before us leads many to regard it as an early Christian hymn that Paul incorporated into his Epistle (see Introduction, 5). But Paul himself was quite capable of a highly poetic style (cf. 1 Cor 13), and may well have composed these exalted lines. Regardless of their precise origin, the passage provides a masterly statement of Christology, and serves well the author's purpose of illustrating supreme condescension.

The exhortation comes first: "Your attitude should be the same as that of Christ Jesus." Here the Greek text could be literally rendered "Keep thinking this among you, which [attitude] was also in Christ Jesus." This rendering fits the context better than another suggestion that has been offered: "Have the same thoughts among yourselves as you have in your communion with Christ Jesus" (BAG, p. 874). Believers, of course, cannot duplicate the precise ministry of Jesus but they can display the same attitude.

6 Christ's preincarnate status is then stated. Two assertions are made: He existed in the form of God and he did not regard his existing in a manner of equality with God as a prize to be grasped or held onto. "Being in very nature God" is, literally, "existing in the form of God." The term *morphē* denotes the outward manifestation that corresponds to the essence, in contrast to the noun *schēma* (2:7), which refers to the outward appearance, which may be temporary.

The participle *hyparchōn* ("being" [NIV], in the sense of "existing") is in the present tense and states Christ's continuing condition. To say that he was existing in the essential metaphysical form of God is tantamount to saying that he possessed the nature of God. The phrase is elaborated on by the words "equality with God" (*isa theō*). It should be noted that *isa* is an adverb (not the substantive *ison*), and hence describes the manner of existence. This does not need to be regarded as precisely the same as "the form of God," for one's essential nature can remain unchanged, though the manner in which that nature is expressed can vary greatly through changing times and circumstances.

The noun *harpagmon* ("something to be grasped") has been variously interpreted. Does it mean something that has been seized, or something to be seized? This uncertainty has led to three possibilities: (1) The preincarnate Christ already possessed equality with the Father and resolved not to cling to it. (2) Christ had no need to grasp at equality with God, for he already possessed it. (3) Christ did not reach for his crowning prematurely, as Adam had, but was willing to wait till after his suffering.

Understanding that *harpagmos* can be used passively in the same sense as *harpagma* to mean "prize," the interpreter must look to the context for guidance. That the preexistent state is in view seems evident from the movement of the passage (see also the parallel at 2 Cor 8:9). Inasmuch as he already existed in "the form of God," the mode of his existence as equal with God was hardly something totally future and thus as yet unexperienced but must rather be something he divested himself of. Hence, view 3 above does not fit the context so well as view 1. View 2, though expressing a truth, does not provide an adequate basis for the statements that follow.

7 The description then moves to Christ's incarnate state. Two clauses carry the main thoughts: "[he] made himself nothing" and "he humbled himself" (v.8). The first clause is literally "but himself he emptied"; it uses a verb (*ekēnosen*) that has lent its name to the so-called "kenosis" theories that probe the nature of Christ's "emptying" himself. Although the text does not directly state that Christ emptied himself "of something," such would be the natural understanding when this verb is used. Furthermore, the context has most assuredly prepared the reader for understanding that Christ divested himself of something. What it was the following phrases imply.

The one who was existing in the form of God took on the form of a servant. The word "taking" (*labōn*) does not imply an exchange, but rather an addition. The "form of God" could not be relinquished, for God cannot cease to be God; but our Lord could and did take on the very form of a lowly servant when he entered human life by the Incarnation. It is sometimes suggested that the term "servant" refers to the exalted Servant of Jehovah, but this passage seems intended to emphasize his condescension and humble station. What an example our Lord provides of the spirit of humility (cf. 2:3–5)! Inasmuch as angels also are servants, the statement makes it clear that Christ became part of humanity: "being made in human likeness." The word "likeness" (*homoiōmati*) does not bear the connotation of exactness as does *eikōn*, or of intrinsic form as does *morphē*. It stresses similarity but leaves room for differences. Thus Paul implies that even though Christ became a genuine man, there were certain respects in which he was not absolutely like the other men. (He may have had in mind the unique union of the divine and human natures in Jesus, or the absence of a sinful nature.)

In summation, Christ did not empty himself of the form of God (i.e., his deity), but of the manner of existence as equal to God. He did not lay aside the divine attributes, but "the insignia of majesty" (Lightfoot, p. 112). Mark Twain's novel *The Prince and the Pauper*, describing a son of Henry VIII who temporarily changed positions with a poor boy in London, provides an illustration. Christ's action has been described as the laying aside during the incarnation of the independent use of his divine attributes (A.J. McClain, "The Doctrine of the Kenosis in Philippians 2:5–8," *Grace Journal*, vol. 8, no. 2; reprinted from *The Biblical Review Quarterly*, October, 1928). This is consistent with other NT passages that reveal Jesus as using his divine powers and displaying his glories upon occasion (e.g., miracles, the Transfiguration), but always under the direction of the Father and the Spirit (Luke 4:14; John 5:19; 8:28; 14:10).

8 After describing the fact of the Incarnation, Paul turns to the consideration of the depths of humiliation to which Christ went: "he humbled himself " and went to "death on a cross." The concluding phrase in 2:7 states what Christ actually was; the opening phrase of 2:8 looks at him from the standpoint of how he appeared in the estimation of men. He was "found" by them, as far as his external appearance was concerned (*schēmati*), as a mere man (*hōs anthrōpos*). Outwardly considered, he was no different from other men. Even this was great condescension for one who possessed the form of God, but Christ's incomparable act did not end here. He further humbled himself by "becoming obedient to death." He was so committed to the Father's plan that he obeyed it even as far as death (Heb 5:8). Nor was this all, for it was no ordinary death, but the disgraceful death by crucifixion, a death not allowed for Roman citizens, and to Jews indicative of the curse of God (Deut 21:23; Gal 3:13).

The mention of *staurou* ("cross") connoted probably the cruelest form of capital punishment. Crucifixion had been practiced by the Phoenicians and Persians and was taken over by the Romans. In Rome it was a punishment reserved for slaves and foreigners. (Pierson Parker, "Crucifixion," IDB, A–D, pp. 746, 747.)

9 The final movement of thought in this sublime illustration describes Christ's subsequent exaltation. The nature of this exaltation was God's elevating Christ to the highest position and granting him the name above all names. "Exalted . . . to the highest place" renders the Greek word *hyperypsōsen*, which might be translated "superexalted." The reference is to the resurrection, ascension, and glorification of Jesus following his humiliating death, whereby all that he had laid aside was restored to him and much more besides. Implicit in this exaltation is the coming consummation mentioned in the next verses, when his triumph over sin and his lordship will be acknowledged by every being.

In view of the chronological pattern exhibited in this passage, the giving of "the name" must have been subsequent to the Cross. This would appear to be sufficient to rule out the identity of the name in view as being "Jesus." A more likely identification of "the name" is "Lord," the equivalent many times of the Old Testament "Jehovah," and supported by the thought of v.11. Christ's exaltation is expressly stated as manifesting his lordship in Acts 2:33-36. Another explanation takes "the name" in the sense of position, dignity, or office, similar to the OT use of the word šēm ("name"). Other NT uses of "name" in this sense may be in Ephesians 1:21 and Hebrews 1:4. There are also instances where "the name" is used alone as a reference to God or Christ (see Acts 5:41; 3 John 7). This use had clear precedent in the OT (Lev 24:11, 16, ASV, RSV; 2 Sam 7:13).

10 The purpose of Christ's exaltation is that all beings might bow in acknowledgment of the name that belongs to Jesus (v.10), and confess that Jesus Christ is Lord (v.11). Because of what the name of Jesus represents, a time is coming when every knee shall bow before him in recognition of his sovereignty. The statement is built on the wording of Isaiah 45:23, a verse quoted by Paul in Romans 14:11 also (cf. Rev 5:13). This universal acknowledgment will include angels and departed saints in heaven, people still living on earth, and the satanic hosts and lost humanity in hell.

The form *Iēsou* (Jesus) can be either genitive or dative, allowing the phrase to be rendered either as "at the name of Jesus" or "at the name Jesus." The former appears to be the more probable, inasmuch as the exaltation is said to be at the time when God granted his Son the "name," and this occurred considerably after the name Jesus was given to Christ. Hence, the expression should be understood as "at the name that belongs to Jesus."

The genitives *epouraniōn*, ("in heaven"), *epigeiōn* ("on earth"), and *katachthoniōn* ("under the earth") are either masculine or neuter. If the latter is meant, Paul's statement was intended to include all of creation, animate and inanimate. Undoubtedly this would agree with Paul's teaching elsewhere regarding the submission of all creation to the Son of God (Rom 8:19-22). However, the mention of "knee" and "tongue" certainly suggests personal beings, unless the passage is highly figurative (cf. Ps 148). But since the context is not figurative, the likelihood is that the terms are masculine here.

11 Submission will be expressed not only by bending the knee, but also by verbal confession. The mention of "tongue" and "confess" suggests a restriction to moral beings, but "every" indicates a universal acknowledgment of Christ's sovereignty, even by his enemies. Paul does not imply by this a universal salvation, but means that every personal being will ultimately confess Christ's lordship, either with joyful faith or with resentment and despair.

This ultimate confession that Jesus Christ is Lord is apparently Paul's indication of the "name" granted Jesus at his exaltation following the Cross (v.9). The name "Lord" with all the dignity and divine prerogatives this implies will eventually be recognized by every creature. Of course, the Son in his *nature* was always deity, but the exaltation following the Cross granted him the dignity of station commensurate with his nature and far superior to his humble state while on earth.

"To the glory of God the Father" is Paul's closing doxology to this remarkable Christology. He has never lost sight of the divine order and of the grand scheme in which the incarnation of Christ must be viewed. Recognition of Christ's lordship fulfills the purpose of the Father and so brings glory to God.

This picture of Christ's humiliation and subsequent exaltation was intended by Paul

125

to encourage in his readers an attitude of Christlike humility. If they were to be identified as Christ's followers, they must demonstrate his characteristics. The appeal, however, was not only to a life of lowliness and hardship; it also contained the reminder that victory followed humiliation and that God's glory will ultimately prevail.

Notes

1 The masc.-fem. form τις (tis, "any") in the fourth clause poses the problem of grammatical disagreement with the neuter σπλάγχνα (splanchna, "viscera"). Attempts to solve it have elicited some imaginative explanations. Bengel urged that "joy" be understood with tis as the predicate of each clause: "if bowels and mercies be any joy," etc. (John Albert Bengel, New Testament Word Studies, trans. C.T. Lewis and M.R. Vincent [Grand Rapids: Kregel, repr. 1971], 2:431). Lenski (p. 761) translates: "if any fellowship, (let it be) of spirit; if any (such fellowship), (let it be) tender mercies and compassions!" This separates tis from splanchna and avoids the grammatical disagreement, but at the cost of considerable manipulation. Tis is found in all ancient MSS (including ℵ A B C D E F G K L P) except for a few minuscules, and must be considered the best-attested reading. The most likely conjecture is that the original form was the neuter τι (ti) and that the sigma (ς) was accidentally assimilated early from the following word (splanchna) by a scribal error of dittography (Kennedy, pp. 432, 433; Hendriksen, p. 98 n.). The error must have occurred prior to our earliest extant MSS.

2 The use of ἵνα (hina, "so that") here introduces the content of the injunction, not just the purpose of it. It is one of those instances where the more common telic use of hina is absorbed into the subject of the wish.

Τὸ αὐτὸ φρονῆτε (to auto phronēte, "think the same [thing]"; NIV, "being like-minded") and τὸ ἓν φρονοῦντες (to hen phronountes, "thinking the one [thing]"; NIV, "being one in . . . purpose") mean essentially the same thing. It is usually suggested that the latter is stronger than the former and serves to reinforce the injunction.

Σύμψυχοι (sympsychoi, "one in spirit") may be regarded as an independent item in the series of phrases or as belonging to the words immediately following. Favoring the latter is the conserving of the literary parallelism utilizing four participles in Paul's elaboration (2:2–4)—a parallelism that would otherwise be marred by the intrusion of an additional item that is not a participle.

3 No verb is expressed in the opening part of v.3, perhaps in the interests of preserving the fourfold participial construction. The reader must supply "do" or "doing."

4 The MSS vary between the sing. and pl. forms of ἕκαστος (hekastos, "each") in the two occurrences in this verse. Some have both as singulars; some, both plurals; and others, one sing. and one pl. Inasmuch as the adjective can be used substantively in either sing. or pl., it is not difficult to see how variation could occur. The Nestle text (25th ed.) adopts both plurals; UBS gives the first as sing., the second as pl.

5 The active form φρονεῖτε (phroneite, "think") is found in the major uncials (ℵ A B C* D E F G), and is to be preferred. The passive φρονείσθω (phroneisthō) is the reading of TR and was the basis of the KJV rendering.

6 All the verb forms in this passage are aorists, except for ὑπάρχων (hyparchōn, "being") and εἶναι (einai, "to be"), the two that refer to Christ prior to when he "emptied himself." The use of the two present forms is most appropriate for describing the timeless existence of the preincarnate Christ. Although these two verbs often seem interchangeable, the distinctive sense of each would be assumed in a context where both appear. "In the one instance we have existence as such, in the other we have being in a condition which comports with that existence" (Lenski, in loc.).

The noun μορφή (morphē, "nature") refers to that external form that represents what is intrinsic and essential. It indicates not merely what may be perceived by others, but what is objectively there (J. Behm, Morphē, TDNT, 4:743). In this passage it refers to the intrinsic form (it need not be physical) that belongs to God and by which he manifests himself to other intelligences.

The ending -μος (-*mos*) commonly denotes an action, and thus ἁρπαγμός (*harpagmos*, "to be grasped") originally meant the activity of seizing. It later came to mean what is seized, ἅρπαγμα (*harpagma*), especially denoting plunder or booty. It could also be used in regard to something already possessed with the sense of "utilize" rather than "take" (Werner Foerster, *Harpagmos*, TDNT, 1:473, 474). This is the only appearance of the word in the NT, but the meaning as given above is justifiable grammatically as shown by analogy with other nouns (BAG, p. 108; Hendriksen, in loc.). In non-Christian writings the word appears only in the active sense, but this yields a sense virtually impossible in our passage (BAG, p. 108). The context favors the meaning of a prize or gain Christ was not unwilling to relinquish for a time.

A careful discussion of the possibility that the language of this passage is a deliberate parallel to the first Adam is given by Martin in *Carmen Christi* (pp. 161–164).

7 The verb ἐκένωσεν (*ekenōsen*, "empty") has no genitive with it to name the object of which the person is deprived, but it is modified by two participles λαβών (*labōn*, "taking") and γενόμενος (*genomenos*, "becoming"; NIV, "being made") that effectively show in what sense this emptying occurred.

Μορφὴν δούλου (*morphēn doulou*, "the very nature of a servant") is in obvious contrast to μορφῇ θεοῦ (*morphē theou*, "the very nature of God") in 2:6. Just as the earlier expression indicated the essential or intrinsic nature of God, so *morphēn doulou* refers to Christ's taking of the genuine nature of a servant (in his human nature, of course). There is no room here for Docetism.

Ὁμοιώματι (*homoiōmati*, "likeness") is a synonym of εἰκών (*eikōn*, "image") but differs from it in that it stresses similarity without any need for an inner connection between the original and the copy (J. Schneider, *Homoiōma*, TDNT, 5:191). That Paul uses this term in describing Christ's humanity in order to avoid implying that Christ was sinful is evident not only from 2:7 but also from Rom 8:3 (Schneider, TDNT, 5:195–198).

8 Σχήματι (*schēmati*, "appearance") always denotes the outward form perceptible to the senses. This is true not only of this word, but also of its many derivatives, such as εὐσχήμων (*euschēmōn*), ἀσχήμων (*aschēmōn*), and σχηματίζω (*schēmatizō*), which refer to outward decency in conduct (J. Schneider, *Schēma*, TDNT, 7:954). Frequently this word (and its cognates) are used in contrast to the word-family μορφή (*morphē*, "form") to differentiate external appearance from the form that is intrinsic and essential.

9 The articular form τὸ ὄνομα (*to onoma*) occurs in the major uncials ℵ A B C, and is preferred by most editors. The article is omitted by TR, and is reflected in the KJV "a name." The former is the more likely from the standpoint of intrinsic probability (as well as from the documentary evidence), in view of the use of the article in the following attributive phrase, as well as the thought of the passage, which calls for something particular.

11 MS evidence varies between the aorist subjunctive ἐξομολογήσηται (*exomologēsētai*, "should confess"), found in P[46] B ℵ, and the future indicative ἐξομολογήσεται (*exomologēsetai*, "will confess"), found in A C D and TR. The subjunctive has been adopted by Nestle (25th ed.) and the indicative by UBS. Parallelism with κάμψῃ (*kampsē*, "should bow," v.10) would favor the subjunctive. However, in Koine both subjunctives and indicatives can be used with ἵνα (*hina*, "so that") in purpose clauses, with no demonstrable difference in meaning (BDF, sect. 369, p. 186).

---

3. *Exhortation to Work Out Their Salvation*

2:12-18

> [12]Therefore, my dear friends, as you have always obeyed—not only in my presence, but now much more in my absence—continue to work out your salvation with fear and trembling, [13]for it is God who works in you to will and to act according to his good purpose.

> [14]Do everything without complaining or arguing, [15]so that you may become blameless and pure, children of God without fault in a crooked and depraved generation, in which you shine like stars in the universe [16]as you hold out the word of life—in order that I may boast on the day of Christ that I did not run or labor for nothing. [17]But even if I am being poured out like a drink offering on the sacrifice and service coming from your faith, I am glad and rejoice with all of you. [18]So you too should be glad and rejoice with me.

12 Paul is not rebuking the Philippians, but exhorting them to pursue their Christian progress without undue dependence on his presence. Perhaps he had noted a weakness along this line. Once before in the Epistle he had mentioned their need to be as diligent in his absence as they were when he was present with them (1:27). The obedience of the Philippians is explained by Karl Barth as their obedience to Paul's commands (p. 69). Even if this be so, the thought must involve the commands of God as taught them by Paul. It may be better, therefore, to explain the thought directly as obedience to the commands of God, with Paul involved only secondarily. The Philippians had always obeyed the commands of God implicit in the gospel. This response had occurred first when Paul originally evangelized them, and had been witnessed by him on all of his subsequent visits. But there must be just as careful attention given this matter while Paul was away and especially if his circumstances should prevent a return, for they owed their obedience not merely to him but to their Lord.

The specific exhortation was to work out their own salvation. The biblical concept of salvation needs to be understood in order to comprehend Paul's intent here. Salvation has many aspects, including a present one. Regeneration initiates the believer into a life with obligations. Acknowledging Jesus Christ as Lord obligates the believer to obey him. Hence, working out salvation does not mean "working for" salvation, but making salvation operational. Justification must be followed by the experiential aspects of sanctification, by which the new life in Christ is consciously appropriated and demonstrated. The emphasis on "your" salvation ("your own," KJV) may reflect the circumstance that Paul wished to visit Philippi to advance them spiritually. In the event that he could not, they must not depend on him but must work out their spiritual progress, because the same Lord who would work through Paul also worked in them.

"With fear and trembling" is no contradiction of the joyful spirit permeating this letter. Christian joy is the experience of every believer in God's will, but holy fear of God that trembles at the thought of sin is also the attitude of the careful Christian (James 4:8–10).

13 Paul describes the enablement to carry out the exhortation as being furnished by God himself, who produces in believers both the desire to live righteously and the effective energy to do so. God does not demand of us what we cannot do. Furthermore, the provision from God takes into account our every need. It is not always enough to "will" something, for good intentions are not always carried out. Paul sees believers as having their wills energized by God and then also having the power to work supplied by him.

14 Compliance with Paul's exhortation should be "without complaining or arguing." The first term describes the grumbling discontents among the congregation, and the second depicts the evil reasonings and disputes that usually follow. Are these directed against God or against each other? Neither alternative is foreign to the context. The passage is influenced by Deuteronomy 32:5, and the example of Israel's complaining, which was chiefly against God, was used elsewhere by Paul to instruct the church (1 Cor 10:10). On the other hand, the problem of disunity in the congregation has already been seen in this letter (2:2), and more is to come (4:2). Perhaps the command is sufficiently general to cover both.

Emphasis in the command falls on the word *everything* (literally, "all things"), which is actually the first word of the verse in the Greek text. Most Christians are able to do some things without complaint. It is when we are exhorted to be doing "all things" with a joyful spirit that the difficulty comes. Yet the outworking of our Christian faith in daily life lays this responsibility upon us.

15 The purpose of the exhortation to work out their salvation was that the readers might be pure and uncontaminated light-givers in the world. By regeneration they had already become children of God in nature and position. Now as they progressed in sanctification, they would become "children of God without fault," particularly as viewed by the world around them. By faithfully adhering to the word of God as contained in Scripture and taught them by Paul, their lives would be free from anything blameworthy (*amemptoi*, "blameless"), as well as devoid of matters foreign or improper in the heart (*akeraioi*, "pure"). Their nature as God's children would be clearly evident, with no obvious flaws (*amōma*, "without fault") to disfigure their witness. The apostle is mindful of their location within a corrupt society. In OT language (Deut 32:5) he depicts mankind generally as "a crooked and depraved generation." By "generation" he was probably thinking of mankind as morally the product of one sinful stock (John 8:44), rather than merely a group of contemporaries. Amid this moral blackness, the children of God should stand out as stars at midnight. Believers are the possessors of Christ, the Light of the world (John 8:12), and so are now light-givers to the world (Matt 5:14). "You shine" states the present fact. They are not told to shine, but are reminded that they already do. The challenge was to let the light shine out unhindered.

16 As luminaries in a world of spiritual darkness, they were to "hold out the word of life." The present participle *epechontes* can be understood either as "holding fast" or as "holding forth." Those who regard the preceding clause as parenthetical (e.g., Lightfoot) explain what follows as in contrast to the "crooked and depraved generation" and so adopt the meaning "holding fast the word of life." On the other hand, the figure of "stars" supports the idea of "holding out" or "holding forth," and there is no real reason to treat it as a parenthesis. Furthermore, this latter sense assumes the former, for those who hold out the word of life to others are understood to have first received it themselves. The word of life is, of course, the gospel, which brings eternal life when it is received by faith (John 6:68).

Faithful living by the Philippians will provide Paul with added reason to rejoice when he appears before Christ. "Boast" (*kauchēma*) refers to the occasion or grounds for boasting (see note on 1:26). "The day of Christ" is the time when Christ will return for his church, and when believers will have their works inspected and rewarded (see note on 1:6). Paul wants the content or basis of his boast at that time to be that his labors for the Philippians had not been useless. He desires that all his efforts to win them to Christ and to nurture their faith will be vindicated at Christ's judgment seat by the victorious presence of the Philippian believers. "Run" expresses Paul's energetic activity, and "labor" depicts its toilsome aspects.

17 The prospect of standing before Christ reminded Paul that it might be soon. By the vivid metaphor of a drink offering, he explained that even though he was presently in a dangerous situation that could lead to a martyr's death, it was the climax of his ministry and a cause for rejoicing. Both Jewish and Greek religious practice included the use of wine poured out ceremonially in connection with certain sacrifices (Num 15:1-10; Homer, *Illiad*, 11:775), and it is fruitless and unnecessary to determine which was most influential in Paul's figure. What is important is to see that Paul regarded his own life as a sacrifice in the interests of the spiritual advancement of such persons as the Philippian believers. He used the same metaphor in 2 Timothy 4:6. "The sacrifice and service" employs only one article with the two nouns, and probably is a hendiadys meaning "sacrificial service." The apostle is thinking of their various Christian ministries performed as a spiritual sacrifice to God (4:18; Heb 13:15) and springing from their faith.

Paul was not embittered but was rejoicing in his present labors and sufferings. He was willing not only to endure his present sufferings but also to lay down his life, and the prospect of being with Christ and of having his ministry among the Philippians seen as successful filled him with joy. Enduring his present danger would be a demonstration that he had learned something of the "mind of Christ" (2:5). (As it turned out, he was probably not executed until some years later during a second Roman imprisonment.) Furthermore, he rejoiced not only for his own sake, but jointly with the Philippians as he contemplated his relation to their faith. He was its planter and nourisher, and thus their victories were his also. He conveys this idea not only by the words "rejoice with all of you," but also by the figure depicting his life as being poured out as a sacrifice along with the Philippians' own sacrifice. They were priests together, making spiritual sacrifices to God as a result of their faith in Christ. Their sacrifices consisted of themselves, presented by faithful service during life, and if need be, by a martyr's death.

18 Likewise the Philippians should display the same attitude as Paul. They must not wring their hands, nor bewail their own trials and Paul's. They must learn to find real joy as they work out their salvation and must also learn to share Paul's attitude about his situation.

Notes

---

12 The use of μή (*mē*, "not") is governed by the imperative κατεργάζεσθε (*katergazesthe*, "continue to work out"), rather than the indicative ὑπηκούσατε (*hypēkousate*, "you obeyed"); hence, the intervening phrases regarding Paul's presence and absence must be construed with the exhortation to "work out" rather than with the reference to their previous obedience.

The compound *katergazesthe* may have its distinctive sense here, which looks to the successful accomplishment of a task. Kennedy points to a Pauline instance where both simple and compound forms are used (2 Cor 7:10) and concludes that "*ἐργ*. refers to a process in its mediate workings, while κατεργ. looks solely at the final result" (p. 440).

13 The Greek word-family to which ἐνεργῶν (*energōn*, "working"; NIV, "works") belongs conveys the thought of energy as fully active, effective in reaching its goal. It is not mere resident energy, but energy in operation (William Barclay, *More New Testament Words* [New York: Harper & Brothers, 1958], pp. 46ff.). Hence, Paul depicts God as actively and continually putting forth his energy in believers to insure the accomplishment of their task.

14 The remaining NT uses of the noun γογγυσμός (*gongysmos*, "complaining") have to do with grumbling complaints against others, a factor suggesting that such would also be the case here. However, the analogy with Israel's murmuring makes it inadvisable to rule out the possibility

that the apostle may have in view complaints against God as well. The term διαλογισμῶν (dialogismōn, "arguing") is used in the NT predominantly of evil thoughts, or else of anxious reflection or doubt (G. Schrenk, Dialogismos, TDNT, 2:97, 98).

15 The active verb φαίνω (phainō) means "shine," and the middle form φαίνομαι (phainomai) means either "shine" or "appear" (BAG, p. 859). It does not seem warranted, therefore, to allege that φαίνεσθε (phainesthe) can only be rendered "appear" in this passage. Such uses as in Matt 24:27 and Rev 18:23 are legitimate parallels with the sense of "shine." Φωστῆρες (phōstēres) refers to light-giving bodies, especially the heavenly bodies such as the sun and stars (BAG, p. 880). The metaphorical uses have this as the background.

16 The verb ἐπέχω (epechō) occurs five times in the NT, but in none of the other instances is the sense precisely what is called for in Phil 2:16 (cf. Luke 14:7; Acts 3:5; 19:22; 1 Tim 4:16). Neither "hold fast" nor "hold forth" (or "hold out") fits the other uses. Both of these senses, however, are found in other literature, and the choice must be made on contextual grounds.

17, 18 The verb σπένδω (spendō, "pour out") occurs only twice in the NT, both times as passives and both as metaphors of Paul's suffering and eventual martyrdom (Phil 2:17; 2 Tim 4:6). Although Gr. custom generally called for the liquid offering to be poured on top of the sacrifice and Jewish procedure required it to be poured around it (Jos. Antiq., III.9.4), the preposition ἐπί (epi) is broad enough in meaning to cover both practices (and is so used in LXX of the drink offering, as well as in pagan literature).

In nonbiblical Gr., the word-family of λειτουργία (leitourgia, "service") denoted official service to the political body. It also developed a cultic use, and it was this use that found further development in LXX, where it was used of priestly functions (R. Meyer, Leitourgeō, Leitourgia, TDNT, 4:215-225). Paul is using the term here in harmony with his metaphor of sacrifice. (See also H. Strathmann, Leitourgeō, TDNT, 4:226-231.)

Lightfoot (p. 119) has insisted that συγχαίρω (synchairō) be understood as "congratulate" rather than "rejoice with" in v.17, since the latter would imply the Philippians were already rejoicing and hence the command for them to do so in v.18 would be strange. While admitting the possibility, one may also note that there are other plausible explanations for the meaning "rejoice with" (as in the exposition above). "Congratulate" seems extremely awkward.

III. Two Messengers of Paul to the Philippians (2:19-30)

1. Timothy

2:19-24

> 19I hope in the Lord Jesus to send Timothy to you soon, that I also may be cheered when I receive news about you. 20I have no one else like him, who takes a genuine interest in your welfare. 21For everyone looks out for his own interests, not those of Jesus Christ. 22But you know that Timothy has proved himself, because as a son with his father he has served with me in the work of the gospel. 23I hope, therefore, to send him as soon as I see how things go with me. 24And I am confident in the Lord that I myself will come soon.

19 The somber note sounded in the previous two verses is balanced by the more optimistic tone that follows. Paul planned to send Timothy to Philippi with a report and hoped to come shortly himself. His hope was "in the Lord Jesus." Every believer is "in Christ," and this vital union should influence every thought and activity. Thus Paul loves in the Lord (1:8); grounds his confidence in the Lord (2:24); rejoices in the Lord (3:3; 4:10); and desires that others rejoice in Christ (1:26; 3:1), welcome Christian leaders in the Lord (2:29), and always stand firm in the Lord (4:1). It may

be that Paul was uncertain of the outcome of his case at Rome and therefore the more obviously submitted all his plans and hopes to the lordship of Jesus.

Timothy was named in the opening of the letter (1:1), but his mention here in the third person shows that he was not a co-writer. Paul refers to Timothy and his proposed trip to Philippi with graciousness and delicacy. One might suppose that Paul would have explained that the purpose of the trip was to tell the Philippians about Paul's situation. But he only hints at that idea by the word "also" and by the clause "as soon as I see how things go with me" (v.23), because his main purpose is to hear about the Philippians, though he assumes that his readers will be cheered by a favorable report of him. The spiritual advancement of the churches was always uppermost in Paul's mind.

Paul must have expected Timothy not to remain at Philippi but to bring him word about the church immediately. Conceivably, they could have planned to meet at Ephesus after Paul's release. At least, they were presumably together at Ephesus subsequent to this time (1 Tim 1:3). This would require that before leaving for Philippi, Timothy knew with certainty the date of Paul's release. (Perhaps 2:23 implies this.) Otherwise, Timothy would have been expected to return to Paul at Rome before the apostle left the city.

20 Paul's glowing testimony about Timothy was not to introduce his young associate, for he was already well known at Philippi (see comment on 1:1). It did serve, however, to avert possible disappointment that Paul himself could not come at once and indicated that he had the fullest confidence in his younger associate. "No one else like him" is literally "no one of equal soul" (*isopsychon*). In the light of what follows, it seems best to take the comparison as being between Timothy and Paul's other available associates (so Lightfoot, Beare, Hendriksen), rather than between Timothy and Paul (so Alford). In the matter of "a genuine interest in your welfare," no one that Paul might conceivably have sent had the same interest in the Philippians as did Timothy. How appropriate that two of the pastoral Epistles were later written to him as he exercised his pastoral concerns in another city.

21 These words must be understood in harmony with other statements in the letter. They must not be denied their force, but neither must they be understood with undue harshness. Paul had already noted that some among his acquaintances at Rome were more concerned with furthering their own interests (1:14–17). Yet his reference to them was a temperate one (1:18). Furthermore, he must have been on good terms with many of the brethren who are included in his comment in 2:21, for he conveys their greeting in 4:21. Nevertheless, some restriction in Paul's reference would seem legitimate, for he is surely not including Epaphroditus or Luke or Aristarchus as not seeking the interests of Christ. It is best to regard Paul as referring solely to all those around him who might conceivably have undertaken the trip to Philippi. Some of them he may have asked and they had refused him in favor of their own pursuits. Others he may have considered but not asked because of what he knew about them. Luke and Aristarchus may have been away on other missions and so have been unavailable. That they are not mentioned in 1:1 suggests their absence at the time the letter was written.

22 The proved character of Timothy, however, put him in a class apart. By the thorough test of his repeated presence and ministry in Philippi, as well as by his reputation achieved elsewhere, the Philippian Christians knew him as a man of God (cf. comment on 1:1). Paul also vouches for him on the basis of many years of personal experience. He and the younger Timothy had a father-son relationship. Together they had served Christ for the furtherance of the gospel, beginning with Paul's second missionary journey more than ten years earlier.

23 The Greek sentence begins with *touton* ("this one"), which gathers up all that has just been said regarding Timothy and emphasizes that he is the one to be sent to Philippi. He will not be the bearer of the letter, however, because Paul wants to retain him until he has more definite information about the outcome of his case (":as soon as I see how things go with me"). This implies that Paul thinks there will soon be some kind of legal decision regarding him. This letter will alert the Philippians to Timothy's coming and will also let them know the reason why he did not come with Epaphroditus. They will also know that when Timothy does come, he will be bringing word about the crucial developments in Paul's legal case.

24 Although granting that the decision might go either way (not because his legal grounds were weak, but because justice is not always served in human courts), Paul was still confident that release was in prospect, and that he would fulfill his wish to visit the Philippians (cf. comments on 1:25). This confidence in the Lord must be similar to that implied in 2:19—"I hope in the Lord Jesus. . . ." All the acts, thoughts, and attitudes of Christians should spring from the fact that they are "in the Lord" and are prompted by the Spirit's energy. Everything they do should be consistent with, and submitted to, the Lord's will.

The Book of Acts does not record Paul's release from his Roman imprisonment. Nor does it record his execution at the end of it. But evidence furnished by the pastoral Epistles supports the hypothesis of a release during which Paul did additional traveling in Crete, Asia Minor, Macedonia, and Achaia. There is good reason, therefore, to believe that Paul's hope was realized.

Notes

19 The verb εὐψυχῶ (*eupsychō*) occurs only here in the NT. Its meaning of "be glad, have courage, be cheered" is well established in the papyri. The imperative εὐψύχει (*eupsychei*) is frequently found on grave inscriptions, meaning "farewell" (BAG, p. 330).

20 The tr. "of like soul or mind" for ἰσόψυχον (*isopsychon*) has the support of classical usage, though the word does not appear elsewhere in the NT (BAG, p. 382). With this meaning in view, Lightfoot is probably right in understanding Paul to mean "no one of a mind equal to Timothy," for if Paul had meant "equal to me," he would have said "no one *else*" or "no one except Timothy" (pp. 120, 121). Barth (p. 85) chooses the meaning "close associate," based on the meaning of the word in LXX of Ps 54:13 (Heb.: Ps 55:13). Beare, however, points out that Paul could hardly have been consciously indebted to this LXX passage, inasmuch as the context uses the word in an unflattering way in referring to a betrayer (p. 96). The meaning of "confidant" is advocated by P. Christou ("Isopsuchos, Phil 2:20," JBL, vol. 70 [1951]: 293-296).

21 The name Jesus Christ appears in the order Ἰησοῦ Χριστοῦ (*Iēsou Christou*) in P46, D, and the Alexandrian family (except B), and is adopted in the UBS text. The alternate reading transposes the words to Χριστοῦ Ἰησοῦ (*Christou Iēsou*), and is found in B and TR. This reading was adopted by Nestle (25th ed.).

22 It is possible to understand a shift in Paul's thought after the words ὡς πατρὶ τέκνον (*hōs patri teknon*, "as a son with his father"). The sense would then be: "as a child serves a father, he served with me." Paul is thought to have begun with the concept of a child serving his father, but to have shifted the wording slightly to indicate that in the ministry both he and Timothy were actually serving Christ. He then inserted the words "with me" to show this (Beare, p. 86). But the thought is certainly clear enough if the dative πατρί (patri, "[with] father") is treated as parallel with σὺν ἐμοί (syn emoi, "with me"); hence, "as a child [serves with] a father, he served with me" (Hendriksen, note, p. 136).

23, 24 The verb ἀφοράω (aphoraō), occurring here as the aorist subjunctive ἀφίδω (aphidō), is used one other time in the NT (Heb 12:2). The latter use shows clearly the basic meaning of "look away at something in the distance." This sense may also be implicit in the usage here, as Paul looks ahead to the time when a decision will be reached in his case. The adverb ἐξαυτῆς (exautēs, "immediately"; NIV, "as soon as") occurring at the end of v.23 should probably be construed with πέμψαι (pempsai, "to send"). It was added because Paul did not want to leave the impression that the delay until he should see how things turned out would be a long one.

---

2. Epaphroditus

2:25-30

> 25But I think it is necessary to send back to you Epaphroditus, my brother, fellow worker and fellow soldier, who is also your messenger, whom you sent to take care of my needs. 26For he longs for all of you and is distressed because you heard he was ill. 27Indeed he was ill, and almost died. But God had mercy on him, and not on him only but also on me, to spare me sorrow upon sorrow. 28Therefore I am all the more eager to send him, so that when you see him again you may be glad and I may have less anxiety. 29Welcome him in the Lord with great joy, and honor men like him, 30because he almost died for the work of Christ, risking his life to make up for the help you could not give me.

25 The second of Paul's messengers to Philippi, and the one whose forthcoming trip was the immediate occasion for this Epistle was Epaphroditus (see Introduction, 4). He is mentioned in the NT only in Philippians (2:25; 4:18). There is no reason to identify him with Epaphras of Colosse (Col 1:7; 4:12; Philem 23), though the names are similar. Epaphroditus had brought the Philippians' gift to Paul. He is identified by the apostle in a series of glowing terms. He was "my brother" (ton adelphon), a sharer of spiritual life with Paul and so his brother in Christ. He was a "fellow worker" (synergon), a participant with Paul in the labors of the gospel. Paul said he was also "my ... fellow soldier" (systratiōtēn mou), a sharer of the dangers involved in standing firm for Christ and in proclaiming the gospel. The next terms tell of Epaphroditus's relation to the Philippians. He had acted as their "messenger" (apostolon), the duly appointed and commissioned delegate to convey the Philippians' gift to Paul. (The broader use of the term apostle without the addition of the phrase "of Jesus Christ" is used also of Barnabas [Acts 14:14] and apparently of Silas and Timothy [1 Thess 2:7; cf. 1:1], and James the Lord's brother [Gal 1:19; 1 Cor 15:7]. For this less-restricted use of apostolon, see also 2 Cor 8:23.)

In this capacity Epaphroditus had served as their "minister" (leitourgon), functioning officially on their behalf in performing a sacred service to Paul. The noun leitourgos appears five times in the NT (Rom 13:6; 15:16; Phil 2:25; Heb 1:7; 8:2) and in several of these a priestly sort of ministry is in view. It is used of Christ's priestly ministry in the heavenly tabernacle (Heb 8:2) and of Paul's sacred service in the evangelizing of Gentiles and presentation of them to God (Rom 15:16). Hence, the use in Philippians 2:25 has overtones of a priestly act, that of Epaphroditus's presenting to Paul the Philippians' offering, "an acceptable sacrifice, pleasing to God" (4:18).

Now Paul had decided that Epaphroditus should be sent home to Philippi for the reasons he next explained.

26 The verb *epipotheō* ("to long for") used here of Epaphroditus, was used by Paul regarding his own feelings toward the Philippians in 1:8. It is also used of the Spirit's strong yearning for the total allegiance of man's heart (James 4:5), and of a newborn baby's longing for milk (1 Peter 2:2).

The addition of *adēmonōn* ("distressed") to the mention of Epaphroditus's longings emphasizes the intensity of his feeling. The only other NT uses of this word describe our Lord's emotions in Gethsemane (Matt 26:37; Mark 14:33). The etymology of the word is not certain, although it is most commonly traced to *adēmos* ("away from home") and thus "beside oneself, distressed, troubled." Epaphroditus had become deeply distressed when he learned that the Philippians knew of his illness. One must beware of reading too much between the lines, but it is a fair inference that more is involved than merely mutual concern. The strong word "distressed" and Paul's emphasis on the point that Epaphroditus had really been seriously ill and should be given a hero's welcome may imply that some misunderstanding had arisen in Philippi, and that word of it had gotten back to Rome. Perhaps there were rumors that he was a malingerer, or that he had been more of a burden than a help to Paul.

27 Paul therefore said that Epaphroditus had "indeed" been "ill" and had "almost died." The precise nature of his ailment is not indicated but it was related to his labors in the Lord's service, perhaps from the hazards or the exertions of the journey to Rome (v.30). The illness was so severe that Paul regarded the recovery as an intervention of God. It is clear that even though at times he exercised "the signs of an apostle" (2 Cor 12:12), Paul himself did not miraculously heal Epaphroditus. Apparently not even apostles could do miracles at will, but only when miracles were in God's purpose. In the case of Epaphroditus, God produced the recovery and by so doing displayed his mercy both on Epaphroditus and on Paul. The restoration of health to the sick man spared Paul "sorrow upon sorrow." He felt keenly the misfortunes of his friends, and though he had been distressed over the illness of this courageous emissary, he was spared the additional sorrow that his death would have brought.

28 The verb *epempsa* ("send") is an epistolary aorist and refers to the present sending of Epaphroditus with this letter. In view of the circumstances noted above, Paul was sending him more hastily than he would otherwise have done. If the serious illness and the apparent misunderstanding at Philippi had not occurred, Paul might have retained him longer, perhaps till the end of the trial. This may also have been part of the intention of the Philippians in sending Epaphroditus to Paul. It was important, then, that this letter should accompany Epaphroditus, so that the Philippians would rejoice at his safe return. Paul was concerned also about the feelings of Epaphroditus (v.26). Thus the return of the messenger to the church, along with the true explanation of what had happened, should bring a happy conclusion to the whole affair and satisfy both parties. At the same time, Paul himself would benefit by being relieved from further anxiety, for knowing that his friends were relieved always brought a lessening of his painful concern over problems in the churches.

29 Paul therefore exhorted the Philippians to welcome Epaphroditus with joy as fellow Christians should. He had fulfilled his mission with distinction and deserved an appropriate homecoming. Paul's words imply that more was involved in Epaphroditus's disturbed feelings than simple affectionate concern, otherwise no such urging from the apostle to welcome him would have been necessary. Some sort of alienation had arisen. The church was also to do more than refrain from criticism of Epaphroditus. They were to give him due recognition for his faithful and sacrificial service to Paul.

30 The reason why a genuine welcome was deserved by Epaphroditus was twofold. First, he had been engaged in the work of Christ and had actually risked his life to accomplish it. Second, he had been trying by his labors to make up for the Philippians' absence from Paul, and so they owed him their gratitude. Epaphroditus's close call with death is to be explained in relation to his sickness (v.27), and was not the result of persecution or of adverse judicial proceedings. Furthermore, the ailment was directly due to his Christian labors on behalf of Paul. Perhaps it resulted from the rigors of travel and was compounded by his efforts to continue ministering to Paul in spite of being sick. It was not merely an unavoidable circumstance but was a risking of his life in the interests of his ministry. Paul strongly commended Epaphroditus to the church that had sent him. The church should be grateful, because Epaphroditus had actually been representing them and was doing for Paul what they could not do. Inasmuch as 4:14–18 reveals that the Philippians had done more than other churches for the apostle, the "lack of service" (KJV) here must be the lack of their physical presence with him. This Epaphroditus had supplied by his presence and personal care. This explanation of the "lack" (*hysterēma*) is supported by the use of the same word describing the Corinthians' absence from Paul as compensated for by the coming of Stephanas, Fortunatus, and Achaicus (1 Cor 16:17).

Notes:

---

25 The verb ἡγησάμην (*hēgēsamēn*) is an epistolary aorist, viewing the action from the standpoint of the reader rather than the writer. English would use the present "I think" (NIV) or the perfect "I have thought."

27 The initial καὶ γὰρ (*kai gar*, "for indeed") implies that the previous statement that Epaphroditus had become ill was really an understatement (Lightfoot), since the man had nearly died. So the report of illness that had reached Philippi had not been exaggerated. The phrase λύπην ἐπὶ λύπην (*lupēn epi lypēn*, "sorrow upon sorrow") is sometimes explained as the sorrow of bereavement added to the miseries of his imprisonment (so Martin, *Philippians*, p. 131). The view expressed in the exposition seems preferable, however.

28 In classical and Hellenistic Gr., the word group σπουδάζω-σπουδαῖος (*spoudazō-spoudaios*) means "to make haste" or "be zealous, active, concerned." In LXX the use is largely confined to "haste." Josephus, however, uses it also in the sense of being zealous, concerned, or showing interest. Both senses are found in NT usage. (Gunther Harder, *Spoudazō*, TDNT, 7:559–568.) The comparative adverb σπουδαιοτέρως (*spoudaioterōs*) could have either sense here, but the idea conveyed by "more hastily" may best suit the context, where Paul explains why he is sending Epaphroditus home at this particular time.

Whether πάλιν (*palin*) should be understood with the preceding ἰδόντες (*idontes*) as meaning "having seen him again" or with the following verb χαρῆτε (*charēte*), with the meaning "again you may rejoice," cannot be settled on grammatical grounds. Paul elsewhere uses *palin* both after and before the verb, though he shows a decided preference for placing it before the verb. If that should be the case here, the sense is that the Philippians would once again rejoice over their brother after seeing him returned and in good health.

29 Although the pl. τοὺς τοιούτους (*tous toioutous*, "men like [him]") is used, we need not conclude that the reference is to companions of Epaphroditus, for Paul returns immediately to the sing. in the next verse. The pl. is a generalization, in which the treatment requested by Paul is the sort that is appropriate for all similar cases.

30 The reading τὸ ἔργον Χριστοῦ (*to ergon Christou*, "the work of Christ") is one of several variations among the MSS at this point. This reading has been adopted by Nestle and UBS, and is reflected in KJV, ASV, and NIV. It has the early support of P[46] B G. D and K are similar, differing only by including the article τοῦ (*tou*). The uncials ℵ A P read κυρίου (*kuriou*, "of the Lord") instead of Χριστοῦ, (*Christou*, "of Christ"), and minuscule 1985 has τοῦ θεοῦ (*tou theou*, "of God"). The most interesting variant appears only in C, in which *to ergon* ("the work") stands alone. This rather abrupt usage is paralleled by the terminology in Acts 15:38 and explains how the other variants could have arisen, but its meager documentary support makes it questionable. It is the reading preferred by Lightfoot and Kennedy.

The verb παραβολεύομαι (*paraboleuomai*, "to risk, to expose to danger") appears in a second-century A.D. inscription at Olbia on the Black Sea, honoring a certain Carzoazus, son of Attalus. Deissmann has tr. as follows: ". . . but also to the ends of the world it was witnessed of him that in the interests of friendship he had exposed himself to dangers as an advocate in (legal) strife (by taking his clients' causes even) up to emperors" (Deiss LAE, p. 88).

IV. Warning Against Judaizers and Antinomians (3:1–21)

1. *The Judaizing Danger*

3:1–16

¹Finally, my brothers, rejoice in the Lord! It is no trouble for me to write the same things to you again, and it is a safeguard for you.
²Watch out for those dogs, those men who do evil, those mutilators of the flesh. ³For it is we who are the circumcision, we who worship by the Spirit of God, who glory in Christ Jesus, and who put no confidence in the flesh—⁴though I myself have reasons for such confidence.
If anyone else thinks he has reasons to put confidence in the flesh, I have more: ⁵circumcised on the eighth day, of the people of Israel, of the tribe of Benjamin, a Hebrew of Hebrews; in regard to the law, a Pharisee; ⁶as for zeal, persecuting the church; as for legalistic righteousness, faultless.
⁷But whatever was to my profit I now consider loss for the sake of Christ. ⁸What is more, I consider everything a loss compared to the surpassing greatness of knowing Christ Jesus my Lord, for whose sake I have lost all things. I consider them rubbish, that I may gain Christ ⁹and be found in him, not having a righteousness of my own that comes from the law, but that which is through faith in Christ—the righteousness that comes from God and is by faith. ¹⁰I want to know Christ and the power of his resurrection and the fellowship of sharing in his sufferings, becoming like him in his death, ¹¹and so, somehow, to attain to the resurrection from the dead.
¹²Not that I have already obtained all this, or have already been made perfect, but I press on to take hold of that for which Christ Jesus took hold of me. ¹³Brothers, I do not consider myself yet to have taken hold of it. But one thing I do: Forgetting what is behind and straining toward what is ahead, ¹⁴I press on toward the goal to win the prize for which God has called me heavenward in Christ Jesus.
¹⁵All of us who are mature should take such a view of things. And if on some point you think differently, that too God will make clear to you. ¹⁶Only let us live up to what we have already attained.

1 By the use of "finally" (*to loipon*), Paul seems to be drawing his Epistle to a close. Inasmuch as over forty percent of the letter is yet to come, some assume that a combination of several letters makes up the Epistle, and suggest that 3:1 is the conclusion of one of them (see Introduction, 2). However, the introductory *to loipon* cannot be confined to the one sense of "finally."

Because of the wide variation in the use of this expression by Paul and other writers, in the New Testament and outside, it may be best to understand the meaning here in a nontechnical and very natural way. A speaker may use the word "finally" when he passes the midpoint of an address, and then continue on for a rather long time. This poses no real problem for the English listener, and even less for a Greek reader for whom the expression could also mean simply "furthermore" or "in addition."

On the assumption that the Epistle is a unity, Paul's exhortation to "rejoice in the Lord" should be understood as belonging with what follows. The readers are to maintain the joyful spirit that has characterized this letter, though Paul now goes on to speak of some unpleasant matters. He repeats some of his former instructions ("to write the same things to you again"), but this is "no trouble" to him, for it has in view the worthy goal of safeguarding them from entrapment in wrong doctrine.

How specifically should "the same things" be understood? Surely it does not refer to the command to rejoice, for this would not have been thought to be a troublesome task or a safeguard against something dangerous. Because there has been no earlier warning against Judaizers in this letter, some have referred "the same things" to prior correspondence with the Philippians. This is certainly possible, though little evidence exists to support it. If, however, Paul meant the words to refer to previous warnings against opponents generally, then 1:27–30 would be an earlier instance in this letter.

2 The verses that follow warrant the identification of these opponents with the Judaizers —those who dogged the trail of the apostles and endeavored to compel Gentile converts to submit to circumcision and other Jewish practices in order to be saved. Three epithets designate them. "Dogs" denotes the wild, vicious, homeless animals that roamed the streets and attacked passersby. Used figuratively, it was always a term of reproach (cf. Deut 23:18; 1 Sam 17:43; 24:14; Prov 26:11; Isa 56:10, 11). Jesus used it in reference to opponents of God's truth (Matt 7:6), and Jews often used it similarly of Gentiles. Paul turns the figure back upon the Judaizing teachers and castigates them with the very term they probably used of others. "Men who do evil" is literally "the evil workers" (*tous kakous ergatas*). If the word *workers* is stressed, the epithet may emphasize their energetic labors and perhaps their concentration on performing deeds of law rather than trusting God's grace.

In the last term, "mutilators of the flesh" (NIV), literally "the mutilation" (*tēn katatomēn*), Paul deliberately parodies the Judaizers' insistence on circumcision by sarcastically calling it mutilation. (An even bolder term ["emasculate themselves," NIV] appears in Gal 5:12). For those who had lost the significance of circumcision and insisted on it as a rite for Christians, it was nothing more than a mutilation of the flesh.

3 Paul follows the above warning with an explanation. Christians are the real "circumcision," not the Judaizers who insisted on the physical rite. He refers to those who have received the circumcision of the heart, whether they be Jew or Gentile (Rom 2:25–29; Col 2:11). This concept was no innovation, for the OT spoke of it frequently (Lev 26:41; Deut 10:16; 30:6; Jer 4:4; Ezek 44:7). The Judaizers misunderstood OT doctrine as well as Christian teaching. Elsewhere Paul equates this circumcision performed without hands with the believer's removal from spiritual death to spiritual life (Col 2:11, 13). Thus it is virtually synonymous with regeneration.

Just as Paul characterizes the Judaizing teachers by three terms in the previous verse, so in v.3 he explains the true circumcision by three descriptive clauses. First, such persons worship by the Spirit of God, not by human traditions or some external rite. Second, they glory in Christ Jesus. Satisfaction comes from recognizing that their hope is found in Christ alone, not through meticulous conformity to the external demands of the Mosaic law. They have understood that Christ's sacrifice has fulfilled the law for them. These words of Paul echo Jeremiah 9:23, 24, and are used by him also in 1 Corinthians 1:31 and 2 Corinthians 10:17. Third, they put no confidence in the flesh. This states the negative aspect of the previous positive phrase. "Flesh" (*sarx*) refers to what man is outside of Christ. Paul often uses the term in controversy with Judaizers, especially in Romans and Galatians (e.g., Rom 3:20; 7:18, 25; Gal 2:16; 3:3; 5:19, 24). He teaches that sinful humanity has no grounds for confidence before God, because man unaided is powerless to achieve righteousness before God. The true believer, however, puts all of his trust in Christ and so removes any grounds for human pride or boasting.

4 Paul's personal testimony shows that he is not reacting against the Judaizers because he is jealous of their supposed strengths. In stating that true believers put no confidence in the flesh, he has in mind the contrary teaching of those opponents who stressed the importance of conformity to Jewish practices. For the sake of argument, therefore, he temporarily adopts one of their attitudes ("confidence in the flesh") and shows that his rejection of certain Jewish "advantages" was not because he did not possess them. He used the same approach in writing to the Corinthians, when for the moment he "made a fool" of himself in order to make his point (2 Cor 11:26–12:12). If any one of these opponents should claim an advantage because of his Jewish heritage and practices, Paul wanted it known that in such matters he could stand on equal footing with any Judaizer. He disavowed such as reasons for confidence before God, not because he did not possess them, but because he had found them inadequate to provide the righteousness God requires (cf. vv.7–9).

5 Now he enumerates some of those reasons for confidence in the flesh. First on the list is physical circumcision, perhaps because the Judaizers so greatly stressed it. Proselytes received this rite at the time they adopted Judaism. (Were some of the Judaizing teachers of this sort?) Others submitted to it in adulthood for various reasons (Acts 16:3). But Paul had been circumcised as a Jewish boy in accord with the instruction given to Abraham (Gen 17:12) and in accord with what the law later prescribed (Lev 12:3). Furthermore, he was born of Israelite stock. He was no proselyte; the blood of Jacob flowed in him. He belonged to the tribe of Benjamin, a fact he proudly acknowledged on more than one occasion (Acts 13:21; Rom 11:1). This tribe alone had been faithful to the Davidic throne at the time of the division of the kingdom. It had given the nation its first king, after whom Paul had been named by his parents. By calling himself a "Hebrew of Hebrews," he may have meant he had no mixed parentage but was of pure Jewish ancestry from both parents. The phrase may also refer to his linguistic and cultural upbringing, which involved the Hebrew and Aramaic languages (in distinction from that of the Hellenist Jews), even though he had been born in the Diaspora (Acts 6:1; 22:2, 3).

It is often averred that Paul mentions his connection with Benjamin because that tribe was especially honored among the tribes of Israel. In addition to the distinctions of Benjamin mentioned in the exposition, this patriarch was the only one born in the Promised Land, he was the offspring of Jacob's favorite wife, and the feast of Purim commemorated the national deliverance by Mordecai, a Benjamite. Furthermore, some suggest that this tribe held the post of honor in the armies of Israel ("following you, Benjamin," Judg 5:14). We must recognize, however, that the tribe of Benjamin also had its share of disappointing episodes, King Saul left much to be desired as a spiritual leader. The shameful episode of the Levite and his concubine (Judg 19–20), the kidnapping of women at Shiloh (Judg 21), and the cursing of David by Shimei (2 Sam 16:5–14), are blots upon the name of Benjamin and should caution us against elevating this tribe unduly. Paul's point may simply have been that he was an Israelite by birth—a Benjamite as a matter of fact—and thus was certainly a genuine Jew.

In addition, it had been his own choice to belong to the most orthodox of the Jewish parties, the Pharisees. This party contained the most zealous supporters and interpreters of OT law, and Paul had studied under Gamaliel, its most celebrated teacher (Acts 22:3; cf. 5:34).

6 When measured for its zeal, Paul's pre-Christian life had been noted for promoting Judaism and condemning Christians. He had become the archpersecutor of the church, and his reputation had gone far beyond Jerusalem (Acts 9:13, 21). His had been no half-hearted Judaism. When judged by men in accord with the righteousness the law demands, he had been blameless. As an earnest Pharisee, he had paid meticulous attention to the requirements of the Mosaic law, and no one could have charged him with failure to keep it. Of course, a distinction must be drawn between external conformity to the law in areas where men can judge and inflict legal penalties, and the perfect spiritual conformity to it that God alone can truly assess, and by which "no one will be justified" (Gal 2:16; 3:11).

7 Through his conversion on the Damascus road, Paul had learned to count such "advantages" as liabilities because of Christ. "Whatever" indicates that the previous listing was not exhaustive but illustrative. He once had regarded such things as "profit" (or "gains" —the Greek word *kerdē* is plural) toward his goal of achieving righteousness by the law, but now he has come to the settled conviction that they were actually a detriment. They had not provided him with true righteousness at all. By trusting falsely in human performance, he had not only failed to make any progress toward the righteousness God requires but had also let his Jewish "advantages" drive him to persecute the church, which proclaimed the message of the righteousness of God received by faith, the only kind of righteousness God accepts.

8 "What is more" introduces a clause stressing that Paul's experience on the Damascus road had produced a strong and lasting impression. The merits of Christ counted for everything. By using *panta* ("all things") rather than *tauta* ("these things," v.7), Paul's thought broadens from his Jewish advantages just mentioned to include everything that might conceivably be a rival to his total trust in Christ. The "surpassing greatness" can be understood of Christ in an absolute sense, though it likely includes at least a sidelong glance at the list of supposed advantages he had once trusted in. Christ is far superior to them in every respect—so much so that Paul had cast them away as nothing but rubbish.

For Paul, the knowledge of Christ Jesus as his Lord meant the intimate communion with Christ that began at his conversion and had been his experience all the years since then. It was not limited to the past (as v.10 shows), but was a growing relationship in which there was blessed enjoyment in the present and the challenge and excitement of increasing comprehension of Christ in personal fellowship. In the interests of this sublime goal, Paul had willingly suffered the loss of all those things (*ta panta*) about which he had spoken, and continues to regard them as "rubbish" in order that he might "gain Christ." Although at regeneration a person receives Christ, this is only the beginning of his discovery of what riches this entails. In Christ all the treasures of wisdom and knowledge are hidden (Col 2:3), but to search them out and appropriate them personally requires a lifetime.

9 Paul's desire to "be found in him" probably has an eschatological aspect. Paul wants the divine scrutiny he will undergo at Christ's return to reveal unquestionably that he had been in vital spiritual union with Jesus Christ. For this to be so, it could not be on the basis of a righteousness he could call "my own" (*emēn*), that is, the kind of righteousness one might achieve through general conformity to the Mosaic law. Such might win the admiration of men, but it could never achieve the absolute perfection God requires (Gal 3:10, 11; James 2:10). In strong contrast (*alla*, "but"), to be found in Christ requires the righteousness that has its source not in man but in God who has provided Jesus Christ, the "Righteous One" (Acts 3:14; 1 John 2:1).

This righteousness of God provided in Christ is received by man "through faith" (*dia pisteōs*) and thus man acquires it "by faith" or "on the basis of faith" (*epi tē pistei*). It is not man's achievement as accomplished by doing the law's requirements but is God's provision freely offered men in Christ (Rom 3:20–22). "Faith" is the very opposite of human works; it is the reception of God's work by those who acknowledge the futility of their own efforts to attain righteousness.

10 The phrase "to know him" (NIV, "to know Christ") resumes the thought of v.8 and explains in more detail what is involved in "knowing Christ Jesus." Paul wants to know experientially the power of Christ's resurrection. He is not thinking only of the divine power that raised Christ from the dead, but of the power of the resurrected Christ now operating in the believer's life. This power enables believers to "live a new life" (Rom 6:4) because they have been "raised with Christ" (Col 3:1; Eph 2:5, 6).

Closely associated in the apostle's thought is "the fellowship of sharing in his sufferings." No reference to Christ's expiatory sufferings is meant, for those were Christ's alone. But each believer, by identifying himself with Christ, incurs a measure of Christ's afflictions (Col 1:24). These may be of varying kinds and degrees, both inward and external, as believers find themselves in a world that is hostile because of their allegiance to Christ. Paul has already expressed this thought to the Philippians in 1:29, where he regards suffering in some sense as an inevitable consequence of believing in Christ (cf. Matt 16:24).

"Becoming like him in his death" further elaborates the previous phrase. For a believer to share Christ's sufferings involves such a complete identification with him that it can only be explained as a death to the former life (cf. Rom 6:4–11). The theological import of union with Christ must be experientially demonstrated. This is the process of sanctification and is intended to bring the believer's present state into ever-increasing conformity to Christ (Rom 8:29; 2 Cor 3:18; Phil 3:21). Therefore, those who died with him and rose with him (Col 2:20; 3:1–3) must exhibit this truth by a separation from their old life and a continual walking in the power supplied by Christ's resurrection life.

11 The form of this statement poses a problem for the interpreter, suggesting as it does in many versions that, though Paul is hopeful of experiencing the resurrection, he has some doubt about it. This is difficult to harmonize with his strong affirmations of faith elsewhere (e.g., 1 Cor 15:1–34). Some have explained the expression as an indication of Paul's humility (Muller, pp. 117, 118; Hendriksen, p. 170). Others regard the apparent doubt as relating not to the fact but the manner in which Paul would be involved (Lenski, p. 841). The verse reflects his uncertainty as to whether he would be among the dead to be raised or among the living to be transformed without dying (Walvoord, *Philippians*, p. 88.) But it is also possible to regard the clause as expressing expectation rather than doubt. See the NIV translation "and so, somehow, to attain to the resurrection from the dead."

"The resurrection from the dead" (*tēn exanastasin tēn ek nekrōn*) is not the usual NT expression. Usage of the preposition *ek* ("out of") twice in the expression strongly suggests a partial resurrection "out from" other dead ones. Hence Paul must be thinking not in terms of a general resurrection of righteous and wicked, but of believers only (cf. Rev 20:4–15). Some interpreters have seen this expression as a reference to the "rapture" of living believers (S.L. Johnson, "The Out-Resurrection from the Dead," BS, vol. 110, no. 439 [July, 1953]; Walvoord, *Philippians*, p. 88). However, it is not clear that *exanastasis* means anything other than "resurrection." The only uncertainty in Paul's mind is whether he will participate in the resurrection because he will have died by then, or whether he will receive his transformed body without dying because the Lord might come before he dies (1 Thess 4:14–17).

12 Having stated that his conversion brought about a new assessment of his goals and gave him the overwhelming desire to know Christ ever more fully, Paul then explains how his present life is a pursuit in this new direction. But he does not want to be misunderstood. He is not claiming that his conversion has already brought him to his final goal. He has not already received all he longs for nor has he been brought to that perfect completeness to which he has aspired. Perhaps there were perfectionists in Philippi who had resisted the Judaizers with their emphasis on works and ceremonies by going to the extreme of claiming to have acquired already the consummation of spiritual blessings. Paul understands clearly that he has a continuing responsibility to pursue the purposes Christ had chosen him for. Spiritual progress is ever the imperative Christians must follow.

13 In this statement Paul addresses the Philippians by the endearing title "brothers," as he repeats the thought of v.12. The emphatic *egō emauton* ("I ... myself") might conceivably introduce his response to what some at Philippi were saying about him. Absence of any other indication that Paul was being accused of espousing perfectionism makes it more likely that his emphasis was in contrast with what some Philippians were claiming about themselves. Paul did not regard himself as having obtained the final knowledge of Christ and the fullest conformity to him. Some may have taught that performance of Jewish rites could bring such perfection, but Paul knew it was not so. One thing, therefore, was the consuming passion of his life.

Using the metaphor of a footrace, Paul describes his Christian life as involving the continual forgetting of "what is behind," and the relentless centering of his energies and interests on the course that is ahead of him. "Forgetting" did not mean obliterating the memory of the past (Paul has just recalled some of these things in vv.5–7), but a conscious refusal to let them absorb his attention and impede his progress. He never allowed his

Jewish heritage (vv.5–7) nor his previous Christian attainments (vv.9–12) to obstruct his running of the race. No present attainment could lull him into thinking he already possessed all Christ desired for him.

14 Continuing the metaphor, Paul likens his Christian life to pressing onward to the goal so as to win the prize. In applying the figure, the goal and the prize are virtually identical, though viewed perhaps from different aspects. Paul's goal was the complete knowledge of Christ, both in the power of his resurrection and the fellowship of his sufferings (v.10). When the goal was reached, this prize would be fully his. As Hendriksen expresses it, "goal" rivets attention on the race that is being run, whereas "prize" centers the thought on the glory that follows (p. 175). E.M. Blaiklock concludes that Paul has the chariot races of Rome in mind (*Cities of the New Testament* [London: Pickering & Inglis, 1965], pp. 43, 44). The "upward calling" could then refer to the summons to the winner to approach the elevated stand of the judge and receive his prize. It is possible that the prize is to be understood as the "upward call of God" (NASB), interpreted as the "rapture" of the church. However, the word *klēsis* ("calling") is always used elsewhere by Paul, not in reference to Christ's return but to denote the effective call of God that brings men to salvation (1 Cor 1:26; 7:20; Eph 1:18; 4:1, 4; 2 Thess 1:11; 2 Tim 1:9). The expression *anō klēseōs* ("upward call"; NIV, "called me heavenward") is similar to *klēseōs epouraniou* ("heavenly calling") in Hebrews 3:1, which certainly refers to the divine call to salvation. Hence, it is preferable to regard Paul as speaking of the goal and prize for which believers have been called to salvation in Christ.

15 In concluding this section, Paul exhorts those who are mature to think in harmony with what he has just said, and promises that those who think differently about minor points will be enlightened by God if their attitude is right. "Mature" (NIV; KJV, "perfect") is the correct rendering of *teleioi*, as Paul's other five uses of the term referring to persons attest (1 Cor 2:6; 14:20; Eph 4:13; Col 1:28; 4:12). He does not mean "sinless," but is referring to a certain level of spiritual growth and stability in contrast to infants. By using the word *teleioi* Paul is not making a sarcastic reference to perfectionists. Instead, he is calling those who have progressed in the faith to recognize the truth he has just voiced (cf. 3:13, 14 and also the entire explanation in 3:2–14). If the Philippian believers are lax in their pursuit of spiritual goals or erroneously suppose they have already arrived, they need to understand Paul's declaration. And if they generally agree but still differ on some isolated point, Paul is confident that God will lead them to the truth if their minds are open to his leading.

16 No one, however, must wait for God to reveal the truth on all points before he begins to give himself to spiritual growth. Each believer should exercise fully the degree of maturity he already possesses. "Live up to" is the verb *stoichein* ("to keep in line with") and calls for Christians to maintain a consistent life in harmony with the understanding of God's truth they already have. Paul recognizes that Christians, though proceeding along the same path, may be at different stages of progress and should be faithful to as much of God's truth as they understand.

Notes

1 The adverbial use of τὸ λοιπόν (*to loipon*) with the sense of "in addition" or "furthermore" provides a transition to something new. Near the end of a work, it may have the sense of "finally," but it does not always appear at the close of a letter. Paul uses it elsewhere near the middle, such as at 1 Thess 4:1 (without the article) and 1 Thess 3:1 (with the article). In the former instance, nearly one-half of the letter still remained, and in the latter, fully one-third was yet to be written.

The tr. of the imperative χαίρετε (*chairete*) as "goodbye" by Goodspeed in 3:1 and 4:4 (twice) reflects his view that the present Philippians was not originally a unity (*The New Testament, An American Translation*, [Chicago: Univ. of Chicago Press, 1923]). There are, however, no other clear uses of the verb carrying this meaning in the NT, though it does have this sense in sepulchral inscriptions (E.J. Goodspeed, *Problems of New Testament Translation* [Chicago: Univ. of Chicago Press, 1945], pp. 174, 175). It is frequently used in greetings at the beginning of letters.

2 The use of the noun κύων (*kuōn*, "dog") in the disparaging sense in which it appears throughout the NT must be distinguished from κυνάριον (*kynarion*), the dimunitive form, which denoted the " 'house dog' as distinct from the 'yard dog' or the 'dog of the streets' " (Michel, *Kunarion*, TDNT, 3:1104). Jesus referred to the *kynarion*, or house dog, in his discourse with the Gentile woman (Matt 15:26, 27; Mark 7:27, 28).

Paul's use of κατατομή (*katatomē*, "concision"; NIV, "mutilators of the flesh") is a play on περιτομή (*peritomē*, "circumcision") in v.3. The noun does not occur elsewhere in Scripture but the corresponding verb appears in LXX to denote the pagan practice of cutting the flesh for religious purposes (Lev 21:5; 1 Kings 18:28; Isa 15:2).

3 The preferred reading θεοῦ (*theou*, "of God") is supported by ℵ A B C Dᶜ G K and yields the tr. "who worship by the Spirit of God" (NIV). This seems preferable to another grammatical possibility: "who worship the Spirit of God." Without at all denying the full deity of the Holy Spirit, it is still doubtful whether any instance can be found in Scripture authorizing believers to worship the Spirit directly in distinction from the Father and the Son. Lightfoot (in loc.) shows that the verb λατρεύω (*latreuō*, "to worship") had come to have a technical sense referring to the worship of God, and therefore one does not need to regard πνεύματι θεοῦ (*pneumati theou*, "the Spirit of God") as the object of the verb (i.e., recipient of the worship). The alternate reading θεῷ (*theō*) found in D P and a corrector of ℵ may have been due to failure to recognize that the verb did not necessarily require an object. This alternate reading gives the sense: "worship God by the Spirit/spirit." Following the preferred reading, it is best to regard *pneumati* as a dative (instrumental) of agency (as in Rom 8:14; Gal 5:18; see Dana, H.E. and Mantey, J.R., *A Manual Grammar of the Greek New Testament* [New York: Macmillan, 1946], p. 91). The oldest witness to this passage (P⁴⁶) omits *theou*.

4 The noun πεποίθησις (*pepoithēsis*, "confidence") may have either a subjective or an objective sense and may thus denote confidence or grounds for confidence (BAG, p. 649). Having denied in v.3 that believers have "confidence in the flesh," Paul would hardly have contradicted himself in the very next sentence. It is better, therefore, to regard the noun as being used objectively to refer to the reasons or basis for confidence in the flesh. Of course, Paul had learned through his conversion that regardless of one's advantages in the flesh, flesh cannot win the approval of God.

6 Ζῆλος (*zēlos*, "zeal") may be either masc. or neuter, with no apparent difference in meaning. The neuter accusative occurs here. The use of νόμῳ (*nomō*, "law") without the article is thought by some to refer to the Mosaic law in the abstract sense as a principle of action (Lightfoot, pp. 147, 148). Paul, however, usually means the Law of God as contained in the OT, whether or not the article is employed (W.D. Davies, "Law in the NT," IDB, vol. K–Q, p. 99), and it is at least questionable whether this feature is to be pressed with a term that is virtually a proper name.

144

7 The verb tenses here and in the succeeding verses are important. The imperfect ἦν (ēn, "was") depicts the continuing attitude of Paul regarding his Jewish "advantages" prior to his conversion. The perfect tense ἥγημαι (hēgēmai, "I consider") describes his present settled condition of mind toward those matters that began at the crisis experience when he saw Christ, and that continued unchanged ever since.

8 The combination of the five conjunctions and particles ἀλλὰ μενοῦν γε καὶ (alla menoun ge kai) provides a subtle shading of the thought that English is ill-equipped to translate. "What is more" (NIV) or "more than that" is an approximation. "Ἀλλά [alla] suggests a contrast to be introduced, μέν [men] adds emphasis, while οὖν [oun], gathering up what has already been said, corrects it by way of extending the assertion; γε [ge] can scarcely be translated, representing, rather, a tone of the voice in taking back the limitations implied in ἅτινα ... κέρδη (hatina ... kerdē)." (H.A.A. Kennedy, "Philippians," EGT, 3:452.)

The etymology of σκύβαλον (skybalon, "rubbish") is uncertain, but in usage it was employed of excrement, of scraps or leavings after a meal, or of general refuse. In the NT it appears only here. The less offensive sense of refuse or rubbish fits the context well; however, if Paul is understood to be rising to a crescendo in his explanation, replacement of ζημία (zēmia, "loss") with a bolder term denoting "dung" would not be unlike him (cf. v.2; Gal 5:12).

The purpose clause with ἵνα (hina, "so that") was related to the verb ἡγοῦμαι (hēgoumai, "consider") in the exposition. Another view construes the clause with the aorist verb ἐζημιώθην (ezēmiōthēn, "I have lost"), and thus explains the subjunctive verbs that follow hina as referring to events connected with Paul's conversion (e.g., Lenski, pp. 837, 838). This alternative fits the thought of v.9, which speaks of forensic, not personal, righteousness and provides a legitimate and probably easier explanation of the clause "that I may gain Christ" and what follows. This view, however, makes the clause "and I consider [them] rubbish" parenthetical. In spite of these attractions, the other view is preferable, since it requires no manipulation of the text. There is no clear warrant for seeing any parenthesis in this passage.

9 It is possible that εὑρεθῶ (heurethō) may be used in the general sense of "be shown as" or simply as "be." Note such uses as "Philip was found [εὑρέθη, heurethē] at Azotus" (Acts 8:40) and "if ... we ourselves also are found [εὑρέθημεν, heurethēmen] sinners" (Gal 2:17). Thus, Phil 3:9 would mean "and be in him," without any particular reference to the Second Coming. But the mention of resurrection (v.11) makes the eschatological sense here a natural one.

The possessive adjective ἐμὴν (emēn, "of my own") is more emphatic than μου (mou, "my") would have been and shows that the contrast is intended to be strong between "my own righteousness" and "the righteousness of God."

10 One article is used with δύναμιν (dynamin, "power") and κοινωνίαν (koinōnian, "fellowship"), denoting them as aspects of a single entity—in this case, facets of Paul's concept of what is involved in knowing Christ.

The participle συμμορφιζόμενος (symmorphizomenos, "being conformed"; NIV, "becoming like") has no other NT use, but the cognate σύμμορφος (symmorphos) is used twice, both by Paul and both times in reference to the believer's likeness to Christ (Rom 8:29; Phil 3:21). This word-family differs from its synonyms by denoting the essential form, rather than mere outward appearance, which may be temporary. Paul is thus stating his desire to duplicate in his experience the essence of the Christ-life in an ever-increasing way.

11 Εἴ πως (ei pōs, "if somehow"; NIV, "and so, somehow") occurs four times in the NT (Acts 27:12; Rom 1:10; 11:14; Phil 3:11). In each of these there is some uncertainty about the matter stated, whether regarding its ultimate achievement or the manner in which it will be accomplished. The sense of expectation, however, is stressed by BDF, p. 375. Burton considers the statement an omitted apodosis that is virtually contained in the protasis. The protasis then expresses the object of hope and has nearly the force of a purpose clause (Syntax of the Moods and Tenses [Chicago: Univ. of Chicago Press, 1897], p. 276).

The NT hapax legomenon ἐξανάστασιν (exanastasin, "resurrection") not only has the article, but is followed by a prepositional phrase that is tied to it attributively by a second article. Whether this term is to be differentiated from ἀνάστασις (anastasis) of v.10 or was merely a

145

stylistic variation is debatable. S.L. Johnson suggests that the sense of "rising up" as found in Polybius would fit admirably the rapture of the church, and its greater vividness than *anastasis* also argues for interpreting it as the rapture ("The Out-Resurrection from the Dead," BS, 110:145). Hendriksen argues for the sense of being "raised completely above sin and selfishness" (pp. 169, 170), although there is little NT warrant for such a use of *anastasis* or its cognate (the only time in the NT that *anastasis* does not refer to physical resurrection is in Luke 2:34, a highly figurative passage). The majority view regards the word as denoting physical resurrection, however, on the basis of its cognate, and from the sense of "from the dead," which follows.

12 The aorist indicative ἔλαβον (*elabon*, "I received"; NIV, "I have ... obtained") points to the experience on the Damascus road nearly thirty years before. The perfect tense of τετελείωμαι (*teteleiōmai*, "have ... been made perfect") depicts the settled condition resulting from that previous occurrence. Paul knew that the culmination of his spiritual progress had not occurred at the beginning (nor at any other time in the past), nor had he arrived at such a state since. The present tense of διώκω (*diōkō*, "I press on") denotes the constant pursuit of the goal.

Whether ἐφ᾽ ᾧ (*eph' hō*) should be treated as "because" or "inasmuch as," naming the reason why Paul feels obligated to pursue the goal (same use as in Rom 5:12; 2 Cor 5:4), or as "with a view to which" (NIV, "for which") referring to the unstated object of καταλάβω (*katalabō*, "to take hold"), is uncertain (C.F.D. Moule, *An Idiom Book of New Testament Greek* [Cambridge: Cambridge Univ. Press, 1953], p. 132). Both fit the context easily. The latter use is the best choice in Phil 4:10, and is adopted in KJV, ASV, Ph, NEB, and NIV. The alternative appears in RSV.

13 The MSS vary between the negatives οὐ (*ou*, UBS) and οὔπω (*oupō*, Nestle). The meaning of the passage is not altered, however, because either "not" or "not yet" must be understood in the light of Paul's claim that he does not presently possess, but that he ultimately will.

"One thing I do" reproduces the phrase ἐν δέ (*hen de*), which uses no verb, and the literal sense "but one thing" is even more forceful and dramatic.

14 Of the eleven NT occurrences of κλῆσις (*klēsis*, "calling"), the only non-Pauline uses are Heb 3:1 (dependent upon one's view of authorship) and 2 Peter 1:10. All eleven have reference to the call of God to salvation. The phrase ἐν Χριστῷ Ἰησοῦ (*en Christō Iēsou*, "in Christ Jesus") should be construed with "calling," not with the more remote "I press on."

15 Paul must be using τέλειοι (*teleioi*, "mature") in a different sense from his use of the verb τετελείωμαι (*teteleiōmai*, "made perfect") in v.12. There the reference was to the culminating and complete perfection toward which each believer must strive. The adjective, however, denotes a relative perfection (maturity) that can be a present possession. Other NT writers using the adjective in this way are Matthew (5:48), the writer of Hebrews (5:14), and James (1:4; 3:2).

16 The infinitive στοιχεῖν (*stoichein*) is used here as an imperative (Dana and Mantey, *Manual Grammar*, pp. 216, 217). Although infrequent, this use of an infinitive does occur elsewhere in the NT (Rom 12:15; Tit 2:2). The verb means "to keep step."

A textual variant is reflected in the KJV, which adds the words "let us mind the same thing" (κανόνι, τὸ αὐτὸ φρονεῖν, *kanoni, to auto phronein*). Numerous other minor variations that occur among the MSS at this point may have been influenced by Gal 6:16 and Phil 2:2.

---

2. The Antinomian Danger

3:17-21

> 17Join with others in following my example, brothers, and take note of those who live according to the pattern we gave you. 18For, as I have often told you before and now say again even with tears, many live as enemies of the cross of Christ. 19Their destiny is destruction, their god is their stomach, and their glory is in their shame. Their mind is on earthly things. 20But our citizenship is in heaven. And we eagerly await a Savior from there, the Lord Jesus Christ, 21who, by the power that enables him to bring everything under his control, will transform our lowly bodies so that they will be like his glorious body.

17 In the early years of the church, believers needed practical guides for conduct. So Paul urged the Philippians to join together in imitating his conduct, just as he had done in his exhortation to the church at Corinth—"Follow my example, as I follow the example of Christ" (1 Cor 11:1). Such advice was not egotism, for Paul's emphasis was always strongly christological (e.g., Phil 2:5–8). Furthermore, Paul includes others in this model as he urges his readers to take note of those who were living in conformity with "the pattern we gave you" (v.17)—i.e., the high standard outlined in 3:7–16. Literally, Paul wrote, "you [pl.] have us as a pattern," and the "us" includes not only himself but Timothy and perhaps Epaphroditus also. Hence, he was not claiming a unique superiority.

18 Who were these "enemies of the cross of Christ"? Some regard them as the Judaizers of 3:2, whose emphasis on legalism undermined the effect of the Cross (Lenski, Muller, Barth). Others view them as antinomians, who went to the opposite extreme from the Judaizers and threw off all restraints (Lightfoot, Kennedy, Beare, Hendriksen). By their lawless lives, they too were enemies of the Cross and the new life that should issue from it. Verse 19 is more readily understood of the antinomians.

It is not likely that these men were simply pagans, of whom nothing much better was to be expected. In all probability they were professing Christians, but ones whose lives were so profligate that it was clear to Paul that they had never been regenerated. Presumably, they were not actually members of the Philippian church (the character of the entire Epistle would have been different if "many" such people were in that congregation), but because there were such in the Christian world as a whole, they posed a danger to every church (cf. Rom 16:17, 18; 2 Peter 2:10–22). Paul had already warned of them, perhaps in former visits or letters, and felt real anguish when the churches were threatened with falseness of doctrine or life.

19 The ultimate end for such persons is "destruction" (*apōleia*, the regular NT word for eternal loss, the opposite of *sōtēria*, "salvation"). (See note on 1:28.) "Their god is their stomach." To interpret this as referring to the Judaizers demands relating it to various "kosher" food regulations. It is easier to explain it of sensualists who indulged various physical appetites without restraint (Rom 16:18; 1 Cor 6:13; Jude 11). "Their glory is in their shame." By their indulgence, they actually exulted in what ought to have been shameful to them (Eph 5:12). Those who relate the statement to Judaizers explain the "shame" as a euphemism for one's private parts, specifically the circumcision demanded by the Judaizers. It would be most unusual, however, for Paul to speak of circumcision as a "shame." The final description characterizes the "enemies of the cross of Christ" as continually minding earthly things. Their whole attention is fixed on physical and material interests. They stand in stark contrast to spiritual men, as explained in the following verse.

20 The "our" is emphatic and stresses the distinction between true believers, whose essential relationships belong to the heavenly sphere, and the sensualists just discussed, who are exclusively concerned with earthly things. The Christian's "commonwealth" is in heaven, and for him earthly things must at best be secondary. The Philippians would find this a most apt metaphor, for in a political sense they knew what it was to be citizens of a far-off city (even though most of them had probably never been to Rome) and they were proud of that status (Acts 16:12, 21; see comment on Phil 1:27). On an immeasurably higher plane, believers belong to the "city . . . whose architect and builder is God"

(Heb 11:10), the "Jerusalem that is above" (Gal 4:26), and are themselves "foreigners and strangers on earth" (Heb 11:13; 1 Peter 2:11). As such, their eyes should be heavenward, anticipating the coming of their Savior, who is not a mere earthly emperor but the Lord Jesus Christ. An eager expectation of his return does much to protect the believer from earthly, sensual enticements.

21 Christ at his return will "transform" (*metaschēmatisei*, "change the outward form of ") believers' mortal bodies, so that they will conform to the character of his resurrection body. The present body is described literally as "the body of lowliness" (*to sōma tēs tapeinōseōs*), a description calling attention to its weakness and susceptibility to persecution, disease, sinful appetites, and death. At Christ's coming, however, the earthly, transient appearance will be changed, whether by resurrection of those dead or by rapture of the living, and believers will be transformed and will receive glorified bodies that will more adequately display their essential character (*summorphon*) as children of God and sharers of divine life in Christ. This will be accomplished by the same effective operation (*energeian*) that will ultimately bring all things in the universe under the authority of Christ.

The tr. "vile" (KJV) for *tapeinōseōs* conveys a wrong idea. Emphasis is not on sinfulness, but on lowliness or humble status.

In all NT uses of *energeia* ("power"), the working is from a supernatural source, whether God or Satan. Hence, effective power is in view. (See note on 2:13.)

Notes

17 Because συμμίμηται (*symmimētai*, "fellow imitators") takes an objective genitive, the sense is "join with others in imitating me," not "join with me in imitating Christ."

The verb σκοπέω (*skopeō*) means "look out for," or "notice," and whether the object is to be emulated (as here) or avoided (Rom 16:17) must be gleaned from the context. Paul and his associates had furnished themselves as a τύπον (*typon*, "example") for Christian conduct. The noun τύπος (*typos*, [nom.] "example") denoted originally the visible impression made by the stroke of some instrument, then a pattern or model. In the moral realm it can mean "example" (BAG).

18 Identification of these errorists as having some connection with the Christian movement is strengthened by the use of περιπατοῦσιν (*peripatousin*, "walking"), a term most commonly used by Paul to describe the conduct of Christians.

19 On ἀπώλεια (*apōleia*, "destruction"), see note on 1:28. The idea that αἰσχύνη (*aischynē*, "shame") refers to one's private parts is expressed by JB: " 'Shame' may be only the traditional euphemism for the circumcised member" (p. 343, note). But there is no evidence for this. The primary LXX usage as "disgrace" (TDNT, 1:189) accords better with relegating the passage to antinomians.

The nominative phrase οἱ φρονοῦντες (*hoi phronountes*, literally, "the ones thinking"; NIV, "their mind") is grammatically governed by πολλοί (*polloi*, "many") of v.18.

20 The noun πολίτευμα (*politeuma*, "citizenship") occurs only here in the NT. The cognate πολιτεία (*politeia*, Acts 22:28; Eph 2:12) can mean either "citizenship" (rights and duties of a citizen) or the "commonwealth" itself, but *politeuma* seems limited to the sense of "commonwealth" (BAG, pp. 692, 693; TDNT, 6:535).

The antecedent of ἐξ οὗ (*ex hou*, "from where"; NIV, "from there") is probably οὐρανοῖς (*ouranois*, "heaven"), with the sing. pronoun having a sense of agreement with the noun, which is commonly pl. (as here) in form but sing. in meaning. It is possible, of course, for the sing. *politeuma* to be the antecedent.

Even though σωτήρ (*sōtēr*, "savior") was a title for various gods in pagan cults and was also applied to various human leaders or to the king, as shown on inscriptions, it was used of God in LXX (Ps 24:5; 26:9); hence, Paul did not need to borrow the usage from any pagan source (BAG, p. 808).

21 On the difference between the related words σχῆμα (*schēma*) and μορφή (*morphē*), see comments and notes on 2:6, 8. The difference is relevant here also. Christ will "transform" the outward, earthly appearance. Then the essential person, regenerated with life from God, will exhibit in his glorified body the form that truly reflects his status in Christ. His body will "conform" to Christ's body.

It is questioned whether αυτῷ (*autō*), which is generally regarded as the preferred reading, should be given the rough breathing and treated as reflexive (αὑτῷ, *hautō*) or should be treated as the personal pronoun (αὐτῷ, *autō*). Lightfoot insists that the aspirated form has no place in the NT (p. 157). However, even if the form is left unaspirated, the personal pronoun is often used with a reflexive sense (RHG, pp. 680, 681; BDF, p. 283; E.V. Goetchius, *The Language of the New Testament* [New York: Scribner's, 1965], p. 375).

V. Second Series of Exhortations (4:1–9)

1. *Exhortation to Stand Firm in Unity*

4:1–3

> [1]Therefore, my brothers, you whom I love and long for, my joy and crown, that is how you should stand firm in the Lord, dear friends!
> [2]I plead with Euodia and I plead with Syntyche to agree with each other in the Lord. [3]Yes, and I ask you, loyal yokefellow, help these women who have contended at my side in the cause of the gospel, along with Clement and the rest of my fellow workers, whose names are in the book of life.

1 This verse is another of Paul's subtle transitions, so skillfully blended as to make it difficult to decide whether it should be placed with what precedes or what follows. A good transition, however, fits both segments. Inasmuch as the following statements discuss the need for unity among certain individuals, it is appropriate to treat v.1 (as does NIV) as a general exhortation to the whole church to stand firm in the manner Paul has been outlining in the previous verses (especially 17–21). It is of interest that the same verb *stēkō* ("stand firm") was used also at the beginning of the first series of exhortations in this Epistle (1:27).

The reference to the Philippians as "brothers, you whom I love and long for," shows the strong feeling of intimacy the apostle felt toward these readers. Their description as Paul's "joy and crown" echoes his earlier words to another Macedonian church (1 Thess 2:19). The Philippians were his present joy as he received favorable reports of their spiritual growth, and their presence with Christ at his return would be his future crown when Christ comes to reward his servants. The "crown" (*stephanos*) mentioned here is the wreath of victory or celebration.

2 The apostle turns from his general exhortation to an application of it. Two women, Euodia and Syntyche, are instructed to bring their attitudes into harmony. Paul does not indicate which one was in the wrong but knows that if the attitude of each would be formed "in the Lord," the disharmony would vanish. Repetition of the verb may indicate

the need for separate admonitions because the rift between them had become so great. Paul's method of handling the problem suggests that it was not a doctrinal issue, but a clash of personalities.

3 At this point Paul seeks to enlist the aid of a third party, Syzygus ("yokefellow," NIV), whom he challenges to live up to his name and be a "loyal yokefellow" (*gnēsie syzyge*) by bringing these women together (see note). (Another Pauline play on a personal name occurs in Philem 10, 11.) Inasmuch as Euodia and Syntyche had once labored with Paul, they should be able to do so again. Perhaps they had been among the original group of converts at Philippi, for women had been Paul's first hearers there (Acts 16:13–15). Their Christian labors had been in conjunction with Clement and others of Paul's co-workers. This Clement is not otherwise known to us with certainty. Even though some of these names are not recorded in this letter, Paul knows that their service is not forgotten, for their names are recorded in the Book of Life. The reference is to the register in heaven of those who are saved (Rev 3:5; 17:8; 20:12, 15; 21:27; 22:19; cf. Luke 10:20; Heb 12:23). It does not imply that they and Clement were now dead, though they might have been. Paul's memory of these happy associations prompted his concern that the present disunity might be ended so that faithful Christian activity could proceed and prosper.

Notes

1 The most common NT meaning of στέφανος (*stephanos*) is "wreath." In four instances, it refers to the crown of thorns, and though it was doubtless meant to mock Jesus' regal claims, *stephanos* rather than διάδημα (*diadēma*) was probably used here because Paul referred to a wreath rather than a royal circlet of gold. The majority of uses denotes the wreath bestowed on believers as a reward by Christ. One instance utilizes the term to denote Christ's crown (Rev 14:14), indicating that even here the connotation may be victory rather than rulership.

2 Εὐοδία (*Euodia*) and Συντύχη (*Syntyche*) are women, as the fem. pronouns αὐταῖς (*autais*) and αἵτινες (*haitines*) in v.3 show. These names are common in the inscriptions and there is no warrant for allegorizing them to represent parties in the church.

3 The verb ἐρωτῶ (*erōtō*) usually means "to ask a question" but can mean "to request." This latter sense is employed here as Paul requests assistance in healing the breach between the two women.

Some have objected that "Syzygus," "yokefellow" in NIV, has not yet been found elsewhere as a proper name. Nevertheless, it still provides a better sense for σύζυγε (*syzyge*) than the suggested alternatives. A proper name is to be expected among the proper names given before (Euodia, Syntyche) and after (Clement). To regard the term as a reference to Paul's wife (!) or some other woman runs afoul of the masculine adjective γνήσιε (*gnēsie*, "loyal"). Unless this person were the acknowledged head of the congregation at Philippi who would have been the one to receive the letter, it is difficult to see how the Philippians themselves could have identified this "yokefellow." Identifying this person as Epaphroditus is illogical, since he was with Paul at the moment. If we identify him as Luke, we must assume either that the Epistle emanated from an earlier time (from Ephesus, perhaps) when Luke presumably was there (inferred from the "we" passages in Acts 16:10 and 20:6) or that Luke was at Philippi some of the time Paul was in Rome. There is no evidence for the latter.

The phrase μετὰ καὶ Κλήμεντος (*meta kai Klēmentos*, "along with Clement") should be construed with συνήθλησάν (*synēthlēsan*, "contended with") as denoting that Clement labored with these women, rather than referring it to the more distant συλλαμβάνου (*syllambanou*, "help") as though Paul were trying to enlist Clement and others to join Syzygus in uniting the women. Clement was identified by Origen as the well-known Clement of Rome (A.E. Brooke, *The*

Commentary of Origen on St. John's Gospel [Cambridge: Cambridge Univ. Press, 1896], 1:173, 174, on 1:29), but no evidence is given for his conclusion.

---

2. *Exhortation to Maintain Various Christian Virtues*
4:4–9

> [4]Rejoice in the Lord always. I will say it again: Rejoice! [5]Let your gentleness be evident to all. The Lord is near. [6]Do not be anxious about anything, but in everything, by prayer and petition, with thanksgiving, present your requests to God. [7]And the peace of God, which transcends all understanding, will guard your hearts and your minds in Christ Jesus.
> [8]Finally, brothers, whatever is true, whatever is noble, whatever is right, whatever is pure, whatever is lovely, whatever is admirable—if anything is excellent or praiseworthy—think about such things. [9]Whatever you have learned or received or heard from me, or seen in me—put it into practice. And the God of peace will be with you.

4 From his previous exhortation to unity and from his attempt to correct a case of disunity, Paul proceeds to exhort the church to maintain certain positive Christian virtues. First, believers are to "rejoice in the Lord always" and "again" to "rejoice." The double emphasis on rejoicing may imply that a single injunction might prompt the question "How can we rejoice, in view of our difficulties?" So he repeats the command, because in all the vicissitudes of the Christian life, whether in attacks from errorists, personality clashes among believers, persecution from the world, or threat of imminent death—all of which Paul himself was experiencing at this very time—the Christian is to maintain a spirit of joy in the Lord. He is not immune to sorrow nor should he be insensitive to the troubles of others; yet he should count the will of God his highest joy and so be capable of knowing inner peace and joy in every circumstance.

5 Second, believers are to be gentle to all. The term *epieikēs* ("gentleness") is difficult to translate with its full connotation. Such words as *gentle, yielding, kind, forbearing,* and *lenient* are among the best English attempts, but no single word is adequate. Involved is the willingness to yield one's personal rights and to show consideration and gentleness to others. It is easy to display this quality toward some persons, but Paul commands that it be shown toward all. That would seem to include Christian friends, unsaved persecutors, false teachers—anyone at all. Of course, truth is not to be sacrificed, but a gentle spirit will do much to disarm the adversary.

As an encouragement, Paul now reminds his readers the Lord is near. His reference is to the Parousia (not just Christ's continuing presence with believers). This seems clear from the context of the letter, where 3:20, 21 focused attention on the glorious prospect in view for believers at Christ's return. A similar connection between a longsuffering spirit and the Lord's coming occurs in James 5:8. The statement is a reminder that at his arrival the Judge will settle all differences and will bring the consummation that will make most of our human differences seem trifling.

6 Third, believers should be prayerful instead of anxious. The verb *merimnate* can mean "to be concerned about" in a proper Christian sense (and is so used by Paul in 2:20), but here the meaning is clearly that of anxiety, fretfulness, or undue concern. Paul is not calling for apathy or inaction, for as we make plans in the light of our circumstances, it is our Christian privilege to do so in full trust that our Father hears our prayers for what we need. The answer to anxiety is prayer. "Prayer" (*proseuchē*) denotes the petitioner's attitude of mind as worshipful. "Petition" (*deēsei*) denotes prayers as expressions of need. "Thanksgiving" (*eucharistias*) should accompany all Christian praying, as the supplicant acknowledges that whatever God sends is for his good. It may also include remembrance of previous blessings. "Requests" (*aitēmata*) refers to the things asked for.

7 Having just given us a classic exhortation to pray, Paul attaches to it the beautiful promise that when we turn from anxiety to prayer and thanksgiving, God will give us his own peace. This peace is for those who are already at peace with God through justification by faith in Christ (Rom 5:8). Although some explain *hē hyperechousa panta noun* ("which transcends all understanding," NIV) as meaning that God's peace accomplishes far more than any human forethought or plan might devise, the comparable expression in Ephesians 3:20 shows that the common rendering is preferable. The NIV rendering or the KJV, "which passeth all understanding," well conveys the sense. For the peace of God not only suffices but far surpasses human comprehension. It acts as a sentry to guard the believer's heart (a biblical symbol for the personality in which the mind resides) and the believer's thoughts from all anxiety and despair.

8 Fourth, believers should keep on thinking and doing what is morally and spiritually excellent. This involves centering their minds on exalted things and then (v.9) putting into practice what they have learned from Paul's teaching and example.

Here (v.8) Paul has set forth in memorable words a veritable charter for Christian thought. Although this beautiful list of virtues is not exclusively Christian, we need not suppose that Paul has borrowed it from pagan moralists. All the terms are found in the Greek versions of the OT (LXX or Symmachus), and most of them appear elsewhere in the NT. "True" (*alēthē*) has the sense of valid, reliable, and honest—the opposite of false. It characterizes God (Rom 3:4) and should also characterize believers. "Noble" (*semna*) is used in the NT only by Paul—here and in 1 Tim 3:8, 11; Tit 2:2—and in the latter passages refers to church officers—i.e., a quality that makes them worthy of respect. "Right" (*dikaia*) refers to what is upright or just, conformable to God's standards and thus worthy of his approval. "Pure" (*hagna*) emphasizes moral purity and includes in some contexts the more restricted sense of "chaste." "Lovely" (*prosphilē*) occurs only here in the NT. It appears in LXX (Esther 5:1) and Josephus (Antiq. I.18.12; XVII.6.22) and relates to what is pleasing, agreeable, or amiable. "Admirable" (*euphēma*) occurs only here, though Paul uses the cognate *euphēmia* in 2 Corinthians 6:8. It denotes what is praiseworthy, attractive, and what rings true to the highest standards.

Suddenly Paul changes the sentence structure to conditional clauses—"if anything is. . . ."—a rhetorical device that forces the reader to exercise his own discernment and choose what is "excellent" (*aretē*) and "praiseworthy" (*epainos*). Paul knows that when we continually center our minds on such thoughts as these, we shall live like Christians.

9 Since Paul himself had been their teacher and example, what they had learned from him they were to keep on practicing. The four verbs in this verse form two pairs. The first pair, "learned" and "received," describes the Philippians' instruction by Paul, from whom they had been taught Christian doctrine and Christian living. The next pair, "heard" and "saw," depicts their personal observation of the apostle—both his speech and his conduct. As Martin aptly remarks, in the early days of the church before the NT writings were written or widely circulated, the standards of Christian belief and behav-

152

ior were largely taught by being embodied in the words and example of the apostles (*Philippians*, p. 173). Those who follow this apostolic guidance have the additional promise that God, who provides true peace (v.9; cf. v.7), will be with them.

Notes

4 On χαίρετε (*chairete*, "rejoice"), see note on 3:1.
5 Herbert Preisker notes that ἐπιεικής (*epieikēs*, "gentleness") and cognates are used in LXX and Josephus mostly of a quality of God or some human ruler who possesses sovereignty but chooses to display mildness or leniency. In the NT the noun form is used of Christians who are associated with the divine King, but must also display his gentleness to others (2 Cor 10:1). In Phil 4:5 Christians have a special incentive to display this royal virtue because the Lord is at hand and their promised glory will soon be manifested. (H. Preisker, TDNT, 2:588–590.)
6 Of the nineteen NT uses of μεριμνάω (*merimnaō*, "to be anxious, concerned"), only four occur in a favorable sense, and all of these four are by Paul (1 Cor 7:32, 34; 12:25; Phil 2:20). The rest are used of anxiety, as in the teaching of Jesus on this subject (Matt 6:25, 27, 28, 31, 34). A striking instance of this meaning relates to Martha (Luke 10:41).
  On the precise distinctions among the terms for prayer in v.6, see Trench, pp. 188–192.
7 Lightfoot exemplifies those who interpret ἡ ὑπερέχουσα πάντα νοῦν (*hē hyperechousa panta noun*, "which transcends all understanding") as referring to human device or council. He regards νοῦν as denoting man's planning, which is so frequently characterized by anxiety and is thus greatly inferior to God's provision for man's needs. Lightfoot admits, however, that Ephesians 3:20 supports the other interpretation (p. 161).
  In both OT and NT, καρδία (*kardia*, "heart") denotes the innermost part of a person—the seat of one's mental and spiritual powers. Although it may include the feelings and emotions, its more important function is its role as the moral, volitional, and intellectual center of man. A narrower term is νοῦς (*nous*), tr. "understanding" by KJV and NIV. From the *nous* proceed a person's thoughts (νοήματα, *noēmata*), rendered somewhat inexactly as "minds" by KJV and NIV.
  The verb φρουρέω (*phroureō*, "to guard") can mean a kind of guarding that prevents entrance or exit, as well as the more general meaning of simple protecting or keeping. "The peace of God" is here regarded as a military protector preventing anxieties within or satanic doubts from without.
8 Some regard τὸ λοιπόν (*to loipon*) as a resumption of the previous "final" word in v.1, after a digression. Others see in it a combining of two letters. There is no need to adopt either explanation. The expression "the God of peace" clearly ties v.9 with v.7 as part of the same unit. Hence, *to loipon* may be regarded as Paul's concluding exhortation in this series, before he introduces the topic of the Philippians' gift.
  Dana and Mantey (*Manual Grammar*, p. 247) argue for a special use of εἴ τις (*ei tis*) and treat it as equivalent to ὅ τι (*ho ti*) or ὅς τις (*hos tis*). This yields the rendering "whatever is true . . . noble," etc., giving broader applications of faith following the previous particularized examples.
9 The verbs ἐμάθετε (*emathete*, "you learned") and παρελάβετε (*parelabete*, "you received") are virtually synonymous; the former refers to the acquisition of knowledge, the second has the additional connotation of gaining instruction from a teacher.
  The article with εἰρήνης (*eirēnēs*, "peace") probably points to the former reference in v.7; thus it means "the God of this peace."

VI. The Philippians' Gifts to Paul (4:10–20)

1. *The Recent Gift*

4:10–14

> ¹⁰I rejoice greatly in the Lord that at last you have renewed your concern for me. Indeed, you have been concerned, but you had no opportunity to show it. ¹¹I am not saying this because I am in need, for I have learned to be content whatever the circumstances. ¹²I know what it is to be in need, and I know what it is to have plenty. I have learned the secret of being content in any and every situation, whether well-fed or hungry, whether living in plenty or in want. ¹³I can do everything through him who gives me strength.
> ¹⁴Yet it was good of you to share in my troubles.

10 As Paul begins to conclude his letter, he voices his joy over the Philippians' recent contribution to him. This is probably not his first note of thanks to them, for considerable time had elapsed since Epaphroditus had brought the gift and several contacts with the church at Philippi had already been made (see Introduction, 3). Furthermore, it is doubtful that his expression of gratitude would have been left to the end of the letter (see Introduction, 4). Paul retained a vivid memory of their generous act. "At last" (*ēdē pote*) should not be regarded as a rebuke, but merely as showing that communication had again occurred after a period of no contact. (The usage is similar to that in Rom 1:10.) Paul makes it clear that the fault was not theirs but came from a lack of opportunity. Perhaps no messenger had been available. In addition, the apostle's own circumstances had been highly irregular in recent years, in part, at least, because of imprisonment and shipwreck. Now the demonstration of concern had bloomed again, like plants in the spring.

11 The apostle hastens to make clear that though he undoubtedly had a need, it was not relief of this need that primarily concerned him. He had learned to be content with what God provided, irrespective of circumstances. It is significant that Paul had to "learn" this virtue. Contentment is not natural to most of mankind.

In Stoic philosophy, *autarkēs* ("content") described a person who accepted impassively whatever came. Circumstances that he could not change were regarded as the will of God, and fretting was useless. This philosophy fostered a self-sufficiency in which all the resources for coping with life were located within man himself. In contrast, Paul locates his sufficiency in Christ who provides strength for believers.

12 Paul understood what it was to be in want as well as "to have plenty." The latter may refer to his earlier days as a rising figure in Judaism (Gal 1:14) or to the possibility that he had received a sum of money more recently. On the other hand, the expression may be merely relative. It may be that Paul considered the times he was not suffering privation to be times of plenty (e.g., Acts 9:19, 28; 16:15, 33, 34; 18:3; 21:8). He had learned the secret of trusting God "in every [particular] situation" (*en panti*) and in all situations as a whole (*en pasin*).

13 His was no Stoic philosophy, however. He did not trace his resources to some inner fortitude that would enable him to take with equanimity whatever life brought him. Instead, his strength for "everything" lay in the One who continually empowered him.

The name "Christ," to which we are accustomed through the KJV translation of v.13, does not appear in the most reliable manuscripts, but surely Paul has Christ in mind. The apostle was not desperately seeking a gift from the Philippians, because he knew that Christ would give him the strength for whatever circumstances were in God's will for him.

14 Nevertheless, the Philippians must not feel that their gift had been unnecessary. They had responded properly to his need, and Paul was truly grateful—not so much for what the gift did for him as for the willingness of the Philippians to share with him. They had accepted his affliction as their own and had done something about it.

Notes

10 The aorist indicative ἐχάρην (echarēn, "I rejoiced" may be either ingressive, denoting the historical incident that caused Paul's rejoicing, or it may be epistolary. If the latter, the meaning is "I rejoice" (as in NIV).

This sole NT occurrence of ἀναθάλλω (anathallō) may be either transitive, "you caused your thinking concerning me to bloom again," or intransitive, "you bloomed again in regard to your thinking concerning me" (NIV, "you have renewed your concern for me"). The difference in meaning is slight, with the latter being perhaps a bit more tactful, since it avoids the implication that their previous lack of thought for Paul came from their failure.

The antecedent of ᾧ (hō) may be either the masc. ἐμοῦ (emou), thus yielding "about whom you were also thinking," or else the entire neuter infinitive phrase τὸ ... φρονεῖν (to ... phronein), hence, "concerning which [i.e., your thinking about me] you were also thinking."

11 The neuter phrase ἐν οἷς (en hois) is not indefinite and should not be rendered "in whatever state." It refers to his present circumstances in Rome, "in which circumstances." The elaboration in the next verse, however, applies the principle more generally.

12 Ramsay argues that Paul's trial in Rome would have required considerable money, and observes that Felix apparently thought Paul had access to funds. He suggests that he may have inherited some family wealth (pp. 34–37, 310–313).

The double use of καὶ (kai) is the "both ... and" construction. The irregularity is caused by the repetition of οἶδα (oida, "I know"), but this is apparently for additional emphasis.

It need not be supposed that Paul borrowed the verb μεμύημαι (memuēmai) from the mystery religions. The term was a technical one, "to initiate into the mysteries," but undoubtedly had a general use as well, "to learn the secret" (NIV). If the cultic sense is insisted on, then we must assume that Paul was using it ironically (G. Bornkamm, Mueō, TDNT, 4:828).

13 The form πάντα (panta, "all things") is an accusative of reference after ἰσχύω (ischuō, "I can do"), as in James 5:16. That Christ is to be understood as the one empowering Paul (though MS evidence is against inclusion of the name here) is strongly probable in the light of a similar statement of Paul in 1 Tim 1:12, τῷ ἐνδυναμώσαντί με Χριστῷ Ἰησοῦ τῷ κυρίῳ ἡμῶν (to endynamōsanti me Christō Iēsou tō kyriō hēmōn, "Christ Jesus our Lord, who has given me strength").

14 The adversative πλήν (plēn, "yet") cautions the readers against drawing the conclusion that Paul did not need their gift.

2. The Previous Gifts

4:15-20

> [15]Moreover, as you Philippians know, in the early days of your acquaintance with the gospel, when I set out from Macedonia, not one church shared with me in the matter of giving and receiving, except you only; [16]for even when I was in Thessalonica, you sent me aid again and again when I was in need. [17]Not that I am looking for a gift, but I am looking for what may be credited to your account. [18]I have received full payment and even more; I am amply supplied, now that I have received from Epaphroditus the gifts you sent. They are a fragrant offering, an acceptable sacrifice, pleasing to God. [19]And my God will meet all your needs according to his glorious riches in Christ Jesus.
> [20]To our God and Father be glory for ever and ever. Amen.

15 In order to make it clear that he is not minimizing the Philippians' generosity toward him, Paul recalls some earlier demonstrations of their love for him. When the gospel was first preached to them—approximately ten years before (Acts 16)—they were the only church to contribute to him when he left Macedonia. Some commentators are influenced by the succeeding reference to Thessalonica and explain this passage to mean that Paul received the gift in Thessalonica while on his way from Macedonia to Achaia (Corinth), though Thessalonica is itself in Macedonia. But this seems more awkward than to consider the gift as the one sent him by the Philippians while he was in Corinth (2 Cor 11:9). As he mentions this gift, he also recalls two earlier instances of their generosity when he was in Thessalonica.

Paul does not mean that no other church ever assisted him (cf. 2 Cor 11:8), but that on the specific occasion referred to here no other church had come to his aid. He uses business terminology, "an account of giving and receiving" (*logon doseōs kai lēmpseōs*—NIV, "the matter of giving and receiving"), to depict the situation.

16 Not only had the Philippians sent him a gift when he left Macedonia, but even when he was in Thessalonica, shortly after his departure from Philippi (Acts 17:1), they had made a contribution to him on more than one occasion. Presumably these earlier gifts were small and so were in a different category from the one mentioned in v.15. This is also implied by references in the Thessalonian Epistles showing that Paul earned his living there (1 Thess 2:9; 2 Thess 3:7, 8).

17 Paul's readers must not suppose that he is primarily concerned with their gift as such, but rather in the development of the grace of giving among them. Continuing to use business terminology, he says that he regards such displays as interest accruing (NIV, "credited") to their account. Their spiritual growth was the fruit Paul desired, and to this end he directed his ministry.

18 The financial language continues as Paul says, "I have received full payment and even more." The gifts brought by Epaphroditus (2:25-30) had completely met his needs, and Paul considers this contribution a sacrificial offering to God, made to further the Lord's work by helping his servant (cf. Matt 25:40). "A fragrant offering" (*osmēn euōdias*) is used in Ephesians 5:2 of Christ's sacrificial offering of himself to God on man's behalf. It reflects the Levitical ritual (e.g., Lev 1:9, 13, 17; 2:12 [LXX]). Such offerings pleased God, because they came from obedient hearts.

The verb *apechō* appears regularly in business papyri and ostraca in the sense of

156

receiving in full. It was a technical expression in drawing up receipts. Deissmann cites numerous examples with several photographs and also notes that *apechō* is often combined with *panta* ("all") in receipts, as is done in Phil 4:18 (Deiss LAE, pp. 110–112, 166).

19 In words that countless Christians have relied on as one of the great Scripture promises, Paul now reminds his benefactors that "his" God (*ho theos mou*, "my God") will do what he himself is in no position to do; namely, reimburse his benefactors. This assurance of the divine supply of the Philippians' needs implies that they had given so liberally that they actually left themselves in some real "need" (*chreian*). Yet it is true that those who share generously with others, especially to advance the work of the Lord, are promised a divine supply of anything they might lack because of their generosity (Prov 11:25; 19:17; Matt 5:7).

The preposition *kata* ("according to") conveys the thought that God's supply of the Philippians' need will not be merely from or out of his wealth but in some sense appropriate to or commensurate with it. The phrase *en doxē* ("in glory"; NIV, "glorious") is sometimes construed with *plērōsei* ("will fill"; NIV, "will meet") and tr. "gloriously" (Muller), or in a local sense, perhaps with eschatological tones, "by placing you in glory" (Lightfoot). Word order, however, strongly favors relating it to *ploutos* ("riches"), "his riches in glory," or "glorious riches" (Martin, *Philippians*). By this understanding, we are to think of the heavenly glories that Christ now enjoys as explaining the source of our supply.

20 Small wonder that Paul closes this beautiful passage with a doxology. The glory of God's providential care must always be recognized by his children. Even the eternal ages yet to come will not be sufficient to exhaust the praises that belong to him.

Notes

15 Although the spelling Φιλιππήσιοι (*Philippēsioi*) is apparently a Latin form less common than Φιλιππεῖς (*Philippeis*) or Φιλιππηνοί (*Philippēnoi*), it also appears in the title of this Epistle and in that of Polycarp's Epistle (see W.M. Ramsay, "On the Greek Form of the Name Philippians," JTS, I [1900], p. 116).

The aorist indicative ἐξῆλθον (*exēlthon*, "I set out") does not describe a process of leaving, or being "on the way," but an actual departure. This reinforces the view that Paul is referring to his actual removal from Macedonia to some other place. The mention of Thessalonica in v.16 indicates that the sharing in v.15 is a separate incident.

Even though λόγον δόσεως καὶ λήμψεως (*logon doseōs kai lēmpseōs*, "the matter of giving and receiving") is financial language, it is clearly figurative. Paul surely did not keep books on the gifts of his friends, nor did he list anything in the debit column.

16 Some regard the introductory ὅτι (*hoti*, "because"; NIV, "for") as dependent on οἴδατε (*oidate*, "you know") in v.15, thus making the clause explicative of the preceding assertion. This is grammatically possible, but by no means mandatory, and runs into the objection that the mention of Thessalonica hardly explains Paul's departure from Macedonia. It seems better to regard *hoti* in the loose causal sense as "for" (BAG, p. 594).

The phrase ἅπαξ καὶ δίς (*hapax kai dis*) is literally "once and twice" and could easily be so understood here, since Paul was in Thessalonica only a short time (Acts 17:1–10). It has this literal sense in LXX (Deut 9:13; 1 Macc 3:30), and may also have it in its only other NT occurrence (1 Thess 2:18). A more general understanding as "more than once" without expressing the exact number is also possible (L. Morris, "*Kai Hapax kai Dis*," NovTest, 1:3 [July, 1956], pp. 205-208; L. Morris, *The Epistles of Paul to the Thessalonians* [Grand Rapids: Eerdmans, 1957], p. 58).

17 Οὐχ ὅτι (*ouch hoti*, "not that") is comparable to the same expression in v.11, being a denial of what could have constituted a false conclusion by the readers.

The term λόγον (*logon*, "account") is used in the same financial figure as in v.15. No literal business account is meant, but simply one in which the practical expression of the Philippians' concern for Paul is described as interest accruing to their spiritual investment.

20 The one article with the phrase τῷ δὲ θεῷ καὶ πατρὶ ἡμῶν (*tō de theō kai patri hēmōn*) makes it certain that only one person is meant, one who is both God and Father. Hence, the meaning is "to even our Father."

The concluding ἀμήν (*amēn*) is a transliteration of the Hebrew אָמֵן (*'āmēn*), often used at the close of a doxology (1 Chron 16:36; Neh 8:6). It denotes assent to the doxology as valid (H. Schlier, *Amēn*, TDNT, 1:335-338).

Closing Salutation

4:21-23

> 21Greet all the saints in Christ Jesus. The brothers who are with me send greetings. 22All the saints send you greetings, especially those who belong to Caesar's household.
> 23The grace of the Lord Jesus Christ be with your spirit.

21 It is likely that the remaining words of the Epistle were written by Paul's own hand, after the pattern announced in 2 Thessalonians 3:17 (see also Gal 6:11; Col 4:18). He sends greetings to every believer at Philippi, to be conveyed to them no doubt by the leadership of the church to whom the letter was initially delivered. Paul's associates also send their greetings. They are to be distinguished from the resident Roman Christians who are mentioned in the next verse. These "brothers who are with me" (*hoi sun emoi adelphoi*) include Timothy and perhaps Epaphroditus (1:1; 2:19-30), and possibly even some of those mentioned in 1:14. The inclusion of these greetings is a caution against interpreting 2:21 as an indictment of all Paul's associates except Timothy (see comment on 2:21).

22 "All the saints" refers to members of the church at Rome. Paul also extends special greetings from "those who belong to Caesar's household." This expression denotes those engaged in imperial service, whether as slaves or freedmen, in Rome or elsewhere. Among them may have been the palace guard (1:13). It is most unlikely that Nero's immediate family is meant, but the expression could refer to persons of considerable importance on the emperor's staff. Paul does not say why they were singled out for special mention. Presumably the Philippians would understand. Perhaps some of these government servants had come from Philippi or had once been stationed at that Roman colony.

23 The concluding benediction is exactly the same as Philemon 25 and similar to Galatians 6:18. It invokes on the Philippian church the continuing favor of Christ to be with their spirits. The realization of this benediction would increase the harmony of the congregation by causing the spirit of each believer to cherish the grace of the Lord Jesus

Christ and by bringing a joyous peace among them, fulfilling the apostle's opening wish (1:2).

Notes

21 "All the saints" (NIV) is actually the sing. "every saint" (πάντα ἅγιον, *panta hagion*) and considers the believers separately. The pl. form πάντες οἱ ἅγιοι, (*pantes hoi hagioi*) in the following verse looks at the saints in Rome collectively.

The phrase ἐν Χριστῷ Ἰησοῦ (*en Christō Iēsou*, "in Christ Jesus") can be construed with either ἀσπάσασθε (*aspasasthe*, "greet") or with ἅγιον (*hagion*, "saint"). In favor of the latter is the analogy with 1:1, and the word order.

22 Lightfoot's extended note explains how οἰκία Καίσαρος, (*oikia Kaisaros*, "Caesar's household") is the Gr. terminology for the Lat. *domus* or *familia Caesaris* and includes the whole of the imperial household. From inscriptions (chiefly sepulchral), lists have been compiled of the varied functions of its members. Vast numbers of these imperial servants were foreign slaves, and if the surmise is correct that many of the earliest converts in Rome were drawn from these classes, the mention of such persons by Paul becomes readily understandable (pp. 167, 171–177). Josephus uses the expression *oikia Kaisaros* in the same way (Antiq. 17.5.8).

23 TR has πάντων (*pantōn*, "all") rather than τοῦ πνεύματος (*tou pneumatos*, "spirit").

COLOSSIANS

Curtis Vaughan

COLOSSIANS

Introduction

1. Destination
2. Authorship
3. Place of origin
4. Occasion
5. Purpose
6. Theme
7. Relation to Ephesians
8. Bibliography
9. Outline

1. Destination

Colosse was a small town situated on the south bank of the Lycus River in the interior of the Roman province of Asia (an area included in modern Turkey). Located about a hundred miles east of Ephesus, its nearest neighbors were Laodicea (ten miles away) and Hierapolis (thirteen miles away). Both of these cities, the more important of which was Laodicea, are named in the Epistle as having communities of believers (cf. 2:1; 4:13). Colosse and Laodicea were probably evangelized during the time of Paul's extended ministry in Ephesus (Acts 19:10). During the periods of the Persian and Greek empires, Colosse was a city of considerable importance. Both Herodotus (fifth century B.C.) and Xenophon (fourth century B.C.) speak of this fact, the former calling Colosse "a great city of Phrygia" and the latter describing it as "a populous city, wealthy and large." But the road system was later changed, and a decline in the social and commercial importance of Colosse set in. In Paul's day it was only an insignificant market town. Lightfoot therefore speaks of the Colossian church as "the least important to which any epistle of Paul is addressed."[1]

We have no record of the establishment of the Colossian church; indeed, Colosse is not even mentioned in Acts. All our information about the church, therefore, must be found in this letter and in incidental allusions in the companion letter to Philemon.

2. Authorship

The authenticity of Colossians has sometimes been questioned. Today, however, there is broad agreement that it is, as it purports to be (1:1; 4:18), from the hand of Paul—or that it is at least substantially Pauline. Evidence in support of Pauline authorship comes

---

[1]J.B. Lightfoot, *St. Paul's Epistles to the Colossians and to Philemon* (London: Macmillan, 1879), p. 16.

163

not only from within the Epistle but also from the witness of early Christian writers. Admittedly, the external testimony to Colossians is not equal to that of some other Pauline Epistles; nevertheless, it is quite strong. Allusions to it in Ignatius, Polycarp, and Barnabas are open to question, but Justin (c.100–c.165) seems to have used it. Irenaeus (c.125–c.202), Clement of Alexandria (d. c.215), and Origen (c.185–c.254) explicitly refer it to Paul, and it is cited in Marcion's list (c.146) and in the Muratorian Canon (c.170). Colossians is also found in second-century Old Latin versions. Moreover, it is included in the Chester Beatty codex of the Pauline Epistles (P[46]), which originated in Egypt near the end of the second century. So far as we can determine from extant writings, Colossians was never suspect in ancient times. In fact, the external testimony for it is so ancient and consistent as to obviate any doubts regarding its authenticity.

Pauline authorship appears not to have been seriously questioned until near the middle of the nineteenth century, when T. Mayerhoff disputed the authenticity of Colossians—mainly because of its alleged dependence on Ephesians, which he accepted as genuine. But the relationship of Ephesians and Colossians does not warrant this conclusion. Indeed, a few years after Mayerhoff's work appeared, W.M.L. DeWette reversed this argument, defending the authenticity of Colossians and rejecting Ephesians as the work of a later writer who drew on the former Epistle. F.C. Baur and his pupils denied the Pauline authorship of both Ephesians and Colossians because they thought both Epistles reflected second-century Gnosticism. But it is no longer widely held that the heresy opposed in Colossians is to be identified with the fully developed gnostic systems of the second century. Fresh knowledge of the bewildering variety of syncretistic religious movements of the Graeco-Roman world of the first century has been gained, and arguments such as Baur advanced have in recent years been largely abandoned. H.J. Holtzmann advanced the theory that there was a shortened Pauline Colossians written at the same time as Philemon, but that it was interpolated by a later writer to give it its present form. Holtzmann's theory is not taken seriously today, though C. Masson (*L'Epitre de Saint Paul aux Colossians*, 1950) and P.N. Harrison (*Paulines and Pastorals*, 1964) both adhere to the interpolation theory.

In recent years doubts concerning the authenticity of Colossians have focused on vocabulary (more than fifty words not found elsewhere in Paul's writings and other distinctive Pauline terms not found in Colossians), style (said to be unlike that of the recognized Pauline Epistles, being cumbersome, wordy, and marked by a multiplicity of genitival constructions, participles, and prepositional phrases), and doctrine. Vocabulary is not a great problem, however, for the distinctive vocabulary is most apparent where Paul is dealing with the Colossian problem. Therefore, it is not unlikely that at least some of these words were borrowed from the errorists for purposes of refutation; naturally, then, they would not be used in other totally different contexts. Paul had new things to say in this Epistle and found new ways of saying them. Moreover, the absence of familiar Pauline words such as *justify, believe,* and *salvation* seems less significant when we remember that equally familiar Pauline words are missing from letters such as Galatians. Caird calls the argument from style the "only valid argument against the Pauline authorship of Colossians."[2] Yet the weakness of the argument lies in its failure to apply equally to all of Colossians; parts of the Epistle are generally conceded to have the authentic ring of Paul's style. Moreover, some of the generally accepted letters of

---

[2]G.B. Caird, *Paul's Letters From Prison* in The New Clarendon Bible, gen. ed. H.F.G. Sparks (Oxford: Oxford University Press, 1976), p. 156.

Paul (Romans, 1 Corinthians, and Philippians) have passages that exhibit the same features of style found in Colossians. Bruce feels that the stylistic distinctiveness of Colossians is bound up with the sustained note of thanksgiving that runs through the Epistle, especially through chapter one. He further thinks that the creedal affirmations of 1:12–17 "probably echo the language of primitive Christian confessions of faith."[3] The doctrinal argument is that the Epistle's teachings about Christ—especially the cosmic aspects of his redemptive work—are more fully developed than in other Pauline Epistles. The overall Christology of Colossians, it is sometimes argued, shows such a pronounced similarity to the Logos doctrine of John (John 1:1–18) that it betrays a post-Pauline date. But why could not two apostles share this exalted view of Christ's person and work? Moreover, this doctrine was not entirely new to Paul (cf. Rom 8:19–22; 1 Cor 8:6); it was only given greater prominence and a more systematic exposition in Colossians.

Others argue that such christological passages as 1:15–20 and 2:9ff. reflect an un-Pauline manner of combating false teaching. The terminology of the errorists, for example, is said to be only Christianized, not repudiated. Furthermore, their Gnostic Christology is simply countered by a *radicalized* Gnostic Christology; their Gnostic soteriology, by a *radicalized* Gnostic soteriology. Reference is especially made to the cosmic character of the Christology in the representation of Christ as "the head of the body, the church" (1:18; cf. 2:19). Kümmel answers that "although in comparison with the recognized Pauline letters the idea of Christ as 'the head of the body, the church' . . . is new, it is really not surprising in the framework of Pauline ecclesiology if one notes that in the acknowledged letters . . . Paul knows the concept of Christ's identity with the ἐκκλησία as his 'body' " (1 Cor 1:13; 12:12c; Gal 3:28).[4]

A strong argument for Pauline authorship is the relation of Colossians to Philemon. Both of these books, sent to the same town and in all likelihood conveyed by the same messenger, contain the names of Paul, Timothy, Onesimus, Archippus, Epaphras, Mark, Aristarchus, Demas, and Luke. The consensus of scholarly opinion is that Philemon is incontestably Pauline, and it is the feeling of many NT scholars that this carries over to Colossians. Kümmel sums up his discussion by affirming that "all the evidence points to the conclusion that Colossians . . . is to be regarded as Pauline."[5]

3. Place of Origin

Colossians was obviously written during an imprisonment of Paul (4:10, 18), but the Epistle contains no indication as to the place of imprisonment. Caesarea has from time to time had its advocates, and a few present-day scholars (e.g., E. Lohmeyer, W.G. Kümmel, B. Reicke, J.A.T. Robinson) support the Caesarean hypothesis. It is unlikely that so small a city as Caesarea would have been the center of such vigorous missionary activity as Colossians 4:3, 4, 10–14 seems to suggest. Furthermore, if Colossians was written from Caesarea, how are we to account for Paul's silence about Philip the evangelist, in whose home Paul had been a guest shortly before his arrest (Acts 21:8)? Others (e.g., G.S. Duncan and Ralph P. Martin) argue for Ephesus as the place of origin. But this view has not gained wide acceptance. One of the chief points against it is the lack of

---

[3]E.K. Simpson and F.F. Bruce, *The Epistles of Paul to the Ephesians and to the Colossians*, NIC, p. 171.
[4]Werner G. Kümmel, *Introduction to the New Testament*. Rev. Eng. ed., trans. Howard C. Key (Nashville: Abingdon, 1975), p. 344.
[5]Ibid., p. 346.

clear and certain evidence that Paul was ever a prisoner in Ephesus. Moreover, though Luke was with Paul when Colossians was written (4:14), he was not with the apostle during the Ephesian ministry (note the absence of "we"/"us" at this point in the Acts narrative). The traditional theory, and the one still most generally held, is that Paul was in Rome when Colossians was written.[6] The Epistle should therefore be dated about A.D. 62, during Paul's first Roman imprisonment (cf. Acts 28:30, 31). Perhaps it was written before Ephesians, but surely not much time separated the two Epistles.

4. Occasion

The immediate occasion for the writing of Colossians was the arrival of Epaphras (1:8) in Rome with disturbing news about the presence of heretical teaching at Colosse that was threatening the well-being of the church. The Epistle gives no direct account of the tenets of this strange teaching, and for that reason it is difficult to obtain a clear and consistent understanding of it. Yet from the many allusions to the heresy, we are able to sketch its leading features: (1) It professed to be a "philosophy," but Paul, refusing to recognize it as genuine, called it a "hollow and deceptive philosophy" (2:8). Moulton characterizes it as a "dabbling in the occult."[7] (2) It placed much emphasis on ritual circumcision, dietary laws, and the observance of holy days (2:11, 14, 16, 17). (3) Affirming the mediation of various supernatural powers in the creation of the world and the whole process of salvation, the false teaching insisted that these mysterious powers be placated and worshiped (2:15, 18, 19). As a result of this, Christ was relegated to a relatively minor place in the Colossian system. "One thing is certain as to the 'Colossian Heresy,' " writes H.C.G. Moule. "It was a doctrine of God and of salvation that cast a cloud over the glory of Jesus Christ."[8] (4) Some of the errorists were ascetic (2:20–23), teaching that the body is evil and must be treated as an enemy. (5) The advocates of this system claimed to be Christian teachers (cf. 2:3–10).

From these considerations we may conclude that the Colossian heresy was a syncretistic movement combining at least three separate elements. First, the insistence on legalism, ritualism, and the observance of holy days points to a *Jewish element*. It seems not, however, to have been the Pharisaic Judaism Paul combated in Galatians. Bruce calls it a "native Phrygian variety," something "worse than the simple Jewish legalism" that earlier threatened the Galatian churches.[9]

Second, the system's "philosophical" character, angelolatry, and perhaps ascetic tendencies point to a *pagan element*. This was probably an incipient form of what later became known as Gnosticism, a very complex system that reached its zenith in the second century. This incipient Gnosticism—some use the expression proto-Gnosticism— was essentially a religio-philosophical attitude, not a well-defined system. R.E.O. White speaks of it as "a climate of thought as widespread as evolutionary theory is today."[10] It sought by its oriental myths and Greek philosophy to absorb the various religions with

---

[6]For an able defense of this position see C.H. Dodd, "The Mind of Paul: II," in *New Testament Essays* (Manchester: University Press, 1953).

[7]Harold K. Moulton, *Colossians, Philemon and Ephesians* (Naperville, Ill.: Allenson, 1963).

[8]Handley C.G. Moule, *Colossian Studies* (New York: Hodder & Stoughton, 1898), p. 9.

[9]Simpson and Bruce, *Ephesians and Colossians*, pp. 166, 168.

[10]Reginald E.O. White, *Colossians* in *The Broadman Commentary*, vol. 11 (Nashville: Broadman, 1969), p. 219.

which it came into contact. It lent itself to an air of exclusiveness, cultivating an "enlightened" elite for whom alone salvation was possible. Gnosticism, in all its forms, was characterized by belief in the evil of matter, in mediating beings, and in salvation through knowledge. Beginning with the assumption that all matter is evil, the Gnostics argued that God and matter were therefore antagonistic. Indeed, they contended that God didn't create this world and that he has absolutely no contact with it. However, intellectual necessity did not permit them to break completely the bond between divinity and the material world. They therefore taught that God put forth from himself a series of "aeons" or emanations, each a little more distant from him and each having a little less of deity. At the end of this chain of intermediate beings there is an emanation possessing enough of deity to make a world but removed far enough from God that his creative activities could not compromise the perfect purity of God. The world, they argued, was the creation of this lesser power, who being so far removed from God was both ignorant of and hostile to him. These "aeons"—"offshoots of deity" Martin calls them[11]—were thought to inhabit the stars and rule man's destiny. They therefore were to be placated and worshiped. Paul's references to "thrones ... powers ... rulers ... authorities" (1:16), "power and authority" (2:9), "powers and authorities" (2:15), and "worship of angels" (2:18) are allusions to these supposed intermediate beings.

Belief in the inherent evil of matter made it impossible for the Gnostics to accept the real incarnation of God in Christ. Some of them explained it away by denying the actual humanity of Jesus, holding that he only seemed to be human. The body of Jesus, they taught, was an illusion, a phantom, only apparently real. In their view, Christ was only one of many intermediaries between God and the world, but he was sufficiently related to God to share his abhorrence of any direct contact with matter. The advent of Christ "was a piece of play-acting when God wore a mask of humanity on the stage of human history, giving the appearance of being a man but really being still God-in-disguise."[12] Other Gnostics explained away the incarnation by denying the real deity of Jesus. That is, they stopped short of making a complete identification of the man Jesus with the aeon Christ. Both of these tendencies were perhaps present at Colosse in embryo form and both may be alluded to in the Epistle—for example, in the affirmation that "in Christ all the fullness of the Deity lives in bodily form" (2:9).

Belief that matter is evil also led to a distorted view of the Christian life. Some Gnostics turned to asceticism, others to libertinism. The ascetics felt that they had to free themselves from the influence of matter (the body) by inflicting punishment on their bodies. Those who gave in to license assumed an attitude of indifference to things physical and material, the idea being that only the soul is important and therefore the body may do what it pleases. Indications of both tendencies may be found in the Colossian letter, the former being opposed in 2:20ff. and the latter in 3:5ff.

As its name would indicate, Gnosticism—the word is related to *gnosis*, "knowledge"— taught that salvation is obtained not through faith but through knowledge. The knowledge of which the Gnostics spoke, however, was knowledge acquired through mystical experience, not by intellectual apprehension. It was an occult knowledge, pervaded by the superstitions of astrology and magic. Moreover, it was an esoteric knowledge, open only to those who had been initiated into the mysteries of the gnostic system.

Third, there was a *"Christian" element* in the Colossian error. While at its heart it was

---

[11]Ralph P. Martin, *The Church's Lord and the Christian's Liberty* (Grand Rapids: Zondervan, 1973), p. 5.
[12]Ibid., p. 7.

a combination of Judaism and paganism, it wore the mask of Christianity. It did not *deny* Christ, but it did *dethrone* him. It gave Christ a place, but not the supreme place. This Christian façade made the Colossian error all the more dangerous.

That Paul found it necessary to write this letter to the community of Christians at Colosse is evidence that the false teachers had made a strong impression on them and that the threat to the well-being of the church was real. There are indications, however, that the errorists had not achieved complete success (cf. 2:4, 8, 20). Paul therefore can express gratitude for the Colossian Christians and rejoice over the order within their ranks and in their continued fidelity to Christ (cf. 1:3ff.; 2:5).

5. Purpose

Paul's purpose in writing Colossians was threefold: (1) to express his personal interest in the church, (2) to warn them against reverting to their old pagan vices (cf. 3:5ff.), and (3) to refute the false teaching that was threatening the Colossian church. The last named was undoubtedly Paul's major concern. He met the Colossian false knowledge, not by appealing to ignorance and obscurantism, but by making a plea for the fuller knowledge found in Christ. He confronted the false representation by a positive setting forth of the exalted nature and unmatched glory of Christ.

6. Theme

Colossians proclaims the absolute supremacy and sole sufficiency of Jesus Christ (cf. esp. 1:18; 2:9; 3:11). It is, as Robertson says, Paul's "full-length portrait of Christ."[13] He is God's Son (1:14), the object of the Christian's faith (1:4), the Redeemer (1:14), the image of God (1:15), Lord of creation (1:15), head of the church (1:18), reconciler of the universe (1:20). In him dwells the fullness of the Godhead (2:9), and under him every power and authority in the universe is subjected (2:10). He is the essence of the mystery of God (2:3), and in him all God's treasures of wisdom and knowledge lie hidden (2:3). He is the standard by which all religious teaching is to be measured (2:8) and the reality of the truth foreshadowed by the regulations and rituals of the old covenant (2:17). By his cross he conquered the cosmic powers of evil (2:15), and following his resurrection he was enthroned at the right hand of God (3:1). Our life now lies hidden with God in Christ, but one day both he and we will be gloriously manifested (3:3, 4). In short, the central thought of the Epistle is summed up in the lines of Charles Wesley's hymn:

> Thou, O Christ, art all I want,
> More than all in Thee I find.

7. Relation to Ephesians

From even a casual reading of Ephesians and Colossians one must conclude that they are kindred Epistles. Both the Epistles were written by Paul out of an experience of imprisonment. Both were sent originally to believers in Asia. Both were entrusted to Tychicus, the messenger who was to bear them to their respective destinations (cf. Eph

---

[13]A.T. Robertson, *Paul and the Intellectuals*, rev. and ed. W.C. Strickland (Nashville: Broadman, 1959), p. 12.

6:21; Col 4:7). Moreover, many of the topics treated are common to both (the person of Christ, the church as Christ's body, ethical duties, relationships within the family, etc.). Even the language of the two Epistles is strikingly similar. Wisdom, knowledge, fullness, mystery, principalities, powers—these are just a few of the terms common to the two Epistles. Moulton points out that in Colossians the margin of the English Revised Version has seventy-two references to Ephesians but only eighty-eight to all of the other Pauline Epistles. Goodspeed writes that "three-fifths of Colossians is reflected in Ephesians."[14] We can best account for the similarities of the epistles on the supposition that Ephesians is an expansion by Paul of ideas presented in compact form in Colossians.

There are also significant differences between the Epistles. For instance, there is a difference in emphasis. Both Epistles are concerned with the lordship of Christ and the unity of his body, the church. However, in Ephesians the stress is on the church as the body of Christ; in Colossians the emphasis is on Christ as the head of the church. There is also a difference of style. Colossians is terse and abrupt; Ephesians is diffuse and flowing. Colossians is specific, concrete, and elliptical; Ephesians is abstract, didactic, and general. Finally, there is a difference in mood. Colossians, argumentative and polemical, is a letter of discussion; Ephesians, calm and irenical, is a letter of reflection.

8. Bibliography

Books

Abbott, T.K. *The Epistles to the Ephesians and to the Colossians.* ICC. Edited by S.R. Driver; Alfred Plummer; and C.A. Briggs. Edinburgh: T. & T. Clark, 1897.

Barclay, William. *The Letters to the Philippians, Colossians, and Thessalonians.* The Daily Study Bible. Philadelphia: Westminster, 1959.

Beare, F.W. *The Epistle to the Colossians.* IB. New York: Abingdon, 1955.

Caird, G.B. *Paul's Letters From Prison.* The New Clarendon Bible. Edited by H.F.D. Sparks. Oxford: Oxford University Press, 1976.

Calvin, John. *The Epistles of Paul the Apostle to the Galatians, Ephesians, Philippians and Colossians.* Translated by T.H.L. Parker. Edited by David W. and Thomas F. Torrence. Grand Rapids: Eerdmans, 1965.

Carson, H.M. *The Epistles of Paul to the Colossians and Philemon.* TNTC. Edited by R.V.G. Tasker. Grand Rapids: Eerdmans.

Eadie, John. *Commentary on the Epistle of Paul to the Colossians.* Classic Commentary Library. Grand Rapids: Zondervan, 1957.

Grant, R.M. *Gnosticism and Early Christianity.* 2nd ed. New York: Columbia University Press, 1966.

Kümmel, Werner G. *Introduction to the New Testament.* Rev. Engl. Ed. Translated by Howard C. Key. Nashville: Abingdon, 1975.

Lightfoot, J.B. *St. Paul's Epistles to the Colossians and to Philemon.* London: Macmillan, 1879.

Maclaren, Alexander. *The Epistles of St. Paul to the Colossians and Philemon.* The Expositor's Bible. Edited by W. Robertson Nicoll. New York: Hodder and Stoughton, n.d.

Macphail, S.R. *The Epistle of Paul to the Colossians.* Edinburgh: T. & T. Clark, 1911.

Martin, Ralph P. *Colossians: The Church's Lord and the Christian's Liberty.* Grand Rapids: Zondervan, 1973.

Meyer, H.A.W. *Critical and Exegetical Hand-Book to the Epistles to the Philippians and Colossians and to Philemon.* Meyer's Commentary on the NT. New York: Funk & Wagnalls, 1885.

---

[14]Edgar J. Goodspeed, *The Key to Ephesians* (Chicago: University of Chicago Press, 1956), p. 8.

Moule, C.F.D. *The Epistles of Paul the Apostle to the Colossians and to Philemon.* CGT. Edited by C.F.D. Moule, Cambridge: Cambridge University Press, 1957.

Moule, Handley C.G. *Colossian Studies.* New York: Hodder and Stoughton, 1898.

Moulton, Harold K. *Colossians, Philemon and Ephesians.* Epworth Preacher's Commentaries. London: Epworth, 1963.

Nicholson, W.R. *Oneness with Christ.* Edited by James M. Gray. Grand Rapids: Kregel, 1951.

Peake, A.S. *The Epistle to the Colossians.* EGT. Edited by W. Robertson Nicoll. Vol. 3. London: Hodder and Stoughton, 1903.

Radford, Lewis B. *The Epistle to the Colossians.* WC. London: Methuen, 1931.

Robertson, A.T. *Paul and the Intellectuals.* Revised and edited by W.C. Strickland. Nashville: Broadman, 1959.

Scott, E.F. *The Epistles of Paul to the Colossians, to Philemon and to the Ephesians.* MNT. Edited by James Moffatt. London: Hodder and Stoughton, 1930.

Simpson, E.K., and Bruce, F.F. *Commentary on the Epistles to the Ephesians and the Colossians.* NIC. Grand Rapids: Eerdmans, 1957.

White, R.E.O. *Colossians.* Broadman Bible Commentary. Edited by Clifton J. Allen, Vol. 11. Nashville: Broadman, 1971.

Wilson, R. McL. *Gnosis and the New Testament.* Philadelphia: Fortress, 1968.

Yamauchi, E.M. *Pre-Christian Gnosticism: A Survey of the Proposed Evidences.* Grand Rapids: Eerdmans, 1973.

Articles

Brandenburger, E. "Cross." *The New International Dictionary of NT Theology.* Edited by Colin Brown. Vol. 1. Grand Rapids: Zondervan, (1976), pp. 398–405.

Casey, R.P. "Gnosis, Gnosticism and the NT." *The Background of the NT and its Eschatology.* (In honor of Charles Harold Dodd). Edited by W.D. Davies and D. Daube. Cambridge: Cambridge University Press, (1956), pp. 52–80.

Eicken, E. von; Lidner, H.; Müller, D.; Brown, C., "Apostle." *New International Dictionary of NT Theology.* Edited by Colin Brown. Vol. 1. Grand Rapids: Zondervan, (1976), pp. 127–137.

Schippers, R. "Fullness." *The New International Dictionary of NT Theology.* Edited by Colin Brown. Vol. 1. Grand Rapids: Zondervan, (1976), pp. 728–744.

Schmitz, E.D. "Knowledge." *The New International Dictionary of NT Theology.* Edited by Colin Brown. Vol. 1. Grand Rapids: Zondervan, (1976), pp. 390–406.

Walls, A.F. "Gnosticism." *The Zondervan Pictorial Encyclopedia of the Bible.* Edited by Merrill C. Tenney. Vol. 2. Grand Rapids: Zondervan, (1975), pp. 736–739.

9. Outline

I. Introduction (1:1–14)
   A. Salutation (1:1, 2)
   B. Prayer of Thanksgiving (1:3–8)
   C. Prayer of Petition (1:9–14)

II. The Supremacy of Christ (1:15–23)
   A. The Scope of Christ's Supremacy (1:15–18)
   B. The Basis for Christ's Supremacy (1:19–23)
      1. The fullness of God in Christ (1:19)
      2. The reconciling work of Christ (1:20–23)

III. The Ministry of Paul (1:24–2:7)
   A. A Ministry of Suffering (1:24)

    B. A Ministry of Preaching (1:25–29)
    C. A Ministry of Intercession (2:1–5)
    D. A Ministry of Exhortation (2:6, 7)
 IV. Warning Against Error (2:8–23)
    A. The Error of False Philosophy (2:8–15)
      1. The warning stated (2:8)
      2. The warning justified (2:9–15)
        a. The full deity of Christ (2:9a)
        b. The real humanity of Christ (2:9b)
        c. The complete adequacy of Christ (2:10–15)
    B. The Error of Legalism (2:16, 17)
    C. The Error of Angel Worship (2:18, 19)
    D. The Error of Asceticism (2:20–23)
      1. The Christian's death to the world (2:20–22a)
      2. The human origin of ascetic restrictions (2:22b)
      3. The ineffectiveness of ascetic restrictions (2:23)
  V. Appeal for Christian Living (3:1–4:6)
    A. The Root Principle of the Christian Life (3:1–4)
      1. Seeking the things above (3:1)
      2. Setting the mind on things above (3:2)
      3. The motivations for these actions (3:3, 4)
    B. Guidelines for the Christian Life (3:5–4:6)
      1. Sins of the old life to be abandoned (3:5–11)
        a. Sins to be put to death (3:5–7)
        b. Sins to be put away (3:8)
        c. A sin to be discontinued (3:9a)
        d. The reason: the new self (3:9b–11)
      2. Virtues of the new life to be cultivated (3:12–17)
        a. Expressions of love (3:12–14)
        b. The rule of peace (3:15)
        c. The indwelling of Christ's word (3:16)
        d. The name of Christ (3:17)
      3. Family relationships to be strengthened (3:18–4:1)
        a. The wife's duty to the husband (3:18)
        b. The husband's duties to the wife (3:19)
        c. The duty of children to parents (3:20)
        d. The duty of parents to children (3:21)
        e. The duty of slaves to masters (3:22–25)
        f. The duty of masters to slaves (4:1)
      4. Religious duties to be faithfully performed (4:2–6)
        a. The duty of prayer (4:2–4)
        b. The duty of witnessing (4:5, 6)
 VI. Conclusion (4:7–18)
    A. Commendations (4:7–9)
    B. Greetings (4:10–15)
    C. Instructions (4:16, 17)
    D. Benediction (4:18)

Text and Exposition

I. Introduction (1:1–14)

A. *Salutation*

1:1, 2

¹Paul, an apostle of Christ Jesus by the will of God, and Timothy our brother,

²To the holy and faithful brothers in Christ at Colosse:

Grace and peace to you from God our Father.

Paul follows the standard form of greeting of first century letters but puts a distinctly Christian content into it. He names himself, with appropriate Christian expressions, as the author of the Epistle (v.1), identifies the readers (v.2a), and then expresses the characteristic greeting of grace and peace (v.2b).

1 In designating himself as "an apostle of Christ Jesus," Paul gives his authority for writing. The literal meaning of *apostolos* is "one sent"; but at its deepest level it denotes an authorized spokesman for God, one commissioned and empowered to act as his representative. Such is the meaning of the word when applied to the Twelve (e.g., Luke 6:13), to Barnabas (Acts 14:14), and to Paul. The word is occasionally used in the NT in the weakened sense of "messenger" (e.g., John 13:16; 2 Cor 8:23; Phil 2:25). Here, however, the term is used to designate Paul as a commissioned ambassador for Christ.

Timothy, who was with Paul at the time of writing and is here identified as a "brother" (*adelphos;* i.e., fellow Christian) of Paul, was named as a matter of courtesy. He appears to have had no part in the actual writing of the book (cf. 4:18). (It is true that the first person plural pronoun is occasionally used [1:3, 4, 9], but ordinarily the singular form is found [1:24, 25, 29; 2:1–5; 4:7–18].)

2 In the OT, holiness is ascribed not only to persons (Lev 20:7; Deut 7:6; 2 Kings 4:9, et al.), but also to places (Exod 29:31; Lev 6:16, 26; Deut 23:14; Ps 65:4, et al.) and things (Exod 28:2; 29:6; 30:25; Num 5:17, et al.). This suggests that the root idea in "holy" (*hagios*) is not excellence of character but dedication, the state of being set apart for the work and worship of God. Here the word may mark the Colossian Christians as a part of the people of God, the new Israel (cf. NEB, TCNT, TEV), though NIV does not bring out that idea. NIV, however, is truer to the Greek in retaining the adjectival force of both *hagios* ("holy") and *pistos* ("faithful").

Most commentators think "faithful" (*pistois*) should be interpreted in the sense of believing. It may, however, also imply the secondary sense of loyalty to Christ, a quality especially appropriate for a church under fire.

"Brothers" (*adelphois*), a term of affection used of Christians in every letter of Paul, calls attention to the intimacy of the fellowship of the Christian community. Despite their differences of culture, social status, and racial background, the Colossian believers were bound together by a common bond of love and thus constituted one spiritual family. The word points also to oneness of parentage. Christians are "brothers" because they are spiritually begotten by one Father.

"In Christ," a phrase used by Paul more than 160 times in various forms ("in the Lord," "in him," "in whom," etc.), emphasizes the spiritual position of believers. They are "in Christ" in the sense that they are united with Christ, joined to him as closely as limbs are joined to the body of which they are a part.

The greeting takes the form of a prayer for "grace and peace" to be given the readers. The Greek word for "grace" (*charis*), which here denotes the favor of God, is built on a root that was used of things that produce well-being. *Charis* appears 155 times in the NT, mostly in the writings of Paul. For him it expresses the essence of God's saving activity in Christ, and is not, even in a greeting such as this, to be interpreted as merely a polite cliché.

In our thinking, "peace" usually suggests, as it did for the early Greeks, the opposite of war or the absence of conflict. The NT concept, however, is richer and broader. Among the Jews the word denoted wholeness or soundness and included such ideas as prosperity, contentedness, good relations with others. In this passage spiritual prosperity is perhaps the leading thought of *eirēnē*.

Notes

1 Ἀπόστολος (*apostolos*), built on a root meaning "to send," was first used of a cargo ship or a fleet of ships. Later it denoted the commander of a naval expedition or leader of a band of colonists sent overseas. The LXX employs the word only in 1 Kings 14:6, where it is used of the commissioning and empowering of Ahijah as a messenger of God. In the NT, where the word occurs at least seventy-nine times, it regularly denotes an authorized spokesman—one clothed with the power of the one sending him and serving as his personal representative.

2 Ἅγιος (*hagios*, "holy"), though not primarily an ethical term, does (in the NT) imply a relationship with God and demands conduct that expresses and corresponds to that relationship. Persons consecrated to a God of absolute moral purity must of necessity take on something of his character.

B. *Prayer of Thanksgiving*

1:3–8

> [3]We always thank God, the Father of our Lord Jesus Christ, when we pray for you, [4]because we have heard of your faith in Christ Jesus and of the love you have for all the saints—[5]the faith and love that spring from the hope stored up for you in heaven, and which you have already heard about in the word of truth, the gospel [6]that has come to you. All over the world this gospel is producing fruit and growing, just as it has been doing among you since the day you heard it and understood God's grace in all its truth. [7]You learned it from Epaphras, our dear fellow servant, who is a faithful minister of Christ on our behalf, [8]and who also told us of your love in the Spirit.

The content of this thanksgiving is determined by the condition of the church, and by Paul's relation to it through Epaphras. In these verses we may observe the circumstances and character of the apostle's thanksgiving (v.3) as well as the grounds and occasion for it (vv.4–8). (Appeals for thanksgiving run through Colossians like the refrain of a song [cf. 1:12; 2:7; 3:15, 17; 4:2]. This passage, which expresses the apostle's own gratitude, shows that what he enjoined upon others he himself practiced.)

3 Paul addresses his thanksgiving to God, thus recognizing that he is the one responsible for the virtues and graces of his people and for the ultimate success of the gospel—both of which items are mentioned in the verses that follow.

God is identified as "the Father of our Lord Jesus Christ." At this point the Greek MSS exhibit some variety in wording, but the essential meaning is not radically affected. The suggestion in all the readings is that the God to whom we pray is the God whom Jesus Christ made known to us in his character as Father.

4,5 Verses 4-8 express the grounds and occasion of Paul's thanksgiving. The apostle specifically mentions three things, the first being the good report that had come to him of the well-being of the Colossian Christians. His reference to "hearing" of their spiritual condition is in keeping with the fact that he had not personally visited Colosse (cf. 1:9; 2:1). The source of this information was probably Epaphras (cf. v.8), though we must not rule out the possibility that Paul's reference includes other previous reports of the faith of the Colossians.

The NIV rendering of the first part of v.5 is quite free. A more literal translation is "on account of the hope ..." (*dia tēn elpida ...*). It is a question whether these words are to be construed with "We ... thank God" (v.3), with "your faith ... and ... love" (v.4), or only with "love" (v.4). In the first construction the Colossians' hope (along with their faith and love) is taken as expressing a reason for Paul's gratitude. This is the interpretation found, with some variation, in both Moffatt and Goodspeed. In the second construction, hope is interpreted as a ground for, or an incentive to, faith and love—or, as H.C.G. Moule puts it, "a grand *occasion* to develop them, and call them out into action" (p. 41). This is the interpretation expressed essentially by NIV, though it represents hope as the *source* of the Colossians' faith and love. The third construction, which is only slightly different from the second, is reflected in Weymouth. Grammatically, one can make a case for any one of these, but our preference is for the first. Whatever construction one chooses, however, it is valid to see hope as a part of the total experience of the Colossians that Paul is thanking God for.

The triad of "faith" (v.4a), "love" (v.4b), and "hope" (v.5a) appears with some degree of frequency in Paul's writings (e.g., Rom 5:2-5; 1 Cor 13:13; 1 Thess 1:3; 5:8). "Faith" (*pistis*), which is commitment to, or trust in, another person, is here defined as being "in Jesus Christ." This English phrase sometimes translates a Greek construction (*eis* with an accusative) that denotes Christ as the object on whom faith rests or toward whom it is directed. In this passage the Greek is different (*en* with a locative), pointing to Christ as *the sphere* in which faith operates. As H.C.G. Moule puts it, the phrase speaks of the Colossians' faith as "anchored" in Christ, "resting" in him (p. 37). Ellicott calls it "Christ-centered faith" (p. 112).

"Love" (*agapē*) is the fruit of faith and the proof of its genuineness (cf. Gal 5:6; James 2:14ff.; 1 John 3:14). The Greek word denotes caring love, the love that counts no sacrifice too great for the one loved. (The verb built on the same root is used in John 3:16.) The Colossians' love was expressed toward "all the saints," that is, all the people of God. Such love bespoke the warmth of their fellowship and the depth and breadth of their brotherly concern. Perhaps the apostle was contrasting the broad good will of the Colossians with the narrow exclusiveness of the heretical teachers.

"Hope" (*elpis*) may be either subjective or objective, depending on the context in which the word is found. In the former sense it indicates the emotion or the faculty of hope (e.g., Rom 5:2, 1 Cor 13:13) and suggests joyful expectancy, a sense of certainty and confidence. In its objective sense, which is its use in the present passage, "hope" denotes the thing hoped for (cf. Gal 5:5; 1 Peter 1:3). The reference then is to the glorious reward, that is, the future heavenly blessedness of the people of God.

Paul affirms two things about the hope of the Colossians. First, it is securely "stored up" for them in heaven, like a treasure. Second, the Colossians' knowledge of hope came from hearing "the word of truth," which is here defined as the gospel that had come to them. The reference is to the original proclamation of the gospel message that resulted in the Colossians' conversion. That message, preached by Epaphras, seems to be contrasted tacitly with the more recent and heretical preaching of the Colossian errorists.

6 Having mentioned the gospel as the source from which the Colossians had heard of the Christian hope, Paul is now led to develop the thought of the progress of the gospel in the world. This is brought out in such a way as to suggest that this, as well as the report of the Colossians' welfare, was for Paul a basis for thankfulness. Two ideas are stressed: First, the gospel is a fruit-bearing power wherever it is preached. Perhaps Paul means that the ever-widening scope and deepening influence of the gospel on its recipients is a mark of its authenticity. "All over the world" is not to be taken in strict literalness, as if Paul were saying that the gospel has been preached in every single place. He uses a deliberate exaggeration. Actually the gospel had spread amazingly in the years between Pentecost and the time when Paul wrote this letter and his language, though an overstatement, dramatically calls attention to this. "Producing fruit," which translates a middle voice (*karpophoroumenon*), probably points to "the inward energy of the gospel ... in its adherents" (Peake, p. 498). Lightfoot sees in this word the suggestion that "the Gospel is essentially a reproductive organism, a plant whose seed is in itself" (p. 135). The term is interpreted by TEV in the very general sense of "bringing blessings." "Growing" (*auxanomenon*) denotes the rapid spread of the gospel. Thus the two terms— "producing fruit" and "growing"—speak respectively of the inner working and the outward extension of the gospel. Nicholson, commenting on this, remarks that the gospel "is not like corn, which having borne fruit, dies, even to its roots, but like a tree, which bears fruit and at the same time continues to grow" (p. 35). The tense of both verbs is present, suggesting constant and continuing action.

Second, the gospel conveys the knowledge of "God's grace in all its truth." The phrase "in all its truth" may be intended to suggest that the "gospel" that had been recently introduced to the Colossians by the heretical teachers was a travesty. Their so-called "gospel" was not a message of divine grace; it was a system of legal bondage and human traditions.

7,8 A third item in Paul's expression of thankfulness concerns the work of Epaphras, through whom the Colossians had been instructed in the gospel. We know very little about this man. Outside of the references in this passage (vv.4, 7, 9), his name, which is a shortened form of Epaphroditus, appears only in Colossians 4:12, 13 and Philemon 23. In the former passage we learn that he was a native of Colosse and that he had ministered not only in that city but also in Laodicea and Hierapolis. In Philemon he is described by Paul as his "fellow-prisoner in the cause of Christ Jesus" (Wms). (The Epaphroditus of Philippians 2:25 and 4:18 is not to be identified with the Epaphras of Colossians. The former was a resident of the province of Macedonia; this Epaphras was a resident of the province of Asia.)

Three things are told us in this passage about Epaphras. First, he was Paul's "dear fellow servant" (v.7a). This means that he was, like Paul, a bondslave of Jesus Christ and that Paul looked upon him as a valued comrade in the work. Second, he was "a faithful minister of Christ on our [Paul's] behalf " (v.7b). The thought seems to be that Epaphras had represented Paul, that is, had preached in his stead, in establishing the work at Colosse. There is perhaps the suggestion that Epaphras was himself a convert of Paul (perhaps during the Ephesian ministry) and that Paul had delegated him to take the gospel to the Colossians. Yet as a "minister of Christ," Epaphras had acted not so much under the authority of Paul but under that of Paul's Lord. The Greek word for "minister," rendered "deacon" in Philippians 1:1 and 1 Timothy 3:8, is used here simply in the sense of "one who serves." NEB translates it "a trusted worker." Third, as a messenger from Colosse, Epaphras had communicated to Paul the fact of the Colossians' love (v.8). The reference may be to the love they had for all the people of God (cf. v.4) or to the love they had for Paul. "In the Spirit" means that it was the Spirit of God who had awakened this love in Paul's readers. (This is the only reference to the Holy Spirit in Colossians.)

There were other matters not so favorable that Epaphras must have told Paul about the Colossians, but for the moment the apostle is concerned only with "the bright features in the report" (Scott, p. 16).

Notes

7 NIV translates ὑπὲρ ἡμῶν (hyper hēmōn, "on our behalf "), the reading supported by P[46] and early Alexandrian and Western authorities. This is also the text followed by ASV, RSV, NEB, NAB, et al. The editors of the UBS text, however, prefer ὑπὲρ ὑμῶν (hyper hymōn, "on your behalf "). The former reading has superior Greek evidence but the UBS editors were impressed by "the widespread currency of ὑμῶν in versional and patristic witnesses" (B.M. Metzger, *A Textual Commentary on the Greek New Testament* [New York: United Bible Societies, 1972]). KJV, Mof, and BV represent this reading.

C. *Prayer of Petition*

1:9–14

9For this reason, since the day we heard about you, we have not stopped praying for you and asking God to fill you with the knowledge of his will through all spiritual wisdom and understanding. 10And we pray this in order that you may live a life worthy of the Lord and may please him in every way: bearing fruit in every good work, growing in the knowledge of God, 11being strengthened with all power according to his glorious might so that you may have great endurance and patience, and joyfully 12giving thanks to the Father, who has qualified you to share in the inheritance of the saints in the kingdom of light. 13For he has rescued us from the dominion of darkness and brought us into the kingdom of the Son he loves, 14in whom we have redemption, the forgiveness of sins.

To the thanksgiving of verses 3–8, the apostle adds a fervent petition. He prays that the Colossians may be so filled with the knowledge of God's will (v.9) that they may be enabled to live worthily of the Lord, pleasing him in everything (v.10a). This worthy life involves fruitfulness in every good work (v.10b), growth in (or by) the knowledge of God (v.10c), patience and long-suffering (v.11), and gratitude to God for the blessings of redemption (vv.12–14).

9 The words "for this reason" (*dia touto*), referring back to the entire discussion of vv.3–8, show that the petitionary prayer is Paul's response to the news that had come to him of the Colossians' experience in Christ. He was grateful for what had already happened to them. He prays now for the further enrichment of their lives.

The Greek word (*kai*) in the opening part of v.9 is not expressed in NIV. C.F.D. Moule construes it with the phrase "for this reason" and interprets the entire construction to mean "that is *precisely* why" or "that, in fact, is why" (p. 52). On the other hand, H.C.G. Moule connects *kai* with the pronoun "we," rendering it "we also." The meaning then is "we on our part, meeting your love with a love-prompted prayer" (p. 48). Either way, the word shows that v.9 stands in close connection with the preceding paragraph.

Paul's prayer contains two requests. The first, and the one on which the rest of the prayer is based, is that God might fill the readers with the knowledge of his will through all spiritual wisdom and understanding. Scott thinks that the apostle here "begins to touch gently on his complaint against the Colossians," namely, that with all their devotion they had failed to attain true knowledge, "mistaking windy speculations for a deeper wisdom" (p. 17).

The Greek word for "knowledge" (*epignōsis*), a compound form used in the NT only of moral and religious knowledge, has engendered considerable debate. Armitage Robinson, for instance, concludes that the simple, uncompounded form (*gnōsis*) is the wider word and denotes knowledge in "the fullest sense." The compound form used here he takes to be "knowledge directed toward a particular object" (*Epistle to the Ephesians*, p. 254). Earlier scholars, on the other hand, are inclined to see *epignōsis* as the larger and stronger word. Meyer, for example, defines it as "the knowledge which *grasps and penetrates into* the object" (p. 215). Lightfoot remarks that "it was used especially of the knowledge of God and of Christ as being the perfection of knowledge" (p. 138). The older interpreters who understand the word as denoting thorough knowledge, that is, a deep and accurate comprehension, are probably correct. Such knowledge of God's will is the foundation of all Christian character and conduct.

The will of God in its broadest and most inclusive sense is the whole purpose of God as revealed in Christ. In this passage the term perhaps has special reference to God's intention for the conduct of the Christian life.

To be "filled" with the knowledge of the divine will suggests that such knowledge is to pervade all of one's being—thoughts, affections, purposes, and plans. (The reader should be alert to the unusual emphasis on "fullness" in this Epistle. The recurrence of this idea suggests that the Colossian errorists claimed to offer a "fullness" of blessing and truth not found, they said, in the preaching of Epaphras. Paul answers by stressing the true fullness available in Christ.)

The phrase containing the words "all spiritual wisdom and understanding" is taken by some interpreters as a fuller explanation of "knowledge of his [God's] will" (cf. TEV). The thought then is that knowledge of the divine will consists or takes the form of spiritual wisdom and understanding. NIV interprets the phrase to denote the means by which we acquire knowledge of the will of God (cf. Ph, TCNT, NEB).

"Wisdom" and "understanding" probably should not be treated separately but should be looked on as expressing a single thought, something like practical wisdom or clear discernment. The use of the two words simply gives a certain fullness to the statement and thus deepens its impression on the reader.

10 Paul's second petition, that the Colossians might "live a life worthy of the Lord," is built on, and grows out of, the request for knowledge of the divine will; living a worthy life is thus represented as a result (or purpose) of knowing God's desire for one's life. This suggests that knowledge of God's will is not imparted as an end in itself; it is given with a practical intent. "The end of all knowledge, the Apostle would say, is conduct" (Lightfoot, p. 139).

"Live a life" translates a single word (*peripatēsai*) that literally means "to walk." But it is often used in Scripture to depict life in its outward expression (cf. Col 2:6; 3:7; 4:4, et al.).

To live a life "worthy of the Lord" (*axiōs tou kyriou*) probably means to live a life that is commensurate with what the Lord has done for us and is to us. It may also suggest acting in conformity with our union with Christ and with his purpose for our lives.

The ultimate aim of knowing the will of God and living a worthy life is that the readers "may please him [God] in every way" (lit., "unto all pleasing"). The Greek word for "please" (*areskō*) suggests an attitude of mind that anticipates every wish. In classical Greek it had a bad connotation, denoting, as H.C.G. Moule observes,

> a cringing and subservient habit, ready to do anything to please a patron; not only to meet but to anticipate his most trivial wishes. But when transferred to . . . the believer's relations to his Lord, the word at once rises by its associations. To do anything to meet, to anticipate His wishes is not only the most absolutely right thing we could do. It is His eternal due; it is at the same time the surest path to our own highest development and gain (*Cambridge Bible for Schools*, p. 72).

Verses 10b–14 underline some of the elements in, or constituent parts of, the kind of life that is pleasing to the Lord. The leading ideas, expressed in Greek by four participles, are rendered in English by "bearing fruit" (v.10b), "growing" (v.10c), "being strengthened" (v.11a), and "giving thanks" (v.12). Grammatically, they all modify, and express attendant circumstances of, *peripatēsai*—the word translated "live a life."

"Bearing fruit" renders a present tense (*karpophorountes*), the meaning being that the Christian life is to exhibit continual fruitfulness. The fruit itself consists in "every good work"—or, as NEB puts it, "active goodness of every kind." (Paul lays great stress on good works in his letters [cf. Eph 2:10; Gal 5:5; Titus 1:16; 2:7, 14; 3:8, 15, et al.]. But he represents them as the fruit, not the root, of a right relationship with God.)

The Christian should not only bear the fruit of good works in his life; he should at the same time experience personal spiritual enlargement. This idea is expressed in the words "growing in the knowledge of God." "Growing" (*auxanomenoi*), like "bearing fruit," represents a present tense and puts emphasis on habitual action. The preposition *in* represents the knowledge of God as the sphere or realm in which spiritual growth takes place. It is possible, however, to translate the phrase as "growing *by* the knowledge of God." When rendered like this, the text affirms that the knowledge of God is the means by which the Christian grows. What rain and sunshine are to the nurture of plants, the knowledge of God is to the growth and maturing of the spiritual life.

11 "Being strengthened with all power" expresses a third element in the life pleasing to God. Christians are engaged in moral conflict with the cosmic powers of a darkened world (cf. Eph 6:12), and nothing short of divine empowerment can enable them to stand. "Strengthened," which speaks of continuous empowerment, translates the same root word used in Philippians 4:13: "I can do everything through him who gives me strength."

This empowerment is "according to his [God's] glorious might." That is to say, it is not proportioned simply to our need, but to God's abundant supply. The Greek behind the phrase "his glorious might" (*to kratos tēs doxēs autou*) is more literally rendered "the might of his glory." Though NIV represents a legitimate interpretation, possibly we should retain the literal rendering and understand the thought to be *the might of God's own manifested nature*. In this interpretation "glory" (*doxēs*) stands for the revealed splendor or majesty of God—the sum total of his divine perfections. (Paul uses the word *glory* more than seventy times in his Epistles. Its basic meaning is physical brightness or radiance, but its exact meaning must be determined by its various contexts. In Romans 6:4 Christ is said to have been "raised from the dead through the glory of the Father.")

The twofold issue of such empowerment is "endurance and patience." The first term renders a Greek word (*hypomonēn*) denoting the opposite of cowardice and despondency. Beare defines it as "the capacity to see things through" (p. 158). The second term (*makrothymian*), translated "longsuffering" in KJV, is the opposite of wrath or a spirit of revenge. It speaks of even-temperedness, the attitude that in spite of injury or insult does not retaliate.

It is debatable whether "joyfully" (*meta charas*; lit., "with joy") should be construed with "endurance and patience" (KJV, ASV, RSV, NEB) or with "giving thanks" (NIV.) In the former construction, joy is seen as the pervading element of endurance and patience. Goodspeed renders it "the cheerful exercise of endurance and forbearance." A distinctively Christian quality (cf. Gal 5:22; Phil 1:18; 2:17; 3:1, et al.), joy is often associated in the NT with hardship and suffering.

12 The fourth ingredient, and the crowning virtue, of the worthy Christian life is gratitude. One reason for giving thanks to God is that he has "qualified" believers "to share in the inheritance of the saints." The Greek word for "qualified" (*hikanōsanti*), which basically has in it the thought of making sufficient or competent, may shade into the sense of empowering or authorizing. From its use in this passage we may conclude that in themselves believers have no fitness for sharing in the heritage of God's people. They can experience this only as God qualifies them for such a privilege. The tense of the word is aorist, pointing to the time of the Colossians' conversion. The suggestion is that the qualifying is not a process but an instantaneous act.

To "share in" the inheritance of the saints is to have a portion of the heritage belonging to God's people. There is an obvious allusion to the inheritance of ancient Israel in the Land of Promise and the share of the inheritance each Israelite had. Christians, as the new people of God, also have an inheritance, and each believer has a share allotted to him.

"In the kingdom of light" appears at first to mark the inheritance as future and heavenly (cf. TCNT). But the following verse affirms that Christians have already been rescued from the dominion of darkness and are even now in the kingdom of God's Son. H.C.G. Moule therefore rightly argues that the reference is "properly to the believer's position and possession even now. This Canaan," he explains, "is not in the distance, beyond death; it is about us today, in our home, in our family, in our business, . . . in all that makes up mortal life" (pp. 65, 66).

13 The proof that God has qualified us for a share of the inheritance of the saints is that he has "rescued us from the dominion of darkness and brought us into the kingdom of the Son he loves." "Rescued" translates *errusato*, a word that means to liberate, save, or deliver someone from something or someone; that from which Christians have been rescued is a "dominion of darkness." Luke (22:53) reports Jesus' use of the same phrase at the time of his arrest in Gethsemane. "Darkness" in Scripture is symbolic of ignorance, falsehood, and sin (cf. John 3:19; Rom 13:12). But Paul probably had the Colossian heresy in mind, because the principalities and powers to which the false teachers urged Christians to pay homage are designated by him "the powers of this dark world" (Eph 6:12).

God's action in behalf of his people does not stop with deliverance from the authority of darkness. He has also "brought" them "into the kingdom of the Son he loves." "Brought" translates *metestēsen*, a word that was used in secular literature in reference to removing persons from one country and settling them as colonists and citizens in another country. It might be rendered "reestablished." The tense of the verb points to the time of conversion. The "kingdom" (rule) is not to be interpreted eschatologically. It was for the Colossians a present reality (cf. John 3:3–5). Nor is the kingdom to be interpreted in a territorial sense. That is to say, it is not an area that may be designated on a map; it is the sovereign rule of the Lord Christ over human hearts.

"The Son he loves" translates a phrase (*tou huiou tēs agapēs autou*) that literally reads "the Son of his love." It is a Hebraic way of saying "God's dear Son." The expression is reminiscent of the words of the Father at the baptism and the transfiguration of Jesus.

14 "In whom," which has its antecedent in "the Son" (v.13), affirms that redemption and forgiveness are ours by virtue of union with Christ. "Redemption" (*apolytrōsin*), a term that speaks of a release brought about by the payment of a price, was used of the deliverance of slaves from bondage or of prisoners of war from captivity. "Emancipation" expresses the idea. "We have" teaches that the believer's redemption is a present possession.

Aphesis ("forgiveness") literally means "a sending away." It thus speaks of the removal of our sins from us, so that they are no longer barriers that separate us from God. Redemption and forgiveness are not exactly parallel or identical concepts, but by putting the two terms in apposition to each other, the apostle teaches that the central feature of redemption is the forgiveness of sins.

Notes

13 The "for" of NIV has no exact equivalent in the Gr. text. However, ὅς (*hos*, "who") in this context has a semi-argumentative—almost causal—force, and in light of this the NIV rendering is justified (cf. RHG, pp. 960–62).
14 Between ἀπολύτρωσιν (*apolytrōsin*, "redemption") and τὴν ἄφεσιν (*tēn aphesin*, "the forgiveness") the TR inserts διὰ τοῦ αἵματος αὐτοῦ (*dia tou haimatos autou*, "through his blood"). Support for this reading is quite weak, and this explains the omission of the English equivalent from versions such as ASV, RSV, and NIV. The words are genuine in Eph 1:7, where there is a thought very similar to the one expressed here.

II. The Supremacy of Christ (1:15–23)

The most dangerous aspect of the Colossian heresy was its depreciation of the person of Jesus Christ. To the errorists of Colosse, Christ was not the triumphant Redeemer to whom all authority in heaven and on earth had been committed. At best he was only one of many spirit beings who bridged the space between God and men.

This passage is a part of Paul's answer to this heretical teaching. One of several great Christological declarations in Paul (cf. 2:9–15; Eph 1:20–23; Phil 2:5–11), it proclaims the unqualified supremacy of our Redeemer. Scott says it "represents a loftier conception of Christ's person than is found anywhere else in the writings of Paul" (p. 20). The affirmations of the passage are all the more remarkable when we remember that they were written of One who only thirty years earlier had died on a Roman cross.

It is somewhat arbitrary to separate this passage from what precedes it. So imperceptibly does Paul move from prayer (vv.3–14) to exposition that it is difficult to know exactly where one leaves off and the other begins. In KJV, for instance, everything from v.9 through v.18 is treated as a single sentence. ASV places a period at the end of v.17. NIV, RSV, JB, and NAB, which begin a new sentence (and a new paragraph) with v.15, seem to represent the best construction of the passage.

A. The Scope of Christ's Supremacy

1:15–18

> ¹⁵He is the image of the invisible God, the firstborn over all creation. ¹⁶For by him all things were created: things in heaven and on earth, visible and invisible, whether thrones or powers or rulers or authorities; all things were created by him and for him. ¹⁷He is before all things, and in him all things hold together. ¹⁸And he is the head of the body, the church; he is the beginning and the firstborn from among the dead, so that in everything he might have the supremacy.

Three profound and sweeping statements concerning Christ are made. These show his relation to deity (v.15a), to creation (vv.15b–17), and to the church (v.18). In making these assertions, Paul refuted the Colossian errorists, in whose system angelic mediators usurped the place and function of Christ. His task in earlier correspondence (such as Galatians and Romans) had been to expound the importance of Christ for salvation; in the face of this new teaching at Colosse, he found it necessary to affirm Christ's cosmic significance.

15 In regard to deity, Christ is "the image of the invisible God" (cf. 2 Cor 4:4). In interpreting this statement, we must not understand the apostle to be teaching that Christ is the image of God in a material or physical sense. The true meaning must be sought on a level deeper than this. Nor should we limit the concept to one stage or period of Christ's existence. Some interpreters think Paul's primary reference is to the preincarnate Christ, and the statements of vv.15b, 16, which speak of Christ's relation to creation, do lend some support to this view. Others prefer to think the apostle had in mind the incarnate Christ in his glorified state. Peake, a proponent of this view, says the passage assumes the preexistence of the Son, but its assertions are of the exalted Christ (p. 502). In view of the uncertainty of the matter, it seems best not to limit the concept at all. Christ always has been, is, and always will be the image of God. His incarnation did not make him the image of God, but it did bring him, "as being that Image, within our grasp" (Nicholson, p. 75).

Eikōn, the Greek word for "image," expresses two ideas. One is *likeness*, a thought brought out in some of the versions (e.g., Moff., Am. Trans., Wms., and Knox). Christ is the image of God in the sense that he is the exact likeness of God, like the image on a coin or the reflection in a mirror (cf. Heb 1:3). The other idea in the word is *manifesta-*

tion. That is, Christ is the image of God in the sense that the nature and being of God are perfectly revealed in him (cf. John 1:18). Therefore Paul can boldly say that we have "the light of the knowledge of the glory of God in the face of Christ" (2 Cor 4:6) and that believers, reflecting the Lord's glory, "are being transformed into his likeness with ever-increasing glory" (2 Cor 3:18). Paul's statement leaves no place for the vague emanations and shadowy abstractions so prominent in the gnostic system.

In relation to the universe, Christ is "the firstborn over all creation." Each word of this phrase must be interpreted cautiously. "Firstborn" (*prōtotokos*) is used of Christ, in addition to the passage under study, in Colossians 1:18; Romans 8:29; Hebrews 1:6; and Revelation 1:15. (It is used also in Luke 2:7, but in a different setting.) It may denote either priority in time (cf. Moff., Am. Trans.) or supremacy in rank (NIV). In the present passage perhaps we should see both meanings. Christ is *before* all creation in time; he is also *over* it in rank and dignity. The major stress, however, seems to be on the idea of supremacy.

Some see in the word an allusion to the ancient custom whereby the firstborn in a family was accorded rights and privileges not shared by the other offspring. He was his father's representative and heir, and to him the management of the household was committed. Following this line of interpretation, we may understand the passage to teach that Christ is his Father's representative and heir and has the management of the divine household (all creation) committed to him. He is thus Lord over all God's creation.

16,17 The apostle now states the ground for Christ's dominion over creation: he is firstborn (Lord) over creation *because he made it.* To him it owes its unity, its meaning, indeed its very existence.

Three prepositional phrases define the creative activity of Christ: All things came to be "in [NIV, by] him" (v.16a), "through [NIV, by] him" (v.16b) and "for him" (v.16c). Creation was "in [*en*] him" in the sense that it occurred within the sphere of his person and power. He was its conditioning cause, its originating center, its spiritual locality. The act of creation rested, as it were, in him. Creation is "through" (*dia*) Christ in the sense that he was the mediating Agent through whom it actually came into being. The preposition is frequently used of Christ's redemptive mediation between God and men (cf. Eph 2:18; 1 Thess 5:9, et al.), but the thought here is that the entire life of the universe is mediated from God through Christ (cf. John 1:3, 10). Creation is "for" (*eis*) Christ in the sense that he is the end for which all things exist, the goal toward whom all things were intended to move. They are meant "to serve His will, to contribute to His glory. . . . Their whole being, willingly or unwillingly, moves . . . to Him; whether, as His blissful servants, they shall be as it were His throne; or as His stricken enemies, 'His footstool' " (H.C.G. Moule, p. 78).

"All things," used twice in the verse, translates an expression (*ta panta*) that was sometimes used in the sense of our word "universe." It denoted the totality of things in heaven and on earth, visible and invisible. The reference to "thrones," "powers," "rulers," and "authorities" is perhaps an allusion to the angelic hierarchy that figured so prominently in the Colossian heresy. Paul's mention of these things does not, of course, mean that he recognized the existence of a hierarchy of spirit beings. His words do suggest, however, that whatever supernatural powers there may be, Christ is the One who made them and he is their Lord.

17 Verse 16 has stated the essential reason for Christ's lordship over creation, namely, that he is its creator. Verse 17 is a sort of summing up of the thought of vv.15, 16. But in addition, it rounds out and completes the statement of Christ's relation to creation. "He is before all things, and in him all things hold together." That Christ is "before" all things means primarily that he is before all *in time;* however, the statement is general enough to include also the notion that he is above all in rank. The thought is similar to that of the earlier expression, "firstborn over all creation" (v.15b).

That all things "hold together" in Christ means that he is both the unifying principle and the personal sustainer of all creation. It springs from him and finds in him its common bond and center. He is, to use the words of Lightfoot, "the principle of cohesion" who makes the universe "a cosmos instead of a chaos" (p. 156; cf. Heb 1:3).

18 Paul's third affirmation concerning Christ's supremacy relates to the new creation: "And he is the head of the body, the church" (v.18a; cf. 2:19; Eph 1:22, 23; 4:15). To be the "head" of the church is to be its sovereign. In the figure there may also be the suggestion that Christ is the source of the church's life, but this is not its primary significance. Christ, as Head of the church, is its Chief, its Leader. It is he who guides and governs it. "He" is emphatic, the meaning being that Christ alone—Christ and no other—is Head of the church.

"Church" (*ekklēsia*), which means "assembly" or "congregation," is best interpreted here as a term embracing all the redeemed people of God. The mention of the church as "the body" of Christ suggests at least three things: (1) that the church is a living organism, composed of members joined vitally to one another, (2) that the church is the means by which Christ carries out his purposes and performs his work, and (3) that the union that exists between Christ and his people is most intimate and real. Together they constitute one living unit, each, in a sense, being incomplete without the other.

Verse 18b gives one ground of Christ's headship over the church: "He is the beginning and the firstborn from among the dead." In the Greek the first word is a relative pronoun (*hos*), and in this context is almost equivalent to "because he is" (cf. Moff., and see notes on v.13). The word *beginning* may be interpreted in any one of three ways: as referring to (1) supremacy in rank, (2) precedence in time, or (3) creative initiative. There is, of course, truth in each of these, but it seems best to see in Paul's word the idea of creative initiative. The meaning then is that Christ is the origin and source of the life of the church, the fount of its being (cf. NEB).

"Firstborn" (*prōtotokos*), which in the Greek text is in apposition with "beginning," defines more precisely what Paul means. This term was used earlier (v.15) to point up Christ's relation to creation, and we concluded that it suggested both precedence in time and supremacy in rank. In the present passage the idea of precedence is the more prominent. Thus, the meaning is that Christ was the first to come from the dead in true resurrection life (i.e., never to die again, cf. 1 Cor 15:20). And because he was the first to be born from the dead, he possesses in himself the new and higher life that his people, by virtue of their union with him, now share. Thus, his being the firstborn from the dead is that which establishes his place as the beginning, the origin of the church's life.

The idea of sovereignty, however, is not entirely absent from this passage. Because Christ was the first to be born from the dead, he has the dignity and sovereignty belonging to the Firstborn. Peake, who is a proponent of this view, interprets the passage to mean that "from among the dead [Christ] has passed to his throne, where he reigns as the living Lord" (p. 507).

"So that in everything he might have the supremacy" in one sense is a summary of all that Paul has affirmed from v.15 to this point, but syntactically it must be seen as expressing the purpose of the immediately preceding statement about Christ's being the beginning, the firstborn from the dead. He rose from the dead in order that his preeminence might become universal, extending both to the old creation and to the new. He had always been first, but by his resurrection he entered upon an even wider and more significant sovereignty (cf. Acts 2:26; Rom 1:4).

The word for "he" (*autos*) is normally not expressed in Greek because it is implied in the personal ending of the verb. Here, however, it is expressed, suggesting that preeminence is the exclusive right of Christ. "He himself" or "he alone" is the idea. "Have supremacy" literally means "have the first place"; or perhaps better still, "become first." C.F.D. Moule takes the whole phrase to mean: " 'that he might be alone supreme among all'—sole head of all things" (p. 70).

Notes

15–20 Much scholarly debate has centered on these verses, and it is often asserted that they contain material not composed by the author of Colossians. The discussions offer a bewildering variety of theories, among which are those that see in the passage a formula emanating from the Hellenistic Jewish synagogue and praising the divine Word or Wisdom, those that claim it was a Gnostic hymn celebrating the authority of the World Ruler over the powers of the cosmos, and those that view it as a pre-Pauline Christian hymn incorporated by the apostle into Colossians. My position is that the passage is genuinely Pauline and, whether hymnic or not, presents a true and exalted view of Christ. Brief but helpful critiques of the various theories may be found in Caird (pp. 174–78) and Martin (pp. 40–55).

15 A superficial reading of the KJV ("of all creation") might lead one to conclude that Christ is a part of creation, the first of God's created beings. Such a reading of the phrase, however, is not in keeping with the context, which in the sharpest manner distinguishes Christ from creation. Nor is that understanding of the phrase demanded by the grammar. κτίσεως (*ktiseōs*, "creation") might be construed either as an ablative of comparison ("before creation") or as a genitive. In the latter case, it is either a genitive of reference ("with reference to creation") or an objective genitive ("over creation"), which is the NIV interpretation. Peake points out that in LXX πρωτότοκος (*prōtotokos*, "firstborn") in some instances had altogether lost its temporal significance. He questions whether the word retains any of its temporal sense in this passage.

16 Ἐν (*en*) may here have in it both the ideas of sphere ("in," ASV) and of agency ("by," NIV), but the former is perhaps the more prominent in this verse. The notion of agency is expressed by διά (*dia*) in the latter part of the verse.

The tenses of the verbs are significant: ἐκτίσθη (*ektisthē*, "were created"), an aorist, points to a particular time and views creation as a definite act; ἔκτισται (*ektistai*, "have been created"; NIV, "were created"), a perfect tense, represents creation as a resultant state. "Stand created" might be an apt rendering for the latter form.

17, 18 The contrast in verbs must not be overlooked. Christ *is* (ἐστιν [*estin*], present tense) first in reference to all creation; his resurrection made it possible for him to *become* (γένηται [*genētai*], aorist tense) first with respect to the church (cf. Phil 2:9–11).

B. The Basis for Christ's Supremacy

1:19–23

> 19For God was pleased to have all his fullness dwell in him, 20and through him to reconcile to himself all things, whether things on earth or things in heaven, by making peace through his blood, shed on the cross.

²¹Once you were alienated from God and were enemies in your minds because of your evil behavior. ²²But now he has reconciled you by Christ's physical body through death to present you holy in his sight, without blemish and free from accusation— ²³if you continue in your faith, established and firm, not moved from the hope held out in the gospel. This is the gospel that you heard and that has been proclaimed to every creature under heaven, and of which I, Paul, have become a servant.

Paul has ascribed unique supremacy to Jesus Christ. He has affirmed him to be Image of God, Lord over creation, Head of the church—indeed, preeminent in all things. Verses 19–23 state the grounds—observe the first word of v.19—on which such supremacy is affirmed.

The last phrase of v.18 implies that Christ has unshared supremacy because God has decreed it. "It was," as Calvin says, "so arranged in the providence of God" (p. 154). The present passage states this in different terms, but still puts it within the context of the divine will. Two things that God willed are specifically set forth, one having to do with the fullness of God in Christ (v.19), the other with the reconciling work of Christ (vv.20–23).

1. The fullness of God in Christ (1:19)

19 The subject of the verb translated "was pleased" is uncertain. Some take it to be "Christ." Lightfoot calls this view "grammatically possible" but thinks "it confuses the theology of the passage hopelessly" (p. 159). Others construe the subject to be "fullness" (cf. Moff., Am. Trans., RSV, PH). The NIV understands the passage as affirming an action of God. *God willed* that in Christ all fullness should dwell.

The word for "fullness" (*plērōma*), which Scott calls "perhaps the most difficult" in the Epistle (p. 25), is the focal point of much discussion. The term is found about seventeen times in the NT, but there are only four places in which the meaning is parallel to that of the present passage (Eph 1:23; 3:19; 4:13; Col 2:9). The word seems to have been in current use by the false teachers, and was possibly, though not certainly, employed by them of the totality of supernatural powers ("aeons") that they believed were in control of men's lives. Calvin understands Paul to use it of "fulness of righteousness, wisdom, power, and every blessing," explaining that "whatever God has he has conferred upon his Son" (p. 154). Peake, following Meyer, Eadie, Alford, and others, interprets "fullness" to mean "the fulness of grace, 'the whole charismatic riches of God'" (p. 508; cf. John 1:14). He understands the whole statement "as having reference to the sending of the Son in the incarnation. The Father was pleased that He should come 'with the whole treasure of Divine grace'" (p. 508).

Others interpret "fullness" as a reference to Deity. C.F.D. Moule, for instance, explains it to mean "God in all his fullness," that is, "all that God is" (p. 70). Phillips renders it "the full nature of God"; NEB, "the complete being of God." Lightfoot paraphrases it, "the totality of Divine powers and attributes" (p. 159), the suggestion being that nothing of deity is lacking in Christ. The similar expression found in Colossians 2:9 lends support to this view.

It is significant that Paul says "all" the fullness dwells in Christ. The Colossian errorists perhaps looked upon the many spirit beings they thought of as filling the space between God and the world as intermediaries and taught that any communication between God and the world had to pass through them. They probably included Christ among these supernatural powers, admitting that he was of heavenly origin and that God was in some sense present in him. He was, however, only one aspect of the divine nature and in himself was not sufficient for all the needs of men. Paul, in contrast, declares that Christ is not just one of many divine beings. He is the one Mediator between God and the world, and all, not part, of the attributes and activities of God are centered in him.

"Dwell" translates *katoikēsai*, a verb that suggests permanent residence as opposed to temporary sojourn. Lightfoot thinks Paul was refuting a Colossian notion that the divine fullness had only a transient and incidental association with Christ. In distinction from this, the apostle asserts that it abides in him permanently.

2. The reconciling work of Christ (1:20–23)

20 The Father was pleased "to reconcile to himself all things" through Christ. This statement sustains a close connection with v.19. For one thing, the Greek word for "to reconcile" (*apokatallaxai*) is parallel with the word for "dwell" (v.19), both terms being grammatically dependent on the verb rendered "was pleased" (*eudokēsen*) (v.19). The Father willed that all fullness should dwell in Christ; he also willed to reconcile all things to himself through Christ. "Reconcile," the essential meaning of which is "to change" (from enmity to friendship), suggests the effecting in man of a condition of submission to, and harmony with, God (cf. Rom 5:10, 11; 2 Cor 5:18–20; Eph 2:14, 15). The Greek verb, a double compound form, probably has intensive force: to change completely, to change so as to remove all enmity.

This work of reconciliation is on the widest possible scale, having to do with "all things." Calvin limits "things in heaven" to angels. H.C.G. Moule interprets it similarly but admits that reconciliation affects the angelic world "in a sense as yet known only to the Lord" (p. 88). It is perhaps better to understand the word *heaven* as an inclusive term taking in everything not belonging to the "earth"—perhaps what is sometimes called the "starry heavens." "Things on earth . . . things in heaven" thus denotes everything in God's universe.

One must be careful not to interpret this in such a way as to make it contradict the clear teaching of other Scriptures. Admittedly, the statement might appear, on its surface, to indicate that eventually everything will be brought into a saving relationship with God. Such universalism, however, is contrary to those passages that affirm that apart from personal trust in Christ there is no salvation. Our Lord, in fact, spoke of the impenitent as going away into "eternal punishment" (Matt 25:46). We should therefore understand this statement to be a reference to the cosmic significance of Christ's work, the thought being similar to, but not identical with, that of Romans 8:19–22. There the general sense is that the disorder that has characterized creation will be done away and divine harmony restored. Here perhaps the main idea is that all things eventually are to be decisively subdued to God's will and made to serve his purposes.

21 Verse 20 has presented the general aspect of the reconciling work of Christ ("all things . . ."). Verses 21–23 show how this applies personally and specifically to the Colossians. Prior to their conversion to Christianity they had been "alienated from God," "enemies" in their minds. The former word (*apēllotriōmenous*), which literally means "transferred to another owner," speaks of estrangement from God. The perfect tense of the Greek word denotes a fixed state or condition. The latter word ("enemies" [*echthrous*]) affirms the Colossians' hostility to God. This hostility, Paul explains, affected their

"minds" (*dianoia;* lit., "thought," "disposition," "attitude") and was outwardly expressed in their "evil behavior" (*ergois tois ponērois;* lit., "wicked deeds").

22 God reconciled the Colossians "by Christ's physical body through death." "Physical body" renders *sōmati tēs sarkos* (lit., "body of flesh"). Perhaps Paul deliberately used this rather redundant expression to emphasize (in contradiction to the views of the heretics) the reality of Christ's body. Peake understands Paul to be alluding to and answering "the false spiritualism" of the Colossian heretics. Asserting that reconciliation could be accomplished only by spiritual (angelic) beings, they attached little or no value to the work of Christ in a physical body. In opposition to this, Paul stressed the importance of Christ's physical body.

The result of Christ's reconciling work is the presentation of the Colossians "holy in his sight, without blemish and free from accusation." Some interpreters, perhaps most, take these words as a description of a yet-future presentation to God (at the Judgment Day). And this is the view this passage seems naturally to suggest. There are, however, a number of scholars (e.g., Lightfoot and Beare) who see it as a statement of what God through Christ had already done for the Colossians. In reconciling them, he brought them into his presence, no longer as unhallowed, stained by sin, and bearing the burden of guilt; but "holy" and "without blemish and free from accusation." So the reference is to the standing effected for the believer at the time of and by the death of Christ.

Bruce presents a view in which there is a balance between the present and the future: "The sentence of justification passed upon the believer here and now anticipates the pronouncement of the judgment day; the holiness which is progressively wrought in his life by the Spirit of God here and now is to issue in perfection of glory on the day of Christ's parousia" (p. 213).

"Holy" suggests consecration and dedication (see the discussion of v.2). "Without blemish," which translates a technical sacrificial term (*amōmous*), was used of animals that were without flaw and therefore worthy of being offered to God. The use of this word gives support to the view that in this statement Paul was not thinking about our personal conduct but about our position in Christ. There has never been, nor will there ever be, a Christian life that is without blemish in actual conduct. But Christians' identification with Christ is such that his righteousness and his standing before God are theirs (2 Cor 5:21; 1 John 4:17).

"Free from accusation," like the other two terms, expresses a condition possible only because men are in Christ, covered by and sharing in the benefits of his death for them.

23 Some interpreters, especially some of those who understand the foregoing words as a description of the believers' presentation before God at the time of judgment, explain v.23 as a warning against indolence and complacency. The Colossians, they understand Paul to say, will be thus presented to God only "if [they] continue in [their] faith, established and firm," and so forth. Bruce comments, "If the Bible teaches the final perseverance of the saints, it also teaches that the saints are those who finally persevere —in Christ. Continuance is the test of reality" (p. 213).

Those who take v.22 to be a statement of accomplished fact contend that the words of v.23 are *proof* of a past (and continuing) experience, not a condition of what is future. "No reference," affirms Nicholson, "is here made to the future, no doubt of any kind is insinuated, no threatening danger is implied. The apostle's purpose is simply to state the absolute accomplishment of salvation in the past sufferings of Christ, and the demonstration of it which is furnished to an individual soul in the present existence of his faith" (p. 122).

It is significant for both interpretations that the condition is stated in such a way as to express the apostle's confidence in his readers. "The Greek," writes Radford, "indicates not an uncertain prospect but a necessary condition and an almost certain assumption. . . . Paul is at once insistent and confident; they must [continue], and he is sure that they will" (p. 194).

"Faith" may denote a body of doctrine, but perhaps here, as usual in the NT, it means personal faith, that is, reliance on Christ. Therefore, instead of "the faith" (KJV, ASV, RSV), it should read "your faith" (NIV, NEB). The words that follow "faith" explain what is involved in continuance in faith, namely, being "established and firm, not moved from the hope held out in the gospel." "Established" suggests being founded securely, as on a rock. "Firm" (lit., "settled") depicts a steady and firm resolve.

The "hope held out in the gospel" is in its fullest sense the expectation of ultimate, complete salvation that will belong to believers upon the return of their Lord. There may be an implicit contrast between the certainty of the gospel and the delusive promises offered by the Colossian errorists.

In the closing words of v.23 three statements are made to stress the importance of remaining true to the apostolic gospel: (1) It is the message "that you heard." The reference is to the gospel that had been initially preached to them by Epaphras (cf. 1:7) and was the instrument of their conversion. (2) It has been "proclaimed to every creature under heaven." Its universality is a mark of its authenticity. C.F.D. Moule suggests that the statement does not mean that the gospel had been preached to every individual, but that it had been "heard in all the great centers of the Empire (cf. Rom 15:19–23)" (p. 73). Bruce suggests that Paul was "perhaps indulging in a prophetic prolepsis" (p. 213). Obviously there is an element of hyperbole in the statement. (3) Paul closes with the affirmation that he himself had "become a servant" of the gospel. Paul does not designate himself in this fashion for the purpose of magnifying his office, but to impress on the Colossians that the gospel heard by them from Epaphras and proclaimed in all the world, was the same gospel he preached.

Notes

19 Πλήρωμα (plērōma, "fullness") was a technical term used by second-century Gnostics of the hierarchy of the supernatural beings lying between God and the world. Many present-day scholars think it likely that the word was employed in this sense during Paul's lifetime. We cannot deny that the Colossian errorists made use of the term or that it bore some relation to gnosticism, but only with great caution can we assert that at this early time it contained the connotations of later fully developed Gnostic systems.

The tense of κατοικῆσαι (katoikēsai; NIV, "dwell") is aorist, perhaps having ingressive force and meaning "take up lasting abode." Whether the reference to "taking up" abode marks an action belonging to eternity or to time has been debated. For instance, Findlay argues for the resurrection-ascension of Jesus as the event when the fullness came to reside in the Son. Eph 1:20–23 and 4:8–10 are cited as confirmation of this interpretation. H.C.G. Moule feels that the context points to a time-act, but he adds that in a very real sense the fullness "is eternally in the Son; it does not take up its abode in Him as if it had to begin" (p. 87). Macphail, on the other hand, thinks that the grand sweep of the passage is an argument for taking the term in its widest possible range and understanding an eternal residence of the divine fullness to be meant. This is the view to be preferred. In it the aorist tense may be interpreted not as ingressive but as constative, serving to sum up in a single point the whole action.

22 There is considerable uncertainty about v.22—both the text and the punctuation. Most MSS read ἀποκατήλλαξεν (*apokatēllaxen*, "he reconciled"), though a few have ἀποκατηλλάγητε (*apokatēllagēte*, "you were reconciled"). The passive was preferred by the editors of UBS text (2nd ed.), but the third edition has the active.

Lightfoot makes v.22a (νυνὶ ... θανάτου, *nuni ... thanatou*, "now ... death") a parenthesis and understands παραστῆσαι (*parastēsai*, "to present," v.22b) to be dependent on εὐδόκησεν (*eudokēsen*, "was pleased," v.19). Peake puts a comma at the end of v.20, a period at the end of v.21; ὑμᾶς (*hymas*, "you," v.21) is then the object of ἀποκαταλλάξαι (*apokatallaxai*, "to reconcile," v.20).

III. The Ministry of Paul (1:24–2:7)

This passage, which is somewhat parallel to Ephesians 3:1ff., comes as a sort of digression. Though decidedly autobiographical, it is not so much concerned with Paul the man as with the office he filled. In the course of his discussion, Paul mentions his suffering and its bearing on the Colossians (1:24), his commission to preach and its implications for them (1:25–29), and his personal interest in and concern for them (2:1–5). The passage closes with a direct appeal to the Colossians (2:6, 7).

A. A Ministry of Suffering

1:24

24Now I rejoice in what was suffered for you, and I fill up in my flesh what is still lacking in regard to Christ's afflictions, for the sake of his body, which is the church.

24 This is a much-disputed verse, but the general sense of it is clear. In it the apostle teaches that the sufferings he endured in the course of his work were in the interest of the Colossians, indeed, of the whole church, and in the knowledge of that, he is able to rejoice (cf. Eph 3:13).

"Now" may possibly be both temporal and transitional in force. In its temporal sense, the word indicates that Paul's joy and his suffering were both realities at the time of writing this letter. There may be a note of emphasis in the word (*nun*), viz., "just now, at this very moment." In its transitional sense "now" shows that this paragraph is closely related to the thought of the preceding section, in which Christ's unique supremacy has been expounded. Looked at in this manner, the term is almost equivalent to "therefore" and shows that the thought of Christ's supremacy is a factor in Paul's ability to rejoice in the midst of suffering.

Three things are said in the verse about the sufferings of Paul: First, they are for the sake of other people. The apostle speaks of suffering "for you" and "for the sake of his [Christ's] body." In both phrases the preposition means not "in place of " but "in the interest of." The first phrase alludes to the fact that Paul's bonds and imprisonment had been incurred in the course of bringing the gospel to the Gentiles, to which class the Colossians belonged. The sufferings, therefore, were for their sake in the sense that they shared in the benefit of the ministry that brought on those sufferings. The second phrase affirms that the benefit of Paul's sufferings extends not simply to the Colossians, nor to the Gentile portion of the church only; they in some sense have a bearing on the whole body of Christ. Indeed, the apostle's sufferings contribute even to our well-being, for had he not suffered imprisonment, this letter might never have been written, and we would have been deprived of its message.

Second, Paul's sufferings are identified with the afflictions of Christ. "I fill up in my flesh what is still lacking in regard to Christ's afflictions." These words have evoked a great amount of discussion. Many Roman Catholics, for instance, interpreting the "afflictions" of Christ as Christ's redemptive sufferings, have used this verse as grounds for asserting that Christ's atonement is defective and that the sufferings of the saints are needed to supplement his work on our behalf. But whatever is meant by "what is still lacking in regard to Christ's afflictions," we may be sure that Paul did not regard the death of Jesus as lacking in efficacy (cf. Col 2:11-15). That death was complete, once for all, and wholly adequate to meet man's need. The Roman doctrine, as Lightfoot says, can be imported into this passage only "at the cost of a contradiction to the Pauline doctrine" of the satisfaction of Christ's sacrifice (p. 167).

In Lightfoot's interpretation, the afflictions of Christ are those endured personally by him on earth, but he insists that the reference is to Christ's ministerial afflictions, not his mediatorial redemptive sufferings. The word "afflictions" (*thlipseōn*), he explains, is never employed elsewhere in the NT of the sufferings of Christ on the cross; the reference, then, is to the tribulations our Lord endured in the course of his life and ministry. The sufferings his people endure are a continuation of what he endured, and in that sense they complete his afflictions. "It is a simple matter of fact," writes Lightfoot, "that the afflictions of every saint and martyr do supplement the afflictions of Christ. The Church is built up by repeated acts of self-denial in successive individuals and successive generations. They continue the work which Christ began" (p. 166).

The underlying principle is the believer's union with Christ. That union is so intimate —Christ the Head, his people the body—that he suffers when they suffer (cf. Isa 63:9). His personal sufferings are over, but his sufferings in his people continue (cf. 2 Cor 1:5; Phil 3:10). Perhaps Paul was thinking of Christ's words to him on the Damascus road (Acts 9:4, 5).

"What is still lacking" is not an intimation of deficiency in Christ's own sufferings but a reference to what is yet lacking in Christ's suffering *in Paul.* In his experience as a prisoner the apostle was filling up the sum or quota of suffering yet remaining for him to endure.

Third, they are the sphere of Paul's joy. The sufferings Paul endured for the gospel seem never to have been to him a source of perplexity or of sadness. "You may," writes MacPhail, "occasionally hear the clang of the Roman chain, but you never hear a groan from the brave prisoner" (p. 49).

Paul's attitude had nothing in common with those ascetics of a later time who inflicted torture on themselves in the belief that they would thereby gain merit with God. Paul's joy was not in suffering as such, but in "what was suffered *for you.*" That is to say, it was the distinctive character and circumstances of his sufferings that enabled him to find joy in the midst of them. He saw them as a necessary part of his ministry and knew that they were incurred in the line of duty. (For other NT references to the theme of joy in the face of suffering, see Matthew 5:12; Acts 5:41; Hebrews 10:34.)

B. *A Ministry of Preaching*

1:25-29

25I have become its servant by the commission God gave me to present to you the word of God in its fullness— 26the mystery that has been kept hidden for ages and generations, but is now disclosed to the saints. 27To them God has chosen

to make known among the Gentiles the glorious riches of this mystery, which is Christ in you, the hope of glory.
[28]We proclaim him, counseling and teaching everyone with all wisdom, so that we may present everyone perfect in Christ. [29]To this end I labor, struggling with all the energy he so powerfully works in me.

A second feature of Paul's ministry was the proclamation of God's message. His statement concerning this is of great value to all who wish a better understanding of preaching. The thought revolves around four conceptions: Paul's appointment to the office of preacher (v.25), the message he preached (vv.25b–28a), the method he employed (v.28b), and his ultimate aim (vv.28c–29).

25 Elsewhere Paul speaks of himself as a minister of the gospel (v.23; Eph 3:7), of God (2 Cor 6:4), of Christ (2 Cor 11:23), of a new covenant (2 Cor 3:6). Here he is the church's minister, and as such is bound to toil and suffer in whatever way the church's welfare requires. Suffering is not, then, simply a matter of joy (v.24) but of duty as well. "I" (*egō*), expressed in Greek for emphasis, suggests that Paul was thinking of a ministry peculiar to himself. The word for "minister" (*diakonos*), the same as that used earlier of Epaphras (1:7) and of Paul (1:23), simply means "one who serves."

Paul's appointment to his office was "by the commission God gave" him—literally, "according to the dispensation [arrangement] of God." "Commission" is a free rendering of the word *oikonomian*, which has a rather wide range of meanings. "Plan," "arrangement," "stewardship," "management," "administration,"—these are all possible meanings. The KJV and ASV here translate it "dispensation"; Am. Trans. has "divine appointment"; RSV, "divine office." "Dispensation" ("arrangement") suggests that Paul looked upon his call to the ministry as part of the divine plan for the evangelization of the world; *oikonomia* is in fact sometimes used in Scripture for the plan by which God has ordered the course of history (cf. Eph 1:10, RSV). But *oikonomia*, related to our words "economy" and "economics," is perhaps best rendered here by "stewardship" (cf. Luke 16:2–4). This rendering suggests that Paul conceived of the work to which God appointed him as both a high privilege and a sacred trust (cf. Williams, TCNT, JB). He was a servant of the church, but in the deepest sense he was a steward of God.

The purpose of the apostle's stewardship was "to present the word of God in all its fullness." Some understand this to refer to the geographical extension of the gospel (cf. Rom 15:19). But Paul probably means that his special ministry was to make clear the true nature of the gospel as a divine provision intended for all people.

26 The preceding verse has spoken of Paul's message as "the word of God," a general term that sums up the oral proclamation of the apostles. Verses 26, 27 define the word of God more specifically in terms of a "mystery." A word borrowed from the religious vocabulary of the day, "mystery" (*mystērion*) is used in the NT of truth undiscoverable except by divine revelation (cf. 1 Cor 2:6ff.; 14:51). In Ephesians it is used six times—more often than in any other book of the NT. In 1:9 the term is used of the mystery of God's dealing with the world; in 3:3–9, where it occurs three times, the word has special reference to the inclusion of Gentiles in the privileges and blessings of the messianic salvation; in 5:22 it speaks of the spiritual union of Christ and his church; and in 6:19 it is practically equated with the gospel. In Colossians the word occurs four times (1:26, 27; 2:2; 4:3). Coming from a root that means to initiate, *mystērion* in a general sense denotes a secret. In its various contexts in the NT, however, it ordinarily speaks of an "open secret"; that is, it denotes something that, though once a secret, has now been fully revealed in the gospel.

This mystery, Paul explains, "has been kept hidden for ages and generations, but is now disclosed to his saints." The words express the two characteristics of a mystery in the NT: "hidden for ages and generations . . . now disclosed."

Some interpreters understand "ages" to refer to the ages before the creation of the world; "generations," to the generations of human history. The whole expression is thus equivalent to a declaration that the mystery had been previously concealed from both angels and men. NIV suggests that "ages" and "generations" are used generally to refer to people living in former times. This is perhaps the better interpretation.

To the people of God ("the saints") the truth that was once hidden is now "disclosed." The Greek construction is grammatically irregular, involving a change from a participle ("has been kept hidden," first part of v.26) to an indicative verb ("disclosed," last part of the verse). The sudden shift from participle to indicative may be a reflection of "Paul's intense joy that the long silence has been broken; he is content with nothing short of a definite statement of the glorious fact" (Peake, p. 516).

27 The thought is that God was pleased to reveal to his people how great is the glorious character of the gospel mystery (lit., "the riches of the glory of this mystery"). Paul's frequent use of "riches" suggests that Christ had "opened the door for him to an inexhaustible treasure of goodness (Rom 2:4), glory (Rom 9:23; Eph 1:18; 3:16; Phil 4:19), wisdom (Rom 11:33), and grace (Eph 1:7; 2:7), and every time he explores it he finds something new to take his breath away" (Caird, p. 186). Scott, observing that "glory" in Paul's writings "carries with it the idea of something divine," thinks the whole phrase suggests "richness in divine significance" (p. 33). "Among [lit., in] the Gentiles" defines the sphere in which the wealth of glory has been especially displayed. Paul seems to have been thinking of the wonder of the unfolding of the divine mystery in the conversion of pagan people and in their being drawn into the one body of Christ.

The inner content of the mystery is defined as "Christ in you." (Cf. vv.25, 26, where the mystery is defined as the gospel.) Some scholars read "Christ among you," that is, among you Gentiles (cf. Lightfoot). If the words are understood in this fashion, the mystery consists in the offer of redemption to the Gentiles. They had appeared to be forever excluded from God's favor, but it had been a part of God's secret plan from the beginning that they should be included in the messianic salvation. There is much to be said for this interpretation, but the context requires that we understand the phrase as referring to an inner, subjective experience. The mystery, therefore, long hidden but now revealed is not the diffusion of the gospel among the Gentiles but the indwelling of Christ in his people, whether Jews or Gentiles.

Christ in you is now declared to be "the hope of glory." "Hope" is joyous expectation or anticipation. "Glory" is that which will belong to the Christian in the heavenly state (cf. 3:4; Rom 5:2; 8:17). The general truth is that Christ dwelling in the believer is the ground for certainty of complete salvation. A kindred notion is found in Ephesians 1:13, 14, where the Spirit is designated as "the earnest of our inheritance." In this letter "Christ himself occupies the sphere that Paul elsewhere assigns to the Spirit" (Beare, p. 181).

28 In v.25 Paul has defined his message as "the word of God." In vv.26, 27 he has used the term *mystery*. Here his message is shown to center in the Christ who indwells believers. At the deepest level, therefore, the apostle conceived of his message not as a system or as a collection of rules and regulations, but as a living and glorious Person who is the fulfillment of the deepest hopes of mankind and the source of new life for all his people. "We" is emphatic (like "I" in vv.23, 25) and distinguishes Paul (and his fellow preachers) from the Colossian errorists. "Proclaim" translates *katangellomen*, a word suggesting a solemn or public proclamation. Scholars of an earlier period (e.g., Westcott, Vincent) thought there was in it the notion of proclaiming with authority. Schniewind, who speaks of it as belonging to the "language of mission," asserts that the term includes the idea of "instruction, admonition and tradition" (TDNT, 1:71, 72). It perhaps has a wider significance than the more common word for "preach" (*kērusso*) in Paul's writings (cf. v.23).

"Counseling" (*nouthetountes*) and "teaching" (*didaskontes*) describe two attendant circumstances of Paul's preaching. The former word, used in the Pauline Epistles eight times and only once elsewhere in the NT (Acts 20:31), has to do with the will and emotions and connotes warning. Here it relates to non-Christians, the thought probably being that the apostle sought to awaken each of them to his need of Christ. Some interpreters think the word corresponds to the demand for repentance in the Gospels. "Teaching," which probably refers to a ministry for converts, stresses the importance of instruction in proclaiming the Word. "With all wisdom" seems to express the way the teaching was done.

"Everyone," stated twice in v.28 for emphasis (three times in the Greek text), shows that Paul's gospel was not marred by the exclusiveness that characterized the false teachers. They believed the way of salvation to be so involved that it could be understood only by a select few who made up a sort of spiritual aristocracy. Unlike the errorists, Paul slighted no one. Every person was the object of his direct concern.

The aim of Paul's proclaiming, admonishing, and teaching was to "present everyone perfect in Christ." "Present" (*paristēmi*) refers to the bringing into God's presence at the return of Christ (cf. 1 Thess 2:19–20; 5:23). Only then will God's work in the believer be complete. "Perfect" suggests attainment of the proper end of one's existence. Other versions use such terms as "complete" (NAB), "full grown" (Montgomery), "mature" (RSV). The reference is to maturity in faith and character (cf. Eph 4:13), and it is a prospect held out for "everyone." Such maturity is possible "in Christ," that is, by virtue of the believer's union with Christ.

29 To accomplishing this end Paul gave himself unstintedly. "I labor" translates *kopiō*, a word denoting wearisome toil. Weymouth expresses it, "I exert all my strength." "Struggling" renders the word *agōnizomenos*, which our familiar English "agonize" transliterates. A term from the athletic arena, it signifies intense exertion. This struggle, Paul affirms, is "according to his [God's] working" (*kata tēn energeian autou*). That is to say, the struggle is carried on, not through Paul's own natural powers, but by the supernatural power at work in him. "Working" is the rendering of a Greek term (*energeian*) from which we get the word "energy." It is an energy that "powerfully works" (lit., "energizes") in the apostle. The entire statement shows that through faith in Christ we can link our life with a source of strength that enables us to rise above our natural limitations.

C. *A Ministry of Intercession*

2:1–5

> [1] I want you to know how strenuously I am exerting myself for you and for those at Laodicea, and for all who have not met me personally. [2] My purpose is that they

may be encouraged in heart and united in love, so that they may have the full riches of complete understanding, in order that they may know the mystery of God, namely, Christ, 3in whom are hidden all the treasures of wisdom and knowledge. 4I tell you this so that no one may deceive you by fine-sounding arguments. 5For though I am absent from you in body, I am present with you in spirit and delight to see how orderly you are and how firm your faith in Christ is.

A third feature of Paul's ministry was his pastoral concern for those he served. The concern expressed in these verses arose from Paul's anxiety about the response of the Colossian Christians to the error being propagated by the false teachers. Such an expression of concern is what we would expect from the man who wrote Philippians 3:18. Anyone who shares Paul's exalted concept of Christ (cf. Col 1:15ff.), we may add, can never be indifferent to the inroads of error.

1 The metaphor of the arena is implicit in this verse, the Greek word translated "exerting" (agōna) being built on the same root as the word rendered "struggling" in 1:29 (agōnizomenos). "How strenuously I am exerting myself" freely renders words that literally mean, "how great a struggle I have." "Struggle" (agōna), which denotes strenuous activity, here speaks of deep and earnest solicitude. The powers that wrestled with Paul for the ruin of his work were real and resolute; he therefore had to "meet them, foot to foot, force to force, in Christ" (H.C.G. Moule, p. 118).

The particular struggle Paul had in mind appears to have been that of prayer. At the time he wrote these words he could not move beyond the walls of his "rented house" (Acts 28:30), being continuously held by the chain linking him to a Roman soldier. But even under these circumstances he could engage in the combat of prayer and so exert himself strenuously in behalf of his readers.

This brings before us an aspect of Paul's prayers that we often overlook—namely, that they sometimes involved him in a truly awesome conflict, an intense struggle of the soul. (Cf. the Gethsemane experience of our Lord.)

Paul's agony in prayer was "for," that is, in behalf of, the Colossians. But it was also in behalf of "those at Laodicea and for all who have not met me personally" (lit., "have not seen my face in the flesh"). Laodicea (cf. Introduction, 1) was an important banking center in ancient times. It is mentioned elsewhere in the NT only in Colossians 4:13, 15, 16 and in Revelation 3:14. The wording of v.1, though capable of being interpreted otherwise, seems to suggest that the Colossians and the Laodiceans were among those who had not met Paul personally.

2 Paul's concern for his readers was that "they may be encouraged in heart and united in love." The Greek word for "encouraged" (paraklēthōsin), which literally means "to call to one's side," signifies such ideas as comfort, encouragement, and exhortation, depending on the context in which it is found. Here perhaps it means being strengthened against the onslaught of error.

"United" suggests being "compacted, welded into genuine unity" (H.C.G. Moule, p. 126). The NIV places "united in love" in a coordinate relation to "encouraged in heart." The Greek text, however, employs a participle for "united" (symbibasthentes) and thereby implies that the means by which the strengthening (encouraging) takes place is the readers' being knit together in love (cf. RSV). But NIV does no violence to the essential meaning of the passage.

One consequence of being "encouraged" and "united" is attaining "the full riches of complete understanding." The idea is that heart encouragement and being united in love bring an inward wealth that consists in full or assured understanding. This in turn brings knowledge of "the mystery of God." The word for "knowledge" (*epignōsin*) indicates a depth of full knowledge, perhaps a true knowledge (cf. 1:9). On "mystery," see 1:26.

There is considerable variation in the last part of the Greek text of v.2. Our own preference is to accept the shorter reading (*tou theou, Christou*) and to understand "Christ" to be an appositive defining the mystery. This is the interpretation preferred by most modern scholars and is represented among the versions by ASV, TCNT, NASB, NAB, NIV, etc. The great truth taught is that all that is deepest in God is summed up in Christ.

3 This Christ who is the essence of the mystery of God is described as the One "in whom are hidden all the treasures of wisdom and knowledge." Two thoughts are contained in this statement: First, all the treasures of wisdom and knowledge are in Christ. The false teachers claimed to have, through their relation with a supposed hierarchy of supernatural beings, a higher knowledge than that possessed by ordinary believers. Against this, Paul argues that all wisdom and knowledge are in Christ and that their treasures are accessible to every believer. Second, the treasures of wisdom are in Christ in a hidden way. "Hidden" does not, however, mean that they are concealed but rather that they are laid up or stored away as a treasure.

4 Paul now expresses the reason for his anxious concern: "I tell you this so that no one may deceive you by fine-sounding arguments." The pronoun "this" refers to the utterances of vv.1–3, containing the declaration that all knowledge is stored up in Christ and also Paul's own expression of anxiety about the Colossians. The Greek word for "deceive" (*paralogizētai*) implies leading astray by false reasoning. "Fine-sounding arguments" (*pithanologia*), translated as "persuasive rhetoric" by Lightfoot, has something of the same meaning. It implies the attempt to convince someone by "fast talk" or, to put it colloquially, by handing him "a smooth line." Paul was obviously thinking of the attempt of the errorists to lead the Colossians away from their convictions about Christ.

5 Paul was no indifferent spectator of his readers' problems but had a sincere interest in them. Though not physically with them, he felt his spiritual oneness with them and rejoiced in their orderliness and in the firmness of their faith. "How orderly you are" (lit., "your order") contains a military term (*taxin*) connoting the orderly array of a band of disciplined soldiers. "Firm" translates *stereōma*, a word meaning solidity and compactness. In applying it to the faith of the Colossians, Paul emphasizes the unyielding nature of their faith or, as Eadie puts it, "the stiffness of its adherence to its one object—Christ" (p. 123). Like the word for "orderly," "firm" belonged to military parlance. It may therefore mean something like "solid front" (Lightfoot, p. 176). If this is the imagery Paul intended, he sees the situation of the Colossians as being like that of an army under attack and affirms that their lines were unbroken, their discipline intact, and their "faith in [reliance on] Christ" unshaken.

Notes

2 Another possible meaning for συμβιβάζω (*symbibazō*, "unite") is "instruct"; it is, in fact, always used in LXX in this sense. Compare Moff.: "May they learn the meaning of love."

D. *A Ministry of Exhortation*

2:6, 7

> 6So then, just as you received Christ Jesus as Lord, continue to live in him,
> 7rooted and built up in him, strengthened in the faith as you were taught, and
> overflowing with thankfulness.

NIV represents the two verses comprising this section as introducing the warnings of 2:8ff. rather than as closing out the section on Paul's ministry (begun at 1:24). NEB and JB, as well as the UBS text, support this arrangement. Although it is not a matter of great importance, it would seem best to take these verses as a kind of summary appeal made in light of the preceding discussion—an appeal for the readers to remain true to Christ as Lord. This is the arrangement of ASV and RSV.

6 "So then" (*oun*) shows that Paul makes his appeal in light of the foregoing discussion. The Colossians had received Christ in a certain manner: as the Anointed of God ("Christ"), as the historic Savior ("Jesus"), and as the sovereign ("Lord"). Paul's appeal is that they "continue to live [lit., walk] in him" in the same manner. That is to say, he wants their present and continuous conduct to conform to the doctrine taught them at the beginning, the doctrine they had committed themselves to at conversion.

7 In this verse four participles describe the walk in Christ. The first two, translated "rooted and built up in him," go together. "Rooted" (*errizōmenoi*) is in the perfect tense, suggesting a once-for-all experience, that is, a being permanently rooted. "Built up" (*epoikodomoumenoi*), a present tense, indicates a continual process. "Strengthened" (*bebaioumenoi*), the third participle, is also a present tense. "In the faith" conceives of faith as the body of truth (the faith system) and looks on this as the sphere within which the being "strengthened" takes place. Some versions render it "your faith," suggesting faith in its more usual sense of trust in, and reliance on, Christ. The whole appeal was to be carried out in accordance with what had been taught the Colossians in their initial experience—"as you were taught." The final phrase, "overflowing with thankfulness," uses *perisseuontes*, a favorite word Paul uses more than twenty-six times. Often translated "abound" in KJV, its literal meaning is expressed in NIV—viz., "overflowing" (like a river overflowing its banks). The tense is present, meaning that for believers thanksgiving is to be a continual, habitual thing.

Gratitude, which Lightfoot calls "the end of all human conduct" (p. 177), receives great emphasis in Paul's Epistles. The present passage may imply that those who lack a deep sense of thankfulness to God are especially vulnerable to doubt and spiritual delusion.

Notes

7 KJV reads "abounding therein [i.e., in faith] with thanksgiving," but this rendering is based on an inferior text. NIV follows UBS, which is supported by very strong evidence.

IV. Warning Against Error (2:8-23)

The apostle now makes his most direct attack against "the Colossian heresy." The entire passage bristles with exegetical difficulties, and calls for closer attention to its wording and argument than any other part of the Epistle.

The tone of the passage is both admonitory and affirmative, but admonition is the prevailing note sounded throughout. The affirmations, which mainly concern Christ and his sufficiency (cf. vv.9-15), form the basis on which the warnings are issued and give point and power to them.

It is characteristic of Paul in Colossians to use the vocabulary of his opponents, though, as H. Chadwick has well stated it, "in a different and disinfected sense" (NTS, 1:272). Instances of this in the present passage may be "philosophy" (2:8), "fullness" (2:9), "Deity" (2:9), "powers and authorities" (2:15), "humility" (2:18), "disqualify" (2:18), "self-imposed worship" (2:23).

A. The Error of False Philosophy

2:8-15

8See to it that no one takes you captive through hollow and deceptive philosophy, which depends on human tradition and the basic principles of this world rather than on Christ.
9For in Christ all the fullness of the Deity lives in bodily form, 10and you have this fullness in Christ, who is the head over every power and authority. 11In him you were also circumcised, in the putting off of your sinful nature, not with a circumcision done by the hands of men but with the circumcision done by Christ. 12In baptism you were buried with him and raised with him through your faith in the power of God, who raised him from the dead.
13When you were dead in your sins and in the uncircumcision of your sinful nature, God made you alive with Christ. He forgave us all our sins, 14having canceled the written code, with its regulations, that was against us and that stood opposed to us; he took it away, nailing it to the cross. 15And having disarmed the powers and authorities, he made a public spectacle of them, triumphing over them by the cross.

1. The warning stated (2:8)

8 Paul first warns against being taken captive through a false philosophy. "See to it" alerts the readers to the danger. NEB has "Be on your guard." The singular "no one" leads some interpreters to conclude that Paul had in mind a particular person, perhaps the leader, among the heretical teachers. The words translated "that no one takes you captive" (*mē tis hymas estai sylagōgōn*) use an indicative verb and point to a real, not merely a supposable, danger. The word translated "takes captive" (*sylagōgōn*), which was regularly used of taking captives in war and leading them away as booty, depicts

the false teachers as "men-stealers" wishing to entrap the Colossians and drag them away into spiritual enslavement.

"Through hollow and deceptive philosophy" expresses the means by which the errorists attempted to do this. This is the only occurrence of the word *philosophy* in the NT. It would, of course, be a mistake to conclude that Paul intended his statement to be a condemnation of all philosophy. The word (*philosophia*) is a noble one, literally meaning "love of wisdom." Here, however, because the reference is to the Colossian error, it has a derogatory connotation.

Paul uses three descriptive phrases to characterize this "hollow and deceptive" system, and each constitutes a reason for its rejection. First, it is "after [according to] the tradition of men" (NIV, "depends on human tradition"). By "tradition" (*paradosin*) Paul may mean the mass of oral tradition the Jews had engrafted on the written law. It is more likely, however, that the term refers to various pagan theories current in that day. The apostle asserts that these, not divine revelation, were the bases of the "philosophy" of the Colossian errorists. Second, it was a philosophy that "depends on ... the basic principles of this world." "Basic principles" translates (*stoicheia*), a word of multiple meanings. Originally it denoted the letters of the alphabet, its root meaning being "things in a row." The term then came to be used of the elements ("ABC's") of learning (cf. Gal 4:3, ASV, NASB, NIV; Heb 5:12, ASV, TCNT, NASB, NIV), of the physical elements of the world (cf. 2 Peter 3:10), of the stars and other heavenly bodies (cf. 2 Peter 3:10, Moff., Am. Trans.), and of the elemental spirits, that is, the supernatural powers believed by many ancients to preside over and direct the heavenly bodies (cf. Gal 4:3, RSV, NEB). The sense in the present passage may be either the elements of learning (NIV, "basic principles") or the elemental spirits (RSV).

If the former sense is intended, the whole statement means that the Colossian system, though represented by its proponents as advanced "philosophy," was really only rudimentary instruction, the ABC's of the world—that is to say, it was elementary rather than advanced, earthly rather than heavenly. The rendering "elemental spirits" (cf. RSV, Moff.) is, however, to be preferred. Understood in this manner, the passage means either (1) that the "philosophy" of the errorists was a system instigated by the elemental spirits (perhaps thought of as the powers of evil) or (2) that it was a system having the elemental spirits as its subject matter. The second meaning is more likely the one intended by Paul, for we know from 2:18 that the Colossian heresy made much of the "worship of angels."

Third, it was a system "not after [according to] Christ" (lit. translation). This is Paul's most telling criticism of the teaching at Colosse. The meaning is that the "philosophy" of the heretics did not accord with the truth as it is revealed in Christ. He is the standard by which all doctrine is to be measured, and any system, whatever its claims, must be rejected if it fails to conform to the revelation God has given us in him.

2. The warning justified (2:9-15)

Paul's warning rests on the fact of Christ's unshared supremacy (v.9) and his complete adequacy to meet human need (vv.10-15). Because of who he is and what we find in him, any system "not after Christ" must be wrong. The passage takes up the central phrase of 1:19 ("fullness") and draws out its consequences in relation to the Colossian heresy. Bruce gives his discussion of it the heading "Christ is all—and all you need" (p. 228).

a. *The full deity of Christ* (2:9a)

9a Nearly every word in this statement is significant. "For," linking this and the follow-ing verses to v.8, shows that the warning there rests on what is said here about Christ and his fullness. The phrase "in Christ" (see comment at 1:2), by its position within the sentence, is emphatic, the thought being that in Christ alone the fullness of deity dwells. "Lives" (lit., "dwells") translates *katoikei*, a verb that suggests taking up permanent residence. The tense is present, stating a general truth and denoting continuous action. The full thought, then, is that in Christ the fullness of deity permanently resides, finding in him "a settled and congenial home" (H.C.G. Moule, p. 144). The context suggests that the primary reference is to Christ in his present glorified state. As Robertson puts it, "The fulness of the Godhead . . . dwells 'in the once mortal, now glorified body of Christ' (Ellicott), now 'the body of his glory' (Phil 3:21)" (p. 81).

"Fullness" translates *plērōma*, a word used earlier in 1:19 (see comment there). Here it is defined by the addition of *tēs theotētos* ("of the Deity"). The word *theotētos* is found only here in the NT, though a similar but weaker word (*theiotēs*, denoting divine nature) is found in Romans 1:20. *Theotētos* is an abstract term, meaning not just divine qualities and attributes but the very essence of God—"the whole glorious total of what God is, the supreme Nature in its infinite entirety" (H.C.G. Moule, p. 144).

b. *The real humanity of Christ* (2:9b)

9b The preceding statement (v.9a) corresponds to John 1:1, "the Word was God"; v.9b corresponds to John 1:14, "the Word became flesh." The fullness of deity dwells in Christ "in bodily form," that is, in incarnate fashion. This fullness, to be sure, resided in the preincarnate Word (cf. John 1.1ff.), but not in bodily fashion.

c. *The complete adequacy of Christ* (2:10–15)

10 This statement crowns Paul's argument. Because Christ is fully God and really man, believers, in union with him, "are made full" (ASV), that is, share in his fullness. "In Christ" (lit., "in him"), a phrase denoting vital union with the Savior, is by its position in Greek emphatic.

" 'Ye are made full,' " writes Calvin, "does not mean that the perfection of Christ is transfused into us, but that there are in him resources from which we may be filled, that nothing be wanting in us" (p. 183). Thus, in union with Christ our every spiritual need is fully met. Possessing him, we possess all. There was no need, therefore, for the Colossians to turn to the "philosophy" of the errorists, the ritual of the Mosaic law, or to the spirit-beings worshiped by the pagan world. All they needed was in Jesus Christ. As Charles Wesley put it, "Thou, O Christ, art all I want, / More than all in Thee I find."

Paul goes on to affirm the all-sufficiency of Christ by stating that he is "the head over every power and authority." He is "the head" in the sense that he is the source of life for all that exists and sovereign Lord over it all. Whatever powers there are in the universe, whatever ranks and orders of authority and government, they all owe their being to Christ and are under his lordship. It is important to observe that though Christ is here described as Head, the powers and authorities are not called his body. That distinction is reserved for Christ's people.

11–15 The thought of Christ's sufficiency, expounded in detail in vv.11–15, is now stressed by the mention of three things Christ (or God in Christ) has done for us. These have to do with spiritual circumcision (vv.11, 12), forgiveness of sins (vv.13, 14), and victory over the forces of evil (v.15).

11 In union with Christ, believers have true circumcision, that is, they have found in him the reality symbolized by Mosaic circumcision. The Christian's "circumcision" is defined as "the putting off" of one's "sinful nature" (lit., "the body of the flesh"). The Greek word for "putting off" (*apekdusei*), a double compound, denotes both stripping off and casting away. The imagery is that of discarding—or being divested of—a piece of filthy clothing. "The body of the flesh" has been variously explained, but of the many explanations proposed only two seem worthy of consideration. One understands "body" to be a reference to the physical body, "flesh" to be a descriptive genitive marking the body as conditioned by our fallen nature. Compare TEV: "freed from the power of this sinful body." The other takes "body" to denote something like "mass" or sum total, "flesh" to denote evil nature. Calvin, a proponent of this view, interprets the phrase to mean "accumulation of corruptions" (p. 184). Scott, in similar fashion, defines it as meaning "the whole carnal nature" (p. 44); Beare uses the expression "the whole of our lower nature" (p. 197). NIV seems to reflect this interpretation, and it is to be preferred.

The description of Christian circumcision as "not . . . done by the hands of men" is obviously intended to contrast the Christian's "circumcision" with that required by the Mosaic law (and advocated also by the errorists of Colosse). That (Mosaic) circumcision, which represented the cutting away of man's uncleanness and was the outward sign of one's participation in Israel's covenant with God, was made with hands (i.e., was physical) and affected an external organ of the body. The circumcision that the believer experiences in Christ is spiritual, not physical, and relates not to an external organ but to one's inward being. In short, it is what elsewhere in Scripture is called "circumcision of the heart" (Rom 2:28 cf. Phil 3:3). The tense of the verb ("were . . . circumcised") points to the time of conversion.

12 Here Paul gives a further explanation of the spiritual circumcision he affirmed in the preceding verse. The context suggests that Christian baptism is the outward counterpart to that experience and as such is the means by which it is openly declared. The emphasis of the verse, however, is not on the analogy between circumcision and baptism; that concept, though implied, is soon dismissed, and the thought shifts to that of baptism as symbolizing the believer's participation in the burial and resurrection of Christ (cf. Rom 6:3ff.).

Being "buried" and "raised" with Christ conveys the thought not simply of burying an old way of life and rising to a new kind of life but of sharing in the experience of Christ's own death and resurrection. That Paul did not think of baptism as actually effecting participation in that experience is made clear when he adds that the Colossians were raised through their "faith in the power of God." Baptism, then, is not a magic rite, but an act of obedience in which we confess our faith and symbolize the essence of our spiritual experience. Faith is the instrumental cause of that experience and, apart from real faith, baptism is an empty, meaningless ceremony.

13,14 In the closing words of v.12 Paul has mentioned God's raising Christ from the dead. Now he assures his readers that in Christ they share the resurrection experience. In Christ's case it was a literal bodily resurrection from the dead. In their case, the death was spiritual ("dead in your sins," "uncircumcision," etc.), and the being made alive is also spiritual. (Eventually, of course, believers will experience a bodily resurrection. The resurrection of Christ, who is "the firstfruits" of those who sleep in death, is God's pledge of that.)

The NIV translation "dead in your sins and . . . and in the uncircumcision of your sinful nature" suggests that "sins" and "uncircumcision" are the sphere in which death was manifested. It is perhaps better to follow ASV and understand the Greek to mean dead *through* or *by reason of* trespasses and an uncircumcised (unregenerate or pagan) nature. (The figurative use of the term *uncircumcision* in this passage is quite legitimate and readily understood. Compare Acts 7:51, where it is said of Jews that they were "uncircumcised in heart and ears.")

The first part of v.13 affirms the readers' deadness through trespasses and their being made alive in union with Christ. The last part of the verse (which NIV translates as the beginning of a new sentence) indicates that their being made alive involved the forgiveness of everything that had once alienated them from God. Forgiveness and making alive are in fact "the same act of divine grace viewed under a different but complementary aspect" (Beare, p. 198). The Greek participle translated "forgave" (*charisamenos*), built on the root of the word for "grace," means literally "to grant as a favor." It was sometimes used for the cancellation of a debt (Luke 7:42, 43). Its use here simply points to divine grace as the root principle in forgiveness.

Verse 14 vividly describes the attendant circumstances of forgiveness in Christ. One is the cancellation of "the written code . . . that was against us." The NIV translation "having canceled" suggests that this act is the ground for forgiveness. Perhaps it would be better to translate it "canceling out" and understand the phrase as specifying the act by which the forgiveness was carried out. At any rate, the word expresses one feature of the forgiveness believers experience. The strict meaning of the Greek term is "to wipe out" or "wipe away" (cf. Acts 3:19; Rev 3:5; 7:17; 21:4). In secular literature it was used of blotting out a writing or of abolishing a law.

What is canceled is called "the written code" (*chairographon;* lit., "handwriting," so KJV), an expression used of any document written by hand. Exactly how Paul uses the term is not certain. Scott, for example, points to its use in ancient times for an indictment drawn up against a prisoner, and understands the apostle to be employing the word similarly (cf. Phillips). Barclay calls it "a self-confessed indictment," "a charge-list which, as it were, they themselves had signed and had admitted was accurate" (p. 170). Others point to the use of the word for a note of hand, an IOU. Bruce, for instance, calls it a "signed confession of indebtedness" (p. 238). Either way, the reference is to the Mosaic law; and whether it is interpreted as an official indictment or as a bond of indebtedness, the thought is that God has blotted it out so that it no longer stands against us.

Paul uses three expressions to describe the law: (1) It was "written in ordinances" (lit.). That is to say, it contained "regulations" (NIV) and "legal demands" (RSV; cf. Eph 2:15). (2) It was "against us." That is to say, God's law had a valid claim on us. It was (if we follow the imagery of a "bond") like a promissory note having our signature attached as evidence that we acknowledged its claim and our debt. (3) It "stood opposed to us." This probably suggests that because we could not meet the claims of the law, it was hostile toward us or that it stood as an obstacle in our way.

Verse 14a has asserted that this bond or indictment has been "canceled out"; v.14b now adds that God (or Christ) "took it away, nailing it to the cross." "Took . . . away," the rendering of *ērken,* a perfect indicative, emphasizes abiding results. The bond (the Mosaic law) has been removed permanently, that is, removed so that its claims against us can never again alienate us from God.

Paul's vivid metaphor of nailing the law to the cross has been variously explained. Some think it alludes to an ancient custom dictating that when decrees were nullified, a copy of the text should be nailed up in a public place. On the other hand, Scott, who interprets the "written code" as an indictment, sees here an allusion to the custom of hanging over the head of an executed person a copy of the charge on which he was condemned. When Jesus was crucified, the superscription nailed to his cross contained the words "The King of the Jews." Paul "boldly ignores the real superscription, and imagines the Law as nailed above the cross. This, on the deeper view," explains Scott, "was the charge on which Christ was put to death. He suffered in order to satisfy in our stead 'the indictment which was against us' and has thus set it aside" (p. 47). Others understand the idea to be that the indictment was itself crucified.

To sum up, the great principle asserted in v.14 is the destruction of the law in and by the cross of Christ. The law, however, is viewed in a certain character (i.e., as a bond of indebtedness or as an instrument of condemnation, something that "stood opposed to us").

15 The meaning of nearly every word of this verse is disputed. One of the key issues concerns the interpretation of "powers and authorities." The interpretation preferred here is that which sees these as hostile supernatural powers, the hierarchy of evil. The words include all the spiritual forces of this world that are in rebellion against God, designated elsewhere as "the world-rulers of this darkness" (Eph 6:12, ASV; cf. Col 1:16; 2:8, 19, RSV).

Paul affirms that Christ has "disarmed" these forces of evil. The Greek verb (*apek-dusamenos*), which is in the middle voice, is interpreted by some in the sense of stripping off *from himself,* as though the powers and authorities had attached themselves to the Son of God in determination to bring about his destruction. Christ strips them from himself like a wrestler casting from himself a disabled antagonist. Perhaps it is better to construe the middle as intensive. The meaning then is simply "having stripped," and the object of the action is not "himself" but the powers and authorities. In this interpretation the imagery is that of a conquered antagonist being stripped of his weapons and armor and put to public shame. (A Greek word built on the same root as the word employed here is used in LXX of the "stripping" of enemies in war.) NIV expresses this meaning.

Paul goes on to say that Christ, having thus disarmed the powers and authorities, "made a public spectacle of them." That is to say, he exposed them to public disgrace by exhibiting them to the universe as his captives. The added words, "triumphing over them by the cross," expand this idea. The picture, quite familiar in the Roman world, is that of a triumphant general leading a parade of victory. The conqueror, riding at the front in his chariot, leads his troops through the streets of the city. Behind them trails a wretched company of vanquished kings, officers, and soldiers—the spoils of battle. Christ, in this picture, is the conquering general; the powers and authorities are the vanquished enemy displayed as the spoils of battle before the entire universe. To the casual observer the cross appears to be only an instrument of death, the symbol of Christ's defeat; Paul represents it as Christ's chariot of victory.

Notes

8 "Through hollow and deceptive philosophy" translates Διὰ τῆς φιλοσοφίας καὶ κενῆς ἀπάτης (*dia tēs philosophias kai kenēs apatēs*). The use of a single article and a single preposition with the two nouns suggests that Paul intended his readers to understand the second term ("empty deceit") as explanatory of the first ("philosophy"). That is to say, the so-called "philosophy" of the Colossian heretics is more aptly and precisely described as an empty delusion. NIV's "hollow and deceptive philosophy" expresses this accurately. Phillips paraphrases it "high-sounding nonsense." Moffatt, avoiding the use of the word *philosophy*, renders the phrase "a theosophy which is specious make-believe."

9 Lightfoot, Abbott, and others think the interpretation of σωματικῶς (*sōmatikōs*, "in bodily form") given above is the only tenable one. There are, however, other views. Calvin, followed by Scott and Beare, takes the word to mean something like "substantially," "really," or "genuinely." Peake, following Haupt, interprets it to mean "as a complete and organic whole." Others have suggested "embodied," that is, in the corporate life of the church. Each of these alternatives puts an unnatural strain on the Greek term.

13 Scholars debate whether God or Christ is to be thought of as the subject of συνεζωοποίησιν (*synezōopoiēsin*, "made alive"). Chrysostom, Ellicott, and others argue for Christ as subject; most modern interpreters take God to be the subject. Likewise, they consider God to be the subject of the verbs "forgave" and "having canceled."

B. *The Error of Legalism*

2:16, 17

16Therefore do not let anyone judge you by what you eat or drink, or with regard to a religious festival, a New Moon celebration, or a Sabbath day. 17These are a shadow of the things that were to come; the reality, however, is found in Christ.

16,17 The false teachers at Colosse laid down rigid restrictions with regard to eating and drinking and with regard to the observance of the religious calendar. "Therefore" shows that this and the following warnings grow out of what Paul says of Christ's complete sufficiency in the preceding verses. There is perhaps a special reference to his removal of the law and his triumph over the forces of evil (vv.14, 15). In light of what Christ did, the Colossians were to let no one "judge" their standing before God on the basis of their observance or nonobservance of the regulations of the Mosaic law. In such matters the principle of Christian liberty comes into play (cf. Gal 5:1). Elsewhere Paul insists that under some circumstances Christian freedom should be voluntarily limited by one's respect for the tender conscience of a weaker brother (cf. Rom 14:1ff.; 1 Cor 8:1ff.). This caution is necessary for those inclined to assert their liberty regardless of the damage their actions might bring to another person. But "at Colosse it is precisely Christian liberty that requires to be asserted in the face of specious attempts to undermine it" (Bruce, p. 243). "What you eat or drink" (lit., "eating and ... drinking") is probably a reference to the dietary rules in the Mosaic law about clean and unclean food. It is possible, however, that Paul was not thinking of Jewish law at all, but simply of the peculiar ascetic tendencies of the Colossian heresy. If this line of interpretation is followed, the question is not one of lawful and unlawful foods but of eating and drinking as opposed to abstinence from such things as animal flesh and wine and strong drink. Caird speaks of it as "an asceticism" that was "the product of an exaggerated and puritanical form of Judaism," but he thinks some "allowance must be made for pagan influence" (p. 197). Then he adds that "Paul treats it as an offshoot of Judaism, but it was probably put together by Gentile Christians who looked to the Old Testament to provide the justification for their ascetic principles" (p. 198).

"Religious festival," "New Moon celebration," and "Sabbath day" probably refer to various holy days of the Jewish calendar—annual, monthly, and weekly. The reference to "Sabbath day" points clearly to the Jewish calendar, for only Jews kept the Sabbath. That being the case, "religious festival" and "New Moon celebration" must point primarily to the ritual calendar of the Jews. Paul's thought is that the Christian is freed from obligations of this kind (cf. v.14; Gal 4:9–11; 5:1). No one, therefore, should be permitted to make such things a test of piety or fellowship (cf. Rom 14:1ff.). Christianity, as Eadie explains, "is too free and exuberant to be trained down to 'times and seasons'. . . . Its feast is daily, for every day is holy; its moon never wanes, and its serene tranquillity is an unbroken Sabbath" (p. 177). Moulton's caution, however, is apropos today. He writes, "In past generations this verse might . . . have been gently shown to Sabbatarians. Now they are harder to find. It is not that we have learnt its lesson, but that we care less about worship" (p. 40).

17 All such legal stipulations were but "a shadow [i.e., an anticipation] of the things that were to come." Therefore to cling to the prophetic shadow is to obscure the spiritual reality of which those things were a prefigurement. "The reality" (substance) belongs to Christ. In him, the things to come have come. (The concept of shadow and substance is found also in Hebrews 8:5; 10:1.)

These two verses, writes H.C.G. Moule, are

> an appeal for "Christian liberty," as earnest . . . as [Paul's] appeal to the Galatians "not to be entangled again in the yoke of bondage." But let us note well that the "liberty" he means is the very opposite of licence and has nothing in the world akin to the miserable individualism whose highest ambition is to do just what it likes. The whole aim of St. Paul is for the fullest, deepest and most watchful holiness. He wants his Colossian converts above all things to be holy; that is, to live a life yielded all through to their Redeemer, who is also their Master (p. 171).

Notes

16 Σάββατα (*sabbata*), though plural, is regularly used in the NT in a singular sense—thus "sabbath day" (NIV), not "sabbath days" (KJV).

C. *The Error of Angel Worship*

2:18, 19

18Do not let anyone who delights in false humility and the worship of angels disqualify you for the prize. Such a person goes into great detail about what he has seen, and his unspiritual mind puffs him up with idle notions. 19He has lost connection with the Head, from whom the whole body, supported and held together by its ligaments and sinews, grows as God causes it to grow.

18 Paul's third warning brings before us two of the most puzzling verses in the NT. The Greek expression for "disqualify you" (*hymas katabrabeuetō*) has been rendered in many different ways: KJV, "beguile you of your reward"; Knox, "cheat you"; ASV, "rob you of your prize"; BV, "defraud you of salvation's prize," etc. The literal meaning of the clause is "let no one act as umpire against you," that is, give an adverse decision against you. Perhaps it is only a stronger and more picturesque way of saying, "Let no one judge you" (cf. v.16). The essential meaning is, "Let no one deny your claim to be Christians."

The person attempting to make such judgment is described as one "who delights in false humility and the worship of angels." The context suggests that he seeks to impose these things on the Colossians and that this is the means by which he attempts to disqualify them for their prize. "Delights in" translates a Hebraism not uncommon in LXX, but found nowhere else in the NT. "False humility," translated "self-abasement" in RSV, is thought by some to be a technical term for fasting, since in the OT this was the usual way for one to humble himself before God. Whether this be so or not, the word in this context appears to denote a mock humility. The same word is used in 3:12 in a list of virtues. "Worship of angels" is an allusion to the deference the heretical teachers paid to the hierarchy of spirit-beings who, in their system, filled the whole universe. Perhaps the "humility" and the "worship of angels" were closely related. (In Greek the word for "false humility" and the expression for "worship of angels" are governed by the same preposition.) That is to say, the heretics probably insisted that their worship of angels rather than the supreme God was an expression of humility on their part. Lightfoot writes that "there was an officious parade of humility in selecting these lower beings as intercessors, rather than appealing directly to the throne of grace" (p. 196).

We see a further indication of the method of the false teachers in the words "goes into great detail about what he has seen." The meaning, according to some, is that the heretical teacher *takes his stand* on his (imaginary or alleged) visions (cf. RSV). He "harps" on his visions, claiming more than he can prove. NIV reflects this interpretation. Others think there is an allusion to the initiatory rites of the mystery cults and that Paul is scornfully quoting some of the jargon ("entering in," "what he has seen") used by the heretical teachers. The meaning of the Greek construction is so obscure that many interpreters have resorted to conjectural emendation.

Paul depicts the heretical teacher as inflated with conceit. "His unspiritual mind puffs him up with idle notions." The "unspiritual" (*tēs sarkos;* lit., "of the flesh") mind is a mind dominated by the unrenewed nature, a mind lacking spiritual enlightenment.

19 The false teacher lacks vital contact with Jesus Christ. This is profoundly serious because it is from Christ as Head that "the whole body [the church], supported and held together by its ligaments and sinews, grows." Each believer is thought of as forming a vital connection with Christ the Head. Thus joined to him, they all become the joints and ligaments by which the church is supplied with energy and life. The heretical teacher, without this contact with Christ, cuts himself off from the source of spiritual vitality for God's people and cannot possibly contribute to their growth.

Notes

18 Θέλων ἐν ταπεινοφροσύνῃ (*thelōn en tapeinophrosynē*, "who delights in false humility") is a particularly difficult expression. The noun (*tapeinophrosynē*) must here mean something like "mock humility" (cf. NIV, "false humility"). Θέλων (*thelōn*), a participle, may mean something like "self-imposed" (cf. KJV and ASV, "voluntary"). Its literal meaning is "willing" (cf. NIV, "delighting in"; RSV, "insisting on"). NEB takes the whole phrase to mean "people who go in for self-mortification." NIV is perhaps to be preferred. KJV translates a text that employs a negative and thus changes the meaning entirely: "intruding into those things which he hath not seen." The thought expressed by this reading is that the false teacher deals with mysteries he has no immediate knowledge of. Lightfoot suspects that the Greek text may be corrupted here and proposes that the reading might originally have been a construction that he translates as "treading the void" (p. 197).

D. *The Error of Asceticism*

2:20–23

> 20If you died with Christ to the basic principles of this world, why, as though you still belonged to it, do you submit to its rules: 21"Do not handle! Do not taste! Do not touch!"? 22These are all destined to perish with use, because they are based on human commands and teachings. 23Such regulations indeed have an appearance of wisdom, with their self-imposed worship, their false humility and their harsh treatment of the body, but they lack any value in restraining sensual indulgence.

Paul's fourth and final warning is against asceticism—the imposition of man-made rules as a means of gaining favor with God. For ascetics the body is a thing to be buffeted and punished, a thing to be treated like an enemy. They see the body as evil and conclude that the way to holiness is to deny all the body's desires, refuse its appetites, and cut its needs down to an irreducible minimum. Asceticism was apparently a prominent feature of the Colossian heresy, and in various periods of history it has appealed strongly to misguided people. It was the ascetic spirit that led to the deprecation of marriage, the exaltation of virginity and monasticism, and the devising of endless means of self-torture. Paul condemns asceticism and urges the Colossians to reject it as a way of life.

1. *The Christian's death to the world (2:20–22a)*

20 When one becomes a Christian, his connection with the world of legal and ascetic ordinances is severed. Asceticism, then, is not in keeping with the nature and circumstances of the new life in Christ. For the Christian, all the rules and requirements of asceticism are a kind of anachronism.

The "if " clause is not intended to express doubt or uncertainty. Its force is argumentative, and the meaning is: "Since [because] you died. . . ." The use of this type of conditional clause is Paul's emphatic way of stating something that is unquestionable (cf. 3:1; Phil 2:1, et al.).

"Died" translates an aorist, pointing to the time of the believer's conversion. In the mention of dying and rising (3:1) with Christ, there may be an allusion to Christian baptism (see comments on 2:12); however, baptism only *pictures* the believer's death to an old way of life and his rising to a new life. The actual change is effected when he is joined to Christ by faith. So he enters into fellowship with Christ, and in dying with him is delivered from "the basic principles of this world."

"Basic principles" (*stoicheiōn*) has the same ambiguity that marks it elsewhere (cf. discussion at 2:8). Perhaps it should be understood as a reference to the supernatural powers of evil (cf. RSV), but the passage also yields an acceptable meaning if *stoicheiōn* is interpreted as in the NIV. At any rate, to order life by ascetic rules is to revert to an inferior state supposedly abandoned at the time of conversion. To die to "the basic principles of this world" (or "the elemental spirits of the universe," RSV) is to have all connections with them severed, to be done with them, to be liberated from their authority once for all. (The Greek preposition *apo* ("to") ordinarily means "from," and here perhaps expresses something like "out of the control of.")

"Submit to its rules," which translates a single Greek word (*dogmatizesthe*), recalls v.14, where reference was made to the canceling out of the bond of ordinances (*dogmata*) against us. To permit oneself to be "dogmatized" is to permit life to become a round of rules again.

21 The "rules" Paul had in mind are such decrees as "Do not handle! Do not taste! Do not touch!" The reference is to the dietary restrictions the errorists imposed as a means of attaining salvation. (Caird thinks it more probable that "Paul is ridiculing his opponents by attributing to them a total withdrawal from all worldly contacts: 'Don't handle that, don't taste this, don't touch anything!' If you pursue to its logical conclusion the notion that holiness consists in avoiding contamination, you can only end in avoiding everything.") Some may have been reenactments of the Mosaic law; others were doubtless prohibitions stemming from pagan asceticism. There is a descending order in the terms, the climax being reached in the last word—i.e., "Don't even touch."

22a Parenthetically (cf. RSV) Paul adds that all such things are "destined to perish with use." Dietary restrictions have to do with things made to be used; and with their use they perish, for food ceases to be food once it is eaten. The underlying thought, then, is that the restrictive regulations of the Colossian heresy deal with matters that are temporary and unimportant. Christ, in fact, has made all food clean (Mark 7:19). (NIV seems to represent a different interpretation, the things destined to perish being the rules themselves, not the things forbidden by the rules. But the words "with use" militate against this view.)

2. The human origin of ascetic restrictions (2:22b)

22b Such regulative prohibitions as "Do not handle! Do not taste! Do not touch!" are "based on human commands and teachings." The thought is that the rules of the ascetic are, both in origin and in medium of communication, strictly human.

3. The ineffectiveness of ascetic restrictions (2:23)

23 Ascetic rules masquerade as wisdom. They seem, on the surface, to be reasonable and wise. But what seems to be wisdom is only an appearance of, or pretension to, wisdom. In reality these rules are expressions of "self-imposed worship" and spurious "humility." The RSV renders the first expression "rigor of devotion," but the stress is not on rigor but on the voluntary nature of the act. Calvin defines it as "voluntary service, which men choose for themselves at their own option, without authority from God" (p. 202). The NIV rendering is in line with this thought. The context suggests that the errorists engaged in such "worship" in the hope that they would thereby acquire superior merit before God. The Greek word (*ethelothrēskia*), a rare compound that has not been found in extrabiblical writings and is used in the NT only here, calls to mind the reference to "worship of angels" in v.18.

"Humility" (*tapeinophrosynē*) must in this context refer to a mock humility (cf. v.18). The idea is that asceticism, while parading under the guise of humility, actually panders to human pride. "Harsh treatment of the body" (lit., "unsparingness") is a reference to ascetic torturings of the body. "Lack any value in restraining sensual indulgence" translates a very difficult Greek construction—*ouk en timē tini pros plēsmonēn tēs sarkos*— which has given rise to many different interpretations. The two that have the most to commend them are those expressed in NIV and in Moff.; the latter reads: "but they are of no value, they only pamper the flesh!" (cf. RSV margin). The Greek behind "sensual indulgence" may be more literally translated "indulgence of the flesh," and by "flesh" Paul probably means more than sensuality. See Galatians 5:19-21, where such sins of disposition as arrogance and pride are listed as works of the flesh.

To sum up, v.23 teaches that ascetic rules have the appearance of wisdom for many people in that they seem to be expressions of devotion to God, of humility, and of a commendable discipline of the body. Paul, however, declares that these regulations have nothing to do with real wisdom, and the worship and humility they seem to express are both spurious. His final appraisal is that asceticism is a dismal failure. On the surface it may appear to be the way to spiritual victory, but it actually is not. Christianity is not a religion of prescriptions but of a living relationship with Jesus Christ. This, of course, does not mean that once we are in Christ everything is permissible. That would amount to moral and spiritual anarchy, a thing contrary to the very nature of the new life in Christ. It does mean that the controls of the Christian life spring from within, that genuine piety grows out of inward conviction generated by a consciousness of union with Christ. Indwelt by the Spirit, we walk by the Spirit and thus avoid carrying out the desires of the lower nature (Gal 5:16). Maclaren says it with characteristic force: "There is only one thing that will put the collar on the neck of the animal within us, and that is the power of the indwelling Christ" (p. 255).

V. Appeal for Christian Living (3:1-4:6)

The apostle has refuted both the doctrinal and practical errors of the false teachers and, in the course of doing this, has given a profound exposition of the cosmic significance of Jesus Christ. In the present section, which is practical and ethical in its emphasis, he exhorts his readers to give outward expression in daily living to the deep experience that is theirs in Christ. The Christian life is a life "hidden with Christ in God," but it is still, Paul explains, a life lived out on earth. The Christian must therefore give attention not only to his inward experience with God but also to his outward relations with his fellowman.

A. The Root Principle of the Christian Life

3:1-4

> [1]Since, then, you have been raised with Christ, set your hearts on things above, where Christ is seated at the right hand of God. [2]Set your minds on things above,

not on earthly things. ³For you died, and your life is now hidden with Christ in God. ⁴When Christ, who is your life, appears, then you also will appear with him in glory.

The opening verses of chapter 3 sustain the closest connection with the closing verses of chapter 2. There the apostle reminds the Colossians that ascetic regulations are of no real value in restraining indulgence of the flesh. The only remedy for sinful passions is found in the believers' experience of union with Christ—a union by virtue of which the Christian dies to sin and to the world's way of thinking and doing. The opening verses of the third chapter, representing the positive counterpart of those verses, teach that this death with Christ involves also participation in his resurrection life. This releases into the believer's life a power that is more than adequate as a check against the appetites and attitudes of the lower nature. These four verses, then, point to the believer's union with Christ as the root principle of the whole Christian life. It is the point of departure and the source of power for all that he does.

On the basis of this mystical but real experience with Christ, the Colossians are urged to seek heavenly things (v.1) and set their minds on them (v.2). As a further incentive to doing this, they are reminded that their lives are now securely hidden with Christ in God and thus belong to the invisible realm. Their sphere of being, action, and enjoyment is therefore now totally different from that of their former situation (v.3). Believers' lives, however, will not always be hidden in this way. Now there is concealment, but when Christ appears, there will be a glorious manifestation of who they truly are (v.4).

1. *Seeking the things above* (3:1)

1 To set the heart on (*zēteite;* lit., "seek") things above is to desire and to strive for those things. It is to see to it that one's interests are centered in Christ, that one's attitudes, ambitions, and whole outlook on life are molded by Christ's relation to the believer, and that one's allegiance to him takes precedence over all earthly allegiances. The verb is a present imperative, suggesting a continuing action: "Keep on seeking."

The description of Christ as "seated at the right hand of God" is another implied rejoinder to those who were seeking to diminish Christ's role as mediator, inasmuch as the right hand of God is a metaphor for the place of supreme privilege and divine authority.

2. *Setting the mind on things above* (3:2)

2 NIV interprets the commands of vv.1, 2 as essentially the same. There may, however, be a slight difference. Setting the heart on things above (v.1) is descriptive of the aim, the practical pursuit of the Christian life. Setting the mind (v.2) on things above refers more to inner disposition. Lightfoot comments, "You must not only *seek* heaven; you must also *think* heaven" (p. 209). There is, of course, an intimate connection between the two.

To set the mind on (lit., "think on") things above has, among other connotations, that of giving such things a large place in one's thought life—seeing to it that the bent of the inner nature, the governing tendency of thought and will is toward God. This, of course, does not mean withdrawal from all the activities of this world to engage only in contemplation of eternity and heaven. The verses that follow make it quite clear that Paul expected Christians to maintain normal relationships in this world. "But," as Barclay explains, "there will be this difference—from now on the Christian will see everything in the light and against the background of eternity. . . . He will no longer live as if this world was all that mattered; he will see this world against the background of the large world of eternity" (p. 177).

"Earthly things" are not all evil, but some of them are. Even things harmless in themselves become harmful if permitted to take the place that should be reserved for the things above. In the present passage "earthly things" may be understood to include wealth, worldly honor, power, pleasures, and the like. To make such things the goal of life and the subject of preoccupation is unworthy of those who have been raised with Christ and look forward to sharing in his eternal glory.

3. The motivations for these actions (3:3, 4)

3 One motive for seeking and setting the mind on the things above is the believer's union with Christ in death and in resurrection (2:20; 3:1). Verse 3 in a sense repeats and summarizes this. Paul is implying that since Christians have died with Christ, all that is alien to him should be alien to them.

Death with Christ (2:20) was followed by resurrection with Christ (3:1), and so our lives are indeed "hidden with Christ in God." This suggests not only that the believer's life is secure, but also that it belongs in a very real and profound sense to the invisible spiritual realm. At the present time his connection with God and Christ is a matter of inner experience; one day it will come into full and open manifestation.

4 Another motivation to seeking and setting the mind on the things above is the prospect of the believer's future manifestation with Christ in glory. Christ is called the believer's "life" because he is, quite literally, the essence of his life. It is he who gives him life and nurtures it by his own continuing presence (cf. Rom 8:10).

"Appears," a reference to the return of Christ, translates one of several Greek terms used in the NT for this event: *parousia* (often rendered "coming") speaks specifically of Christ's (future) presence with his people; *epiphaneia* ("manifestation," "appearance"; cf. "epiphany") relates to the visibility and splendor of his coming; *apokalypsis* ("revelation") denotes the inner meaning of the event. *Phaneroō*, the word Paul uses here, emphasizes the open display of Christ at his coming. Paul's teaching is that when Christ is thus manifested, believers also "will appear with him in glory." "The veil which now shrouds your higher life from others, and even partly from yourselves, will be withdrawn. The world which persecutes, despises, ignores now, will then be blinded with the dazzling glory of the revelation" (Lightfoot, p. 210).

Notes

1 NIV takes οὗ ὁ Χριστός ἐστιν ἐν δεξιᾷ τοῦ Θεοῦ καθήμενος (*hou ho Christos estin en dexia tou theou kathēmenos*, "where Christ is seated on the right hand of God") as a single thought. It is possible that the participle (καθήμενος, *kathēmenos*, "sitting") should be understood as expressing a separate idea. The things above are "where Christ is," and he is there as One "seated [*kathēmenos*] at the right hand of God."

B. *Guidelines for the Christian Life* (3:5-4:6)

Paul has reminded his readers of their vital union with Christ and the power and encouragement this gives to holy living. The present passage (3:5-4:6) shows in a practical way how this principle of union with Christ is to be applied in daily life. In short, the apostle teaches that the Christian's experience in Christ calls not simply for regulating the old earthbound life but for digging out its roots and utterly destroying it. In this way the new life in Christ will have full control over the believer. The underlying thought is: Let the life that is in you by virtue of your union with Christ work itself out and express itself in all your thoughts, actions, and relationships. Union with Christ, explains Caird, is "the supreme reality," but it is "a reality of status not yet fully worked out in experience. Believers [are] like immigrants to a new country, not yet completely habituated to its ways of life. They [have] accepted citizenship in a new world and must learn to live in it" (p. 204).

1. *Sins of the old life to be abandoned*

3:5-11

> 5Put to death, therefore, whatever belongs to your earthly nature: sexual immorality, impurity, lust, evil desires and greed, which is idolatry. 6Because of these, the wrath of God is coming. 7You used to walk in these ways, in the life you once lived. 8But now you must rid yourselves of all such things as these: anger, rage, malice, slander, filthy language. 9Do not lie to each other, since you have taken off your old self with its practices 10and have put on the new self, which is being renewed in knowledge in the image of its Creator. 11Here there is no Greek or Jew, circumcised or uncircumcised, barbarian, Scythian, slave or free, but Christ is all, and is in all.

Paul speaks forthrightly about the demands of the new life and our urgent need to repress all the degrading tendencies of the old nature. The three imperatives of the paragraph ("put to death," v.5; "rid yourselves," v.8; and "do not lie," v.9) are the pegs on which the thought hangs.

a. *Sins to be put to death* (3:5-7)

5 In principle the Colossians had, in becoming Christians, died with Christ (cf. 2:20;3:3). Now they are charged to make this death to the old life real in everyday practice. As Caird puts it, "The old life is dead; they must let it die. The indicative of faith must be matched by the imperative of ethics" (p. 203). The verb *nekrōsate*, meaning literally "to make dead," is very strong. It suggests that we are not simply to suppress or control evil acts and attitudes. We are to wipe them out, completely exterminate the old way of life. "Slay utterly" may express its force. The form of the verb (aorist imperative) makes clear that the action is to be undertaken decisively, with a sense of urgency. Both the meaning of the verb and the force of the tense suggest a vigorous, painful act of personal determination. Maclaren likens it to a man who while working at a machine gets his fingers drawn between rollers or caught in the belting. "Another minute and he will be flattened to a shapeless bloody mass. He catches up an axe lying by and with his own arm hacks off his own hand at the wrist. . . . It is not easy nor pleasant, but it is the only alternative to a horrible death" (p. 275).

"Whatever belongs to your earthly nature" is defined by the list of sins placed in apposition with it in this verse. Paul is calling, then, not for the maiming of the physical body, but for the slaying of the evil passions, desires, and practices that root themselves in our bodies, make use of them, and attack us through them.

His catalog of sins is a grim one, and all of the sins, with the possible exception of the last, have to do with sexual vice. "Sexual immorality" translates *porneia*, the most general Greek word for illicit sexual intercourse. Originally it denoted the practice of consorting with prostitutes; eventually it came to mean "habitual immorality."

"Impurity" (*akatharsia*), though sometimes used of physical impurity (Matt 23:27), here has a moral connotation. Including uncleanness in thought, word, and act, it has a wider reference than "sexual immorality" (*porneia*).

The word for "lust" (*pathos*), which essentially means "feeling" or "experience," was used by classical Greek writers to refer to any passive emotion, whether good or bad. Later it came to be specially used of violent emotions. In the NT, where it *always* has a bad sense, it means uncontrolled desire. The phrase following (*epithymian kakēn*, "evil desires") is similar but perhaps more general in meaning.

The Greek word for "greed" (*pleonexian*) is a compound form whose root meaning suggests a desire to have more. It has a much wider significance than its English equivalent. Souter's *Lexicon*, calling it "a word active in meaning and wide in scope," defines it as "greediness, rapacity, entire disregard of the rights of others." Caird sees it as "the arrogant and ruthless assumption that all other persons and things exist for one's own benefit" (p. 205). Some interpreters think the context supports the view that greed for sex is the meaning here. But it may be better to retain the more usual meaning and understand it as a ruthless desire for, and a seeking after, material things. This attitude is identified with "idolatry" because it puts self-interest and *things* in the place of God. (Cf. Romans 1:18ff., where the visible degradation of pagan life is represented as proof that the wrath of God is being poured out upon those who have rebelled against his rule in their lives.)

6,7 Paul now mentions two factors that point to the impropriety of the sins listed in v.5 existing in the lives of the Colossian believers. First, they are sins that incur "the wrath of God." Some understand the "wrath of God" (*orgē tou Θεου*) as referring to a general principle in life—that is, we reap what we sow and can never escape the consequences of our sin. It is better, however, to interpret Paul's term as meaning the eschatological wrath of God. "Is coming," a present tense, may represent God's judgment upon sin as already on the way, but more likely the present tense depicts more vividly the certainty with which God's judgment will fall on the disobedient. Second, the sins mentioned in v.5 are those that characterized the pre-Christian experience of the Colossian believers: "You used to walk in these ways, in the life you once lived" (v.7). The two verbs—"used to walk" and "lived," both past tenses—emphasize that this kind of life belongs to the past and that the Christian should be done with it. "Used to walk" (*periepatēsate*), an aorist tense in Greek, has summary force—i.e., it gathers up their whole life as pagans and focuses it in a point; "lived" (*ezēte*), an imperfect tense, stresses the course and habit of their existence. "Walk" calls attention to outward conduct; "live," to the attitudes and feelings from which that conduct flows.

b. *Sins to be put away* (3:8)

8 Whereas the sins of v.5 had to do with impurity and covetousness, the catalog of v.8 concerns sins of attitude and speech. "But now" marks an emphatic contrast. The imagery in "rid yourselves" is that of putting off clothes—like stripping off from oneself a filthy garment. Perhaps the term has both a forward and a backward reference, but it seems mainly to point forward (note NIV punctuation).

The first three terms—"anger," "rage," "malice"—speak of sins of disposition. Scholars are not in agreement on the distinction, if any, between the words for "anger" (*orgē*) and "rage" (*thymos*). The view perhaps most widely held looks upon *orgē* as the settled feeling of anger, and *thymos* as the sudden and passionate outburst of that feeling. Others, however, take the opposite view. In the LXX the terms are virtually synonymous. "Malice" (*kakia*), a general term for badness, seems here to denote a vicious disposition, the spirit that prompts one to injure his neighbor. "Slander" (KJV, "blasphemy") renders a word (*blasphēmia*) that denotes insulting and slanderous talk—here, against one's fellowman.

The Greek for "filthy language" (*aischrologia*) may denote either filthy or abusive speech, and the authorities are divided as to its meaning here. Weymouth, following Lightfoot, combines both ideas: "foul-mouthed abuse."

c. A sin to be discontinued (3:9a)

9a Some think the sin of falsehood is singled out for special mention because in it more frequently than in anything else we manifest ill-will toward our fellowmen. At any rate, the fact that the sin of lying is given separate treatment makes the condemnation of it more emphatic. The verb (*pseudesthe*), unlike those in vv.5, 8, is present imperative, which with the negative forbids the continuance of the act. It might therefore be rendered, "Stop lying."

d. The reason: the new self (3:9b–11)

9b,10 Grammatically there is a strict connection between these verses and the prohibition against lying; probably, however, there is a sense connection with the total thought of vv.5–9a. The essence of it is that the Christian has had a radical, life-changing experience in which he has put off the old self with its practices (i.e., habits or characteristic actions) and has put on the new self. The metaphor again is one of clothing. The "old self" (i.e., the old, unregenerate self; RSV, "old nature") is like a dirty, worn-out garment that is stripped from the body and thrown away. The "new self" (i.e., the new, regenerate self; RSV, "new nature") is like a new suit of clothing that one puts on and wears. The picturesque language gives vivid expression to a great truth, but one must be careful not to press the imagery too far, for we are painfully aware that the old nature is ever with us.

The new self is described as "being renewed in knowledge." The essential thought is that the new self (new nature) does not decay or grow old but by constant renewal takes on more and more of the image of its Creator. "Being renewed" (*anakainoumenon*) is present tense, expressing a continuous process of renewal. "Knowledge," which is represented either as the goal (object of *eis*) or as the sphere (NIV) of this process, denotes true knowledge (cf. 1:9).

11 The various groups mentioned reflect distinctions of national privilege ("Greek or Jew"), legal or ceremonial standing ("circumcised or uncircumcised"), culture ("barbarian, Scythian," the former denoting persons who did not speak Greek [that is, foreigners], the latter thought of as the lowest of the barbarians), and social caste ("slave or free"). In the realm of the new self—that is, where the image of God is truly reflected—these distinctions have no real significance (cf. Gal 3:28). Differences, to be sure, remain in the Christian community, but not in such a way as to be barriers to fellowship. To the extent that Christians do permit them to be barriers, they are acting out of character.

"Christ is all, and is in all" suggests that Christ is *the* great principle of unity. In him all differences merge, all distinctions are done away. C.F.D. Moule, who thinks the phrase ought not to be too precisely analyzed, looks on it as "a vigorous and emphatic way of saying that Christ is 'absolutely everything.' " Loyalty to him must therefore take precedence over all earthly ties (p. 121).

Notes

9 For the idea of renewal see Rom 12:2; 1 Cor 4:16. For the thought of creation in the "image" of God see Gen 1:26–28.

2. Virtues of the new life to be cultivated

3:12–17

> 12Therefore, as God's chosen people, holy and dearly loved, clothe yourselves with compassion, kindness, humility, gentleness and patience. 13Bear with each other and forgive whatever grievances you may have against one another. Forgive as the Lord forgave you. 14And over all these virtues put on love, which binds them all together in perfect unity.
> 15Let the peace of Christ rule in your hearts, since, as members of one body, you were called to peace. And be thankful. 16Let the word of Christ dwell in you richly as you teach and counsel one another with all wisdom, and as you sing psalms, hymns and spiritual songs with gratitude in your hearts to God. 17And whatever you do, whether in word or deed, do it all in the name of the Lord Jesus, giving thanks to God the Father through him.

a. Expressions of love (3:12–14)

12 The Christian has already put on the new self (the regenerate nature, v.10). Now he must clothe himself with the garments that befit the new self. "Clothe yourselves" (*endysasthe*) should be compared with "put to death" (*nekrōsate,* v.5) and "rid yourselves" (*apothesthe,* v.8). Those terms express the negative, this verse the positive aspects of the Christian's reformation of character. The tense of *endysasthe,* an aorist imperative, speaks of an action to be undertaken with a sense of urgency.

Paul's appeal is based on this threefold fact: Christians are chosen of God, set apart by and for God, and loved by God. The three terms—*chosen, holy* and *dearly loved*—signify essentially the same great fact, but under different aspects. Used in the OT of Israel, they emphasize the favored position now enjoyed by Christians as the heirs of Israel's privileges.

Verse 12b contains a pentad of great Christian virtues: "compassion, kindness, humility, gentleness and patience." They point to those qualities of life which, if present in the community of believers, will eliminate, or at least reduce, frictions. All of them are manifestations of love, which is mentioned in v.14 as the crowning virtue. "Compassion" (*splanchna oiktirmou*) betokens pity and tenderness expressed toward the suffering and miserable. The word for "kindness" (*chrēstotēs*) combines the ideas of goodness, kindliness, and graciousness. Ellicott defines it as "sweetness of disposition" (p. 181). In Romans 11:22 it is contrasted with "severity," and in Galatians 5:22 it is listed as a fruit of the Spirit. "Humility" and "gentleness," which are related terms, were not considered virtues by the pagan world. The NT, however, deepened and enriched their meanings and made them two of the noblest of Christian graces. Humility (*tapeinophrosynē*), which originally meant servility, came to denote a humble disposition—"the thinking lowly of ourselves because we are so" (Ellicott, p. 182). "Gentleness" (*prautēs*) the opposite of arrogance and self-assertiveness, is the special mark of the man who has a delicate consideration for the rights and feelings of others. C.F.D. Moule aptly defines it as "willingness to make concessions" (p. 123). It is mentioned in the NT as a characteristic of Christ (Matt 11:29), a fruit of the Spirit (Gal 5:23), a distinctive trait of those who belong to Christ (Matt 5:5), and so on. "Patience" (*makrothymia;* lit., "longsuffering") denotes the self-restraint that enables one to bear injury and insult without resorting to hasty retaliation. It is an attribute of God (Rom 2:4) and a fruit of the Spirit (Gal 5:22).

13 Two Greek participles (*anechomenoi,* "bear with" and *charizomenoi,* "forgive") expand the thought of patience. Paul uses them to show that Christians who are truly patient will manifest this attitude by (1) a willingness to bear with those whose faults or unpleasant traits are an irritant to them and (2) a willingness to forgive those they have grievances against. "Bear with" suggests the thought of putting up with things we dislike in others. "Forgive," a word used in 2:13 of God's action toward us, has the sense of forgiving freely.

14 The final article in this description of Christian attire is "love" (*agapē,* the distinctive Christian term for caring love; cf. commentary on 1 Cor 13). All the virtues listed in vv.12, 13 are, on the highest level, manifestations of love; but love is larger than any one of them, indeed, larger than all of them combined. The mention of love as a separate "article of clothing" is therefore not superfluous.

b. *The rule of peace* (3:15)

15 Those who see this verse as a continuation of the appeal for loving concern (v.14) among Christians are inclined to interpret "peace" to mean peace among the members of the Christian community. Those who understand it as introducing a new idea interpret "peace" as inward "heart" peace. Eadie defines it as "that calm of mind which is not ruffled by adversity, overclouded by sin or a remorseful conscience, or disturbed by the fear and the approach of death" (p. 247). Perhaps we should not limit the word but should understand it as including peace in the largest sense. It is the peace "of Christ" because it is the peace he gives—peace that comes by way of obedience to him (cf. John 14:27).

The word for "rule" (*brabeuō*), an expressive term used only here in the NT, originally meant "to act as umpire." Scholars are not agreed whether in Paul's time the word retained the connotation of a contest or simply had the general sense of administering, ruling, or deciding. In 2:18 Paul used a compound form of it. Here it means that in all inner conflicts as well as in all disputes and differences among Christians, Christ's peace must give the final decision. We are to do nothing that would violate that peace.

"And be thankful" (*kai eucharistoi ginesthe*) is added not as an afterthough but because gratitude is intimately associated with peace. The meaning probably is that we are to be grateful for the peace Christ bestows on us (which is the main idea of the verse). Thankfulness for this peace becomes an incentive for preserving it. It may be that the injunction should be taken in its broadest sense: Be thankful—both to God and to men. Such gratitude surely promotes peace and harmony within a fellowship. The verb *ginesthe* ("be") may be rendered "become," the implication being that it is a habit (present tense) that must be acquired. Knox: "Learn, too, to be grateful."

c. The indwelling of Christ's word (3:16)

16 All the preceding appeals (with the possible exception of that in v.15) have to do largely with duties Christians owe one another. Verses 16, 17 focus attention on matters that have to do more directly with the personal life. Even here, however, the thought of our duty to others is not entirely absent.

"The word of Christ" (*ho logos tou Christou*) probably refers to the gospel, that is, the message *about* Christ. It may, however, refer to Christ's teaching—a message *from* Christ—recorded or remembered by his apostles. To "let the word of Christ dwell in you richly" is to let it "have ample room" (BV) or "remain as a rich treasure" (Wey.) in the heart. Thus we are to submit to the demands of the Christian message and let it become so deeply implanted within us as to control all our thinking.

The correct punctuation of the remainder of v.16 is uncertain. NIV (along with most other modern versions) construes "with all wisdom" with "teach" and "counsel". The thought is that under the influence of the word of Christ Christians are to do two things: (1) Making use of every kind of wisdom, they are to teach and admonish one another. (2) Using psalms, hymns, and spiritual songs, they are to sing with gratitude in their hearts to God.

No rigid distinctions should be made between "psalms," "hymns," and "spiritual songs." Paul is simply emphasizing the rich variety in Christian song. Essentially the three terms heighten the idea of joyousness called for in the passage. If any differences are made, "psalms" may be taken to refer to the OT psalter, "hymns" and "spiritual songs" to distinctly Christian compositions. The great periods of renewal in Christendom have always been accompanied by an outburst of hymnology. Armitage Robinson describes the apostolic age as "characterized by vivid enthusiasm" and as "a period of wonder and delight. The floodgates of emotion were opened: a supernatural dread alternated with an unspeakable joy" (*St. Paul's Epistle to the Ephesians*, p. 168). Robertson writes that Christian hymns "demand two things above all else. They must express real emotion of the heart, adoration and worship. They must do it in a way worthy of our Saviour God" (p. 113).

d. The name of Christ (3:17)

17 Here Paul gives us a kind of summary. There are various ways of interpreting "do it all in the name of the Lord Jesus." Some understand the meaning to be that everything a Christian does is to be undertaken *in dependence on the Lord* (cf. Moff.). Others think it means that everything a Christian does is to be done *in recognition of the authority of Jesus' name*. Still others take "in the name of the Lord Jesus" to mean "as followers of the Lord Jesus" (cf. Am. Transl.). This last interpretation reflects the thought that to act in the name of a person is to act as his representative. The last two interpretations are both acceptable, but the third is the preferred. Bruce appropriately points out that "the NT does not contain a detailed code of rules for the Christian . . . . Codes of rules, as Paul explains elsewhere, are suited to the period of immaturity when he and his readers were still under guardians. . . . What the NT does provide is those basic principles of Christian living which may be applied to all situations of life as they arise" (p. 285). The words under consideration enunciate such a principle. Maclaren writes that the name of Christ "hallows and ennobles all work. Nothing can be so small but this will make it great, nor so monotonous and tame but this will make it beautiful and fresh" (p. 333).

"Giving thanks" points to an essential accompaniment of acting in the name of the Lord Jesus—viz., that in everything we do we are to retain a sense of God's goodness and are to be careful to thank him.

Notes

14 Some take τελειότητος (teleiotētos, "bond") to be an appositive genitive. The meaning is then "the bond that is [or consists in] perfection." Peake, who adopts this view, says, "When love binds all Christians together the ideal of Christian perfection is attained" (p. 541). Others construe the genitive as attributive. The meaning is then that love is "the bond characterized by perfectness," that is, the perfect bond—in the sense that it embraces and completes all the other virtues.

3. Family relationships to be strengthened

3:18–4:1

18Wives, submit to your husbands, as is fitting in the Lord. 19Husbands, love your wives and do not be harsh with them. 20Children, obey your parents in everything, for this pleases the Lord. 21Fathers, do not embitter your children, or they will become discouraged. 22Slaves, obey your masters in everything; and do it, not only when their eye is on you and to win their favor, but with sincerity of heart and reverence for the Lord. 23Whatever you do, work at it with all your heart, as working for the Lord, not for men, 24since you know that you will receive an inheritance from the Lord as a reward. It is the Lord Christ you are serving. 25Anyone who does wrong will be repaid for his wrong, and there is no favoritism. 4:1Masters, provide your slaves with what is right and fair, because you know that you also have a Master in heaven.

Several observations are in order as we approach this important paragraph. First, we may see it as applying specifically to the general principle Paul set down in v.17. Second, the emphasis of the whole passage is on duties, not rights. (The rights, to be sure, are clearly implied, but the stress does not fall on them.) Third, the duties are reciprocal—that is, not all the rights are on one side and all the duties on the other. Fourth, the entire passage is remarkably similar to Ephesians 5:22–33, though it is much briefer. The chief difference is that in Ephesians, where Paul unfolds the Christian philosophy of marriage, he introduces a rather extended and beautiful statement about the church as the bride of Christ.

217

a. The wife's duty to the husband (3:18)

18 The one duty Paul enjoins on the wife is submission, an attitude that recognizes the rights of authority. His main thought is that the wife is to defer to, that is, be willing to take second place to, her husband. Yet we should never interpret this as if it implies that the husband may be a domestic despot, ruling his family with a rod of iron. It does imply, however, that the husband has an authority the wife must forego exercising. In areas where one must yield—e.g., in the husband's choice of a profession or of a geographical location for doing his work, the primary submission devolves upon the wife.

Three things may be said about a wife's subjection to her husband. First, the context shows that the wife's attitude is prompted and warranted by her husband's unselfish love. Second, the form of the verb (*hypotassesthe*, middle voice) shows that the submission is to be voluntary. The wife's submission is never to be forced on her by a demanding husband; it is the deference that a loving wife, conscious that her home (just as any other institution) must have a head, gladly shows to a worthy and devoted husband. Third, such submission is said to be "fitting in the Lord." The verb has in it the thought of what is becoming and proper. The phrase "in the Lord" indicates that wifely submission is proper not only in the natural order but also in the Christian order. The whole thing, then, is lifted to a new and higher level.

b. The husband's duties to the wife (3:19)

19 The ancient world was a man's world, and even among the Jews the wife was often little more than chattel. Paul's counsel in the present passage is in striking contrast to this. Caird's comment is again apropos: "Jew and Gentile alike assumed that the head of a household would wield an authority which others were bound to obey. Paul does not openly challenge this assumption, but he modifies both the authority and its acceptance by the Christian principle of mutual love and deference, so that both are transformed" (p. 208).

Paul speaks of two responsibilities of the husband—one positive and the other negative. Positively, Paul urges husbands to "love [*agapate*] your wives." This of course is their supreme duty. *Agapaō* does not denote affection or romantic attachment; it rather denotes caring love, a deliberate attitude of mind that concerns itself with the well-being of the one loved. Self-devotion, not self-satisfaction, is its dominant trait. Negatively, Paul urges husbands not to be "harsh" with their wives, using a word that suggests a surly, irritable attitude. Perhaps the colloquialism "don't be cross with" best expresses the meaning.

c. The duty of children to parents (3:20)

20 The one obligation Paul places on children is obedience to their parents. "Obey" (*hypakouete*) implies a readiness to hear and carry out orders; the child is to listen to and carry out the instructions of his parents. The verb is in the present tense, indicating that such action is to be habitual.

Two things are said about the obedience children owe their parents. First, it is to be complete: "in everything." Paul, of course, sets this in a Christian context. He is dealing with the Christian home and presupposes Christian attitudes on the part of parents. Second, the obedience of children to their parents "pleases the Lord." The meaning is that in the Christian order, just as in the order under the law or in the natural realm, obedience to parents is pleasing to God. The obedience of children is not, therefore, based on accidental factors, nor does it depend essentially on the parents' character. It is an obligation grounded in the very nature of the relationship between parents and children. It is, as the parallel passage in Ephesians (6:1–3) clearly states, a thing that is right in itself. It is therefore especially pleasing to God when believing children are careful to fulfill this duty.

d. The duty of parents to children (3:21)

21 The specific mention of "fathers" suggests that the father as head of the household has a special responsibility for training the children. No slight toward the mother is intended. Paul would surely have recognized her rights and the power of her influence in the home. It is possible that "fathers" as used here has the broad meaning of "parents." (Cf. Heb 11:23, where the same Greek word [*paterōn*] is used of the parents of Moses.)

Fathers are not to "embitter" (*erithizō*) their children. The sense is that they are not to challenge the resistance of their children by their unreasonable exercise of authority. Firm discipline may be necessary, but it must be administered in the right spirit. Parents should not give in to fault-finding, nor always be nagging their children. Wey translates, "Do not fret and harass your children." Ph has "don't over-correct." Knox says, "And you, parents, must not rouse your children to resentment."

Paul gives the reason for this counsel; viz., "or they will become discouraged." Parents can be so exacting, so demanding, or so severe that they create within their children the feeling that it is impossible for them to please. The Greek word (*athymeō*) has in it the idea of "losing heart" and suggests going about in "a listless, moody, sullen frame of mind" (Lightfoot, p. 227). "The twig," writes Eadie, "is to be bent with caution, not broken in the efforts of a rude and hasty zeal" (p. 262). Paul may have had in mind the regimen of "don'ts" that loomed so large in the Colossian heresy.

e. The duty of slaves to masters (3:22–25)

22 Slavery, with all its attendant evils, was not only universally accepted in ancient times but also considered a fundamental institution, indispensable to civilized society. More than half the people seen on the streets of the great cities of the Roman world were slaves. And this was the status of the majority of "professional" people such as teachers and doctors as well as that of menials and craftsmen. Slaves were people with no rights, mere property existing only for the comfort, convenience, and pleasure of their owners. (Cf. vol.1, "The Cultural and Political Setting of the New Testament" by Arthur A. Rupprecht.) Paul deals with the duty of slaves in the context of the family because slaves were considered a part of the household.

It is a matter of concern to some that neither Paul nor the other apostles denounced slavery and demanded its immediate overthrow. The apostles, however, were not social reformers; they were first and foremost heralds of the good news of salvation in Christ. Then again, the church was a very small minority in the Roman world, and there was no hope that its stance on the matter of slavery would influence Roman policies. We should be careful to understand, though, that they did not condone slavery. Indeed, they announced the very principles (such as that of the complete spiritual equality of slave and master) that ultimately destroyed the institution of slavery.

The one duty Paul presses upon slaves is complete obedience—i.e., "in everything." He was obviously thinking of the Christian household and thus did not have in mind orders contrary to the principles of the gospel. They were not, of course, to obey such orders; no matter what their position in life, the Christians' highest duty is to God, and all lesser duties must give way to this. The latter part of the verse insists that obedience of slaves is to be sincere and ungrudging, and rooted in "reverence for the Lord." "Sincerity of heart" (lit., "singleness of heart") translates *en haploteti kardias,* a phrase that implies the absence of all base and self-seeking motives.

23 Slaves are to see their service as a service rendered not to men but to the Lord. This would transform the most menial responsibilities and give dignity to all of their work.

24 Slaves are reminded of the reward that will be theirs for serving faithfully in Christ's name. "Receive" translates *apolempsesthe,* which here combines the ideas of receiving what is due and receiving in full (cf. Rom 1:27, where it is used in the sense of retribution). On "inheritance," see 1:12.

25 This verse, set in contrast to the preceding, shows that wrong will be punished, because "there is no favoritism" with God. Doubtless Paul meant it as a warning to Christian slaves not to presume on their position before God and think that he would overlook their misdeeds. In the parallel passage in Ephesians it is the master who is reminded that there is no partiality with God, while here it is the slave. In Ephesians, masters are not to think that God is influenced by social position; in the present passage, slaves are not to act unscrupulously just because they know men treat them as irresponsible chattel.

The entire passage about the duty of slaves (vv.22–25) may seem completely irrelevant to our day. It contains, however, this enduring principle: Christians, whatever their work, are, like slaves in Paul's day, to see it as a service rendered to the Lord. This is what motivates them to give honest, faithful, ungrudging work in return for the pay they receive. Moreover, it imparts a sense of dignity in work, regardless of how unimportant it may seem.

f. *The duty of masters to slaves* (4:1)

4:1 Now Paul turns to the duty of masters toward their slaves in terms of dealing justly and equitably with them—"what is right and fair." Though in the Roman world slaves had no rights, Paul does not hesitate to teach that duty is not all on the side of slaves. Masters also have obligations. Maclaren observes that Paul did not counsel masters to give their slaves "what is kind and patronising. He wants a great deal more than that. Charity likes to come in and supply wants which would never have been felt had there been equity. An ounce of justice is sometimes worth a ton of charity" (p. 352).

His reason for their being completely fair with their slaves is a compelling one: "because you know that you also have a Master in heaven." It is to God that Christian masters are accountable for how they treat their slaves. Both bow alike before one Master, with whom there is no "favoritism."

Notes

---

21 Some manuscripts have παροργίζετε (*parorgizete*, "provoke to anger") instead of ἐρεθίζετε (*erethizete*, "provoke"; NIV, "embitter"). The KJV follows this variant, but it is a patently inferior reading, having probably been inserted from Eph 6:4, where it is genuine.

---

4. Religious duties to be faithfully performed

4:2–6

²Devote yourselves to prayer, being watchful and thankful. ³And pray for us, too, that God may open a door for our message, so that we may proclaim the mystery of Christ, for which I am in chains. ⁴Pray that I may proclaim it clearly, as I should. ⁵Be wise in the way you act toward outsiders; make the most of every opportunity. ⁶Let your conversation be always full of grace, seasoned with salt, so that you may know how to answer everyone.

The immediately preceding paragraph (3:18–4:1) consisted of a series of special appeals based on the several relationships in the Christian household. Now Paul returns to counsel that applies to the entire church. Most of what he says relates to the personal devotional life (vv.2–5), but the section closes with an appeal for wise behavior toward non-Christians (vv.5, 6). Maclaren therefore aptly remarks that the injunctions given in this paragraph touch "the two extremes of life, the first of them having reference to the hidden life of prayer, and the second and third to the outward, busy life of the market place and the street. . . . Continual prayer is to blend with unwearied action" (p. 354, 355).

a. The duty of prayer (4:2–4)

2 Here is a general appeal for prayerfulness. The word for "devote yourselves" (*proskartereite*), used ten times in the NT, is translated in a variety of ways in KJV; e.g., "continue," "continue instant," "continue steadfastly." Built on a root meaning "to be strong," it always connotes earnest adherence to a person or thing. In this passage it implies persistence and fervor (cf. Acts 1:14; 2:46; 6:5; Rom 12:12).

"Being watchful" (*grēgorountes*; lit., "keeping awake") suggests constant spiritual alertness. So Christians must be watchful and active in prayer, alive in the fullest sense, never careless or mechanical, dull and heavy (cf. Matt 26:41; Mark 14:38; 1 Thess 5:6; 1 Peter 5:8). "Being thankful" refers to the spirit in which prayers should be offered. "Maintain your zest for prayer by thanksgiving" (Moff.).

3,4 This is Paul's request for prayer for himself while he was imprisoned in Rome. His concern was that he and his associates might have opportunities for witnessing ("that God may open a door for our message") and that Paul might make clear ("proclaim") the great secret ("mystery"; cf. Col 1:26; 2:2 with Eph 1:9; 3:1) of redemption in Christ in a worthy manner. There was no selfish motive behind this prayer; Paul's consuming interest was for the advancement of the gospel, not for his own blessing.

b. *The duty of witnessing* (4:5, 6)

These verses, with their call for discreet behavior in an unbelieving society, may reflect the fact that charges of misconduct on the part of Christians were being circulated. Therefore the Colossian Christians should be all the more cautious, living in so exemplary a way as to give the lie to such slander.

Actually Paul makes two appeals—one having to do with how Christians are to live (v.5), the other relating how they are to speak (v.6). Careful attention to these matters will not only remove unfounded suspicions about Christians but also further the acceptance of the gospel.

5 To "be wise in the way you act toward outsiders" is to show practical Christian wisdom in dealing with secular society. Paul's words imply that believers are to be cautious and tactful so as to avoid needlessly antagonizing or alienating their pagan neighbors. In a positive sense, they also imply that believers should conduct themselves so that the way they live will attract, impress, and convict non-Christians and give the pagan community a favorable impression of the gospel. (See 1 Cor 5:12, 13; 1 Thess 4:12; 1 Tim 3:7 for other passages where unbelievers are designated as "outsiders.")

The verb in the statement "make the most of every opportunity" is a market term that meant "to buy out," "purchase completely" (*exagorazomenoi*). So Christians, as an expression of practical wisdom, must buy up and make the most of every opportunity for witnessing to the faith. (It may be appropriate at this point to recall the parables of the hidden treasure and the pearl of great price in Matthew 13.) The word translated "opportunity" is *kairos*, which essentially denotes a point of time in contrast to duration, which is the idea in *chronos*. *Kairos*, however, is sometimes used for significant time, God's time, or opportunity, and this appears to be the sense to be preferred in the present passage.

6 Like his Lord and also like James the brother of the Lord, Paul knew how important the way Christians speak is (cf. Matt 12:36; Eph 4:24; Titus 2:8; James 3:1–12). Here he may well have had in mind the relation of the right kind of speech to witnessing. So their speech, he reminds the Colossians, must be always full of "grace" and "seasoned with salt." "Grace" (*charis*), which in the NT usually denotes divine favor, seems here to be used in the broader sense of "pleasantness," "attractiveness," "charm," "winsomeness." These ideas are all implicit in the word.

"Seasoned with salt" may mean that Christian conversation is to be marked by purity and wholesomeness. Some, however, understand "salt" in the sense of that which gives taste or flavor (cf. NEB, "never insipid"). Among the ancient Greeks "salt" (*halas*) might designate the wit that gives zest and liveliness to conversation. Here "hallowed pungency" may be its meaning. C.F.D. Moule writes that "loyal godliness" is not to be confused "with a dull, graceless insipidity" (p. 135).

The remainder of v.6 tells why we should cultivate this kind of speech: "so that you will know how to answer everyone." Conversation must be appropriate for each person we speak to.

VI. Conclusion (4:7–18)

The body of the letter, in which Paul has met head-on the false teachers threatening the church at Colosse, is complete. By a masterful exposition of the sovereign lordship and complete sufficiency of Jesus Christ, Paul has refuted their so-called "philosophy" with all its attendant errors (1:15–2:23); he has set forth the nature of the Christian life, calling attention to its springs of power, its heavenly aspirations, and its distinguishing characteristics (3:1–17); he has shown how the lofty principles of the gospel must affect relationships within Christian households (3:18–4:2); and he has earnestly exhorted his readers to pray (4:2–4) and given them practical advice for living in the pagan world (4:5, 6). Now all that remains is for him to mention some personal matters.

A. *Commendations*

4:7–9

> 7Tychicus will tell you all the news about me. He is a dear brother, a faithful minister and fellow servant in the Lord. 8I am sending him to you for the express purpose that you may know about our circumstances and that he may encourage your hearts. 9He is coming with Onesimus, our faithful and dear brother, who is one of you. They will tell you everything that is happening here.

7 These commendations, given to insure their welcome by the Colossian church, concern two men: Tychicus (vv.7, 8) and Onesimus (v.9). The former, who is described by Paul as "a dear brother" and "a faithful minister and fellow servant in the Lord," was probably the bearer of both this letter and the one we know as Ephesians (cf. Eph 6:21, 22). He was a native of the province of Asia and was earlier selected to be one of the two delegates of the churches who were to accompany Paul on his last visit to Jerusalem, probably as custodians of the offering that was given by the churches for the needy in Jerusalem (Acts 20:4; 24:17; Rom 15:25, 26; 1 Cor 16:1; 2 Cor 8; 9).

"Dear brother" (*agapētos adelphos*) shows that Tychicus was a much-loved fellow Christian. "Faithful minister" (*pistos diakonos*) may identify him as a loyal servant of Christ, but more likely the expression marks his relation to Paul. Wey. renders it "trusted assistant." Earlier Paul had used the same noun (*diakonos*) of Epaphras (1:7) and of himself (1:23). "Fellow servant" (which, like "minister," is qualified by "faithful") speaks of Tychicus as a bondslave of Christ with himself and others (*syndoulos*). The prefix *syn* ("fellow") before *doulos* ("bondslave") affirms Paul's sense of comradeship with him. In 1:7 Paul had called Epaphras his dear *syndoulos*.

8 Paul explains that he had a twofold purpose in sending (*epempsa*, an epistolary aorist, best translated into English by a present tense) Tychicus to the Colossians—viz., "that you may know about our circumstances and that he may encourage your hearts." Some think that the wording of this verse suggests that Paul had made a special point of including Colosse in the itinerary of Tychicus.

9 Accompanying Tychicus was Onesimus, the runaway slave who in the providence of God had met Paul in Rome and had apparently been led to Christ by him. (Cf. the commentary on Philemon in this volume.) Paul is now sending Onesimus back to Colosse —with no mention of his past, but with the heart-warming phrase that he is now "one of you."

B. *Greetings*

4:10–15

> [10]My fellow prisoner Aristarchus sends you his greetings, as does Mark, the cousin of Barnabas. (You have received instructions about him; if he comes to you, welcome him.) [11]Jesus, who is called Justus, also sends greetings. These are the only Jews among my fellow workers for the kingdom of God, and they have proved a comfort to me. [12]Epaphras, who is one of you and a servant of Christ Jesus, sends greetings. He is always wrestling in prayer for you, that you may stand firm in all the will of God, mature and fully assured. [13]I vouch for him that he is working hard for you and for those at Laodicea and Hierapolis. [14]Our dear friend Luke, the doctor, and Demas send greetings. [15]Give my greetings to the brothers at Laodicea, and to Nympha and the church in her house.

10,11 In vv.10–15 six persons join in sending greetings to the Colossian church. Three of them—Aristarchus, Mark, and Jesus Justus—were Jewish Christians. Aristarchus, a native of Thessalonica who had been arrested at the time of the riot in Ephesus (Acts 19:29), accompanied Paul to Jerusalem (Acts 20:4) and later on was with him on the journey from Caesarea to Rome (Acts 27:2). Here Paul calls him his "fellow prisoner" (*synaichmalōtos*). The term may be interpreted either literally or spiritually (i.e., one who, along with Paul, had been taken captive by Christ). Mark, called here "the cousin of Barnabas," wrote the gospel that bears his name. He appears in the NT with some frequency, and we know more about him than about any of the others mentioned in this passage (cf. Acts 12:12, 25; 13:13; 15:37–39; 1 Peter 5:13). Of Jesus Justus we know nothing beyond the mention of his name here.

There is a note of pathos in Paul's remark about these three: "These are the only Jews among my fellow workers for the kingdom of God." He felt keenly his alienation from his countrymen (cf. Rom 9:3; Phil 1:15–17). But these three, he adds, "have proved a comfort to me." "Proved" (*egenēthēsan*), an aorist tense, may point to a particular crisis when they stood by Paul. "Comfort" (*parēgoria*), used only here in the NT, is the word from which "paregoric" comes and denotes relief of pain.

12 Epaphras, mentioned in 1:7 as the founder of the Colossian church and as Paul's representative, is here described as "one of you" (cf. v.9) and as "a servant [bondslave] of Christ Jesus." Paul reminds the Colossians that Epaphras was continually wrestling (*agōnizomenos;* cf. 1:29 for the same word) for them in his prayers. He was concerned that they stand firm, mature, and fully convinced in relation to everything God wills. Undoubtedly he had in mind the danger of their wavering under the influence of the heretical teaching at Colosse.

13 Paul confirms Epaphras's anxiety for the Colossians and assures them that "he is working hard for [them] and for those at Laodicea and Hierapolis." "Working hard" is a free translation of *echei polyn ponon,* a phrase the key word of which (*ponon*) suggests heavy toil to the extent of pain. Here it may refer to the emotional distress Epaphras had experienced in reference to the people at Colosse.

Laodicea and Hierapolis were cities near Colosse. The former, which lay ten miles downstream to the west of Colosse, was situated on a plateau to the south of the River Lycus. On the other side of the river, six miles north of Laodicea, was Hierapolis. Laodicea was a city of great wealth and boasted a medical school. Names of its physicians appear on coins as early as Augustus. The church at Laodicea received the sternest denunciation of all the seven churches of Asia in the Book of Revelation. The name *Hierapolis* suggests the city owed its initial importance to religion. (The Greek word *hieros* means "holy," "sacred.") There were hot mineral springs in the area. After the death of Alexander the Great in 323 B.C., these cities, together with most of Asia Minor, came under the control of the Seleucid kings of Antioch. Antiochus III (233–187 B.C.) settled a large number of Jews in the area. In 190 B.C. this particular part of southwest Phrygia was ceded to the king of Pergamum; and Attalus III bequeathed his whole kingdom to Rome. Upon his death in 133 B.C., the whole district became the Roman province of Asia.

14 Luke and Demas are mentioned next; no descriptive phrase is used of Demas. (Cf. Philemon 24 and 1 Timothy 4:10 for the only other NT references to him.) Of Luke, Paul says very little. Interestingly enough, however, much of what we know about Luke is derived from this casual reference. It is here that we learn that Luke was a physician, and the context suggests that he was a Gentile (cf. v.11). The adjective *dear* confirms what is implied in Acts; namely, that Luke—assuming that he was author of Acts—was a trusted friend of Paul.

15 Greetings for the Christian "brothers" of Laodicea, for "Nympha," and for "the church in her house." A transliterated Greek name, "Nympha" may be either masculine or feminine, depending on the position of the accent mark. The versions differ. KJV and ASV interpret it as a man's name (Nymphas). NIV and NEB have "Nympha," a woman's name. The decision (i.e., whether to construe the name as masculine or as feminine) is made largely on the basis of the pronoun used with "house." At this point, however, the Greek MSS exhibit a variety of readings. Instead of "her" house (NIV, RSV, NEB), some texts have "his" house (cf. KJV); others, "their" house (cf. ASV). The femine pronoun represents perhaps the true reading. Numerically the MS evidence for it is slight, but the overall attestation is very strong.

The reference to the church in Nympha's "house" is significant. There were, of course, no church buildings in apostolic times, and in the NT, "church" always designates an assembly of believers, never the place where they met.

The location of Nympha's "house-church" is uncertain, though the context implies that it was in the vicinity of Laodicea. Some have suggested that it was in Hierapolis, a city near both Colosse and Laodicea (see Introduction, 1).

Notes

10 Ἀνεψιός (*anepsios*) was understood in the sense of "nephew" by the KJV translators, but the word did not take on this meaning till after the NT age.

C. *Instructions*

4:16,17

[16]After this letter has been read to you, see that it is also read in the church of the Laodiceans and that you in turn read the letter from Laodicea.
[17]Tell Archippus: "See to it that you complete the work you have received in the Lord."

These final instructions relate to three matters: the Colossian Epistle (v.16a), the epistle from Laodicea (v. 16b), and advice to Archippas (v.17).

16 After reading this letter, the Colossian Christians were to see to it that it was read also in the Laodicean church. Perhaps they first made a copy of it to keep for themselves and then sent the original to the Laodiceans. In return, the Colossians were to read "the letter from Laodicea." It has been conjectured that this is the epistle we know as Ephesians, but that seems highly unlikely. The most obvious conclusion is that Paul wrote to the Laodicean church an epistle that has not been preserved. A similar reference to a lost letter is in 1 Corinthians 5:9 (cf. Introduction, 1, and also the commentary on 1 Cor 5:9).

17 Archippus, to whom Paul sent a special message, appears again in Philemon 2. From the context there some think he was a member of Philemon's household. Indeed, many commentators think he was Philemon's son. The present verse implies that he had some ministerial responsibility in the Colossian church, though Paul gives no definite information about it. Perhaps he was serving as pastor in the absence of Epaphras.

Paul tells the Colossian church to instruct Archippus to "complete" the work assigned him. Some commentators, assuming that this charge implies a degree of failure on the part of Archippus, interpret Paul's words as a rebuke. But we cannot be sure that censure was what Paul meant. This could have been his way of letting the church know that Archippus had his full support.

D. *Benediction*

4:18

[18]I, Paul, write this greeting in my own hand. Remember my chains. Grace be with you.

18 When a stenographer's services were used to write a letter (as perhaps was Paul's custom; cf. Rom 16:22), it was normally the stenographer's task to compose the final greeting. Apparently, however, Paul regularly wrote the benediction in his own hand (cf. 2 Thess 3:17). So here at the end of this letter, he took the stylus and signed the letter in his own hand.

The letter ends as it began, with the simple but profound prayer: "Grace be with you."

1 THESSALONIANS
Robert L. Thomas

1 THESSALONIANS

Introduction

1. Background
2. Unity
3. Authorship and Canonicity
4. Date
5. Place of Origin and Destination
6. Occasion
7. Purpose
8. Theological Values
9. Bibliography
10. Outline

1. Background

First Thessalonians is understood by many to be the earliest of the Pauline Epistles. One may see a special appropriateness in this because these five chapters reveal so much of Paul's mind and heart. They contain a number of his characteristic doctrinal emphases and show the depth of his feeling for the Christians in Thessalonica.

Having been hindered by divine intervention from going south into the province of Asia and north into Bithynia (Acts 16:6, 7), Paul arrived at Troas probably in late March or early April of A.D. 49. From Troas, the westernmost city of Asia Minor, he was directed in a vision to cross the Aegean Sea into Macedonia and to take the gospel there for the first time (Acts 16:9). That he did (Acts 16:10, 11) was one of the crucial events in history because through it the gospel moved to the west and the evangelization of Europe began. Arriving at the port of Neapolis after a two-day voyage, the missionary party of Paul, Silas, Luke, and Timothy left almost immediately on the single-day journey of ten miles toward the larger city of Philippi to the north.

The successful mission at Philippi (Acts 16:12–40) lasted about two months. Then, leaving Luke and possibly Timothy behind, Paul and Silas left Philippi under pressure from the city officials and went westward toward Thessalonica, a major center about one hundred miles or a five-day walk away. It must have been a painful journey because of what they had suffered while in prison at Philippi (Acts 16:22–24; 1 Thess 2:2). En route they followed the famous Egnatian Way, which crossed Macedonia from east to west, and passed through Amphipolis and then through Apollonia (Acts 17:1). These two cities were apparently not suitable points for evangelism, so Paul and Silas continued to Thessalonica, a city founded by the Macedonian general Cassander in 315 B.C. and named after the step-sister of Alexander the Great.

At Thessalonica they found the circumstances suitable for settling down to preach for a time. The city was of good size, perhaps only about a third smaller than Salonika, its present-day counterpart, which has a population of about 300,000. Its location was conducive to commerce. It had a good natural harbor at the head of Thermaic Gulf and east of the mouth of the Auxius River. Traffic to and from the rich agricultural plains in the interior fed through this port and in both directions on the Egnatian Way. The city attracted sufficient Jewish merchants of the dispersion to account for the presence of a well-established synagogue within it (Acts 17:1).

Thessalonica was a free city ruled by its own council of citizens. Since 146 B.C. it had been the seat of Roman government for all Macedonia, earning for itself the description "the mother of all Macedon." The city was administered by five or six "officials" known as "politarchs" (Acts 17:6). For some years the accuracy of this title in Luke's account of the events was questioned; now it is universally conceded on the basis of nineteen inscriptions that clearly show the use of "politarch" in Macedonian governmental organization.[1]

Paul thought of Thessalonica as the next suitable place for planting the gospel. The presence of a synagogue offered an obvious place to begin (Acts 17:1–4). So he pursued his approach of proving from the OT that the Messiah must suffer and be raised and that Jesus is this Messiah. In the meantime, he could readily follow his own trade of manufacturing the goat's-hair cloth that was a prominent part of the local economy (cf. Acts 18:3; 1 Thess 2:9; 2 Thess 3:8). For three consecutive Sabbaths Paul spoke in the synagogue, but met with the usual Jewish resistance. Luke's description of the events may be interpreted as meaning that the resistance forced him to leave the city immediately.[2] On the other hand, we may understand that he continued his work in the city for some time after it was terminated in the synagogue.[3]

Three points make the latter alternative more probable: (1) Paul engaged in gainful employment at Thessalonica (1 Thess 2:9; 2 Thess 3:8). Two to three weeks are not sufficient time for settling into a trade and freeing converts from the burden of supporting their missionaries. Besides, Paul used his working as proof of his self-sacrifice for them, something he could hardly have done during a limited stay. (2) Upon his departure from Thessalonica, he left a thriving church—not one still in the throes of separation from the local synagogue. Indeed, by the time he left, this church included many Gentiles fresh from their heathen idolatry (1 Thess 1:9). They could not have been won through a synagogue ministry. (3) Before leaving, Paul had received at least two special gifts from Philippi a hundred miles or five days away. It is difficult to crowd all this into two or three weeks.[4]

A good number of Jews, God-fearing Gentiles, and prominent women responded to the synagogue ministry, including Jason at whose home Paul was entertained (Acts 17:4–9). Many others, principally Gentiles, became Christians in the weeks following (1 Thess 1:9). Numbered among the converts in the city were probably Aristarchus and Secundus (Acts 19:29; 20:4; 27:2) and perhaps Gaius (Acts 19:29) and Demas (2 Tim 4:10). After approximately three months, the Christian assembly was of considerable size, and the Jews became unbearably jealous. So they instigated riots to force the politarchs to rule against the Christians, whom they accused of upsetting society and opposing Caesar's decrees (Acts 17:5–9). Jason and several other Christians were brought in for a hearing. The city officials, however, stood firm under pressure and eventually let Jason and the others go. Though not personally involved in this incident,

---

[1]J.A. Thompson, *The Bible and Archaeology* (Grand Rapids: Eerdmans, 1972), pp. 388, 389.

[2]Donald Guthrie, *New Testament Introduction* (Downers Grove, Ill.: Inter-Varsity, 1970), p. 568.

[3]George Ogg, *The Odyssey of Paul* (Old Tappan, N.J.: Revell, 1968), pp. 121, 122.

[4]Willi Marxen, *Introduction to the New Testament* (Philadelphia: Fortress, 1968), p. 33.

Paul, Silas, and perhaps Timothy (if by now he had joined them from Philippi) knew it was time to leave so as to avoid bringing additional hardship on their brothers in Christ (Acts 17:10).

From Thessalonica they traveled west for two and a half days (fifty miles) to Berea. Here their synagogue ministry was favorably received for about seven weeks. It might have continued even longer if adversaries from Thessalonica had not heard of their success and come to disrupt their preaching. At this point Paul was forced to go on to Athens, but since Silas and Timothy had not been so conspicuous, they were able to remain at Berea (Acts 17:11–15).

The Berean brothers conducted Paul all the way to Athens, going first to the nearby coast (Acts 17:14) and then catching a ship for a one-week voyage to the city. A three-hundred mile overland trip to Athens, as certain Western and Byzantine readings imply,[5] is not probable. Paul's physical condition and his personal safety were too much a concern for his escorts to have taken this risk.[6] The party probably arrived in Athens late in October, A.D. 49.

Paul gave the returning Bereans instruction to have Silas and Timothy join him immediately at Athens (Acts 17:15), which they did (1 Thess 3:1). The two were then sent back to Macedonia, Timothy's responsibility being to encourage the Thessalonian Christians and bring back a report about them. If Timothy joined Paul at Athens by late November, it would have been about three months since Paul had left Thessalonica. He had become quite concerned about the converts there and at great personal sacrifice commissioned Timothy to strengthen them and find out how they were faring under persecution (1 Thess 3:1–5). Silas was probably sent on a similar mission to Philippi.

While the two men were away, Paul had a relatively fruitless ministry at Athens (Acts 17:16–34). Leaving there, he went to another Achaian city, Corinth, where he enjoyed a spiritually prosperous eighteen-to-twenty-month ministry. If the stay in Athens was about two months, his arrival in Corinth must have been in December, A.D. 49, or January, A.D. 50. If we allow time for Timothy's round trip to Thessalonica on foot and also time for his ministry in Thessalonica, then he and Silas probably returned to Paul from Macedonia in the spring of A.D. 50 (Acts 18:5; 1 Thess 3:6, 7). Timothy's report on Thessalonica was so encouraging that Paul wrote 1 Thessalonians almost immediately.

Luke's accuracy in describing Thessalonian history has been questioned on three counts.[7] The claim that Acts does not account for the presence of Gentile converts fresh from idolatry (1 Thess 1:9) is met by observing that Acts allows for a longer ministry than just two or three weeks in the synagogue (Acts 17:1–9). Subsequently, Paul's ministry became more oriented to the Gentiles. It is also claimed that 1 Thessalonians 3:4 indicates no persecution in connection with the founding of the church, contrary to Acts 17:5–8. This objection can be met by questioning whether 3:4 as well as 1:6 and 2:14, does not mean that Paul and his helpers experienced such trouble from the beginning. Verse 4 of chapter 3 could just as well speak of tribulations continuing into the future as of their beginning in the future. A third objection to the account in Acts 17:1–9 concerns its limitation of the length of Paul's stay to the time necessary for three Sabbath appearances. First Thessalonians necessitates a much longer period. This is not a valid criticism, however, because, as shown above, Acts allows for the longer period.

---

[5]F.F. Bruce, *The Acts of the Apostles* (London: Tyndale, 1952), p. 330.
[6]Ogg, *Odyssey of Paul*, p. 124.
[7]Marxen, *Introduction to the New Testament*, pp. 32, 33.

2. Unity

The unity of 1 Thessalonians has not been strongly questioned. Minor objections have been raised to 2:14–16 or some part of it. This passage is suspected of being a gloss added after the siege of A.D. 70.[8] No manuscript basis can be found for this supposition, nor is it necessary to assign the words to anyone but Paul. His situation is sufficient to account for an uncharacteristic outburst against his fellow Jews. Also to see direct reference in 2:14–16 to Jerusalem's fall is unfounded.

Another question about the unity of the Epistle involves two thanksgivings (1:2ff.; 2:13ff.) and two prayers (3:11–13; 5:23). These supposedly signal the beginnings and endings of what were originally two epistles. However, the various schemes proposed for a division of 1 Thessalonians into two epistles have not been persuasive.[9]

3. Authorship and Canonicity

Pauline authorship of 1 Thessalonians has not been successfully challenged. Only extremists such as the Tübingen scholars have questioned it. Morton belongs in this category.[10] Ancient testimony favors Paul. The canons of Marcion and Muratori have the Epistle among Paul's works. Irenaeus quotes it by name, and Tertullian and Clement of Alexandria acknowledge it as Pauline. Its recognition as canonical came quite early throughout Christendom, as attested by its inclusion in the Old Latin and Old Syriac versions.[11]

4. Date

Paul's initial visit to Corinth probably terminated shortly after Gallio became proconsul in that city (Acts 18:11–18). An inscription at Delphi in central Greece dates a proclamation of Roman Emperor Claudius some time early in A.D. 52. The inscription calls Gallio proconsul of Asia at the time, probably meaning that he had begun his term in the summer of 51. Paul's trial before Gallio appears to have come when he was new to the city, because the Jewish accusers tried to take advantage of his inexperience (Acts 18:12, 13). Paul's departure from Corinth was therefore in the late summer or early fall of A.D. 51. Since he spent eighteen to twenty months in Corinth (Acts 18:11, 18), we may reckon that he arrived there from Athens late A.D. 49 or early A.D. 50.

Timothy joined him from Thessalonica a few months later (see Background). After Paul's departure from the Thessalonian city, news about the Christians there had spread far and wide (1 Thess 1:8, 9). Also, a number of converts to Christ had died (1 Thess 4:13). From the late summer of A.D. 49 till the spring of A.D. 50 is enough time for these things to have happened, as well as for Timothy to have completed his mission. Hence, we may place Paul's writing of 1 Thessalonians some time in the spring of A.D. 50.

---

[8]Moffat, EGT, 4:11, 29.

[9]Ernest Best, *A Commentary on the First and Second Epistle to the Thessalonians* (New York: Harper, 1972), pp. 30–35.

[10]A.Q. Morton and James McLemon, *Paul, the Man and the Myth* (New York: Harper, 1966), pp. 93, 94.

[11]Guthrie, *New Testament Introduction*, p. 567.

5. Place of Origin and Destination

In light of the foregoing discussion under "Background," there is little doubt that Paul was at Corinth when he wrote 1 Thessalonians (Acts 18:5; 1 Thess 3:6). Suppositions as to an Ephesian origin fail to explain the presence of all three men—Paul, Silas, and Timothy—when the letter was written. Silas is not known to have been with Paul and Timothy after the initial Corinthian mission (Acts 18:5).[12] As for the traditional destination of Thessalonica, it has never been seriously challenged.

6. Occasion

Elements of Timothy's report (1 Thess 3:6, 7) undoubtedly prompted Paul to write 1 Thessalonians. The most significant of these included (1) encouraging words as to the spiritual stamina of the Thessalonian converts in the face of fierce opposition (3:6–10), (2) an alarming report of efforts to undermine Paul's reputation and question his sincerity (2:1–12, 17–20), (3) confusion and discouragement in regard to the return of the Lord and the part of the dead in it (4:13–5:11), and (4) areas of individual and community life that needed improvement (4:1–12; 5:12–22).

7. Purpose

In response to Timothy's report, Paul had three chief aims in writing the Epistle: (1) to express satisfaction and thanks to God for the healthy spiritual condition of the church (1:2–10), (2) to make a strong case against the false insinuations against himself and his associates (2:1–3:13), and (3) to suggest specific ways in which already strongly Christian behavior of the Thessalonians could be improved as they continued to seek God-approved holiness (4:1–5:24).

8. Theological Values

The two Thessalonian Epistles contribute much toward our understanding of Paul's theological outlook. In them he touches briefly on a number of themes: the doctrine of inspiration and authority of Scripture (1, 2:13; 2, 2:15; 3:6, 17); the doctrine of one true God (1, 1:9) existing in three Persons (1, 1:1, 5, 6; 4:8; 5:19; 2, 1:1, 2; 2:13); the doctrine of Jesus Christ's deity (1, 3:11, 12; 2, 2:16, 17); the doctrine of salvation based on Christ's death (1, 4:14; 5:9, 10; 2, 2:13, 14) and the believer's union and identification with Christ (1, 1:1; 5:5; 2, 1:1); and the doctrine of sanctification as relates to personal purity (1, 4:3–8), love (1, 4:9, 10), vocational diligence (1, 4:11, 12; 5:12–15; 2, 3:6–15), motivation (1, 5:16–18), and other areas. Also by his example he teaches important lessons on discipling others (1, 2:1–12, 17–20; 3:1–5) and prayer (1, 3:11–13; 5:23, 24; 2, 1:11, 12; 2:16, 17; 3:5, 16).

Far and away the largest theological contribution of the Epistles lies in what they say about eschatology. Perhaps the best way to summarize this is to survey Paul's use in the Epistles of various terms and themes relating to the end time. "Coming" or "presence"

---

[12]Marxen, *Introduction to the New Testament,* pp. 33, 34.

(*parousia*) is the most frequent term, sometimes referring to an examination of Christians before the Father and Christ (1, 2:19; 3:13; 5:23), sometimes to the moment of the Lord's meeting Christians in the air (1, 4:15; 2, 2:1), and sometimes to Christ's triumphant conquest of "the lawless one" (2, 2:8). From all this the dead in Christ will not be excluded (1, 4:13–18). "Revelation" (*apokalupsis*) occurs only once (2, 1:7) and spans the entire period beginning with the Lord's coming from heaven for the saints till his appearance on earth to put down those who do not know God and those who do not obey the gospel of Christ. Between these two points is a time of God's "wrath" (*orgē*) on earth (1, 1:10; 2:16; 5:9). This outworking of God's "vengeance" (*ekdikēsis*) against earth's rebels (2, 1:8) is the initial phase of the day of the Lord and may come at any moment (1, 5:2, 3). It will mean "tribulation" (*thlipsis*) to the unrepentant (2, 1:6)—a "sudden destruction," comparable to a pregnant woman's labor pains, that will culminate in "eternal destruction" or separation from the returning Lord and his glory (1, 5:3; 2, 1:9). While suffering through the period of wrath, the rebels will unite in a great apostate movement (*apostasia*) and support the rise of a great figure who advocates opposition to God's laws (2, 2:3, 4). They will be captivated by his deluding words and activities (2, 2:9–11). His high point in opposing God will be the abomination "that makes desolate" (Dan. 12:11) in the rebuilt Jerusalem temple (2, 2:4).

The "righteous judgment" (*dikaia krisis*) of God assures a devastating penalty against the ungodly, but also guarantees that believers will be counted worthy of God's kingdom (*basileia*) (1, 5:24, 2, 1:5), find rest from hardships (2, 1:7) and experience salvation and glory in lieu of the terrible fate awaiting their persecutors (1, 1:10; 5:9; 2, 1:7, 10, 12; 2:13, 14). Hence, they have every reason to persevere because they anticipate a deliverer who at any moment may summon them to meet him in the air (1, 1:10; 4:15–17; 5:4, 9; 2, 1:4–10). Anticipating that the Lord will return soon does not, however, release Christians from their usual everyday responsibilities. On the contrary, they must continue working and providing for their own support (1, 4:11, 12; 5:14; 2, 3:6–15).

9. Bibliography

Auberlen, C.A., and C.J. Riggenbach. *The Two Epistles of Paul to the Thessalonians* (Lange's Commentary), tr. by John Lille, New York: Scribner, Armstrong and Co., 1868.

Bailey, John, and James Clark. "I and II Thessalonians," *IB*, Vol. 11, 1955.

Best, Ernest. *A Commentary on the First and Second Epistles to the Thessalonians* (Harper's New Testament Commentaries). New York: Harper and Row, 1972.

Charles, R.H. *Eschatology*. New York: Schocken Books, 1963.

Ellicott, Charles J. *St. Paul's Epistles to the Thessalonians*. London: Longman, Green, Longman, Roberts and Green, 1880.

Frame, James Everett. *The Epistles of St. Paul to the Thessalonians* (ICC). Edinburgh: T. & T. Clark, 1912.

Fuller, Reginald H. *A Critical Introduction to the New Testament*. London: Gerald Duckworth, 1966.

———. *The Mission and Achievement of Jesus*. Chicago: Alec R. Allenson, Inc., 1954.

Guthrie, Donald. *New Testament Introduction*. Downers Grove, Ill.: Inter-Varsity, 1970.

Hendriksen, William. *I and II Thessalonians* (New Testament Commentary). Grand Rapids: Baker Book House, 1955.

Hiebert, D. Edmond. *The Thessalonian Epistles. A Call to Readiness*. Chicago: Moody Press, 1971.

Hogg, C.F., and W.E. Vine. *The Epistles of Paul the Apostle to the Thessalonians*. Glasgow: Pickering and Inglis, 1929.

Jeremias, J. *Unkown Sayings of Jesus,* tr. by Reginald H. Fuller. New York: Macmillan, 1957.

Kümmel, W.G. *Promise and Fulfillment,* tr. by Dorothy M. Barton. Naperville, Ill.: Alec R. Allenson, Inc., 1957.

Lenski, R.C.H. *The Interpretation of St. Paul's Epistles to the Colossians, to the Thessalonians, to Timothy, to Titus and to Philemon.* Columbus, Ohio: The Wartburg Press, 1946.

Lightfoot, J.B. *Notes on the Epistles of St. Paul.* Grand Rapids: Zondervan (1957 reprint), 1895.

Lünemann, Gottlieb. *Critical and Exegetical Handbook to the Epistles of St. Paul to the Thessalonians* (Meyer's Commentary), tr. by Paton J. Gloag. Edinburgh: T. & T. Clark, 1885.

Manson, T.W. *Studies in the Gospels and Epistles.* Manchester: University of Manchester, 1962.

Marxen, Willi. *Introduction to the New Testament,* tr. by G. Buswell. Philadelphia: Fortress, 1968.

Milligan, George. *St. Paul's Epistles to the Thessalonians* (ICC). London: Macmillan, 1908.

Morris, Leon. *The First and Second Epistles to the Thessalonians* (NIC). Grand Rapids: Eerdmans, 1959.

Olshausen, Hermann. *Biblical Commentary on St. Paul's Epistles to the Galatians, Ephesians, Colossians, and Thessalonians.* Edinburgh: T. & T. Clark, 1851.

Perrin, Norman. *The New Testament, An Introduction.* New York: Harcourt Brace Jovanovich, 1974.

10. Outline

    I. Salutation (1:1)

   II. Thanksgiving for the Thessalonians (1:2–10)

     A. The Manner of Giving Thanks—Praying (1:2)

     B. The Circumstances of Giving Thanks—Remembering (1:3)

     C. The Cause for Giving Thanks—Knowing (1:4–10)

       1. The impressions of the missionaries (1:4, 5)

       2. The effect on the Thessalonians (1:6–10)

         a. Their transformation (1:6, 7)

         b. Their witness (1:8–10)

  III. Vindication Before the Thessalonians (2:1–3:13)

     A. Vindication Through Methods (2:1–12)

       1. Preaching, replete with power (2:1, 2)

       2. Preaching, removed from untruth (2:3, 4)

       3. Preaching, reinforced by godly concern (2:5–12)

         a. Evidenced by the absence of lower motives (2:5–7a)

         b. Evidenced by the presence of higher motives (2:7b–12)

     B. Vindication Through Their Thanksgiving (2:13–16)

       1. For the ready acceptance of the Word of God (2:13)

       2. For their endurance under persecution (2:14–16)

     C. Vindication Through Their Separation (2:17–3:13)

       1. Desire to go to them (2:17–20)

       2. Sending Timothy to them (3:1–5)

       3. Delight over their progress (3:6–10)

       4. Seeking direction for them (3:11–13)

  IV. Exhortation to the Thessalonians (4:1–5:22)

     A. Exhortation Regarding Personal Needs (4:1–12)

       1. Continual improvement (4:1, 2)

       2. Sexual purity (4:3–8)

       3. Filial love (4:9, 10)

       4. Individual independence (4:11, 12)

     B. Exhortation Regarding Eschatological Needs (4:13–5:11)

       1. The dead in Christ (4:13–18)

       2. The day of the Lord (5:1–11)

         a. The coming of the day (5:1, 2)

         b. Unbelievers and the day (5:3)

         c. Believers and the day (5:4–11)

     C. Exhortation Regarding Ecclesiastical Needs (5:12–22)

       1. Responsibilities to the leaders (5:12, 13)

       2. Responsibilities to all (5:14, 15)

       3. Responsibilities to oneself (5:16–18)

       4. Responsibilities to public worship (5:19–22)

   V. Conclusion (5:23–28)

     A. Petition for the Thessalonians (5:23, 24)

     B. Reciprocation by the Thessalonians (5:25–27)

     C. Benediction (5:28)

Text and Exposition

I. Salutation

1:1

¹Paul, Silas and Timothy,

To the church of the Thessalonians, who are in God the Father and the Lord Jesus
Christ:
Grace and peace to you.

1 This salutation follows the form Paul used in all his Epistles and is in the same style
as that of other letters of his time. It contains three elements: the writer, the recipient,
and the greeting or salutation proper.

The first element of this particular salutation contains not one, but three names: Paul,
Silas (Silvanus), and Timothy. "Paul" is a Greek name meaning "little." In Acts Luke
preserves the Hebrew name "Saul" up to the point of the apostle's encounter with the
Roman official Sergius Paulus (Acts 13:9) and also when he reports Paul's calling himself
"Saul" when he retold his experience on the Damascus Road (Acts 22:7, 13; 26:14).

Obviously absent is the official title "apostle" Paul used in all his other Epistles to
churches except 2 Thessalonians and Philippians. A reasonable explanation of this is that
no note of authority was necessary in letters addressed to the Macedonian churches,
where his apostolic position never seems to have been questioned as it was elsewhere
(e.g., Galatia, Corinth). This is not to say that there was no opposition to Paul in Thessalonica. On the contrary, that there was opposition is evident from his self-vindication (1
Thess 2–3). The opposition, however, never became overt as in other places and never
specifically attacked his right to apostleship.

The second name included among the writers is that of Silas. The spelling found in
v.1 is actually "Silvanus," probably the Roman transliteration of the Jewish name given
the Greek transliteration "Silas." In Acts, Luke consistently uses "Silas" (Acts 15:22, 27,
32, 34, 40; 16:19, 25, 29; 17:4, 10, 14, 15; 18:5); Paul always uses "Silvanus" (2 Cor 1:19;
2 Thess 1:1). At any rate, this colleague of Paul was most likely a Jew by birth, a gifted
prophet, and highly esteemed among the Jerusalem Christians (Acts 15:22, 32). That he
inclined toward the Hellenistic wing of Palestinian Christianity is supported on several
grounds, such as, his hearty concurrence with the Jerusalem Council's decision concerning Gentile believers (Acts 15:22–32), his Roman citizenship (Acts 16:37), and his being
chosen as Paul's fellow worker on the second missionary journey (Acts 15:40–18:6). After
the mission in Corinth, we find no further word of Silas's connection with Paul. He
probably became associated with Peter, especially in the composition and sending of
1 Peter (1 Peter 5:12).

As an associate in the founding of the Thessalonian church, he endured cruel beatings,
imprisonment, and pursuit by an angry mob (Acts 16:23–25; 17:5). Silas was known for
his absolute reliability and his faithfulness in risking his life in the service of Christ (Acts
15:25–27).

Paul's other colleague at this time was Timothy. This young man, having helped in
Philippi, had apparently remained behind when Paul had left that city (Acts 16:40). His
name is not included in the account of the founding of the Thessalonian church (Acts
17:1–10), but he presumably joined Paul and Silas at Thessalonica later. (For further
information about Timothy, see the commentaries on 1 and 2 Timothy.)

The second element in the salutation is the reference to the recipient of the letter—
"the church of the Thessalonians who are in God the Father and the Lord Jesus Christ."
Ekklēsia ("church," "assembly") was the term applied to many types of public gatherings in the ancient Roman world, whether civil or religious. From this general sense,
which is found also in LXX, there developed the technical meaning of an assembly of
believers in Christ. The development of a technical meaning did not come at once,
however. In fact, the earliest occurrence of the word in Acts is in 5:11 (*ekklēsia* in TR
at Acts 2:47 is not found in more reliable MSS). Some have suggested that by the time
this first Epistle was written, the word was still general and needed qualifying ("in God
the Father and the Lord Jesus Christ") to distinguish it from other assemblies in the city
(Frame, pp. 68, 69). They argue in this connection that Paul saw no need to identify
ekklēsia thus in his later salutations (cf. also 1 Thess 2:14). But, contrary to this explanation, James used the word at an earlier date (c. A.D. 47) without qualification (James 5:14).

Some have not admitted this narrower scope of *ekklēsia*, on the grounds that the NT
church is merely a development of the OT church and that they find in Acts 7:38 and
Hebrews 2:12 a technical use of *ekklēsia* for God's people in the OT (cf. Deut 4:10; 23:2
and elsewhere in LXX where the word depicts Israel as a community). This reasoning,
however, does not allow for the special use of the word in the NT in its preponderant
reference to people from all races in the body of Christ beginning with Pentecost. This
people is always distinguished from Israel and her ongoing purpose in God's plan.

In general usage, *ekklēsia* had lost some of its etymological force of "called out." Yet
there is good possibility that something of this meaning pertains to the special group
composing the Christian church (Acts 15:14; Rom 9:24). They are "called out" from
previous relationships so as to constitute a body with special relation to God (cf. 1 Cor
10:32).

Sometimes *ekklēsia* designates all Christendom and is a synonym for the body of
Christ (Col 1:18, 24). At other times it is a particular assembly in a particular location
(Rom 16:5; 1 Cor 16:19; Col 4:15). Elsewhere, as here, it denotes all the assemblies in
a single city (Rom 16:1; 1 Cor 1:2).

"In God the Father and the Lord Jesus Christ" tells of the spiritual quality of the
believers. The translation of the phrase by the relative clause "who are in God the
Father" gives more particularized information as to which *ekklēsia* Paul addresses within the city. It is not a pagan or nonreligious assembly (cf. "God the Father"). It is not
a Jewish assembly (cf. "the Lord Jesus Christ"). It is distinctly "in Christ Jesus" (2:14).
Being in union with the Father and Christ meant a new sphere of life, on an infinitely
higher plane.

It should not be overlooked that the deity of the Son is taught here. Combining "God
the Father" and "the Lord Jesus Christ" under one preposition demonstrates Jesus'
equality with the Father and consequently his deity. To deny this fact (Best, p. 63) is
to approach v.1 in an unnatural way, especially in light of *kyriō* ("Lord"—frequently
used in reference to deity) and *Christō* ("Christ"—the title of Israel's divine Messiah).

"Grace to you and peace" (the Greek word order) recalls the normal Greek and
Hebrew greetings. Paul coined a slight variation to connote the deepened Christian
meaning. *Charis* ("grace") goes beyond *chairein* ("greetings"; cf. Acts 15:23; 23:26;
James 1:1) in highlighting unmerited benefits given by God to the believer in Christ.
Through grace lost men are saved from their sins in the eyes of a holy God by a
transaction completely free of charge. Grace, however, does not cease at the point of
salvation. It continually issues in privileges. These the writer wishes for his readers.

One of these benefits is reflected in "peace" (cf. Judg 19:20) but with a deeper meaning than among the ancient Hebrews. Differences separating God from his creatures had for centuries worked against peaceful relationships, but with the entrance of grace in its fullness through the coming of Christ (John 1:17) the ultimate basis for resolving this conflict and establishing harmony between God and man was laid. Because of this harmony man can also enjoy inward wholeness and tranquility.

Notes

1 The adjectival function of ἐν θεῷ πατρὶ καὶ κυρίῳ Ἰησοῦ Χριστῷ (en theō patri kai kyriō Iēsou Christō, "in God the Father and the Lord Jesus Christ") could have been shown more clearly with τῇ (tē, "the [one]") introducing it. This would have made perfectly clear its relationship to τῇ ἐκκλησίᾳ (tē ekklēsia, "the church"). It is doubtful that the gen. Θεσσαλονικέων (Thessalonikeōn, "of the Thessalonians") is of sufficient import to carry the weight of this phrase. Without the article, however, the function is almost the same, the only difference being added emphasis on unity and closeness as the text stands (Lightfoot, pp. 7, 8; Milligan, p. 4; Frame, pp. 69, 70). An adverbial force for the phrase is dubious—i.e., understanding a word like χαίρειν (chairein, "greetings") or γράφουσι (graphousi, "writing") before the phrase. The former is excluded by the χάρις (charis, "grace") to follow. The latter idea of "writing in God the Father..." is unparalleled elsewhere in Paul.

The phrase ἀπὸ θεῷ πατρὸς ἡμῶν καὶ κυρίου Ἰησοῦ Χριστοῦ (apo theō patros hēmōn kai kyriou Iēsou Christou, "from God our Father and the Lord Jesus Christ") following εἰρήνη (eirēnē, "peace"), while finding support in a few strong MSS, cannot be accepted here (but cf. 2 Thess 1:2). The reading that closes v.1 with eirēnē finds stronger support geographically and chronologically among the witnesses. It is therefore preferred.

II. Thanksgiving for the Thessalonians (1:2–10)

A. The Manner of Giving Thanks—Praying

1:2

2We always thank God for all of you, mentioning you in our prayers.

2 It was Paul's practice to begin his letters by thanking God for his readers. The only exception is the letter to the Galatians, where indignation and disappointment ruled out gratitude. The Thessalonians, however, did not disappoint him. Paul found much in their lives to be grateful for. In fact, he kept on being grateful, as the present tense of the verb "thank" and the adverb "always" show. Paul was not alone in gratitude. The pronoun "we" includes Silas and Timothy as sharing his appreciation. The verb must be understood as genuinely plural because the names of Paul's two colleagues immediately precede it. Of course, the first person plural need not always refer to more persons than the writer. There is such a thing as the editorial "we" in Paul's style (cf. 2:18; 3:1).

By thanking God at the beginning of the epistle, Paul lifts the thought above the human level and rises above the conventional opening of letters of his time. He is not trying to win the Thessalonians over by rhetorical flattery (cf. 2:5). On the contrary, he is sincerely trying to give the ultimate credit to the One from whom spiritual progress comes. When Christians realize their complete dependence on God and keep this in clear focus, then and only then are they capable of moving on to greater spiritual exploits such as those spoken of later in this Epistle (Milligan, p. 5).

"All of you" expresses Paul's desire not to exclude any of the Thessalonian believers. Every single one of them, no matter how obscure, had certain qualities worth thanking God for.

The latter part of v.2 is the first of three participial phrases that elaborate on the thanksgiving. "Mentioning you in our prayers" tells how Paul and his colleagues expressed their thanks. *Mneian poiein* ("making mention") is never used by Paul except in conjunction with prayer. Making mention of his readers at prayer times enabled him not only to thank God for their progress, but also to intercede for their advancement in the gospel. The full meaning of "in our prayers" is "on the occasion of our prayers." Paul is pointing to the times when, as he prayed with Silas and Timothy, they had remembered the Thessalonian believers one by one with gratitude and intercession.

Notes

2 The case for connecting περὶ πάντων (*peri pantōn*, "for all") with μνείαν ποιούμενοι (*mneian poioumenoi*, "making mention") instead of with εὐχαριστοῦμεν (*eucharistoumen*, "we give thanks") is quite unimpressive, as the finite verb clause would be stripped of its major content in favor of the subordinate participial clause. Hence, a comma should come after ὑμῶν (*hymōn*, "you"), not after πάντοτε (*pantote*, "always").

B. *The Circumstances of Giving Thanks—Remembering*

　　1:3

　　　　3We continually remember before our God and Father your work produced by faith, your labor prompted by love, and your endurance inspired by hope in our Lord Jesus Christ.

3 The *mnēmoneuontes* ("remembering") clause in v.3 tells us the occasion when Paul and his colleagues thanked God. This was whenever they recalled the threefold nature of the Thessalonians' progress—a recollection so frequent as to be "continual." Of course, Paul does not mean that they thought of nothing but the Thessalonians. He rather uses the hyperbolic "continually" to indicate intense interest.

The words "before our God and Father" show the sincerity of this remembrance in prayer. Some in the Thessalonian church had questioned Paul's motives in dealing with them. So at the very outset, he dispels this suspicion and confronts it more directly in chapters 2–3 (cf. "God is our witness," 2:5, and "You are witnesses, and so is God," 2:10; cf. 3:9). To interpret "before our God and Father" (which comes at the end of v.3 in the Greek word order) in connection with "hope in our Lord Jesus Christ," as some have done, is to see in the phrase the heavenly scene where Christian hope will be culminated. While favored by the Greek word order, this interpretation fails to explain why Paul would leave the relation of the phrase introduced by *emprosthen* ("before") to *elpidos* ("hope") so ambiguous when he could have clarified it by an additional article (*tēs*) before the preposition. Hence, the phrase is best taken as an adverbial modifier with *mnēmoneuontes* ("remembering"; NIV, "remember").

The substance of what Paul and his colleagues remember about the Thessalonians is summed up in three words: "work," "labor," and "endurance." In turn, these three reflect three qualities of Christian character: "faith," "love," and 'hope." (For other appearances of this familiar combination of graces, see 5:8; 1 Cor 13:13; Gal 5:5, 6; Col 1:4, 5; Heb 6:10–12; 10:22–24; 1 Peter 1:21, 22.) The exact nature of the first expression, "work produced by faith," has been identified as being either direct missionary work (cf. 1:8), acts of goodness toward others (cf. 4:9, 10), or loyalty to Christ in the face of severe persecution (1:6; 3:3–4, 8; cf. Best, p. 68). Though the second possibility overlaps the "labor prompted by love," it is probably an overrefinement to eliminate any one of these three from the scope of "work produced by faith." Faith manifests itself on a very broad front, so "work" should be left as general as possible.

For Paul to appreciate works is not surprising. Even in Romans, so notable for its repudiation of any system of justification by works (Rom 3:20, 21, 28; 4:4–6), Paul finds occasion to speak of *ergon* as the essential fruit of the believing life (Rom 2:7; 13:3; 14:20; cf. 1 Cor 3:14; Eph 2:10; Titus 3:1). This emphasis sets him in alignment with James regarding Christian living and the absolute necessity of works' accompanying faith to prove its vitality (James 2:14–26). Indeed, wherever genuine faith is present, it works (Gal 5:6).

Ergou ("work") looks specifically at the work performed. It is the end product. Love's result, *kopou* ("labor"), approximates the meaning of *ergou* but with a distinctive connotation of extraordinary effort expended. Coupled with the product of faith, therefore, is the wearisome toil by which love expends itself. So great is its concern for the object that love does not stop with ordinary effort, but goes the second mile and even beyond for the sake of another. "Labor" sometimes expended itself in providing financial support to sustain a Christian outreach (1 Cor 4:12; 2 Thess 3:8; cf. 1 Thess 2:9). This idea, however, is not prominent in 1:3, where the labor is more distinctly spiritual service— either beneficial efforts to help the sick and hungry or intense devotion to spreading the gospel despite intense persecution (Hendriksen, p. 48), or both (cf. 1 Cor 3:8; 15:10, 58; 2 Cor 10:15; Gal 4:11; Phil 2:16; 1 Thess 3:5). As with faith, so with love, a broad application is probably best. However it showed itself, one thing is certain: a great spirit of self-sacrifice was present, because this is inseparable from Christian love.

The supreme example of such loving self-sacrifice comes from no less than God the Father (John 3:16; 1 John 4:10) and his Son Jesus (John 13:34; 15:12). This is no mere emotional response prompted by the desirability of, or affinity for, the person loved, though feeling certainly is not absent from it. It is ultimately traceable to the will of the one who loves. He determines to love and does so no matter what the condition of the one loved. Such is God's love for man and so must the Christian's love for others be if "labor" for their good is to result. Remembering this attainment of their readers, Paul and his helpers had additional cause for thanking God.

"Endurance" (*hypomonē*) is the third visible fruit that evoked thanksgiving. This is an aggressive and courageous Christian quality, excluding self-pity even when times are hard. Difficulties endurance must cope with consist of trials encountered specifically in living for Jesus Christ. Endurance accepts the seemingly dreary "blind alleys" of Christian experience with a spirit of persistent zeal. It rules out discouragement and goes forward no matter how hopeless the situation. Such endurance is possible only when one is "inspired by hope in our Lord Jesus Christ." "Hope" (*elpis*) is the only adequate incentive for this heroic conduct. Christian anticipation looks to future certainties surrounding the return of "our Lord Jesus Christ." This confidence about the future braces the child of God to face all opposition while persevering and continuing in the spread of the gospel. Jesus' return and the encouragement it is to believers are major themes in both Thessalonian Epistles (1 Thess 1:10; 3:13; 4:13–5:11; 5:23; 2 Thess 1:4, 7, 10; 2:16).

These three Christian virtues—faith, love, and hope—occupied a large place in early analyses of Christian responsibility. The expectation was that in every life faith would work (Gal 5:6; James 2:18), love would labor (Rev 2:2, 4), and hope would endure (Rom 5:2–4; 8:24, 25). This threefold balance probably arose even before Paul's doctrinal stance had matured and perhaps came from the teachings of Christ himself (A.M. Hunter, *Paul and His Predecessors* [London: SCM Press Ltd., 1961], pp. 33–35). Paul's Thessalonian readers had fulfilled this expectation in everyday experience. Upon every remembrance of this success, he and his companions were moved to express gratitude to God.

Notes

---

3 Whether to understand ἀδιαλείπτως (*adialeiptōs*, "continually") (v.2 of Gr. text) with the previous ποιούμενοι (*poioumenoi*, "making [mention]") clause or with the subsequent μνημονεύοντες (*mnēmoneuontes*, "remembering") presents a difficult choice. The connection of the adverb with prayer elsewhere in Paul (especially Rom 1:9; cf. 1 Thess 2:13; 5:17) argues for the former connection. The cognate adjective's relation to μνείαν (*mneian*, "remembrance") in 2 Tim 1:3 does the same. Yet its immediate juxtaposition with *mnēmoneuontes* and the presence of the ἐπί (*epi*, "on," "in" [v.2]) phrase as another temporal qualification of *poioumenoi* tip the balance in favor of rendering the adverb with v.3: "continually remember."

The ἔμπροσθεν (*emprosthen*, "before") phrase of v.3 resembles the one in 3:9 more than those in 2:19 and 3:13. The latter carry special local connotations because of the forensic nature of their contexts. The idea of personal presence is not required in contexts where the phrase is designed to bring solemnity of expression as here. Furthermore, to read "before our God and Father" with "hope in our Lord Jesus Christ" results in a cumbersome accumulation of phrases quite uncharacteristic of Paul (Best, p. 70). Hence the connection with *mnēmoneuontes* is preferred.

C. The Cause for Giving Thanks—Knowing (1:4–10)

1. The impressions of the missionaries

1:4, 5

> 4Brothers loved by God, we know that he has chosen you,
> 5because our gospel came to you not simply with words, but also with power, with the Holy Spirit and with deep conviction. You know how we lived among you for your sake.

4,5 The wisdom of beginning a new paragraph at v.4 seems debatable, for it is a third participial clause modifying the subject of *eucharistoumen* ("we thank") (v.2) and in parallel with the subordinate clauses of vv.2b, 3. If v.2b supplies the manner of thanksgiving and v.3 the occasion, v.4 gives its ultimate cause. Intuitive knowledge of the

Thessalonian believers' having been selected by God was the source of the missionaries' constant prayer of thanksgiving.

A touch of tenderness, the first of many in these two Epistles, punctuates Paul's acknowledgment of the election of the Thessalonians. "Brothers" denotes the spiritual brotherhood into which all disciples of the Lord Jesus have been inducted (cf. Matt 12:46–50; Mark 3:31–35; Luke 8:19–21). That this form of address, a partial carryover from Judaism (cf. Acts 2:29, 37; 3:17), became very frequent in early Christianity is attested by twenty-eight occurrences in these two Epistles. It fell into relative disuse during the third century (A. Harnack, *The Expansion of Christianity in the First Three Centuries* [London: Williams and Norgate, 1905], pp. 9, 10, 31, 32). The affectionate vocative "brothers" is intensified when "loved by God" is added to it. Only here is this exact phrase used, though its near equivalent, "loved by the Lord," describes these same readers in 2 Thessalonians 2:13. More often Paul uses *agapētoi* ("beloved," "loved"), the verbal adjective, rather than *ēgapēmenoi* ("beloved," "loved"), the participial form (e.g., 1 Cor 10:14, 15:58). But with the adjective only once does he identify God as the one who loves (Rom 1:7). The participle in the present verse lays more emphasis than the adjective on the active exercise of God's love as already consummated and resulting in a fixed status of being loved (perfect tense).

Though God is specifically identified as the agent in loving, the agent of choosing (*tēn eklogēn*, "he has chosen," NIV) is not named. However, the obvious inference is that God had chosen them. "Loved by God" is suitable assurance that he also chooses, since his love and election are inextricably bound together (Rom 11:28; cf. 11:5).

"He has chosen" stands for *eklogēn*. This is God's sovereign choice of certain individuals, including the Thessalonian believers, prior to Adam's appearance on earth (cf. Eph 1:4). Some would locate God's choice of the Thessalonians at their conversion or thereafter by defining the elect as "those who are continuing in faith and who are persevering in obedience" (Arnold E. Airhart, "I and II Thessalonians," *Beacon Bible Commentary* [Kansas City, Mo.: Beacon Hill Press of Kansas City, 1965], 9:443). Yet Paul speaks of their election as a thing of the past, not as dependent on any human response, whether initial faith or subsequent faithfulness. To deny the pretemporal nature of this selection makes the word refer to historical circumstances surrounding the Thessalonians' conversion to Christ. But this unnaturally forces on *eklogē* ("selection," "choosing") an inappropriate meaning (Hiebert, p. 51) and necessitates positing an unprecedented second phase of divine election. For Paul to write concerning a knowledge his readers already knew him to possess, i.e., the details of their conversion, is too much of a truism to carry the emphasis resting on v.4. It is much better to allow *eklogēn* a setting prior to history. Knowledge of this prior choice by God was the root of Paul's thanksgiving.

Paul cannot leave unproved so direct a statement regarding election. So vv.5–10 give two grounds for the knowledge just asserted. The former of these relates to the experience of the missionaries themselves (v.5). They had sensed an unusual divine moving such as occurred only in special cases.

Interpretations that have assigned *hoti* ("because," v.5) an epexegetic force (i.e., giving additional information) see vv.5ff. as detailing the historical occasion and manner of election. Most persuasive among the evidences for this interpretation is Paul's practice elsewhere of assigning an objective force to *hoti* wherever he utilizes the *eidenai ti hoti* ("know something that") combination, as he does in vv.4, 5 (Rom 13:11; 1 Cor 16:15; 2 Cor 12:3, 4; 1 Thess 2:1; cf. Acts 16:3) (Lightfoot, p. 12). Aside from the difficulty in making this understanding of *hoti* ("that") agree with meaning given *eklogēn* ("chosen") in v.4, this idea misconstrues vv.5ff. in that these verses do not primarily deal with the

Thessalonians' conversion experience. In fact, v.5 does not directly relate to the Thessalonians but rather to Paul and his colleagues and vv.6–10 go beyond the conversion experience and its immediate sequel. It is better, therefore, to favor a causal *hoti*. Paul does follow up *eidenai ti* with a causal *hoti* at times, as witnessed by Romans 8:28, 29, though admittedly his syntax there is not exactly analogous with the present passage.

Instead of writing, "We came to you," the apostle puts the messengers in the background by saying, "Our gospel came to you." The message deserved foremost attention. Eight times in two Epistles *euangelion* ("gospel") is used to refer to the good news of salvation through Christ. Once the "good news" is unqualified by any modifier (1 Thess 2:4). Three times it is called "the gospel of God" (1 Thess 2:2, 8, 9), God being the author of the gospel (ablative of source). Twice it is "the gospel of Christ [or our Lord Jesus]" (1 Thess 3:2; 2 Thess 1:8), Christ being named as topic of the gospel message (objective genitive). The other two occurrences (1 Thess 1:5; 2 Thess 2:14) use "our gospel," meaning "the gospel we preach" (subjective genitive). Paul makes no claim to having originated the gospel (cf. 1 Cor 15:1–11; cf. Hunter, *Paul and His Predecessors*, p. 15). He claims only to be a staunch proclaimer of the glad tidings from the Father concerning his Son.

This gospel made its way to the Thessalonians through the missionaries in a fourfold manner. It came, first of all, "with words" or, literally, "in word" (*en logō*). This is obvious, since words are basic to intelligent communication. But the gospel's coming was not "simply" in word; speaking was only a part of the whole picture. Their preaching was not mere hollow rhetoric but contained three other ingredients essential to the outworking of God's elective purpose.

The first is "power" (*dynamei* [dat.]). Not to be confused with *dynameis*, the plural of *dynamis*, which means "miracles" (1 Cor 12:10; Gal 3:5), the singular does not specify supernatural manifestations but neither does it exclude them. This verse primarily points to the inward power with which the speakers were filled as they gave the message, a power that might show itself in a variety of ways. This made the speakers aware of God's special involvement in the gospel and its presentation.

The second ingredient of the spoken word is a person, for the message came "with the Holy Spirit." This Person certainly was behind the power just named. Yet he is much greater and more versatile than just the subjective power he produces. He is part of the Godhead (contrast Best, p. 75; Turner, *Syntax*, Vol. III of Moulton's *Grammar of NT Greek* [Edinburgh: T. & T. Clark, 1963], p. 175). He supplies a sense of divine reality to the spoken message.

Growing out of his special activity is a third ingredient of the spoken word. "With deep conviction" (*plērophora pollē*) means that the preachers possessed perfect assurance as to the truth and effectiveness of their message. *Plērophoria*, at one point meaning "fullness," developed a NT connotation of "full assurance" or "confidence" (MM, pp. 519, 520). Such subjective certainty, sensed by Paul and his associates, served as a major ingredient of this first proof that these readers had been chosen by God.

"You know how we lived among you for your sake" draws on the Thessalonians' innate awareness of what Paul and Silas and Timothy became while with them, so as to substantiate what sort of inner transformation God had wrought. Throughout the Epistle Paul carries his readers along with him by such expressions as "you know how" (*kathōs oidate*), which he uses as a precaution against those who might disagree (cf. 2:2, 5; 3:4). The quality of life shown by the missionaries had in itself been sufficient vindication of their sincerity and of the message they preached. Their attitudes were completely unselfish ("for your sake").

Notes

4,5 The only difference in construction between Romans 8:28, 29 and the present use of εἰδέναι τι ὅτι (*eidenai ti hoti,* "to know something because") is the replacing of a noun (τὴν ἐκλογήν, *tēn eklogēn*) as direct object by an objective ὅτι (*hoti,* "that") clause. The second *hoti* in Romans 8:28, 29 is causal. Though not an exact parallel, the structure is similar enough to refute the generalization that Paul *always* follows *eidenai ti* with an objective *hoti.*

In v.5 two appearances of ἐν (*en* "in;" NIV, "with," "among")—before πληροφορίᾳ (*plērophoria,* "conviction") and before ὑμῖν (*hymin,* "you")—have weak MS support. The sense of the verse is not greatly affected by their absence.

2. *The effect on the Thessalonians* (1:6–10)

a. *Their transformation*

1:6, 7

> 6You became imitators of us and of the Lord; in spite of severe suffering, you welcomed the message with the joy given by the Holy Spirit.
> 7And so you became a model to all the believers in Macedonia and Achaia.

6,7 The second proof of election lies in the effect of the gospel on those evangelized (vv.6–10): (1) They "welcomed the message" and were converted. (2) They did so "in spite of severe suffering." (3) In difficult circumstances they had a joy that could only be "given by the Holy Spirit." (4) They rapidly became "imitators" of Paul and also the Lord. (5) They grew to a point of becoming a "model to all the believers in Macedonia and Achaia." So complete a transformation rapidly accomplished happens only when God's elective purpose is at work in people.

At the beginning of v.6 the *kai* ("and" or variants thereof) has not been translated. But here *kai* followed by *hymeis* ("you") means "and you on your part" and introduces a new point in Paul's explanation of how he knew God had chosen the Thessalonians (v.4). In a relatively short time they "became imitators." *Egenēthēte,* "became," is the same verb and tense as *egenēthēmen,* "we lived," in v.5. Now their life style was completely different from what it was before the gospel came to them, because their conversion led them to imitate Paul and his companions. Paul repeatedly encouraged this wholesome following of examples (1 Cor 4:16; 11:1; Gal 4:12; Eph 5:1; Phil 3:17; 4:9; 1 Thess 3:12; 2 Thess 3:7, 9). He did not hesitate to present himself as one to be copied, because he had patterned his own life after Christ's (1 Cor 11:1). So he added "and of the Lord" in 1:6. The notion of imitating God and Christ applies especially to *holiness* (1 Peter 1:15, 16), *love* (Matt 5:43–48; Luke 6:36; John 13:34; 15:12) and *suffering* (Matt 16:24, 25; Mark 10:38, 39; Luke 14:27; John 15:18–20; 1 Peter 2:18–21)—three areas touched upon later in Thessalonians: holiness in 3:13; 4:3, 7; love in 3:12; 4:9, 10; and suffering in 3:2–4.

Spiritual advance was possible for the Thessalonians only after they first "welcomed the message" preached by the missionaries ("words," v.5, and "message," v.6, both are from *logos* ["word"]). Even after their conversion, their response to the message was just as enthusiastic, though this reponse entailed "severe suffering." "Suffering" or "tribulation" (*thlipsis*) plays a large part in these letters (1 Thess 1:6; 3:3, 4, 7; 2 Thess 1:4, 6,

7) because persecution was so common (Acts 17:5-9) and grew so intense as to be comparable to the bitter opposition by the Jews against the Lord Jesus and the Judean church (1 Thess 2:14-16). There was no extreme to which Christ's enemies would not go in making life miserable for Christians. Yet instead of misery the Thessalonians displayed a "joy given by the Holy Spirit." Such a response defies natural explanation. The same One who gave Paul and his companions power for proclaiming the gospel (v.5) dwelt within those who received the gospel and transformed them with joy.

The greatest attainment for these new Christians was becoming for others what Paul and his companions had been for them (v.7). They had become "a model" to Christians throughout Greece. *Typon* ("model") suggests an exact reproduction. Christians in Philippi, Berea, Athens, Corinth, and elsewhere in the Grecian provinces of Macedonia and Achaia did well to look to Thessalonica.

Notes

6,7 Whether the aorist participle δεξάμενοι (*dexamenoi*, "welcoming") is antecedent to or simultaneous with ἐγενήθητε (*egenēthēte*, "you became") should be clarified. If it is simultaneous, the participial phrase defines the nature of their imitation (Frame, p. 82; Lightfoot, p. 14). Syntactically this is possible, but it results in much too narrow a definition of μιμηταί (*mimētai*, "imitators"). Doubtless the Thessalonians' cordial reception of the message (*logos*) was part of their imitation subsequent to conversion, but this could not exhaust it as the above discussion of "imitators" shows. It is thus preferable to assign an antecedent force to the aorist participal and understand the clause as "after you received the message. . . ."

Θλίψει (*thlipsei*, "suffering") is used rarely outside biblical Gr. Its secular usage as "pressure" quickly became more frequent in LXX and the NT and took on a metaphorical connotation of "affliction"—the lot of God's people in this world. In the NT it has a general usage referring to any tribulation suffered by Christians (1:6; John 16:33), but it also has a special eschatological force in reference to the period just before Christ's return (Matt 24:21; cf. Dan 12:1).

For Christ to be referred to as "the Lord" instead of "Jesus" is not nearly so difficult as Best makes it (Best, pp. 77, 78). Artificial schemes for distinguishing the image of Christ, supposedly constructed in the imagination of the early church, from the historical Jesus are unworthy of serious exegetical consideration by those who are convinced of the infallibility of Scripture.

The sing. τύπον (*typon*, "model") in v.7 is a more likely reading than the pl. τύποι (*typoi*) because of diversified geographical support among ancient sources. It is also the more difficult reading. A copier would hardly have changed a pl. to a sing., but the converse is not true.

b. *Their witness*

1:8-10

> 8The Lord's message rang out from you not only in Macedonia and Achaia—your faith in God has become known everywhere. Therefore we do not need to say anything about it, 9for they themselves report what kind of reception you gave us. They tell how you turned to God from idols to serve the living and true God, 10and to wait for his Son from heaven, whom he raised from the dead—Jesus, who rescues us from the coming wrath.

8-10 In describing how the Thessalonians were a model Christian community and giving further proof of the effect of the gospel on them, Paul gives another indication of their election (cf. v.4): their vigorous propagation of their faith. Using the same Greek term (*logos*) that is translated "words" in v.5 and "message" in v.6, Paul now adds an ablative *tou kuriou* ("of the Lord") to specify the source of the message. Their progress was remarkable in that what Paul and his companions had preached (v.5) and the Thessalonians had received (v.6), they were now sharing on the widest scale possible. *Ho logos tou kuriou* ("the word [NIV, "message"] of the Lord," an OT equivalent of the Lord's utterance; cf. Isa 38:4, 5) is used extensively in Acts to describe the spreading gospel message (Acts 8:25; 13:44, 48, 49; 15:35, 36; 16:32; 19:10, 20). Paul affirms that these converts played a substantial part in this ever-widening scope of Christian witness.

With Thessalonica as the starting point ("from you"), the message "rang out" (v.8) as brass instruments that keep on sounding. The figure is of an echo that continues indefinitely (perfect tense, *eksēchētai*, "rang out') and implies the persistence of the testimony over an ever-increasing expanse—"not only in Macedonia and Achaia . . . everywhere." Here Greece is viewed as a single territory rather than two separate provinces (cf. also v.7). This contrasts (*all'*, "but," a word implied by the dash but not translated in the NIV, though found in the Greek of v.8) with "everywhere" or "in every place" (*en panti topō*). So impressed is Paul with how far the gospel had progressed through the Thessalonians' faithful witness that he obviously indulges in a kind of hyperbole. "Everywhere" is clearly not worldwide in scope; in writing to the Romans some five years later, Paul implied that Spain had not yet been evangelized (Rom 15:19, 20, 24). (For similar Pauline hyperboles see Rom 1:8; 2 Cor 2:14; Phil 1:13; Col 1:6.) Part of the Thessalonians' outreach stemmed from their location on the Egnatian Way and the Thermaic Gulf with access by sea to the whole Mediterranean world (Milligan, p. 12; Lightfoot, pp. 15, 16; Hiebert, p. 64). But the largest factor was their diligence in communicating their faith to others. This was probably reported to Paul by Silas and Timothy on returning from Macedonia (Acts 18:5; 1 Thess 3:6) and by Aquila and Priscilla from as far as Rome (Acts 18:2).

So carried away with the Thessalonians' witness was Paul that instead of ending his sentence of v.8 in a grammatically acceptable way at *en panti topō* ("everywhere"), he added, "Your faith in God has become known." News of this believing relationship constituted part of "the Lord's message" that had issued from them. It had gone forth and remained (*ekselēluthen*, perfect tense) so that Paul and his companions did not need to speak of it, though Paul later referred to it (cf. 2 Cor 8:1, 2).

Instead of Paul's telling others what had happened in Thessalonica, others were giving him a twofold report about this Macedonian city. First, they described how Paul, Silas and Timothy had entered the city (cf. v.5). Second, this church had turned to God from idols (v.9). Here Paul, who most often refers in a positive way to conversion as believing (cf. 1:7) uses a word for turning away from error and toward God ("turned," *epistrepsate*; cf. Acts 14:15; 26:18, 20; 2 Cor 3:16). His mention of idols shows the Thessalonians' Gentile origin, since idol worship did not dominate the Jews after the Babylonian exile. At the same time, it raises the question as to whether these are the same "God-fearing Greeks" (Acts 17:4) who were among the original converts. Normal expectation would be for "God-fearers" to already have separated themselves from idolatrous paganism because of affiliation, though loose, with a Jewish synagogue. Yet their release from past darkness may not have been total till secured by their relationship to God through Jesus Christ. Also probably included were additional Gentile converts who had no previous contact with Judaism.

Two purposes in the Thessalonians' turning to God are given: "to serve [*douleuein*—a verb related to *doulos,* "slave"] the living and true God" (v.9) and "to wait for his Son from heaven" (v.10). Such service to God speaks of utter devotion and recognition of his rightful lordship over mankind. He alone is worthy of this, for he is "living," in contrast to lifeless idols, and "true," in contrast to counterfeit representations of himself.

The second purpose, "to wait for his Son from heaven," strikes a doctrinal note prominent throughout the remainder of the Epistle. Paul's second missionary journey as gauged by his preaching at Thessalonica and as reflected in these two Epistles stressed eschatological events surrounding the return of Jesus Christ from the Father's right hand in heaven (cf. Acts 17:7; 1 Thess 2:19; 3:13; 4:15; 5:2, 23; 2 Thess 2:1, 8). Primitive Christianity universally held that the resurrected and ascended Christ would return and their expectancy of this event implied its nearness (Best, p. 83). For Paul to include himself and his readers among those to be rescued from wrath at this future moment (cf. "us," v.10) shows that they expected this to happen before death. Had Jesus never been raised from the dead, he could never return, but since he had been raised, his future reappearance is guaranteed by that very resurrection (just as is his divine sonship, Rom 1:4).

It is not some mystical spirit but the historical personage "Jesus" who will return as rescuer ("who rescues," *ton rhuomenon,* is a timeless substantive denoting one of his characteristics) of living Christians from the period of divine wrath at the close of the world's present age of grace. Used technically, as it so frequently is in the NT, "wrath" (*orgēs*) is a title for the period just before Messiah's kingdom on earth, when God will afflict earth's inhabitants with an unparalleled series of physical torments because of their rejection of His will (Matt 3:7; 24:21; Luke 21:23; Rev 6:16, 17). That the wrath is pictured as "coming" or "approaching" carries out effectively the force of the present participle *erchomenēs.* It is already on its way and hence quite near (Frame, p. 89). Throughout the Epistle, the events of Jesus' future coming are imminent (cf. "we who are still alive, who are left," 4:15, 17). So near was the world to being plunged into an unexpected time of trouble (cf. 1 Thess 5:2, 3) that it was on the brink of disaster. Such was the outlook of early Christendom and such is always a proper Christian anticipation.

Rather than fearing this time, however, Christians find an incentive to persevere (cf. "endurance inspired by hope," 1:3), because for them it will mean rescue rather than doom. Not even the stepped-up persecution of Christ's followers that will mark this future period will touch them, for their deliverer will remove them from the scene of these dreadful happenings.

It has been accurately observed that much of the terminology in vv.9b, 10 differs from normal Pauline usage (Hiebert, p. 66; Best, pp. 85, 86). Whether these differences can be attributed to Paul's incorporation of reports from others (Hiebert, p. 66) or to his adoption of "a pre-Pauline statement of the Church's faith" (Best, p. 86) cannot be determined with certainty. Perhaps both explanations contain elements of truth. In this his earliest Epistle Paul may not as yet have formulated his own theological vocabulary as he did later and so may have been dependent on statements that came to him from others (cf. 1 Cor 15:1–5).

Notes

8 The ἐν τῇ (*en tē,* "in [the]") appearing before "Achaia" in some MSS should be omitted in agreement with most editors. Its omission is more difficult to explain, as a scribe would more

likely have added it intentionally from v.7 than omitted it unintentionally. Yet the omission is not so difficult as to be impossible. Two proper nouns governed by the same *en tē* (before "Macedonia") present Greece as a unit in contradistinction to ἐν παντὶ τόπῳ (*en panti topō*, "in every place").

Placing a full stop after κυρίου (*kyriou*, "Lord") or Ἀχαΐα (*Achaia*) (see NIV, v.8) is questionable. While we must grant that the sentence as it stands is irregular, it is not beyond Paul's impetuous style to write such an anacoluthon. His emotional makeup often prompted him to vary from usual syntax. Perhaps a preferable rendering of the verse would be, "For the Lord's message rang out from you not only in Macedonia and Achaia, but everywhere your faith toward God has become known, so that we do not need to say anything about it."

10 Not much can be concluded regarding Paul's use of the pl. οὐρανῶν (*ouranōn*, "heavens"), since he uses the noun's sing. and pl. about equally (eleven sing. and ten pl.). The Heb word for "heaven"—שָׁמַיִם (*šāmayim*)—is pl. and Paul knew a plurality of heavenly spheres (2 Cor 12:2), but in these same Epistles he conceives of Christ's return from a singular οὐρανοῦ (*ouranou*; cf. 1 Thess 4:16; 2 Thess 1:7; so Milligan, pp. 14, 15). Apparently these are two ways to think of heaven, either as its components or as a single entity.

It is quite possible that Paul substitutes τῆς ἐρχομένης (*tēs erchomenēs*, "the coming"; i.e., on its way) for John the Baptist's τῆς μελλούσης (*tēs mellousēs*, "the coming") (Matt 3:7; Luke 3:7) to show a greater degree of imminence. For John this wrath was not an "any-moment" possibility, even though quite near. For Paul, however, prophetic events to precede the wrath had now been fulfilled (cf. 1 Thess 2:15, 16). This future wrath should be distinguished from the present wrath of God currently being poured out against rebellious humanity (Rom 1:18-32).

III. Vindication Before the Thessalonians (2:1-3:13)

A. *Vindication Through Methods* (2:1-12)

1. *Preaching, replete with power*

2:1, 2

> [1]You know, brothers, that our visit to you was not a failure. [2]We had previously suffered and been insulted in Philippi, as you know, but with the help of our God we dared to tell you his gospel in spite of strong opposition.

1,2 Having explained so fully why he and his colleagues were thankful (1:2-10), Paul now takes up one of the main purposes for writing the Epistle—a lengthy vindication of the missionaries' character and ministry (chs. 2-3). *Gar* ("for") in 2:1, though not translated in NIV, forms a bridge between the chapters. It marks 2:1-16 as an expansion of chapter 1—probably 1:5-10 especially, since 2:1-12 looks into Paul's coming to Thessalonica and his conduct there (cf. 1:5, 9a) and 2:13-16 turns our attention to the Thessalonians' response (cf. 1:6-8, 9b, 10).

Yet chapter 2 does not just go over the same ground. In chapter 1 Paul's coming and the peoples' response show a knowledge of election (1:4). But in chapter 2 the same themes establish Paul's defense against insinuations about his alleged ulterior motives.

The identity of Paul's Thessalonian opponents is a puzzle difficult to piece together. Suggestions have included heretical pseudo-apostles as found in Corinth and Galatia, Judaizers, spiritual enthusiasts, Gnostics, and Jews (Best, p. 16). Also whether they were within the church or outside it remains a mystery. A possible reconstruction sees the Jews as continuing adversaries of Paul, even after he left Thessalonica (cf. 2:14-16), for they were so intent on destroying the work he had started that they persistently hurled accusations at him and labeled him another self-seeking religious propagandist. How they distorted his teaching to accuse him of treason while he was yet in the city (Acts 17:7) shows an abiding animosity toward him. Subjected to a constant barrage of accusations, Thessalonian Christians may easily have begun to question Paul's sincerity. There is no evidence of organized opposition within the church, yet Timothy apparently brought back news (3:6) that some uncertainty had arisen within it as to whether Paul's concern for it was genuine. This is not to say that his relations with the readers of the Epistle were no longer cordial (cf. 3:6), but symptoms of estrangement had appeared that could have led to an open rift unless treated immediately.

In light of this development, Paul again addresses his readers affectionately ("brothers," v.1) and reminds them of conditions throughout his initial visit. Special concern that his readers recall certain matters for themselves is evident in the recurrence of "you know" (vv.1, 2, 5, 11; cf. "you remember," v.9, and "you are witnesses," v.10). In v.1 particularly he points to their awareness by the intensive *autoi:* "you yourselves know."

What they are called to witness regarding the "visit" or "entrance" (*eisodon,* cf. 1:9) is that it "was not a failure." "Failure" renders the Greek adjective *kenē,* whose meaning has received much discussion. Some have referred it to the results of their ministry (Best, pp. 89, 90), but this idea would have been conveyed by *mataios* (Milligan, p. 16; Ellicott, p. 15; Lightfoot, p. 18; Frame, p. 92). Another suggestion is "empty-handed," i.e., greedy for gain (Hendriksen, p. 60). The ideas of "false," i.e., under false pretenses, and "aimless," i.e., without specific purpose, have also been suggested (Hiebert, pp. 79, 80). The greatest probability, however, rests with assigning the word a qualitative force, "void of content," "empty," since v.2 in presenting the other side speaks of their boldness and earnestness in ministry. This conclusion also agrees with 1:5, of which the present section is a resumption. The character of their ministry "was" and continues to be (*gegonen,* 2:1, perfect tense) real and courageous.

The opposite of the empty ministry denied in v.1 is one where no obstacle or threat is sufficient to deter the speaker of God's gospel (2:2. In Philippi, Paul and Silas had been beaten and severely flogged; they had been put in prison with their feet in stocks (Acts 16:22–24) and possibly otherwise cruelly mistreated because they had rescued a slave girl in the name of Jesus Christ. They had also been insulted by being arrested unjustly, stripped of their clothes, and treated like dangerous fugitives. Their Roman citizenship had been violated, and for this Paul demanded restitution (Acts 16:37). Still staggering from these injuries and indignities, the two came to Thessalonica. Under such conditions, most people would have refrained from repeating a message that had led to such violent treatment, but not these men. With God's help, they mustered sufficient courage to declare in this new city their gospel from God. *Eparrēsiasametha,* "we dared," richly describes how they boldly spoke out despite the same potential dangers as faced in Philippi.

Here again they encountered "strong opposition." *Agōni,* represented in the text above by "opposition," pictures an athlete's struggle to gain first place in a race or contest. Paul's conflict may have been inward (cf. Col 2:1), but most likely it came from outward persecutions and dangers originated by his Jewish opponents (cf. Phil 1:30), since inner strivings cannot equal the tempo of persecution set earlier in v.2. Though Luke does not directly mention "strong opposition" in Thessalonica (Acts 17:1–10), it is clear from the present Epistle that such did come. In spite of it, however, Paul's inner help from God produced a continuing proclamation of the gospel. Such earnestness plainly shows sincerity.

Notes

1,2 προπαθόντες (propathontes, "having previously suffered") and ὑβρισθέντες (hubristhentes, "having been insulted") are preferably understood as concessive rather than temporal, even though the καί (kai, "and") preceding the former in TR is not genuine. The bold speech of the apodosis is attained despite the condition expressed in the protasis.

2. Preaching, removed from untruth

2:3, 4

3For the appeal we make does not spring from error or impure motives, nor are we trying to trick you. 4On the contrary, we speak as men approved by God to be entrusted with the gospel. We are not trying to please men but God, who tests our hearts.

3,4 Not only was the preaching of Paul and his companions filled with power and earnestness when they evangelized Thessalonica (vv.1, 2), but wherever they went it was above suspicion of any kind (vv.3, 4). The boldness just described was possible because ("for," v.3) God, who tests man's motives, had approved their fitness to preach the gospel.

"Appeal" hints at the gently persuasive form of Paul's preaching. Whether hortatory or consolatory, paraklēsis ("appeal") always addresses the will in quest of a favorable decision, but the intellect is not excluded. Persuasion, however, is of various types, both wholesome and otherwise. Paul and his fellow workers had apparently been accused of appealing on wrong grounds. The damage from this accusation he is quite anxious to repair.

First to be corrected was the claim that his appeal arose from "error" or self-delusion. Planēs ("error") at times has an active sense of "deceit," a meaning indistinguishable in the present verse from dolō ("trying to trick you"). Here, however, it should be assigned its passive meaning of "error" as usual in the NT. Paul's message agreed perfectly with truth.

He answers his opponents further in the matter of "impure motives" or "impurity" (akatharsias). Some have defended a general definition of "impurity" by saying that a more specialized sense of sexual impurity is too abrupt and out of place in the present discussion (Best, p. 93). They add that Paul is never accused elsewhere of this sin of immorality (Findlay, CGT, p. 37; Lenski, p. 246). Whatever specialization may lie in its scope, it is argued, is limited to covetousness (cf. 2:5), which at times allegedly is covered by akatharsia (Hauck, TDNT, 3:428–429). Yet a more restricted meaning of sexual impurity has much in its favor. A casual reference to such in this pagan environment would have shocked no one (cf. 4:3–8; Milligan, p. 18; Lightfoot, pp. 20, 21). Doubtless, Paul's enemies were attacking him on many fronts, including this sin so prevalent among traveling religious teachers. Constant use of akatharsia for sexual sins in all literature of the time is persuasive for giving it the same meaning here (Frame, p. 95). The apostle disclaims anything of this type as a motive for his missionary activities.

He further denies any attempt to use deceit so as to trick his listeners. He was neither guilty of self-deceit (planēs, "error") nor of deceiving others (dolō, "guile,"; NIV, "trying to trick you") though he was accused of doing so on more occasions than this (cf. 2 Cor 4:2; 12:16). He made no empty promises and followed no humanly devised schemes. In seeking intelligent decisions from his hearers, he presented facts in their true light.

The true state of the missionaries was one of openness and honesty to the point that an omniscient God had found them worthy to declare his gospel (v.4). To be "approved by God" (perfect tense, *dedokimasmetha*) entails a process of testing, success in completing the tests, and a consequent state of endorsement by God. After calling Paul on the Damascus road, God subjected him to necessary rigors to demonstrate his capability for his assigned task. Having thus prepared him, he committed to him the gospel message for proclamation among Gentiles such as these readers. On the basis of this commission, the missionary team spoke wherever they went. They did nothing superficial just "to please men." Ultimately, they sought God's approbation. This kind of goal excluded anything ulterior or hidden from the eyes of him "who tests our hearts." The scrutiny of a God, who is able to sound the depths of every thought (cf. Rom 8:27 as to God's awareness of all men's thoughts), is Paul's ultimate court of appeal in summoning evidence for his absolute sincerity.

3. Preaching, reinforced by godly concern (2:5–12)

a. Evidenced by the absence of lower motives

2:5–7a

> [5]You know we never used flattery, nor did we put on a mask to cover up greed—God is our witness. [6]We were not looking for praise from men, not from you or anyone else.
> [7]As apostles of Christ we could have been a burden to you. . . .

5–7a Godly concern for his listeners underscores more forcefully than anything else the legitimacy of Paul's missionary methods (2:5–12). In turning to discuss his sincere care, he initially dispenses with the notion that he was moved by lower motives. *Gar* ("for," untranslated in text above but introducing v.5 of Greek text) explains how his general policy (vv.3, 4) was applied in Thessalonica. As in vv.1, 2 and 3, 4 Paul begins in a negative vein by denying allegations against his character (vv. 5–7a) before presenting the true picture (vv.7b–12; cf. *alla*, which introduces the positive side in each case, vv.2, 4, 7).

In the first of three denials, he calls his readers to verify his complete abstinence from any word used for flattering purposes. The insidious practice of saying nice things to gain influence over others for selfish reasons is what *kolakeias* ("flattery") denotes in classical writings (Milligan, p. 19; Lightfoot, p. 23). Paul seeks their own confirmation that he "never" (*oute . . . pote*) was guilty of this.

Second, he denies putting on the kind of mask that greed wears. "A mask to cover up greed" (v.5) renders *pleonexias* ("greed") as an objective genitive and may imply that the missionaries were greedy, but did not seek to hide it. This is out of harmony with Paul's defense that would not admit to greed. A more appropriate sense comes from a subjective genitive, "a pretext such as covetousness would use" (Ellicott, p. 19; Milligan, p. 20). Only God could verify inner freedom from greed. So Paul calls on God as witness (*theos martys*, v.5). The greed of which he was accused includes more than just avarice or love of money, which would be *philargyria* (cf. 1 Tim 6:10). *Pleonexia* is self-seeking of all types, a quest for anything that brings self-satisfaction. It grows out of complete disinterest in the rights of others—an attitude foreign to Paul and his helpers.

Third, Paul disavows the desire for "praise from men" (v.6). *Doxa*, most frequently rendered "glory" in the NT, here carries its classical force of "good opinion" or "honor." The world of Paul's time was filled with wandering philosophers, prophets of other religions, magicians, false prophets, and others seeking not only financial gain, but also the prestige of a good reputation. Divine approval (cf. v.4), not public esteem, was what motivated Paul and his companions, whether in Thessalonica or elsewhere.

Grammatically, the first part of v.7, *dynamenoi en barei einai hōs Christou apostoloi* ("as apostles of Christ we could have been a burden to you"), goes with the preceding and is required to complete the sense of v.6. *Dynamenoi* is concessive, "though we could have been." Paul, Silas, and Timothy could legitimately have claimed the dignity associated with their apostolic office. (*Apostoloi* is used here in a nontechnical sense that covers others besides eyewitnesses of Christ's resurrection; cf. 2 Cor 8:23; Phil 2:25.) *En barei* ("a burden") has primary reference to apostolic dignity. Such a prestigious connotation is to be preferred over understanding a material burden as the meaning. Verse 9 implies the right of the servant of Christ to receive support from converts; but v.7a speaks of authoritative position, in contrast both to seeking "praise" as they might have done (v.6) and to giving "gentle" treatment as they actually did (v.7b). The important position of Paul and his colleagues as Christ's representatives earned for them the right to receive special respect, but they did not stand on this right. So this is further evidence that they were not prompted by lower motives.

Notes

5 The genitive κολακείας (*kolakeias*, "of flattery") with λόγῳ (*logos*, "word") has been analyzed in several ways: ablative of source, "a word that comes from flattery"; genitive of description, "a flattering word"; and genitive of apposition, "a word that is flattery." Yet a subjective genitive is more to the point: "the word that flattery uses," in that the other genitive πλεονεξίας (*pleonexias*, "of greed") is also subjective (Ellicott, p. 19; Lightfoot, p. 23; Frame, p. 97).
6 Ζητοῦντες . . . δόξαν (*zētountes . . . doxan*," looking for praise") is a participial phrase of manner describing how the missionaries did not undertake their Thessalonian ministry. Paul does not say he never received honor from men or that he had no right to receive it. He does, however, deny that he required such from his converts (Frame, pp. 98, 99).
7 Placing Χριστοῦ (*Christou*, "Christ") before ἀπόστολοι (*apostoloi*, "apostles") calls special attention to whose apostles they were. This was the key to the importance of their position. Apostleship in itself is meaningless apart from the prestige of the sender (Ellicott, p. 20).

b. *Evidenced by the presence of higher motives*
2:7b–12

7bbut we were gentle among you, like a mother caring for her little children. 8We loved you so much that we were delighted to share with you not only the gospel of God but our lives as well, because you had become so dear to us. 9Surely you remember, brothers, our toil and hardship; we worked night and day in order not to be a burden to anyone while we preached the gospel of God to you.

10You are witnesses, and so is God, of how holy, righteous and blameless we were among you who believed. 11For you know that we dealt with each of you as a father deals with his own children, 12encouraging, comforting and urging you to live lives worthy of God, who calls you into his kingdom and glory.

7b The godly concern of Paul and his helpers was proved by their higher motives (7b–12) as well as by their freedom from lower motives (5–7a). With the "but" of v.7, the apostle takes up a positive description the Thessalonians were bound to agree with because of their own observations—"you remember" (v.9); "you are witnesses" (v.10); "you know" (v.11). While intermingling with these Macedonians as equals (*en mesō hymōn*, "among you," is intensive), Paul and his helpers were gentle, not authoritarian (v.7). They put aside their rights of being respected and playing a dominating part and demonstrated the utmost tenderness, comparable to that of a mother nursing her own children. *Trophos* means a nurse, but often as here refers to the mother herself. "Her" (*heautēs*) is emphatic and marks this close relationship. The figure implies a special effort to protect and to provide for every need, even to the extent of great sacrifice.

8 The manner of gentle treatment was a willingness to "share with you not only the gospel of God but our lives as well." "We loved you so much" represents a rare word of uncertain derivation (*homeiromenoi*), but the general thrust is clear. The missionaries knew a constant "yearning for" (cf. Job 3:21, LXX) these people, so much so that they found it a continual delight (*eudokoumen*, "we were delighted") to share their whole being with them. "Lives" (*psychas*) conveys more than just their physical lives; in the depths of their being they cared "because [the Thessalonians] had become so dear" to them. An even stronger relationship of love developed as the ministry continued—a relationship like that of a nursing mother with her child.

9 Verse 9 recalls the long hours of extreme toil and hardship by which the missionaries supported themselves while preaching. *Gar* ("surely") looks back to "we were delighted to share ... our lives" (v.8; cf. Lightfoot, p. 26; Ellicott, p. 22). The gentleness of v.7 (Frame, p. 102) is too distant to be included through the *gar,* and the endearing close of v.8 (Lenski, p. 253) is too subordinate grammatically to merit support by this conjunction. So Paul is taking the single item of self-support as evidence of his broader concern for the Thessalonians.

"Toil" (*kopon*), translated "labor" in 1:3, emphasizes the fatigue they incurred in expending themselves, while "hardship" (*mochthon*) highlights external difficulties encountered in the process. As in 2 Thessalonians 3:8, the combination describes the apostles' efforts at providing their own upkeep, an example much needed by some they were writing to (1 Thess 4:11, 12; 5:14; 2 Thess 3:6–15). They worked at night as well as during the day while proclaiming the gospel (2:9b). Paul's work was probably tentmaking (Acts 18:3), though it may have been the production of tent material from animal hair or skins (Hiebert, pp. 98, 99). Part of a Jewish child's upbringing was learning a trade, and Paul was no exception to this. He received some financial help from the Philippian church while he was in Thessalonica (Phil 4:15, 16), but not enough to permit him to stop working. Apparently his wages were so low that he needed gifts to enable him to take some time off for preaching (Acts 18:5; Best, p. 104). Though missionary service includes the right to support from others (1 Cor 9:3ff.), Paul does not seem to have used that right in Thessalonica, Corinth (1 Cor 4:12; 2 Cor 11:8), Ephesus (Acts 20:34, 35), and elsewhere.

By this "around-the-clock" diligence Paul lifted the burden of support from his converts. His central purpose was to give them the gospel of God. From this nothing should detract, and making the gospel "free of charge" (1 Cor 9:18) eliminated charges of selfish motives.

10 Paul appeals to the Thessalonians as witnesses of "how holy, righteous and blameless we were among you who believed." God also is called to attest to whatever was hidden to human eyes. *Hosiōs* ("holily") highlights religious piety while *dikaiōs* ("righteously") pertains principally to moral conduct. From the negative side, Paul and his companions were "blameless," untainted by fault in their dealings. All this was for the sake of the believers (*tois pisteuousin*).

11 A further comparison (*kathaper*, translated "for" in NIV) enlivens Paul's expression of concern. Changing from a mother's tender care in v.8 to a new metaphor, Paul is now a father dealing with his own children individually (*hena hekaston hymōn*, "each of you"). Christians need fatherly teaching and advice as well as motherly care.

12 The fatherly treatment included encouragement, comfort, and urging. "Encouraging" (*parakalountes*) can in some contexts signify a note of comfort, but here it has the hortatory flavor of "admonishing." "Comfort" is covered by the second participle (*paramythoumenoi*). "Urging" (*martyromenoi*) adds a note of authority. These actions were more than mere requests. Their goal was a worthy life style. "Live lives" represents the figure of "walking around" (*peripatein*), a common way of designating conduct in both biblical and nonbiblical Greek (Best, p. 107). In reference to the Christian life, it relates primarily to the moral sphere. Conduct should be on the plane of God's standards.

The call of God into His kingdom and glory is an incentive to a high quality of life. The articular present participle *tou kalountos* ("calls," NIV) probably has a substantival force with little attention to a continuing call (cf. Best, pp. 107, 108; Hiebert, pp. 105, 106), since God's character as a caller is indicated by a comparable construction in 5:24 and Paul uses *kaleō* only in the aorist and perfect indicative, never in the present. This participle displays no duration but looks back to the initial call of these readers, which in Paul is always effectual (Lightfoot, p. 29). In one sense God's kingdom is already present (Matt 12:28; 13:1–52; Rom 14:17; 1 Cor 4:20; Col 1:13), but ultimate realization of the messianic kingdom with its future glory is in view here (cf. Acts 17:7). As frequently in the Thessalonian literature, those Paul is addressing are pointed to the bliss ahead as incentive to godly living now. "Glory" is that unhindered manifestation of God's presence in which believers will share (Rom 5:2; 8:18).

Notes

7 The textual choice between ἤπιοι (*ēpioi*, "gentle") and νήπιοι (*nēpioi*, "babies") is difficult. External evidence for *nēpioi* is much stronger than for *ēpioi*. Yet Paul never used νήπιος (*nēpios*, "baby") of himself, and a radical inversion of metaphor that transforms the apostle so quickly from a baby to a mother nurse is too violent even for Paul (cf. Gal 4:19, which only approaches this in suddenness). On the other hand, *ēpioi* is an appropriate sequel to v.7a. Understanding that the n of *nēpioi* could have arisen by dittography, *ēpioi* is slightly preferable. This dictates that a full stop be placed after ἀπόστολοι (*apostoloi*, "apostles"), a comma after ὑμῶν (*hymōn*, "you") and another full stop after τέκνα (*tekna*, "children"). This allows the comparative ὡς (*hōs*, "as") clause to amplify the *ēpioi* (Metzger, *The Text of the NT*, [New York: Oxford, 1968], pp. 230–233; Metzger, *A Textual Commentary of the Greek NT*, [New York: U.B.S., 1971], pp. 629–630; Hiebert, pp. 93–95).

8 Of the various suggested etymologies for ὁμειρόμενοι (*homeiromenoi*, "longing for") BAG, p.

568; Frame, p. 101; Lightfoot, pp. 25, 26), none has gained widespread acceptance. The verb's rarity makes it hard to trace. Nonetheless, the general meaning is clear from its context here, in Job 3:21 (LXX), and Psalm 62:2 (Symmachus).

Whether Paul received contributions from Philippi once or more than once is obscured by difficulty with the phrase καὶ ἅπαξ καὶ δίς (kai hapax kai dis, "both once and twice"; NIV, "again and again") in Philippians 4:16 (cf. 1 Thess 2:18). Either way, the effect on the meaning in the present context is not great (Best, p. 104). It does appear from the present discussion that Paul spent an extended period in this city in which case multiple offerings are very likely.

10 The force of the dative τοῖς πιστεύουσιν (tois pisteuousin, "the ones believing") is probably that of advantage. A locative of sphere is not probable. A dative of reference is too general. Since he emphasizes in this section such devotion to his readers, advantage provides the best analysis.

11, 12 It is possible to construe the three participles as indicatives, e.g., παρακαλοῦντες (parakalountes, "encouraging") as παρακαλοῦμεν (parakaloumen, "we encouraged") (Frame, p. 104). But the rarity of this in Paul argues against it. Rather than inserting a verb completely foreign to the context, such as "we dealt" or "we admonished," to govern ἕνα ἕκαστον (hena hekaston, "each one") (Lightfoot, pp. 28, 29), ἐγενήθημεν (egenēthēmen, "we were," v.10) can more naturally extend its force into vv. 11, 12 (Ibid.).

The articular present participle carries mainly a substantival sense (RHG, pp. 892, 1108, 1109). Hence, it is precarious to build anything on the progressive nature of the aktionsart of such as καλοῦντος (kalountos, "calling"; NIV, "who calls") since nothing in the context especially warrants it.

B. Vindication Through Their Thanksgiving (2:13–16)

1. For the ready acceptance of the Word of God

2:13

> 13And we also thank God continually because, when you received the word of God, which you heard from us, you accepted it not as the word of men, but as it actually is, the word of God, which is at work in you who believe.

13 Having already thanked God in 1:2, 3 for their progress, Paul now does so again by alluding to 1:5–10, which describes specifically how the Thessalonians so rapidly entered on a Christian way of life (1:6–10; cf. discussion of 2:1, 2). Now he cites their ready acceptance of the Word of God (cf. 1:6)—not in proof of their election as in chapter 1, but to show the reason for his sincere gratitude for them.

Because of the deep personal commitment he and his helpers had to the work at Thessalonica (dia touto, "because of this," untranslated in NIV, connects v.13 with vv.1–12), Paul could write, "We also thank God continually." "Also" here connotes "on our part." The missionary team's reaction to the Thessalonians' ready response to the word was incessant thanksgiving. The spotlight now shifts from the evangelizers (vv.1–12) to those evangelized (vv.13–16) (Milligan, p. 28; Lightfoot, p. 30; Frame, pp. 106, 107).

The cause of thanksgiving having already been given (vv.1–12, as stipulated by dia touto), hoti in v.13 does not add another cause ("because" in NIV), but rather introduces the content of thanksgiving ("we also thank God continually that. ..."; so Best, pp. 109, 110). The prayer of thanks not only referred to an objective reception (paralabontes, "[having] received"), but also a subjective acceptance (edexasthe, "you accepted"). The latter, a wholehearted welcome, indicated their high estimate of God's word (Ellicott,

p. 27; Lightfoot, p. 30; Frame, p. 107). This was the word they had heard preached by the missionaries (*akoēs par' hēmōn*, "you heard from us"), but ultimately it was the word from God (*tou Theou*). To accentuate the word's ultimate source, Paul bluntly states that they were not accepting "the word of men" ("as" in NIV is not in the Greek text), but what it "actually" was—"the word of God." Their appraisal of what they heard was accurate. Here is indication of Paul's consciousness of his own divinely imparted authority (cf. 1 Cor 14:37). His preaching was not the outgrowth of personal philosophical meanderings, but was deeply rooted in a message given by God himself (cf. *logos*, 1:5, 6, 8). What had been delivered to him through others (e.g., 1 Cor 11:23; 15:1, 3) and from the Lord directly (e.g., 1 Thess 4:15), he passed on to others. Such traditions were in turn taught to still others. Some teachings, such as the Thessalonian Epistles, were in written form, and became part of the NT canon (cf. 2 Tim 2:2; 2 Peter 3:15, 16).

Once received, this Word of God becomes an active power operating continually in the believer's life. When it is at work in those "who believe," there is a change in behavior and constant fruitfulness.

Notes

13 To seek an antecedent of τοῦτο (*touto*, "this"; with διά = "because of this," "therefore") in 2:1 (Best, pp. 109, 110), in 2:1–4 (Frame, p. 106) or in the ὅτι (*hoti*, "that," "because") clause of 2:13 (Lenski, p. 262) misses the underlying motive of the present paragraph. A desire to vindicate his ministry continues to control Paul's reasoning through chapter 3. He thus presents thanksgiving as another indication of his guileless interest in them. *Touto* therefore sums up what vv.1–12 has told about the missionaries' self-giving ministry.

Ἐνεργεῖται (*energeitai*, "is at work") is middle voice. Used actively in the NT, it always describes supernatural activity, principally God's. Since it is middle here, however, "the word," not "God," is the antecedent of its subject ὅς (*hos*, "which") (Armitage Robinson, *Ephesians*, [London: James Clarke & Co.], pp. 241–247).

2. *For their endurance under persecution*

2:14–16

14For you, brothers, became imitators of God's churches in Judea, which are in Christ Jesus. You suffered from your own countrymen the same things those churches suffered from the Jews, 15who killed the Lord Jesus and the prophets and also drove us out. They displease God and are hostile to all men 16in their effort to keep us from speaking to the Gentiles so that they may be saved. In this way they always heap up their sins to the limit. The wrath of God has come upon them at last.

14 Some see "for" as confirming the continued working of God's word (v.13; Ellicott, p. 28) while others see it as confirming the fact of the Thessalonians' belief (v.13; Olshausen, *Biblical Commentary* [Edinburgh: T. & T. Clark, 1851], 7:415). It is best, though, to regard it as confirming the principal statement of v.13—their ready acceptance of the Word (Best, p. 112). Welcoming the Word and enduring sufferings because of it often go together (cf. 1:6). While the working of the Word continued (v.13) up to

the point of Paul's writing, the stature of the Thessalonians as "imitators" had already been established in the past (*egenēthēte*, "you . . . became"; cf. *egenēthēte*, 1:6). Imitation "of God's churches in Judea" differs, however, from imitating Paul and the Lord (1:6). Deliberate imitation of sufferings for sufferings' sake is an unworthy Christian objective, but imitation of a Christian life style is legitimate and desirable. Persecution inevitably arises from the outside when a Christian patterns his life after the Lord.

Paul tenderly reminds these brothers that they were not the first to be afflicted. "God's churches in Judea, which are in Christ Jesus" had been the first and through faithful endurance had become an example of what Jesus had predicted about the suffering entailed in discipleship. Lest there be any doubt as to whom they were following, these are distinguished from all pagan assemblies by being identified as "God's" and from all Jewish churches by being specified as those "in Christ Jesus." Apparently the way these earliest Jewish Christians handled themselves had become widely known, even before Luke wrote Acts about A.D. 62. Paul's sympathy toward and harmony with Judean Christianity, whose bitter opponent he had been before conversion, is hereby assured, and the unity of all Christians, no matter what ethnic background or geographical locality, underlies this description of their common experience in suffering. Hearty acceptance of the Word, which is so often accompanied by adversity, is the very thing that insures one against falling away when adversity arises (cf. Matt 13:20, 21; Luke 8:13).

Both the Thessalonian churches and the churches in Judea suffered persecution from fellow-countrymen. For the Thessalonians these were predominantly Gentiles, though Jews also had been instrumental in stirring up opposition in that city (Acts 17:5–9). For the Judean churches, opposition had come from those of a Jewish background who, of course, were also strong advocates of the Jewish religion that Christianity so strongly threatened.

15,16 Mention of "the Jews" (v.14) furnishes Paul an occasion to digress slightly and deliver a violent criticism of this persecuting element among them. Such harsh language is markedly out of character for Paul as we know him from his other writings. He is renowned for his desire to see the salvation of these his blood relatives (Rom 9:1–3; 10:1), regardless of how much he had suffered personally at their hands (2 Cor 11:24, 26). So "un-Pauline" is the passage that some have supposed that all or part of it was added at a later time (Bailey, IB, 11:279, 280). Yet there is not the slightest shred of hard evidence for deletion. Exactly what provoked this sudden outburst cannot be known with certainty. An accumulation of hostile acts probably played a part. The writer had been chased out of Damascus (Acts 9:23–25) and Jerusalem (Acts 9:29, 30) by his own people not very long after his conversion. His message was rejected and his party driven out of Pisidian Antioch by them (Acts 13:45, 46, 50). At Iconium the Jews poisoned people's minds against Paul and Barnabas and ultimately forced them out (Acts 14:2, 5, 6). They made a special journey to Lystra to instigate an uprising that produced Paul's stoning and being left for dead (Acts 14:19). Jewish opposition continued to hound the missionary band into the second journey, specifically at Thessalonica, again producing Paul's exit (Acts 17:5, 10). Even now as Paul pens these words from Corinth, a united attack has been mounted against him by the city's Jewish residents (Acts 18:6, 12, 13). Couple with this the present plight of the Thessalonian Christians (1 Thess 3:3), ultimately traceable to Jewish opponents, and it is no wonder that Paul uses the occasion to recount their consistent opposition to the Lord Jesus.

The acme of the Jews' opposition is their part in the death of the Lord Jesus. Hence,

Paul places this crime first among their offences (v.15). By persuasion of the Jewish leaders, the Roman authorities crucified Jesus (John 19:16; 1 Cor 2:8). Though joint responsibility was shared by Gentiles and Jews (Acts 4:27), at this point Paul lays guilt for the crime on Israel. The aggravated nature of the injustice is implied by the way Paul separates *ton kyrion* ("the Lord") from the human name "Jesus" (*ton kyrion apokteinantōn Iēsoun*, "the Lord killing [i.e.,] Jesus"). It was none less than the exalted Lord of glory against whom this heinous crime was committed.

In the wording above, "the prophets" (v.15) are grouped with "the Lord Jesus" as murder victims of the Jews. This is a possible interpretation in that many, though not all, the OT prophets died in this way. Also, it is an oft-sounded note in biblical writings (1 Kings 19:10; Matt 23:31, 35, 37; Luke 13:34; Acts 7:52; Rom 11:3). More important in this connection is Jesus' parable of the vineyard in which killing some of the servants [prophets] is preliminary to killing the son (Matt 21:35–39; Mark 12:5–8). On the other hand, a very probable case can be made for connecting "the prophets" with "us" in this verse and translating "drove out the prophets and us" (Milligan, p. 30). If the parable of the vineyard furnishes a valid background, connecting "the prophets" here in v.15 with "the Lord Jesus" is unsatisfactory in that a chronological order is not observed and not all the servants in the parable are slain. Of greater import in the parable is the idea of the persecution of the servants [prophets]. In fact, Luke's account (Luke 20:9–16) does not even mention killing the servants. It is anticlimactic to name OT prophets in series after the Lord Jesus, but to list them alongside Paul's missionary band furnishes excellent reason for the past action of "drove . . . out" (aorist participle, *ekdiōxantōn*), since it is doubtful that Paul in this generalized description is thinking only of the single instance of their being forced out of Thessalonica. Furthermore, it helps vindicate the missionaries by placing them alongside the honored OT prophets.

Paul concludes v.15 by listing two more characteristics of the Jewish antagonists. "They displease God and are hostile to all men." The former is clearly an understatement, since they were militantly opposed to God. Their zeal for God was not guided by knowledge (Rom 10:2). So by opposing God's Messiah so strenuously, they became God's adversaries. This could not help but produce hostility to all men—a hostility arising not from a supposed racial superiority, but one manifested in stubborn resistance to admitting Jesus' messiahship.

This is proved by their "effort to keep us from speaking to the Gentiles so that they may be saved" (v.16). The Jews were quite resistant to having Jesus' messiahship and saving work proclaimed among themselves (Acts 4:18–21; 5:27, 28, 40), but Paul's Gentile mission provoked even more indignation, because it implied God's forsaking of Israel (cf. Acts 13:46, 48–50; 17:4, 5; cf. also Rom 11:11, 25). The saving purpose of Gentile preaching was what the Jews sought to eliminate. "They always heap up their sins to the limit" is the outcome of killing the Lord Jesus and all their subsequent adverse actions. Grammatically, the sentence sees the Jews with this aim, but consciously it was God who contemplated the ultimate outcome (cf. Rom 1:20; so Milligan, p. 31; Ellicott, p. 31). The figure of "heap up" or "fill to the full" (*anaplērōsai*) points to a well-defined limit of sin appointed by divine decree. When this point is reached, divine chastisement becomes inevitable. After generations of repeated apostasies and rebellion, Israel had arrived. The climax had come especially with rejection of the Messiah himself, and their already-fixed judgment was biding its time till its direct consequences were released.

"The wrath of God" is none other than the eschatological wrath for which the whole world is destined just before Messiah's kingdom (cf. 1:10) (Reginald H. Fuller, *The Mission and Achievement of Jesus* [Chicago: Alec R. Allenson, Inc., 1954], p. 26). A more general definition, such as the present outpouring of wrath (Rom 1:18), cannot satisfy the wrath's definiteness (*hē orgē*, "the wrath") in a letter so eschatologically oriented as this (Best, p. 119). In bringing Paul's excursus regarding the Jews to its logical climax, the meaning required is the future day of wrath. It is, to be sure, God's wrath, though "of God" (supplied in NIV) is not in the Greek.

If the wrath is yet future, why does Paul speak of it as happening in the past (*ephthasen*, "has come")? The best explanation of the aorist tense of the verb comes from comparing the only other NT combinations of *phanō epi* ("come upon")—Matt 12:28; Luke 11:20—where Jesus speaks of the kingdom's arrival in comparable terminology. The unique force of this verb connotes "arrival upon the threshold of fulfilment and accessible experience, *not* the entrance into that experience" (K.W. Clark, "Realized Eschatology," JBL, [Sept 1940], 59:379). Just as the kingdom reached the covenant people at Christ's first coming without their enjoying "the experience ensuing upon the initial contact" (Ibid., p. 379), so the wrath that will precede that kingdom has come before the Jews' full experience of it. All prerequisites for unleashing this future torrent have been met. God has set conditions in readiness through the first coming and the rejection of Messiah by this people. A time of trouble awaits Israel just as it does the rest of the world, and the breaking forth of this time is portrayed as an "imminent condemnation" by *ephthasen ep'* ("come upon") (Ibid., p. 380). As soon as human conditions in the progress of God's program warrant, the Jews with the rest of the non-Christian world will be plunged into this awful future turmoil. "At last" should probably be replaced by the footnote alternative "fully," the latter meaning that the issue is now settled. The determination cannot be reversed, the obstinate blindness of the Jewish people furnishing obvious proof of this (cf. John 13:1 for this sense of *eis telos* ["the full extent"] to describe Christ's irrevocable love).

Notes

15 Additional support for associating τοὺς προφήτας (*tous prophētas*, "the prophets") with τὸν κύριον Ἰησοῦν (*ton kurion Iēsoun*, "the Lord Jesus") may be cited. The position of the initial καί (*kai*, "and") just before *ton kurion* accords better with a correlative force: "both the Lord Jesus and the prophets." Also Christ's association (in Acts 7:52) with the prophets in suffering adds to the case. The chief deficiency with making this connection, however, is that one cannot justify placing "the Lord Jesus" prior to "the prophets." This order is neither logical nor chronological. Coupled with the aorist tense of ἐκδιωξάντων (*ekdiōxantōn*, "chasing out"; NIV, "drove . . . out") which most likely would have been present tense if the missionaries alone were in view, the case for associating OT prophets with NT Christian disciples in this verse is more convincing (cf. Matt 5:12).

16 God's displeasure with the Jews was already evident in the teachings of Christ (Matt 21:43; 23:38; 24:15–28; 27:25; Mark 11:14, 20; Luke 21:5–24; 23:27–31). That ἡ ὀργή (*hē orgē*, "the wrath") was already being carried out as a foreshadowing of punishments to come has been one explanation for the definiteness of wrath in 2:16 (Hendriksen, p. 73). *Orgē* is also used of God's present anger with the Jews nationally in Rom 9:22 (Hogg and Vine, p. 49). It is impossible to deny a present manifestation of God's wrath against both Jews and Gentiles, but predominantly in the NT and in 1 Thess particularly, God's wrath refers narrowly to a specific future period of limited duration. Such a meaning is required in 2:16.

Explanations for the aorist ἔφθασεν (*ephthasen*, "has come") have been multiplied. Some have taken it as constative and historical, pointing back either to OT times (Lenski, pp. 273, 274) or to the crucifixion (Hiebert, p. 120; Lightfoot, p. 35) or to some event or events in the more recent past such as Jewish misfortunes under Caligula, Claudius, or even Titus. But the Epistle was written long before A.D. 70 (Moulton, *Grammar*, 1:135; Milligan, p. 32; W.G. Kümmel, *Promise and Fulfilment* [Naperville, Ill.: Alec R. Allenson, Inc., 1957], p. 106). Because of the eschatological force of ὀργή (*orgē* "wrath"), however, all these are untenable. Others have taken the aorist to be prophetic (R.H. Fuller, p. 26; Morris, p. 92). The prophetic aorist as a Greek parallel to the Hebrew prophetic perfect is an established usage, but it is expected more in a grammatical framework characterized by other Semitisms (cf. Luke 1:51–53). The best explanation is a constative aorist, pointing to a past arrival but an arrival only in a potential or positional sense. Such a potential presence of the wrath accords with the Epistle's emphasis on an imminent breaking forth of end time events, one of which is the well-known trouble of Israel before Messiah's return (Best, pp. 120–121).

C. Vindication Through Their Separation (2:17-3:13)

1. Desire to go to them

2:17-20

> [17]But, brothers, when we were torn away from you for a short time (in person, not in thought), out of our intense longing we made every effort to see you. [18]For we wanted to come to you—certainly I, Paul, did, again and again—but Satan stopped us. [19]For what is our hope, our joy, or the crown in which we will glory in the presence of our Lord Jesus when he comes? Is it not you? [20]Indeed, you are our glory and joy.

17 Turning from his digression about the Jews, Paul continues to stress deep feeling for the Thessalonians. He pictures himself in contrast ("but") to the persecutors just mentioned (2:14–16). The affectionate "brothers" prepares for heartfelt words about his leaving them—a painful experience because of a consuming attraction for them, like that of a child who has prematurely lost his parents (cf. *aporphanisthentes*, "were torn away from you"). This graphic word combines the idea of separation with the mental anguish accompanying it. After only a brief absence ("for a very short time"), he wants to be with them. "We made every effort" (*perissoterōs espoudasamen*) conveys a depth of feeling amounting to zeal, a zeal heightened by separation. Added to this deep emotion already portrayed is his "intense longing" (*pollē epithumia*).

Paul's warm words about his feeling for the Thessalonians may reflect rumors that he did not really care for them. Apparently some had said he had no interest in coming back to them and had come the first time only to satisfy selfish ambition.

18 Therefore, as if he were not satisfied with his already-overwhelming expressions of his feeling toward the Thessalonians, Paul proceeds to proof of a longing to see them. It is his personal inclination and purpose ("we wanted"). Here Paul's use of *thelō* ("wish," "will") better accords with his strong desire to return to the Thessalonians than *boulomai*, which relates more to decision after deliberation. The tug on his heart is manifest in the words "certainly I, Paul." Though Timothy and Silas had already returned to Thessalonica, Paul's failure to do so did not come from lack of intention; he had attempted another visit several times.

What can hinder such intense desire? It must be nothing less than Satanic hindrance. The hindrance was probably not the demands of missionary work elsewhere, since it is not the enemy's purpose to encourage such work. Restraint by civil officials in Thessalonica and opposition from local Jews are other possibilities, but these would hardly be sufficient to prevent Paul's return. A more plausible identification of the hindrance might be his illness (cf. 2 Cor 12:7), even though this would require the "us" to refer only to Paul. Of course, Paul did not attribute all changes in plans to Satan. He saw some doors as being closed by God's intervention. In fact, it was the Spirit's intervention that had led to the gospel's original proclamation in Thessalonica and surrounding Macedonia (cf. Acts 16:6–10).

The real existence of a personal and supernatural devil is incontrovertible. His present activity in opposing God is only a foretaste of heightened opposition to be launched in the future through his special human representative just prior to Jesus' personal return to earth (2 Thess 2:3–12).

19 Paul's rhetorical questions tie the Thessalonians into Paul's anticipation of the Lord Jesus' coming and presence. They will bring him joy and be a victor's wreath for him to glory in at that future moment of truth. As always with Paul, this is a boasting or glorying in what God has done (cf. 1 Cor 1:31), not in personal accomplishment (Rom 3:27; 4:2; cf. 2 Cor 1:14; Phil 2:16).

Interrupting his own question, he anticipates the answer: "Is it not you?" The untranslated *kai* ("even") in this answer heightens the effect of his statement: Is it not [in fact] you?" This is Paul's answer to those who say he did not care for the Thessalonian Christians. The future event Paul is looking toward is identical with the appearance of every Christian before the *bema* ("judgment seat") of Christ (2 Cor 5:10), where the works of every Christian will be evaluated. Because of his converts' evident spiritual attainments, Paul feels that this will be an occasion of joy and victory.

"When he comes" translates the literal meaning—"in [or at] his presence [or coming]." Here the noun is *parousia*, which in extrabiblical Greek sometimes meant a ruler's visit to a certain place. *Parousia* comes from two words: "to be" and "present." It may point to the moment of arrival to initiate a visit or it may focus on the stay initiated by the arrival. In the NT the word applies to the return of Jesus Christ. The various facets of this future visit are defined by the contexts in which *parousia* appears. In this instance it is Jesus' examination of his servants subsequent to his coming for them (4:15–17) that is in view.

20 Finally, Paul declares that the Thessalonians are his "glory and joy." Not only will they be this when Christ returns; they are so right now. So he silences the insinuations about his lack of concern for his converts.

Notes

17 Δέ (*de*, "but," "now") at the beginning of v.17 has been understood by some as simply continuative, rather than adversative (Best, p. 124; Hiebert, p. 122). The great difference between the attitude closing the previous paragraph and the one described in this paragraph speaks more strongly in favor of contrast than continuation, (Frame, p. 117; Milligan, p. 33).

18 Morris, after rejecting the idea that ἅπαξ καὶ δίς (*hapax kai dis*, "once and twice"; NIV, "again and again") is a Latinism, finds its source in LXX. The English meaning most suitable for the idiom, he writes, is "more than once." This is better than "repeatedly," which is too strong, or "once or twice," which is too weak (Leon Morris, ΚΑΙ ΑΠΑΞ ΚΑΙ ΔΙΣ, NovTest [1956]:1:205–208).

---

2. Sending Timothy to them

3:1-5

> [1]So when we could stand it no longer, we thought it best to be left by ourselves in Athens. [2]We sent Timothy, who is our brother and God's fellow worker in spreading the gospel of Christ, to strengthen and encourage you in your faith, [3]so that no one would be unsettled by these trials. You know quite well that we were destined for them. [4]In fact, when we were with you, we kept telling you that we would be persecuted. And it turned out that way, as you well know.
>
> [5]For this reason, when I could stand it no longer, I sent to find out about your faith. I was afraid that in some way the tempter might have tempted you and our efforts might have been useless.

1-5 Paul now sought another way to dull the pain of separation from his beloved Thessalonians. So he sent Timothy, a valuable companion and effective servant, to serve in his place and bring back word about their afflictions and satanic temptation (3:1–5).

1 Paul gives as his reason for doing this: "We could stand it no longer." "Stand" (*stegontes*, literally "cover") does not refer to concealment of his feelings. That is the very thing he does not do. Rather, the verb has the metaphorical meaning of "hold out against." He was at this point unable to continue in ignorance of how his precious converts were faring in persecution. His personal trials meant far less to him than those he suffered vicariously for his beloved in Christ.

Paul's sincerity is again demonstrated by his willingness to do without his cherished co-worker Timothy ("to be left by ourselves") in a strange city dominated by pagan philosophy and animosity toward the gospel (cf. Acts 17:16–34). But was Paul actually alone? Some have thought that "we" and "ourselves" imply Silas's presence even after Timothy's departure because plural pronouns elsewhere in the letter include others besides Paul (cf. 1:2; Best, p. 131; Hiebert, p. 132). Yet his use of "us" in 2:18 may well have been in a singular sense in light of the "I, Paul" in the same verse. Also, v.5 picks up the plural of v.1 with the singular "I." For Paul to have used "we" in v.1 in any other than a singular sense would have defeated his apologetic desire to express his loneliness. If his long-time companion Silas had still been in Athens, there would have been little deprivation in Paul's not having Timothy with him. He would not be "alone" (*monoi*, v.1) in the real sense of the word unless Silas too was away (Morris, *NIC*, pp. 98, 99).

2 Some are troubled by the problem of harmonizing Timothy's movements with those recorded in Acts 17–18. Luke does not speak of Silas's and Timothy's response to Paul's invitation to come to him quickly (Acts 17:15)—i.e., while he was still in Athens. He does, however, tell of their joining him after his move to Corinth (Acts 18:5). Some have therefore surmised that either this passage in 1 Thessalonians or the account in Acts is historically inaccurate. Yet the supposition is unnecessary. Both books are quite accurate. The reconciliation lies in Luke's decision to omit the visit of Silas and Timothy to Athens. Actually, they did come to Paul while he was in Athens and then were again sent to the Macedonian cities, Timothy going to Thessalonica in accordance with v.1. With Silas's departure prior to or simultaneous with Timothy's departure, the apostle was subjected to an almost intolerable state of loneliness until their subsequent return (Acts 18:5; 1 Thess 3:6). And he was willing to endure this only for the sake of benefitting the Thessalonians and satisfying his thirst for news of them.

Timothy was valuable not only to Paul, but also to Christians more generally, for he was their "brother and God's fellow worker in spreading the gospel of Christ." Timothy was a spiritual brother in the truest sense and an effective servant of God, and for Paul to choose him to go to Thessalonica demonstrates again his genuine concern for the Christians there.

Timothy's mission was "to strengthen and encourage" them in their faith, as Paul himself usually did (Acts 14:22; 15:32, 41; 18:23; Rom 1:11; 16:25; 1 Thess 3:13; 2 Thess 2:16, 17; 3:3). Dependence on God in faith was their only recourse in adversity. They could remain faithful only as they let him supply inner strength. Paul had a continuing concern for the Thessalonians' faith (cf. 3:10).

3 Timothy told them not to be "unsettled by these trials." "Trials," more specifically "afflictions" or "tribulations" (*thlipsesin*), are the stiffest test of faith. Such is the lot of Christ's followers (e.g., John 16:33). Yet these trials are not to be identified with the end-time tribulation just before the Messiah's return (Best, p. 135), which will mark the culmination of God's wrath against the ungodly (Matt 24:21; 1 Thess 2:16; 5:9; 2 Thess 1:6). The trials Paul speaks of here are part of the church's immediate experience, some of them having already happened (cf. v.4).

"Unsettled" (*sainesthai*) describes a state of being shaken or disturbed. In some contexts the same word connotes being lured away through deceptive means, but its other meaning of "unsettled" or "disquieted" better suits this discussion.

Paul had already told them that trials are an inevitable part of Christian experience (3:3; cf. Acts 14:22). Timothy was to reinforce this warning.

4 Christians are marked out for trials. The repeated warnings about persecution had already been substantiated. Prior to the writing of 1 Thessalonians things had "turned out that way" (*egeneto*). So there could be no confusion with the end time tribulation before the *parousia*, for these were the common day-by-day tribulations that befall the disciple just as they did the Master (cf. John 15:18–16:4).

5 In this situation, Paul, speaking now only of himself at this point ("I"; cf. v.1), was constrained to find out through Timothy the state of their faith. He knew that "the tempter" (Satan; cf. Matt 4:3) had been at work among them and that God permits the enemy this activity. What Paul did not know about the Thessalonians, however, was whether or not the tempter's solicitations had been successful, making his work and that of his colleagues "useless."

Notes

2 The reading συνεργόν τοῦ θεοῦ (*sunergon tou theou*, "God's fellow worker") is preferred by some in lieu of διάκονον τοῦ θεοῦ (*diakonon tou theou*, "God's servant") as being more difficult and best explaining the origin of the other readings (Metzger, *The Text of the NT*, pp. 241, 242). "God's fellow worker" is no more difficult than "God's servant," however, in view of 1 Cor 3:9.

Since superior MS support rests with *diakonon tou theou*, it is the more probable choice. Since *diakonon* later became a secondary ecclesiastical office, some copyist may have balked at applying this title to Timothy and substituted "fellow worker."

5 The distinction between the indicative ἐπείρασεν (*epeirasen*, "tempted") and the parallel subjunctive γένηται (*genētai*, "became"; NIV, "might have been") should be high-lighted. The fact of temptation no doubt existed; consequently, an indicative appears in the former clause. The issue of temptation was unknown, however, until the return of Timothy. A potential mood, the subjunctive, was therefore appropriate. Happily, the missionaries' labor was not "useless."

---

3. Delight over their progress

3:6–10

> 6But Timothy has just now come to us from you and has brought good news about your faith and love. He has told us that you always have pleasant memories of us and that you long to see us, just as we also long to see you.
> 7Therefore, brothers, in all our distress and persecution we were encouraged about you because of your faith. 8For now we really live, since you are standing firm in the Lord. 9How can we thank God enough for you in return for all the joy we have in the presence of our God because of you?
> 10Night and day we pray most earnestly that we may see you again and supply what is lacking in your faith.

6–10 Timothy finally returned from his Thessalonian mission with an opposite report from what Paul had feared. This cheering news greatly encouraged Paul and moved him to thanksgiving and prayer.

6 "Just now" shows that Timothy's arrival from Thessalonica immediately preceded the composition of the Epistle and probably provided its chief motivation. This arrival is the same as that in Acts 18:5, when Timothy and Silas came at approximately the same time. This substantiates the earlier conclusion that Paul was actually separated from both Timothy and Silas for a time (cf. 3:1). Doubtless he was refreshed by the return of his two associates, though by now he had moved from Athens to Corinth, where new Christian fellowship had developed.

Rather than using a neutral verb in speaking of Timothy's report (cf. *apangellousin*, "they relate," 1:9), Paul chooses the verb usually reserved for gospel preaching (*euangelisamenou*, "bringing good news"). Only here and in Revelation 10:7 does it refer to anything other than the good news of salvation. That Paul places Timothy's report in this exalted category shows his high estimate of the Thessalonians.

The report was both spiritual and personal. Spiritually, they had progressed in faith and love; their trust in God had been sufficient for their difficulties. Yet room for improvement remained (cf. v.10). Likewise their progress in loving others was uplifting news, though even here there was also room for growth (cf. 3:12; 4:9, 10). The absence of hope from the triad of faith, love, and hope (cf. 1:3; 5:8) is not significant. Faith and love adequately describe wholesome Christian development (cf. Gal 5:6; Eph 1:15; 3:17; 6:23; Col 1:4; 2 Thess 1:3).

Timothy's report of the kindly feelings of the Thessalonians toward him ("pleasant memories," "long to see us") assured Paul that they had not written him off as an exploiter, disinterested in their welfare. They still maintained a warm spot for him, matching his own tender longing to see them (cf. 2:17; 3:10).

7 The report helped Paul in his adversity (cf. Acts 18:6, 9, 10, 12, 13). He faced physical privations ("distress," *anagkē*) and suffering inflicted by his antagonists ("persecution," *thlipsei*). Like all Christians (3:3, 4), he was called to suffer persecution (cf. 2 Tim 3:12). It was their faith that encouraged Paul. Since they were willing to depend on God for help against impossible obstacles, Paul himself had an additional incentive to do this; in fact, he regularly derived personal encouragement from other believers (Rom 1:12; 2 Cor 7:4, 13; Philem 7).

8 The news Timothy brought rejuvenated Paul—"for now we really live." This was not a mysterious "communication of life within the Christian community," growing out of a relationship sustained "in the Lord" (contra Best, pp. 142, 143). Paul had been given a new lease on life. To know they continued "standing firm in the Lord," unmoved by affliction and unshaken by his detractors, was enough to stimulate Paul to renewed activity.

9 The result was thanksgiving to God. Paul found words inadequate to express his appreciation for what had happened in their lives. The change in Paul's mood was radical; "all our distress and persecution" (*pasē tē anagkē kai thlipsei hēmōn*, 3:7) has now become "all the joy we have" (*pasē tē chara hē chairomen*) because of the steadfastness of the Thessalonians. His was no superficial happiness but heartfelt and sincere joy "in the presence of our God."

10 Along with his rejoicing, Paul prayed continually for the Thessalonians. "Night and day" does not mean once in the evening and once in the morning, nor that he did nothing else but pray. It rather points to the extreme frequency of his prayers, while "most earnestly" refers to the intensity of his prayers.

The thrust of Paul's petitions for the Thessalonians is twofold: first, "that we may see you" (cf. 2:18 and 3:6); second, "to supply what is lacking in your faith." This shows his desire to correct, restore, and equip them in respect to faith. They have already been commended for "their work produced by faith" (1:3). Yet they had room for additional growth, and Paul felt his presence could foster it.

Notes

7 Διά (*dia*) is more precisely tr. "through" than "because of," since it is followed by the genitive rather than the accusative case. Very rarely does the preposition with the genitive express cause, but it does quite frequently denote means, which is very appropriate in this context. Hence, faith is seen as the instrument through which encouragement is imparted.

8 It is rare for ἐάν (*ean*, "if") to be followed by a present indicative such as στήκετε (*stēkete*, "stand"), the reading preferred to the weakly attested present subjunctive in v.8. Paul's choice of a present indicative rather than a more normal aorist subjunctive has the effect of expressing certainty that his readers will continue to stand firm from this point on.

4. Seeking direction for them

3:11–13

11Now may our God and Father himself and our Lord Jesus clear the way for us to come to you. 12May the Lord make your love increase and overflow for each other and for everyone else, just as ours does for you. 13May he give you inner strength that you may be blameless and holy in the presence of our God and Father when our Lord Jesus comes with all his holy ones.

11–13 A transitional "now" introduces a subject that is not unrelated to v.10, in which Paul had spoken of his two petitions for the Thessalonians. Here they are elaborated on. God is addressed indirectly in the third person, in keeping with an Epistle addressed to men (cf. 5:23; 2 Thess 2:16; 3:5, 16).

11 Paul recognizes the uselessness of personal efforts toward a revisit unless God "clears the way." At the moment, the path of return is untravelable (cf. 2:18), but Paul prays for the removal of the barriers. Two persons viewed as one (cf. John 10:30) possess power to open the way to Thessalonica once again; "our God and Father himself and our Lord Jesus" is the compound subject of a singular verb (*kateuthunai*, "may [He] clear")—probably an indication of the unity of the Godhead (Ellicott, p. 46). Even if the deity of Jesus is not to be seen in such a grammatical feature (Best, p. 147), it must be understood, since only God is worthy to be addressed in prayer. "Himself" (*autos*), the word with which Paul opens this prayer, very possibly refers to both Father and Son, once again implying the one essence of these two persons (cf. 2 Thess 2:16) (Frame, pp. 136, 137).

In any event, it is futile to argue that the early church only gradually came to look upon Jesus as God. Indeed this is a truth endorsed prior to Pentecost (cf. Matt 16:16) and one that is foundational to the church's existence (cf. Matt 16:18). The Father and Son in their unity can grant this request, which they eventually did. Paul returned to the Macedonian province approximately five years later (Acts 19:21; 20:1; 1 Cor 16:5; 2 Cor 2:13) and in all likelihood made a point of visiting Thessalonica.

12,13 Paul's second petition pertains to "what is lacking" in their faith (cf. v.10), specifically the outworking of that faith in a growing love. Since "Lord" refers to Jesus in vv.11, 13 and likewise in all Paul's writings for the most part, it is best interpreted in this way here.

12 The petition is offered to the Lord Jesus alone, as Paul seeks the enlargement (*pleonasai*) and abundance (*perisseusai*) of the Thessalonians. Combined, the two words mean "increase you to overflowing." Paul prays this for them, not because they lacked love (4:9, 10a; cf. 4:1a), but because continual increase in selfless devotion to others (*perisseusai*, ["overflow"] and *perisseuein mallon*, ["do so more and more," 4:10b]; cf. *perisseuēte mallon*, ["do this more and more," 4:1b]) is always a need for Christians.

In line with the consistent NT emphasis, the prime objects of love are fellow Christians ("each other"; cf. John 13:34, 35; Rom 13:8; 1 Thess 4:9; 1 Peter 1:22; 1 John 3:11, 23). But love also reaches beyond the circle of Christians to all other people ("everyone else"). Jesus warned against a narrow conception of one's "neighbor" (Matt 5:43–48; Luke 10:25–37; cf. Matt 19:19; 22:39; Mark 12:31). Daringly, Paul sets himself as a standard of love to be emulated ("just as ours does for you"), a step he could take only because of his imitation of Jesus (cf. 1:6), who is the ultimate standard (John 13:34; 15:12).

13 The goal of Paul's prayer for the Thessalonians is that the Lord will grant them "inner strength" to be "blameless" in holiness "in the presence of our God and Father" when the Lord Jesus returns. He looks forward to the time of final accounting. An overflow of love (v.12) is the only route to holy conduct in which no fault can be found (v.13). For unless love prevails, selfish motives inhibit ethical development by turning us toward ourselves and away from God and blameless living. The holiness that belongs to God is the ideal we must seek (cf. Lev 19:2; 1 Peter 1:16).

The final accounting Paul alludes to will take place in the personal "presence of our God and Father." The local force of *emprosthen* ("in the presence of") obtains whenever this preposition relates appearance before a judge (Matt 27:11; 25:32; Luke 21:36; 2 Cor 5:10; contrast 1 Thess 1:3; 3:9; 1 John 3:19) (cf. BAG, p. 256). Earlier Paul has made "our Lord Jesus" the judge at this scene (1 Thess 2:19). This is no contradiction. The unity of the Father and Son, just seen in v.11, allows a joint judgeship. The *bēma* of Christ (2 Cor 5:10) is also the *bēma* of God (Rom 14:10), because Christ in his present session is with the Father in his heavenly throne (Rev 3:21; cf. Rom 8:34; Heb 1:3; 10:12). This hearing will take place at the future "visit" (*en tē parousia*, "in the coming") of the Lord Jesus (cf. 2:19). For the Thessalonians Paul prays for a favorable verdict at that time.

Others present at this reckoning will be "all his holy ones." Their identity has been variously taken either as that of angels or of redeemed human beings, or both angels and redeemed human beings. The last possibility can be eliminated in that Paul would hardly include two such diverse groups in the same category. That angels alone are meant is unlikely in light of NT usage of *hagioi* ("holy ones"). Universally in Paul and perhaps the entire NT (Jude 14 is debatable) it is a term for redeemed humanity, though usage in LXX and later Jewish literature differs. The redeemed are elsewhere associated with Christ at his return (2 Thess 1:10). Since human beings are the objects of judgment and their holiness is what is in focus (cf. "blameless and holy"), it is entirely appropriate to identify "the holy ones" as other Christian people joined with the Thessalonian Christians before the *bēma* of God and Christ.

Certain matters about the time "when our Lord Jesus comes" require clarification. For example, what relation does this event bear to the predicted future wrath (1:10; 2:16; 5:9) and the meeting of the saints with the Lord in the air (4:15-17)? If this is Christ's coming (*parousia*) prior to the period of wrath, it is identifiable with the meeting of 4:15-17. This interpretation, however, encounters obstacles. "With all his holy ones" is one of them. The redeemed cannot come with him until he has first come for them. To interpret "all his holy ones" as the spirits of the dead in Christ is not a satisfactory answer to the difficulty because some of those in Christ will not yet have died. "All" would not therefore be accurate because of the exclusion of this latter group. Furthermore, the readers were not yet assured that their dead would participate in the *parousia* (Best, p. 153).

If this is Christ's coming after the wrath, difficulties of a different type are encountered. Foremost among these is a disregard for the contextual emphasis on the judgment of saints. By the time of his return to earth after the wrath, this reckoning will have already taken place in heaven (i.e., *emprosthen tou theou kai patros hēmōn*, "in the presence of our God and Father"). It is to Christ's earlier return in the air (4:15-17) that the *bema* of God and Christ relates.

In resolving this difficulty, we must consider the scope of *parousia* as indicated in these Epistles (see Introduction, pp. 233, 234). The complexity of the term *parousia* demands that it include an extended visit as well as the arrival initiating that visit. This is provided for adequately in the rarer meaning of *parousia,* "presence" (cf. 1 Cor 16:17; 2 Cor 10:10; Phil 2:12). Included in this visit is an evaluation of the saints (cf. 2:19; 5:23), which is the aspect in view here in v.13. This judgment cannot be completely dissociated from Christ's coming in the air (4:15–17), because this advent marks its initiation. Yet it must be conceived of as a session in heaven in some measure separate from the arrival itself. At this juncture the degree to which Christians have attained a "blameless and holy" character will be divinely ascertained.

Notes

11 Αὐτός (*autos,* "himself") introduces prayers of this type also in 5:23; 2 Thess 2:16; 3:16. It refers once to the Father alone (5:23) and once to the Lord Jesus alone (2 Thess 3:16). In 2 Thess 2:16 the subject is a compound one as in 3:11, but with the Son preceding the Father. This pattern of usage implies that the pronoun extends to both members of the compound subject. The sense is probably "our God and Father and our Lord Jesus himself" rather than "our God and Father himself."

A compound subject governing a sing. verb is well known, but this is ordinarily found only when the verb precedes or stands between the subjects (Turner, *Syntax,* pp. 313, 314). Aside from v.11 and 2 Thess 2:16, 17, the only time Paul has a sing. verb following a compound subject is 1 Cor 15:50, another instance where the two subjects constitute a unit. Hence, unity in the Godhead best explains the sing. κατευθύναι (*kateuthynai,* "may [he] clear") in v.11.

13 Ἔμπροσθεν (*emprosthen,* "in the presence of") at times has nonlocal connotations, as in 1:3 and 3:9 of this Epistle. Yet a judicial hearing requires actual proximity to the judge. So here the preposition requires a location before the Father in heaven.

IV. Exhortation to the Thessalonians (4:1–5:22)

A. *Exhortation Regarding Personal Needs* (4:1–12)

1. *Continual improvement*

4:1, 2

1Finally, brothers, we instructed you how to live in order to please God, as in fact you are living. Now we ask you and urge you in the Lord Jesus to do this more and more. 2You know what instructions we gave you by the authority of the Lord Jesus.

1 Paul now urges the Thessalonians on to greater spiritual attainments outlined in 3:10–13. His exhortations, introduced by "finally" (*loipon oun*—"finally therefore"; NIV includes the *oun,* "therefore," in the "finally"), however, are logically based on more than 3:10–13. The drastic change to a new line of thought implies that all of chapters 2 and 3 are in view. "Since our relations with you have been such as they have, since we have labored so much among you, since you have suffered for the gospel's sake, since there is yet progress to be made, since we have maintained a continuing prayerful

interest in you, we ask you, brothers, and urge you in the Lord Jesus . . ." (Lightfoot, p. 51; Ellicott, p. 58; Frame, p. 141).

"Finally" shows that the series of admonitions launched here will be the final part of the letter. With Paul a final word may be brief (2 Cor 13:11; Phil 4:8; 2 Tim 4:8) or extended (Phil 3:1; 2 Thess 3:1) as here. "Brothers" again shows his tenderness in approaching delicate subjects.

The nature of Paul's appeal is conveyed in "ask" (erōtōmen) and "urge" (parakaloumen). Since erōtōmen is used alone later in these Epistles ("We ask," 2 Thess 2:1), it is best not to equate the two words, but to understand the former as a gentle, friendly request and the latter as an authoritative apostolic plea. Paul frequently uses parakaloumen ("urge") when turning from the didactic portions of his Epistles to the outcome of his teaching (e.g., Rom 12:1; Eph 4:1). Such urging is more than a request, but less than a command (Best, p. 155). It conveys a kind of diplomatic authority and is absent from Paul's sharpest Epistle, Galatians. The words "in the Lord Jesus" are the context of the exhortations that are to follow.

The Thessalonians had already been given instruction about how they must "live in order to please God." Paul again views the Christian life as a "walk" ("live," peripatein; cf. 2:12). He might have immediately requested compliance with earlier instruction, but in the Greek word order he interrupts himself before doing so, lest he appear to be condemnatory. As always he gives credit where it is due, in this case recognizing the substantial progress that has been made. (cf. his previous commendations—1:3, 6–10; 3:6, 8).

Yet the realization of the ultimate goal of pleasing God and receiving his commendation (3:13) entailed continual improvement. "Do this more and more" (perisseuēte), though referring to the overflow of love Paul had prayed for (3:12) and was to urge (4:10), here relates to other dimensions of the Christian life as well (4:3 ff.; cf. 3:10).

2 So Paul stimulates his converts' memory of what he and his companions had told them. He characterizes their previous ministry as a delivering of "commands" (parangelias; NIV, "instructions"). These were binding because they were given "by the authority of the Lord Jesus."

Notes

1 An established Hellenistic Gr. formula is illustrated here: (1) a verb in the first person, παρακαλοῦμεν (parakaloumen, "we urge"), (2) a vocative, (3) a prepositional phrase, ἐν Κυρίῳ Ἰησοῦ (en Kyriō Iēsou, "in the Lord Jesus"), and (4) substance of what is requested (cf. ἵνα [hina, "in order to"] clause) Bjerkelund, Parakalō, cited by Best, pp. 154, 155).

A second hina is required to resume the first because of the extraordinary length of the parenthesis begun at the first καθώς (kathōs, "as"). It is sometimes Paul's style to deviate from his initial structure in order to interject an additional thought. In this case the second hina marks his return to the thought he began with the first hina (Lightfoot, p. 52; Frame, p. 142; Milligan, p. 46).

2. Sexual purity

4:3-8

> ³It is God's will that you should be holy; that you should avoid sexual immorality; ⁴that each of you should learn to control his own body in a way that is holy and honorable, ⁵not in passionate lust like the heathen, who do not know God. ⁶and that in this matter no one should wrong his brother or take advantage of him. The Lord will punish men for all such sins, as we have already told you and warned you. ⁷For God did not call us to be impure, but to live a holy life. ⁸Therefore, he who rejects this instruction does not reject man but God, who gives you his Holy Spirit.

3 The Greek text uses a *gar*, "for instance," (untranslated in NIV) to introduce some needed exhortations about sexual behavior. Christian holiness, says Paul, requires total abstinence from *porneias* ("sexual immorality," "fornication"). The word requires broad definition here as including all types of sexual sins between male and female. A year or two earlier a Christian council in Jerusalem had ruled decisively on a related issue affecting Gentile Christians (cf. Acts 15:20). It is not clear whether the Thessalonians were guilty of fornication, so common among the pagans (v.5). Though Paul may have had in mind the temptation to indulge in it, his strong words probably imply some overt transgressions. Pagan moral corruption looked upon fornication either indifferently or favorably. That the Thessalonians slipped into it after their conversion would not have been strange (Ellicott, p. 51; H. A. W. Meyer, *Acts*, p. 61; Lightfoot, p. 53). While Paul had congratulated them on their faith (cf. 1:3), this does not mean that there was no occasional misbehavior, even this kind, within the church (cf. 1 Cor 1:4-9; 5:1-5; 6:12-20).

4 The positive side of holiness requires one to "learn to control his own body" or "learn to live with his own wife" (cf. footnote in NIV; also note below). Some have resolved the uncertainty over the exact meaning of the Greek by referring *skeuos* (literally, "vessel"; NIV, "body") to the human body, a meaning that seeks support from Paul's usage in Romans 9:22, 23 and 2 Corinthians 4:7. But this overlooks the figurative nature of this term from the ceramics trade in its other two contexts. It also strains the meaning of *ktasthai*, which can only with great difficulty be understood as "control." Taking *skeuos* to be a wife may therefore be preferable. *Ktasthai* may in this way be given its natural meaning of "acquire." Or it may mean "keep on acquiring" or "live with" in the sense of cultivating a wife's favor, i.e., the couple should not be unduly separated and thus strain their marital relationship (cf. 1 Cor 7:2-5). Use of *skeuos* as "wife" is loosely paralleled in 1 Peter 3:7. A wholesome marriage was thus Paul's antidote for "sexual immorality." "Holy and honorable" describe the way to maintain the right kind of marriage, holiness being due God (4:3; cf. 3:13) and honor due the wife (Lightfoot, p. 55).

5 The pagans (i.e., the Gentiles), those with no inkling of the law of Moses or Christian practice, know nothing of this holy and honorable behavior. Their guiding principle is "passionate lust" because they "do not know God." Such reprehensible behavior is a consequence of their refusal to respond to God's revelation of himself (Rom 1:18-32). "Who do not know God" is a familiar Pauline expression for the Gentile world (Gal 4:8;

271

2 Thess 1:8; cf. Ps 79:6; Jer 10:25). Once removed from that realm into the church of God (cf. 1 Cor 10:32), a believer is obligated to maintain much higher standards.

6 Wronging and taking advantage of a brother, probably a Christian brother, are other violations of holiness. Though some have taken "this matter" to be business dealings, the emphasis of the context shows it to be sexual transgression. (Business dealings would require a plural, *pragmata*, "matters"). To have relations with a woman outside marriage is not just a trespass against God's law. It also defrauds some fellow Christian who eventually will take this woman as his own wife, or perhaps has already done so—an especially heinous sin because the one robbed is a spiritual relative of the robber. Paul does not allude to the other injustice, which is quite obvious. The woman herself is an object of cruel abuse in such a situation. This too is especially repulsive in a Christian setting.

A reason for complying with the standards set forth in vv.4, 5 relates to the Lord Jesus' future punishment of "all such sins." (*Dioti*, "because" in Gr. NT, shows the verse to be motivational.) Paul is not speaking of a present vengeance (1 Cor 5:1–5; 11:30–32), but of the future judgment of Christians at the *parousia* (2:19; 3:13; 1 Cor 3:10–17)—a judgment to be carried out by Christ (John 5:22; 2 Cor 5:10) in association with God the Father (Rom 14:10; 1 Thess 3:13). Paul's initial expedition to Thessalonica had informed and solemnly warned them of these dire consequences. We do not know what prompted him to put in writing this admonition about judgment. Perhaps urgency required stern words.

7 Another reason for compliance is the nature of God's calling. As in 2:12, this is God's effectual call, mediated through gospel preaching (2 Thess 2:14). Those who, having been called, have responded have not been inducted into a life of sexual impurity, but into a holy life (cf. 3:13; 4:3, 4). They now belong to a community with values different from those of "the heathen" (v.5) among whom they formerly lived.

8 Still another reason for compliance with the standards set forth in vv. 4, 5 is that they are God-given. Therefore rejection of them means rejecting not man, but God, "who gives [us] his Holy Spirit," who is inseparable from the kind of holy living demanded in this paragraph. (The Greek word order places special emphasis on "holy.")

Notes

4 In v.4 ἑαυτοῦ (*heautou*, "himself"; NIV, "his own body") is emphatic in meaning and by position (Blass-Debrunner, p. 148; Turner, p. 190). This furnishes additional reason for referring σκεῦος (*skeuos*, "vessel") to a wife. "*His own* wife" is meaningful, but little is gleaned from one's controlling "*his own* body."

6 Deciding how τὸ μὴ ὑπερβαίνειν κ. τ. λ. (*to mē huperbainein k. t. l.*, literally, "not to go beyond ...") relates to the preceding infinitival clauses is not simple. It is probably not parallel to them because of its article. If it were the purpose of previous actions, the article would have been τοῦ (*tou*, "of the"). Hence, it probably reverts to ὁ ἁγιασμός (*ho hagiasmos*, "holiness") of v.3 and introduces an example of sanctification even more specific than that in vv.3b, 4. This is a sample of the social injustice of fornication (Ellicott, p. 53).

8 There is some MS support for an aorist participle δόντα (*donta*, "having given") rather than a present διδόντα (*didonta,* "giving"). Yet it is not nearly so strong as that for the present. The aorist probably was prompted by the customary NT practice of referring to the Spirit's initial coming to the believer. The present may refer to God's character as giver (Best, p. 172), or it may look on his giving as a perpetual fortifying against uncleanness (Lightfoot, p. 58). The latter is more suitable to the context.

---

3. *Filial love*

4:9, 10

> [9]Now about brotherly love we do not need to write to you, for you yourselves have been taught by God to love each other. [10]And in fact, you do love all the brothers throughout Macedonia. Yet we urge you, brothers, to do so more and more.

9,10 "Now about" (*peri de*) is a frequent Pauline formula for introducing a new subject (4:13; 5:1; cf. 1 Cor 7:1, 25; 8:1; 12:1; 16:1, 12). In Corinthians the formula indicates answers to written questions, but here Paul responds to different elements of Timothy's oral report about Thessalonica (1 Thess 3:6). In vv.9, 10a he acknowledges their practical compliance with a responsibility to "love the brothers." "Brotherly love" (*philadelphia*), an expression for attachment to one's blood relatives in secular speech, was taken over by Christianity because of the close ties within the spiritual family of God. Paul views further writing on the subject as superfluous in that they are "taught by God" to do it. "Taught by God" (*theodidaktoi*), a rare term, does not refer to any single teaching such as an OT passage (Lev 19:18), the teaching of Jesus (John 13:34), or a prophetic revelation to the church through Paul or anyone else. It rather describes a divine relationship through the indwelling Holy Spirit (4:8; cf. John 6:45). At conversion, believers become lifelong pupils as the Spirit bears inner witness to the love within the Christian family (cf. Rom 5:5; Gal 5:22). No external stimulus is necessary. Mutual love among Christians is an inbred quality.

Proof of this inner instruction was visible in the Thessalonian's love for all Christians of their province. Any contacts they had with churches in Berea and Philippi are unknown except for the implications of these verses. Very possibly, groups of believers had sprung up in other parts of the province since the beginning of Paul's Macedonian mission (Acts 16:9–12). With some allowance for Paul's hyperbolic "all," it is safe to assume that a goodly proportion of the believers in the province had been touched by the Thessalonians' unselfish concern. Otherwise, the missionary zeal reflected in 1:8 lacks clear substantiation.

As exemplary as the Thessalonians had been (1:3; 3:6), however, further progress remained a goal for them (3:12). Paul's repetition of v.1 in "we urge you, brothers, to do so more and more" (a number of the Greek words are identical or nearly so) shows v.10b to be a particularization of the general admonition of v.1. "More love" is always a potentiality for Christians because the ultimate, the example of Christ himself (John 13:34; 15:12), is infinite and can only be approached, not fully reached.

Notes

9 The verb ἐστε (este, "are"; NIV, "have been") is present in sense as well as form. It does not have a perfect force ("have been"). It was the Thessalonians' continuing experience after Paul's departure, just as much as while he was there, to be taught of God to love one another. Hence, "you yourselves *are* taught by God" more suitably represents the meaning.

4. Individual independence

4:11, 12

11Make it your ambition to lead a quiet life, to mind your own business and to work with your hands, just as we told you, 12so that your daily life may win the respect of outsiders and so that you will not be dependent on anybody.

11,12 These verses stand in close grammatical connection with v.10b. Yet the logical connection is not immediately obvious (Ellicott, p. 58). From the subject of love, Paul apparently changes to something quite different—viz., the importance of industry and individual responsibility in Christian living. The two are not completely unrelated. Nothing disrupts the peace of a Christian community more than the unwillingness of members to shoulder their part of the responsibility for it (Hiebert, p. 180). To disturb tranquility violates the love that permeates a truly Christian community. More specifically, some members of the Thessalonian church appear to have taken advantage of the liberality of other Macedonian Christians (cf. 2 Cor 8:1–5) in accepting financial help while making no effort at self-support (Lightfoot, p. 60).

We do not know the reason for this idleness. Though Paul had already spoken out against the lack of industry ("just as we told you") and though he now writes of it again, the condition later grew worse (2 Thess 3:6–15). Since these two Thessalonian Epistles are so strongly eschatological, it is quite probable that the condition stemmed from their misapplying truths about the Lord's return to their daily living. Christians must never evade their daily responsibilities under the pretense of proclaiming or preparing for Christ's return. To do so is to distort this great hope.

11 That restlessness may have been a problem for the Thessalonians is implied by Paul's exhortation—"make it your ambition to lead a quiet life." Another exhortation, "mind your own business," implies that a meddlesome spirit that often goes with restlessness was troubling them. Busybodies were active (2 Thess 3:11) and needed a reprimand. But the exhortation goes beyond telling them to stay out of other people's affairs; it also implies the necessity of keeping one's own affairs in order. Still another exhortation, "work with your hands," implies that idleness was a problem among the Thessalonians. In a Greek culture that degraded manual labor, Christianity joined with Judaism in viewing it as an honorable pursuit. Most of the Thessalonian believers earned their living with their hands. Paul tells them to continue supporting themselves and thus avoid the pitfalls of idleness (Ellicott, p. 59; Frame, p. 162).

12 These exhortations find a twofold result. For their conduct to "win the respect of outsiders," the Christians in Thessalonica must eliminate restlessness, meddlesomeness,

274

and idleness (v.11). Even "outsiders," so called because they have no connection with Christ and hence are outside the family of God—cf. 1 Cor 5:12, 13; Col 4:5; 1 Tim 3:7—recognize winsome conduct. On the other hand, they are repelled by those who do not carry their share of social responsibility. Closely associated with the importance of a good testimony is the need not to "be dependent on anybody." Of course, independence in an absolute sense is neither possible nor even desirable. We must understand Paul's admonitions not to be dependent in the light of the situation described in vv.11, 12a.

Notes

11 καί (*kai*, "and") begins v.11 and connects φιλοτιμεῖσθαι (*philotimeisthai*, "to strive eagerly"; NIV, "make it your ambition"), πράσσειν (*prassein*, "to do"; NIV, "to mind") and ἐργάζεσαι (*ergazesthai*, "to work") in parallel with περισσεύειν (*perisseuein*, "to do so more and more," v.10). All are dependent on παρακαλοῦμεν (*parakaloumen*, "we urge," v.10). The need to apply *perisseuein* to the preceding topic of love and the radical subject change in v.11 require a new paragraph at v.11, even though grammatically vv.11, 12 are a unit with v.10b.

"Make it your ambition" applies only to "lead a quiet life" and does not carry its force over to "mind your own business" or "work with your hands." It appears most natural to apply the καθώς (*kathōs*, "just as") clause to all three responsibilities rather than just the last.

12 Μηδενός (*mēdenos*, "no one, nothing"; NIV, "not . . . anybody") is probably masc., not neuter, in that a masc. focuses on an abuse of brotherly love more clearly and constitutes a better parallel to the masc. πρὸς τοὺς ἔξω (*pros tous eksō*, "of outsiders") in the other half of the clause.

B. *Exhortation Regarding Eschatological Needs* (4:13–5:11)

1. *The dead in Christ*

4:13–18

> 13Brothers, we do not want you to be ignorant about those who sleep, or to grieve like the rest of men, who have no hope. 14We believe that Jesus died and rose again and so we believe that God will bring with Jesus those who sleep in him.
> 15According to the Lord's own word, we tell you that we who are still alive, who are left till the coming of the Lord, will certainly not precede those who have fallen asleep. 16For the Lord himself will come down from heaven, with a loud command, with the voice of the archangel and with the trumpet call of God, and the dead in Christ will rise first. 17After that, we who are still alive and are left will be caught up with them in the clouds to meet the Lord in the air. And so we will be with the Lord forever.
> 18Therefore encourage each other with these words.

13–18 Another issue raised by Timothy's report requires clarification: the part of the Christian dead in Christ's *parousia* (his coming). Paul discusses this new subject in one of the classic NT passages on the Lord's return (vv.13–18). The lack of knowledge of the Thessalonians concerning the part their fellow Christians who had died will have when the *parousia* occurs led him to write this reassuring paragraph.

13 Paul's words "we do not want you to be ignorant" as usual mark what follows for special attention. Here they introduce the correction of false impressions (cf. Rom 11:25; 1 Cor 10:1; 12:1). The Thessalonians had concluded that "those who sleep" would miss the victories and glory of the Lord's return. "Those who sleep" (*tōn koimōmenōn*) is an expression chosen in lieu of the "the dead" (v.15) because of death's temporary nature for Christians (cf. 1 Cor 7:39; 11:30; 15:6, 18, 20, 51; cf. also John 11:11). Though the pagans used "sleep" as a metaphor for "death," it is especially appropriate for Christians because of their assured bodily resurrection. Paul had previously taught the Thessalonians about the resurrection. On the basis of the resurrection our Christian "hope" has objective reality. That this sleep refers to the physical body and not to man's spirit is clear for several reasons. Death for Paul did not mean a state of unconscious repose, but a condition of being with Christ (Phil 1:23). Also the expression "dead in Christ" (v.16) is meaningless in connection with soul sleep, for a nonexistent sleeper can hardly be in union with Christ. Paul viewed "those who sleep" as continuing their relationship with Christ in heaven while their bodies were in the grave. The essential issue is not the fact of bodily resurrection, but what part, if any, those so raised will play in the *parousia*.

Paul wanted to deliver his readers from the grief experienced by "the rest of men" (cf. "outsiders," v.12). Non-Christians sorrow out of pity for the departed who have ventured into an unknown realm. For Christians, however, there should be no sorrow on behalf of believers who are dead. Grief on behalf of the living and the loss sustained when a loved one dies is legitimate for Christians (Phil 2:27), but that kind of grief is not in view here. Those who have died are better off than those left behind and will be equal participants in future resurrection and the glory of Christ.

14 For Christians, relief from sorrow is related to what the future holds. Just as "Jesus died and rose again," so will "those who sleep in him" be raised when God brings them to heaven with Jesus at his *parousia*. The fact of Jesus' death and resurrection guarantees as its sequel the eventual resurrection of the dead in Christ. This is similar to the guarantee of his return in 1:10.

It is significant that Paul does not refer to Jesus' death as "sleep." The difference between Jesus' experience and that of believers is that he really endured actual separation from God for the world's sins. Because of his real death Christian death has been transformed into sleep (Milligan, p. 57).

Though we might expect Paul to write "God will raise" instead of "God will bring with Jesus," he used the latter because of an unexpressed connection in his mind between the two ideas. To be brought with Jesus presupposes rising from the dead as part of the process (v.16). This is what had been taught the Thessalonians. Yet their ultimate anticipation is not just that of being raised, but that of being "with Jesus" (4:14; cf. 4:17; 5:10). Beyond resurrection this is the consummating desire of Christians. But even more is in store for Christians. The words "God will bring" point to a continuing movement heavenward after the meeting in the air (v.17), until the arrival in the Father's presence (3:13; cf. John 14:2, 3). A more detailed analysis of the process follows (*gar*, v.15).

15-17 The authority that validates Paul's affirmation ("we believe") in v.14 is nothing less than "the Lord's own word" (*logou kyriou*, "the word of the Lord"; cf. 1:8). Various attempts have been made to identify this source more specifically. Some say Jesus spoke the words while on earth, their substance being recorded later in such places as Matthew 24:30, 31 and John 6:39, 40; 11:25, 26. Similarities between this passage in 1 Thessalonians and the gospel accounts include a trumpet (Matt 24:31), a resurrection (John 11:25,

26), and a gathering of the elect (Matt 24:31) (Robert Gundry, *The Church and the Tribulation* [Grand Rapids: Zondervan, 1973], pp. 104, 135). Yet dissimilarities between it and the canonical sayings of Christ far outweigh the resemblances (Olshausen, p. 138; Lightfoot, p. 65; Moffatt, p. 37; Hendriksen, p. 114). Some of the differences between Matthew 24:30, 31 and 1 Thessalonians 4:15–17 are as follows: (1) In Matthew the Son of Man is coming on the clouds (but see Mark 13:26; Luke 21:27), in 1 Thessalonians ascending believers are in them. (2) In the former the angels gather, in the latter the Son does so personally. (3) In the former nothing is said about resurrection, while in the latter this is the main theme. (4) Matthew records nothing about the order of ascent, which is the principal lesson in Thessalonians. Distinctions between this and the Johannine passages are just as pronounced, if not more so.

Another suggestion has it that this is a saying of Jesus not contained in the canonical Gospels. Acts 20:35 is cited as another quotation of a non-Gospel saying (Moffatt, p. 37). It is further speculated that a saying like this may have come as a sequel to Jesus' repeated predictions of his disciples' martyrdom (Matt 10:28; 24:9; Mark 8:34; 10:39, 40; 13:12, 13; John 16:2). Such could have raised the issue of the disadvantage in martyrdom as compared with surviving to the *parousia* (Jeremias, p. 67). Though possible, this suggestion is not probable. Because of its relevance to early Christian circumstances, such a saying of Jesus would hardly have been passed over by the Gospel writers (Milligan, p. 58).

For Paul to have claimed this special authority for his own personal utterances does not adequately explain the definiteness of the expression "the Lord's own word" (Best, p. 190). Or for him to have drawn the saying from a Jewish or early Christian apocalyptic writing is not likely. The closest extrabiblical approximation to 4:15–17 is 4 Esdras 7:28, but 4 Esdras came at the end of the first century or in the early second century, too late for Paul to have known it (R.H. Charles, *Apocrypha and Pseudepigrapha* [London: Oxford, 1913] 2:552–553).

"The Lord's own word," therefore, is probably a direct revelation to the church through one of her prophets, Paul himself or possibly some other. The NT prophet's function was to instruct and console believers (cf. v.18 with 1 Cor 14:31), utilizing predictions about the future in the process (Acts 11:27, 28; 21:11). Since these elements are prominent here and since 1 Corinthians 15:51 classifies this subject as "mystery" revelation, which is the character of prophetic utterances, this explanation of Paul's external authority is quite satisfactory (Best, pp. 191–193; Hiebert, pp. 196, 197). Nowhere in these Epistles are the addressees reminded of having heard this teaching previously, though they were fully informed about the day of the Lord (1 Thess 5:2). How they could have been uninformed about this detail of the *parousia* (v.13) is not disclosed. Conceivably it could have been a special revelation to Paul for the sake of answering their question through Timothy, or it might have been a revelation received at another time since Paul's departure from the city. Whenever it came, it was now the privilege of the Thessalonians to know certain details about departed believers' part in the *parousia*.

The first part of Paul's prophetic revelation in vv.15–17 tells what will not happen. Believers "who are still alive, who are left to the coming of the Lord," will not go to meet him before the dead in Christ do so (v.15). When Paul uses "we," he apparently places this event within his own lifetime. How then can it be explained that the *parousia* did not precede Paul's death? To theorize that Paul was mistaken and to consider biblical inspiration in the light of such errors (James Denney, *Expositors Bible* [Hodder and Stoughton, n.d.], pp. 175–177) is to ignore Paul's avoidance of date setting (1 Thess 5:1,

2). In view of Jesus' teaching about our not knowing the day or hour of his coming (Matt 24; 36; cf. Acts 1:7), surely Paul would not limit it to his own lifespan.

Another possibility is to understand the participles *zōntes* and *perileipomenoi* as being hypothetical and meaning "if we live, if we remain." Yet rarely, if ever, can attributive participles function in such an adverbial and conditional sense. Furthermore, this sense would hardly fit the same two words in v.17 (Best, p. 195).

Some have also been proposed that Paul used less-than-honest means to prepare the Thessalonians for the Lord's return. With a good motive he proposed a time limit, though he knew Christ's word to the contrary (Matt 24:36). Aside from Paul's rejection of the unethical practice of making the end justify the means (Rom 3:8), this proposal conflicts with 1 Thessalonians 5:1, 2.

Others have suggested that Paul simply establishes two categories—those alive and those asleep. Since he did not fit into the latter, he took his place with the former. His presence in one or the other is inconsequential, however (Ellicott, pp. 62, 63; Hogg and Vine, pp. 138–140; Hiebert, p. 196). By entertaining the possibility of his own death before the *parousia*, as he did elsewhere (2 Cor 5:9; Phil 1:21ff.; 2:17; 2 Tim 4:6), Paul could not have meant more than to establish two categories here (Auberlen and Riggenbach, p. 76). While somewhat plausible, this view fails to explain the emphatic *hēmeis* ("we," v.15) or tell us why Paul used the first person instead of the third (Best, p. 195).

More feasible is the solution that sees Paul setting an example of expectancy for the church of all ages (Lightfoot, p. 67). Proper Christian anticipation includes the imminent return of Christ. His coming will be sudden and unexpected, an any-moment possibility. This means that no divinely revealed prophesies remain to be fulfilled before that event. Without setting a deadline, Paul hoped that it would transpire in his own lifetime. Entertaining the possibility of his own death (2 Tim 4:6–8) and not desiring to contravene Christ's teaching about delay (Matt 24:48; 25:5; Luke 19:11–27), Paul, along with all primitive Christianity, reckoned on the prospect of remaining alive till Christ returned (Rom. 13:11; 1 Cor 7:26, 29; 10:11; 15:51, 52; 16:22; Phil 4:5). A personal hope of this type characterized him throughout his days (2 Cor 5:1–4; Phil 3:20, 21; 1 Tim 6:14; 2 Tim 4:8; Titus 2:11–13). Had this not been the Thessalonians' outlook, their question regarding the dead in Christ and exclusion from the *parousia* would have been meaningless. They were thinking in terms of an imminent *parousia*, expecting to see it before death (Best, p. 183). An intervening period of messianic woes or birthpangs was not their anticipation (Best, p. 184), for such intense persecution would have meant probable martyrdom, and in that case they would have had doubts about their own participation in the *parousia*. Hence, Paul believed and had taught his converts that the next event on the prophetic calendar for them was their being gathered to Christ.

This teaching about a future *parousia* that will be a cosmic and dateable event in world history is as valid for the twentieth century as it was for the first. It is not to be explained away as an event outside history because of the alleged limited cosmological framework of early Christian minds (cf. Best, pp. 360–370). Just as God intervened in history through his Son's first coming, so he will do at his return.

The principal assertion of v.15, then, concerns those who are alive and anticipating Christ's momentary return, as was Paul, and their relation to "those who have fallen asleep." The former group "will certainly not precede" the latter. This strong assertion alleviates the Thessalonians' apprehension about their dead.

The positive chronology of vv.16, 17 supports this strong statement (cf. the *gar* ["for"] at the beginning of v.16). Without any intermediary, "the Lord himself will come down from heaven" (v.16), where he has been since ascending to the Father's right hand. In so doing, he will issue "a loud command," such as one given by a person with authority.

The purpose is to awaken "those who have fallen asleep." Associated with the command will be "the voice of the archangel," probably Michael's (Jude 9) and "the trumpet call" (cf. 1 Cor 15:52). As a sequel to this movement from heaven, "the dead in Christ" will rise before anything else occurs. Far from being excluded from the *parousia*, they will be main participants in the first act of the Lord's return. This word of comfort must have brought great relief to the Thessalonians and it has certainly done so for innumerable Christians after them.

Only "after that" (v.17) will living Christians "be caught up" for the meeting with Christ. The interval separating the two groups will be infinitesimally small by human reckoning. Yet the dead in Christ will go first. They will be the first to share in the glory of his visit. Then the living among whom Paul still hoped to be (cf. "we") will be suddenly snatched away (*harpagēsometha*, "caught up"; cf. Acts 8:39; 2 Cor 12:2, 4; Rev 12:5). This term in Latin, *raptus*, is the source of the popular designation of this event as the "rapture." So sudden will it be that Paul likens it to a blinking of the eye (1 Cor 15:52). In this rapid sequence the living will undergo an immediate change from mortality to immortality (1 Cor 15:52, 53), after which they will be insusceptible to death.

Together with the resurrected believers, they will ascend, be enshrouded in the clouds of the sky (cf. Acts 1:9), and meet the Lord somewhere in the interspace between earth and heaven ("air," *aera*).

The nature of this "meeting" (*apantēsin*, v.17) deserves comment. Some feel that the technical force of the word obtains—i.e., a visitor would be formally met by a delegation of citizens and ceremonially escorted back into their city (Best, p. 199). On this basis, they contend that Christians go out to meet the Lord and return with him as he continues his advent to earth. Advocates of this proposal see this connotation in two other NT usages of the word (Matt 25:6; Acts 28:15, 16) (George Ladd, *The Blessed Hope* [Grand Rapids: Eerdmans, 1956], p. 91; William C. Thomas, *The Blessed Hope* [William C. Thomas, 1972], pp. 5, 6). Whether or not this is true is debatable. Even if it were true, Christ would not necessarily be escorted back to earth immediately (Gundry, pp. 104, 105). Usage of the noun in LXX as well as differing features of the present context (e.g., Christians' being snatched away rather than advancing on their own to meet the visitor) is sufficient to remove this passage from the technical Hellenistic sense of the word (Moulton, *Prolegomena*, p. 14, n. 4; Best, p. 199). A meeting in the air is pointless unless the saints continue on to heaven with the Lord who has come out to meet them (Milligan, p. 61). Tradition stemming from Jesus' parting instructions fixes the immediate destination following the meeting, as the Father's house, i.e., heaven (John 14:2, 3) (John Walvoord, *The Thessalonian Epistles* [Grand Rapids: Zondervan, 1967], p. 70).

The location is secondary, however, in light of the final outcome. To "be with the Lord forever" represents the fruition of a relationship begun at the new birth and far outweighs any other consideration of time and eternity.

18 With this word of assurance, Paul gives a basis for his converts to "encourage [*parakaleite*] each other."

Notes

13 The δε ... περι (*de ... peri*, "now about") signals a new subject (cf. 4:9; 5:1). The difference between the present participle κοιμωμένων (*koimōmenōn*, "sleeping") and the aorist κοιμηθέντας (*koimēthentas*, "having slept," vv.14, 15) is probably the perspective represented in

each statement. The former pictures "those falling asleep from time to time," while the latter looks back from the vantage point of the *parousia* when all Christian death will be a thing of the past (Hiebert, pp. 188, 193).

14 Ἀνέστη (*anestē*, "rose again") is used by Paul only here, in v.16, and in Eph 5:14 for rising from the dead. He customarily uses some form of ἐγείρω (*egeirō*, "to rise") though his favorite noun for "resurrection" is ἀνάστασις (*anastasis*).

Διὰ τοῦ Ἰησοῦ (*dia tou Iēsou*, "in" or "through Jesus") poses a syntactical question. Whether it connects with "will bring" or with "those who sleep" is the crux of the issue. Since the former possibility entails a tautologous "God will bring through Jesus with him" and since the symmetry of the two clauses is best maintained by the latter ("Jesus died" with "those who sleep through Jesus" and Jesus "rose" with "will bring with Him"), the latter connection is preferred (Lightfoot, p. 64; Hendriksen, p. 112). "Sleeping through [or in] Jesus" signifies what death has become to the Christian because of Jesus' death and resurrection. It assumes the temporary character of sleep.

17 "With" is from ἅμα σύν (*hama syn*, "together with"). Whether to understand ἅμα (*hama*) as depicting local coherence ("together") or temporal correspondence ("at the same time") is a matter to be resolved. Most helpful in reaching a conclusion is an understanding of ἔπειτα (*epeita*, "then"; NIV, "after that"). Together with πρῶτον (*prōton*, "first," v.16), this particle indicates a temporal sequence, the living being caught up after the dead have been raised. For *hama* to have the sense of "at the same time" would make the sentence self-contradictory. Hence, local coherence, "together with," best represents the meaning of *hama syn*.

---

2. The day of the Lord (5:1–11)

a. The coming of the day

5:1, 2

> ¹Now, brothers, about times and dates we do not need to write to you, ²for you know very well that the day of the Lord will come like a thief in the night.

1 With the perplexity about the dead in Christ resolved, Paul turns to a new subject (cf. *peri de*, "now about") yet not one completely distinct from the previous one. It is wrong to say that the two are so different as to be in contrast (Ryrie, "The Church and the Tribulation: A Review," BS, April-June, 1974, p. 75; Ellicott, p. 67). But it is equally wrong to see this as a simple continuation of the same subject (W.C. Thomas, p. 7). The proper interpretation recognizes a shift in thought, but not without some connection with the foregoing (Walvoord, p. 81; Gundry, p. 105). The direct and affectionate address "brothers" marks the new discussion as an addition prompted by Timothy's report of the Thessalonians' situation. The nonarrival of the *parousia* had created another perplexity for them (Best, p. 203).

Despite their ignorance about the dead in Christ (4:13), they had received prior instruction regarding other eschatological matters. "We do not need to write to you" is Paul's attestation to this fact. "Times and dates" (*tōn chronōn kai tōn kairōn*) are well-known words describing the end times from two perspectives. The former conceives more of elapsed time and hence a particular date or dates when predictions will be fulfilled. The latter word, while including some reference to extent of time, gives more attention to the character or quality of a given period, i.e., what signs will accompany the consummating events. The two words together have this same eschatological connotation in Acts 1:7; 3:19–21. The latter word very frequently refers to this future period (Dan 9:27, LXX; Mark 13:33; Luke 21:8, 24; Eph 1:10; 1 Tim 6:15; Titus 1:3; Heb 9:10; Rev 1:3; 11:18; 22:10) (Ellicott, p. 67; Milligan, p. 63; Lightfoot, pp. 70, 71). During his first visit Paul had effectively communicated the basic features of precise times and accompanying circumstances of future events.

2 For this reason he could say to the Thessalonians, "You know very well" the features of the day of the Lord. "Very well" translates *akribōs*, a word of precision. Paul is not sarcastically alluding to their own claim, but conceding that their previous learning on this subject had been adequate, definite, and specific, ultimately including even pertinent teachings of Christ (Matt 24:43; Luke 12:39) (Lightfoot, p. 71; Ellicott, p. 68).

The focus is on "the day of the Lord." A theme for extensive biblical attention, this "day" has multiple characteristics. It is so associated with the ultimate overthrow of God's enemies (Isa 2:12) that *hēmera* ("day") sometimes means "judgment" (1 Cor 4:3). It will be a day of national deliverance for Israel and a day of salvation (1 Thess 5:9), but it will also be a day when God's wrath puts extended pressure on his enemies (Isa 3:16–24; 13:9–11; Jer 30:7; Ezek 38–39; Amos 5:18, 19; Zeph 1:14–18; 1 Thess 1:10; 2:16; 5:9). By using "day of the Lord" terminology to describe the great tribulation, Christ includes the tribulation within the day of the Lord (cf. Matt 24:21 with Jer 30:7; Dan 12:1; Joel 2:2). This time of trial at the outset of the earthly day of the Lord will thus not be brief, but comparable to a woman's labor before giving birth to a child (Isa 13:8; 26:17–19; 66:7ff.; Jer 30:7, 8; Micah 4:9, 10; Matt 24:8; 1 Thess 5:3) (Pentecost, *Things to Come* [Findlay, Ohio: Dunham, 1958], p. 230; McClain, *The Greatness of the Kingdom* [Grand Rapids: Zondervan, 1959], pp. 186–191). Growing human agony will be climaxed by Messiah's second coming to earth, a coming that will terminate this earthly turmoil through direct judgment. He cannot personally appear on earth, however, until this preliminary period has run its course. Armageddon and the series of tribulation visitations prior to it are inseparable from each other (Rev 6–19). If Christ's triumphant return to earth (Rev 19:11–21) is part of the day of the Lord, as all admit, so special divine dealings preparatory to it must also be part of it. God's eschatological wrath is a unit. It is quite arbitrary to hypothesize two kinds of future wrath, one prior to the day of the Lord and another within it (cf. Gundry, pp. 46, 54).

But this earthly wrath does not pertain to those in Christ (v.9). Their meeting with Christ will be "in the air" and separate from God's dealing with those on earth. The only way to hold that this meeting with Christ in the air is an imminent prospect is to see it as simultaneous with the beginning of the divine judgment against earth. Only if the rapture coincides with the beginning of the day of the Lord can both be imminent and the salvation of those in Christ coincide with the coming of wrath to the rest (v.9) (Walvoord, p. 81).

Were either the rapture or the day of the Lord to precede the other, one or the other would cease to be an imminent prospect to which the "thief in the night" and related expressions (1:10; 4:15, 17) are inappropriate. That both are any-moment possibilities is why Paul can talk about these two in successive paragraphs. This is how the Lord's personal coming as well as the "day's" coming can be compared to a thief (2 Peter 3:4, 10; Rev 3:3, 11; 16:15). *Erchetai* ("will come") is a vivid futuristic present (cf. John 14:3) to portray the day as already on its way with an arrival anticipated any time (cf. 1:10). "In the night" is a detail of the simile not given in other NT usages. It simply names the usual time for thievery, i.e., under cover of darkness. Such unexpectedness will mark the tribulation's inauguration.

The Thessalonians were now instructed about these matters, though later they were to be deceived regarding them (2 Thess 2:1, 2). Yet even with their present knowledge they had difficulty in applying the truths in a practical way while waiting for the day. So Paul seeks to alleviate this difficulty.

Notes

2 The anarthrous ἡμέρα κυρίου (hēmera kyriou, "day of the Lord") may be understood as a proper title, since it is already anarthrous in LXX usage. Absence of the articles may also be traced to a Semitic source, the construct state (Moule, *An Idiom Book of NT Greek*, p. 117). More probably, however, it is explainable by a qualitative emphasis: "a day of such character that belongs to the Lord" (Milligan, p. 64).

b. *Unbelievers and the day*

5:3

3While people are saying, "Peace and safety," destruction will come on them suddenly, as labor pains on a pregnant woman, and they will not escape.

3 The surprise beginning of the day of the Lord has a twofold impact. For those who are not in Christ and therefore unprepared, the consequences are far from cheerful. "People," "them," and "they" are identified only when v.4 contrasts them with the "brothers" who are the addressees. The "nonbrothers" compose an unbelieving world against whom the devastation of the coming day will be unleashed. Just as disaster overtakes the unsuspecting householder when set upon by a robber, so catastrophe will overcome the living who are spiritual outsiders.

They will be priding themselves on their secure life styles. "Peace" characterizes their inward repose, while "safety" reveals their freedom from outward interference (Ellicott, p. 69; Frame, p. 181). Yet at the moment that tranquility seemingly reaches its peak, "destruction will come on them suddenly." "Destruction" means utter and hopeless ruin, a loss of everything worthwhile (Milligan, p. 65; Frame, p. 182), causing the victims to despair of life itself (Rev 9:6). Without being totally annihilated, they are assigned to wrath and denied the privileges of salvation (v.9).

Comparing the beginning of this period with a period of labor pains just before childbirth makes vivid the unexpectedness with which the former comes (cf. Isa 13:8, 9; Jer 4:31; Hos 13:13; Mic 4:9). Pain is certainly involved in both (Isa 66:7) as are certainty and nearness, but "suddenly" points most prominently to the absence of any forewarning. Tribulation will suddenly become worldwide, rendering it impossible for non-Christians to escape.

Notes

3 Evidence for exchange of material between Paul and Luke sometime during their long association is prominent here as it is in several other passages (cf. 1 Cor 11:23–26 with Luke 22:19, 20;

1 Cor 15:5 with Luke 24:34; 1 Tim 5:18 with Luke 10:7) (Lightfoot, p. 72). Luke 21:34, 36 contains a number of verbal similarities to the present verse: cf. ἐπιστῇ (*epistē* "come on") with ἐφίσταται (*ephistatai*, "comes on"), αἰφνίδιος (*aiphnidios*, "suddenly") in both, ἡ ἡμέρα (*hē hēmera*, "the day") with ἡμέρα (*hēmera*, "day," v.2), ἐκφυγεῖν (*ekphugein*, "to escape") with ἐκφύγωσιν (*ekphugōsin*, "will escape"). A pronounced eschatological emphasis is also in both, though Luke uses the thought more in relation to the preparation of God's people. The ultimate source of the words was undoubtedly Jesus himself.

---

c. *Believers and the day*

5:4–11

> ⁴But you, brothers, are not in darkness so that this day should surprise you like a thief.
> ⁵You are all sons of the light and sons of the day. We do not belong to the night or to the darkness. ⁶So then, let us not be like others who are asleep, but let us be alert and self-controlled. ⁷For those who sleep, sleep at night, and those who get drunk, get drunk at night.
> ⁸But since we belong to the day, let us be self-controlled, putting on faith and love as a breastplate, and the hope of salvation as a helmet.
> ⁹For God did not appoint us to suffer wrath but to receive salvation through our Lord Jesus Christ.
> ¹⁰He died for us so that, whether we are awake or asleep, we may live together with him. ¹¹Therefore, encourage one another and build each other up, just as in fact you are doing.

4 In contrast to the non-Christians referred to in v.3 as "them" and "they," and in v.6 as "others," are the believers in Thessalonica whom Paul affectionately calls "brothers." Continuing the figure of night (v.2), "darkness" refers to the realm of wickedness and the darkened understanding and ignorance of impending doom that go with it (Ellicott, p. 70; Frame, p. 183). Such symbolical language occurs quite widely in nonbiblical and biblical writings (Best, p. 209; Conzelmann, TDNT, 7:428, 429, 431–433, 441–445; cf. Deut 28:29; Job 19:8; 22:10, 11; 30:26; Ps 11:2; 74:20; 82:5; Isa 42:6, 7; Jer 13:16; Matt 10:27; John 3:19; 8:12; Rom 13:12; 2 Cor 4:6; Eph 4:18; 5:8, 11; 1 John 1:5, 6). In reassuring his converts, Paul declares without qualification that those in Christ belong to a realm different from that of the world.

Growing out of this assertion that believers will not participate in darkness is the promise of their non-participation in "the day" of the Lord. It will not overtake them by surprise—"like a thief" overtakes his victim. As v.5 explains, their position in Christ guarantees their deliverance from this.

5 Paul's assertion, "you are all sons of the light and sons of the day," rules out dwelling in darkness. "All" brings reassurance that none are excluded. The fainthearted may take heart as may those others who have been confused about the *parousia* (cf. 4:11, 12; 5:14) (Frame, p. 184).

To reinforce his point, Paul returns to the negative side. Putting light and day in inverse order, he excludes himself along with all Christians from the night of moral insensitivity (cf. "sons of the light" . . . "darkness"; "sons of the day" . . . "night"). By a casual change from "you" to "we" he takes his place with his readers in accepting the exhortation of v.6. This dulls the edge of what would otherwise be a sharp rebuke (Frame, p. 185).

"The day" has no reference to the eschatological day of the Lord, as the anarthrous construction attests, but is used metaphorically in association with spiritual light (Lightfoot, p. 73). Verse 5 guarantees the readers' participation in a spiritual environment entirely different from that of non-Christians.

6 This provides a solid basis ("so then," *ara oun*) for the ethical behavior Paul now urges on the Thessalonians. It is a life style free from moral laxity. *Katheudōmen* ("let us not sleep") represents the ethical insensitivity that besets people of the other realm ("like others," *hoi loipoi*; cf. 4:13). While it is impossible for the day of the Lord to catch Christians unprepared, it is possible for them to adopt the same life style as those who will be caught unawares. Paul urges his readers not to let this happen.

Conduct in keeping with "the light" and "the day" also includes alertness. Inattention to spiritual priorities is utterly out of keeping for those who will not be subject to the coming day of wrath. Though the Thessalonians were, if anything, overly watchful to the point of neglecting other Christian responsibilities (4:11, 12; 2 Thess 3:6–15), they were not to cease watching altogether.

Apparently self-control was a great need. *Nēphō* ("to be self-controlled") is found with *grēgoreō* ("to be alert," "to watch") in a noneschatological context in 1 Peter 5:8. Its usage in 1 Peter 1:13 and 4:7 is eschatological. *Nēphō* denotes sobriety. To counteract what might become a state of wild alarm or panic, Paul urges self-control as a balance for vagaries arising from distorted views of the *parousia*. Undue eschatological excitement was a serious problem; spiritual sobriety was the cure.

7 To explain his exhortation in v.6, Paul appeals to everyday experience. Sleep and drunkenness are most often associated with the night. So he illustrates his figurative use of "sleep" in v.6 by referring to the normal habit of sleep and uses "drunkenness" to point up his reference to sobriety.

8 Here Paul resumes his exhortation but drops for the moment the need for alertness, speaking only of sobriety as a countermeasure against "spiritual" drunkenness. The idea of belonging to the realm of "spiritual" daylight goes back to vv.4, 5 and becomes the motivation for self-controlled action. So Paul goes on to describe "self-control" in figurative language drawn from Isaiah 59:17 (cf. Eph 6:14–17). Though the breastplate and helmet were Roman military apparel, lexical similarity to the Isaiah passage points to the OT as the probable source for the reference to them here.

The relation of this soldierly figure of speech to sobriety has been a puzzle. Frame suggests soberness as a prerequisite to effective vigilance by a sentry on duty (Frame, p. 187). Yet vigilance is covered in the earlier word on alertness. Obviously, intoxication prevents effective duty as a sentry, and this thought may supply the answer. To be armed against wild excitement with its disregard of normal Christian responsibilities requires soberness. Paul had earlier spoken of the need for calmness (4:11, 12). The Thessalonians had already made significant progress in faith and love (1:3; 3:6), but additional improvement was still needed (3:10; 4:1, 10). So the breastplate of faith and love could furnish protection from the problems mentioned in 5:14. To these Paul added the indispensable helmet of the hope of salvation (cf. 1:10). These three (faith, love, and hope) strengthened them for their present trials (1:3) and doubts (5:14). The Thessalonians could confidently anticipate a future deliverance not to be enjoyed by those in darkness (v.3), but assured to those in the realm of light (vv.4, 5). Self-control consists of balancing future expectations with present obligations. The well-equipped soldier wears both a breastplate and a helmet.

9 Paul now summarizes the reason for this guaranteed salvation. Negatively, "God did not appoint us to suffer wrath." Without question, this wrath is future and specific, being identified with the messianic era just prior to his reappearance (1:10; 2:16) and with the sudden destruction mentioned in v.3. "Appoint" (*etheto*) is used regularly for God's sovereign determination of events (Milligan, p. 69). When God vents his anger against earth dwellers (Rev 6:16, 17), the body of Christ will be in heaven as the result of the series of happenings outlined in 4:14–17 (cf. 3:13). This is God's purpose.

The positive side of this purpose is that believers will "receive salvation through our Lord Jesus Christ." "Receive" represents the noun *peripoiēsin* that some have translated actively as "gaining," "winning," or "acquiring" (Hiebert, p. 223; Hendriksen, p. 128; Best, p. 217) and others have interpreted passively as "possession" or "adoption" (Lightfoot, p. 76). The former meaning injects human effort into procuring future salvation and emphasizes alert activity. Yet the thought of "acquiring one's own slavation" conflicts with God's unconditional appointment of believers to salvation. Furthermore, the incompatibility of the word's usual active meaning of "preservation" (or "preserve") with future salvation is obvious. And in view of the cognate verb *peripoieō* with its technical connotation of divine action in God's procuring a people for himself, taking *peripoiēsin* passively becomes more plausible. Also the antithetical *orgēn* ("wrath") clearly implies divine activity. As Christians have been elected (1:4), they have also been adopted. For them to be possessed by God as his very own is synonymous with the future salvation to come "through our Lord Jesus Christ." In this divine operation, human diligence is not a factor. Therefore, in the certainty of this provision the Thessalonians could find relief from the frantic activity and panic that had been disturbing their tranquil anticipation of the future.

10 This verse is noteworthy. Here for the first time in all Paul's writings, he states the specific means by which Jesus Christ procures our salvation: "He died for us." In four key Epistles (Rom, 1 and 2 Cor, Gal), Paul laid prime emphasis on this about five years later. But only here in the Thessalonian letters does he mention the death of Christ, though it had undoubtedly been presented as the basis of all his teaching about salvation (cf. Acts 17:2, 3). Though the purpose of the letters does not call for an extended discussion of the death of Christ, here it is important in establishing the definite historical basis of our salvation. His death was "for us" or "on our behalf"—i.e., it was the sole condition in procuring as God's peculiar possession a people destined for salvation when the rest of the world is plunged into the wrath of the future day.

So sufficient is Christ's death that it brings assurance of future life with all obstacles removed. In fact, this was the very reason he died. It is conceivable, though highly improbable, that "awake" and "asleep" actually refer to physical conditions (cf. Luke 17:34). *Katheudō* ("asleep," NIV) has this literal sense in v.7.

A more plausible suggestion takes "awake or asleep" as metaphorical terms for the living and the dead. This is consistent with Paul's discussion in 4:13–18 and matches Jesus' use of *katheudō* ("sleep") in raising Jairus' daughter (Matt 9:24). Yet this use of *katheudō* is rare. Only with difficulty can one explain its substitution for the metaphorical *koimaō* ("sleep") of the previous section (4:13, 14, 15). Furthermore, *grēgoreō* ("to be awake") is never used metaphorically for physical life in the Greek Bible (Milligan,

p. 70) or in any literature (Oepke, TDNT, 2:338–339). Paul's word for "to live" is *zaō* (4:15, 17). To assign this metaphorical sense to "awake" or "asleep" is not probable because it makes v.10 a needless repetition of what is already proved in 4:13–18.

An explanation that is exegetically preferable and of less difficulty takes *grēgorōmen* ("we are awake") and *katheudōmen* ("we are asleep") in an ethical sense as in v.6. Since future salvation has been so fully provided by Christ's finished work, it cannot be cancelled by lack of readiness. Moral preparedness or unpreparedness does not affect the issue one way or the other. Though at first this suggestion seems to nullify Paul's earlier exhortation to alertness (v.6), it must be acknowledged that this meaning for *grēgoreō* is well established in other places besides the present paragraph (Matt 24:42; 25:13; Mark 13:35, 37; Rev 3:3; 16:15) (Hogg and Vine, p. 172; Oepke, TDNT, 2:338). This conclusion also recognizes the established meaning of *katheudō* in the present context and accords with the strong case for the secure position of the believers (5:4, 5, 9).

There still remains, however, a serious obstacle to this ethical meaning of "awake or asleep," namely its seeming nullification of the exhortation of vv.6–8. Yet this is a problem only if these exhortations are understood as relating just to watchfulness. We have not, however, found this to be the case. The Thessalonians were already watchful and Paul warns them against extremes of overreaction. "Self-control" or "soberness" (vv.6, 8) serve as a complementary emphasis. Paul seeks to restore a proper balance between future anticipations and present obligations. In helping the Thessalonians, therefore, he had to calm their fears by convincing them of their participation in the *parousia* regardless of their degree of watchfulness. Every contingency has been met through the work done at Calvary by God himself. Christians need not fear missing the Lord's return, because they are "sons of the light and sons of the day" (vv.4, 5). Their enjoyment of the future resurrection life in union with Christ is certain.

11 With such a guarantee, the Thessalonians are now equipped to "encourage one another and build each other up." As in 4:18, *parakaleite* ("encourage") has more a consolatory than a hortatory meaning. Here is an unconditional pledge to strengthen even the weakest in faith. It can also build up another Christian. *Oikodomeite* ("build ... up") was later to become one of Paul's favorite ways of writing about growth in the church (Eph 2:20–22; 4:12). An intellectual grasp of the provisions Paul has been describing leads to individual as well as collective growth of the body of Christ. Paul is quick to acknowledge progress along this line: "just as in fact you are doing." Yet he also looks forward to even greater attainments (cf. 4:1).

Notes

4 In v.4 ἵνα (*hina*) has one of its rarer uses—i.e., it expresses result rather than purpose, since the *hina* clause cannot be a purpose of their not being left in darkness (Milligan, p. 76; Lightfoot, p. 73; Frame, p. 183).

The accusative pl. reading of κλέπτας (*kleptas*, "thieves") rather than the nominative sing. κλέπτης (*kleptēs*, "thief"), while finding some respectable MS support, cannot be accepted because that external support is not as substantial as for the other reading and because of the harsh reversal of the figure of v.2 whereby the thief becomes the one startled by the arrival of daylight (v.4) rather than the one causing the surprise (v.2). Possibly the form *kleptas* arose as a scribe unintentionally copied the ending of the preceding ὑμᾶς (*humas*).

5 The two uses of υἱοί (huioi, "sons") are figurative and stem from a Semitic idiom denoting individuals with a quality of what is denoted by the genitive of descriptions that follow (Robertson, RHG, p. 496; Turner, p. 207; Blass-Debrunner, p. 89). Though not repeated with νυκτός (nyktos, "of night") and σκότους (skotous, "of darkness") and ἡμέρας (hēmeras, "of the day") (v.8), the force of huioi should probably be understood (Blass-Debrunner, p. 89).

7 A difference in meaning between μεθυσκόμενοι (methuskomenoi, "those who get drunk") and μεθύουσιν (methuousin, "are drunk"; NIV "get drunk") is denied by some (Best, p. 212), but it is probably wiser to allow the former an inceptive force, "get drunk," and the latter a progressive meaning, "are drunk," so as to maintain careful distinctions between synonyms (BAG, p. 500; Hiebert, p. 220).

8 The aorist participle ἐνδυσάμενοι (endusamenoi, "putting on") is simultaneous with the present νήφωμεν (nēphōmen, "let us be self-controlled"), because the antecedent relationship does not yield good sense. This combination gives the aorist an ingressive force, while the present subjunctive carries the idea of continuation after the initial act: "let us take up the armor and continue to wear it" (Best, p. 215).

9 The greatest problem in taking περιποίησιν (peripoiēsin, "obtainment"; NIV, "receive") passively is the genitive σωτηρίας (sotērias, "of salvation") associated with it (Auberlen and Riggenback, p. 85). When the noun is taken actively, the genitive is one of object, but the solution is not quite so obvious with the passive sense of "possession." In light of other considerations discussed above, however, and in light of the reasonable sense derived from a genitive of apposition, the passive sense is the better conclusion.

10 The reading ὑπέρ (hyper, "on behalf of"; NIV, "for") rather than περί (peri, "concerning") is preferable. The idea of benefit is more specific this way. Peri has too narrow MS support geographically to be taken as a serious possibility, even though the few MSS that do support it are impressive.

The adverb ἅμα (hama, "together") should be understood in the same local sense as in 4:17. It is a reinforcement of σύν (sun, "with") to emphasize union with Christ.

11 While generally equivalent to ἀλλήλους (allēlous, "one another"), εἰς τὸν ἕνα (heis ton hena, "each other") has a stronger individualizing effect. The total body is edified only as each member of it experiences growth.

C. Exhortation Regarding Ecclesiastical Needs (5:12–22)

1. Responsibilities to the leaders

5:12, 13

> 12Now we ask you, brothers, to respect those who work hard among you, who are over you in the Lord and who admonish you. 13Hold them in the highest regard in love because of their work. Live in peace with each other.

12,13 No more effective way of carrying out mutual edification (v.11) can be found than Paul's closing exhortations for improvement within the assembly (vv.12–22). Heading the list are the exhortations regarding the proper attitude toward leaders (vv.12, 13). They are introduced as a request from a friend ("we ask," erōtōmen, v.12; cf. 4:1). The request includes "respect" (eidenai, v.12) and "hold[ing] them in highest regard" (hēgeisthai, v.13), both of which represent rare verb nuances. The former verb (eidenai) directs respect toward the leaders who function in three areas: the first more general and the last two definitive of the first. "Those who work hard among you" is reminiscent of Paul and his colleagues with their unselfish toiling to support themselves while sharing the gospel with the Thessalonians (2:9). It is appropriate for those who follow them in leadership to do the same. Thus they become local exmples of how love works hard (1:3) in contrast to the problem group within the church that was doing practically nothing (4:11) (Frame, p. 193).

Paul points to two of the many areas where the hard work of the leaders was evident: "who are over you in the Lord who admonish you." The participle *proistamenous* ("who are over you") probably stipulates what is already implied by the existence of such a request as this: the presence of some form of church government in this early assembly. It was the responsibility of these leaders to "stand over" the rest of the assembly in the Lord. A secondary sense of "care for" (*proistēmi*) is also involved here and in the other uses of the verb (Rom 12:8; 1 Tim 3:4, 5, 12; 5:17) because ruling in a Christian way entails sincere interest in the welfare of those who are ruled (cf. Matt 20:26–28; 1 Peter 5:2, 3). Yet the element of "caring for" cannot erode the authority of the office and the need to "respect" the office (Reicke, TDNT, 6:701, 702). Anarchy is always wrong, particularly among Christians. If any tendency to it existed in Thessalonica, it must be rooted out. Where believers are united with Christ, respectful submission to Christian leaders is service to the Lord. The leaders were charged with guiding the congregation, and their decisions were binding (cf. Heb 13:17). It is also notable that this authority was not vested in one person. Such singular authority belonged only to an apostle (Denney, pp. 204–207; Lightfoot, p. 79).

A second phase of the leaders' hard work was "admonishing" the rest of the assembly. Admonishing is correction administered either by word or deed. It implies blame on the part of the one admonished. Naturally, it arouses resentment, since discipline is never pleasant. Still the apostle presents admonition as necessary for the congregation and requires respect for those who exercise it.

The group whose functions are thus described quite probably correspond to the elders (*presbyteroi*) and overseers (*episkopoi*), whose qualifications are described in more detail later in the pastoral Epistles (1 Tim 3:1–2; 5:17; Titus 1:5). Such leadership existed in local congregations from the earliest days of the Christian church (Acts 11:30; 14:23).

Another part of Paul's "request" regarding leadership is that leaders to be held "in highest regard in love" (v.13). Here is another unusual verbal nuance. *Hēgeisthai* here connotes "esteem" or "hold in high regard" rather than its more usual meaning of "consider." The context requires a specialized sense (Milligan, p. 72), though the more neutral meaning is possible: "consider them worthy of being loved" (Ellicott, p. 76; Olshausen, p. 452). This latter, however, injects without warrant the thought of worthiness. The exhortation is to hold these leaders in esteem "beyond all measure" (*hyperekperissōs*). No reservations are allowable. Rulers in the local assembly must be held "in the highest regard" (NIV) and given wholehearted support, and this in a spirit of "love." A suitable reason for this high appreciation is "their work" (v.13).

Concluding the brief exhortation about leadership is a general command for leaders as well as for those they lead: "Live in peace with each other." That Paul included such a command shows that relations were not all they could have been. Perhaps there was trouble between the idle and those who were admonishing them. But no matter who was to blame, there had to be peaceful relations. Leaders were to guard against abusing their authority; idlers were not to disregard those over them in the Lord.

Notes

12 The three participles represent three functions of the same group, not three distinct functioning groups. Grammatically this is shown by the single article τούς (*tous,* "the") governing all three and unifying them into a single concept.

2. *Responsibilities to all*

5:14, 15

> 14And we urge you, brothers, warn those who are idle, encourage the timid, help the weak, be patient with everyone. 15Make sure that nobody pays back wrong for wrong, but always try to be kind to each other and to everyone else.

14 A new and stonger set of brief commands begins with "And we urge you, brothers." "We urge" is more authoritative than Paul's previous "we ask" (5:12; cf. 4:1). Coupled with this stronger word are the imperative verbs in vv.14, 15 instead of the volitionally weaker infinitives in vv.12, 13.

Some early church fathers, beginning with Chrysostom, saw these strong directives as addressed to the leaders, thus counterbalancing those just given to the rest of the people (Best, p. 228). Such a distinction, however, finds more difference between the leaders and the led than is justified at this point in church history (Hogg and Vine, p. 181). It also overly restricts "brothers," which must broadly designate the whole Christian community. Furthermore, Romans 12:14–17, a section similar to 1 Thessalonians 5:15, is directed to the whole Roman church, not just to its leaders.

"Warn those who are idle" translates the same Greek word as "admonish" in v.12 (*noutheteite*). Christians in general, not just a limited few, are responsible for corrective measures. The entire local body copes with practical situations by advising an errant brother. The only ones excused from the obligation to warn are those in need of warning, in this case described as "those who are idle." *Ataktous* ("idle") describes those who are disorderly in conduct, but since disorderly conduct is so intertwined with idleness, the latter meaning very quickly associated itself with the word (cf. 2 Thess 3:6, 7). A certain amount of unbecoming behavior had already appeared in the Thessalonian church (4:11, 12).

"Encourage the timid" concerns a different need. Words of comfort (*paramutheisthe,* the word translated "comfort" in 2:12) to the "timid" or "fainthearted" are also needed. In the light of what Paul wrote in chapter 4, those who needed comfort were both troubled over their friends who had died in Christ (4:13) and confused about what the *parousia* held for themselves (5:1–11). Within this letter Paul has given ample information for removing these misgivings.

"Help the weak" almost certainly relates to moral and spiritual debility. Whether it was weakness in shrinking from persecution (3:3–5), yielding to temptations to immorality (4:3–8), or some other kind of weakness cannot be precisely determined. It may well have been weakness in exercising full Christian liberty in doubtful matters as was the case in other churches that included people from a pagan background (Rom 14:1–15:6; 1 Cor 8–10). Whatever it was, however, the strong in faith were responsible to support those who were weak.

Summing up the previous three commands is a fourth general one: "Be patient with everyone." *Makrothumeite* ("be patient") is sometimes translated "be long-suffering." It pictures the even-tempered response of one who is slow to anger. Dealing with the idle, the timid, and the weak requires this special disposition because they so often refuse to respond immediately to constructive counsel. Yet these are not the only ones requiring patient treatment. All Christians ("everyone") at one time or another provoke dissatisfaction through thoughtless or even intentionally hurtful acts. They too need patient treatment. The same patience is required toward non-Christians, but reference to them is not specific until v.15.

15 When tempers run short, the whole group (*horate*, pl.) has the responsibility for seeing that no member "pays back wrong for wrong." The natural tendency to retaliate and inflict injury for a wrong suffered must be strongly resisted, no matter what the injury. Apparently the Christian stand against retaliation crystalized very early, no doubt being formulated from principles established by Jesus in his Sermon on the Mount (Matt 5:38–42). Jesus refuted a false scribal inference drawn from Exodus 21:23, 24 (cf. Lev 24:19, 20; Deut 19:21). "An eye for an eye, and a tooth for a tooth" was originally intended to restrain people from going beyond equal retaliation in punishment for social wrongs against the community. The scribes had distorted the commandment's purpose by using it to justify personal revenge. What had been given as restrictive law had through human traditions been transformed into a permissive rule. In speaking out against this tradition, Jesus emphatically set the tone for his followers in forbidding personal revenge altogether.

That this lesson took firm hold is evidenced not only in the present verse, but also in Romans (12:17–21), where Paul treats the subject in more detail. Peter also shows the influence of this teaching (1 Peter 2:19–23; 3:9). Nonretaliation for personal wrongs is perhaps the best evidence of personal Christian maturity.

In v.15 Paul gives a constructive alternative to retaliation: "Always try to be kind to each other and to everyone else." *Diōkete* ("pursue"; NIV, "try") is immeasurably more than halfhearted effort. Eager expenditure of all one's energies is none too much in seeking *to agathon* ("the good"; NIV, "to be kind"). In place of wrong, injury, or harm dictated by a vengeful spirit, Christians must diligently endeavor to produce what is intrinsically beneficial to others, whether other Christians ("each other") or unbelievers ("everyone else"). The seriousness of the abuse suffered is no issue. Some Thessalonians doubtless had been victims of unjustified harsh treatment, but regardless of this, a positive Christian response is the only suitable recourse. The welfare of the offender must be the prime objective.

3. *Responsibilities to oneself*

5:16–18

> [16]Be joyful always; [17]pray continually; [18]give thanks in all circumstances, for this is God's will for you in Christ Jesus.

16 Compliance with the social regulations of vv.12–15 is impossible apart from personal communion with God. So Paul turns to the believer's inner life. In the exhortation "Be joyful always" he voices a theme that is characteristic of the NT writings. While this probably goes back to the teaching of Jesus in the Sermon on the Mount (Matt 5:10–12), it recurs both in the historic (Acts 5:41; 16:25) and epistolary writings (e.g., Phil 1:18; 4:4). The uniqueness of Christian joy lies in its emergence under the most adverse circumstances. Paul states the paradox succinctly in 2 Corinthians 6:10: "sorrowful, yet always rejoicing" (cf. 2 Cor 12:10). The Thessalonian Christians had already suffered with joy (1 Thess 1:6) as had Paul himself (3:9). The challenge is for this joyful outlook to become constant ("always"). From a human perspective they had every reason not to be joyful—persecution from outsiders and friction among themselves. Yet in Christ they are to be more and more joyful.

17 Intimately related to constant joy is incessant prayer—the only way to cultivate a joyful attitude in times of trial. Uninterrupted communication with God keeps temporal and spiritual values in balance. *Adialeiptōs* ("continually"; cf. Rom 1:9; 1 Thess 1:2, 3; 2:13) does not mean some sort of nonstop praying. Rather, it implies constantly recurring prayer, growing out of a settled attitude of dependence on God. Whether words are uttered or not, lifting the heart to God while one is occupied with miscellaneous duties is the vital thing. Verbalized prayer will be spontaneous and will punctuate one's daily schedule as it did Paul's writings (3:11-13; 2 Thess 2:16, 17).

18 A final member of this triplet for personal development is "Give thanks in all circumstances." No combination of happenings can be termed "bad" for a Christian because of God's constant superintendence (Rom 8:28). We need to recognize that seeming aggravations are but a temporary part of a larger plan for our spiritual well-being. Out of this perspective we can always discern a cause for thanks. In fact, failure to do this is a symptom of unbelief (Rom 1:21).

"For this is God's will for you in Christ Jesus" justifies all three brief commands. Rejoicing, praying, and giving thanks do not exhaust God's will but are vital parts of it. "In Christ Jesus" is a significant qualification of God's will because only here can inner motives be touched. Paul's earlier rule, the Mosiac law, was strong on outward conformity, but was helpless to deal with human thoughts. It could not dictate an inner attitude even though it was a perfect expression of God's will (Best, p. 236). In union with Christ, together with an accompanying inward transformation (2 Cor 5:17), however, compliance with God's standards can extend to motives. These three commands penetrate the innermost recesses of human personality—the spring from which all outward obedience flows. If the source is contaminated, fulfillment of God's will in outward matters is impossible. Such is the note sounded by the Lord Jesus in his own teaching (Matt 5-7). The true victories in life are won by Christians who are joyful, prayerful, and thankful.

4. *Responsibilities to public worship*

5:19-22

> **19**Do not put out the Spirit's fire; **20**do not treat prophecies with contempt. **21**Test everything. Hold on to the good. **22**Avoid every kind of evil.

19 At this point Paul shifts from the personal life to communal worship (vv. 19-22). "Do not put out the Spirit's fire" alludes to the Holy Spirit as a burning presence (cf. 2 Tim 1:6). In particular, this is his impartation of specialized capabilities for ministry to others in the body of Christ. In his discussions of spiritual gifts elsewhere (Rom 12:6-8; 1 Cor 12:8-10, 28-30; Eph 4:11) Paul distinguishes eighteen such special abilities. Only nine of them, however, involve speaking publicly (apostleship, prophecy, discerning of spirits, kinds of tongues, interpretation of tongues, evangelism, teaching, pastor-teaching, and exhorting). Since apostleship in the narrower sense was not present in Thessalonica, it, along with the nonspeaking gifts, could not have been the one in question here. When Paul commands, "Stop putting out the Spirit's fire," as v.19 might literally be translated, he advocates the cessation of something already being practiced. It is possible that other gifts in addition to prophecy (cf. v.20) had been abused, with the result that the more sober-minded leadership had overreacted and prohibited Spirit manifestations altogether. In 1 Corinthians 14, Paul dealt with the wrong use of tongues. But the need in Thessalonica was apparently different. Rather than allowing the error to continue as the Corinthians had done, the leadership in Thessalonica had completely repressed some gifts, with a resulting loss of spiritual benefit. Paul forbids such repression. The proper course is to allow gifted ones to share in a decent and orderly fashion what the Spirit can do through them for edification of the body of Christ (1 Cor 14:12, 26, 40). Control is necessary, but overcontrol is detrimental. So it is the responsibility of leadership and the whole community to find the right balance.

20 From Paul's next prohibition, "Do not treat prophecies with contempt," it appears that the Christians at Thessalonica like those at Corinth (1 Cor 14:1) had underrated the gift of prophecy. The directive may literally be translated "Stop treating prophecies with contempt." These were separate utterances of those who in their prophetic office proclaimed the will and command of God as well as predicted the future (Acts 11:28). Benefits from these utterances could build up a local church (1 Cor 14:3).

Apparently, however, certain "idle" brothers (v.14; cf. 4:11, 12) had misused this gift by falsifying data regarding the Lord's return. This had soured the remainder of the flock against prophecy in general. Their tendency now was not to listen to any more prophetic messages, but to discount them in view of counterfeit utterances they had heard. Once again Paul warns against overreaction and urges the church to give prophecies their proper place in edifying its members (cf. v.11).

21 To balance the two prohibitions, Paul stipulates that all charismatic manifestations be tested with a view to accepting what is valid and disallowing what is not (vv.21, 22). "Everything" is subject to the limitation of vv.19, 20, i.e., the exercise of spiritual gifts. The mere claim to inspiration was not a sufficient guarantee, because inspirations were known at times to come from below (1 Cor 12:2) as well as from above (Lightfoot, p. 84). Some have found in these words of Paul an allusion to a saying of Jesus preserved by a number of church fathers, including Clement of Alexandria and Origen. Origen wrote, "Be ye approved money changers" (*ginesthe trapezitai dokimoi*). To this Clement adds a thought about money changers "who reject much, but retain the good" (Jeremias, *Unknown Sayings of Jesus*, pp. 89–93). Followers were thus figuratively warned against accepting false prophets. Paul probably knew this saying, but the absence of "money changers" from 1 Thessalonians 5:21, 22 probably indicates that he did not have this quotation specifically in mind.

The nature of the test is not specified, but suggestions are forthcoming from related passages. In 1 John 4:1ff., as well as probably 1 Corinthians 12:3, the test is theological in nature, having to do with a proper view of Jesus as the Christ and Lord. In 1 Corinthians 12:10 and 14:29 discernment is a specific spiritual function in combination with the gift of prophecy. It consists of an ability to discern whether another prophetic spokesman has given a genuinely inspired utterance. But perhaps these two tests are too specialized for the present context, and preference should be given a more general criterion of whether a positive contribuion to the body's edification and mutual love has been made.

Testing like this will identify some spiritual activities as attractive and conducive to a growing love and to Christian power (5:11; 1 Cor 13; 14:3-5, 12, 26; so Frame, p. 207). These are genuine gifts and should be clung to tenaciously. In a very similar discussion about five years later for "hold on to the good" (*to kalon katechete,*) Paul substituted "cling to what is good" (*kollōmenoi tō agathō,* Rom 12:9). Both speak of determined tenacity to retain the beneficial. This church had been remiss (19, 20). "Good" in Thessalonians describes what is outwardly attractive and therefore beneficial and in Romans what is inherently good and therefore bound to be beneficial also.

22 Allowance must also be made for professed spiritual manifestations that do not contribute but rather detract from the development of the local body. Paul designates this category by *pantos eidous ponērou* ("every kind of evil"). The expression lends itself to varying interpretations. *Eidous* ("kind"), in keeping with its predominant NT meaning (Luke 3:22; 9:29; John 5:37; 2 Cor 5:7) may denote "appearance." Or in accord with the obvious antithesis between this and v.21, it may mean "kind" or "species." The latter meaning (as in NIV) is preferable because spiritual gifts could hardly with any credibility assume the "appearance of evil," but they could be a "species of evil" falsely attributed to the Holy Spirit.

Ponērou ("of evil") likewise presents two options: if it is taken as an adjective qualifying *eidous,* the phrase is "evil kind," or taken as a substantive, a practical equivalent of the noun *ponērias,* the phrase is "kind of evil." Though the anarthrous adjective in Paul is more frequently adjectival in force, the nature of the present contrast with *to kalon* (v. 21) resolves this particular issue in favor of the substantival use adopted by NIV.

Paul very clearly intends an antithesis with v.21 here. "Hold fast" (*katechete,* v.21) to the good, but "hold yourselves free from" (*apechesthe;* NIV, "avoid," v.22) every kind of evil that tries to parade as a genuine representation of the Spirit (Hiebert, p. 249). Only then can maximum benefit for the body of Christ in local worship be achieved.

Notes:

21 A contrast is indicated by an adversative δέ (*de,* "but," untranslated in above text). The conjunction is genuine, the progress of development being such as to demand a connective at that point (Lightfoot, p. 84). Several worthy MSS including ℵ and A omit it, but evidence for its inclusion (B D 33) is quite substantial. The omission may have arisen by the conjunction's being assimilated with the initial letter of the following word δοκιμάζετε (*dokimazete,* "test") (Metzger, *A Textual Commentary on the Greek NT,* p. 633).

V. Conclusion (5:23–28)

A. Petition for the Thessalonians

5:23, 24

23May God himself, the God of peace, sanctify you through and through. May your whole spirit, soul and body be kept blameless at the coming of our Lord Jesus Christ. 24The one who calls you is faithful and he will do it.

23 Having concluded his assorted suggestions for practical improvement, Paul looks to God to grant these objectives in the light of the Lord's return (cf. 3:12, 13). Sexual purity (4:3–8), brotherly love (4:9, 10), personal independence (4:11, 12), understanding the *parousia* (4:13–5:11), respect for leaders, love for other people, rejoicing, prayer, thankfulness, and concern for public worship (vv.12–22) are possible only through God. "I have simply told you all these things to do," Paul is saying, "but God alone has power to make your efforts a success."

Paul addresses God as the giver "of peace" (cf. 1 Cor 14:33), who has provided for a harmonious relationship between himself and man through Christ's death. At this point, following exhortations that imply at least a trace of disharmony (4:6, 10–12; 5:12–22), he invokes God's intervention as peacemaker.

Throughout the Epistle Paul has been concerned with sanctification (3:13; 4:3, 4, 7, 8). Now he prays that God will sanctify (separate to himself) the readers of the Epistle "through and through." *Holoteleis* ("through and through") speaks of the ultimate maturity of Christian character. It presents the qualitative side of spiritual advance in its final perfection. Toward this goal sanctification is directed.

The quantitative objective of the prayer is in *holoklēron* ("whole"; cf. James 1:4, where similar adjectives describe qualitative and quantitative spiritual development). Wholeness pertains to three parts of the human make-up, "spirit, soul and body." Paul petitions that this wholeness may be "kept" or "preserved" and that it may be "blameless at the coming of our Lord Jesus Christ."

The question arises as to how Paul conceives of man in the words "spirit, soul and body." Among the various explanations of this expression are these four:

1. Paul intends no systematic dissection of human personality. Instead, he uses a loose rhetorical expression emphasizing the totality of personality and reinforcing "through and through" and "whole" (H.W. Robinson, *The Christian Doctrine of Man* [Edinburgh: T. and T. Clark, 1926], pp. 108–109). This view leans heavily on comparable expressions in Deuteronomy 6:5; Mark 12:30; and Luke 10:27 (e.g., "with all your heart, with all your soul, with all your mind and with all your strength," Mark 12:30). What it fails to explain, however, is why Paul did not use this already well-known formula for completeness, if that is what he meant. It also cannot explain why he included man's material part ("body"), which the alleged analogous passages do not include. It is contrary to Paul's acknowledged careful use of words to attribute such a rhetorical device to him (Ellicott, p. 84; Hiebert, p. 252).

2. Another explanation makes "spirit" and "soul" interchangeable and sees each of them as referring to man's immaterial substance. "Body" then completes the picture by referring to man's material part: "your whole spirit (i.e., soul) and body." This sees man as dichotomous. Two terms for the same immaterial substance simply view it according to its two functions, relationship to God and relationship to the lower realm of sensations, affections, desires, etc. (Strong, *Systematic Theology*, p. 483). Defense of this approach lies in the way Paul parallels *pneuma* ("spirit") with *psychē* ("soul") in Philippians 1:27 and speaks at times of man's make-up as bipartite (2 Cor 7:1). Also, body and soul (or spirit) together sometimes describe the whole man (Matt 10:28; 1 Cor 5:3; 3 John 2) (Strong, p. 483). The weakness in the above arguments is evident, however, because Paul sometimes parallels *pneuma* with *sarx* ("flesh," "body"), with which it cannot be identical (2 Cor 2:13; 7:5, 13). Clear-cut distinctions between *psychē* and *pneuma* indicate they cannot be used interchangeably (Cremer, *Theological Lexicon of New Testament Greek*, pp. 504–505). In addition, it is doubtful whether Paul would pray for man's

functional capabilities, as this view holds, rather than two substantial parts of man's make-up.

3. Others try to escape a threefold division by dividing the last sentence of v.23 either into two independent parts (Hendriksen, p. 150) or else by joining "may your whole spirit" with the first part of the verse (Stempvort, cited by Best, p. 243). The former alternative requires inserting words that are not in v.23b, while the latter is unnecessarily complicated and causes prohibitive grammatical difficulties (Best, p. 243). To fill out the sense of either of these explanations, words must also be omitted.

4. That Paul saw man as a threefold substance in this verse has been generally recognized since the early fathers. The symmetrical arrangement of three nouns with their articles and their connection by means of two "ands" (*kai*) renders this the most natural explanation. This becomes a "distinct enunciation of three component parts of the nature of man" (Ellicott, p. 84). That Paul elsewhere does not make such a distinction (Best, pp. 242–244; Hendriksen, pp. 146–147) is no argument against trichotomy. It is always possible that Paul has been misunderstood elsewhere. It is also conceivable that he did not endeavor to make specific distinctions in other letters as he does here. That Paul possibly depends on liturgical formulation and attaches no special meaning to these separate terms (Dibelius, cited by Best, p. 244) is also inconclusive speculation. To object that this interpretation reads in the trichotomy of secular psychology (Schweizer, TDNT, 6:435) neglects Paul's occasional acceptance of portions of secular philosophy that were valid. He simply incorporated them into a divinely inspired framework (Ellicott, p. 84). A trichotomous understanding of 5:23 has so much to commend it that other interpretations cannot compete without summoning arguments from elsewhere. The difference between the material part ("body") and the immaterial parts ("spirit" and "soul") is obvious. Paul's pronounced distinction between *psychikos* ("natural"; NIV, "without the spirit") and *pneumatikos* ("spiritual") (1 Cor 2:14, 15; 15:44), his differentiation of *pneuma* ("spirit") and *egō* ("self") or *nous* ("mind"), parts of *psychē* ("soul") (Rom 7:17–23; 1 Cor 14:14), and other writers' distinguishing of *pneuma* and *psychē* (James 3:15; Jude 19) argue heavily for a substantial, not just a functional, difference between the two immaterial parts (Hiebert, p. 252; Schweizer, TDNT, 6:436; Lightfoot, p. 88).

The spirit (*pneuma*) is the part that enables man to perceive the divine. Through this component he can know and communicate with God. This higher element, though damaged through the fall of Adam, is sufficiently intact to provide each individual a consciousness of God. The soul (*psychē*) is the sphere of man's will and emotions. Here is his true center of personality. It gives him a self-consciousness that relates to the physical world through the body and to God through the spirit. This analysis of man had been Paul's training in the OT and no impressive evidence has surfaced to eradicate such a picture here (Milligan, p. 78; Olshausen, p. 457). Yet, it must be confessed, much unresolved mystery remains regarding the interrelationships between man's different parts, including the body. How one affects the other is fully understood only by him who is the Creator.

For such a composite creature Paul therefore prays, seeking an unblamable wholeness in the presence "of our Lord Jesus Christ" (23; cf. 2:19; 3:13).

24 To Paul, utterance of a prayer was not the end, but only the means to it. One who asks God for something can anticipate the fulfillment of his request because of God's character: "The one who calls you is faithful." He who issues an effectual call can be absolutely relied on to carry out his call, including among other things the sanctification and preservation prayed for in v.23. Faithfulness is the characteristic of God that determines that he will do the very thing Paul has prayed for. In his pretemporal selection of the Thessalonian church (1:4; 2:12), God had already determined to do so in his own counsels. This, however, did not render prayer for them superfluous, as human effort and application also have their place in carrying out the purposes of God.

Notes:

23 All three nouns of v.23 are governed by ὁλόκληρον (holoklēron, "entire") even though it agrees in gender with the first. The Greek adjective usually agrees with the nearest member of a compound expression. Strictly speaking, this adjective probably should not be understood attributively as in the tr. "your whole spirit, soul and body." Taking it as a predicate adjective is more faithful to the anarthrous form: "May your spirit and soul and body be preserved entire" (ASV). The singular number is no problem since it may view man as unity (cf. 3:11) or else the number, like the gender, may be determined by the nearest member of the compound expression.

The question of how to relate the adverb ἀμέμπτως (amemptos, "blameless") is also pertinent. To let it describe the manner of keeping (tērētheiē, "may be kept") is not convincing. In all likelihood it supplements the sense of ὁλόκληρον (holoklēron, "entire"): "blamelessly whole" or "whole, beyond reach of complaint."

B. *Reciprocation by the Thessalonians*

5:25–27

25Brothers, pray for us. 26Greet all the brothers with a holy kiss. 27I charge you before the Lord to have this letter read to all the brothers.

25 Following his prayer, Paul offers his readers opportunity to reciprocate along three lines. First, he requests prayer for himself and his fellow missionaries.

The scope of "brothers" presents two possibilities. On the one hand, because the phrase "all the brothers" of vv.26, 27 seemingly limits the addressees to church leaders, the tendency could be to limit v.25 accordingly. Yet how strict a distinction is made between leaders and followers in vv.26, 27, as well as in the rest of the letter? Certainly vv.12, 13 address the congregation at large and even tend to exclude leadership. In each case where "brothers" is found earlier in the Epistle, the whole church is included. Hence, Paul probably follows his customary policy of requesting prayer from the total body, not just from a limited few (Rom 16:16; 1 Cor 16:20; 2 Cor 13:12).

Paul depended on his converts' spiritual support (Rom 15:30; Eph 6:19; Phil 1:19; Col 4:3; 2 Thess 3:1; Philem 22). So now he asks for a continuing place in their prayers (v.17), similar to the place they have been given in his (23, 24). Good textual support indicates that "also" should be added at the end of v.25, the thought being to pray for the Pauline group in addition to others for whom they prayed.

26 A second closing request is for all the brothers to be greeted with a holy kiss. Paul's usual "one another" (Rom 16:16; 1 Cor 16:20; 2 Cor 13:12; cf. 1 Peter 5:14) is replaced

this time by an expression that may imply that the request is addressed to leaders only. This need not distinguish leaders from the rest of the assembly, however, as the Epistle will eventually find its way to all (v.27). In the meantime those receiving it first were to greet the rest (Moffatt, p. 43). The symbol of greeting was "a holy kiss" (v.26). This was not a kiss of respect as was used in ancient times to honor men of authority. Neither was it cultic as though copied from an ancient mystery religion. It most closely parallels the use of a kiss among members of the same family as a token of their close relationship. Christians have come into the family of God, which knows even closer ties than those of any human family (Matt 12:46–50). It was quite appropriate that a symbolic greeting be adopted. It was to be "holy" (*hagiō*), i.e., such as is becoming to saints (*hagiois*, 3:13). This may have been the custom of men kissing men and women kissing women so as to forestall any suspicion of impropriety. A Jewish synagogue practice, it could easily have found its way into early Christian assemblies.

27 The third parting word is more than just a request. The formula "I charge you before the Lord" shows an unusual concern on Paul's part regarding the possibility of his letter's not being read. Invoking an oath and switching to the first person singular indicate his urgency. He may have feared that the contents of the letter might be limited to those interested in a particular issue, e.g., those who had fallen asleep in Christ (4:13–18) (Ellicott, p. 86). Perhaps he was aware that some were already at work attributing wrong teaching to his name and authority (2 Thess 2:2) (Hogg and Vine, p. 216; Lightfoot, p. 91). Or he could have feared a breakdown in communications between the church's leadership and some of the communicants within the church (4:11, 12; 5:12, 13) (Frame, p. 217). Very probably Paul sensed the far-reaching import of the teaching of the Epistle and its binding authority as part of a canon of Scripture (1 Cor 14:37). Whatever the case, this charge has implications of divine punishment for failure to comply. The first recipients of the letter, probably the church leaders, were bound under oath "to have this letter read to all the brothers."

Obviously it was to be read aloud, in line with the classical meaning of *anaginōskō* ("read"). Under restrictions of limited educational privilege, not all participants in Christian circles were able to read for themselves. The further limitation of insufficient copies and expense of writing materials prohibited distribution to all. The only solution was to give the Epistle a place in public worship alongside the OT Scripture, the consequence of which would eventually be ecclesiastical recognition of its authority as an inspired book.

Notes

25 The reading of καί (*kai*, "also") is probably to be accepted. External attestation favors it slightly. It is doubtful that Colossians 4:3 could have prompted its inclusion, but it is possible that there was a scribal omission in some MSS when its reference to 5:17 was overlooked (Metzger, *Textual Commentary*, p. 633).

27 The double accusative ὑμᾶς τὸν κύριον (*humas ton kurion*, "you [before] the Lord") following ἐνορκίζω (*enorkizō*, "I charge") names the persons bound by the adjuration ("you") and the one to whom accountability is due ("the Lord"). Necessity for two objects stems from the causative nature of *enorkizō*; "I cause you to swear by the Lord" hence becomes "I adjure you by the Lord" (BDF, pars. 149, 155.7).

The aorist of ἀναγνωσθῆναι (*anagnōsthēnai*, "to have ... read") cannot be pressed into restricting Paul's meaning to one public reading. A constative aorist easily provides for regular reading as a standard practice. This latter was the sense understood by early Christianity.

The textual suggestion that "all the brothers" should be "all the holy brothers" rests basically upon TR authority. Coupled with the weakness of this external support is the internal improbability that so significant a term as ἁγίοις (*hagiois*, "holy") could have been dropped by copyists (Metzger, *Textual Commentary*, pp. 633, 634).

C. Benediction

5:28

28The grace of our Lord Jesus Christ be with you.

28 This customary benediction was probably added in Paul's own handwriting (cf. 2 Thess 3:17, 18). His distinctive farewell was always built around his favorite concept, grace, which replaced the usual epistolary farewell (cf. Acts 15:29). This trait is distinctive in his Epistles whether the benediction be longer (2 Cor 13:13 [13:14 in KJV, NASB, and others]) or shorter (Col 4:18; 1 Tim 6:21; 2 Tim 4:22; Titus 3:15). The primacy of grace resulting from the saving work of "our Lord Jesus Christ" was a constant theme as the apostle sought the welfare of those he served (cf. 1:1).

Notes

28 The absence of ἀμήν (*amēn*, "amen") from reliable representatives of both Alexandrian and Western text types indicates that it was probably added when the book was used in liturgical settings (Metzger, *Textual Commentary*, p. 634). It was habitual to close the portion read with "Amen," signifying accord with the content.

Subscripts found in various textual sources locate the writing of the Epistle either in Athens or Corinth. The former possibility must be a scribal inaccuracy drawn from a misunderstanding of 1 Thess 3:1. Historical data in Acts 17–18 determine that Corinth is the place of origin (cf. Introduction, p. 233).

2 THESSALONIANS

Robert L. Thomas

2 THESSALONIANS

Introduction

1. Background
2. Unity
3. Authorship and Canonicity
4. Date
5. Place of Origin and Destination
6. Occasion
7. Purpose
8. Theological Values
9. Bibliography
10. Outline

1. Background

Paul's interest in his Thessalonian converts did not terminate with the dispatch of the first Epistle. His ministry was one of continual discipling of those he had won to Christ. This second letter was written only slightly later than 1 Thessalonians.

The background of 2 Thessalonians is therefore the same as that of 1 Thessalonians (see Introduction, pp. 229–231) with only slight additions. While he was still in Corinth, Paul received further word about this church's condition. Through what channel the report came is not known, but its content was sufficiently important to prompt him to write 2 Thessalonians.

2. Unity

The division of 2 Thessalonians into two letters (1:1–12 + 3:6–16 and 2:13, 14 + 2:1–12 + 2:15–3:5 + 3:17, 18) has been proposed, but it has not received substantial support. As with 1 Thessalonians, this theory is built largely on the presence of two thanksgivings (1:3ff.; 2:13f.) and two prayers (3:16, 18). The proposal of the division of 2 Thessalonians rests on an assumption that Paul never deviated from a stereotyped literary pattern. But this has never been proved. Even if it were true, the proposals for what that pattern is can be used against the theories they allegedly support. (Best, pp. 45–50). No manuscript authority for questioning the unity of 2 Thessalonians has ever been found. We may therefore safely conclude that it has been preserved in its original form.

3. Authorship and Canonicity

The external evidence for the Pauline authorship of 2 Thessalonians is stronger than for 1 Thessalonians. Possible references to it are found in the Didache and Ignatius, and Polycarp has two passages that are almost assuredly from the Epistle. Justin Martyr also clearly refers to it. In addition, the witnesses cited for 1 Thessalonians (cf. p. 232) add their support to the Pauline authorship of 2 Thessalonians and an early recognition of its canonicity (Milligan, pp. lxxvi–lxxvii).

Yet various objections to Pauline authorship have been offered on internal grounds:

1. The one objection most widely used finds in 2 Thessalonians an eschatology different from that of 1 Thessalonians, one that represents a Christian perspective that arose after the destruction of Jerusalem in A.D. 70 (Marxen, p. 42; Reginald H. Fuller, *A Critical Introduction to the New Testament* [London: Gerald Duckworth, 1966], p. 57; Norman Perrin, *The New Testament, An Introduction* [New York: Harcourt Brace Jovanovich, 1974], p. 120). The principal difference cited is emphasis on premonitory signs of the *parousia* in 2 Thessalonians in contrast to 1 Thessalonians' presentation of the event as something that may come at any moment. The notes below, however, explain in detail why this disagreement is not present. A right understanding of the several phases of the *parousia* and of the meaning of 2 Thessalonians 2:3, shows the harmony between the two Epistles. The apostasy and the man of lawlessness (2, 2:3) come after the initial phase of the *parousia* when Christ comes for his own, so there is no disagreement. Differing circumstances at the two writings called for emphases on different aspects of end-time events in the two Epistles.

2. Paul's authorship of 2 Thessalonians is also questioned because of its different view of the last judgment. A reversal of fates, with the persecutors receiving tribulation and the persecuted relief (2 Thess 1:5ff.), is not paralleled in Paul's acknowledged writings (Fuller, p. 58). This kind of thinking is alleged to belong to a generation later than Paul's (Rev 16:5–7; 19:2) (Perrin, p. 120). This objection sterotypes Paul's thinking unreasonably to the point of prohibiting him from expressing his eschatology in added dimensions. Far from belonging to a later generation, vengeance in connection with the Lord's return is traceable to Jesus himself (Luke 21:22) and to the OT (Isa 66:15). Paul simply developed it in 2 Thessalonians more than elsewhere. Furthermore, end-time tribulation and judgment for earth's inhabitants along with relief to Jesus' followers has its part in Jesus' teaching also (Matt 24:15–22; 25:31–46). In fact, Paul elsewhere understands the same twofold judgment of the two groups (Rom 2:5–10). Second Thessalonians is therefore in agreement with Pauline perspectives and fits quite well into the Pauline canon.

3. Another objection is that it is post-Pauline to assign divine attributes and functions to Christ (2 Thess 2:16; 3:5 with 1 Thess 3:11–13) (Fuller, p. 58). This difference in the prayers of the two Epistles reveals that 2 Thessalonians could not have been written during Paul's lifetime (Perrin, p. 120). To affirm, however, that Paul never believed in the deity of Christ is precarious. Even 1 Thessalonians sees him as a source of divine grace (1:1; 5:28), as one to whom prayer is properly addressed (3:11, 12), and, in addition, one to whom future accountability must be given (2:19). These are divine prerogatives that can be ignored only by a determined predisposition to the contrary. Both 1 and 2 Thessalonians rest staunchly upon a high view of Christ's person.

Other objections to the Pauline authorship of 2 Thessalonians include its difference in tone from 1 Thessalonians; its greater use of the OT, indicating Jewish rather than Gentile readers; and similarities to 1 Thessalonians so pronounced as to make the second Epistle unnecessary (Guthrie, pp. 572, 573). The harsher tone is adequately accounted for if Paul is dealing with a worsening situation in the second letter. Increased use of the OT is easily explainable for Gentile Christians who quite soon after conversion became conversant with it. Similarities to 1 Thessalonians are not so numerous as to make 2 Thessalonians a mere carbon copy. There are also differences. The combination of similarities and differences is such as to render Pauline authorship quite reasonable (ibid.).

None of these arguments based on internal considerations is sufficient to overthrow the Epistle's self-claims and the strongly attested traditional view of Paul's authorship.

4. Date

If one accepts the accuracy of the Acts account, 2 Thessalonians must have been written during Paul's stay in Corinth because Paul, Silas, and Timothy are not known to have been together after that. The conditions are still generally the same as those represented in 1 Thessalonians. First Thessalonians must have come earlier because its autobiographical portions leave no room for correspondence between Paul's departure from the city and the Epistle itself (Marxen, p. 41).

Some efforts to prove 2 Thessalonians earlier than 1 Thessalonians have been made: (1) In 2 Thessalonians trials are said to be at their height, whereas in 1 Thessalonians they are past (T.W. Manson, *Studies in the Gospels and Epistles* [Manchester: University of Manchester, 1962], p. 269). Yet 1 Thessalonians 3:4 is easily understood to indicate trials as present in that Epistle too. (2) In 2 Thessalonians internal difficulties (3:6–15) are a new development, but in 1 Thessalonians they are already well known (4:11, 12; 5:14) (Manson, p. 272). These phenomena, however, can be explained differently. The situation had become more aggravated in 2 Thessalonians, necessitating extended discussion. In 1 Thessalonians only a passing mention was required for a problem that had not yet become serious. (3) Three didactic sections of 1 Thessalonians, each introduced by *peri de* ("now about") correspond to questions raised by 2 Thessalonians (1 Thess 4:9–12 with 2 Thess 3:12; 1 Thess 4:13–18 with 2 Thess 2:1–12; 1 Thess 5:1–11 with 2 Thess 2:1–12) (Manson, pp. 274–277). While interesting, these correspondences may be just as easily explained by postulating the traditional order for the Epistles.

If efforts to prove 2 Thessalonians earlier fail, a date shortly after 1 Thessalonians is most probable for the writing of 2 Thessalonians, perhaps late in the summer of A.D. 50.

5. Place of Origin and Destination

Like 1 Thessalonians, this second Epistle also originated at Corinth. As far as is known, Silas and Timothy were not together with Paul at any later time (cf. Acts 18:5; 2 Thess 1:1). Berea and Philippi have been suggested as possible destinations of this letter. The former is considered plausible because of the favorable reception the Jews gave Paul and his companions in that city and the larger place of the OT in 2 Thessalonians. The suggestion of Philippi is supported by references in Polycarp, who seemingly names it as the destination of several passages in 2 Thessalonians (Best, pp. 40, 41). The difference in OT usage between 1 and 2 Thessalonians has already been accounted for without assigning a different destination (see Authorship and Canonicity). Polycarp's reference to Philippi probably arose through confusion of one Pauline Epistle with another; he was thoroughly familiar with Paul's writings and quoted from memory. Other passages imply that he knew of only one Philippian Epistle and that was certainly the same as the one currently known by that title (ibid.).

6. Occasion

Second Thessalonians was apparently prompted by three main developments: (1) Persecution of the Christians had grown worse and was leaving victims at the point of despair. (2) A pseudo-Pauline letter and other false representations were on the point of convincing believers that the end time was already present because of their increased suffering. (3) The nearness of Christ's return had been misused as a basis for shirking vocational responsibilities even more than at the time of 1 Thessalonians. This problem had become quite severe.

7. Purpose

To meet the needs that occasioned the Epistle Paul pursued three broad purposes: (1) He provided an incentive for the Thessalonians to persevere a little longer by describing the reward and retribution issuing from the future judgment of God (1:3–10). (2) He clarified prominent events belonging to the day of the Lord to prove the falsity of claims that the day had already arrived (2:1–12). (3) He issued detailed instructions covering disciplinary steps the church was to take in correcting those who refused to work (3:6–15).

8. Theological Values

(Cf. Introduction to 1 Thessalonians, pp. 233–234.)

9. Bibliography

(See Bibliography for 1 Thessalonians, pp. 234–235.)

10. Outline

    I. Salutation (1:1, 2)

   II. Assurance of Repayment at God's Righteous Judgment (1:3–12)

      A. Thanksgiving for Present Perseverance (1:3–10)

        1. Healthy development (1:3–5a)

        2. Righteous judgment (1:5b–10)

          a. Categorization of participants (1:5b–7a)

          b. Circumstances of fulfillment (1:7b)

          c. Consideration of repayment (1:8–10)

            1) Alienation (1:8, 9)

            2) Glorification (1:10)

      B. Prayer for Future Acceptance (1:11, 12)

  III. Assurance of Noninvolvement in the Day of the Lord (2:1–17)

      A. The False Claim (2:1, 2)

      B. The True Condition (2:3–12)

        1. Defiance—yet to come (2:3, 4)

        2. Delay—presently in effect (2:5–7)

        3. Deception and destruction—after the delay (2:8–10)

        4. Delusion and divine judgment—because of present recalcitrance (2:11, 12)

      C. The Truth's Continuance (2:13–17)

        1. Thanks for divine deliverance (2:13, 14)

        2. Call to doctrinal adherence (2:15)

        3. Prayer for practical compliance (2:16, 17)

  IV. Encouragement to Gainful Employment for the Present (3:1–15)

      A. Prayerful Preparation for Encounter (3:1–5)

        1. Prayer for Paul (3:1, 2)

        2. Prayer for the people (3:3–5)

      B. Proper Solution for Idleness (3:6–15)

        1. Previous instruction and example (3:6–10)

        2. Renewed instruction (3:11, 12)

        3. Corrective separation (3:13–15)

   V. Conclusion (3:16–18)

      A. Prayer for God's Peace and Presence (3:16)

      B. Personalized Benediction (3:17, 18)

Text and Exposition

I. Salutation

1:1, 2

> [1]Paul, Silas and Timothy, to the church of the Thessalonians, who are in God our Father and the Lord Jesus Christ: [2]Grace and peace to you from God the Father and the Lord Jesus Christ.

1,2 After a period of probably several months, new reports from Thessalonica reached Paul while he and his missionary party were still in Corinth. These reports were such as to lead him to write a second Epistle. Conditions reflected in 2 Thessalonians are similar to those in the first letter, though in some ways problems had become worse. In this second letter he sent to the Thessalonian church Paul provides solutions for a new set of circumstances.

The salutation is identical with that of the first letter (cf. exposition of 1 Thess 1:1) except for two additions. The first is "our" in the expression "God our Father" (v.1). This relates the fatherhood of God to Christians rather than to Jesus. (However, see note below.) The latter aspect of God's fatherhood is in view elsewhere (2 Cor 1:3; Eph 1:3; 1 Peter 1:3).

The second addition is the phrase "from God the Father and the Lord Jesus Christ" (v.2). Comparable phrases identifying the sources of "grace and peace" occur in all other Pauline superscriptions except 1 Thessalonians 1:1. The words make explicit what is already implicit—viz., that God is ultimately the only source of grace and peace. Two persons of the Godhead are specified: the Father and the Son. To Paul, Jesus was Deity in the fullest sense. This is the only justification for placing his name beside the Father's as co-author of the unmerited favor and harmonious relationship pronounced in this greeting.

Notes

2 There is textual evidence for reading "from God our Father," ℵ and A from the Alexandrian text-type being in support of including the possessive pronoun "our." Since this is the Pauline pattern wherever this source phrase is used, however, how could the pronoun ἡμῶν (hēmōn, "our") ever have been omitted by substantial authorities B (Alexandrian) and D (Western)? Copyists would hardly have omitted it in light of its presence in 1:1 and other Pauline salutations. Yet they may easily have been influenced to add it to bring the expression into line with practice elsewhere. Therefore, it probably was not present in the autograph.

II. Assurance of Repayment at God's Righteous Judgment (1:3–12)

A. *Thanksgiving for Present Perseverance* (1:3–10)

1. *Healthy development*

1:3–5a

> [3]We ought always to thank God for you, brothers, and rightly so, because your faith is growing more and more, and the love every one of you has for each other is increasing.
> [4]Therefore, among God's churches we boast about your perseverance and faith in all the persecutions and trials you are enduring.
> [5]All this is evidence that God's judgment is right. . . .

3 As is his practice in every Epistle but Galatians, Paul begins his remarks by thanking God for the spiritual progress of those he is writing to. Here his appreciation is marked by a feature found nowhere else except later in this same Epistle—he was obligated to express gratitude for what God had done in their lives. "We ought" appears only here and in 2:13 in connection with his thanksgiving and gives a glimpse into how Paul conceived of his duty to God. This unusual reference to responsibility, thought by some to be prompted by the readers' remarkable progress or by a special need among them (Lenski, p. 376; Hiebert, p. 279), should be limited to a special personal duty to God (Rom 1:14; 1 Cor 9:16, 17), because the Greek verb (*opheilō*, "ought"), implies an exclusive personal responsibility. "And rightly so" later in the verse refers to the readers' sterling performance amid persecutions (Milligan, p. 86; Lünemann, p. 184). Paul never ceased feeling a compulsion to give gratitude to God for what Christ had done. His post-conversion service was invested as a partial repayment for the personal debt he incurred when God gave him salvation.

"And rightly so" supplies a second reason for thanksgiving. "Just as it is fitting," the literal meaning, is not intended to limit the thankfulness (contra Lenski, p. 376), but stipulates the nature of response that caused appreciation (Best, pp. 249, 250). Paul habitually gave credit where credit was due. The conduct of his readers "under fire" was so commendable that he could not refrain from doing so again.

So great is Paul's excitement over their progress that he gives some details: "because your faith is growing more and more, and the love every one of you has for each other is increasing." Faith and love comprehend the total Christian walk (cf. 1 Cor 16:13, 14; 2 Cor 8:7; Gal 5:6; Eph 1:15; 3:17; 6:23; 1 Thess 3:6). The absence of "hope" from this combination is not overly significant. It does not hint at a lack of hope (Morris, NIC, p. 195; Hiebert, p. 281). Nor is it to be concluded that "hope" is represented in the "perseverance" of v.4. Paul rather uses two qualities instead of three (cf. 1 Thess 1:3) to designate Christian virtue and progress.

"Faith," an area commended in the first Epistle (1:3), was one where improvement was needed. The apostle's earlier prayer (1 Thess 3:10) had in view a return visit to strengthen the believers in this respect. Apparently, however, their faith had grown during his absence. They also needed to grow in "love," a quality he had already commended them for (1 Thess 1:3, 4:9, 10). For this too, Paul had prayed (1 Thess 3:12). It is no wonder, then, to find him rejoicing over their growth in faith and love.

4 In further reference to this radical improvement Paul says, "among God's churches we boast about your perseverance and faith." "We ourselves" would better translate the emphasis of the Greek text. But why this stress on the missionaries ("we ourselves")? Was Paul intimating that those who establish a church normally do not brag about that church (Morris, NIC, pp. 195, 196)? Or was he simply pointing to their own boasting in addition to that by others (Lenski, p. 379)? He more probably meant to contrast the missionaries' boasting with the Thessalonians' self-evaluation, since the Greek text places the intensive first person (*autous hēmas*, "we ourselves") in juxtaposition with the second person (*hymin*, "you"). At least some of these Christians felt inferior because of failures (1 Thess 5:14) and so were not inclined to boast. Paul speaks to this discouragement when he says, "As far as we are concerned your progress has been tremendous, so much so that we boast about it to other churches." The churches to which Paul had boasted were probably more widespread than in the vicinity of Corinth (contra Henry Alford, *The Greek Testament*, 3:285; Milligan, p. 87). Churches everywhere had heard this report, either through letter or through personal contact with those visiting Paul in Corinth. This did not necessarily include every single church, of course, but represents a relatively widespread dissemination of the news (cf. 1 Thess 1:8) (Hogg and Vine, p. 222; Hendriksen, p. 156).

The boasting pertains to "your perseverance and faith in all the persecutions and trials you are enduring." "Perseverance" is the attitude that accepts trying circumstances without retarding progress (cf. comment on "endurance" in 1 Thess 1:3). Accompanying the perseverance of the Thessalonians was their "faith" or, perhaps better, their "faithfulness." While "faith" is the common meaning of *pistis* in Paul's writings (Morris, NIC, p. 196), the present context justifies the less frequent sense of "faithfulness" or "fidelity," which Paul also makes use of (Rom 3:3; Gal 5:22; Titus 2:10) (Lünemann, p. 188). Their tenacious loyalty to Christ in spite of fierce adversity is what Paul finds so remarkable. "Persecutions" (*diōgmois*) are sufferings incurred because of faith in Christ, while "trials" (*thlipsesin*) are troubles of any kind. The believers were "enduring" (*anechesthe*) these—but only for the time being; in God's plan such conditions were not to be permanent.

5 Instead of beginning a new paragraph, "all this is evidence that God's judgment is right" should probably be read with the end of v.4. The subject of Paul's boasting—i.e., their perseverance and faithfulness—is proof positive of God's righteous judgment. That he gives strength enough to face all the persecutions and trials victoriously shows that his "judgment is right" (Hendriksen, p. 155).

Withstanding *present* pressures demonstrates the rightness of God's *future* judgment. Some have seen present judgment in this reference because *endeixis* ("sign," "proof"), a cognate of *endeigma* ("evidence"), usually speaks of something already in force and because Peter views present suffering as a phase of God's judgment (1 Peter 4:17) (Auberlen and Riggenbach, p. 115; Olshausen, *Biblical Commentary*, 7:463). Yet subsequent descriptions (vv.6–10) relate so integrally to future accountability with the accompanying thought of reward for sufferers and retaliation against offenders that an understanding of present judgment is practically impossible (Hiebert, p. 285; Moffatt, EGT, 4:45; Lightfoot, p. 100). Quite clearly Paul uses a corresponding term (*dikaiokrisias*, "righteous judgment") in Romans 2:5 with this future sense (Frame, p. 226). The fact is that righteous judgment in 1:5a sets the tone for five and one-half verses about what is to come. The persecuted must understand clearly its twofold nature.

Notes

3 The use of ὀφείλω (opheilō, "ought") rather than δεῖ (dei, "it is necessary") probably shows that Paul's feeling of obligation at this point is unrelated to the Thessalonians' response. That he would use the same word again in 2:13, where the behavior of the Thessalonians is only remotely in view, increases the likelihood that here he is thinking strictly of his own debt to God.

To take the καθώς (kathōs, "as") clause (lit., "as it is fitting") as purely comparative implies a Pauline reluctance to "go all out" in his thanksgiving for them. The causal sense of kathōs is well established (Rom 1:28; 1 Cor 1:6; 5:7; Eph 1:4; Phil 1:7) (Robertson, RHG, p. 968; BDF, p. 236). It is much better when the comparison is allowed to take a causal flavor. From the standpoint of the Thessalonians' receptivity, it was incumbent upon Paul to express gratitude to God.

4 An additional reason for giving αὐτοὺς ἡμᾶς (autous hēmas, "we ourselves") a sense contrasted to ὑμῖν (hymin, "you") comes from 1 Thess 4:9 where the emphatic αὐτοὶ ... ὑμεῖς (autoi ... hymeis, "you ... yourselves") is antithetic to a supplied ἡμᾶς (hēmas, "us") with the infinitive γράφειν (graphein, "to write") (Frame, p. 223). This reflects a possible Pauline pattern of placing first and second person pronouns in such proximity for sake of contrast. In other cases where the intensive pronoun is used with the first person, it implies contrast (Rom 7:25; 9:3; 15:14; 2 Cor 10:1; 12:13) (Best, p. 251).

Used only here in the NT, ἐγκαυχᾶσθαι (enkauchasthai, "boast") governs two ἐν (en, "in") phrases, the former one specifying the object of boasting and the latter the place of boasting. The association of πίστεως (pisteōs, "faith") with ὑπομονῆς (hypomonēs, "perseverance"), διωγμοῖς (diōgmois, "persecutions"), θλίψεσιν (thlipsesin, "trials") and ἀνέχεσθε (anechesthe, "you are enduring") argues strongly for allowing its exceptional meaning of "faithfulness." Paul boasts about tangible perseverance. To have pisteōs refer to intangible faith does not furnish a suitable parallel. It must be the visible fruit of faith—faithfulness. Paul's habitual use of πιστός (pistos) for "faithful" lends further support to the choice of "faithfulness" instead of "faith" (1 Cor 1:9; 10:13; 2 Cor 1:8; 1 Thess 5:24; 2 Thess 3:3; 2 Tim 2:13) (Lünemann, p. 188).

5a The syntactical arrangement of ἔνδειγμα ... τοῦ θεοῦ (endeigma ... tou theou, "evidence that God's judgment is right") is difficult to decipher with assurance. Probably the best evidence favors taking ἔνδειγμα (endeigma, "evidence") as accusative in apposition with the whole idea behind ὑπομονῆς (hypomonēs, "perseverance") and πίστεως (pisteōs, "faith," "faithfulness," v.4). The difference in case is explained by Paul's consolidation of the whole expression introduced by the genitives of v.4 into a single concept (Lightfoot, p. 100). The case of endeigma is accusative, in agreement with a precedent in classical literature (Milligan, pp. 87, 88) and elsewhere in Paul (Rom 12:1).

2. Righteous judgment (1:5b–10)

a. Categorization of participants

1:5b–7a

> [5] ... and as a result you will be counted worthy of the kingdom of God, for which you are suffering. [6]God is just: He will pay back trouble to those who trouble you [7]and give relief to you who are troubled, and to us as well. ...

5b–7a The remainder of this section (vv.5b–10) expands on what God's future righteous judgment is. Paul first describes what it will mean to victims of present persecution (v.5b). He then points out the fate of persecutors (v.6), following this with a second look at what will happen to the persecuted (v.7a).

5b Future reckoning assures a future recognition of the worthiness of those suffering for the sake of the kingdom of God. This recognition will be God's pronouncement of fitness. It will not be self-earned but a gracious divine impartation resulting from the decision to believe in the Lord Jesus (1:3, 10; 2:13; 1 Thess 1:8), who himself earned the believer's forgiveness of sins and eternal life by dying a sacrificial death (1 Thess 5:10). The worthiness of the Thessalonian believers had already been established before persecutions came. Their firm stand in the face of persecutions (v.4) confirmed their relationship to God and was a pledge that their worthiness will be openly declared by God himself. Believers in Thessalonica were not the only ones suffering this kind of treatment. "For which you *also* [*kai*, v.5, untranslated in text above] are suffering" reminds the readers of something they already knew well—an experience they had in common with Paul, Silas, Timothy, and others (Acts 17:5; 1 Thess 2:2; cf. 2 Thess 3:2). With opposition behind them, all who are Christ's at his *parousia* will be welcomed into the messianic kingdom on the ground of their God-given worthiness.

6 On the other hand, it is well known how God will pay back those responsible for troubling Christians. They will be repaid proportionately for the suffering they have caused God's people. This is only right ("just") in God's eyes and is the reason this future judgment is called "righteous" (NIV, "right," v.5). In return, the antagonists will receive "trouble" (*thlipsin*), a term not further defined at this point. In v.9 another expression, "everlasting destruction," adds insight into these consequences. *Thlipsin* is a word often translated "tribulation." It is the present lot of Christians to undergo tribulation (v.4; 1 Thess 3:4). For the rest of the world, however, tribulation will be future and far greater in intensity (Matt 24:21; cf. Rev 3:10). In his first Epistle to this church, Paul described this period in relation to its source—viz., God's wrath (1:10; 2:16; 5:9). But here he speaks of it from the standpoint of circumstances that engulf the victims. After the period of tribulation has passed, these troublers will be denied entrance into the messianic kingdom that has welcomed the faithful followers of Christ (v.5; Matt 25:41, 46).

7a The other side of God's justice is full bestowal of rest on those who have been "persecuted" ("troubled"), a reward awaiting Paul and his co-workers also ("and to us as well"). This will be the relief from tension and suffering that is the portion of all who become Christ's disciples. Their rest and bliss in the future state (cf. Acts 3:19, 20; Rev 14:13) are guaranteed by the justice of God. A sublime anticipation thus helps suffering Christians to maintain unwavering perseverance and faithfulness (cf. v.4).

Participants in God's righteous judgment fall into these two classes: For one, the future holds the most severe threat. Though their domination is tolerated for the present, when the proper time comes, the roles will be reversed. The second class, though under the heel of the other for the moment, will become the overcomers who will enjoy all privileges in God's kingdom.

Notes

5b Here εἰς τό (*eis to*, "for the,"; NIV, "as a result") cannot introduce a purpose clause as it commonly does, because future judgment can hardly have as its objective the accomplishment of the believer's worthiness. Being counted worthy might be considered a result of God's judgment, but *eis to* introducing a result clause normally must modify a verb and this clause modifies a noun (κρίσεως, *kriseōs*, "judgment"). The most probable solution is to assign *eis to* a substantival function expanding the meaning and implications of τῆς δικαιας κρίσεως (*tēs dikaias kriseōs*, "righteous judgment," v.5a). The same function is performed by *eis to* infinitive combinations in 1 Thess 2:12; 4:9 (Milligan, p. 26; Moulton, *Prolegomena*, p. 219). Details about judgment in subsequent verses (e.g., δίκαιον, *dikaion*, "just," v.6) confirm this conclusion.

It is conceivable that the καί (*kai*, "also") views present suffering as a companion of future glory (Acts 14:22; Rom 8:17; 2 Cor 1:7; Phil 3:10; 2 Tim 2:12) (Lightfoot, p. 101; Ellicott, p. 98). Yet this contrast has already been made in vv.4, 5a and grouping the Pauline missionary staff with the Thessalonian sufferers has more point in v.5b (cf. μεθ' ἡμῶν, *meth' hēmōn*, "with us," v.7) (Best, p. 256). Paul's trying experiences at Corinth were very much the same as earlier (Acts 18:6, 12, 13) (Frame, p. 227).

---

b. *Circumstances of fulfillment*

1:7b

> [7] ... This will happen when the Lord Jesus is revealed from heaven in blazing fire with his powerful angels.

7b "When the Lord Jesus is revealed" (lit., "at the revelation of the Lord Jesus") identifies the time of God's righteous judgment. This second advent will occasion a "paying back" (v.6) of both the troublers and the troubled.

As defined by these Epistles, the objects of Christ's revelation are twofold. On the one hand, he will appear to those who are in Christ. It will be an appearance that means rest (1:7a) when he comes "from heaven" (cf. 1 Thess 4:16) to meet the dead and living in Christ in the air (1 Thess 4:17) and gather them to himself (2 Thess 2:1). This begins their unending fellowship with him (1 Thess 4:17; 5:10) and participation in his glory (2 Thess 1:10, 12). Paul hoped to be alive at this time ("and to us as well;" cf. "we who are still alive, who are left," 1 Thess 4:15, 17).

The other group on whom God's righteous judgment and the revelation of the Lord Jesus will make their impact are "those who trouble you" (v.6). The consequences for these will be prolonged and painful. Christ will not be unveiled personally to them at first, but will begin by subjecting earth's rebels to a period of intense "trouble." The human misery of those days is and will be without parallel in the annals of history (Dan 12:1; Mark 13:19). It will grow into a dominant factor during the time of "the rebellion and the man of lawlessness" (2:3). As the period runs its course, it will witness the abomination of desolation (2:4; cf. Dan 9:27; 11:31, 36; 12:11; Matt 24:15) and the Satanic deception of an unbelieving world (2:9, 10). All this is the initial phase of God's vengeance ("he will punish," v.8; lit., "rendering vengeance,") against a world that persists in rebellion (cf. Luke 21:22; Rev 6:10; 19:2).

As the period draws to its close, the Lord Jesus will be revealed personally to culminate this vengeance with "everlasting destruction" and exclusion from the Lord's presence and glory (v.9). Paul's concept of what the future holds for the lost is bleak. It is a day of wrath and revelation of the righteous judgment of God (Rom 2:5; 1 Thess 1:10; 2:16; 5:9) just before the revelation of Christ's glory in the world (Oepke, TDNT, 3:583).

Afflicted Christians, on the other hand, are offered the brightest anticipation. They look forward to the Lord Jesus' revelation from heaven and not to increased trouble and intensified persecution from the man of lawlessness (2:3, 4). Their incentive to persevere is the prospect of immediate rest "when the Lord Jesus is revealed." They will not be present for the apostasy (2:3), the rule of the lawless one (2:3, 4) or his "counterfeit miracles, signs and wonders" (2:9), because their promised rest in heaven will have begun by then. This is a marked contrast to their persecutors' fate. With a hope like this there is ample reason to continue in faithfulness to the Lord.

The "blazing fire" of his coming recalls the glory of OT theophanies (Exod 3:2; 19:18; 24:17; Deut 5:4; Ps 18:12; Isa 30:27–30; Dan 7:9, 10). It will be a revelation of glory in which the saints will share (1:10, 12). The Lord Jesus will be accompanied by "his powerful angels" (lit., "angels of his power"), who will draw on his power for their part in the revelation.

Many have chosen to limit *apokalypsei* ("revelation," "appearance") to a single event, identifying it with Christ's return to earth at the close of the tribulation. The role of "his powerful angels" in the revelation favors this understanding in the light of Matthew 24:30, 31; 25:31. It is more persuasive, however, to explain *apokalypsei* as a complex of events, including various phases of end-time happenings. The present context associates the word with Christ's coming for his own as well as his coming to deal with opponents. Since the primary thrust of vv.5–10 is to encourage suffering Christians, the meaning of *apokalypsei* for them should receive the emphasis. God's dealings with the rest of the world are included only to enhance the "relief" experienced by believers at the righteous judgment of God.

Notes

7b Δυνάμεως (*dynameōs*, "of power"; NIV, "powerful") is best understood as an objective genitive modified by αὐτοῦ (*autou*, "his"), giving the meaning "the angels of his power." The tr. "his powerful angels" treats *dynameōs* as a descriptive genitive, which makes the position of *autou* awkward (Lightfoot, p. 102; Milligan, p. 89). This rendering, moreover, unnecessarily reduces the prominence of "power" in a setting where it deserves emphasis.

If πυρὶ φλογός (*pyri phlogos*, "blazing fire") referred strictly to a purifying effect, it would find its most natural connection with v.8 rather than v.7. The more positive understanding of it as picturing glory is better, necessitating its attachment to the previous clause. Besides, to begin a participial clause with a prepositional phrase is quite rare.

c. Consideration of repayment (1:8–10)

1) Alienation

1:8, 9

> 8He will punish those who do not know God and do not obey the gospel of our Lord Jesus. 9They will be punished with everlasting destruction and shut out from the presence of the Lord and from the majesty of his power....

8 Two types of repayment to be meted out at the righteous judgment of God deserve consideration in light of the Christian's present trouble. One is toward the troublers

(vv.8, 9) and the other toward the troubled (v.10). "He will punish" is literally "rendering vengeance." The word stem for vengeance is the same as that for "right" (v.5) and "just" (v.6). It has no overtones of selfish vindictiveness or revenge, but proceeds from the justice of God to accomplish appropriate punishment for criminal offenses.

Recipients of God's avenging judgment will be in two groups: "those who do not know God and [those who] do not obey the gospel of our Lord Jesus." Those coming from a Gentile background constitute the former class. They are "without God in the world" (Eph 2:12; cf. Gal 4:8; 1 Thess 4:5), being estranged from him (Rom 1:18–32). The comparable use of the expression in Jeremiah 10:25 makes the Gentile identification even more convincing. That the immediate context does nothing to prepare for separate allusions to Gentiles and Jews (Morris, p. 204) is not sufficient reason for rejecting evidence in favor of distinguishing the two groups. It is appropriate for Gentile persecutors at Thessalonica to be singled out in both Epistles (1 Thess 2:14) because of this church's history (Acts 17:5). Gentiles without any background in OT teaching about God are nonetheless culpable for their persecution of Christians.

The other group, those who do not obey the gospel of our Lord Jesus, are well-versed in OT Scriptures because of their Jewish backgrounds. Here Paul uses an apt description of unbelieving Jews, found also in Romans 10:16, where the same terminology again designates Abraham's physical descendants (cf. Rom 10:3). These are the persecutors against whom such strong feelings were evident in his first Epistle (1 Thess 2:14–16). That Jews are occasionally called those who do not know God (John 8:54, 55) and Gentiles are called those who are disobedient to God (Rom 11:30) (Morris, p. 204) is interesting but not adequate to erase the clear impression that Paul in the present verse makes an ethnic distinction. Jews, like Gentiles, had been adamant in their opposition to Christians in Thessalonica and its vicinity (Acts 17:5, 13). Because of this, when the wrath of God makes itself felt at the revelation of the Lord Jesus, both classes of humanity will face dreaded agonies.

9 The most sobering experience of all will culminate God's righteous judgment against his enemies: "They will be punished with everlasting destruction"; literally, "they will pay the penalty, everlasting destruction." A price must be paid in return for the suffering inflicted on God's people and that price is none other than "everlasting destruction." *Olethros* ("destruction") does not refer to annihilation, which cannot be "everlasting" (Hendriksen, p. 160). The word in LXX and NT usages never has this meaning but rather turns on the thought of separation from God and loss of everything worthwhile in life (Schneider, TDNT, 5:169; Morris, p. 205). Just as endless life belongs to Christians, endless destruction belongs to those opposed to Christ (Matt 25:41, 46).

The consequences of permanent separation from God come out forcibly in the phrase "from the presence of the Lord" (cf. Isa 2:10, LXX). Banishment from the Lord's presence is what Jesus taught about punishment (Matt 7:23; 8:12; 22:13; 25:30; Luke 13:27). Words cannot adequately express the misery of this condition. On the other hand, those in Christ can anticipate the very opposite: "we will be with the Lord forever" (1 Thess 4:17).

Some have questioned whether the parallel phrase, "from the majesty of his power," can likewise signify separation (Olshausen, p. 467). If "majesty" (lit., "glory") be visible manifestations proceeding from his power (lit., "strength"), there is no problem in understanding how this expression also describes the anguish of separation. Instead of enjoying that glory or majesty, an uncrossable gulf will preclude access for those destined to everlasting punishment (cf. Luke 16:24–26).

Notes

---

8 A repeated article before μὴ ὑπακούουσιν (mē hypakouousin, "not obeying") is in itself substantial indication that two distinct classes are intended. Other passages where two articles appear with expressions designating the same group are for one reason or another not parallel to this construction (cf. 1:10; Rom 4:12). Also, synonymous parallelism in poetic writings is not the same as this usage (cf. Ps 35:11). These are two distinct classes who make up the larger group of "those who trouble you" (v.6).

9 It is possible to assign a causal meaning to ἀπό (apo, "from"; cf. Matt 13:44; Luke 12:57), but this is a relatively infrequent NT meaning (Frame, p. 235) and presents a thought repetitious of vv.7, 8 (Lünemann, p. 195). To see the two phrases as sources from which eternal destruction proceeds is also possible (Olshausen, p. 467), since comparable meanings of the preposition are found in Acts 3:20 and 1 Thess 1:8 (Hogg and Vine, p. 234). But this explanation also goes over the same ground as vv.7, 8 (Hiebert, p. 292). The spatial sense of apo is normal and therefore preferable in the present verse (cf. Acts 5:41; Rev 12:14; 20:11) (Best, p. 263). Distance from eternal blessedness is most potent in describing eternal punishment.

As compared with δύναμις (dynamis), ἰσχύς (ischys) stresses power or ability in action. Its word group emphasizes utilization of capacity, whereas the dynamis group is more a subjective ability, not necessarily actualized. Here it is the Lord's "power" exerted, not just potential (Marvin R. Vincent, The Epistles to the Philippians and to Philemon [ICC], p. 145; Grundmann, TDNT, 3:397).

---

2) Glorification

1:10

10on the day he comes to be glorified in his holy people and to be marveled at among all those who have believed. This includes you, because you believed our testimony to you.

10 Thankfully, another side of God's repayment remains, that of glorification. "On the day he comes" further defines "when the Lord Jesus is revealed" (v.7). Literally, it is composed of two distinct parts: "when he comes" and "in that day." The latter of these is placed emphatically at the very end of v.10 in the Gr. text. "That day" is a frequent OT designation for the day of the Lord (cf. Isa 2:11, 17). In the present verse it solemnly emphasizes a time coincident with "when he comes" as it does repeatedly in the NT (Mark 13:32; 14:25; Luke 21:34; 2 Tim 1:12, 18; 4:8) (Milligan, p. 92). Earlier Paul has disclosed how the day of the Lord will encompass in its initial stage a period of wrath and tribulation. The tribulation will be climaxed when Jesus Christ returns personally to judge and to inaugurate his reign on earth. In v.10, however, Paul has in view an event at the very beginning of the day and before the wrath—the meeting of Christ with his saints in the air (1 Thess 4:17; 2 Thess 1:7a; 2:1). This is the moment of reward for those who have faithfully persevered in all their persecutions and trials (v.4).

The substance of their reward will be participation in the glory and marvel of the Lord's return. In a unique sense he is the glory and the object of wonder, but he purposes to share these "in [the midst of] his holy people and ... among all those who have believed." Psalm 89:7 is the source of the phrase "in his holy people." It speaks of "a God greatly feared in the council of the holy ones." Here is a glorified assembly. Christ's glorification belongs to Christians also. Along with the mutual experience of wonder "among all those who have believed," the fact that we will be glorified constitutes more than sufficient incentive to endure life's present trials (cf. Rom 8:17, 18; 9:23).

"Those who have believed" becomes very personal as Paul adds "because you believed our testimony to you." These words remind the troubled readers that they themselves will participate in the glory and amazement of that day—i.e., "because at a decisive moment you personally appropriated the gospel to yourselves, you can live with the sustaining hope and certainty of knowing you are included." Enjoyment of the future glory of Christ's coming is the leading idea of the chapter (Lightfoot, p. 105) and a prime incentive for faithfulness.

Notes

10 Whether ἐν (en, "in") stipulates cause (Best, p. 264; Frame, p. 237) or sphere (Lünemann, p. 196; Robertson, *Word Pictures*, 4:44) in its first two occurrences is debated. A causal force is an established possibility in Paul and the rest of the NT (Turner, *Syntax*, p. 253). The causal usage is thought by some to be required in the parallel case of v.12. Yet this draws attention away from the Lord by attributing the glory of the occasion to "his holy people." The more usual locative force of the preposition allows the saints participation in the glory but recognizes Christ as its focal point.

An issue revolves about τοῖς ἁγίοις (tois hagiois, "holy people") similar to the one with τῶν ἁγίων (tōn hagiōn, "holy ones") in 1 Thess 3:13. Here as there, these are redeemed people, not angels. Contextual emphasis on persecuted believers, as well as the use of ἀγγέλων (aggelōn) for angels in v.7, makes this even clearer.

The aorist τοῖς πιστεύσασιν (tois pisteusasin, "those who have believed") has been understood by some as written from the standpoint of Christ's return when belief will be past (Ellicott, p. 102). But it is better to explain the aorist in terms of the precise moment when faith in "our testimony" was initiated. This conclusion is dictated by the ἐπιστεύθη (episteuthē, "you believed") immediately following and by the same verb's aorist usage elsewhere in Paul (1 Cor 15:2, 11; 2 Cor 4:13) (Lightfoot, p. 104; Milligan, p. 92; Best, p. 266).

The textual variant of ἐπιστώθη (epistōthē, "you were persuaded") instead of ἐπιστεύθη (episteuthē, "you believed") has external evidence too slight to merit serious consideration. It probably arose through failure to notice the ὅτι (hoti, "because") clause's proper connection with the rest of the verse.

Lenski chooses to connect the final ἐν (en, "in" ["in that day"]) phrase of v.10 with μαρτύριον (martyrion, "testimony") rather than to allow it to resume the ὅταν (hotan, "whenever") earlier in the verse. "In connection with," a meaning for en required by this view, is so rare that it is better to follow the more usual temporal meaning. The eschatological force of "that day" requires the phrase to resume and solemnly repeat the anticipation of "when he comes."

B. *Prayer for Future Acceptance*

1:11, 12

> [11]With this in mind, we constantly pray for you, that our God may count you worthy of his calling, and that by his power he may fulfill every good purpose of yours and every act prompted by your faith. [12]We pray this so that the name of our Lord Jesus may be glorified in you, and you in him, according to the grace of our God and the Lord Jesus Christ.

11 Not content with the certainty of coming glorification, Paul now prays for its realization. Human minds wrestle with the problem of praying for something already fixed in the unalterable purpose of God. Yet has not Paul already done this in these Epistles (1 Thess 3:12, 13; 5:23)? Is it not God's pleasure for saints to cooperate with his ongoing program? (Phil 2:12, 13). For example, the NT closes on the note of John's prayer for the already certain return of the Lord Jesus (Rev 22:20).

The purpose of Paul's prayer is "that our God may count you worthy of his calling." This probably corresponds to their worthiness for the kingdom mentioned in v.5. No uncertainty of ultimate acceptance is implied in the prayer. Uncertainty would undercut, not build, assurance for the fainthearted. Though the worthiness of the Thessalonian believers was confirmed (v.5), certainty in the security of God's purposes does not diminish the need to keep on praying. Ultimate salvation rests on the sure foundation of God's faithfulness (1 Thess 5:24), but until its actual accomplishment, Paul continues praying for it (Hogg and Vine, p. 237).

"His calling" is usually regarded by Paul as a past decree (Rom 11:29; 1 Cor 1:26) (Milligan, p. 93; Best, p. 268). To construe it like this here could imply the possibility of falling away from it (Lünemann, p. 198; Frame, p. 239). Yet such cannot happen to those already assured of a future worthiness (v.5) based solely on the grace of God (v.12). It is reassuring to know that God's call is made effective quite apart from human merit (cf. Gal 1:13–15). Instead of limiting the call to what happened before the foundation of the world, the present emphasis on Christ's return (v.10) and the eschatological kingdom of God (v.5) argues for extending the scope of "calling" to include its future outworking at God's righteous judgment (v.5).

Paul's other prayer objective is for God to "fulfill every good purpose [lit., 'every resolve for goodness'] of yours and every act prompted by your faith." "Goodness" is part of the fruit of the Spirit (Gal 5:22). Paul prays for the kind of desire that produces goodness—i.e., the active quality that constantly pursues what is right and beneficial for others. "Every act prompted by your faith" is what he had witnessed in them previously (cf. "work produced by faith," 1 Thess 1:3). What they had already attained was important, but room for growth was still there (cf. 1 Thess 3:10; 4:1). Realization of these objectives can come only "by his power," i.e., that of him the prayer is addressed to.

12 Here Paul states the purpose of his prayer—the glorification of Christ in the believers and they in him (cf. Isa 66:5). This is an intermediate step toward the final recognition of the Lord's own worthiness and majesty and the saints' participation in these things with him. "Name" is a reference to the dignity, majesty, and power of the Lord's revealed character.

Several have chosen to understand "in you ... in him" causally: "because of you ... because of him" (Frame, p. 241; Best, pp. 271, 272); i.e., glory comes to the Lord because of the saved and to the saved because of the Lord. It is unnecessary to resort to this rare meaning of en ("in"), however. The more common locative meaning allows us to see this as the "en of mystic indwelling" (Robertson, RHG, pp. 587, 588). A technical expression initiated by Jesus (John 15:4; 17:21), this was taken up by Paul and developed more completely (Rom 6:11, 23; 1 Cor 1:5; 2 Cor 13:4; et al.). The thought is that of reciprocity resting on the union of the Lord with his people. They are to share the future moment of glorification together—as a unit.

Elsewhere Paul shows a continuing zeal to exclude merit from the salvation process (cf. Rom 4:16; 11:5, 6; Eph 2:5, 8); so here also grace is the source of everything (Lightfoot, p. 107). Grace is from both Father and Son as in the salutation. We pray for such things as these and our prayers are answered in harmony with the working of God's grace.

Notes

11 The antecedent of ὅ (ho, "which"; NIV, "this") is not immediately apparent. Some identify it as the entirety of vv.5–10. Future glorification of the Lord in his saints (v.10) is another possibility because of proximity, but this is only a subordinate part of the very involved sentence in vv.3–10. The most probable antecedent is worthiness for the kingdom mentioned in v.5. All intervening material is a digression and development of this thought. Confirmation of this choice is found in the way καταξιωθῆναι (kataxiōthēnai, "be counted worthy," v.5) is picked up by ἀξιώσῃ (axiōsē, "may count . . . worthy," v.11) (Hogg and Vine, p. 237).

The presence of the first καί (kai, "and," "also") of v.11 (untranslated in NIV here) deserves clarification. "We also constantly pray" is sometimes understood as contrasting hope and expectation (v.10) with the prayer of this verse (Ellicott, p. 103). Morris says it joins the apostle's prayers with those of the Thessalonians (Morris, p. 209). Still others see it as connecting prayer with the earlier thanksgiving (v.3), boasting (v.4), testimony (v.10), or some combination of these (Hiebert, p. 295; Frame, p. 238). A further viewpoint accords with NIV in attributing no significance at all to the kai (Best, pp. 267, 268). Its position before προσευχόμεθα (proseuchometha, "we pray") probably indicates a new activity, something done along with the thanksgiving of v.3. Thus, εὐχαριστεῖν ὀφείλομεν (eucharistein opheilomen, "we ought to thank," v.3) and proseuchometha ("we pray," v.11) are the controlling grammatical features of vv. 3–12.

Some have preferred to give ἀξιώσῃ (axiōsē, "may count worthy") the meaning "make worthy" (Foerster, TDNT, 1:380; BAG, pp. 77, 78). Whether this meaning is lexically demonstrable may be questioned, however, especially in NT usage (Ellicott, pp. 103, 104; Lightfoot, p. 105). Giving καταξιωθῆναι (kataxiōthēnai, "to be counted worthy") a judicial sense in v.5 probably indicates that the same should be done for axiōsē in v.11. This agrees with the verb's predominant meaning of "esteem worthy" in the NT (1 Tim 5:17; Heb 3:3; 10:29) (Hogg and Vine, p. 237; Frame, p. 240; Milligan, p. 93).

"Every good purpose" takes ἀγαθωσύνης (agathōsunēs, "of goodness") as a genitive of description. Factors favoring such an interpretation are minimal. Agathōsunēs, a very meaningful and prominent noun, is robbed of its fulness by being construed as a subordinate adjective, "good." Εὐδοκίαν (eudokian) has the force of "resolve" (Hendriksen, p. 163) and unless agathōsynēs is seen as an objective genitive, the goal of the resolve is left undefined. "Resolve for goodness" therefore makes better sense (Best, p. 270).

12 The definiteness of the second κυρίου (kyriou, "Lord") diminishes the probability that τοῦ (tou, "of the") governs it as well as the preceding θεοῦ (theou, "God"). In other words, Paul names the Father as well as the Son. This is not a case to use the grammatical principle of one article governing two nouns connected by καί (kai, "and") to demonstrate the deity of Christ as is Titus 2:13 or 2 Peter 1:1 (Robertson, RHG, p. 786).

III. Assurance of Noninvolvement in the Day of the Lord (2:1–17)

A. *The False Claim*

2:1, 2

¹Concerning the coming of our Lord Jesus Christ and our being gathered to him, we ask you, brothers, ²not to become easily unsettled or alarmed by some prophecy, report or letter supposed to have come from us, saying that the day of the Lord has already come.

1,2 The hortatory words "we ask you, brothers" are identical in the Greek with "now we ask you, brothers" of 1 Thessalonians 5:12. This formula provides a transition from what Paul has been saying about the day of the Lord to an acute problem related to it.

The problem has to do with the events he has just described. It is "concerning" or "on behalf of" the Lord's coming and the saints' gathering to him that Paul now writes. In the interest of truth about this vital hope, we must set down accurately certain features of "the day of the Lord" as a corrective to what some were falsely claiming.

He must explain what he means by "the coming of our Lord Jesus Christ and our being gathered to him" or else the solution to the problem cannot be grasped. *Episynagōgēs* ("being gathered") defines what part of the *parousias* ("coming") Paul has in mind. This is the great event he has described more fully in 1 Thessalonians 4:14–17—i.e., the gathering of those in Christ to meet him in the air en route to the Father in heaven. This begins the day of the Lord. What relationship this happening bears to the tribulation phase of the day of the Lord so frequently mentioned in these Epistles is important. Some limit the *parousia* to a single event and insist that it comes after the tribulation (Morris, pp. 151, 152; Gundry, pp. 113, 114). It is hardly possible, though, to explain the variety of relationships belonging to *parousia* in these Epistles if it is understood only as a single event. Even the meaning of the word suggests a longer duration.

Another problem is encountered if the *parousia* that initiates the day of the Lord is considered only the single event of Christ's return to earth following the tribulation. If Paul had given oral or written instruction to this effect, the false claim that the day of the Lord was already present could hardly have alarmed these Christians. According to this scheme, the day of the Lord could not begin without Christ's personal reappearance. His continued absence was obvious to all.

Yet the claim *was* made and accepted to the extent that the church was troubled. This implies Paul had not taught that a one-phase *parousia* after the period of wrath will begin the day of the Lord. He had told them that the coming of the Lord to gather his saints into heaven would initiate both the tribulation and the day of the Lord. They were promised immediate "rest" (1:7) and glorification with Christ (1:10), not increased persecution.

The false instruction had, however, denied them an imminent "rest." They would first have to undergo the severe persecution of the tribulation and possibly even suffer martyrdom before Christ's coming, according to these misrepresentations. They were even told that their current suffering indicated the arrival of the expected tribulation. Second Thessalonians 2:3, 4, 8–12 speaks of this future period in terms quite similar to those of Revelation 13 and 17. The man of lawlessness has a number of affinities with the beasts of Revelation, enough to show that the two books describe the same period (R.H. Charles, *Eschatology* [New York: Schocken Books, 1963], p. 441n). Though 2 Thessalonians does not specifically mention the beast's war with the saints and their martyrdom, Revelation 13:7, 10 declares it explicitly. If this is a possibility for the church, why did Paul at no point teach this kind of anticipation? The answer must lie in the removal of Christians (including the Thessalonian believers) from earth before this persecution. It is another group of God's people, following the church's translation, who must face the terror of this archenemy.

Despite their "persecutions and trials" (1:4) these Thessalonian Christians were not living in the day of the Lord as they had been erroneously told. A right understanding of "being gathered to him" reveals that they could not be so enmeshed, because for them Christ's *parousia* will antedate the awful period to come. In fact, their "being gathered to him" will be the event that signals the day's beginning.

As their friend and brother, Paul respectfully requests (*erōtōmen*, "we ask," v.1; cf. 1 Thess 4:1) them not to become "unsettled or alarmed" (v.2). This might easily happen if they were led to believe that somehow the glorious coming had passed them by. "Unsettled" means "to be shaken from your sensibleness [lit., mind]." Distorted teaching had alarmed them. Paul cautioned them against hastily (*tacheōs*, "easily" [NIV]) adopting something other than the instruction he had previously given them (cf. v.15). Teaching that seemed to have come from Paul had reached them through various avenues. One was the spiritual gift of prophecy or something related to it (lit., "spirit," v.2). There were prophets in this church (cf. 1 Thess 5:19, 20) and *pneuma* ("spirit") is a name for this gift and others (cf. 1 Cor 14:12). Whatever the specific medium, the teaching was represented as having Paul's authority.

Another avenue for the false teaching was the spoken word ("report," *logou*). Though this did not claim the direct inspiration of prophecy, it too was based on an allegedly Pauline foundation. The same basis was claimed for a third medium of communication ("letter"). Someone had apparently misrepresented Paul's views in an epistle bearing his name, a mistake he intends to rectify in any future correspondence (cf. 3:17, 18). It is not clear whether the readers had been misguided through one or all three channels, but in any case Paul denounces them all.

The false teaching consisted in the claim "The day of the Lord has already come [Gr., 'is present']" (v.2). *Enestēken* ("is present") does not denote imminence, but actual presence. These readers who knew about the day (1 Thess 5:2) knew that its earlier phase would be a time of heightened persecution for the saints. Their suffering had already been so severe that someone tried to convince them that the period was already in progress, even though the Lord had not yet come to gather them to heaven (Auberlen and Riggenbach, p. 126; Moffatt, EGT, 4:47; Hogg and Vine, p. 245; Morris, p. 217; Hiebert, p. 304). They knew of the time of trouble and the Lord's return to culminate it (1:7–9). They had been led to believe, however, that his coming for them would spare them the anguish of that hour (1 Thess 5:9). But here were people telling them, with Paul's apparent backing, that such a deliverance was not to be.

Therefore they were in great need of an authentic word from Paul assuring them that they had understood him correctly in his first Epistle. They needed to know that the *parousia* (coming) of Christ for his church would mark the beginning of the future day of trouble and consequently that the day had not yet arrived. To accomplish this, Paul proceeds to describe features, obviously not yet present, that will characterize the day's early stages.

Notes

1 The choice of ὑπέρ (*hyper*, "on behalf of") rather than περί (*peri*, "concerning") implies that Paul was speaking "in the best interests of" the παρουσία (*parousia*, "coming"). *Hyper* adds the idea of advocacy not found in *peri* (Ellicott, p. 106; Lightfoot, p. 108).

Arguments favoring the review that a posttribulational rapture is implied in this verse refer to a cognate verb of ἐπισυναγωγῆς, (*episynagōgēs*, "being gathered") that is used for a gathering of the elect following the tribulation in Matt 24:29–31 and to the noun itself along with its cognate verb in LXX to describe the regathering of dispersed Jews to Palestine after the tribulation (cf. Isa 52:12) (Best, p. 274). But these are not sufficient to overthrow the inability of advocates of posttribulationalism to show a satisfactory relationship between believers' being gathered to Christ at the *parousia* and the presence of the day of the Lord (v.2). In vv.1, 2 the gathering must be the event that signals the opening of the day. If that day opens with the tribulation, as it obviously will (cf. discussion of 5:2), the gathering must come at the beginning of the tribulation.

2 Ἐνέστηκεν (enestēken, "is present") in all its other NT uses marks something as already present (Rom 8:38; 1 Cor 3:22; 7:26; cf. Gal. 1:4; 1 Tim 3:1; Heb 9:9). The present tense is thus the word's acknowledged meaning (Frame, pp. 248, 249).

B. *The True Condition* (2:3–12)

1. *Defiance (yet to come)*

2:3, 4

> 3Don't let anyone deceive you in any way, for that day will not come until the rebellion occurs and the man of lawlessness is revealed, the man doomed to destruction. 4He opposes and exalts himself over everything that is called God or is worshiped, and even sets himself up in God's temple, proclaiming himself to be God.

3 Paul supplements his request in v.1 with a prohibition: "Don't let anyone deceive you in any way." Apparently those who willfully and maliciously troubled the Thessalonian believers had done this by deceiving anyone who would listen to them regarding the day of the Lord. Paul warns his readers not to be taken in by these speculations, whether through "prophecy, report or letter" (v.2) or "in any way." Paul does not say what moved these promoters of error. Perhaps a misunderstanding of grace led them to teach that Christians must earn their part in the *parousia* by persevering through severe suffering. Whatever it was, Paul is determined to prove that his readers were not in the day of the Lord.

His proof of the day's nonpresence consists of citing two phenomena that had not yet occurred. The text does not explicitly say whether these will come before the day of the Lord or immediately after it begins, because the Greek sentence is not complete, but it presupposes something to be added from the previous verse; i.e., "that day will not come" (NIV) or "that day is not present" (cf. note). Grammatically similar constructions elsewhere (Matt 12:29; Mark 3:27; John 7:51; Rom 15:24) show these two happenings are conceived of as within the day of the Lord, not prior to it. The day of the Lord had not yet arrived because these two conspicuous phenomena that will dominate the day's opening phase had not yet happened.

Some wonder how the failure of these two to arrive can be a proof of the nonarrival of the day. The answer lies in understanding Paul's reference to these phenomena as his way of identifying the very earliest stage of this eschatological period. The readers had not missed the rapture (1 Thess 4:15–17) and were not in the day of the Lord (v.2) because these two clear indicators of the day's presence had not yet appeared (cf. Introduction to 1 Thess, pp. 233–234).

Let us put it this way. Suppose the government of some country should announce, "In the near future on a date known only to us, Christianity will be suppressed. To mark the official beginning of this policy, on the appointed day the largest church in the country will be demolished and its pastor required to renounce Christianity publicly. Thereafter, all who admit they are Christians will be placed in jeopardy of imprisonment." At that time a foreigner might arrive in that country, having heard nothing more than that

Christianity would be cruelly suppressed. He would doubtless find some Christians already experiencing certain hardships and, in his ignorance of the timing of the actual beginning of the policy of suppression, might assume that it was already in effect. A citizen who knew the details of the policy would have to tell him, "The period of suppression of Christianity is not yet present, because the largest church in the country has not yet been demolished and its pastor has not yet renounced Christianity publicly."

So far there is no logical problem. But some who have problems with the pretribulational view of the rapture ask, "How can the nonarrival of two events ('the rebellion' and the revealing of 'the man of lawlessness,' v.3) that initiate the day of the Lord, a period that will come after the believers have been raptured—how can the nonarrival of these events prove to the confused Thessalonian believers (who are to be raptured and thus will not be in the day of the Lord) that they are not actually in that day?" The answer still is that the absence of the phenomena demonstrates the nonpresence of the day of the Lord. Obviously, had "the rebellion" and the revealing of "the man of lawlessness" already taken place when Paul was writing this letter, then the teaching of the priority of the rapture to "the day of the Lord" would have been called into question. But here in 2 Thessalonians 2 Paul is not discussing the timing of the rapture. He is simply reassuring his readers that "the day of the Lord" had not come. Nor does he at any place in this context (2 Thess 2:1–12) tell his readers that they will at some future time "see" the two initial phenomena of "the day of the Lord." Had he said that, there would indeed be a problem. But he did not speak of the Thessalonians' actually seeing the phenomena. He simply stressed the present nonarrival of the phenomena.

To sum up, let us return to the analogy of the newcomer to the country facing the suppression of Christianity. Suppose now that, arriving after the initial announcement, he is a short-term visitor due to leave before the official beginning of the anti-Christian policy. The answer to his confusion about being in the country with the policy already in effect would be corrected by his realizing that the largest church would have to be destroyed and its pastor publicly renounce Christianity before suppression of Christianity began. And this would be a valid answer, even though he would not be present when these things took place.

The troubled at Thessalonica could take heart in knowing they had not missed the gathering of those in Christ at the *parousia* (v.1). Their present persecutions were not identifiable with those to be inflicted by the man of lawlessness on a later group of saints after the eschatological day begins.

A closer look at the two phenomena accompanying the day of the Lord illuminates the characteristics of that day. "The rebellion" represents *apostasia*, from which the English word *apostasy* comes. Usage in LXX and elsewhere in the NT gives this word a religious connotation (Josh 22:22; 2 Chron 29:19; 33:19; Jer 2:19; Acts 21:21). It points to a deliberate abandonment of a former professed position. Attempts to identify the apostasy Paul is speaking of here with some past or present movement are futile because of its contextual association with the Lord Jesus' second advent (v.1). An illustration of this kind of apostasy was that of faithless Jews just before the Maccabean uprising (Dan 8:23ff.; 11:36f.) (Hendriksen, p. 169). A similar defection of professing Christians is elsewhere anticipated (Matt 24:11, 12, 24; 1 Tim 4:1ff.; 2 Tim 3:1–5; 4:3, 4; 2 Peter 2:1–22; 3:3–6; Jude 17, 18). After the catching away of those in Christ (1 Thess 4:17), all who are truly in him will be gone. Conditions will be ripe for people, especially those who call themselves Christian but are not really such, to turn their backs on God in what they do as well as in what they already have in thought. Then their insincerity will demonstrate itself outwardly. This worldwide anti-God movement will be so universal as to earn for itself a special designation: "*the* apostasy"—i.e., the climax of the increasing apostate tendencies evident before the rapture of the church.

Following and in conjunction with the apostasy will come the unveiling of a mighty figure embodying everything opposed to God. His whereabouts before his unveiling are not given. He will be alive for years before his unveiling, but his dramatic public presentation will occur after the rebellion begins.

Paul characterizes him in three ways. First, as "the man of lawlessness," he is the epitome of opposition to the laws of God. Satan so indwells and operates through him that his main delight will be in breaking God's righteous laws. Second, he is called "the man doomed to destruction"—literally, "the son of perdition." The Hebrew idiom "son of" indicates character or destiny. He belongs to a class so destined. The same expression describes Judas Iscariot (John 17:12), another member of this class. It does not, however, identify this later "son of perdition" with Judas.

4 Third, this individual "opposes and exalts himself over everything that is called God or is worshiped." His direct and determined opposition to the true God will be a leading feature of the continuing apostasy. It will be especially marked by removal of the symbolic articles from the Jerusalem temple. The man of lawlessness will occupy the holy precincts in order to accept and even demand worship that is due God alone. This evidently is a Jewish temple to be rebuilt in Jerusalem in the future. Dependence of these words on Daniel 9:26, 27; 11:31, 36, 37; 12:11 (cf. Matt 24:15; Mark 13:14) demands such a reference. There is no impressive evidence for understanding *naon* ("temple") in a nonliteral sense. The well-known "abomination that causes desolation" is sometimes regarded as a person and sometimes as an act of desecration by that person (Mark 13:14) (Hubbard, *Wycliffe Bible Commentary*, p. 1364). The act of desecration to which this verse looks will transpire half-way through the seventieth prophetic week of Daniel 9:24–27, when the covenant made earlier with the Jewish people is broken. This will mark the climax of this lawless one's career. Historically, a foreshadowing of this blasphemous intrusion happened when Antiochus Epiphanes desecrated the temple in Jerusalem just before the Maccabean revolt.

The lawless man's identity has been studied by many throughout the Christian era. Some deny that he is a historical person. They write off the terminology as detached from history and mythically oriented like the Jewish apocalyptic writings by which Paul was strongly influenced (Best, p. 289; J. Julius Scott, "Paul and Late-Jewish Eschatology—A Case Study, 1 Thessalonians 4:13–18 and 2 Thessalonians 2:1–12," JETS, (Summer, 1972), (15:139–141). But closer scrutiny of the parallels between late-Jewish eschatology and Paul's words reveals more by way of difference than similarity (Scott, pp. 141, 142).

The relationship of this apocalyptic portion of 2 Thessalonians to Christ's *parousia* (coming) confirms the impression that Paul must be referring to a single historical personage. Quests for such a person in the past and present have proved fruitless. Resemblances to Antiochus Epiphanes, Nero, Diocletian, one of the popes, and others may be admitted. But fulfillment of all details of the prophecy must await the future period of this man's prominence. It is futile to suppose that Judas Iscariot, Antiochus Epiphanes, or Nero will be brought back to life to fill this role. "The man of lawlessness" will be a new historical figure whom Satan will energize to do his will in the world. As "man of God" in the OT regularly designates a divine prophet, the present "man of lawlessness" designates a false prophet, probably to be identified with the second beast of Revelation

13 (Rev 13:11ff.; 16:13; 19:20; 20:10) (Best, pp. 283, 284, 288). His primary function will be to preside over the religious apostasy in cooperation with the beast out of the sea (Rev 13:1ff.), who leads political opposition to God. As God's chief opponent in Jerusalem whose background is probably Jewish (cf. Dan 11:36, 37), the lawless one will give religious leadership to complement the dominance of his associate over governments of the world's nations.

The presence of such an apostasy and counterfeit god will not escape international observation. The nonpresence of these things when Paul wrote proves his thesis regarding the nonarrival of the day of the Lord.

Notes

3 The preference of most English translations for a future tense apodosis in v.3 is probably explained by the frequency of that tense with conditional clauses with ἐάν (ean, "if"; with μὴ [mē, "not"] = "if not," "unless"; NIV, "until"). Circumstances here justify a present tense in the apodosis, however, the carry-over thought from ἐνέστηκεν (enestēken, "is present") (v.2) being a prime consideration (cf. Robertson, RHG, p. 1019). Other NT combinations of ἐάν ... πρῶτον (ean ... prōton, "if ... first") (Matt 12:29; Mark 3:27; John 7:51; Rom 15:24) reveal preference elsewhere for a present-tense apodosis under similar circumstances. They also reveal that actions of the conditional clause are included within the scope of the apodosis. These other passages show that πρῶτον (prōton, "first") in the protasis does not indicate priority to the apodosis, but priority to another action contained in (or implied by) the protasis—i.e., the rebellion precedes the revelation of the lawless one. All this confirms what is necessitated by Paul's viewpoint throughout the rest of these Epistles: the parousia for the church and the launching of the day of the Lord can come at any moment. The apostasy and the revelation of the man of lawlessness are not necessary preludes to them, but follow the church's gathering to Christ and lie within the day of the Lord.

Whether to read ἀνομίας (anomias, "lawlessness") or ἁμαρτίας (hamartias, "sin") presents a choice between two "harder" readings. The former is harder because of its rarer use by Paul (Metzger, *Textual Commentary*, p. 635). It is also harder because its meaning is narrower and less certain (Best, p. 283). On the other hand, hamartias is harder because anomias in v.7 presupposes an earlier anomias (Metzger, p. 635). Better MS and versional support for reading anomias tips the weight of probability against hamartias.

4 The ἐπί (epi, "over") phrase must be read with ἀντικείμενος (antikeimenos, "opposing") as well as with ὑπεραιρόμενος (hyperairomenos, "exalting himself"). Otherwise, the direction of opposition in the former is left unstated. So a hostile sense of "against" rather than one of position ("above") is preferable for the preposition. This is an accepted meaning of the word wherever hostility is in the context (John 13:18) (Alford, *The Greek Testament*, 3:289; Robertson, RHG, p. 602).

Figurative meanings of ναός (naos, "temple") elsewhere, including its reference to the church (1 Cor 3:16; 2 Cor 6:16; Eph 2:21) and possible allusions to the heavenly temple where God is (Heb 8:1-4; 9:23, 24; Rev 15:5), fall short of the literal significance required by the present passage. A human being can take his seat in none of these others. The article with naon (accusative) is a further indication that the Jerusalem temple of the God of Israel is intended (Olshausen, p. 482; Lünemann, p. 211).

2. Delay (presently in effect)

2:5-7

> 5Don't you remember that when I was with you I used to tell you these things? 6And now you know what is holding him back, so that he may be revealed at the proper time. 7For the secret power of lawlessness is already at work; but the one who now holds it back will continue to do so till he is taken out of the way.

5 A note of impatience may be detected in Paul's question. If the Thessalonian believers had recalled Paul's oral teaching, disturbing elements in the newly arisen false system could have been eliminated. Paul was certain about their previous familiarity with the substance of vv.3, 4 because he had personally (sing. "I," v.5) given them this information.

6 So he can declare, "You know what is holding him back." "Now" should be connected with "what is holding him back" to indicate that "holding back" is a present phenomenon. To katechon ("what is holding back") is a neuter title for this restraining force. The word recurs in the masculine in v.7 where it is translated "who ... holds it back."

Proposed identifications of to katechon have been multiple. Because of inability to explain the neuter-masculine combination, such suggestions as the preaching of the gospel, the Jewish state, the binding of Satan, the church, Gentile world dominion, and human government are improbable. To identify to katechon with a supernatural force or person hostile to God is difficult in a paragraph such as this because the restrainer is limiting Satan (vv.7-9), not cooperating with him (Best, pp. 298-301). A popular understanding since early times has been that this is a reference to the Roman Empire (neuter) and its ruler (masc.) (See George Ladd, NT Theology [Grand Rapids: Eerdmans, 1974], pp. 530, 560). Paul had several times benefited from the intervention of the Roman government (Acts 17:6ff.; 18:6ff.). In other writings he limits the role of human government to its dealing with wrong-doing (Rom 13:1, 3) (Milligan, p. 101). Though preferable to some other solutions, this explanation is disappointing in several ways. To predict the demise of the Roman Empire (cf. v.7) is very uncharacteristic of Paul (Frame, p. 260). Then too, the Roman emperors sometimes precipitated anti-Christian activities rather than restrained them (Auberlen and Riggenbach, p. 139; Hogg and Vine, p. 260). Elimination of this solution is sealed when we remember that the Roman Empire has long since ceased to exist, and the appearance of Christ or the lawless one has yet to take place (Hogg and Vine, p. 259).

It is evident that the restrainer, to accomplish his mission, must have supernatural power to hold back a supernatural enemy (v.9). God and the outworking of his providence is the natural answer (Ladd, The Blessed Hope, p.95). Reference to God is favored by the restrainer's harmony with divine purpose and a divine timetable ("at the proper time," v.6) (Hiebert, p. 313; Delling, TDNT, 3:460, 461).

Yet to say that God is the restrainer is not quite enough to explain the variation in gender. To one familiar with the Lord Jesus' Upper Room Discourse, as Paul undoubtedly was, fluctuation between neuter and masculine recalls how the Holy Spirit is spoken of. Either gender is appropriate, depending on whether the speaker (or writer) thinks of natural agreement (masc. because of the Spirit's personality) or grammatical (neuter because of the noun pneuma; see John 14:26; 15:26; 16:13, 14) (Robertson, RHG, pp. 208, 209). This identification of the restrainer with deep roots in church history (Alford, 3:57, 58) is most appealing. The special presence of the Spirit as the indweller of saints will terminate abruptly at the *parousia* as it began abruptly at Pentecost. Once the body of Christ has been caught away to heaven, the Spirit's ministry will revert back to what he did for believers during the OT period (Ryrie, p. 113). His function of restraining evil through the body of Christ (John 16:7-11; 1 John 4:4) will cease similarly to the way he terminated his striving in the days of Noah (Gen 6:3). At that point the reins will be removed from lawlessness and the Satanically inspired rebellion will begin. It appears that *to katechon* ("what is holding back") was well known at Thessalonica as a title for the Holy Spirit on whom the readers had come to depend in their personal attempts to combat lawlessness (1 Thess 1:6; 4:8; 5:19; 2 Thess 2:13).

God has a "proper time" for the lawless one's revelation just as he does for the revelation of the Lord Jesus from heaven (1:7). No one knows that time, since it is part of the future day of the Lord (1 Thess 5:2; 2 Thess 2:2, 3). Until the gathering of saints (2:1), the Spirit will continue his restraining work.

7 Further clarification ("for") is in order. The "secret power [or, mystery] of lawlessness" was already evident in such things as their own persecutions (1:4), but lawlessness will be open when the rebellion arrives and the lawless one is unveiled (2:3, 8). The secrecy and limitation is attributable to "the one who now holds it back." Upon his removal, the rebellion will break out.

Notes

6 It is necessary to take νῦν (*nun*, "now") temporally and connect it with "what is holding him back" to balance off the ἐν τῷ αὐτοῦ καιρῷ (*en tō autou kairō*, "at the proper time") in the last part of the same verse. A temporal *nun* connected with οἴδατε (*oidate*, "you know") and answering to ἔτι (*eti*, "when") of v.5 does not render a satisfactory sense (Lightfoot, p. 114; Moffatt, EGT, 4:49). An inferential *nun* can also be excluded because of conflict with another conjunction, καί (*kai*, "and") at the beginning of v.6.

"Hold back" or "restrain" is the more plausible choice for the meaning of κατέχω (*katechō*) because the atmosphere of conflict pervades the passage. "Hold fast" and "hold sway," though legitimate for the verb elsewhere, cannot satisfy the obvious antagonism in the present discussion.

Other suggestions as to the identity of τὸ κατέχον (*to katechon*, "what is holding ... back") include Michael, Elijah, the apostles, the saints in Jerusalem before its destruction, the Mosaic law, Paul, and Seneca. Some feel it fruitless to attempt identification, either because we are too far removed from the original situation (Morris, pp. 226, 227) or because the whole passage is so apocalyptic that it defies identification of single individuals within it (Best, p. 301). All the above positions either have very slight foundations or else shy away from an issue where exegetical data can be brought to bear. That the ongoing conflict between God and Satan lies behind specific naming of the restrainer and the man of lawlessness is quite clear. Varying forms and stages of the Spirit's ministry among men adequately explain how God in the person of the Spirit can be removed; i.e., the Spirit terminates a form of God's special presence.

7 Since μόνον (*monon*, "only"; NIV, "but") pertains to a limitation of "the secret power of lawlessness," the better choice is to connect it with ἕως (*heōs*, "till") to indicate the terminal point of restraint: "only until the one who now holds it back is taken out of the way." Ὁ κατέχων ἄρτι (*ho katechōn arti*, "the one who now holds ... back") stands prior to the *heōs*, separating it from *monon*, to give the words an appropriate emphasis in the clause (Auberlen and Riggenbach, p. 129; Frame, pp. 264, 265).

3. Deception and destruction (after the delay)

2:8-10

> 8And then the lawless one will be revealed, whom the Lord Jesus will overthrow with the breath of his mouth and destroy by the splendor of his coming. 9The coming of the lawless one will be in accordance with the work of Satan displayed in all kinds of counterfeit miracles, signs and wonders, 10and in every sort of evil that deceives those who are perishing. They perish because they refused to love the truth and so be saved.

8-10 Departure of the restrainer is the cue for the revelation (v.8) and coming (v.9) of the lawless one. His revelation, already mentioned in v.3 in conjunction with the rebellion and in v.6 as being delayed until the proper time by the restrainer's presence, is of Satanic origin, though admittedly it can happen only by God's permission. Satan's present efforts to effect unhindered lawlessness are frustrated by divine restraint (v.7), but through cessation of the Spirit's indwelling ministry to the body of Christ, his lawless one will be granted a future interval to do his worst.

8 After this time has elapsed, the Lord Jesus will personally come to earth to slay (*anelei*, "overthrow," NIV) the lawless one "with the breath of his mouth" and abolish (*katargēsei*, "destroy," NIV) him "by the splendor of his coming." By putting the lawless one to death, the Lord will also bring to a stop his program of deceiving the world. "The breath of his mouth" could be a figurative reference to a word spoken by Christ, but a literal sense is quite satisfactory. The breath of God is a fierce weapon according to the OT (Exod 15:8; 2 Sam 22:16; Job 4:9; Ps 33:6; Isa 30:27, 28) (Milligan, p. 103; Best, p. 303). "The splendor of his coming" is his other means of conquest. Probably "the appearance of his coming" does more justice to *epiphaneia*, since in the Pastoral Epistles it is practically equivalent to *parousia* as a name for his coming (1 Tim 6:14; 2 Tim 1:10; 4:1, 8; Titus 2:13). This "appearance" phase of the *parousia* differs from the "gathering" phase (v.1). It concludes and climaxes the tribulation instead of beginning it. The visible presence of the Lord Jesus in the world will put an immediate stop to an accelerated diabolical program.

9,10a That Satan is the root of the lawless one's deception is explicit in a further elaboration. *Energeian* ("work") in the NT is reserved for supernatural activities. A superhuman person will utilize the supernatural means of "miracles, signs and wonders." These remarkable phenomena, which in the past have been used so effectively in laying a foundation for the church (Acts 2:22, 43; 4:30; 5:12; 6:8; 7:36; 14:3; 15:12; Rom 15:19; 2 Cor 12:12; Heb 2:4), will be redirected to purposes of deceit. They will not be "counterfeit" (see text) but genuine supernatural feats to produce false impressions, deluding people to the point of accepting the lie as truth (cf. v.11). The motivation of the lawless one is to deceive. "Every sort of evil that deceives" is literally "every deceit of unrighteousness"—i.e., every sort of deceit that unrighteousness produces. It is the nature of unrighteousness to palm itself off as righteousness (Hiebert, p. 317). "Those who are perishing" will be particularly vulnerable to trickery. Not only will they confuse unrighteousness with righteousness; they will also attribute deity to this lawless one (v.4).

10b Their blindness will be self-imposed because of a prior refusal to "love the truth and so be saved." They lack a positive committal to the gospel. This is just as blamable as indifference or even antagonism toward the truth. The right choice could have brought them salvation and deliverance from the lawless one's devices, but they elected not to receive God's salvation.

Notes

8 Alexandrian and Western witnesses—including uncials, versions, and fathers—provide support for reading Ἰησοῦς (Iēsous, "Jesus"). This support is stronger than that of the authorities omitting this human name of the Lord. Thus, "the Lord Jesus" is the correct translation.

External evidence supporting ἀνελεῖ (anelei, "will remove," "will destroy"; NIV, "will overthrow") is also quite impressive. The other readings ἀνέλοι (aneloi, "consumed," "destroyed"), ἀναλοῖ (analoi, "consumes," "destroys") and ἀναλώσει (analōsei, "will consume," "will destroy"), though quite interesting, cannot muster sufficient MS authority for their inclusion (Metzger, *Textual Commentary*, p. 636).

Paul's preoccupation with the glory of Christ's return (1:7, 9, 10) supports the rendering of ἐπιφανείᾳ (epiphaneia) by "splendor." Still, the redundancy that would result in Titus 2:13 where it is used in combination with δόξα (doksa, "brightness") more probably excludes the notion of "brightness" from the word. It merely describes the visibility of his *parousia* (coming). The glory of it is frequently described elsewhere.

9 The time perspective of this verse is set by the future tenses of v.8. Ἐστιν (estin, "is"), though a present tense, has the *parousia* as its point of reference. Ψεύδους (pseudous) is probably not a genitive of description, "counterfeit," telling the intrinsic quality of the miracles (contra Lenski, p. 426). Emphasis on deceit and "the lie" in the next two verses shows these to be miracles "leading to a lie" (Ellicott, p. 116). A genitive of the object is therefore preferable.

10 "Every sort of evil that deceives those who are perishing" properly makes ἀδικίας (adikias, "of unrighteousness"; NIV, "of evil") a genitive of the subject (or ablative of source). This is deceit wrought by or proceeding from unrighteousness (Hendriksen, p. 185; Best, p. 307). This supplies the best contextual sense and is normal with a genitive following ἀπάτη (apatē, "deceit") (Mark 4:19; Heb 3:13) (Frame, p. 270).

Refusal "to love the truth" is not quite the same as refusing the truth. Loving the truth is a very positive dedication to the gospel. One can refuse to love the truth without refusing the truth. This positive commitment furnishes a suitable opposite to εὐδοκήσαντες τῇ ἀδικίᾳ (eudokēsantes tē adikia, "having delighted in unrighteousness," v.12), which is a commitment at the other extreme (Lightfoot, p. 117; Best, p. 308).

---

4. Delusion and divine judgment (because of present recalcitrance)

2:11, 12

> [11]For this reason God sends them a powerful delusion so that they will believe the lie [12] and so that all will be condemned who have not believed the truth but have delighted in wickedness.

11 By covering again the same ground in vv.11, 12 as in vv.9, 10, Paul reemphasizes the fate of rejectors of the truth and adds more information about them. Already he has shown Satan's part in getting them to believe lies and bewildering them with deceitful measures and he has shown their refusal to love the truth. Because they deliberately reject God, he himself will send "them a powerful delusion so that they will believe the

lie." This "working of error" will be supernatural in character (*energeian*, cf. v.9) so as to prove irresistible to rebellious humanity. "Powerful delusion" is another way of referring to the lie (v.9) and deceit (v.10) already predicted. God will create false belief to make them "believe the lie." This is their only alternative because they have refused to love the truth (v.10). They will be completely defenseless against the false claims of the lawless one (v.4) and his perversion of the true gospel. The Satanic promise that deceived Eve (Gen 3:5) will find its ultimate fulfillment in the end-time master of deceit (Auberlen and Riggenbach, p. 132). They will mistake someone else and his lying promises for God and his truth.

12 The ultimate consequences for them will be condemnation. Failing to appropriate the truth of the gospel, they willingly choose wickedness instead. They cannot blame circumstances. Retrospect will show their own wrongly directed personal delight to be the cause of God's adverse judgment against them (cf. 1:9). What an incentive this powerful passage is for non-Christians to turn to God before the rebellion and delusion arrive.

Notes

11 The present tense of πέμπει (*pempei*, "sends") has a future significance because the point of reference is the coming period of the lawless one's activity. After his future revelation (v.8), the rest of the paragraph takes on this as-if-present perspective (cf. ἐστὶν [*estin*, "is" v.9]) (Best, p. 304).

Ἐνεργείαν (*energeian*, "working"; NIV, "powerful") is a supernatural operation as in v.9, but this time traceable to God rather than Satan. The genitive πλάνης (*planēs*, "of error"; NIV, "delusion") immediately following is objective, "a working that enhances and develops error," as evidenced in the εἰς τό (*eis to*, "so that") clause.

C. *The Truth's Continuance* (2:13–17)

1. *Thanks for divine deliverance*

2:13, 14

> 13But we ought always to thank God for you, brothers loved by the Lord, because from the beginning God chose you to be saved through the sanctifying work of the Spirit and through belief in the truth. 14He called you to this through our gospel, that you might share in the glory of our Lord Jesus Christ.

13 Paul is thankful that God chose some to believe the truth and to be delivered from delusion and from divine judgment. He and his co-workers can rejoice in looking forward to salvation for themselves and their converts, an anticipation drastically different from the outlook for those awaiting perdition (cf. v.10). The salvation viewed from its human side in 1:3ff. is now seen as an undertaking of God.

For Paul to address these "brothers" as those "loved by the Lord" (cf. 1 Thess 1:4) is appropriate, because God chose them to be saved. "From the beginning" refers to their pretemporal election (cf. 1 Thess 1:4). Paul usually places God's prior choice of men to salvation (v.13) alongside their historical call (v.14; cf. Rom 8:30) (Hendriksen, p. 188). This salvation is what will elude those who refuse to love the truth (v.10). It entails present benefits and also future deliverance from the doom that will befall the lost at Christ's return (cf. 1:6, 8, 9; 2:8–12). God's choice operates in the realm of belief in the truth and of the Spirit's sanctifying work. The role of the Spirit in sanctification looms large for Paul (Rom 15:16; 1 Cor 6:11, 12; 1 Thess 4:7, 8) as it does for Peter (1 Peter 1:2) (Best, pp. 314, 315). The sphere of God's choice of believers for salvation is also marked by its faith-in-truth emphasis. Belief in the truth is the means of the beginning and continuing relationships of salvation (cf. vv.10–12).

14 God has fulfilled his foreordained purpose by calling the chosen to this salvation "through our gospel." The good news of divine truth conveyed through Paul's preaching was the means through which God called these Thessalonian converts at a particular point in time. What God purposed in eternity was carried out in history that the future might bring them a share "in the glory of our Lord Jesus Christ." God's design was to make them adopted ones who participate in Christ's glory at the *parousia* (coming) (cf. 1:10, 12). As God's purchased possessions, they will be granted this matchless privilege. They do not earn it or in any other way acquire it for themselves. It is accomplished solely by God, as is all else referred to in this context (vv. 13, 14).

Notes

---

13 The choice between the variants ἀπαρχήν (*aparchēn*, "firstfruits") and ἀπ' ἀρχῆς (*ap' archēs*, "from the beginning") is difficult. The latter has a slight edge in external support, being found in both Western and Alexandrian text-types. It is a hard reading because of the absence of the phrase from Paul's other writings. On the other hand, *aparchēn* is extremely difficult, because without an explanatory genitive, it renders no satisfactory sense in the verse (Best, p. 313). "Firstfruits" points to a larger group, but no group can be found among which these believers were first. Hence, *ap' archēs* has been chosen as the correct reading.

A locative instead of an instrumental force has been chosen for ἐν (*en*, "in") because the clause names an act in eternity past. To render the preposition by "through" (NIV) unduly anticipates the historical call of v.14. The means of their call is expressed in the διά (*dia*, "through") phrase v.14, while the ἐν (*en*, "in") phrase of v.13 indicates the spiritual state in which God chose them to salvation (Ellicott, p. 220).

14 Whether to take περιποίησιν (*peripoiēsin*, "acquisition"; NIV, "share") actively (Hendriksen, p. 128; Hiebert, p. 223) or passively (Lightfoot, p. 76) recalls the discussion of 1 Thess 5:9. An active sense in a setting that so strongly emphasizes God's part in the total salvation process is inappropriate, to say the least. More congruity is obtained by omitting the element of personal attainment that the active meaning of *peripoiēsin* would convey. Human responsibility comes in v.15, but vv.13, 14 are devoted to what God has done. The meaning of "acquired possession" is therefore preferred over "acquiring" for *peripoiēsin*. This necessitates taking δόξης, (*doxēs*, "of glory") as a genitive of apposition.

---

2. Call to doctrinal adherence

2:15

> 15So then, brothers, stand firm and hold to the teachings we passed on to you, whether by word of mouth or by letter.

15 "So then" turns the discussion to a practical responsibility derived from God's elective purpose (vv.13, 14). Against a background of such an imminent world crisis as described in vv.1–10, the beneficiaries of God's saving work cannot afford to lapse into lethargy, but must respond with loyal steadfastness ("stand firm") and keep a firm hold on the traditions ("teachings") taught them by Paul and his associates. A continuing stability and firm grasp on basic Christian doctrines would have alleviated the instability and alarm that prompted the writing of this Epistle (cf. v.2). They had received instructions about ethical matters (1 Thess 4:1, 2; 2 Thess 3:6), but the particular data needed at this point is doctrinal, as shown by Paul's reference to "our gospel" in v.14 (cf. 1 Cor 15:3–5) (Best, p. 317). Paul himself had been a recipient of Christian traditions subsequent to his conversion. Through divine revelation he had originated other traditions (1 Thess 4:15). These he had passed on to his converts both "by word of mouth" and "by letter" in his previous contacts with them. In light of their inclusion in God's saving purpose (vv.13, 14), he commands them to remain unmovable and cling tenaciously to these doctrines.

3. *Prayer for practical compliance*

2:16, 17

> [16]May our Lord Jesus Christ himself and God our Father, who loved us and by his grace gave us eternal encouragement and good hope, [17]encourage and strengthen you in every good deed and word.

16,17 The prayer that closes chapter two is in slight contrast (*de*, v.16, untranslated in NIV) to the appeal of v.15. Paul and his co-workers cannot in themselves make the appeal effective. Only God himself, who initially chose them, (vv.13, 14) can do that. Addressing his prayer to the first two persons of the Trinity, Paul names the Son before the Father (contra 1 Thess 3:11), probably in line with the Son's worthiness of equal honor with the Father and his special prominence in the chapter's emphasis on future salvation and glory. Yet the two persons are one God as shown by several structural features in vv.16, 17: (1) The pronoun *autos* ("himself," v.16) is singular and probably should be understood as emphasizing both persons—"our Lord Jesus Christ and God our Father himself" (cf. 1 Thess 3:11). (2) "Loved us and . . . gave us" (v.16) represents two singular participles whose actions are applicable to both the Son and the Father. The singular number is explained by Paul's conception of the two persons as one God. (3) "Encourage and strengthen" (v.17) are likewise singular in number though they express the action of a compound subject. This grammatical feature is attributable to the oneness of essence among the persons of the Godhead (cf. John 10:30). Paul conceived of Jesus Christ as God in the same full sense as he conceived of God the Father. No other explanation of this unusual combination of grammatical features is satisfying.

Reminding himself and his readers of why God has every reason to answer this prayer, Paul notes that the Son and the Father "loved us" and graciously "gave us eternal encouragement and good hope." Evidence of this can be seen in the incarnation and death of Jesus Christ, which are so often referred to in terms of God's loving and giving (John 3:16; Rom 5:5, 8; 8:35, 37; Gal 2:20; 1 John 4:10). Because of God's love displayed in Christ, the present readers had a source of unending encouragement to offset their persecutions and accompanying doubts.

Paul prays that the encouragement provided in the crucifixion and resurrection of

Christ may be appropriated inwardly—literally, "encourage your hearts"—as a motivation for giving them strength for "every good deed and word." Disquiet regarding the coming of the Lord (v.2) was the need to be met. As God undertakes their cause, they can "stand firm and hold to the teachings" (v.15).

Notes

16 To put the emphasis of αὐτός (*autos*, "himself") on the Son alone (and on the Father alone in 1 Thess 3:11) presents an unbalanced picture, as though Paul expected one person to answer one prayer and another to answer the other. The best way to solve this imbalance is to take the pronoun as extending to both persons in each case (cf. note on 1 Thess 3:11).

Galatians 1:1 presents a comparable situation of a singular participle following "Jesus Christ and God the Father," when the participle goes only with the latter of the two persons. Yet it is questionable whether Galatians 1:1 is parallel, since the participial expression "who raised him from the dead" cannot logically modify "Jesus Christ." The same is not true here. Both the Son and the Father have loved (Rom 8:35–39). Both the Son and the Father have given (Rom 8:32; Gal 2:20). In light of the stress in this verse on the unity of the Godhead, it is more plausible to refer the participles to both Persons (Frame, p. 286; Hiebert, p. 327).

IV. Encouragement to Gainful Employment (3:1–15)

A. *Prayerful Preparation for Encounter* (3:1–5)

1. *Prayer for Paul*

3:1, 2

¹Finally, brothers, pray for us that the message of the Lord may spread rapidly and be honored, just as it was with you. ²And pray that we may be delivered from wicked and evil men, for not everyone has faith.

1 Eschatological matters were Paul's main concern in writing 2 Thessalonians. "Finally" indicates that these have in the main been dealt with. Yet an important and related matter needs to be discussed before the letter ends. Before discussing it, Paul makes one of his typical requests for prayer (cf. Rom 15:30, 31; Eph 6:18, 19; Col 4:3; 1 Thess 5:25; Philem 22). "Spread rapidly" (*trechē*) relates to the idea of running. Paul also desired that the gospel be "honored." This speaks of triumph. As more people receive the good news, victories are won and God is glorified. "Spread rapidly and be honored" does not apply to isolated victories or a single great triumph but to a continuing progress—viz., the word is to "keep on running and keep on being honored." "Just as it was with you" recalls the amazing success of the message in Thessalonica (cf. 1 Thess 1:5, 6, 8; 2:13). Paul wanted this repeated in other communities where he would preach Christ.

2 Again, Paul asked prayer for deliverance "from wicked and evil men." "Wicked" labels them as capable of outrageous and harmful acts against others. "Evil" speaks of persons not only themselves thoroughly corrupted but intent on corrupting others and drawing them into their own slide toward perdition. Who were they? Suggestions have ranged from heretics like Hymenaeus and Alexander (1 Tim 1:20) (Chrysostom) to hypocrites and false brothers more generally (Zwingli, cited by Auberlen and Riggenbach, p. 150). It has also been suggested that they were unbelievers, both Jewish and Gentile, since both Paul and his readers had encounters with each group (Acts 16:19–24; 1 Thess 2:15; 2 Thess 1:8) (Best, p. 326). A more pointed identification, however, ties these "wicked and evil men" to unbelieving Jews in Corinth where Paul was encountering opposition as he wrote (Acts 18:5, 6, 12, 13). This is confirmed by the definiteness of the expression (definite article *tōn*) and by the use of an aorist tense of the verb "may be delivered," suggesting one particular act of deliverance (Hendriksen, p. 195; Best, p. 325). As Paul wrote this second Epistle, he was facing a severe crisis in Corinth.

Evil men exist because "not everyone has faith." This understatement effectively highlights the large number of those who have not responded to the gospel by believing in Christ. That the persecutors had had the opportunity to believe but had rejected it accounts for their vicious reaction against the message and those who preached it.

Notes

1 A καί (*kai*, "and," "also," "even"), untranslated here in NIV, adds a thought to the last clause: "just as it *also* was with you"—i.e., Thessalonica was not the only place where the word had received a good response (Ellicott, p. 124).
2 The suggestion that "faith" in this verse has the sense of the body of Christian teaching, i.e., "the faith" (Morris, p. 246), finds support in the ordinary usage of ἡ πίστις (*hē pistis*, "the faith") in the NT (Lightfoot, p. 125). Yet the present context does not criticize noncompliance with orthodox doctrine, but unwillingness to embrace Jesus' messiahship in a personal way. So here the better understanding of "faith" is its subjective sense of "trust" (Hiebert, p. 332; Best, p. 326).

2. Prayer for the people

3:3–5

> ³But the Lord is faithful, and he will strengthen and protect you from the evil one. ⁴We have confidence in the Lord that you are doing and will continue to do the things we command. ⁵May the Lord direct your hearts into God's love and Christ's perseverance.

3 In contrast with the widespread lack of faith among men (v.2) is the faithfulness of the Lord Jesus. He can be relied on to "strengthen [2:17] and protect" Christians "from the evil one." Here is assurance of inner security and an outward protection from the author of evil whose activity is so prominent in these letters (1 Thess 2:18; 3:5; 2 Thess 2:9). *Phylaxei* ("protect") is often used of military protection against a violent assault. Jesus' faithfulness provides a defense against even the touch of the enemy (cf. 1 John 5:18).

4 The faithfulness of the Lord is supplemented by the faithfulness of his people. So Paul can add, "We have confidence in the Lord that you are doing and will continue to do the things we commanded." This rendering does not translate the phrase *eph' hymas* ("about you" or "concerning you") after the clause "we have confidence." Paul has

confidence in Christian people. In them union with Christ counteracts the weakness of human nature. Paul and his co-workers could rely on the Thessalonian believers to do what they had been taught (cf. 1 Thess 4:2). By this favorable opinion, he paves the way for further instruction (cf. 3:6–15).

5 Paul realizes that the Lord's help is indispensable. That he has complimented them (v.4) does not imply that they are self-sufficient. Therefore he requests the Lord to direct them into a fuller appreciation of God's love for them and Christ's perseverance on their behalf. To comply with Paul's command to discipline the idle (vv.6–15) will be difficult. So the strongest possible motivation—recollection of God's love and Christ's endurance of suffering—will undergird the discipline of idle believers.

Notes

3 "The evil one" takes τοῦ πονήρου (tou ponērou) as masc., a reference to Satan. Though neuter adjectives appear in Rom 12:9 and 1 Thess 5:22, the masc. form of this word outnumbers the neuter by four to one in the NT (Lightfoot, pp. 125–127), strongly favoring the masc. in these Epistles where the devil is prominent (1 Thess 2:18; 3:5; 2 Thess 2:9).

4 Paul's confidence about the Thessalonians ἐφ' ὑμᾶς (eph' hymas, "about you") regarded them as "in the Lord" and so he was protected from the disappointment due to fickle human nature (Best, pp. 328, 329). An ἐπί (epi, "about") phrase is often construed as the object of πείθω (peithō, "to be confident") (Matt 27:43, 2 Cor 2:3) (Frame, pp. 295, 296).

5 "Love toward God" and "patient waiting for Christ" have sometimes been advocated as translations of τὴν ἀγάπην τοῦ θεοῦ (tēn agapēn tou theou) and τὴν ὑπομονὴν τοῦ Χριστοῦ (tēn hypomonēn tou Christou) (Alford, 3:295; Hiebert, p. 336). This takes the genitives as objective. Contextually this is acceptable, but it is unlikely because Paul usually refers to our human love for God by the verb ἀγαπάω (agapaō, "to love") and because ὑπομονή (hypomonē) in its other uses by Paul never has the sense of "patient waiting." He generally uses the genitive with ἀγάπη (agapē, "love") subjectively, and this satisfies the present sentence quite well. Also, the frequent teaching of a suffering Messiah and his perseverance (Heb 12:1–3; 1 Peter 2:21) argues for a subjective genitive in τοῦ Χριστοῦ (tou Christou, "of Christ") (Milligan, p. 112; Hendriksen, p. 198).

B. *Proper Solution for Idleness* (3:6–15)

1. *Previous instruction and example*

3:6–10

> 6In the name of the Lord Jesus Christ, we command you, brothers, to keep away from every brother who is idle and does not live according to the teaching you received from us. 7For you yourselves know how you ought to follow our example. We were not idle when we were with you, 8nor did we eat anyone's food without paying for it. On the contrary, we worked night and day, laboring and toiling so that we would not be a burden to any of you. 9We did this, not because we do not have the right to such help, but in order to make ourselves a model for you to follow. 10For even when we were with you, we gave you this rule: "If a man will not work, he shall not eat."

6 Now Paul comes to his command regarding the idle. That he invokes "the name of the Lord Jesus Christ" shows the urgency of the command. Every brother who remains idle is to be denied the privilege of associating with his fellow Christians. "Idle" translates a word meaning "disorderly" (cf. 1 Thess 5:14). The disorder defined by the remainder of the paragraph is loafing, being remiss in daily work and conduct. This is contrary to the "teaching" ("tradition") that Paul had given them earlier (cf. 1 Thess 4:11, 12; 5:14). No excuse could justify such misconduct. Paul therefore advocates the drastic discipline of keeping away from the "idle."

7–9 Paul himself was not idle. His readers could verify this claim ("you yourselves know," v.7; cf. 1 Thess 2:1; 3:3; 4:2; 5:2). In imitating Paul, they would be imitating the Lord himself (1 Thess 1:6) because Paul's life was so carefully patterned after his Lord's. He did not loaf at Thessalonica (v.7b), nor depend on others to supply him with free food (v.8a). He supported himself in spite of much fatigue ("laboring," v.8) and many obstacles ("toiling," v.8; cf. 1 Thess 2:9) in order to relieve the new Christians in Thessalonica of the burden of maintaining him.

Paul did not have to exert himself so tirelessly. As an apostle, he had "the right to such help" (v.9; cf. 1 Cor 9:4ff.; 1 Thess 2:7) from his converts. He decided, however, to forego this privilege and leave an example for them to imitate.

10 Paul reinforced his example by this definite command. From a very early time denying food to the lazy was a traditional form of discipline in the church. (Note Genesis 3:19.)

Notes

6 Παρελάβοσαν (parelabosan, "they received") is preferred over παρελάβετε (parelabete, "you received') because of its stronger external support. It is also the harder reading because of the change from the second to third person and is therefore the reading that best explains the origin of the alternative readings (Metzger, *Textual Commentary,* p. 367).
8 "Eat anyone's food" is literally "eat bread from anyone." "Eat bread" is a Semitic idiom for eating any kind of food. It should probably not be broadened to include one's total living (contra Morris, p. 253; Hiebert, p. 342). Paul claims nothing regarding his living accommodations with Jason (Acts 17:7) beyond payment for his own meals. What the apostle did for housing is not stated here.

2. *Renewed instruction*

3:11, 12

> ¹¹We hear that some among you are idle. They are not busy; they are busybodies. ¹²In the name of the Lord Jesus Christ, we command and urge such people to settle down and earn the bread they eat.

11,12 Here the previously given rule (v.10) is repeated because of reports that the problem of loafing had recurred. People who came from Thessalonica to Corinth had reported this. Some of their number had stopped working, even since receiving the corrective of 1 Thessalonians 4:11, 12 and 5:14. They were using the extra time to interfere in other people's affairs. *Periergazomenous* ("they are busybodies," v.11) graphically shows them to be meddling in the lives of others.

"In the Lord Jesus Christ" (cf. note on v.12) Paul commanded such people to settle down and earn the bread they eat (v.12). He uses the common union of believers with Christ as ground for his appeal. He might well have addressed the idle ones pejoratively as "you loafers," but instead he tactfully refers to them as "such people," doubtless hoping to lead them back to earning their own food. Thus, order would replace the disruption caused by their idleness and meddling. The tense of the verb implies that they were to work steadily, not occasionally or spasmodically.

Notes

11 Ἀκούω (*akouō*) is one of the special verbs that take on a perfective force in the present (cf. Luke 9:9) (BDF, par. 322). This is the probable force here. Paul had recently heard about the problem, so he proceeds to deal with it.
12 "In the name of the Lord Jesus Christ" appears to be identical with a comparable phrase in v.6, but this is not so. The literal rendering in v.12 is "in the Lord Jesus Christ." Hence the emphasis in this verse is not on authority as in v.6, but on union with Christ: "by virtue of our union with the Lord Jesus Christ we as fellow members of Christ command and urge such people . . ." (cf. Hendriksen, p. 203). This sets a tone of gentleness for v.12. Had Paul wanted to convey authority, he would have reused the formula "in the name of" (Best, p. 341).

3. Corrective separation

3:13-15

13And as for you, brothers, never tire of doing what is right.
14If anyone does not obey our instruction in this letter, take special note of him. Do not associate with him, in order that he may feel ashamed. 15Yet do not regard him as an enemy, but warn him as a brother.

13-15 Paul now describes how the Thessalonian Christians should deal with loafers who disobey his instructions. First, they are urged to keep on doing right. *Enkakēsēte* ("tire") implies the possibility of their losing heart in struggling with their idle brothers. Exemplary conduct serves as a constant reprimand to wrongdoers and is an incentive for them to turn from their delinquency. Included in "doing what is right" is generosity toward those in need. Yet to keep on supporting those who have nothing because they refuse to work is wrong (v.10).

So the Thessalonians should deal firmly yet charitably with the mistakes of their brothers. Anyone refusing to comply with the work ethic set out in this letter was not to be associated with, so that he might be ashamed of his behavior. He was not to be expelled from the church like the sinning brother referred to in 1 Corinthians 5. In Corinth the offense was so flagrant as to bring disrepute on the whole church. In Thessalonica, however, the lapse was not yet so aggravated as to bring the reproach of the pagans on the church. Here the erring brother was allowed to continue in the meetings, but probably was denied participation in such things as the love feast and the

Lord's Supper. Certainly he was not to be given food, because this would make the community appear to condone his offense. *Mē synamignysthai* ("do not associate") implies "let there be no intimate association [with him]" (Frame, p. 309).

To sum up, the recalcitrant idler was not to be treated as an enemy cut off from all contacts, but was allowed to continue in a brotherly status. So lines of communication were kept open for continued warnings about his behavior.

Notes

---

13 Καλοποιοῦντες (*kalopoiountes*, "doing what is right") has been taken to mean "doing good" to others (Best, pp. 341, 342). This is the meaning in Gal 6:9, with the sense of giving financial help, but it is difficult so to understand v.13. Here Paul's emphasis is the very opposite—viz., that of disciplining loafers by witholding food from them. So it is a better choice to render the participle more generally as "acting correctly" or "doing what is right" (Milligan, p. 116; Hiebert, p. 348).

14,15 The meaning of "do not associate with him" can hardly be pressed to include formal excommunication. Συναναμίγνυσθαι (*synanamignysthai*) is not a word for official action. A limited social ostracism is much more in order (Hendriksen, p. 306). If this discipline proves unsuccessful, however, formal excommunication might follow (cf. Matt 18:17; 1 Cor 5:11). Continued treatment of the offenders as "brothers" indicates they were not to be denied fellowship altogether.

V. Conclusion (3:16–18)

A. *Prayer for God's Peace and Presence*

3:16

16Now may the Lord of peace himself give you peace at all times and in every way. The Lord be with all of you.

16 "Now" (or perhaps more accurately "but") once again marks a transition from command and exhortation to prayer. The prayer recognizes that ultimately God alone can bring about compliance with what Paul has asked of his readers. "Yet without the Lord's help all your efforts will be in vain" is the thought behind this petition. "The Lord of peace" alone can make harmony among believers a reality. While this is, first and foremost, peace with God, it provides the ground for believers' peace with one another (Eph 2:14–18; cf. 1 Thess 5:23). "At all times" asks that there be no break in the flow of Christ's peace (cf. John 14:27; 16:33; Col 3:15); "in every way" asks that the prevalence of peace continue no matter what the outward circumstances. "The Lord be with all of you" requests what was previously guaranteed for Christians. His promise never to leave or forsake his own provides the assurances of this (Heb 13:5). Here is an instance of the cooperation of prayer in fulfilling what God's purpose predetermines (cf. 1:11, 12).

B. *Personalized Benediction*

3:17, 18

17I, Paul, write this greeting in my own hand, which is the distinguishing mark in all my letters. This is how I write.
18The grace of our Lord Jesus Christ be with all of you.

17,18 Paul was dictating to an amanuensis up to 3:17 (cf. Rom 16:22; 1 Cor 16:21; Col 4:18). At this point he took the pen into his own hand to add a closing greeting. Though he undoubtedly did this quite frequently, he has called attention to it only here, in 1 Corinthians 16:21, and in Colossians 4:18. The greeting in his own hand, "which is the distinguishing mark" in all his letters (v.17), includes also the benediction of v.18. Apparently Paul followed this practice consistently, expecting churches where he had served to recall his distinctive handwriting. It was particularly needed in this Epistle as a deterrent against any future attempt to forge a letter in his name (cf. 2:2). The practice was customary in ancient times (Frame, p. 312). When Paul says "in all my letters" (v.17), he does not mean just the letters previous to this, for he was also to follow this procedure later. Neither is the expression to be limited only to books found in the NT, because he is known to have written other Epistles besides these (cf. 1 Cor 5:9). The handwriting furnished a key by which his Thessalonian readers could recognize a spurious Epistle bearing his name.

Even when Paul did not call attention to it, a closing benediction came in his own hand. "The grace of our Lord Jesus Christ be with all of you" or a near equivalent is found at the close of all Paul's writings. In the autographa (the original MSS) they were all in Paul's handwriting, though most of his Epistles may have been written through amanuenses. The present benediction agrees verbatim with that of 1 Thessalonians 5:28 except for the "all" added here. Significantly, no one was excluded from Paul's good wishes toward this church, not even those he had rebuked at various points.

Notes

17,18 That Paul here inaugurates the policy of a self-written greeting because of the problem of 2:2 (Alford, 3:298, 299) cannot be substantiated, since only two of his remaining ten Epistles (1 Cor; Col) have this kind of greeting (Lünemann, p. 254). That it was a policy to follow only in his future Thessalonian correspondence (Eadie, *A Commentary on the Greek Text of the Epistles of Paul to the Thessalonians* [London: Macmillan, 1877], p. 323) would require a future tense of εἰμί (*eimi*, "to be") rather than the present tense ἐστίν (*estin*, "is") (3:17). It apparently was a widespread custom in ancient letter writing for the author to do this at the close of the letter. In the present instance there was a particular occasion for calling attention to it—viz., to guard Christians from being misled in the future as they had been in the past (cf. 2:2).

1 TIMOTHY

Ralph Earle

1 TIMOTHY

Introduction 1 and 2 Timothy

1. Authorship
2. Date
3. Place of Origin
4. Destination
5. Purpose
6. Summary
7. Theological Values
8. Canonicity
9. Special Problems
10. Bibliography for Pastoral Epistles
11. Outline of 1 Timothy

First Timothy, Titus, and Second Timothy—probably written in that order and commonly called the pastoral Epistles—form a rather closely knit unity. They are somewhat distinct from Paul's other ten Epistles and share common problems of authorship and date. It is logical, then, to treat them together in a single introductory article. For a fuller treatment of Titus, however, see the Introduction to that Epistle.

1. Authorship

The four Gospels and Acts are all anonymous. In connection with these, we are faced with the question of authorship, but not of genuineness. But since all three pastoral Epistles begin with Paul's name, the matter of authorship involves the crucial problem of whether or not they are genuine. We must therefore investigate this subject at some length.

Four arguments commonly raised against the Pauline authorship of the pastoral Epistles need to be answered.

1) *Historical.* The events in the pastoral Epistles do not fit into the account in Acts. Nowhere in Acts do we read about Paul preaching in Crete and leaving Titus there (Titus 1:5). Nor does his leaving Timothy at Ephesus fit into the Acts account. On these points all scholars agree.

But was Paul put to death at the end of his Roman imprisonment described in the closing verses of Acts? This is assumed by many scholars, and so they say that Paul could not have written these epistles.

The answer is that Paul was released from his first Roman imprisonment and made further journeys, during which he wrote First Timothy and Titus. It was during a later imprisonment that he wrote Second Timothy.

There is considerable evidence for this position. Clement of Rome (A.D. 95) says that

Paul went "to the extreme limit of the west."[1] For a man living in Rome, this would mean Spain. The Muratorian Canon (c. A.D. 200) says that the apostle "departed for Spain." Paul had written to the Romans that he planned to go past them to that country (Rom 15:24, 28). Here we have the statement that he carried out this purpose, and this would have to be after his first Roman imprisonment—as any careful reading of Acts will show.

The most definite statement comes from Eusebius. He writes:

> Paul is said, after having defended himself, to have set forth again upon the ministry of preaching, and to have entered the city [Rome] a second time, and to have ended his life by martyrdom. Whilst then a prisoner, he wrote the Second Epistle to Timothy, in which he both mentions his first defence, and his impending death.[2]

2) *Ecclesiastical.* In the pastoral Epistles we read about bishops, elders (presbyters), and deacons. It is claimed by scholars that this shows a more advanced church organization than existed during the lifetime of Paul.

But a careful reading of Titus 1:5–9 shows that "elders" and "bishops" are terms used interchangeably. And in Philippians 1:1 Paul addresses the "bishops and deacons" in the church at Philippi.

Very different is the situation in the Epistles of Ignatius (c. A.D. 115). Here each local church has one bishop, several presbyters and several deacons. The evidence is clear that the pastoral Epistles reflect the type of church organization known to Paul, rather than the type Ignatius was familiar with. Thus, a second-century date for the Pastorals, as held by many today, seems unrealistic.

3) *Doctrinal.* A third argument against Pauline authorship is the claim that the doctrinal emphases of the Pastorals are different from those in Paul's previous Epistles, especially the recurring use of the expression "sound doctrine" (2 Tim 4:3; Titus 1:9; 2:1). Kümmel makes much of this. But he admits that "the Jewish-Christian Gnostic heresy which the Pastorals combat is ... quite conceivable in the lifetime of Paul."[3] He also states, "The Pauline origin of the Pastorals was not challenged from the time of their recognition as canonical writings toward the end of the second century till the beginning of the nineteenth century."[4]

Paul opposes Gnostic ideas in his Epistle to the Colossians. The error of the nineteenth century critics was their belief that these did not exist until the second century. Today it is generally acknowledged that Gnostic ideas had already penetrated Judaism before the advent of Christianity. But that there is no evidence of a pre-Christian Gnostic system has been fully demonstrated by Edwin M. Yamauchi in his recent scholarly study, *Pre-Christian Gnosticism.*[5]

4) *Linguistic.* The most serious argument against the genuineness of the pastoral Epistles is their difference in style and vocabulary from Paul's earlier writings. This is the main point stressed today by negative critics.

Harrison found 175 words used nowhere else in the NT and 130 non-Pauline words

---

[1]Clement 5.

[2]*Ecclesiastical History* (A.D. 326) 2:22.

[3]Feine-Behm-Kümmel, *Introduction to the New Testament* (Abingdon, 1966), p. 267.

[4]Ibid., p. 261.

[5]Grand Rapids: Eerdmans, 1973.

shared by other NT writers. Working with a word-per-page method, he found an abrupt, sharp rise in new words in the Pastorals. So he concluded that Paul could not have written these later Epistles.[6]

These statistics have carried great weight with many twentieth century scholars. Guthrie answers: "But numerical calculations cannot with the limited data available from Paul's letters take into account differences of subject-matter, differences of circumstances and differences of addressees, all of which may be responsible for new words."[7] Cambridge statistician Yule declared that samples of about ten thousand words are necessary as a basis for valid statistical study.[8] This, of course, we do not have in the case of the Pastorals. Bruce M. Metzger asserts that Harrison's use of the statistical method has proved to be unsound.[9]

In recent years several scholars have been suggesting that Luke was the amanuensis (secretary) who actually composed the pastoral Epistles for Paul. Moule writes, "My suggestion is, then, that Luke wrote all three Pastoral epistles. But he wrote them during Paul's lifetime, and, in part but only in part, at Paul's dictation."[10] The careful student can discover a considerable number of significant Greek words that occur in both Luke-Acts and the Pastorals but nowhere else in the NT. It appears that amanuenses were sometimes given considerable liberty in writing manuscripts, and we know that Paul was in the habit of using amanuenses for the actual writing of his Epistles (Rom 16:22).

In his volume on the pastoral Epistles (in ICC, 1924), Walter Lock comes out emphatically for the genuineness of these letters. He notes that there are many points of contact between the Pastorals and Paul's farewell address to the Ephesian elders (Acts 20:17–38): "The evidence of Church writers is the same as for the other letters of St. Paul." He also declared that the doctrinal background is essentially Pauline.[11] Moreover, Lock and Guthrie point out the Lucan language in the Pastorals.[12]

Perhaps more significant is the fact that J.N.D. Kelly of Oxford, in his 1963 volume in "Harper's New Testament Commentaries," gives adequate answers to all the negative arguments we have noted. After a careful reappraisal of the whole situation, he concludes that the evidence "tips the scales perceptibly ... in favour of the traditional theory of authorship."[13] W.J. Lowstuter wrote in the *Abingdon Bible Commentary* (p. 1276) that, taken altogether, the evidence is favorable to the Pauline authorship.

2. Date

The date of Paul's first Roman imprisonment was perhaps A.D. 59–61. (Some say 60–62, others 61–63 or 62–64.) The early church unanimously testifies that Paul was put to death by Emperor Nero, who committed suicide in June of A.D. 68. Since Paul asked Timothy to come to him "before winter" (2 Tim 4:21), it is obvious that the second

---

[6]P.N. Harrison, *The Problem of the Pastoral Epistles* (London: Oxford University Press, 1921).

[7]Donald Guthrie, *New Testament Introduction: The Pauline Epistles* (Chicago: InterVarsity, 1961), p. 221.

[8]G.U. Yule, *The Statistical Study of Literary Vocabulary* (Cambridge, 1944).

[9]Expt, 70:91–94.

[10]C.F.D. Moule, "The Problem of the Pastoral Epistles: A Reappraisal," in *Bulletin of John Rylands Library*, vol. 47 (March, 1965), p. 434.

[11]p. xxv.

[12]Ibid., p. xxix; Guthrie, *New Testament Introduction*, p. 235.

[13]p. 34.

Epistle to Timothy was written not later than A.D. 67. It may have been as early as 65. This means that 1 Timothy and Titus were probably written between 62 and 66. If we assume omitted details in the Acts account, earlier dates might be possible.

3. Place of Origin

First Timothy 1:3 seems to indicate that Paul was in Macedonia when he wrote that Epistle. Second Timothy was written from prison in Rome, shortly before the apostle's death. We have no clear indication as to where the Epistle to Titus was written.

4. Destination

Titus was on the island of Crete when Paul wrote to him (Titus 1:5). Timothy was at Ephesus when the apostle wrote him the first Epistle (1 Tim 1:3). Presumably he was still there when Paul wrote the second Epistle.

5. Purpose

These Epistles are called "pastoral" because they are addressed to pastors of churches to outline their pastoral duties. These responsibilities were twofold: to defend sound doctrine and maintain sound discipline. This double emphasis is especially obvious in the Epistle to Titus, but it appears in all three letters.

To be more specific, Paul says he had urged Timothy to "stay on in Ephesus so that you may command certain men not to teach false doctrines any longer" (1 Tim 1:3). The apostle also deals with numerous problems that would arise in the church and gives advice as to how they should be handled.

The occasion and purpose of 2 Timothy are stated more fully. Paul is in prison at Rome, awaiting his expected execution. He longs to see his "son" Timothy (1:4). He is getting cold in the dungeon and urges Timothy to come before winter (4:21) and bring the warm coat Paul left at Troas, and his books and parchments (4:13). He wants to study.

6. Summary of 1 and 2 Timothy

Paul begins his First Epistle to Timothy by warning him against false teachers, who seem to have been Judaizers (1:3–11). He thanks "Christ Jesus our Lord" for his amazing grace to him, "the worst of sinners" (1:12–20). Chapter 2 is taken up with instructions for public worship, chapter 3 with the qualifications of the overseers and deacons in the church. In Chapter 4 Paul gives personal instructions to Timothy, again warning him against false teachers (vv.1–5) and admonishing him to maintain sound doctrine and sound discipline (vv.6–16). Chapter 5 deals mainly with the place of widows in the church (vv.3–16) and the treatment of elders (vv.17–20). Chapter 6 has instructions for slaves (vv.1, 2) and more warnings against false teachers (vv.3–5) and the love of money (vv.6–10). After a personal charge to Timothy (vv.11–16), Paul gives special instructions to the rich (vv.17–19).

The second Epistle is much more personal, written near the close of Paul's life. He talks more directly to Timothy than in the first letter, urging him to maintain the spiritual glow (1:1–7) and to be a faithful partner of his in suffering for the gospel (1:8–2:13). Again the apostle warns against the false teachers (2:14–19) and urges Timothy to be a noble servant of Christ (2:20–26). The third chapter contains a description of conditions in the last days (vv.1–9). Then the aged apostle gives his final charge to his son in the faith (3:10–4:5) and his own testimony (4:6–8). The Epistle closes with personal remarks about the current situation (4:9–18) and the final greetings (4:19–21) and benediction (4:22).

Because these two letters were written primarily to an individual whom Paul loved dearly, they provide us with some valuable insights into his life and character. Yet, through his associate Timothy, Paul is speaking to the entire church at Ephesus, and indeed to the whole church of Jesus Christ today.

7. Theological Values

There is a strong OT background here. It is reflected in the use of the phrase "God our Savior," which occurs five times in the Pastorals (1 Tim 1:1; 2:3; Titus 1:3; 2:10; 3:4) and nowhere else in Paul's Epistles. It is found in Jude 25, and a similar expression, "God my Savior," occurs in a hymn that is full of OT language (Luke 1:47). But we also find in the Pastorals the typically Pauline emphasis on "our Savior, Christ Jesus" (2 Tim 1:10), "Christ Jesus our Savior" (Titus 1:4), and "Jesus Christ our Savior" (Titus 3:6). Also the significant Pauline expression "in Christ" occurs seven times in 2 Timothy and twice in 1 Timothy.

Furthermore, the fact that salvation is through God's grace rather than our own good works is clearly asserted (2 Tim 1:9; Titus 3:5). Closely allied to this is the teaching that eternal life comes by faith in Jesus Christ (1 Tim 1:16).

More precisely than anywhere else it is stated: "For there is one God and one mediator between God and men, the man Christ Jesus" (1 Tim 2:5). It is also declared that this Mediator gave himself "as a ransom for all men" (v.6). Here the doctrine of the atonement comes through clearly. By his coming, Christ "has destroyed death and has brought life and immortality to light through the gospel" (2 Tim 1:10).

The divine inspiration of the Scriptures is stated in the Pastorals more forcefully than anywhere else in the NT. We read, "All Scripture is God-breathed and is useful for teaching, rebuking, correcting and training in doing what is right" (2 Tim 3:16).

The pastoral Epistles are primarily practical rather than theological. The emphasis lies rather on the defense of doctrine than on its explication or elaboration. The distinctively doctrinal passages comprise only a small part of the whole; Timothy and Titus had already been instructed.

8. Canonicity

Guthrie states that the external attestation for the Pastorals—the testimony of the early church fathers—"is as strong as that for most of the other Epistles of Paul, with the exception of I Corinthians and Romans."[14] The pastoral Epistles were known and used by Polycarp, Justin Martyr, and Irenaeus—all of the second century.

---

[14]Guthrie, *New Testament Introduction*, p. 199.

The one negative note is found in the heretic Marcion (c. A.D. 140), but then he rejected the whole Bible except ten Pauline Epistles and a mutilated copy of Luke's Gospel.

The first "orthodox" NT canon was the so-called Muratorian Fragment (c. 170–200), the opening part of which is broken off. After mentioning Paul's letters to seven different churches, it says, "But he wrote one letter to Philemon, and one to Titus, and two to Timothy from affection and love." From this time until the rise of negative criticism in the nineteenth century, there seems to have been no question about the acceptance of the pastoral Epistles as Pauline and as a part of the inspired NT Scriptures.

9. Special Problems

In most of Paul's Epistles he is apparently concerned about the work of the Judaizers in hindering the progress of the gospel. The mention of "myths and endless genealogies" (1 Tim 1:4) may refer to Judaistic or Gnostic emphases, or both. But when Paul says that the troublemakers want to be "teachers of the law" (v.7), he is evidently talking about Judaizers. (See also Titus 1:14.)

There also seems to be a combination of Gnosticism and Judaism in those who "forbid people to marry, and order them to abstain from certain foods" (4:3). The first of these prohibitions arose from a false asceticism, based on the Gnostic idea that all matter is evil.

Another troublesome topic concerned who should be enrolled as widows. Paul deals with this at some length and gives specific instructions about their qualifications (1 Tim 5:3–16).

10. Bibliography for Pastoral Epistles

Alford, Henry. *The Greek Testament.* 4 vols. Revised by E.F. Harrison. Chicago: Moody, 1958 (1861).

Barclay, William. *The Letters to Timothy, Titus and Philemon.* Philadelphia: Westminster, 1960.

Barrett, C.K. *The Pastoral Epistles.* Oxford: Clarendon, 1963.

Bernard, J.H. *The Pastoral Epistles.* Cambridge: Cambridge University Press, 1899.

Easton, B.S. *The Pastoral Epistles.* New York: Scribner's, 1947.

Erdman, Charles R. *The Pastoral Epistles of Paul.* Philadelphia: Westminster, 1923.

Fairbairn, Patrick. *Commentary on the Pastoral Epistles.* Grand Rapids: Zondervan, 1956 reprint, (1874).

Falconer, Robert. *The Pastoral Epistles.* Oxford: Clarendon, 1937.

Feine, Paul, and Behm, Johannes. *Introduction to the New Testament.* Completely reedited by W.G. Kümmel. Translated by A.J. Mattill. Nashville: Abingdon, 1966.

Guthrie, Donald. *The Pastoral Epistles.* Grand Rapids: Eerdmans, 1957.

Harrison, Everett F. *Introduction to the New Testament.* Grand Rapids: Eerdmans, 1964.

Hayes, D.A. *Paul and His Epistles.* New York: Methodist Book Concern, 1915.

Hendriksen, William. *New Testament Commentary: Pastoral Epistles.* Grand Rapids: Baker, 1957.

Hiebert, D. Edmond. *An Introduction to the Pauline Epistles.* Chicago: Moody, 1954.

Kelly, J.N.D. *A Commentary on the Pastoral Epistles.* New York: Harper & Row, 1963.

Lenski, R.C.H. *Interpretation of St. Paul's Epistles to the Colossians, to the Thessalonians, to Timothy, to Titus and to Philemon.* Columbus, Ohio: Wartburg, 1937.

Lock, Walter. *A Critical and Exegetical Commentary on the Pastoral Epistles.* Edinburgh: T. & T. Clark, 1924. On the Greek text.

Lowstuter, W.J. "The Pastoral Epistles." *Abingdon Bible Commentary*. Nashville: Abingdon, 1929.

Scott, E.F. *The Pastoral Epistles*. New York: Harper and Brothers, n.d. (1936).

Simpson, E.K. *The Pastoral Epistles*. Grand Rapids: Eerdmans, 1954.

Vine, W.E. *An Expository Dictionary of New Testament Words*. 4 vols. Westwood, N.J.: Revell, 1940.

Zahn, Theodor. *Introduction to the New Testament*, vol. 2. Grand Rapids: Kregel, 1953 reprint, 1909.

11. Outline of 1 Timothy

    I. Salutation

    II. Timothy's Task at Ephesus (1:3–11)
        1. Suppression of False Teachers (1:3–7)
        2. The Purpose of the Law (1:8–11)

    III. Thanksgiving to God (1:12–17)
        1. God's Abundant Grace (1:12–14)
        2. The Worst of Sinners (1:15–17)

    IV. Timothy's Responsibility (1:18–20)

    V. Worship and Conduct (2:1–3:16)
        1. Prayer (2:1–7)
        2. Men (2:8)
        3. Women (2:9–15)
        4. Overseers (3:1–7)
        5. Deacons (3:8–13)
        6. The Mystery of Godliness (3:14–16)

    VI. Special Instructions to Timothy (4:1–16)
        1. False Asceticism (4:1–5)
        2. Superiority of the Spiritual (4:6–10)
        3. Pastoral Duties (4:11–16)

    VII. Special Groups in the Church (5:1–6:2)
        1. The Older and the Younger (5:1, 2)
        2. Widows (5:3–16)
        3. Elders (5:17–25)
        4. Slaves (6:1, 2)

    VIII. The Danger of the Love of Money (6:3–10)

    IX. Paul's Charge to Timothy (6:11–16)

    X. Closing Instructions (6:17–21)
        1. Admonitions to the Wealthy (6:17–19)
        2. Admonition to Timothy (6:20, 21a)
        3. Farewell (6:21b)

Text and Exposition

I. Salutation

1:1, 2

> [1]Paul, an apostle of Christ Jesus by the command of God our Savior and of Christ Jesus our hope,
> [2]To Timothy my true son in the faith:
> Grace, mercy and peace from God the Father and Christ Jesus our Lord.

1 In keeping with the custom of that day, every one of Paul's thirteen Epistles begins with his name (*Paulos*). Born a Roman citizen (Acts 22:27, 28), he had been given the Latin name "Paulus" in addition to his Jewish name Saul. At the beginning of his Gentile mission the apostle adopted the habit of using his Roman (Latin) name (Acts 13:9), and this is what we find in all his letters.

In all but four of his Epistles—Philippians, 1 and 2 Thessalonians, and Philemon—Paul identifies himself as "an apostle." The Greek *apostolos* literally means "one sent on a mission." This was the title that Jesus gave to his first twelve disciples (Luke 6:13). After the death of Judas Iscariot, Matthias was elected to take his place (Acts 1:23–26). Later the term was extended to take in Paul and Barnabas (Acts 14:14), the first two missionaries to the Gentile world. Paul uses it at the beginning of his Epistles to underscore the fact that he is writing with apostolic authority.

He was "an apostle of Christ Jesus." That is, Christ had commissioned and sent him as a missionary. It was not by his own choice but "by the command of God ... and of Christ Jesus." Paul was very conscious of his divine call to the apostolic ministry. He had evidently expected to be a Jewish rabbi, but God had other plans for his life. Only the firm assurance of this could have carried him through all his hardships.

Some have asked why Paul mentioned his apostolic authority in writing to his two faithful colleagues. He understandably omitted this item in his letters to the loving, loyal churches at Thessalonica and Philippi and in his brief personal note to Philemon. But why does he include it in his Epistles to Timothy and Titus?

The answer seems to be that the apostle intended these letters to be read to the local church congregations. He knew that both his recipients were being challenged by false teachers and he wanted to strengthen the hands of these two pastors.

The expression "God our Savior" occurs five times in the Pastorals and nowhere else in Paul's Epistles. Besides this passage, it is found in 2:3 and in Titus 1:3; 2:10; 3:4. Elsewhere in the NT we find it only in Jude 25. A similar phrase, "God my Savior, occurs in Luke 1:47, in a hymn that is characterized largely by OT language. We have already noted in the Introduction the view held by a number of scholars that Luke acted as Paul's amanuensis in the writing of the pastoral Epistles. If so, he may have had some influence on the apostle's language at this point. It may be, too, that Nero's claim to the title "Savior of the world" caused Paul to assert emphatically that the only real Savior is God, the Supreme Being.

Another unique feature is the designation of Christ as "our hope," although Paul elsewhere calls him "the hope of glory" (Col 1:27). In the early second century, Ignatius borrowed the phrase, speaking of "Jesus Christ our hope" (*Epistle to the Trallians*, ch. 2). He is our only hope.

2 The Epistle is addressed to Timothy (*Timotheos*), "my true son in the faith." Elsewhere Paul refers to him as "my son whom I love, who is faithful in the Lord" (1 Cor 4:17) and says, "Timothy has proved himself, because as a son with his father he has served with me in the work of the gospel" (Phil 2:22).

The word *true* (*gnēsios*) means "genuine, true-born." Perhaps the thrust here is two-fold: Timothy was a true believer and he was also a genuine convert of Paul's ministry.

We first meet Timothy in Acts 16:1–3. There we are told that on Paul's second missionary journey he found at Lystra a young disciple named Timothy, the son of a Jewish Christian mother and a Greek father. Paul was so impressed with the young man that he asked him to join the missionary party. It seems clear that Timothy had been converted under Paul's preaching at Lystra on the first missionary journey (about A.D. 47). He had matured so well as a Christian that only two years later (A.D. 49) he was ready to become an apprentice to the great apostle. He became one of Paul's most trusted helpers, so that the apostle could write, "I have no one else like him, who takes a genuine interest in your welfare" (Phil 2:20). The life of Timothy is a constant challenge to every young Christian to imitate his devotion and faithfulness.

After the name of the writer (v.1) and the recipient (v.2a) comes the greeting (v.2b). In all ten of Paul's previous Epistles the greeting is twofold—"grace and peace." Here and in 2 Timothy it is "grace, mercy and peace." These all come to us "from God the Father and Christ Jesus our Lord."

Two things may have suggested the addition of "mercy" (which is not found in the best Greek text of Titus 1:2). One would be Timothy's frail health (see 5:23). As a loving father, the apostle wishes mercy for his son. The other would be the difficulties that Timothy was encountering at Ephesus. He was in need of God's mercy and help.

"Grace" (*charis*) is a favorite word with Paul, occurring nearly one hundred times in his Epistles. First meaning "gracefulness" and then "graciousness," it is used in the NT for the "divine favor" that God bestows freely on all who will believe.

"Peace" has always been the typical greeting of the East. It is one of God's best gifts to men. In a world of war and hate this term becomes particularly significant. In Christ we have peace of heart and mind.

Notes

1 The word ἀπόστολος (*apostolos*) occurs eight times in the Gospels (six of those in Luke), thirty times in Acts, thirty-two times in Paul's Epistles (including five in the Pastorals) and eight times in the rest of the NT. In most cases it refers either to Paul or to the Twelve.

Twice in this verse we have the name "Christ Jesus." In the earlier Epistles of Paul, as in the Epistles of James, Peter, John, and Jude, the order is more frequently "Jesus Christ," which may be interpreted as meaning "Jesus the Messiah." But in Paul's later Epistles "Christ Jesus" becomes the dominant expression, particularly in the Pastorals. The emphasis here is more on the title ("Christ" means "Anointed One") than on the personal name.

Surprisingly, σωτήρ (*sōtēr*, "Savior") is found only twenty-four times in the NT ("salvation" 44 times). Of these, ten are in the pastoral Epistles and five in 2 Peter. Apparently the term came into prominent use in the later period, perhaps because of its false use by Nero (see Exposition), under whom both Peter and Paul were executed.

2 Aside from 1 Tim 1:2 and Titus 1:4, γνήσιος (*gnēsios*, "true," "genuine") is found only twice in the NT (2 Cor 8:8; Phil 4:3). But it is found frequently in the papyri in the sense of "genuine." It "becomes an epithet of affectionate appreciation" (MM, p. 129). That is its use here.

The addition of "mercy" has been cited as evidence against the Pauline authorship of the

Pastorals. But Simpson cogently observes: "A copyist would have surely avoided such a deviation from precedent" (p. 26).

We are apt to think of ἔλεος (*eleos*, "mercy"), as indicating God's attitude toward the sinner in bringing him to a place of repentance and forgiveness. But the word has broader connotations. In LXX it is used to tr. the Heb. term that means "lovingkindness" or "steadfast love." This is probably the full import here.

II. Timothy's Task at Ephesus (1:3–11)

1. *Suppression of False Teachers*

1:3–7

> ³As I urged you when I went into Macedonia, stay there in Ephesus so that you may command certain men not to teach false doctrines any longer ⁴nor to devote themselves to myths and endless genealogies. These promote controversies rather than God's work—which is by faith. ⁵The goal of this command is love, which comes from a pure heart, a good conscience and a sincere faith. ⁶Some have wandered away from these and turned to meaningless talk. ⁷They want to be teachers of the law, but they do not know what they are talking about or what they so confidently affirm.

3 When Paul went into Macedonia—at exactly what time we do not know—he urged Timothy to "stay [*prosmenō*, 'remain still'] there in Ephesus." As noted in the Introduction, it appears that Paul was released from his first Roman imprisonment of two years, recorded at the close of Acts, and that he made another visit to Ephesus. There he discovered some conditions that needed extended attention. So he left Timothy as pastor of this important church.

3b, 4a What was the problem that concerned Paul? We find the answer here in the purpose for which Timothy was to remain: "that you may command certain men not to teach false doctrines any longer nor to devote themselves to myths and endless genealogies." The church has always had false teachers—they appeared on the scene in the very first generation, within thirty-five years of the church's birth at Pentecost (A.D. 30–65).

What was the nature of these "false doctrines"? What is meant by "myths and endless genealogies" (*genealogiai*)?

There are two possible answers. In the first place, the reference could be to the vagaries of Gnosticism, with its endless genealogies of aeons between God and man. But v.7 suggests that these were Jewish teachers, who were caught up in the mythological treatment of OT genealogies. Titus 1:14 speaks of "Jewish myths." There is abundant evidence that both these features were found in the Judaism of that day, especially in its apocalyptic literature.

4b Paul declares that such teachings "promote controversies rather than God's work—which is by faith." The word translated "work" is *oikonomian*, which literally means "stewardship" but is often rendered "dispensation." Simpson aptly remarks, "The divine dispensation of truth does not beget fable-spinning but faith. . . . By faith we stand, not by weaving webs of whimsical fancies" (p. 28).

5 The "goal" or "end" (*telos*) of "this command"—literally, "the command"—"is love." It may be seriously questioned whether the translation limiting it to "this command" is fully justified. We would agree with Walter Lock when he comments: "Primarily, the charge which Timothy has to give ... but the last [preceding] words ... have carried the mind on to the whole scheme of salvation, and perhaps extend the meaning more widely—the end of all Christian moral preaching, the whole moral charge which is given to God's stewards" (p. 10). That is, the highest goal of true religion is love—*agapē*, the unselfish love of full loyalty to God and boundless goodwill to our fellowmen. This must be our ultimate goal in life.

This love comes "from a pure heart, a good conscience and a sincere faith." Our hearts must be cleansed from self-centeredness if we are going to obey the first and second commandments enunciated by Jesus (Matt 22:37–40). Then we must maintain a good conscience if love is to function properly. And all this is based on "sincere" (literally, "unhypocritical") faith. All love comes from God and it comes to us only as we are united to him by faith.

6 Unfortunately, some at Ephesus had missed the mark (*astochēsantes*) and had turned to "meaningless talk" (*mataiologian*, "empty chatter"—only here in the NT). They were doing much talking, but saying nothing of value. Simpson calls them "wordmongers."

7 Paul scores these would-be teachers of the Law rather heavily. His verdict: "They do not know what they are talking about or what they so confidently affirm." Their self-confidence was empty pretense. Simpson comments, "These whipper-snappers have an exchequer of words, but no fund of insight" (p. 29). They were what Philo called "syllable-squabblers."

8 Having identified the false teachers at Ephesus as self-appointed teachers of the Law, the apostle now points out the purpose of the Law. He says that "the law"—probably here meaning the Mosaic law—"is good if a man uses it properly." Here the KJV rendering preserves the play on words in the Greek—"law" (*nomos*) ... "lawfully" (*nomimōs*).

Notes

3 "To teach false doctrines" is all one word in Greek, ἑτεροδιδασκαλεῖν (*heterodidaskalein*, lit., "to teach differently"), found only here and in 6:3, and never found outside of Christian writings. Paul may well have coined the term as a contrast to the claim of these false leaders that they were νομοδιδάσκαλοι (*nomodidaskaloi*, "teachers of the law," v.7). Actually they were teaching something "different" (*heteros*).

4 Our word *myth* comes directly from the Greek μῦθος (*mythos*). At first this meant simply a story or narrative. But finally it became equivalent to the Latin *fabula*, "a fable" or "fiction."

"Controversies" translates ἐκζητήσεις (*ekzēteseis*, only here in NT and found only in Christian writings). It means "useless speculations" (BAG).

"Godly edifying" (KJV) is based on an inferior reading, οἰκοδομίαν (*oikodomian*, "act of building"), rather than οἰκονομίαν (*oikonomian*, "administration").

5 "Conscience" comes from the Latin—*cum*, "with," and *scio*, "know." So it literally means "a knowing together"—the exact meaning of the Gr. word here, συνείδησις (*syneidēsis*). Among the Greeks it meant "self-consciousness," which was primarily an intellectual matter. It was the Jews, along with the Stoics, who introduced a moral content into the term, so that "consciousness" became "conscience."

2. The Purpose of the Law

1:8-11

> 8We know that the law is good if a man uses it properly. 9We also know that law is made not for good men, but for lawbreakers and rebels, the ungodly and sinful, the unholy and irreligious; for those who kill their fathers or mothers, for murderers, 10for adulterers and perverts, for slave traders and liars and perjurers —and for whatever else is contrary to the sound doctrine 11that conforms to the glorious gospel of the blessed God, which he entrusted to me.

9a "Law" in this verse is without the definite article and so probably refers to law in general. The apostle indicates that the purpose of law is not to police good men but bad men. In other words, we need law for the punishment of criminals and the protection of society. He says that law is not appointed "for good men"—literally, "for a righteous person." Rather, it is intended to deal with those who are unrighteous.

The list that follows is typically Pauline (cf. Rom 1:24-32). It starts with more general terms, in three pairs: "lawbreakers and rebels, the ungodly and sinful, the unholy and irreligious." These represent attitudes or states of mind. "Lawbreakers" is literally "lawless"—that is, those who ignore the law. The Greek word translated "rebels" literally means "not subject to rule," and so "insubordinate." The word for "ungodly" means one who is deliberately guilty of "irreverence." The adjective "irreligious" means "profane" (KJV) in the sense of having no sense of the sacred—a common sin of secular society.

9b,10a "For those who kill their fathers . . . mothers" translates only two words in Greek (*patrolōais . . . mētrolōais*). The two terms (found only here in the NT) are constructed, respectively, of the words for "father" and "mother" with the verb meaning "to smite." So J.H. Bernard writes, "The rendering of A.V. and R.V. 'murderers of fathers' is, no doubt, legitimate, but it is not the sin of *murder*, but of *dishonouring parents*, which is here uppermost in the writer's thought, and the wider translation is justified by the usage of the words elsewhere. For this extreme and outrageous violation of the Fifth Commandment the punishment of death was provided in the Mosaic law (Ex. xxi.15)" (p. 27). The fact that "murderers" immediately follows perhaps lends some support to "smiters of fathers and smiters of mothers" as the correct translation here. This is favored by Alford, Fairbairn, Simpson, and others.

Paul goes on to say that law is made for adulterers and "perverts." The last term is *arsenokoitais*, which means "male homosexuals." The word occurs only once elsewhere in the NT, in 1 Corinthians 6:9, where it is stated that "homosexual offenders" will not inherit the kingdom of God. Despite its condonation by some church leaders today, homosexuality is categorically condemned in both the OT and NT. It is the peculiar sin for which God destroyed Sodom and Gomorrah. It is widely recognized as one of the causes for the downfall of the Roman Empire, and its rapid increase today in Europe and North America poses a threat to the future of Western civilization.

"Slave traders" is *andrapodistais*, which may be translated "kidnapers." The Jewish rabbis specifically applied the eighth commandment, "Thou shalt not steal," to kidnaping—a crime that has greatly increased in the last few years. Philo, a Jew of the first century, makes this interesting observation: "The kidnaper too is a kind of thief who steals the best of all the things that exist on the earth" (*Spec. leg.* 4:13).

We have noted that "smiters of fathers" refers to the fifth commandment. The terms that follow relate to the sixth, seventh, eighth, and ninth commandments. So these items cover most of the second table of the Decalogue.

10b,11 Lest he miss any other important item, Paul adds, "And for whatever else is contrary to the sound doctrine that conforms to the glorious gospel of the blessed God which he entrusted to me." The one Greek word for "is contrary to" literally means "lies opposite," and so "opposes" or "resists."

"Sound" is one of the key words of the pastoral Epistles. Here it is the verb *hygiainō* (from which comes "hygienic"), which occurs eight times in the Pastorals and only four times elsewhere in the NT. (The adjective *hygiēs* is found in Titus 2:8). The verb means *"be in good health, be healthy* or *sound"* (BAG, p. 839). Both words are used with reference to physical health in the Gospels. But the ethical, metaphorical usage here is widely paralleled in Greek literature.

Does "sound" mean "healthy" or "healthful"—that is, conducive to good health? A.T. Robertson supports the latter, as do Patrick Fairbairn and J.H. Bernard. But Lock says that it does not mean "wholesome" (p. 12), although this is the translation in Wey and NEB.

Perhaps this is a false antithesis. It may be a question not of either/or but of both/and. E.F. Scott points out that this phrase, "sound doctrine," fits in with its previous context (vv.3-10) and its following context (v.10). He writes, "As contrasted with all morbid types of belief, the gospel is healthy.... Law is a sort of medicine, only to be applied where the moral nature is diseased; Christian teaching is a healthy food for healthy people, a means of joy, freedom, larger activity" (p. 10).

"That conforms to the glorious gospel of the blessed God" is literally "according to the gospel of the glory of the blessed God." Fairbairn felicitously observes, "The gospel of God's glory is the gospel which peculiarly displays His glory—unfolds this to the view of men by showing the moral character and perfections of God exhibited as they are nowhere else in the person and work of Christ" (p. 90).

Paul declares that this gospel was "entrusted to me." Again and again he makes this assertion (see 1 Cor 9:17; Gal 2:7; 1 Thess 2:4). It amazed him that God should have placed such trust in him—the one who had formerly opposed the gospel and persecuted the church (cf. vv.12-14). The last clause of this paragraph is therefore a fitting introduction to the next section, in which he thanks God for choosing him.

Notes

9 "Murderers" translates the compound ἀνδροφόνοις (*androphonois*, lit., "men-killers." It is found only here in NT.
10 The question as to whether ἀνδραποδισταῖς (*andrapodistais*)—only here in NT—should be tr. "slave traders" or "kidnapers" is difficult to decide. Hendriksen comments that "it clearly refers primarily to 'slave-dealers' (the word ἀνδράποδον means slave) and then, by extension, to all 'men-stealers' or 'kidnapers'" (p. 69).
Διδασκαλία (*didaskalia*, "teaching") is used (in the NT) only by Paul, except in a quotation from Isa 29:13 (Matt 15:9; Mark 7:7). It occurs fifteen times in the Pastorals and four times in his other Epistles. Originally it meant the act of teaching, and then a body of doctrine. It is evidently used in the latter sense here.

III. Thanksgiving to God (1:12–17)

1. *God's Abundant Grace*

1:12–14

> [12]I thank Christ Jesus our Lord, who has given me strength, that he considered me faithful, appointing me to his service. [13]Even though I was once a blasphemer and a persecutor and a violent man, I was shown mercy because I acted in ignorance and unbelief. [14]The grace of our Lord was poured out on me abundantly, along with the faith and love that are in Christ Jesus.

12 Usually the thanksgiving in Paul's Epistles follows the salutation. But in this case the apostle has inserted between them a statement of his purpose in leaving Timothy at Ephesus. Now we find the familiar expression of thanks. In previous Epistles it was usually to God; here it is to "Christ Jesus our Lord." The lordship of Jesus finds increasing emphasis in Paul's later Epistles.

It is Christ who has "given me strength" (*endynamōsanti me*). This could be translated, "who has empowered me." This was because the Lord "considered" or "counted" (KJV) him faithful, "appointing me to his service." The last word is *diakonia*, which basically means "service" but is also used in a somewhat technical sense in the NT. Probably "putting me into the ministry" (KJV) is also a satisfactory translation.

13 Formerly Paul had been "a blasphemer." This probably means that in his opposition to the new movement he cursed the name of Jesus. Now he realized that this was blasphemy, because Jesus was divine.

Paul was also "a persecutor." This fact is documented abundantly in Acts 8:3; 9:1, 2, 4, 5; 22:4, 5; 26:9–11; Galatians 1:13. In his zeal to protect Judaism, the young Saul believed that he must destroy Christianity.

Still worse, he was "a violent man." This is one word, *hybristēn*. This term, found only here and in Romans 1:20, is much stronger than "injurious" (KJV). It refers to insolence and violence (cf. Acts 8:3).

Paul is fond of trilogies, and this is another example. Lock summarizes it this way: "A triad (as so often in St. Paul) with perhaps an ascending scale rising from words to acts of authorized persecution and of illegal violence" (pp. 14, 15).

In spite of this, he was "shown mercy" because he "acted in ignorance and unbelief." Paul was sincere in believing he was serving God in acting this way. When brought before the Sanhedrin in Jerusalem, he had testified, "I have fulfilled my duty to God in all good conscience to this day" (Acts 23:1). This apparently included his pre-Christian life.

14 It was more than mercy that Paul received from God. He declares, "The grace of our Lord was poured out on me abundantly, along with the faith and love that are in Christ Jesus." This is another of the apostle's great trilogies. "Grace" provided his salvation, "faith" appropriated it, and "love" applied it.

354

Notes

14 "Was poured out on me abundantly" translates one word in Gr.: ὑπερεπλεόνασε (*hyperepleonase*, "exceedingly abounded"). Paul is fond of compounds with ὑπέρ (*hyper*, "above"). This one is found only here in the NT. Bunyan found here his title for *Grace Abounding to the Chief of Sinners.*

2. The Worst of Sinners

1:15–17

> ¹⁵Here is a trustworthy saying that deserves full acceptance: Christ Jesus came into the world to save sinners—of whom I am the worst. ¹⁶But for that very reason I was shown mercy so that in me, the worst of sinners, Christ Jesus might display his unlimited patience as an example for those who would believe on him and receive eternal life. ¹⁷Now to the King eternal, immortal, invisible, the only God, be honor and glory for ever and ever. Amen.

15,16 "Here is a trustworthy saying" is literally "faithful the word" (*pistos ho logos*). This formula is found only in the pastoral Epistles (see 3:1; 2 Tim 2:11; Titus 3:8). Here and in 4:9 we find the added words: "that deserves full acceptance." The repeated formula is always attached to a maxim (relating either to doctrine or practice) on which full reliance can be placed. The saying here is "Christ Jesus came into the world to save sinners." This is the Good News, the heart of the gospel.

Paul felt that of all sinners he was "the worst"—literally, "first" or "chief." This was because he had persecuted Christ's followers so vigorously. As far as morality was concerned, young Saul had been a strict Pharisee, living a life that was blameless before the Law. But in his case as chief sinner, Christ's "unlimited patience" had been displayed as an example to all who would believe in Jesus and thus receive eternal life. Paul's life was a powerful demonstration of divine grace.

17 This verse is typical of Paul's habit of breaking out spontaneously into praise. We find briefer doxologies at 6:16 and 2 Timothy 4:18, as well as extended ones in Romans 11:36; 16:27; Galatians 1:5; Ephesians 3:21 and Philippians 4:20.

Notes

15 The term πιστός (*pistos*, "faithful" or "trustworthy") is found eleven times in 1 Tim and three times each in 2 Tim and Titus—a total of seventeen times in the Pastorals. It is obviously a key word in these three Epistles.

17 "King eternal" is lit. "King of the ages," a phrase found in Tobit 13:6, 10.

IV. Timothy's Responsibility

1:18–20

> ¹⁸Timothy, my son, I give you this instruction in keeping with the prophecies once made about you, so that by following them you may fight the good fight, ¹⁹holding on to faith and a good conscience. Some have rejected these and so have shipwrecked their faith. ²⁰Among them are Hymenaeus and Alexander, whom I have handed over to Satan to be taught not to blaspheme.

18,19 "Instruction" is the same word, *parangelia*, that is translated "command" in v.5. It means "instruction, charge, command." The aged apostle is giving his son in the faith a solemn charge "in keeping with the prophecies once made about you"—perhaps at the time of Timothy's ordination or of his induction into missionary work. "Once made" is *proagousas*, "leading to" or "going before." So the phrase has sometimes been translated, "according to the prophecies leading me toward you," or "predictions leading up to you." They seem to have been prophetic utterances that pointed Timothy's way into the ministry. Because of these he was to "fight the good fight [lit., 'war the good warfare'] holding on to faith and a good conscience." Paul was much concerned that he and his colleagues should have a good conscience always. Some have rejected this "and so have shipwrecked their faith."

20 Paul names two who have been shipwrecked: Hymenaeus and Alexander. The former is mentioned again as a heretical teacher in 2 Timothy 2:17. Two Alexanders are spoken of in connection with Ephesus. The first was a Jew (Acts 19:34). The second is "Alexander the metalworker," who did Paul a great deal of harm (2 Tim 4:14). He may be the one intended here.

The apostle had handed these two ringleaders "over to Satan to be taught not to blaspheme." The language here is similar to that found in 1 Corinthians 5:5, where it seems to indicate excommunication from the church. The purpose was to jolt the offender into repentance, induced by the fearful thought of being turned over to Satan's control. Bernard observes, "It is certainly a *disciplinary* or *remedial* and not a merely *punitive* penalty in both cases" (p. 36).

V. Worship and Conduct (2:1–3:16)

1. Prayer

2:1–7

> ¹I urge, then, first of all, that requests, prayers, intercession and thanksgiving be made for everyone—²for kings and all those in authority, that we may live peaceful and quiet lives in all godliness and holiness. ³This is good, and pleases God our Savior, ⁴who wants all men to be saved and to come to a knowledge of the truth. ⁵For there is one God and one mediator between God and men, the man Christ Jesus, ⁶who gave himself as a ransom for all men—the testimony given in its proper time. ⁷And for this purpose I was appointed a herald and an apostle—I am telling the truth, I am not lying—and a teacher of the true faith to the Gentiles.

1 Chapter 2 of 1 Timothy consists of instructions for public worship. The apostle was concerned that divine worship should be carried on in Ephesus most effectively and helpfully.

So he says, "I urge." The verb used here (*parakaleō*) may be translated "beseech" or "exhort." It indicates the urgency of Paul's admonition.

"First of all" probably emphasizes primacy in importance rather than in time (Guthrie). The most essential part of public worship is prayer.

In the NT we find seven different Greek nouns used for prayer. Four of them occur in this verse.

The first is *deēseis*, which is found nineteen times. Translated here as "requests" (KJV, "supplications"), it basically carries the idea of desire or need. All true prayer begins in a sense of need and involves a deep desire, although it should never stop there. God wants us to bring our "requests" to him, and he always has a listening ear.

The second word is *proseuchē*. It is the most general word for prayer, occurring thirty-seven times. Regularly translated as "prayer," it always signifies praying to God. It is used for both private and public prayers. The context suggests that here Paul had the latter in mind, although the former is certainly not excluded.

The third word, *enteuxis*, is found in the NT only in 1 Timothy (here and in 4:5). Translated here as "intercession," it seems to be used there in a more general way for prayer. The Greek word was used in the sense of "conversation" and then of "petition." Perhaps it suggests the idea that prayer should be a conversation with God.

Trench (p. 190) says that it implies "free familiar prayer, such as boldly draws near to God." Origen, the greatest Bible scholar of the early church, taught that the fundamental idea of *enteuxis* was boldness of access to God's presence.

This, again, is one aspect of successful, satisfying prayer. We must come to God with full confidence and enter into close communion with him in a conversational atmosphere if we wish to experience depth and richness in our prayer life. And only he who really communes with God in private can edify others in his public prayers.

The fourth word is *eucharistia*, from which we get "eucharist." The Lord's Supper, or Holy Communion, should always be a time of "thanksgiving." And "giving of thanks" (KJV) should be a part of all our praying. Thanking God for what he has done for us in the past strengthens our faith to believe that he will meet our needs in the future. Trench observes that this is the one aspect of prayer that will continue throughout eternity, where it will be "larger, deeper, fuller than here" (p. 191), because there the redeemed will know how much they owe their Lord.

2 Prayers of these varied types are to be made "for everyone" (v.1), but especially "for kings and all those in authority." The term *basileus* ("king") was applied in that day to the emperor at Rome, as well as to lesser rulers. When it is remembered that the Roman emperor when Paul wrote this Epistle was the cruel monster Nero—who later put Paul and Peter to death—it will be realized that we should pray for our present rulers, no matter how unreasonable they may seem to be. Prayer for "all those in authority" in various levels of government should have a regular place in all public worship.

The purpose of this is very logical and significant: "that we may live peaceful and quiet lives in all godliness and honesty." The fact that we are permitted to assemble peaceably for public worship is dependent on our rights under law—law as upheld and enforced by our legislators, administrators, and judicial leaders. We ought to pray for them, and also thank God for them.

The Greek adjective translated "peaceful" occurs only here in the NT. It means "quiet, tranquil." The basic idea is that of "restfulness unmarred by disturbance" (Vine, p. 34). The word for "quiet" (only here and in 1 Peter 3:4) "suggests the stillness that accompanied restfulness, in contrast to noisy commotion and merely bustling activity" (ibid.). Marvin Vincent says of these two terms: "*Ēremos* denotes quiet arising from the absence of outward disturbance; *hēsychios* tranquility arising from within" (Vincent, 4:217).

The word for "godliness" basically means "piety" or "reverence." The man who is irreverent is living an ungodly life.

"Holiness" is more accurate than "honesty" (KJV), which reflects an archaic sense no longer associated with that term. The Greek word *semnotēs* suggests "reverence, dignity, seriousness, respectfulness, holiness, probity" (BAG). Elsewhere in the NT it occurs only in 3:4 ("respect") and Titus 2:7 ("seriousness"). It is one of a considerable list of terms found only in the pastoral Epistles.

3,4 Such a life is "good"—*kalos* also means "beautiful, excellent"—and pleasing (acceptable) to God our Savior (cf. 1:1). He "wants all men to be saved and to come to a knowledge of the truth." This statement is in accord with John 3:16 and with the declaration in 2 Corinthians 5:14, 15 that Christ died for all. Salvation has been provided for all, but only those who accept it are saved. Vine writes, "Salvation is universal in its scope but conditional in its effect" (p. 35).

"Knowledge" (*epignōsis*) may also be translated "recognition." The compound noun means "precise and correct knowledge" (Thayer). "Knowledge of the truth" is both the root and fruit of salvation. Paul here sounds a frequent note of the Pastorals—true knowledge saves from error.

5 This is one of the most significant verses of the NT. It declares first of all that "there is one God." This is a primary affirmation in the OT, in opposition to the many polytheisms of that day. Monotheism is the basic premise of both Judaism and Christianity.

But then comes a difference. For Christianity goes on to assert that "there is one mediator between God and men, the man Christ Jesus."

The Greek word for "mediator," *mesitēs*, occurs only once in LXX (Gr. tr. of the OT). Job was frustrated by the fact that God was not a man with whom he could converse. In despair he concluded, "Neither is there any daysman [*mesitēs*] betwixt us, that might lay his hand upon us both" (Job 9:33). Christ is the answer to this ancient cry for help.

The basic meaning of *mesitēs* is "one who intervenes between two, either in order to make or restore peace and friendship, or to form a compact, or for ratifying a covenant." Thayer goes on to say that Christ is called the mediator between God and men "since he interposed by his death and restored the harmony between God and man which human sin had broken" (*Lexicon*, p. 401).

To be of any use, a bridge across a chasm or river must be anchored on both sides. Christ has closed the gap between deity and humanity. He has crossed the grand canyon, so deep and wide, between heaven and earth. He has bridged the chasm that separated man from God. With one foot planted in eternity, he planted the other in time. He who was the eternal Son of God became the Son of Man. And across this bridge, the man Christ Jesus, we can come into the very presence of God, knowing that we are accepted because we have a Mediator.

6 This Christ "gave himself as a ransom for all men." The word for "ransom," *antilytron*, occurs only here in the NT. It means "what is given in exchange for another as the price of his redemption" (Thayer). In the first century the simple word *lytron* was used for the ransom price paid to free a slave. So Christ paid the ransom to free us from the slavery of sin. Because of this we are rightfully his possession.

Jesus gave his life as a ransom "for all men." The Greek word translated "for" means "on behalf of." Christ died on behalf of all people, but only those who accept his sacrifice are actually set free from the shackles of sin.

This message of the redemptive death of Christ was the distinctive apostolic witness—

"the testimony given in its proper time." The last phrase is literally "in its own appointed times." Christ's sacrifice for sin took place at God's appointed hour. The Twentieth Century New Testament translates the whole clause: "This is the fact to which we are to bear our testimony, as opportunities present themselves."

7 For the purpose of giving this witness, Paul was "appointed"—literally, "placed, set"—"a herald and an apostle." The term *kēryx* ("herald") was used for "*a messenger* vested with public authority, who conveyed the official messages of kings, magistrates, princes, military commanders, or who gave a public summons or demand, and performed various other duties" (Thayer, p. 346). In the NT it signifies "God's ambassador, and the herald or proclaimer of the divine word" (ibid.). So the "preacher" (KJV) is one who makes a public proclamation for the King of kings. He is not to air his own opinions or debate other people's ideas but proclaim the Word of God. What a glorious privilege and what an awesome responsibility! No wonder Paul says "*I* [emphatic *egō* in Gr.] was appointed." Perhaps he is thinking "even I"—the one who blasphemed Christ and persecuted the church (see 1:12-14).

The word *apostle* (*apostolos*) has been discussed in connection with 1:1. It is almost equivalent to "missionary," which comes from the Latin. But probably it means here Christ's authoritative representative as a leader of the church.

Paul adds, "I am telling the truth, I am not lying." This implies that some of the church members at Ephesus were challenging his apostolic authority, as had happened at Corinth (2 Cor 10:10).

Paul was not only a herald and an apostle but also "a teacher of the true faith to the Gentiles." This was his special assignment from the Lord (Acts 9:15). Though he was "a Hebrew of the Hebrews" (Phil 3:5) and brought up a strict Pharisee, he had been born in Tarsus, one of the three main centers of Greek learning (after Athens and Alexandria), and was therefore suited to this assignment. The Christian leaders at Jerusalem agreed that he should evangelize the Gentiles (Gal 2:9).

Notes

3 We have already observed in connection with 1:1 that the use of "God our Savior" may point toward Luke as being the one who actually composed the pastoral Epistles under Paul's supervision. In this verse we find an additional item possibly pointing in the same direction. "Pleases God our Savior" is literally "acceptable"—ἀπόδεκτος (*apodektos*), only here and in 5:4—"in the presence of" (ἐνώπιον, enōpion) "God our Savior." The preposition *enōpion* is found twenty-two times in Luke's Gospel and fifteen times in Acts (not at all in Matthew or Mark and only once in John). Elsewhere it occurs very infrequently except in Revelation, where it is used thirty-six times. Martin McNamara shows that "in the presence of God" is a phrase that was adopted in the Aramaic Targums of the OT (*Targum and Testament* [Eerdmans, 1972], pp. 93-97).

6 Of ἀντίλυτρον (*antilytron*) Vine writes, "The word *antilutron*, a ransom, denotes an equivalent (or adequate) ransom price (from *anti*, corresponding to, and *lutron*, a ransom, from *luō*, to loose ...). The prefix *anti* expresses that the ransom is equivalent in value to that which is procured by it. It indicates the vicarious nature of the expiatory sacrifice of Christ in His death" (p. 39).

Walter Lock (p. 28) suggests that the "testimony" may include "the whole chain of witnesses," that is, "(a) The law and the prophets pointing to it, cf. Ro 3²¹.... (b) The witness of the Lord Himself in His Life (cf. 6¹³ and John 18³⁷).... (c) The witness which the writer and all future teachers have to give, cf. 1 Co 1⁶, 2 Th 1¹⁰."

2. Men

2:8

8I want men everywhere to lift up holy hands in prayer, without anger or disputing.

Getting back specifically to the matter of public worship, the apostle wants "men
everywhere to lift up holy hands in prayer, without anger or disputing." The last word
is translated "doubting" in KJV, a meaning that was adopted by several of the early
church fathers. But the context seems to favor "disputing," a sense that the Greek word
dialogismos clearly has in Romans 14:1 and Philippians 2:14.

Lifting up one's hands in prayer is often mentioned in the OT (e.g., 1 Kings 8:22; Pss
141:2; 143:6). It is a natural gesture, indicating earnest desire. The word "holy" is not
the more common *hagios* but *hosios*, which means "devout, pious, pleasing to God"
(BAG).

Lock says of the expression "lifting up holy hands" that it "combines the idea of moral
purity . . . with that of consecration" (p. 30). We cannot pray effectively unless our lives
are clean and committed.

Concerning "anger," Jeremy Taylor many years ago observed, "Anger is a perfect
alienation of the mind from prayer" (quoted by Bernard, p. 44). And Bernard says about
"disputing": "In our prayers we leave our differences behind us" (ibid.).

Notes

KJV has "will" in vv.4, 8; NIV, "want." But in the Gr. the former uses θέλω (*thelō*), while the
latter uses βούλομαι (*boulomai*). Thayer writes: "As respects the distinction between βούλομαι
and θέλω, the former seems to designate the will which follows deliberation, the latter the will
which proceeds from inclination" (p. 286). But Cremer says: "Both words are, upon the whole, used
synonymously" (p. 143). (So BAG, p. 145).

3. Women

2:9-15

9I also want women to dress modestly, with decency and propriety, not with
braided hair or gold or pearls or expensive clothes, 10but with good deeds, appropriate for women who profess to worship God.
11A woman should learn in quietness and full submission. 12I do not permit a
woman to teach or to have authority over a man; she must be silent. 13For Adam
was formed first, then Eve. 14And Adam was not the one deceived; it was the
woman who was deceived and became a sinner. 15But women will be kept safe
through childbirth, if they continue in faith, love and holiness with propriety.

9,10 The first clause of v.8 reads literally: "I desire therefore the men to pray in every
place." In v.9 Paul says, "Likewise also women." The use of the definite article with men
and not with women may suggest that the apostle was laying down the pattern that
public worship should be conducted by the men. Now he proceeds to tell how women
should conduct themselves in church services.

First, they are to "dress modestly." This is a compact translation that represents the thought correctly. In the Greek there is a play on words: *kosmein heautas . . . en katastolē kosmiō.* The verb *kosmeō* (cf. the English word "cosmetic") means first "put in order" and then "adorn, decorate" (BAG). The adjective *kosmios* (in NT only here and in 3:2) means "orderly, decent, modest" (A-S, p. 255). *Katastolē* (only here in the NT) is "attire," though it sometimes had the wider sense of outward appearance or deportment. The full expression signifies: "adorn themselves in modest clothes." This is a much needed admonition today.

The word for "decency" is *aidōs* (only here in the NT). The translation "shame-facedness" (KJV) is both inaccurate—as every scholar agrees—and unfortunate. Paul is not urging women to go around looking ashamed of themselves, with faces averted or veiled. Bernard says that the Greek word "signifies that modesty which shrinks from overstepping the limits of womanly reserve" (p. 45). This should apply to both dress and deportment, although the rest of the verse suggests that the primary reference here is to one's clothing (as indicated in NIV).

Women are also to dress with "propriety." The Greek word (*sōphrosynē*) means "soundness of mind, good sense" (A-S). It could be translated "sound judgment," or as we might say today, "good judgment." Vine makes the timely observation: "What the apostle had in view in the present passage was the snare of the extreme forms of current fashions" (p. 43).

"Braided hair" is one word in Greek—*plegma*, which means something woven or braided. But clearly "hair" is understood. This is shown by a comparison with 1 Peter 3:3, where "hair" is expressed in the Greek. These two passages are very similar, a coincidence that is all the more striking since there was probably no collusion between the authors.

The Christian woman is not to adorn herself with "gold or pearls or expensive clothes" so as to draw attention to herself. At worst, this is what the prostitutes did. At best, it shows pride and self-centeredness, both of which are contrary to the spirit of Christ. Such dress is especially unbecoming in church.

Rather, Christian women are to adorn themselves "with good deeds, appropriate for women who profess to worship God." The Greek literally says "through good deeds." That is the way we express our faith. This thought is more dominant in the pastoral Epistles (occurring a dozen times) than in Paul's earlier letters—perhaps because the need for such emphasis became more apparent.

11,12 The teaching of these two verses is similar to that found in 1 Corinthians 14:33–35. There Paul tells the women that they are not allowed to talk out loud in the public services; here he says that they are to "learn in quietness and full submission." Titus 2:5 suggests that he means a wife is to be submissive to her husband. But it may well have the wider application of "submission to constituted authority, i.e., the officials and regulations of the Church" (Ramsay, quoted in Lock, p. 32).

The attitude of the Greeks toward women's place in society was not altogether uniform. Plato gave them practical equality with men. But Aristotle thought their activities should be severely limited, and his views generally prevailed. Plutarch (*Moral Essays,* p. 785) sounds much the same note as Paul does here.

The expression "full submission" needs to be treated intelligently. Vine offers this helpful comment: "The injunction is not directed towards a surrender of mind and conscience, or the abandonment of the duty of private judgment; the phrase 'with all subjection' is a warning against the usurpation of authority, as, e.g., in the next verse" (p. 45).

Specifically Paul says, "I do not permit a woman to teach or to have authority over a man." Some have even said that the apostle's prohibition excludes women from teaching Sunday school classes. But he is talking about the public assemblies of the church. Paul speaks appreciatively of the fact that Timothy himself had been taught the right way by his godly mother and grandmother (2 Tim 1:5; 3:15). The apostle also writes to Titus that the older women are to train the younger (Titus 2:3, 4). Women have always carried the major responsibility for teaching small children, in both home and church school. And what could we have done without them!

The word *silent* translates *en hēsychia*, exactly the same phrase that is rendered "in quietness" in v.11. Quietness is an important Christian virtue. Paul was especially opposed to confusion in the public services of the church (1 Cor 14:33).

13,14 The apostle adds that the wife's role of submission to her husband is inherent in creation. Adam was created first, and then Eve.

The story is told in Genesis 2:21–23. The Lord God made Eve from a rib taken from Adam. Matthew Henry pointed out beautifully the implication of this description: "The woman ... was not made out of his head to rule over him, nor out of his feet to be trampled upon by him, but out of his side to be equal with him ... and near his heart to be beloved" (*Commentary*, 1:20). This expresses perfectly the ideal of a happy married life. The husband who has this concept will usually find his wife eager to please him.

Paul makes one further point. It was the woman who was deceived by Satan and who disobeyed God (cf. Gen 3:1–6). Since she was so easily deceived, she should not be trusted as a teacher.

15 This verse is obviously a difficult one to explain. Thousands of godly women have *not* been "kept safe through childbirth."

The passage literally reads, "But she will be saved through the childbirth, if they continue in faith. . . ." The verb *sōzō* ("save") is used in the NT for both physical healing (mostly in the Gospels) and spiritual salvation (mostly in the Epistles). Perhaps it carries both connotations here. The wife may find both physical health and a higher spiritual state through the experience of bearing and rearing children. "They" probably means "women" (so NIV), though it could possibly refer to the husband and wife.

Three interpretations of this verse have been suggested. The first emphasizes the use of the definite article with "childbirth" and suggests that the reference is to the birth of Christ, through whom salvation has come to the world. Lock, Ellicott, and some other good modern commentators favor this meaning, but Bernard dismisses it almost with scorn: "The interpretation must be counted among those pious and ingenious flights of fancy, which so often mislead the commentator on Holy Scripture" (pp. 49, 50).

A second interpretation is closely related to this. It connects the statement here with Genesis 3:15. The seed of the woman would crush the serpent's head and bring salvation to mankind.

The third interpretation is suggested by Vine. He writes, "By means of begetting children and so fulfilling the design appointed for her through acceptance of motherhood ... she would be saved from becoming a prey to the social evils of the time and would take her part in the maintenance of the testimony of the local church" (p. 47). This fits best with the context and the main emphasis of this Epistle.

Notes

9 Of σωφροσύνη (*sōphrosynē*, "propriety"), found in the NT only three times (here, v.15, and Acts 26:25), Trench writes, "It is that habitual inner self-government, with its constant rein on all the passions and desires, which would hinder the temptation to this from arising, or at all events from arising in such strength as should overbear the checks and barriers which *aidōs* opposed to it" (p. 72).

The word πλέγμα (*plegma*, "braided") is found only here (in the NT). But a cognate term is used with τριχῶν (*trichōn*, "hair") in 1 Peter 3:3.

12 "To have authority over" is αὐθεντεῖν (*authentein*, only here in the NT). It comes from αὐθέντης (*authentēs*, "one who acts on his own authority").

13 "Formed" is the Greek verb πλάσσω (*plassō*, only here and in Rom 9:20). It signifies to form or mold. The cognate adjective πλαστός (*plastos*) gives us our word "plastic"—something molded.

---

4. Overseers

3:1–7

¹Here is a trustworthy saying: If anyone sets his heart on being an overseer, he desires a noble task. ²Now the overseer must be above reproach, the husband of but one wife, temperate, self-controlled, respectable, hospitable, able to teach, ³not given to much wine, not violent but gentle, not quarrelsome, not a lover of money. ⁴He must manage his own family well and see that his children obey him with proper respect. ⁵(If anyone does not know how to manage his own family, how can he take care of God's church?) ⁶He must not be a recent convert, or he may become conceited and fall under the same judgment as the devil. ⁷He must also have a good reputation with outsiders, so that he will not fall into disgrace and into the devil's trap.

This paragraph gives the qualifications for overseers in the church. The requirements are spelled out specifically. For a list similar to that of vv.2–7, see Titus 1:6–9.

1 "Sets his heart on" may well be translated "aspires to" (*oregetai*). "Being an overseer" is one word, *episkopē*. It comes from *episkopeō*, which literally means "look upon," and so "oversee, care for." So the concrete noun *episkopos* (v.2) means "overseer" and the abstract noun *episkopē* (v.1) means "office of overseer" (cf. KJV, "the office of a bishop"). The word is used in this sense in one other passage in the NT (Acts 1:20).

The apostle says that one who aspires to the position of overseer in the church "desires a noble task"—and, we might add, a place of heavy responsibility. One needs to be sure that such a desire is not an expression of carnal pride, but that rather it reflects a deep consecration to the work of the church.

2 As we have just noted, *episkopos* means "overseer." It is translated that way in KJV in Acts 20:28. Elsewhere in the NT it is rendered "bishop" (Phil 1:1; 1 Tim 3:2; Titus 1:7; 1 Peter 2:25). Our word *episcopal*, of course, comes from it. But Titus 1:6, 7 seems to suggest that "elder" (*presbyteros*) and "bishop" (*episkopos*) were the same person. An even more definite proof of this is found in Acts 20. In v.17 we read that Paul sent for the "elders" (*presbyterous*) of the church at Ephesus. But in v.28 he calls them "overseers" (*episkopous*). So there were several bishop-elders in each local church. That suggests something far different from the diocesan "bishop" in the ecclesiastical struc-

ture of our day. So it seems best to translate *episkopos* as "overseer" rather than "bishop."

Since the subject of ecclesiastical organization bulks larger in the pastoral Epistles than anywhere else in the NT (see Introduction), it has called for rather extended treatment. Philippians 1:1 mentions the "overseers" (*episkopoi;* KJV, "bishops") and "deacons" (*diakonoi*) in the church at Philippi. The fact that "elders" are not mentioned gives added support to the evidence of the Pastorals that the same leaders in each local congregation were called both elders and overseers.

Now we come to the specific qualifications of an "overseer." Fifteen are listed in vv.2-7. The first is that he must be "above reproach." This is one word in the Greek, the double compound *anepilēmptos* (only here and in 5:7; 6:14). Literally it means "not to be laid hold of." N.J.D. White says it describes "one against whom it is impossible to bring any charge of wrong doing such as could stand impartial examination" (EGT, 4:111). Because it stands at the head of the list, Lock suggests that it means: "Not liable to criticism as he would be if he failed in any of these qualities" (p. 36).

The second qualification is that he must be "the husband of but one wife." The same was required of deacons (v.12). Some have interpreted this as meaning "married only once." By the end of the second century this interpretation was being promulgated, under the influence of an asceticism that led to clerical celibacy in the Roman Catholic Church. Bernard defends this view emphatically. He writes of the phrase here: "It excludes from ecclesiastical position those who have been married more than once" (p. 52). But most commentators agree that it means monogamy—only one wife at one time—and that the overseer must be completely faithful to his wife.

The third qualification is "temperate." The word *nēphalios* in classical Greek meant "not mixed with wine." In later writers it came to have the broader sense of "temperate" or "sober." One of a considerable number of words found only in the pastoral Epistles, it occurs again in v.11 and in Titus 2:2.

The fourth qualification is "self-controlled." *Sōphronos* (in the NT only here and in Titus 1:8; 2:2, 5) means "of sound mind." So it carried the sense of "self-controlled" or "sober-minded."

Fifth in the list is "respectable." This is the same word, *kosmios,* that is translated "modestly"—literally, "with modesty" in 2:9. "Of good behaviour" (KJV) is obviously a rather free rendering. The basic meaning of the word is "orderly." But Greek writers used it in the sense of "respectable" or "honorable." That fits well here.

The sixth qualification is "hospitable." The word *philoxenos* (found again in Titus 1:8; 1 Peter 4:9) literally means "loving strangers." Christians traveling in the first century avoided the public inns with their pagan atmosphere and food that had already been offered to idols (cf. 1 Cor 8). So they would seek out a Christian home in which to stop for the night. A valuable by-product was that believers from widely scattered areas would get to know each other, thus cementing lines of fellowship. So hospitality was an important Christian virtue in that day. Even in our modern hotel-motel age it can have its place.

The seventh item is "able to teach" (*didaktikos,* "didactic," only here and in 2 Tim 2:24). Vine makes this helpful comment: "Not merely a readiness to teach is implied, but the spiritual power to do so as the outcome of prayerful meditation in the Word of God and the practical application of its truth to oneself" (p. 51).

3 The eighth qualification for an overseer is that he must not be "given to much wine." The last four words represent one word in Greek, *paroinos* (literally, "beside wine"), "lingering with the cup." It is one of several terms found only here and in the parallel list in Titus (1:7). Aristotle's use of this and related words suggests that it meant "tipsy" or "rowdy." It is a sad commentary on the culture of that day that such a warning would have to be given concerning church overseers.

Ninth on the list is "not violent"—literally, "not a striker" (*mē plēktēn*, only here and in Titus 1:7). The person who is given to wine is apt to become involved in drunken brawls.

This verse has four negative items and one positive one, "gentle" (*epieikēs*, five times in the NT). This is the word that Matthew Arnold translated "sweet reasonableness." E.K. Simpson says: "*Epieikēs* defies exact translation ... *Gracious, kindly, forbearing, considerate, magnanimous, genial,* all approximate to its idea" (p. 51).

The eleventh item is "not quarrelsome" (*amachos*, only here and in Titus 3:2). The word literally means "abstaining from fighting" or "noncombatant." Here it is used in the metaphorical sense of "not contentious." A contentious leader is a sad feature in any church.

Number twelve is "not a lover of money"—all one word in the Greek, *aphilargyros* (only here and in Heb 13:5). The love of money (cf. 6:10) is one of the greatest dangers confronting every Christian worker. One who finds that he can make big money in part-time secular work is apt to be diverted from an effective ministry.

4,5 Verses two and three list a dozen qualifications for overseers (most of them a single adjective in Greek). Now we come to three more that are stated at greater length. The first of these covers two verses. The overseer of the church must be one who can "manage his own family well." His children must be obedient and respectful. This implies that the overseer would normally be a married man.

In v.5 Paul makes the logical point, in the form of a question, that if one cannot "manage" (KJV, "rule") his own house, he should not be expected to take proper care of God's church. It is an argument from the lesser to the greater, and the case is clear and incontrovertible. (In this passage "church" clearly means a local congregation.)

6 The overseer must not be "a recent convert" (KJV, "a novice"). The Greek word (only here in the NT) is *neophytos* ("neophyte") an adjective that literally means "newly planted." Here it is used metaphorically, as a substantive, for a new convert.

The reason for this prohibition is spelled out in the rest of the verse. There is danger that such a person might "become conceited." This is the verb *typhoō* (only here and in 6:4; 2 Tim 3:4). It comes from *typhos*, "smoke," and so literally means to "wrap in smoke." But in the NT it is always used metaphorically in the passive in the sense of being "puffed up" with pride.

When this happens, the person will "fall under the same judgment as the devil." We believe that only God is uncreated and so it is he who created all life. But we also know (Gen 1) that God pronounced "good" all that he created. It follows, then, that Satan was created by God as a good creature. It is generally assumed that Satan is a fallen archangel, and that the cause of his fall was pride. All proud people are subject to the same judgment as he.

7 The fifteenth and last qualification of an overseer that is given here is that he must "have a good reputation with outsiders"—literally, "a good testimony from those outside." When a leader in the church has a bad reputation in the community, it often brings irreparable damage to the local congregation and indeed to the entire cause of Christ.

A church leader must have a good reputation "so that he will not fall into disgrace and into the devil's trap"—literally, "the snare of the devil." This could be taken as the snare in which the devil was caught, that is, pride. But most commentators feel that it means the snare or trap which the devil lays for unsuspecting Christians. This is clearly the meaning in 2 Timothy 2:26—"escape from the trap of the devil, who has taken them captive to do his will."

Paul's careful concern for the right choice of leaders in the church, and the extensive qualifications listed here, should serve as guidelines for those who are charged with the responsibility of such selection today. Attention at this point could save much grief.

Notes

1 The familiar formula "Here is a trustworthy saying" (cf. 1:15) was applied by Chrysostom and others—both ancient and modern—to the end of the previous chapter. But probably NIV is correct in indicating that it applies to what follows (the last part of v.1).

2 For "the husband of but one wife"—lit., "a husband of one wife"—Lock lists no fewer than five distinct interpretations: a bishop must (1) be a married man; (2) not be a polygamist; (3) be a faithful husband, having no mistress or concubine; (4) not divorce one wife and marry another; (5) not marry a second time after the wife's death. He properly rejects the first and last, but supports the other three. The word *but* is added before "one wife" in NIV apparently to avoid the possibility of taking the passage as condemning all second marriages, but it may be doubted whether it succeeds in doing this.

3 The thoughtful reader who compares the KJV rendering of this verse with NIV or NASB will wonder at the wide divergence. The reason is that KJV is based on TR, a Greek text derived from a few late MSS of the Middle Ages, while modern translations are from the Textus Criticus, which is formed from the earliest Gr. MSS that come from the third, fourth, and succeeding centuries.

4,5 "Family" is literally "house," (*oikos*), as in KJV. But here, as in many other places, it clearly means "household." In those days it often included a man's servants, as well as his wife and children.

4 For the meaning of σεμνότης (*semnotēs*, "respect"), see the comments on 2:2.

6,7 Bernard (pp. 56, 57) takes "the devil"—τοῦ διαβόλου (*tou diabolou*, "the slanderer")—as referring to a human accuser or slanderer, who passes judgment on the overseer or catches him in a trap. But παγὶς τοῦ διαβόλου (*pagis tou diabolou*) in 2 Tim 2:26 clearly refers to the "snare of the devil" and should be taken that way here.

5. Deacons

3:8-13

8Deacons, likewise, are to be men worthy of respect, sincere, not indulging in much wine, and not pursuing dishonest gain. 9They must keep hold of the deep truths of the faith with a clear conscience. 10They must first be tested; and then if there is nothing against them, let them serve as deacons.

11In the same way, their wives are to be women worthy of respect, not malicious talkers but temperate and trustworthy in everything.

12A deacon must be the husband of but one wife and must manage his children and his household well. 13Those who have served well gain an excellent standing and great assurance in their faith in Christ Jesus.

In vv.1–7 we find the qualifications for the overseers of the church. Here in vv.8–13 are the qualifications for deacons.

8 The word *deacon* comes from the Greek *diakonos*. The simple meaning of this word is "servant," and it is used that way many times in the Gospels. Specifically, it was used by Josephus and other writers of that period for those who wait on tables.

This leads us to chapter 6 of Acts. The apostles as overseers of the church in Jerusalem did not have time to take care of the material needs of the poorer members, such as the widows. They said, "It would not be right for us to neglect the ministry of the word of God in order to wait on tables" (Acts 6:2, where the verb *diakoneō* is used). So the church chose seven men to assume this responsibility, while the apostles gave their attention to public "prayer and the ministry of the word" (v.4). Although the term *deacon* is not used in this connection, it would seem that these men were the forerunners of the deacons in the church.

The term is first used in a technical sense in Philippians 1:1. That Epistle is addressed to "all the saints in Christ Jesus at Philippi, together with the overseers and deacons"— those in charge of the spiritual life of the church and those who supervised its material affairs. This distinction of two groups with differing functions is prominent in the pastoral Epistles.

Paul says that the deacons, like the overseers, are to be men "worthy of respect." This is one word in Greek, the adjective *semnos* (cf. the noun *semnotēs* in 2:2 and 3:4). Vine says of this term: "No English word exactly conveys the meaning of *semnos*, which combines the thoughts both of gravity and dignity," or, as Moule points out, "both of seriousness of purpose and self-respect in conduct" (p. 55).

In the second place, the deacons are to be "sincere"—literally, "not double-tongued." The adjective *dilogos* (only here in the NT) has the idea of saying something twice, with the bad connotation of saying one thing to one person and something else to another. Bunyan typically speaks in *Pilgrim's Progress* of "the parson of our parish, Mr. Two-Tongues." Metaphorically, the word means "insincere," and "not insincere" becomes "sincere."

The third qualification is "not indulging in much wine." This is a longer and stronger expression than that found in v.3 in relation to the overseers.

Item number four is "not pursuing dishonest gain" (*mē aischrokerdeis*, only here and in Titus 1:7). The adjective is compounded of *aischros* ("base, shameful") and *kerdos* ("gain") and so means "fond of dishonest gain."

9 KJV gives a literal rendering of this verse: "Holding the mystery of the faith in a pure conscience." The word *mystērion* was used in that day for a secret that was unknown to the masses but disclosed to the initiated. In the NT it signifies the secret of salvation through Jesus Christ, which is revealed by the Holy Spirit to all who will believe. Today the word *mystery* implies knowledge withheld; in the Bible it indicates truth revealed. That is the reason for the change in translation.

Probably "the faith" is to be taken in an objective sense, referring to the truths of the Christian religion, rather than as subjective, having to do with one's personal faith in Christ.

This Epistle has a strong emphasis on a pure conscience as well as a pure faith. We have already had the expression "a good conscience" twice (1:5, 19). Vine writes, "A pure conscience is that which has been cleansed by the blood of Christ, Heb. 10:22, and is exercised to avoid offence towards God and men, Acts 24:16" (p. 56).

10 Deacons "must first be tested" (KJV, "proved"). The verb *dokimazō* has three stages: (1) test, (2) prove by testing; (3) approve as the result of testing. Perhaps all three are in mind here. Before men were accepted as deacons they had to prove themselves before the community. Then they could serve as deacons, "if there is nothing against them"— literally, "being not called in" (*anenklētos,* "not called to account," and so, "irreproach-able").

11 In the Greek language the same word, *gynē,* is used for "woman" and "wife." Since this single word is found here for "their wives," there are three possible interpretations as to what group Paul is talking about.

NIV follows KJV in assuming that these women were the wives of the deacons. The main argument against this is that the word for "their" is missing in the Greek. Yet Vine feels that this meaning is "probable."

Some have suggested that he is speaking of women in general. But the context of vv.8–12 would seem to rule this out.

White argues strongly that the reference is to deaconesses, of whom Phoebe (Rom 16:1) is an example (EGT, 4:115, 116). He would take these as a separate group of church officials. The same view is maintained by Bernard (pp. 58, 59) and Lock (pp. 40, 41). We know that there were deaconesses in the church in later centuries; but whether there was such an order in the first century is debatable.

Hendriksen takes somewhat of a mediating position. He writes,

> They are a group by themselves, not just the wives of the deacons nor *all* the women who belong to the church. . . . On the other hand, the fact that no special and separate paragraph is used in describing their necessary qualifications, but that these are simply wedged in between the stipulated requirements for deacons, with equal clarity indi-cates that these women are not to be regarded as constituting a third order in the church, the office of 'deaconesses,' on a par with and endowed with authority equal to that of deacons (pp. 132, 133).

In spite of this weight of scholarly opinion, we are still inclined to favor the idea that the reference is to "their wives." Paul talks about the qualifications of the deacons in vv.8–10 and again in vv.12, 13. It would seem natural to assume that he is talking about their wives in v.11.

He says that these women—whoever they are—must, "in the same way" as the dea-cons, be "worthy of respect." This is the same adjective (*semna,* fem.) as in v.8 (masc.).

They are also not to be "malicious talkers." This is one word in Greek, the adjective *diabolos,* which means "slanderous, accusing falsely." It can well be translated here as "slanderous." But most versions take it as a substantive (e.g., "slanderers," KJV). This note was a needed warning in the early church, and is still needed today.

For a discussion of "temperate," see the comments on v.2. It was necessary that the wives as well as the husbands have this virtue.

"Trustworthy in everything" is a comprehensive requirement. Church workers must not be lax in taking care of their assigned duties.

12 Now Paul returns to the specific qualifications of deacons. He says that the deacon, like the overseer (v.2), must be the husband of one wife. He must also "manage his children and his household well" (cf. v.4). The Greek word for "household" (*oikos*) is the same as that translated "family" in v.4.

13 Those who serve well in their assigned duties in the church are gaining (present tense) for themselves (*heautois*) "an excellent standing" (KJV, "a good degree"). The noun *bathmos* (only here in the NT) literally means "a step," and so metaphorically "standing" or "rank." Some think this suggests promotion to a higher rank (e.g., overseer). Others think it means great respect in the eyes of the church. Still others would relate it to good standing in God's sight. Probably the best interpretation is a combination of the last two.

"Great assurance" in relation to men or in relation to God? Again, why not both? Often a both/and interpretation is more reasonable than an either/or, and is certainly more fruitful. Christian workers should have "an excellent standing and great assurance" in relation to both God and their fellowmen.

Notes

8 William Barclay (*More New Testament Words* [New York: Harper, 1958], pp. 144, 145) writes, "*Semnos* is the word which describes the man who carries himself towards other men with a combination of dignified independence and kindly consideration.... The Christian should be *semnos*; he should ever display in his life the majesty of Christian living."

11 *Diabolos*, usually with the definite article, is tr. "devil" some thirty-five times in the NT. Only here (and possibly in vv.6, 7; see comments there) and in 2 Tim 3:3 and Titus 2:3 is it used of human beings as slanderers. Judas is called "a devil" in John 6:70.

13 The noun παρρησία (*parrēsia*) first meant "freedom or plainness of speech." Then it came to be used more generally for "courage, confidence, boldness." BAG tr. it here as "joyousness" or "confidence" toward God that is the result or accompaniment of faith (p. 636).

6. The Mystery of Godliness

3:14–16

14Although I hope to come to you soon, I am writing you these instructions so that, 15if I am delayed, you will know how people ought to conduct themselves in God's household which is the church of the living God, the pillar and foundation of the truth. 16Beyond all question, the mystery of godliness is great:

> He appeared in a body,
> was vindicated by the Spirit,
> was seen by angels,
> was preached among the nations,
> was believed on in the world,
> was taken up in glory.

14,15 Paul was hoping to visit Timothy soon. But just in case he was delayed, he was writing to his young associate so that Timothy might know "how people ought to conduct themselves in God's household." The KJV rendering "how thou oughtest to behave thyself" is out of keeping with the context. The apostle is laying down rules for church members and their leaders. This is a summary of what we find in chapters 2, 3.

"The house of God" (KJV) might well be taken by readers as meaning a church building; so "God's household" is a more adequate translation. This is "the church of the living God." The language of v.5 suggests that the primary reference is to the local congregation, although the general church of Jesus Christ may also be in view.

This church is "the pillar and the foundation of the truth." The idea of "pillar" is that of support, which is further strengthened by "foundation" or mainstay (*hedraiōma*, only here in the NT). Taken together, these two terms emphasize the certainty and firmness of "the truth" that is revealed in God's Word. The meaning of this clause is well expressed by Lock: "Each local Church has it in its power to support and strengthen the truth by its witness to the faith and by the lives of its members" (p. 44).

16 "Beyond all question" (KJV, "without controversy") is *homologoumenōs*, "confessedly." Found only here in the NT, it may be translated "by common agreement" or "by common profession." The "mystery of godliness" is "the revealed secret of true religion, the mystery of Christianity, the Person of Christ" (Lock, p. 44). It is particularly the incarnate Christ who is revealed here in the striking credal statement that follows.

In KJV the first word of the creed is "God" (*theos*). But the oldest Greek MSS have *hos*, "he who" as the subject of "appeared." The verb (*phaneroō*) means, in the active voice, "make visible, clear, manifest, or known." The eternal Son of God, existing as pure spirit, was made visible, was manifested, in his incarnation. "Incarnation" is from the Latin and literally means "in flesh," which is exactly what the Greek has here (*en sarki*).

In the second place, Christ "was vindicated by the Spirit"; "the Redeemer's profound claims are vindicated on the basis of His Deity" (Simpson, p. 61). Christ's miracles, climaxing in his resurrection, were demonstrations of his deity, sure evidences that he was the sinless Son of God. (The word *vindicated* is *edikaiōthē*, usually tr. "justified.")

The third line of this credal hymn reads, "was seen by angels." This may refer to the fact that during his earthly ministry angels watched over him (Matt 4:11; Luke 22:43).

The fourth statement is that he "was preached among the nations." The Greek *ethnesin* literally means "nations" but is often translated "Gentiles" (KJV), as distinct from Jews. This preaching among the Gentiles took place, of course, after Christ's death. It will be noted that what was preached was not a theory or even a creed, but a Person. Paul declared, "We preach Christ" (1 Cor 1:23).

In the fifth place, he "was believed on in the world" (*kosmos*). This follows closely from the previous line, for the true preaching of Christ produces faith in him on the part of many hearers.

The last statement is that he "was taken up in glory." The same verb (*analambanō*) is used of Christ's ascension in Acts 1:2. This was the climax of his earthly ministry. Preaching Christ means preaching his life, death, resurrection, and ascension as the glorified Lord.

Notes

16 In the earliest Gr. MSS of the NT "God" is usually written in abbreviated form. Instead of θεός (*theos*) we find ΘC. This could easily be confused with the relative pronoun OC, meaning "who." Most scholars agree that the pronoun is more probably the original reading. But the meaning is much the same, as the antecedent could well be "God" (v.15). Even if it is taken as "Christ Jesus" (v.13), his deity is clearly implied here.

VI. Special Instructions to Timothy (4:1–16)

1. *False Ascetism*

4:1–5

> [1]The Spirit clearly says that in later times some will abandon the faith and follow deceiving spirits and things taught by demons. [2]Such teachings come through hypocritical liars, whose consciences have been seared as with a hot iron. [3]They forbid people to marry and order them to abstain from certain foods, which God created to be received with thanksgiving by those who believe and who know the truth. [4]For everything God created is good, and nothing is to be rejected if it is received with thanksgiving, [5]because it is consecrated by the word of God and prayer.

1 This chapter consists of special instructions given to Timothy on various subjects. Verses 1–5 discuss the matter of ascetic teachings.

The Holy Spirit says "clearly"—*rhētōs* means "expressly" or "explicitly"—that in later times some people will "abandon" the faith. The verb means "to withdraw." For this passage BAG gives "fall away, become apostate."

Instead of being led by the Holy Spirit, these apostates give their attention to deceiving spirits and the teaching of "demons." Since this last word occurs only here in the pastoral Epistles, we might pause to look at it. KJV has "devils," and British scholars still use this term (cf. NEB). But in the Greek there is a clear distinction between *daimonion* ("demon," often in the pl.) and *diabolos* ("devil," regularly in the sing.). The NT clearly teaches that there are many "demons" but only one "devil." The plural of *diabolos* occurs only in the Pastorals (1 Tim 3:11; 2 Tim 3:3; Titus 2:3), where it is used for human "slanderers."

The expression "in later times" is not as strong as the phrase "in the last days" (2 Tim 3:1). The conditions that Paul is discussing here evidently took place during his lifetime.

2 The apostle uses strong language in describing the teachers of the false doctrines he is about to mention. He declares that they are "hypocritical liars" (*en hypocrisei pseudologōn*, "speaking falsely in hypocrisy"). This implies that they know better. They have deliberately forsaken the faith. They are men whose consciences "have been seared as with a hot iron"—all one word in Greek: *kekaustēriasmenōn*, "branded with a red-hot iron." They have been "seared in their own conscience," so that they have become unfeeling about their willful wrongdoings. Some commentators, however, feel that the meaning is that they have been branded as sinners, as the slaves of Satan.

3 Paul mentions two of their false teachings: "They forbid people to marry and order them to abstain from certain foods." This ascetic emphasis crept into the church in the first century and was widely felt in the second century, under the influence of Gnosticism. The Gnostics taught that all matter is evil; only spirit is good. So all physical pleasure is sin. Holiness was identified with asceticism. This was the error that the Jewish sect of the Essenes had made, and it cropped up early in Christianity.

What these false teachers forgot is that marriage "is ordained by God," as we are reminded at weddings. God clearly established marriage as the normal thing in human society. Those who commend celibacy as being more holy or religious are promoting the heresy of Gnosticism, not the teaching of the NT. Paul uses powerful language (v.2) to describe those who forbid people to marry—as some still do.

The idea of abstaining from certain foods goes back, of course, to the Mosaic law. But Christ has freed us from the Law (Gal 5:1–6). We are no longer under its restrictions regarding certain kinds of food, "which God created to be received with thanksgiving by those who believe and who know the truth." Only those"whose faith is weak" avoid eating meat and restrict themselves to a vegetable diet (Rom 14:1, 2). In spite of this, some still advocate and practice vegetarianism in the name of Christianity. Paul deals much more severely with this heresy in 1 Timothy than he did in Romans. Evidently the false teaching of asceticism was spreading in the church and the apostle struck out forcefully against it as a negation of our freedom in Christ—which is true Christianity.

4,5 The simple fact is that "everything God created is good." This is an echo of the first chapter of Genesis, where the statement "God saw that it was good" occurs no fewer than five times (vv.10, 12, 18, 21, 25). It is true that vegetarianism may have prevailed before the flood (cf. Gen 2:9, 16), but God clearly told Noah that animals could be eaten as food, as well as vegetables and grains (Gen 9:3).

Paul declares that "nothing is to be rejected [*apobleton*, 'thrown away,' only here in NT] if it is received with thanksgiving." This perhaps underscores the importance of "offering thanks" always before we eat, and this is reinforced by v.5: "because it is consecrated by the word of God and prayer." The Greek for "consecrated" is *hagiazetai*, "made holy." Lock writes, "It becomes holy to the eater; not that it was unclean in itself, but that his scruples or thanklessness might make it so to him" (p. 48). "The word of God" may suggest the use of Scripture phrases when saying grace at the table. White thinks it may also mean "a scriptural prayer; a prayer in harmony with God's revealed truth" (EGT, 4:122).

2. *Superiority of the Spiritual*

4:6-10

> 6If you point these things out to the brothers, you will be a good minister of Christ Jesus, brought up in the truths of the faith and of the good teaching that you have followed. 7Have nothing to do with godless myths and old wives' tales; rather, train yourself to be godly. 8For physical training is of some value, but godliness has value for all things, holding promise for both the present life and the life to come.
> 9This is a trustworthy saying that deserves full acceptance 10(and for this we labor and strive), that we have put our hope in the living God, who is the Savior of all men, and especially of those who believe.

6 Paul tells Timothy that if he calls the attention of "the brothers" (believers) to these truths, he will be a good "minister" (*diakonos*, "servant," but probably carrying here the modern technical connotation of "minister"). To be "a good minister of Christ Jesus" should be the aim of every pastor today.

Timothy had been "brought up [*entrephomenos*, 'trained up' or 'nurtured,' only here in the NT] in the truths [*logois*, lit., 'words'] of the faith." His earliest training was in Judaism, but he had been converted as a young man to Christianity. He had "followed" its teachings. The Greek verb *parakoloutheo* comes from *akoloutheo*, "follow," and *para*, "beside." So it suggests that he had "closely followed" the teachings of the new religion.

7,8 "Godless myths and old wives' tales" is literally "profane and old-womanish myths." The second adjective, *graodes* (only here in the NT) means "characteristic of old women." The reference is to "tall tales" such as elderly women love to tell children. That is the way Paul describes the Jewish legends of his day (cf. Titus 1:14).

Instead of giving himself to these, Timothy is admonished: "Train yourself to be godly." The word for "train" (KJV, "exercise") is *gymnaze.* "Physical training" (KJV, "bodily exercise") rather clearly refers to athletic discipline. Some think that in view of the earlier verses ascetic discipline may also be included. But would the apostle assign any worth to it? The Greek word for "training" is *gymnasia,* from which we get "gymnasium."

Paul concedes that physical training "is of some value." KJV says "profiteth little," which is probably too derogatory. The Greek *pros oligon* could be translated "for a little time"—that is, for this life. "For all things" would then suggest "for all time," or forever. Literally, the passage says that bodily gymnastics are beneficial (*ōphelimos,* "useful, profitable") "for a little." This certainly does not mean that physical exercise is of no value. But spiritual exercise is far more important, for it has value for eternity—"holding promise for both the present life and the life to come."

9,10 Again we find the formula, "This is a trustworthy saying that deserves full acceptance" (cf. 1:15). The consensus of commentators is that this refers to the preceding statement (v.8). The NIV rendering follows the punctuation of UBS, which connects v.9 with v.10. This is the interpretation of NEB, which puts a colon at the end of v.9 and begins v.10 with a quotation mark. But even NEB follows most of the other versions in translating *hoti* ("that," after parenthesis in NIV) as "because." The NIV treatment of the first clause of v.10 (making it parenthetical) is unique. But this is perhaps logical if we connect v.9 with v.10.

"Labor" and "strive" are both strong terms in the Greek. The first verb (*kopiaō*) means "grow weary" and so in the NT "work with effort, toil." The second (*agōnizō,* "agonize") was used for competing in an athletic contest. So it meant "struggle" or "strive." Just as athletes exert what seems to be their last ounce of energy to win a race, so Paul was giving the ministry all he had.

God is "the Savior of all men, and especially of those who believe." This statement has provoked much discussion. In what sense is he the Savior of all men? To interpret this in terms of universal salvation would be contrary to the whole tenor of Scripture.

Hendriksen explains at considerable length how God is the Savior of all people in the general sense of watching over them and delivering them. But it seems best to adopt the more familiar interpretation that God is potentially the Savior of all men, because of Calvary, but actually the Savior of those who believe.

Notes

6 The best Gr. text, based on the earliest MSS, has "Christ Jesus" rather than "Jesus Christ." The order of these two words is much confused in the MSS, due in part to the custom of abbreviating them, using only the first and last letters. In the Gr. the last letters are the same and the first letters look more alike than in English.

9 For the last clause of this verse Hendriksen prefers, "as it holds promise of life both for the present and for the future" (p. 152).

10 "Suffer reproach" (KJV) has very little MS support in the Gr. It translates ὀνειδιζόμεθα (*oneidizometha*). But ἀγωνιζόμεθα (*agōnizometha,* "strive") is clearly the correct reading.

3. Pastoral Duties

4:11–16

11Command and teach these things. 12Don't let anyone look down on you because you are young, but set an example for the believers in speech, in life, in love, in faith and in purity. 13Until I come, devote yourself to the public reading of Scripture, to preaching and to teaching. 14Do not neglect your gift, which was given you through a prophetic message when the body of elders laid their hands on you. 15Be diligent in these matters; give yourself wholly to them, so that everyone may see your progress. 16Watch your life and doctrine closely. Persevere in them, because if you do, you will save both yourself and your hearers.

11 "Command" and "teach" are both in the present tense of continuous action. Timothy is to keep on doing these two things. He is to exercise his authority as pastor.

12 Timothy was urged to conduct himself in such a way that no one would look down in a condescending way on his youthfulness. The word for "youth" (KJV) is *neotēs*, "used of grown-up military age, extending to the 40th year" (Lock, p. 52). Timothy was probably about thirty years old at this time.

On the positive side, he was to be "an example." The word *typos* (cf. "type") meant "a figure, image" and then ethically "an example, pattern." Timothy was to present the proper image of the Christian and he was to be a pattern for other believers to follow. This is an awesome responsibility that one accepts on entering the ministry.

He was to be an example in "speech" (*logos*, "word"), in "life" (*anastrophē*, "manner of living," not "conversation," KJV), and in "love" (*agapē*), "faith" (*pistis*), and "purity" (*hagneia*, only here and in 5:2). These are all vital constituents of Christian living. Carelessness in any one of these areas can spell failure and even disaster.

13 Until Paul came, Timothy was to devote himself "to the public reading of Scripture." The Greek simply says "to the reading," but the NIV rendering is undoubtedly correct. The early church followed the example of the Jewish synagogue in publicly reading the Scriptures at every service.

He was also to give himself to "preaching" (*paraklēsis*, lit., "exhortation"). This is an important part of every pastor's duties. He must not only read the Word of God to his people but also exhort them to obey it.

The third important function of the pastoral ministry is "teaching" (*didaskalia*). The people need instruction in Christian living, and the pastor should give it to them.

14 Paul has some more advice to give his younger colleague: "Do not neglect your gift" (*charismatos*). The term *charisma* occurs sixteen times in Paul's Epistles and only once elsewhere in the NT (1 Peter 4:10). It comes from the root *charis*, "grace," and so means "*a gift of grace, a free gift,* especially of extraordinary operations of the Spirit in the apostolic church but including all spiritual graces and endowments" (A-S, pp. 479, 480).

The verb *ameleō*, "neglect," is not used elsewhere by Paul. It literally means to be careless about something. Bernard rightly observes: "To neglect God's gifts, whether of nature or of grace, is a sin" (p. 72).

This gift was "given you through a prophetic message"—literally, "through prophecy" (*prophēteia*)—when "the body of elders"—one word in Greek, *presbyterion*—"laid their hands on you." We are not told when or where this happened. Lock thinks that this

374

ceremony took place at Ephesus when Paul left Timothy there (p. 54). We find similar references in 1:18 and 2 Timothy 1:6.

15 "Be diligent" is *meleta*. The verb *meletaō* comes from *meletē*, "care." So it literally means "care for." It was used frequently by Greek writers of that period in the sense of "practice, cultivate, take pains with," and that is the meaning assigned to it in this passage by BAG. But it can also mean "think about, meditate upon" (cf. KJV), as it does in the only other place where it occurs in the NT, in a quotation from LXX (Acts 4:25; NIV, "plot"). Bernard prefers the translation "ponder these things" for our passage (p. 73).

There is a play on words here in the Greek that does not come through in English. In v.14 Paul says, "Do not neglect" (*amelei*, *melō* with *a*-negative). In v.15 he says, "Be diligent" (*meleta*). What he is saying is "Don't be careless about your gift, but be careful about your pastoral duties."

"Give yourself wholly to them" (also in KJV) is literally, "Be in these things" (*toutois isthi*). NASB puts it well: "Be *absorbed* in them." But NIV represents the thought accurately.

The purpose of this was that everybody might see Timothy's "progress." The term *prokopē* (only here and in Phil 1:12, 25) was "a favourite word in Stoic writers of a pupil's progress in philosophy" (Lock, p. 54). Timothy was to make progress in his own spiritual life and in his effectiveness in the ministry.

16 "Watch your life and doctrine closely." This is a good way of representing the Greek, which says, "Give attention to yourself and to the teaching." The first thing that every Christian worker must watch is himself, not only his outward life but also his inner thoughts and feelings. No matter how straight a person may be in his doctrine or how effective he may be in his teaching, if there is a flaw in his inner or outer life, it will ruin him. This is where many ministers have failed tragically. While he is watching over others, the pastor must keep an eye on himself.

"Persevere" is *epimene*, which literally means "stay" or "remain" and then figuratively (as here), "continue, persist in, persevere." Paul is saying to Timothy, "Stay right in there; keep on doing the things I have called your attention to."

By so doing, the pastor will save both himself and his hearers. For a soul-winner to save others and lose his own soul is an unmitigated tragedy. For one to save his own soul and have his hearers lost is no less tragic. We must give attention to both.

VII. Special Groups in the Church (5:1–6:2)

1. *The Older and the Younger*

5:1, 2

> [1]Do not rebuke an older man harshly, but exhort him as if he were your father. Treat younger men as brothers, [2]older women as mothers, and younger women as sisters, with absolute purity.

1 "Do not rebuke an older man harshly." The reason for adding the modifier "harshly" to "rebuke" (KJV) is that the verb *epiplēssō* (only here in the NT) literally means "strike at." Older men are to be treated with gentleness and kindness.

"Older man" is better than "elder" (KJV), since the latter term has a technical use in the pastoral Epistles for an overseer in the church. That "older man" is the correct meaning is shown by the parallel in v.2: "older women."

"Exhort" and "intreat" (KJV) are both correct translations of *parakaleō*, which also means "encourage." Goodspeed puts it well: "But appeal to him as to a father."

The "younger men" are to be treated as brothers. Grammatically, the verb *exhort* carries through to the end of v.2.

As a young man, Timothy was to treat the "older women" as mothers. Even today in that part of the world an elderly woman is greeted as "mother." Fortunate is the young pastor who has godly "mothers in Israel" in his congregation.

In relation to "younger women," a needed caution is added. They are to be treated as sisters—because the Christians are all one family in the Lord—but "with absolute purity." The pastor who does not heed this warning will soon be in trouble. BAG translates "with all propriety."

2. *Widows*

5:3–16

3Give proper recognition to widows who are left all alone. 4But if a widow has children or grandchildren, these should learn first of all to put their religion into practice by caring for their own family and so repaying their parents and grandparents, for this is pleasing to God. 5The widow who is all alone puts her hope in God and continues night and day to pray and to ask God for help. 6But the widow who lives for pleasure is dead even while she lives. 7Give the people these instructions, too, so that no one may be open to blame. 8If anyone does not provide for his relatives, and especially for his immediate family, he has denied the faith and is worse than an unbeliever.

9No widow may be put on the list of widows unless she is over sixty, has been faithful to her husband, 10and is well-known for her good deeds, such as bringing up children, showing hospitality, washing the feet of the saints, helping those in trouble and devoting herself to all kinds of good deeds.

11As for younger widows, do not put them on such a list. For when their sensual desires overcome their dedication to Christ, they want to marry. 12Thus they bring judgment on themselves, because they have broken their first pledge. 13Besides, they get into the habit of being idle and going about from house to house. And not only do they become idlers, but also gossips and busybodies, saying things they ought not to. 14So I counsel younger widows to marry, to have children, to manage their homes and to give the enemy no opportunity for slander. 15Some have in fact already turned away to follow Satan.

16If any woman who is a believer has widows in her family, she should help them and not let the church be burdened with them, so that the church can help those widows who are really in need.

3 "Give proper recognition to" is explicatory of "honour" (KJV). The verb *timaō* comes from the noun *timē*, which means first "price" or "value" and then "honor" or "reverence." In view of the following context, it could possibly mean "give proper compensation to" widows in real need. "Who are left all alone" is literally "who are really [*ontos*] widows." Goodspeed catches the thought: "Look after widows who are really dependent."

4 The case is different with widows who have children or "grandchildren" (*ekgona*, only here in the NT). In explanation of "nephews" in KJV, the *Oxford English Dictionary* (7:91) notes that in the seventeenth century (when KJV appeared) the term *nephew*

376

was commonly used for a grandson, though that meaning is now obsolete. Paul is saying here that if a widow has children or grandchildren, they are to take care of her.

"To put their religion into practice by caring for their own family" is literally "to show piety toward [*eusebein*] one's own household." This would be shown especially by "repaying"—literally, "to give" (*apodidonai*) "recompenses" (*amoibas*, only here in the NT)—to their "parents and grandparents" (*progonois*). This word (only here and in 2 Tim 1:3) may mean either parents or ancestors (literally, "born before")—hence the dual translation in the NIV. BAG translates the whole clause, "make a return to those who brought them up." This is "pleasing" (or, "acceptable") to God.

The Jewish synagogues gave careful attention to the care of their widows, and the early church followed that custom (Acts 6:1). This was due to the fact that in the culture of those days a widow could not ordinarily find any employment and so would need financial support. Today, with insurance income, social security, and job opportunities, the situation is very different. But each church should still see that no widow in its congregation is left destitute. Christian love demands this, and it is especially appropriate in view of the NT concept that all believers are one in Christ, fellow members of the family of God. We should care for each other.

5 This verse gives the characteristics of a true Christian widow. She is first identified as "the widow who is all alone"—literally, "the one who is a real widow and left all alone" (*memonōmenē*, perfect passive participle of *monoō*, "leave alone," only here in the NT). This means that she is childless.

Such a woman puts her hope in God, for she has no earthly hopes. So she "continues night and day to pray and ask God for help"—literally, "continues in her supplications and her prayers night and day." One is reminded of the widow Anna, who was eighty-four years old. We are told that "she never left the temple but worshiped night and day, fasting and praying" (Luke 2:37).

6 In contrast with that picture is this statement: "But the widow who lives for pleasure is dead even while she lives." The expression "lives for pleasure" is one word in Greek, the verb *spatalaō*. It means to live luxuriously or self-indulgently. White comments, "The modern term *fast*, in which the notion of prodigality and wastefulness is more prominent than that of sensual indulgence, exactly expresses the significance of this word" (EGT, 4:129).

7 Timothy is to "give the people these instructions." *Tauta parangelle* can have the stronger meaning, "command these things," but perhaps NIV is best. The purpose of the instruction is "that no one may be open to blame"—literally, "that they may be irreproachable" (*anepilēmptoi*).

8 Paul speaks strongly on this matter of caring for the needy. He declares that if anyone does not "provide for" (*pronoeō* lit., "think of beforehand," and so "take thought for") his own (relatives) and especially those of his own family, "he has denied the faith and is worse than an unbeliever." White observes, "The Christian who falls below the best heathen standard of family affection is the more blameworthy, since he has, what the heathen has not, the supreme example of love in Jesus Christ" (EGT, 4:129).

9,10 Having defined who a real widow is—one bereft of all relatives to take care of her—Paul now restricts the matter further. He gives instructions that no widow under sixty years of age should be "put on the list" (*katalegō*, only here in the NT, "enrolled"). It seems evident that an official list of widows was kept by each church and that only these received material support.

The further stipulation is made that she must have "been faithful to her husband"—literally, the "wife of one man." This is exactly the same sort of expression as is found in the qualifications for overseers (3:2) and deacons (3:12). As we noted there, only scholars with strong ascetic or ecclesiastical bias insist that this means "only once married." Verse 14 shows that widows were not forbidden to remarry.

To qualify for enrollment, a widow must also be well known for her good deeds. Several of these are spelled out. The first is "bringing up children"—one word in Greek, the verb *teknotropheō* (only here in the NT). This would most naturally refer to her own children but could include the care of orphans. The second is "showing hospitality." This is also one word in Greek, *xenodocheō* (only here in the NT)—literally, "welcome strangers" (cf. *philoxenos* in 3:2). The third item is "washing the feet of the saints." This was an important courtesy whenever guests entered a house. So this function belonged to that culture.

The verse closes with two more general duties: "helping those in trouble and devoting herself to all kinds of good deeds" (lit., "to every good deed"). This is the kind of a life that the widows were expected to live if they were going to be supported by the church. They were to be helpers, not troublemakers.

11,12 Regarding the widows under sixty years of age, Paul says, "Do not put them on such a list." This is all one word in Greek—*paraitou*, "refuse" or "reject." He goes on to tell why: they are overwhelmed by their feelings and want to marry. "Their sensual desires overcome their dedication" is all one word in Greek, *katastrēniasōsi* (only here in the NT). The verb means "become wanton against." Lock says it here suggests that they "grow physically restless and so restive against the limitations of Christian widowhood" (p. 60). In a similar vein, Bernard comments, "The metaphor is that of a young animal trying to free itself from the yoke, and becoming restive through its fulness of life" (p. 82).

If they do marry, they incur "judgment" (*krima*), or "condemnation" (but not "damnation," KJV). This is because they have "broken" (*ēthetēsan*, "disregarded" or "set aside") their first "pledge" (*pistis*, which may indicate "solemn promise" or "oath"). Lock thinks this means "the original impulse of faith which led her to join the widows; or more exactly 'the first troth' or 'promise of allegiance' made when she joined " (ibid.). It would seem that they promised to be devoted only to Christ.

13 Another risk with younger widows is that "they get into the habit of being"—one word, *manthanousi*, "learn" (to be)—"idle" or inactive. Instead of working, they go from house to house as "gossips"—the adjective *phlyaroi* (only here in the NT), "gossipy, foolish." In their visits to homes they pick up private matters and spread them abroad. This is always a snare to those who go from home to home or church to church.

"Busybodies" is the adjective *periergoi*, "paying attention to things that do not concern one, meddlesome" (BAG). The related verb, *periergazomai*, occurs in 1 Thessalonians 3:11.

As gossips and busybodies, these younger widows were "saying things they ought not to." This always happens when people talk too much. The consequences of this meddling in other people's business can be tragic.

14 In view of these dangers, Paul writes, "So I counsel [*boulomai*] younger widows"— "widows" is not in the Greek but probably is implied by the context—"to marry, to have children [*teknogonein*], to manage their homes" (*oikodespotein*). These last two compound verbs are found only here in the NT. Paul is dealing with new situations and he employs new terms.

The reason for the injunction to marry is that these younger women may "give the enemy no opportunity for slander." The word for "enemy" means "the adversary" (*antikeimenō*), one who opposes. It is generally agreed that the reference here is to a human adversary, not to Satan (who is mentioned in the next verse), although some think it may mean the devil (BAG).

The word for "slander" is *loidoria* (only here and 1 Peter 3:9). It is a strong term meaning "abuse" or "railing." Paul fears that the unfortunate conduct of younger widows might bring serious reproach on the church.

15 He goes on to say that some of them have already turned away to follow "Satan." This is a Hebrew word taken over into Greek and English. Since its literal meaning is "the adversary," it may be that the "enemy" (adversary) of the previous verse is Satan.

16 "Woman who is a believer" is one word in Greek, *pistē*, the feminine of the adjective *pistos*, "believing." "In her family" is not in the Greek, but of course is implied. The woman believer who has widows dependent on her (cf. NASB) "should help them and not let the church be burdened with them." This will free the church to help "those widows who are all alone—literally, "those who are really widows" (cf. v.3).

Notes

7 The adjective ἀνεπίλημπτοι (*anepilēmptoi*, "without blame") is found only in 1 Tim (see 3:2; 6:14). It is compounded of *a*-negative and the verb ἐπιλαμβάνω (*epilambanō*, "lay hold of"). It suggests that there should be nothing in the Christian's life that anyone can seize upon for censure.

8 Τὴν πίστιν (*tēn pistin*, "the faith") is used here in an objective sense, as elsewhere in the Pastorals, for Christianity or the body of Christian doctrine. This fact has been cited as an argument against Pauline authorship. But Paul uses this expression in the same way in his prison Epistles (Eph 4:5; Phil 1:27; Col 2:7).

16 KJV "man or woman" is based on the reading πιστὸς ἢ πιστή (*pistos ē pistē*, "believer [masc.] or believer [fem.]"), found in the late Gr. MSS. Most textual critics prefer the shorter reading πιστὴ (*pistē*, "believer" [fem.], א,A,C,), although the translators of NEB chose the longer reading, on the internal argument that this charge would not be laid on women alone (R.V.G. Tasker, *The Greek New Testament*, p. 441).

3. Elders

5:17–25

[17]The elders who direct the affairs of the church well are worthy of double honor, especially those whose work is preaching and teaching. [18]For the Scripture says, "Do not muzzle the ox while it is treading out the grain," and "The worker deserves his wages." [19]Do not entertain an accusation against an elder unless it is brought

by two or three witnesses. 20Those who sin are to be rebuked publicly, so that the others may take warning.

21I charge you, in the sight of God and Christ Jesus and the elect angels, to keep these instructions without partiality, and to do nothing out of favoritism.

22Do not be hasty in the laying on of hands, and do not share in the sins of others. Keep yourself pure.

23Stop drinking only water, and use a little wine because of your stomach and your frequent illnesses.

24The sins of some men are obvious, reaching the place of judgment ahead of them; the sins of others trail behind them. 25In the same way, good deeds are obvious, and even those that are not cannot be hidden.

17 In 5:1 *presbyteros* is clearly used in its literal sense of "older man." Here it is just as clearly used in its technical sense of "elder."

"Direct the affairs of the church" is literally "preside over" or "rule" (*proestōtes*). It was the responsibility of these earliest church officials (cf. Acts 14:23) to supervise the work of the local congregation.

Those who performed their functions well were worthy of "double honor." Since the word for "honor" (*timē*) was used in the sense of a price paid for something, it has been suggested that here it might be translated "honorarium" (BAG). But that raises the problem of "double"—double what was paid to the widows, or double what the other elders received? The NEB has: "reckoned worthy of a double stipend." Williams softens it a bit perhaps by translating it "considered as deserving twice the salary they get." Bernard's suggestion is helpful: "*Double* honour, i.e. *ample* provision, must be ensured for them; *diplē* is not to be taken as equivalent to 'double of the sum paid to widows,' or in any similiar way, but without any definite numerical reference" (p. 85). Perhaps we should allow both "honor" and "honorarium," as Paul may have intended both.

Highest honor is to be given to "those whose work is preaching and teaching"— literally, "those laboring in word and teaching." Some have found here a distinction between ruling elders and teaching elders. But this is doubtful. Probably it means that some elders gave themselves to preaching and teaching in addition to their regular duties. Such was the case with Stephen and Philip as deacons (Acts 6–8).

18 This verse, as well as the preceding discussion of support for widows (vv.3–16), suggests definitely that the "double honor" for elders was to be a financial remuneration. Quoting Deuteronomy 25:4 (as he does in 1 Cor 9:9) and Luke 10:7, Paul makes the point that the workman should receive compensation.

As usual, Paul quotes the OT as "Scripture." But does the introductory formula, "For the Scripture says," apply also to the second quotation? Bernard and others think not. But White (EGT, 4:135) seems to favor it, and Lock allows the possibility that this may be "the earliest instance of the Lord's words being quoted as "Scripture'" (p. 63).

19,20 Paul sounds a salutary warning: "Do not entertain [*paradechou*, 'receive, admit'] an accusation [*katēgorian*, tr. 'charge' in Titus 1:6] against an elder unless it is brought by two or three witnesses." The last part of this verse is almost a quotation from Deuteronomy 19:15 (cf. Deut 17:6). An accusation concerning an individual was not to be admitted as a charge against him unless it was supported by two or three witnesses. Paul appealed to this same principle in 2 Corinthians 13:1. Any accusation brought before him by the church at Corinth would have to be "established by the testimony of two or three witnesses."

The context suggests that "those who sin" (v.20)—literally, "are sinning" (present participle)—refers to presbyters. Such offenders Timothy is to rebuke "publicly"—literally, "before all" (*enōpion pantōn*). Does this mean before the whole church or only before the other elders? The next clause seems to favor the latter: "so that the others"— *hoi loipoi*, "the rest"—"may take warning"—literally, "may have fear" (*phobon echōsi*). "The rest" would normally be the other presbyters.

21 "Charge" is "solemnly charge" (*diamartyromai*, an intensive compound). The mention of "elect angels" is typical of Paul (cf. 3:16; 1 Cor 4:9).

Timothy is solemnly charged to keep these instructions without "partiality" (*prokrimatos*, "pre-judging, prejudice," only here in the NT). He is to do nothing out of "favoritism" (*prosklisin*, "inclination"). The verb *prosklinō* was used in the sense of to "make the scale incline one way or another." Timothy was not to permit his personal prejudices to tip the scales of justice.

22 What is meant by "the laying on of hands"? Lock and White feel that the context favors the idea of laying hands of reconciliation on repentant fallen elders when they are received back into the communion of the church. Eusebius (4th century) says of heretics who repented: "The ancient custom prevailed with regard to such that they should receive only the laying on of hands with prayers" (*Ecclesiastical History*, vii.2). Martin Dibelius and Hans Conzelmann adopt this interpretation in their volume on the pastoral Epistles in the new "Hermeneia" series.

On the other hand, J.N.D. Kelly in the "Harper's New Testament Commentaries" says, "The command *Don't be in a hurry to lay hands on anyone* almost certainly refers to ordination" (p. 127). This is the view of exegetes such as Chrysostom and Theophylact. Theodoret (5th century) wrote, "For one ought first to inquire into the life of him on whom hands are to be laid (or who is ordained), and so to invoke on him the grace of the Spirit" (quoted in Fairbairn, p. 223). Most recent versions and commentaries favor the interpretation that this passage prohibits hasty ordination. That fits in well with the main discussion of this chapter. And the laying on of hands in these epistles seems to be regularly associated with ordination (cf. 4:14; 2 Tim 1:7).

But what about "Do not share in the sins of others"? If Timothy ordained an elder, he thereby became in a measure a surety for this person's character and thus was implicated in any sins the man might commit. So the young superintendent is warned, "Keep yourself pure"—primarily by being cautious about ordaining candidates. Of course, the more general application to the whole of life may well be intended also.

23 Apparently for medicinal purposes, Timothy is told not to restrict himself to drinking water but to "use a little wine because of your stomach [Greek *stomachon*] and your frequent illnesses." The word for wine (*oinos*) is sometimes used in LXX for "must," or unfermented grape juice (Thayer, p. 442). Furthermore, it is generally agreed that the wine of Jesus' day was usually rather weak and, especially among the Jews, often diluted with water. Moreover, safe drinking water was not always readily available in those eastern countries.

24,25 The sins of some men are "obvious." The adjective *prodēlos* literally means "evident beforehand" (cf. KJV) and so "clearly evident." These sins precede a man to judgment. The less obvious sins of others "trail behind them"—but finally catch up! Similarly, good deeds are "obvious" (v.25, same Greek word), "and even those that are not cannot be hidden."

What does this have to do with avoiding hasty ordination? Apparently the sense is that some men's sins are so evident that there is no question about rejecting them as candidates. Their sins precede them to judgment—first Timothy's judgment and finally divine judgment. The sins of others do not show up so soon but careful investigation will discover them.

In the same way, the good deeds of qualified candidates will be easily seen. Those that seem less obvious will still appear on further search; they cannot be hidden.

4. Slaves

6:1, 2

> ¹All who are under the yoke of slavery should consider their masters worthy of full respect, so that God's name and our teaching may not be slandered. ²Those who have believing masters are not to show less respect for them because they are brothers. Instead, they are to serve them even better, because those who benefit from their service are believers, and dear to them. These are the things you are to teach and urge on them.

1 The word for "servants" (KJV) is *douloi*, which is correctly rendered "slaves." This is further emphasized by the phrase "under yoke" (*hypo zygon*). Putting it together, we have "all who are under the yoke of slavery."

It is claimed that half the population of the Roman Empire in the first century was composed of slaves. Several times in the NT we read of the conversion and baptism of entire households (e.g., Acts 16:15; 1 Cor 1:16). So there were many Christian slaves at that time. They were admonished to "consider their masters worthy of full respect [literally, 'all honor,' *pasēs timēs*] so that God's name and our teaching may not be slandered." Paul was always concerned that the conduct of Christians should be such as to bring glory to God and not reproach on his name and on the gospel.

2 Not all Christian slaves had "believing masters." But those who did were not "to show less respect for them"—all one word in Greek, *kataphroneitōsan*, "think down on, despise." Instead, they were to serve them even better, realizing that they were benefiting their brothers in Christ. This would give added incentive to their service. The masters were "dear to them" (*agapētoi*, "beloved").

Notes

1,2 The word used here for "masters" of slaves is not the usual one in the NT, κύριος (*kyrios*, "master," "lord"), which occurs about 750 times and refers to masters of slaves at least seven times (e.g., Eph 6:5, 9; Col 3:22; 4:1). Here it is δεσπότης (*despotēs*), which occurs only ten times in the NT. It is used five times for masters of slaves (1 Tim 6:1, 2; 2 Tim 2:21; Titus 2:9; 1 Peter 2:18). Otherwise it is used as a title for God or for Christ. Both words are very common in LXX, sometimes together (e.g., Gen 15:2, 8, "Lord God"), and Philo held them to be syononymous.

Should βλασφημῆται (*blasphēmētai*) be translated "slandered" or "blasphemed" (KJV)? The word means the former when directed toward man and the latter when directed toward God. Part of the problem is ἡ διδασκαλία (*hē didaskalia*), which literally means "the teaching." This can be taken as referring either to "our teaching" (NIV) or "*his* doctrine" (KJV). This is the problem of the ambiguity of the definite article in Greek. It could go either way.

Is "because they are brothers" nonrestrictive (KJV, ASV) or restrictive (RSV, NAB, JB, NEB, NASB)? The latter, making the relationship the possible cause of a lack of showing respect, seems to give the better sense.

In the last part of v.2 we cannot be certain whether πιστοί (*pistoi*) should be tr. "faithful" (KJV) or "believers" (NIV). Since it is the same word that is tr. "believing" (KJV, NIV) in the first part of the verse, the latter is preferable.

NIV ends this paragraph with "These are the things you are to teach and urge [παρακάλει, *parakalei*, 'exhort'] on them." (The last two words are not in the Gr.) UBS places this with the next paragraph. This arrangement is followed by RSV and NEB, making it a general command, rather than one directed particularly to slaves. Either way makes good sense.

VIII. The Danger of the Love of Money

6:3-10

3If anyone teaches false doctrines and does not agree to the sound instruction of our Lord Jesus Christ and to godly teaching, 4he is conceited and understands nothing. He has an unhealthy interest in controversies and arguments that result in envy, quarreling, malicious talk, evil suspicions 5and constant friction between men of corrupt mind, who have been robbed of the truth and who think that godliness is a means to financial gain.

6But godliness with contentment is great gain. 7For we brought nothing into the world, and we can take nothing out of it. 8But if we have food and clothing, we will be content with that. 9People who want to get rich fall into temptation and a trap and into many foolish and harmful desires that plunge men into ruin and destruction. 10For the love of money is a root of all kinds of evil. Some people, eager for money, have wandered from the faith and pierced themselves with many griefs.

3-5 "Teaches false doctrines" (KJV, "teach otherwise") is *heterodidaskalei* (cf. 1:3, the only other place where it occurs in the NT). "Agree to" is *proserchetai*, "come to." Elsewhere in the NT this verb always describes the movement of a body to a place. But in later Greek it came to be used for the assent or consent of the mind. "Sound" is a participle of the verb *hygiainō*, "be healthy," found (in the NT) only in the Pastorals in a metaphorical sense (cf. 1:10). "Instruction" is literally "words" (*logois*). But *logos* can be translated many ways.

Having defined the false teacher in v.3, Paul goes on to describe him in vv.4, 5. Bluntly he declares that such a person "is conceited and understands nothing." The word for "is conceited" (KJV, "proud") is *tetyphōtai*, the perfect passive (indicating a fixed state or condition) of *typhoomai* (cf. 3:6), "puffed up."

Although he understands nothing, the false teacher "has an unhealthy interest"—one word, *nosōn* (only here in the NT), "being sick" (mentally), "having a morbid craving for" (BAG)—"in controversies and arguments." The first of these two nouns is *zēteseis*. It basically means "investigation," and so in the pastoral Epistles (cf. 2 Tim 2:23; Titus 3:9) the investigation of religious and theological problems. But the context suggests that here it indicates "debates" or "disputes." "Arguments" is *logomachias* (only here in the NT), "word-battles," or disputes about words. White observes, "The heretic spoken of is a theorist merely; he wastes time in academic disputes; he does not take into account things as they actually are" (EGT, 4:141). A morbid craving for controversies and arguments is not the sign of good health, either psychologically or spiritually. Even well-intentioned theological discussions sometimes have a tendency to degenerate into mere word-battles or exercises in semantics.

"That result in" is literally "out of which come" (*ex hōn ginetai*). Five things are mentioned as the result of the disputes and arguments. The first two are "envy" and "quarreling" (*eris*, "strife"). These two also occur together in Romans 1:29 and Galatians 5:21. Envy always produces quarreling and strife.

"Malicious talk" is *blasphēmiai* (pl.). When directed against God, it means "blasphemy," but when directed against men, as here, it means "abusive speech" or "slander." "Evil suspicions" is *hyponoiai ponērai*. The first of these words (only here in the NT) means "surmisings." The combination could also be "evil conjectures" or "false suspicions" (BAG).

The fifth result is spelled out at considerable length, comprising all of v.5. "Constant friction" is *diaparatribai* (only here in the NT). It means "mutual irritations" or "incessant wranglings," and so "constant friction." This is found in the relations between "men of corrupt minds" (*diephtharmenōn anthrōpōn ton noun*). The compound form of this verb and the fact that it is a perfect passive participle suggest that it means "thoroughly corrupted or depraved." These men "have been robbed of the truth." This expresses well the force of the verb. White says that *apostereō* "conveys the notion of a person being deprived of a thing to which he has a right. . . . The truth was once theirs; they have disinherited themselves. The A.V., *destitute of*, does not assume that they ever had it" (EGT, 4:142). These men think that godliness is "a means to financial gain"—all one word in Greek, *porismos* (only here and v.6). It literally means "a procuring," and so "a means of gain."

6 Although "godliness," or "piety," should never be used as a means to secure financial gain, it is nevertheless true that "godliness with contentment is great gain." The word for "contentment" (*autarkeia*) was used in classical Greek in a philosophical sense for "a perfect condition of life, in which no aid or support is needed" (Thayer). In the only other passage in the NT where this word occurs (2 Cor 9:8) it is used objectively for "a sufficiency of the necessities of life." But here it is used subjectively for "a mind contented with its lot," and so "contentment" (EGT, 4:142). The closest parallel passage in thought is Philippians 4:11, where the adjective *autarkēs* is employed. Contentment is one of the greatest assets of life.

7,8 The reason we should be content is that "we brought nothing into the world, and we can take nothing out of it." That is, "nothing the world can give is any addition to the man himself" (White, EGT, 4:143).

So if we have food and clothing, we should be content with these things. The words for "food" (*diatrophas*) and "clothing" (*skepasmata*) are both plural and are found only here in the NT. The ordinary word for food in the NT is *trophē*. But the compound occurs in the literature of that time. The term *skepasma* comes from *skepazō*, the verb meaning "to cover." So it could mean both clothing and shelter. But Josephus uses it clearly in the sense of clothing alone (*Antiq.*, xv.9.2).

9 Those who "want," or are determined (*boulomenoi*), to be rich fall into temptation and "a trap" (*pagis*, "trap" or "snare") and into many desires that are "foolish" ("senseless") and "harmful." The adjective *blaberos* (only here in the NT) comes from the verb *blaptō*, which means "hurt" or "injure," and so this means "hurtful" or "injurious." "Plunge" is *bythizousi*, "plunge into the deep" (*bythos*), as a sinking ship in the sea (cf. Luke 5:7, the only other place where this verb occurs in the NT). Wrong desires plunge men into "ruin" (*olethron*) and "destruction" (*apōleian*). Both words mean "destruction," but the

second is somewhat stronger. Thayer says that it is used in particular for "the destruction which consists in the loss of eternal life," and so means "eternal misery" or "perdition" (cf. KJV). Lock observes, "The combination (found here only) is emphatic, 'loss for time and eternity'" (p. 69).

10 The first part of this verse is often quoted—though sometimes misquoted as "Money is the root of all evil." Rather, it is "the love of money" (*philargyria*) that is "a root" of "all kinds of evil"—literally, "all the evils." (The Greek has no definite article before "root.")

"Eager" is the present participle of the verb *oregō* (cf. 3:1)—always "reaching after, grasping at" money. This is the curse of too much of modern living. Some Christians, unfortunately, have been trapped in this way. They have "wandered" (*apeplanēthēsan*, "been led astray," only here and Mark 13:22) from the faith. In straying from the straight path, they have been caught in the thorn bushes and have "pierced themselves with many griefs" (*odynais*, only here and Rom 9:2). Another translation is: "They have pierced themselves to the heart with many pangs" (BAG).

Some have questioned the validity of the first part of this verse. But this proverbial statement echoes what had already been said by both Greek and Jewish writers. Fairbairn gives this helpful interpretation: "The sentiment is, that there is no kind of evil to which the love of money may not lead men, when once it fairly takes hold of them" (p. 239).

Notes

5 "Supposing that gain is godliness" (KJV) is not a correct translation. The noun εὐσέβειαν (*eusebeian*, "godliness") has the definite article, whereas πορισμόν (*porismon*, "gain") does not. The rule in Gr. grammar is that in such cases the noun that has the article is the subject.

The last clause of this verse in KJV is not found in the early Gr. MSS. It is almost certain that it was added by a later scribe, perhaps because he felt that it was needed to complete the grammatical sense of this very long sentence.

7 UBS has ὅτι (*hoti*, "because") at the beginning of the second clause. Though this reading is found in some of the very earliest MSS, it is given only a "C" rating because it does not seem to fit. This is one of the unsolved problems of textual criticism.

8 Bernard says that ἀρκεσθησόμεθα (*arkesthēsometha*, "we will be content") is "not imperatival, but future, with a slightly *authoritative* sense" (p. 96).

IX. Paul's Charge to Timothy

6:11-16

11But you, man of God, flee from all this, and pursue righteousness, godliness, faith, love, endurance and gentleness. 12Fight the good fight of the faith. Take hold of the eternal life to which you were called when you made your good confession in the presence of many witnesses. 13In the sight of God, who gives life to everything, and of Christ Jesus, who while testifying before Pontius Pilate made the good confession, I charge you 14to keep this commandment without spot or blame until the appearing of our Lord Jesus Christ, 15which God will bring about in his own time—God, the blessed and only Ruler, the King of kings and Lord of lords, 16who alone is immortal and who lives in unapproachable light, whom no one has seen or can see. To him be honor and might forever. Amen.

11 Paul begins by saying, "But you"—the "you" is emphatic (placed first) in the Greek. Then he addresses Timothy as "man of God." This is a common designation for prophets in the OT (e.g., 1 Sam 9:6; 1 Kings 12:22; 13:1). There has been considerable discussion as to whether it carries that connotation here or is used as a general title for all Christians. The only other place in the NT where it occurs is in 2 Timothy 3:17. Even there it is not absolutely clear whether it is used in a particular or general sense. J.N.D. Kelly says of the expression: "It connotes one who is in God's service, represents God and speaks in his name, and admirably fits one who is a pastor" (p. 139). That seems to be a reasonable interpretation.

"Pursue" (*diōke*) means "keep on pursuing," make these things your lifelong pursuit. Then Paul names six Christian virtues. Only the last two are different from KJV. We have already noted that *hypomonē* means "endurance," not "patience." *Praupathia* (only here in the NT) may equally well be translated "meekness" (KJV) or "gentleness."

12 "Fight the good fight" is *agōnizou ton kalon agōna*, "agonize the good agony." The related verb and noun come from the verb *agō*, which means "lead" or "bring." From this was derived the noun that we have here, *agōn*. It meant first "a gathering," especially for "games" (the sports events in the various Greek cities). Then it was used for the athletic competitions themselves. Similarly, the verb *agōnizō* meant "to enter a contest; contend in the gymnastic games"; and then more universally, "to contend with adversaries, fight" (Thayer). In the NT both words are used to describe the struggles of the Christian life. The background of the words suggests exerting every ounce of energy to win. Paul uses this same combination of words again in 2 Timothy 4:7.

Timothy is told to take hold of the eternal life to which he was called "when you made your good confession"—literally, "and professed the good profession" or "confessed the good confession" (*hōmologēsas tēn kalēn homologian*). But the repetition of a cognate noun after the verb is an ancient custom that is not idiomatic today. BAG suggests for this passage "made the good profession of faith." Probably the reference is to Timothy's confession of faith in Christ at the time of his baptism, when "many witnesses" were no doubt present.

13,14 Typically, Paul appeals to God, who "gives life to" (*zōogonountos*, "preserves alive") everything, and to Christ Jesus, "who while testifying before Pontius Pilate made the good confession." It is in their sight that he solemnly charges Timothy to keep "this commandment," literally, "the commandment" (*tēn entolēn*), possibly broader than the immediate context here. He is to keep it "without spot" (*aspilon*, "spotless, unblemished") "or blame" (*anepilēmpton*, lit. "without reproach"; cf. 3:2).

There has been much discussion as to whether these two adjectives modify "commandment" or "you." Elsewhere in the NT they are applied to persons, but here they are more closely attached to "commandment." Perhaps the best way is to try to combine the two ideas. White comments, "If Timothy 'keeps himself unspotted' (Jas. i.27) and 'without reproach,' the *entolē*, so far as he is concerned, will be maintained flawless" (EGT, 4:147).

Timothy is to keep the commandment until the "appearing" of our Lord Jesus Christ. *Epiphaneia*, "manifestation, appearance," occurs five times in the pastoral Epistles (cf. 2 Tim 1:10; 4:1, 8; Titus 2:13) and only once elsewhere in the NT (2 Thess 2:8, "splendor"). It is found in late Greek writers and in the inscriptions of that period for a visible manifestation of an invisible deity. It is also used frequently in the LXX for manifestations of God's glory. In 2 Timothy 1:10 it refers to the first coming of Christ. Elsewhere it is used only for the Second Coming.

This is one of three words in the NT for the return of our Lord. *Apokalypsis*, "revelation" ("apocalypse"), is found eighteen times, but not in the Pastorals. The most common word (24 times) is *parousia*, "presence," which also does not occur in the pastoral Epistles.

15,16 God will "bring about" (*deixei*, "show, exhibit, display") this Second Coming "in his own time." The use of this verb in John 2:18 (see NIV there) suggests that the return of Christ will be God's final proof to the world that Jesus is the Son of God and Savior.

The word for "time" (pl. here) is *kairos*, which means a fixed or definite time. In the NT it is often used eschatologically (in a prophetic sense) for God's appointed time, especially in relation to the Second Coming and the future judgment.

The last part of v.15 and all of v.16 form a doxology, such as we often find in Paul's Epistles (cf. 1:17; 2 Tim 4:18). Much of the language is derived from the OT (see note below).

God is first described as "the blessed and only Ruler." The last word is *dynastēs* (cf. "dynasty"). Elsewhere in the NT it is found only in Luke 1:52 ("rulers") and Acts 8:27 ("important official"). BAG translates it here as "Sovereign." It indicates a "possessor of power" (Cremer, *Lexicon*, p. 221).

The next two titles, "King of kings and Lord of lords," are applied to Christ twice in Revelation (17:14; 19:16). They are used for God in the OT (Dan 4:34, LXX; cf. Deut 10:17; Ps 136:3).

God alone is "immortal"—literally, "the only one having immortality" (*athanasia*, only here and 1 Cor 15:53, 54). The Greek word comes from *a*-negative and *thanatos*, "death." So it means "not subject to death."

The idea of immortality is not clearly expressed in the OT (see note below). But the NT teaching is that God alone has inherent immortality; ours is derived from him. It is in the resurrection that the true believer receives an immortal body (1 Cor 15:53), so that the whole man, body and soul, becomes immortal.

We are next told that God lives in light "unapproachable" (*aprositon*, only here in the NT). Philo uses this adjective for Mount Sinai when it was covered with God's glory (*de Vita Mosis* iii.2). Josephus, like Paul, applies it to God (*Antiq.* iii.5.1). The declaration is added here that no person has ever seen God or can see him. This truth is stated in the OT (Exod 33:20) and repeated in the New (John 1:18).

The doxology ends with the ascription: "To him be honor and might forever. Amen." It is typical of Paul to inject a doxology in the midst of a discussion (cf. 1:17; Rom 1:25; 11:36).

Notes

15,16 For a complete list of "Apostolic Doxologies" see B.F. Westcott, *The Epistle to the Hebrews*, pp. 464, 465. William Hendriksen (pp. 205, 206) gives a number of OT parallels to each phrase of this doxology.

16 Besides ἀθανασία (*athanasia*), the idea of "immortality" is expressed in the NT by ἀφθαρσία (*aphtharsia*, lit., "incorruption" and ἄφθαρτος (*aphthartos*, "incorruptible"). The adjective ἀθάνατος (*athanatos*, "immortal") is not found in the NT. All four words are used in the apocryphal books of LXX, but none of them occurs in the canonical books of LXX. This concept evidently developed in the inter-testamental period.

The word κράτος (*kratos*, "might") is common in NT doxologies (cf. 1 Peter 4:11; 5:11; Jude 25; Rev 1:6; 5:13).

X. Closing Instructions (6:17–21)

1. *Admonitions to the Wealthy*

6:17–19

> [17]Command those who are rich in this present world not to be arrogant nor to put their hope in wealth, which is so uncertain, but to put their hope in God, who richly provides us with everything for our enjoyment. [18]Command them to do good, to be rich in good deeds, and to be generous and willing to share. [19]In this way they will lay up treasure for themselves as a firm foundation for the coming age, so that they may take hold of the life that is truly life.

17 In vv.17–19 we find admonitions to the wealthy. Timothy is to command them not "to be arrogant" (*hypsēlophronein*, only here in the NT). This verb means "to be high-minded, proud, haughty." Bernard comments, "The pride of purse is not only vulgar, it is sinful" (p. 101). It is evident that in the wealthy city of Ephesus there were some church members who had money.

Timothy is to warn them not to put their hope in "wealth, which is so uncertain"— literally, "uncertainty" (*adēlotēti*, only here in the NT) "of riches" (*ploutou*). The uncertainty of wealth has been commented on from ancient times. It takes to itself wings and flies away (Prov 23:5). Even great fortunes have disappeared almost overnight.

One should instead put his hope in God (cf. Ps 52:7). He is the one who "richly provides us with everything for our enjoyment." The last word is *apolausin* (only here and Heb 11:25). This strong compound suggests that physical pleasure is in itself not sinful, but divinely ordained when sought within the structure of God's will. White rightly observes, "No good purpose is served by pretending that God did not intend us to enjoy the pleasurable sensations of physical life" (EGT, 4:149). Such an attitude comes from Gnosticism, not the NT (see 4:1–5).

18 The wealthy are to use their money "to do good" (*agathoergein*, only here and Acts 14:17); they are "to be rich in good deeds" (*en ergois kalois*). Wealth imposes a heavy responsibility on its possessor. The greater our means for doing good, the greater our obligation. What an opportunity wealthy people have for benefiting the needy!

So they are to be "generous" (*eumetadotos*, only here in the NT). This adjective is compounded of *eu*, "good, noble," and the verb *metadidōmi*, "give a share of." They are also to be "willing to share"—one word, the adjective *koinōnikos* (also only here). It comes from *koinōnia*, "fellowship, communion." It may therefore suggest that wealthy Christians should share their hearts as well as their money. This combination is what pleases God and imparts a double blessing to the recipient. Bernard comments, "A kind heart as well as a generous hand is demanded of the rich" (p. 102). Paul rejoiced that the generous Macedonians first gave themselves (2 Cor 8:1–5). It is easier to give money than to give ourselves, but love requires both.

19 By following these instructions the well-to-do will "lay up treasure" (*apothēsaurizontas*, only here in NT) "as a firm" (*kalon*, "good") "foundation for the coming age." This is in line with Jesus' teaching in Matthew 6:19–21: "Do not store up (*thēsaurizete*) for yourselves treasures (*thēsaurous*) on earth. . . . But store up for yourselves treasures in heaven. . . . For where your treasure (*thēsauros*) is, there your heart will be also." In contrast to the uncertainty of earthly riches (v.17) will be the "firm foundation" (v.19) of treasure laid up in heaven.

The purpose of this is that they may take hold of "the life that is truly life"—literally, "the truly life" (*tēs ontōs zōēs*). In place of *ontōs* ("really, truly") the late, medieval MSS have *aiōnou*, "eternal" (cf. KJV). We have already found *ontōs* used in connection with widows (5:3, 5, 16). There is no question but that it is the correct reading here.

2. Admonition to Timothy

6:20,21a

> [20]Timothy, guard what has been entrusted to your care. Turn away from godless chatter and the opposition of what is falsely called knowledge, [21]which some have professed and in so doing have wandered from the faith.

20 Paul concludes with a personal admonition to Timothy: "Guard what has been entrusted to your care" (*tēn parathēkēn phylaxon*, lit., "guard the deposit"). The noun *parathēkēn*—literally, "what is placed beside," and so a "deposit" or "trust"—occurs elsewhere in the NT only in 2 Timothy 1:12, 14. Here the context suggests that it means the sound doctrine that had been entrusted to Timothy. Simpson comments, "The deposit he is to guard can be nothing else than 'the revelation of Jesus Christ' in all its fulness" (p. 92).

Timothy is to turn away from "godless chatter" (*bebēlous kenophōnias*).The first word, an adjective, means "unhallowed, profane." The second, a noun, (only here and 2 Tim 2:16), compounded of *kenos*, means "empty" and *phōneō*, "talk aloud." So it means "empty talk, babbling." This is how Paul characterizes what the false teachers were saying.

"Opposition" is *antitheseis* (only here in the NT; cf. "antithesis"). The noun literally means "a placing over against," and so the plural here signifies "contrasts." It is true that the term in Paul's day commonly meant "opposition." But Lock is probably right in thinking that there the term (pl.) means "rival theses, sets of antitheses." These could have been "the Gnostic contrasts between the O.T. and the New, which found their fullest expression in Marcion's 'Antitheses' " or, "more probably" the arguments of Jews (p. 76). This is what Hort indicates when he suggests that it means "the endless contrasts of decisions, founded on endless distinctions, which played so large a part in the casuistry of the Scribes as interpreters of the Law" (*Judaistic Christianity*, p. 140).

The "opposition" consisted of "what is falsely called knowledge." "Falsely called" is the compound adjective *pseudōnymos* (cf. "pseudonymous"), found only here in the NT. It means "under a false name." "Knowledge" is *gnōsis*. We have already seen that several times in this Epistle Paul is combating the false teachings of Gnosticism—those who professed a superior *gnōsis* and believed that salvation comes to those who have this secret, intellectual treasure. But, as noted above, Paul may be here warning against the teachings of both Gnostics and Judaizers.

21 This is the kind of false gospel that some have "professed" (*epangellomenoi*, cf. 2:10).

In doing so they "have wandered" (aorist of *astocheō*, "miss the mark"), have deviated from the faith.

3. *Farewell*

6:21b

Grace be with you.

The closing benediction is "Grace be with thee" (KJV) in the late MSS. But most of the early MSS have "Grace be with you" (pl.). This would include the church along with Timothy.

2 TIMOTHY

Ralph Earle

Outline

     I. Salutation (1:1, 2)

    II. Thanksgiving (1:3–7)

        1. Timothy's Heritage (1:3–5)

        2. God's Gift to Timothy (1:6, 7)

   III. Suffering for the Gospel (1:8–18)

        1. Plea to Timothy (1:8)

        2. Paul's Testimony (1:9–12)

        3. Paul's Admonition (1:13, 14)

        4. Paul Deserted (1:15)

        5. Paul Befriended (1:16–18)

   IV. Three Symbols of the Christian (2:1–7)

        1. Introduction (2:1, 2)

        2. The Soldier (2:3, 4)

        3. The Athlete (2:5)

        4. The Farmer (2:6, 7)

     V. Suffering and Glory (2:8–13)

   VI. Contrasts in the Church (2:14–26)

        1. True and False Teachers (2:14–19)

        2. Noble and Ignoble Vessels (2:20, 21)

        3. The Kind and the Quarrelsome (2:22–26)

  VII. Characteristics of the Last Days (3:1–9)

        1. Love of Money and Pleasure (3:1–5)

        2. Depraved Living and Thinking (3:6–9)

 VIII. Persecution and Steadfastness (3:10–17)

        1. All Christians Persecuted (3:10–13)

        2. The Adequacy of Scripture (3:14–17)

   IX. Preach the Word (4:1–5)

    X. Paul's Final Testimony (4:6–8)

   XI. Paul's Final Plea (4:9–13)

  XII. Human Opposition and Divine Support (4:14–18)

 XIII. Closing Greetings, Farewell (4:19–22)

Note: For introduction to 2 Timothy, see pp. 341–347.

Text and Exposition

I. Salutation

1:1, 2

> ¹Paul, an apostle of Christ Jesus by the will of God, according to the promise of life that is in Christ Jesus,
>
> ²To Timothy, my dear son:
>
> Grace, mercy and peace from God the Father and Christ Jesus our Lord.

This salutation is very similar to the one found at the beginning of 1 Timothy. There Paul identifies himself as "an apostle of Christ Jesus by the command of God," here as "an apostle ... by the will of God." In this second Epistle he adds, "According to the promise of life that is in Christ Jesus." All spiritual life comes to us only "in Christ." And the more fully and consciously we live in him, the richer that life becomes.

In the first Epistle Paul greeted Timothy as "my true son in the faith." Here it is "my dear (*agapētos,* "beloved") son." Paul had a warm affection for his young convert and colleague. The greeting (v.2b) is exactly the same as that in 1 Timothy (see comments there). Everything we have comes to us from God through Christ.

Notes

---

1 Paul begins five of his Epistles (cf. 1 Cor 1:1; 2 Cor 1:1; Eph 1:1; Col 1:1) with this identification: "Paul, an apostle of Christ Jesus by the will of God" (Παῦλος ἀπόστολος Χριστοῦ Ἰησοῦ διὰ θελήματος θεοῦ, *Paulos apostolos Christou Iesou dia thelēmatos theou).* He was God's called man.

For the expression "promise of life" (ἐπαγγελίαν ζωῆς, *epangelian zōēs)* see 1 Tim 4:8.

II. Thanksgiving (1:3–7)

1. Timothy's Heritage

1:3–5

> ³I thank God, whom I serve, as my forefathers did, with a clear conscience, as night and day I constantly remember you in my prayers. ⁴Recalling your tears, I long to see you, so that I may be filled with joy. ⁵I have been reminded of your sincere faith, which first lived in your grandmother Lois and in your mother Eunice, and I am persuaded, now lives in you also.

3 In his first Epistle, before stopping to thank God, Paul talked to Timothy about the urgent task that faced him at Ephesus. But here he follows his regular custom (except in Galatians) of having a thanksgiving right after the greeting. Paul was serving God "as my forefathers did." He appreciated very much his religious heritage (cf. Acts 22:3; 24:14), and so today should all those who have been brought up in a Christian environment.

The apostle served God "with a clear"—literally, "clean" or "pure" (*kathara)* "conscience." (For this last word, see the note on 1 Tim 1:5.) Acts 23:1 implies that he had maintained a clear conscience even in his earlier years.

"Night and day" Paul was "constantly" (*adialeipton*, "unceasingly") remembering Timothy in his prayers (cf. Rom 1:10; 1 Thess 1:2; 3:6). He must have had a large heart to carry such a loving concern for so many people. It is true that letter writers of that period sometimes mentioned that they were always remembering their correspondents. But Paul put a new Christian dimension into these epistolary conventions.

4 "Long" is a strong compound verb, *epipotheo* (only here in the Pastorals; "long for, desire"). Recalling Timothy's tears, probably at the time of their last parting, Paul had an intense longing to see his son in the faith, that he might be "filled with joy." One of the fascinating aspects of Pauline studies is the very real humanity of this man of God. Paul was a stalwart soldier, but he had a tender heart.

5 "I have been reminded" is literally "having received a reminder" (*hypomnēsin labōn*). The noun *hypomnēsis* (only here and 2 Peter 1:13; 3:1), Bernard says, "is an act of the memory prompted from without" (p. 108). J.A. Bengel wrote, "Some external occasion, or a message from Timothy, had brought his faith to Paul's remembrance" (*Gnomon of NT*, 4:291).

"Sincere" is literally "unhypocritical" (*anhypokritou*). "Grandmother" is *mammē* (only here in the NT). In classical Greek it was a child's name for its mother, like our "mama." But in later Greek it means "grandmother." "Eunice" literally means "good victory." Timothy had a godly mother and grandmother.

Notes

---

3 Instead of Paul's usual verb εὐχαριστέω (*eucharisteō*, "I thank"), he begins his thanksgiving here and in 1 Tim 1:12 with χάριν ἔχω (*charin echō*, lit., "I have thanks"). This more literary expression (Simpson, p. 121) may well reflect the fact that Luke, the highly educated Greek physician, was his amanuensis (cf. Luke 17:9; Heb 12:28).

"I serve" is λατρεύω (*latreuō*), not used elsewhere in the Pastorals. In the NT it is used only for serving or worshiping God, and occurs most frequently in Hebrews.

Πρόγονοι (*progonoi*) occurs elsewhere in the NT only in 1 Tim 5:4, where it refers to one's immediate parents or grandparents. Here it is used in the more remote sense of "ancestors" ("forefathers"). It is an adjective meaning "born before."

For δεήσεσιν (*deēsesin*, "prayers") see the note on 1 Tim 2:1.

Bernard thinks that "night and day," which comes at the very end of the verse in Gr., goes with "longing to see you" at the beginning (in the Gr.) of v.4. Lock agrees, but White connects it with "remember." The Gr. allows either.

---

2. *God's Gift to Timothy*

1:6, 7

6For this reason I remind you to fan into flame the gift of God, which is in you through the laying on of my hands. 7For God did not give us a spirit of timidity, but a spirit of power, of love and of self-discipline.

6 Because of his sincere faith and spiritual heritage, Timothy is urged to "fan into flame" (*anazōpyrein*, only here in the NT) "the gift (*charisma*) of God, which is in you through the laying on of my hands" (see comments on 1 Tim 4:14). This would most naturally be taken as the time of Timothy's ordination. Concerning "gift," Bernard writes, "The *charisma* is not an ordinary gift of God's grace, such as every Christian may seek and obtain according to his need; but it is the special grace received by Timothy to fit him for his ministerial functions" (p. 109). (It should be remembered that *charisma* comes from *charis*, "grace.")

General Booth, the founder of the Salvation Army, once sent this message to those under him: "The tendency of fire is to go out; watch the fire on the altar of your heart." Anyone who has tended a fireplace fire knows that it needs to be stirred up occasionally.

7 Paul is fond of making a negative statement and then following it with three positive ideas, thus giving the introduction and three points of the outline for a textual sermon (cf. Rom 14:17). Here he says that God has not given us a spirit of "timidity" (*deilia*, "cowardice," only here in the NT), but rather a spirit of "power" (*dynamis*), of "love" (*agapē*) and of "self-discipline" (*sōphronismos*, "self-control," only here in the NT). This is a significant combination. The effective Christian worker must have the power of the Holy Spirit (cf. Acts 1:8). But that power must be expressed in a loving spirit, or it may do damage. And often the deciding factor between success and failure is the matter of self-discipline.

This is one of the several passages in these two Epistles that hint at Timothy's naturally timid nature. He had been brought up by his mother and grandmother, and now Paul was taking the place of a father to him.

III. Suffering for the Gospel (1:8-18)

1. *Plea to Timothy*

1:8

> [8]So do not be ashamed to testify about our Lord, or ashamed of me his prisoner. But join with me in suffering for the gospel, by the power of God.

8 In view of the spirit that has been divinely given to Timothy (cf. v.7), he is urged not to be ashamed "to testify about our Lord." Since "do not be ashamed" is in the aorist, not present, tense, Paul is not implying that Timothy was already guilty of doing this. But apparently he felt that his young colleague needed to have his courage strengthened.

Paul also urges Timothy not to be ashamed of "me his prisoner." The aged apostle was now a prisoner of the emperor (probably Nero) and facing almost certain death. Timothy must not be so fearful as to be ashamed to visit Paul in prison.

Instead, he is told: "Join with me in suffering"—all one word, *synkakopathēson* (only here and in 2:3). It is compounded of *patheō*, "suffer"; *kakos*, "bad"; and *syn*, "together." So it means "bear evil treatment along with," "take one's share of ill-treatment" (A-S).

Notes

8 "To testify about our Lord " is τὸ μαρτύριον τοῦ κυρίου ἡμῶν (*to martyrion tou kyriou hēmōn,* lit., "the testimony of our Lord"). White takes *tou kuriou* as subjective genitive: "*testimony borne by our Lord,* His words, His ethical and spiritual teaching" (EGT, 4:156). Bernard, however, prefers treating it as objective genitive: "*about* our Lord." Lock agrees. This is almost equivalent to "the gospel" (cf. Rom 1:16).

Lock says of συγκακοπάθησον (*synkakopathēson,* "join ... in suffering"): "not found in earlier writers; probably coined by St. Paul, who frequently coins compounds of σύν out of his deep sense of the close 'withness' of Christians with each other and with Christ" (p. 86). (TDNT, 5:937 does not give any earlier occurrence.) A-S has twelve pages treating words beginning with σύν (*syn,* "with"). A large proportion of these are found only in Paul's Epistles. He believed in "togetherness"! "For the gospel" means "for the sake of the gospel," that is, because of preaching it. It is only "by the power of God" that Timothy will be able to suffer for the gospel.

2. Paul's Testimony

1:9–12

> 9who has saved us and called us to a holy life—not because of anything we have done but because of his own purpose and grace. This grace was given us in Christ Jesus before the beginning of time, 10but it has now been revealed through the appearing of our Savior, Christ Jesus, who has destroyed death and has brought life and immortality to light through the gospel. 11And of this gospel I was appointed a herald and an apostle and a teacher. 12That is why I am suffering as I am. Yet I am not ashamed, because I know whom I have believed, and am convinced that he is able to guard what I have entrusted to him for that day.

9 Paul says that God "saved us and called us to a holy life"—or "with a holy calling" (*klēsei hagia*). Lock says of this phrase: "Mainly 'with a calling to be holy' ... but with the further thought of God's holiness which we have to imitate" (p. 87). We are called to holiness (1 Thess 4:7).

The next part of this verse is as Pauline as Romans—"not because of anything we have done" (lit., "not according to our works") "but because of his own purpose and grace ... given us in Christ Jesus." This is Paul's doctrine of grace that is central to his theology.

"Before the beginning of time" is literally "before times eternal" (*pro chronōn aiōn-iōn*). Lock comments, "The grace of God is embodied in Christ Jesus: we only gain it through union with Him, and it was given to Him by God long before we were born" (ibid.).

10 This grace has now been "revealed" (*phanerōtheisan,* "manifested"). Thayer says that *phaneroō* means "*to make manifest or visible or known* what has been hidden or unknown" (p. 648). How has this grace been made known? "Through the appearing of our Savior, Jesus Christ." The word "appearing" is *epiphaneia.* Elsewhere in the NT (2 Thess 2:8; 1 Tim 6:14; 2 Tim 4:1, 8; Titus 2:13) it refers to Christ's second coming. But here it obviously refers to the first coming. It was at his first coming that Christ "destroyed death" through his own death on the cross (cf. Heb 2:14). He has also "brought life and immortality [*aphtharsia,* 'incorruptibility'] to light through the gospel." That is,

the preaching of the gospel has offered men life and immortality. This is the good news Christ came to bring.

11 For the proclamation of this gospel Paul was appointed "a herald and an apostle and a teacher." We find the same three functions, together with exactly the same introductory formula in Greek in 1 Timothy 2:7 (see comments there).

12 Paul's appointment as a preacher of the gospel had cost him much in "suffering" and persecution. But he was not ashamed. Why not? "Because I know whom I have believed [not just 'what I have believed'] and am convinced [same verb as 'persuaded' in v.5] that he is able to guard what I have entrusted to him for that day." For "what I have entrusted to him" (lit., "my deposit") see the comments on 1 Timothy 6:20.

What was this deposit? As Lock says, "He does not define or limit; it will include his teaching . . . his apostolic work, his converts . . . his life which has been already in God's keeping and which will remain safe there even through death" (p. 88).

Notes

11 The added phrase "of the Gentiles" in KJV is not in ℵ our oldest Gr. MS for this passage (4th century), nor A (5th century). It was probably imported here from 1 Tim 2:7.
12 Παραθήκη (*paratheke*, "deposit") is found only in these two verses and in 1 Tim 6:20. Lock has an excellent additional note on this (pp. 90–92). He says that it "always implies the situation of one who has to take a long journey and who deposits his money and other valuables with a friend, trusting him to restore it on his return" (p. 90). Paul was preparing for his last long journey, and he was depositing his gospel (a body of truth) with Timothy. This fits vv.13, 14. With regard to v.12 Lock has this comment: "The life which at first was God's deposit with us becomes our deposit with God" (p. 92).

3. Paul's Admonition

1:13, 14

13What you heard from me, keep as the pattern of sound teaching, with faith and love in Christ Jesus. 14Guard the good deposit that was entrusted to you—guard it with the help of the Holy Spirit who lives in us.

13 "Pattern" is *hypotyposin*. Elsewhere in the NT it occurs only in 1 Timothy 1:16, where it is translated "example." What Timothy had heard from Paul he was to keep as the pattern of "sound" (*hygiainonton*) "teaching" (*logon*, lit., "words"). But this was to be done "with faith and love in Christ Jesus." The only way to keep doctrine is to both live and proclaim·it with faith and love.

14 Timothy was to "guard the good deposit" ("that was entrusted to you" is not in the Greek, but implied). This was evidently the gospel that Paul had entrusted to Timothy to preach and the doctrine he was to preserve. How could he do this? Only "with the help of the Holy Spirit who lives in us." It has been well said that the Holy Spirit is the great Conservator of orthodoxy. (See note on v.12 for *paratheke*, "deposit.")

4. *Paul Deserted*

1:15

> ¹⁵You know that everyone in the province of Asia has deserted me, including
> Phygelus and Hermogenes.

15 The term *Asia* in the NT does not mean the continent, as now, but rather the Roman
province of Asia, at the west end of Asia Minor. It was made into a province by the
Romans about 133 B.C. and Ephesus finally became its capital.

On his third missionary journey Paul had spent three years in Ephesus (Acts 20:31),
longer than anywhere else. While he was there, the preaching of the gospel reached
every part of the province (Acts 19:10). There is deep pathos, then, in this verse: "You
know that everyone in the province of Asia has deserted me"—i.e., turned away from
me. Paul singles out two men for special mention among the deserters, perhaps because
they were well known to Timothy. But of "Phygelus and Hermogenes" we know nothing
further.

When did the Christians of Asia turn away from Paul? Perhaps it was when he was
arrested and taken to Rome for his second and final imprisonment. If so, one can
understand the "tears" (v.4) Timothy shed at that time.

5. *Paul Befriended*

1:16–18

> ¹⁶May the Lord show mercy to the household of Onesiphorus, because he often
> refreshed me and was not ashamed of my chains. ¹⁷On the contrary, when he was
> in Rome, he searched hard for me until he found me. ¹⁸May the Lord grant that
> he will find mercy from the Lord on that day! You know very well in how many ways
> he helped me in Ephesus.

16–18 In contrast to the attitudes and actions of the majority was the kindness of
Onesiphorus. He had lived up to his name, which means "help-bringer" (cf. Onesimus,
"helpful," "useful," Philem 10, 11). Onesiphorus had often "refreshed" (*anepsyxen,* only
here in the NT) Paul and had not been ashamed of the apostle's chains, as the others
had been. When he went to Rome, Onesiphorus had "searched hard" for Paul until he
finally found him. There were many prisoners in Rome, and it was not an easy task to
locate this particular one. Paul prays that mercy may be shown to Onesiphorus "on that
day"—presumably the day of judgment. Then he adds that Timothy knew very well how
this faithful Christian had often helped Paul when the latter was in Ephesus.

Those must have been lonely hours for the aged apostle in prison, facing almost certain
death and forsaken by his friends. It is difficult for us to understand why God's servants
who have given themselves in sacrificial service to others should suffer like this at the
end. But Paul knew that the glory of the next life would repay it all.

IV. Three Symbols of the Christian (2:1–7)

1. *Introduction*

2:1, 2

> ¹You then, my son, be strong in the grace that is in Christ Jesus ²And the things
> you have heard me say in the presence of many witnesses entrust to reliable men
> who will also be qualified to teach others.

1,2 After exhorting Timothy to "be strong in the grace that is in Christ Jesus," Paul sounds his frequent note in the Pastorals about preserving and transmitting the tradition of truth (cf. 1:13, 14). "Entrust" (v.2) is *parathou*, which is related to *parathēkē* (see note on v.12). The deposit that Timothy had received from Paul he was to pass on to "reliable men who will also be qualified to teach others."

2. *The Soldier*

2:3, 4

> [3]Endure hardship with us like a good soldier of Christ Jesus. [4]No one serving as a soldier gets involved in civilian affairs—he wants to please his commanding officer.

3 "Endure hardship" is *synkakopathēson* (see comments on 1:8). One aspect of the Christian life is that it is a warfare against the forces of evil. So Timothy must be "a good soldier of Christ Jesus." Paul uses this figure especially for ministers of the gospel (Phil 2:25; Philem 2).

4 No one "serving as a soldier" (*strateuomenos*) gets involved in "civilian affairs"— literally, "the affairs" (*pragmateiais*, "business, occupations," only here in the NT) "of the [this] life." The verb "gets involved" is *empleketai* (only here and 2 Peter 2:20). In the active voice *emplekō* means "weave in, entwine." In the passive, as here, it is used metaphorically in the sense of "be involved, entangled in." The soldier has to lay aside all secular pursuits, and the Christian minister must be willing to do the same.

"His commanding officer" is literally "the one who enrolled him as a soldier" (*to stratologēsanti*, only here in the NT). When Christ has enrolled us as full-time soldiers in his army, we should seek to please him by giving ourselves to his service without distraction.

3. *The Athlete*

2:5

> [5]Similarly, if anyone competes as an athlete, he does not receive the victor's crown unless he competes according to the rules.

5 Paul is fond of both military and athletic metaphors. The Christian, and especially the minister, must be spiritually a good soldier and a good athlete. "Competes as an athlete" is *athlē*, found (in the NT) only in this verse (twice). We have already noted a similar verb in 1 Timothy 6:12 (see comments there). The verb here is used for competing in an athletic contest in the arena.

"Receive the victor's crown" is also one word, *stephanoutai* (only here and Heb 2:7, 9). The Greek has two words for crown: *diadēma* ("diadem," Rev 12:3; 13:1; 19:12), which means a royal crown; and *stephanos*, the victor's wreath given to the winner in an athletic contest. Hence the full translation here of the verb *stephanoō*.

The winning athlete does not receive this crown unless he competes "according to the rules"—one word in the Greek, *nomimōs*, "lawfully" (only here and 1 Tim 1:8). The man who breaks the rules is disqualified.

4. *The Farmer*

2:6, 7

> 6The hard-working farmer should be the first to receive a share of the crops. 7Reflect on what I am saying, for the Lord will give you insight into all this.

6 The Christian ministry can also be compared to farming. The pastor must sow the seed and cultivate the growing plants. Paul says, "The hard-working farmer should be the first to receive a share of the crops." The emphasis here is on "hard-working" (*kopiōnta*, "toiling"). Bernard puts it well: "The main thought is that labour, discipline, striving are the portion of him who would succeed in any enterprise, be he soldier or athlete or farmer" (p. 118).

7 Paul winds up this section by saying, "Reflect on what I am saying." If Timothy does this, he will understand what it is all about. The three similes that Paul uses here—soldier, athlete, farmer—are found together in 1 Corinthians 9:6; 7:24–27. The closest parallel between these two Scriptures is in the case of the athlete, who must go into strict training if he is going to win the prize. So a Christian must have intense devotion and firm self-discipline if he is to win out for the Lord.

V. Suffering and Glory

2:8–13

> 8Remember Jesus Christ, raised from the dead, descended from David. This is my gospel, 9for which I am suffering even to the point of being chained like a criminal. But God's word is not chained. 10Therefore I endure everything for the sake of the elect, that they too may obtain the salvation that is in Christ Jesus, with eternal glory.
> 11Here is a trustworthy saying:
> If we died with him,
>   we will also live with him;
> 12if we endure,
>   we will also reign with him.
> If we disown him,
>   he will also disown us;
> 13if we are faithless,
>   he will remain faithful,
>   for he cannot disown himself.

8 Now Paul urges Timothy to keep on remembering (present tense) Jesus Christ. "Raised from the dead" emphasizes his deity; "descended from David," his humanity (cf. Rom 1:3, 4). It is not the dead Christ that Timothy is to contemplate, but the risen living Lord. This is Paul's gospel ("good news").

9 For preaching this gospel, Paul is suffering. The Greek literally says, "I am suffering evil . . . as an evil-doer" (*kakopathō . . . hōs kakourgos*). He was "chained like a criminal." But he rejoices that "God's word is not chained." The preacher is in prison, but the Word of God is still moving on and transforming lives.

10 Because of this, the apostle patiently endures (*hypomenō*) everything for the sake of the "elect." The adjective *eklektos* (lit., "chosen") comes from the verb *eklegō*, "choose." Thayer says that this is used "of Christians, as those whom he [God] has set apart from among the irreligious multitude as dear unto himself, and whom he has rendered, through faith in Christ, citizens in the Messianic kingdom" (p. 197). The important qualification here is "through faith in Christ." E.F. Brown says: "The elect are those whom God has already chosen or those whom He will choose for admission into the Christian Church. . . . It does not mean 'chosen to final salvation,' as is shown by the words which follow" (*The Pastoral Epistles*, "Westminster Commentaries," p. 67).

The whole purpose of Paul's ministry was that people might "obtain the salvation that is in Christ Jesus." The ultimate goal of this salvation is "eternal glory." But from beginning to end it is all in Christ.

11–13 For the opening formula see the comments on 1 Timothy 1:15. Some scholars think it goes with the preceding verse, but it seems more reasonable to apply it to what follows. In these three verses we find what is usually thought to be an early Christian hymn. It is in the typical form of Hebrew poetic parallelism—four "if" clauses, each followed by a balancing conclusion. The first two are positive, the other two negative.

"If we died with him" is in the aorist tense, (*synapethanomen*), indicating a crisis (EGT, 4:163). Paul spells this out in Romans 6:3–6. It is only as we die with Christ, by identification with him in his death, that we can have spiritual life in him. "We will also live with him" does not refer to our future resurrection, but to our present life in Christ. The parallel is Romans 6:8, 11. Right here and now we are to count ourselves "dead to sin but alive to God in Christ Jesus." The Pauline formula is "You have to die to live."

Then Paul goes on to say, "If we endure, we will also reign with him." The verb "endure" is in the present tense of continuous action (*hypomenomen*). It is only as we keep on enduring to the end that we will be saved in time of persecution (Matt 10:22; cf. context.).

The third proposition is negative: "If we disown him" (aorist tense, *arnēsometha*), "he will also disown us." This is a serious warning. We cannot reject Christ without being rejected ourselves.

"If we are faithless" is in the present tense (*apistoumen*), indicating a settled state of refusing to believe in Jesus and obey him. But whatever we do, "he will remain faithful, for he cannot disown himself." God's faithfulness is eternal.

Notes

12,13 It may be wondered why NIV changed the familiar "deny" to "disown." The reason is that "deny" means primarily "to declare untrue; assert the contrary of, contradict," whereas "disown" means "to refuse to acknowledge or accept as one's own" (*American Heritage Dictionary*). Thus, "disown" was more accurate when applied to persons as its object.

VI. Contrasts in the Church (2:14–26)

1. True and False Teachers

2:14–19

14Keep reminding them of these things. Warn them before God against quarreling about words; it is of no value, and only ruins those who listen. 15Do your best to present yourself to God as one approved, a workman who does not need to be ashamed and who correctly handles the word of truth. 16Avoid godless chatter, because those who indulge in it will become more and more ungodly. [17]Their teaching will spread like gangrene. Among them are Hymenaeus and Philetus, [18]who have wandered away from the truth. They say that the resurrection has already taken place, and they destroy the faith of some. [19]Nevertheless, God's solid foundation stands firm, sealed with this inscription: "The Lord knows those who are his," and, "Everyone who confesses the name of the Lord must turn away from wickedness."

14,15 In these two verses Paul challenges Timothy to be an approved workman. He is to "keep on reminding" the believers of "these things," the things about which Paul has been speaking. He is also to warn them before God against "quarreling about words"— *logomachein* (only here in the NT; cf. *logomachia*, 1 Tim 6:4). Fighting over mere words is a waste of time; "it is of no value." It only brings ruin (*katastrophē*, "catastrophe," only here in the NT) to the listeners.

"Do your best" is *spoudason*, which literaly means "make haste," and so "be zealous or eager." "Study" (KJV) is obviously too narrow a term, usually referring today to the studying of books. The true meaning is "make every effort."

"Who does not need to be ashamed" is one word, the compound adjective *anepaischynton* (only here in the NT), literally "not to be put to shame." White suggests that the combination here means "a workman who has no cause for shame when his work is being inspected" (EGT, 4:165).

"Who correctly handles" is *orthotomounta* (likewise only here in the NT)—"holding a straight course" in the word of truth. The renowned Syrian exegete Theodoret (c. 393–c. 458) applied the verb to "a plowman who drives a straight furrow." BAG says "Found elsewhere independently of the NT only in Prov 3:6; 11:5, where it is used with *hodous* and plainly means 'cut a road across country (that is forested or otherwise difficult to pass through) in a straight direction,' so that the traveler might go directly to his destination.... Then *orthotomein ton logon tēs alētheias* would perhaps mean *guide the word of truth along a straight path* (like a road that goes straight to its goal), without being turned aside by wordy debates or impious talk" (p. 584). The context suggests that Paul is warning against taking the devious paths of deceiving interpretations in teaching the Scriptures.

16–18 In these three verses the apostle describes heretical teachers. He warns Timothy to "avoid" ("shun") godless "chatter" (*kenophōnias*, "empty sounds," only here and 1 Tim 6:20). Lock paraphrases this: "But to all these irreligious and frivolous hair-splittings give a wide berth" (p. 97). For they *prokopsousin*—"will cut forward," or "advance"—"to more of ungodliness" (so the Greek). Probably "they" means the false teachers, as suggested in NIV.

Paul goes on to say that their "teaching [*logos*] will spread"—literally, "will have pasture" (*hexei nomēn*). The noun *nomē* is found (in the NT) only here and in John 10:9 ("pasture"). But Bernard notes that it "is often used by medical writers of the 'spreading' of a disease, as here" (p. 123). "Gangrene" is *gangraina* (only here in the NT), used by medical writers of that day for a sore that eats into the flesh.

Hymenaeus is probably the one mentioned in 1 Timothy 1:20. Nothing is known about Philetus. These had "wandered away [*ēstochēsan*, see 1 Tim 1:6; 6:21] from the truth." Specifically, they said that the resurrection had already taken place, and thereby they were destroying, or "subverting," the faith of some people. They were evidently explaining the resurrection in a spiritual sense, equating it with regeneration, or the new birth.

First Corinthians 15 is Paul's extended answer to this false teaching, which was propagated by some in the church at Corinth.

19 In this verse the apostle emphasizes the solid foundation of truth. He declares that in spite of the subversion, God's "solid" (*stereos*) foundation "stands firm" (*hestēken*). Lock says that the foundation is "either Christ Jesus and his Apostles (cf. 1 Cor 3:11; Eph 2:20; Rev 21:14): or, more widely, 'the Church' (cf. 1 Tim 3:15); or 'the truth,' 'the deposit'" (p. 100). Bernard favors "the church," which stands firm inspite of the waywardness of some of its members.

The foundation is "sealed with this inscription"—literally, "having this seal" (*echōn tēn sphragida tautēn*). White comments, "The one seal bears two inscriptions, two mutually complementary parts or aspects: (a) The objective fact of God's superintending knowledge of His chosen; (b) the recognition by the consciousness of each individual of the relation in which he stands to God, with its imperative call to holiness" (EGT, 4:167).

Notes

14 Καταστροφῆ (*katastrophē*) is found also in 2 Peter 2:6 (TR) but not in the best Gr. text.
19 The first quotation is taken from Num 16:5. The second one is not an exact quotation from the OT, but is probably also related to Korah's rebellion (cf. Num 16:26).

2. Noble and Ignoble Vessels

2:20, 21

> [20]In a large house there are not only articles of gold and silver, but also of wood and clay; some are for noble purposes and some for ignoble. [21]If a man cleanses himself from the latter, he will be an instrument for noble purposes, made holy, useful to the Master and prepared to do any good work.

20,21 Having drawn at some length the contrast between true and false teachers (vv.14–19), Paul now points up a second contrast—that between noble and ignoble vessels. Both will be found in the church.

"In a large house," where a wealthy man lives, "there are not only articles of gold and silver, but also of wood and clay." The word translated "articles" is *skeuē* (plural). The noun *skeuos* literally means "a vessel, jar, or dish." Plutarch (Caes. 48.7) speaks of four kinds, as here.

"Of gold" is the adjective *chrysa*, from the noun *chrysos*, "gold." One of the most eloquent preachers in the early church was a man named John who was called Chrysostom—*chrysos*, "gold," and *stōma*, "mouth"—John of the Golden Mouth. He was certainly "a vessel unto honour" (KJV).

Some less eminent articles were "of silver." But others were of "wood"—for example, wooden bowls for holding flour—or "clay" (*ostrakina*, cf. "*ostraca*," a term used in archaeology for fragments of ancient pottery).

Some of these, apparently the ones made of gold and silver, are "for noble purposes"—literally, "for honor" (*eis timēn*)—and some "for ignoble" (*eis atimian*, "for dishonor").

We find the same two expressions in Romans 9:21. In the verses that follow there we find that the former vessels are "objects of his [God's] mercy, whom he prepared in advance for glory" (v.23), whereas the latter are "objects of his wrath—prepared for destruction" (v.22). On the basis of this, as well as the context here in 2 Timothy, some scholars feel that the articles for ignoble purposes are the false teachers in the church (vv.16–18), who are destined for eternal destruction. In that case, "if a man cleanses himself from the latter" (v.21) means that Timothy must expel from the church the ignoble members.

Another interpretation is less drastic. It holds that in "a large house"—the visible church or a local congregation—there are members who are prepared for "noble purposes" and others who are fitted for more menial tasks. Both have their place and function in the church. Verse 21 would then mean that the individual who cleanses himself from "the latter" (*toutōn*, "these things," perhaps false teachings) will be "an instrument for noble purposes" (*skeuos eis timēn*). He will be "made holy" (*hēgiasmenon*, "sanctified"), "useful to the Master" (*euchrēston tō despotē*) "and prepared to do any good work."

Both of these interpretations seem valid. Since we cannot be sure which one Paul had in mind, perhaps we should make both applications.

Notes

20 Some of the early church fathers held that the "large house" was the world. But it seems much more logical to take it as being the church.

20,21 Martin Dibelius and Hans Conzelmann write, "We are not dealing with a problem of those who are less gifted, but with the seducers and the seduced. This interpretation is demanded by the context." They paraphrase v.21 like this: "Even though these vessels for disreputable use ... are present in the house, nevertheless be sure that you yourself remain a vessel for honorable use ... by cleansing yourself of these—perhaps ... the actions designated as 'disreputable'" (*The Pastoral Epistles*, "Hermeneia," p. 113).

3. *The Kind and the Quarrelsome*

2:22–26

> 22Flee the evil desires of youth, and pursue righteousness, faith, love and peace, along with those who call on the Lord out of a pure heart. 23Don't have anything to do with foolish and stupid arguments, because you know they produce quarrels. 24And the Lord's servant must not quarrel; instead, he must be kind to everyone, able to teach, not resentful. 25Those who oppose him he must gently instruct, in the hope that God will give them a change of heart leading them to a knowledge of the truth, 26and that they will come to their senses and escape from the trap of the devil, who has taken them captive to do his will.

The last of the three "contrasts in the church" is that between kind people and quarrelsome people (vv.22–26). Unfortunately, both types are in the visible, organized church.

22 Timothy was still a rather young man, probably in his early thirties, and so the aged apostle warns him: "Flee the evil desires of youth" (*neōterikas*, only here in the NT). The

verb "flee" is in the present tense of continuous action; he must keep on fleeing youthful lusts. But he must keep on pursuing (*diōke*, present imperative) the positive virtues. It is not enough to run away from wrong; we must run after what is good. To do this is the only way to escape temptations to evil (cf. Rom 12:21).

Timothy was to pursue four things: "righteousness, faith, love and peace." The first three of these are mentioned in a similar context in 1 Timothy 6:11. Although Timothy must purge the church of false teachers, he had to be careful to promote "love and peace" among the Christian believers committed to his care. "Faith" (*pistis*) may also be translated "faithfulness." Both ideas fit well here.

23 "Don't have anything to do with" is one word, *paraitou* (cf. 1 Tim 4:7). "Foolish" is the adjective *mōros* (cf. "moron"): "1. properly of the nerves, *dull, sluggish*. . . . 2. Of the mind, *dull, stupid, foolish*" (A-S, p. 299). "Stupid" is *apaideutos* (only here in the NT), "uninstructed, ignorant." "Arguments" is *zēteseis*, "questionings, debates." *Paraitou* is a strong verb: "refuse," not merely "avoid" (KJV). White gives the force of it: "Such questions will be brought before you: refuse to discuss them" (EGT, 4:168). Sometimes the wise pastor has to do this. Why? Because "they produce quarrels" (*machas*, "fights"). These tend to divide the church and so destroy it.

24 "The Lord's servant"—every Christian, but particularly the pastor of a church—must not "quarrel" (*machesthai*). Rather, he must be "kind" (*ēpios*, "gentle") to everyone, "apt to teach" (*didaktikon*, only here and 1 Tim 3:2), "not resentful" (*anexikakon*, only here in the NT). It means "bearing evil without resentment" (BAG). This is the attitude that Christians must have toward those who oppose them.

25,26 And so Paul goes on to say that the good minister must "gently instruct" ("in meekness") "those who oppose him"—*tous antidiatithemenous* (only here in the NT). He does this in the hope that God will give them "a change of heart" (*metanoia*, "repentance"), leading to "a knowledge" (*epignōsis*, "full knowledge") of the truth. He hopes that "they will come to their senses and escape" (v.26). This is all one word in the Greek: *ananēpsōsin*. The verb (*ananēphō*) literally means "return to soberness." Thayer says that this passage indicates "to be set free from the snare of the devil and to return to a sound mind ['one's sober senses']" (*Lexicon*, p. 40).

Notes

23 On this verse Bernard says, "The irrelevancy of much of the controversy then prevalent among Christians seems to have deeply impressed St. Paul; again and again he returns to this charge against the heretical teachers, that their doctrines are unprofitable and vain, and that they breed strife about questions either unimportant or insoluble" (p. 126).

26 "Who has taken them captive" is literally "having been taken captive by him" (ἐζωγρημένοι ὑπ' αὐτοῦ, *ezōgrēmenoi hyp' autou*). The verb *zōgreō* occurs only here and in Luke 5:10, where it means "catch alive."

"His will" is τὸ ἐκείνου θέλημα (*to ekeinou thelēma*, "the will of that one"). The change from *autou* (his) to *ekeinou* (that) leads Bernard to think it is "God's will" in rescuing them from the devil's trap. But Dibelius and Conzelmann say, "Both pronouns . . . refer to the devil" (p. 114). We agree.

VII. Characteristics of the Last Days (3:1–9)

1. *Love of Money and Pleasure*

3:1–5

> ¹But mark this: There will be terrible times in the last days. ²People will be lovers of themselves, lovers of money, boastful, proud, abusive, disobedient to their parents, ungrateful, unholy, ³without love, unforgiving, slanderous, without self-control, brutal, not lovers of the good, ⁴treacherous, rash, conceited, lovers of pleasure rather than lovers of God—⁵having a form of godliness but denying its power. Have nothing to do with them.

1 The expression "in the last days" (*en eschatais hēmerais*) comes from the OT (e.g., Isa 2:2; Mic 4:1). In Peter's quotation of Joel 2:28 on the day of Pentecost (Acts 2:17) it clearly refers to the whole messianic age, for he declared that the prophecy was being fulfilled that very day. Hendriksen insists that the phrase has that meaning here (pp. 281–283). But it seems more natural to take it as applying especially to the last days of this age, before the Second Coming, as in 2 Peter 3:3 and Jude 18. This does not at all deny that these conditions have been and will be present throughout the church age. It is simply to say that the characteristics enumerated here will be more intensive and extensive as the end approaches.

Paul declared that in the last days "there will be [*enstēsontai*, 'will be upon us'] terrible times." The adjective *chalepos* ("terrible") occurs only here and in Matthew 8:28, where it is used for the "violent" demoniacs. It means "hard to bear, troublesome, dangerous" (Thayer).

2–4 In these three verses we find a list of no fewer than eighteen vices that will characterize people in the last days. These conditions have always existed in some measure but they have become more marked in recent decades. "Lovers of themselves" is *philautoi* (only here in the NT, "selfish"). "Lovers of money" is *philargyroi* (only here and Luke 16:14, "avaricious"). The cognate noun *philargyria* ("love of money") is found in 1 Timothy 6:10.

Men will also be "boasters" (*alazones*, "imposters" or "braggarts," here and Rom 1:30). They will be "proud" (*hyperēphanoi*, lit., "showing oneself above others"). Originally used in a good sense in Greek literature for truly superior persons, this word soon took on the bad connotation that it always has in the NT: "with an overweening estimate of one's means or merits, despising others or even treating them with contempt, haughty" (Thayer, p. 641). Bernard translates these two words as "*boastful, haughty,* the former term referring specially to *words,* the latter to *thoughts*" (p. 130).

"Abusive" is *blasphēmoi* ("evil-speaking, slanderous"). And it may well be questioned whether children and young people were ever more "disobedient to their parents" than they are today.

The next four adjectives all begin with *a*-negative. *Acharistoi* (only here and Luke 6:35) is the opposite of being thankful. *Anosioi,* "unholy" (only here and 1 Tim 1:9) describes the person who has no fellowship with God and so is living a merely "secular" life. *Astorgoi* ("without love") is found elsewhere (in the NT) only in Romans 1:31, where several of these terms are included in a list of vices. It literally means "without family affection." *Aspondoi,* "unforgiving" (only here) originally indicated "without a treaty or covenant" and so "irreconcilable."

"Slanderous" is *diaboloi*. This usually occurs in the NT as a substantive with the definite article and is translated "the devil." But the adjective connotes "prone to slander" or "accusing falsely."

The next three adjectives also begin with *a*-negative. *Akrateis* (only here in the NT), " 'without self-control' . . . in the widest sense, but more particularly in regard to bodily lusts" (Bernard, p. 130). The adjective literally means "without strength." So it describes the weak man who is easily led into sin. *Anēmeroi*, "brutal" (only here in the NT) means "not tame, savage, fierce." *Aphilagathoi* ("not lovers of the good") has not been found elsewhere in Greek literature. But its meaning is clear from its composition: *a*-negative, *philos* ("lover") and *agathos* ("good").

"Treacherous" is *prodotai*, a noun meaning "traitor" or "betrayer." It is used for Judas Iscariot (Luke 6:16). "Rash" is *propeteis* (only here and Acts 19:36). Literally it meant "falling forward, headlong." Metaphorically it came to mean "hasty, rash, reckless." *Tetyphōmenoi*, "conceited," is the perfect passive participle of typhoō, found elsewhere in the NT only in 1 Timothy 3:6; 6:4 (see comments there).

"Lovers of pleasure rather than lovers of God" is a play on words: *philēdonoi* . . . *philotheoi*. Both words are found only here in the NT. They describe those who put self in the place of God as the center of their affections—a commentary on *philautoi* (v.2).

5 Yet they are religious—"having a form of godliness but denying its power" (v.5). Timothy is told to "have nothing to do" (*apotrepou*, "turn away from," only here in the NT) with such hypocrites.

2. Depraved Living and Thinking

3:6–9

> 6They are the kind who worm their way into homes and gain control over weak-willed women, who are loaded down with sins and are swayed by all kinds of evil desires, 7always learning but never able to acknowledge the truth. 8Just as Jannes and Jambres opposed Moses, so also these men oppose the truth—men of depraved minds, who, as far as the faith is concerned, are rejected. 9But they will not get very far because, as in the case of those men, their folly will be clear to everyone.

6,7 In the first five verses of this chapter Paul has been pointing out the characteristics of those who love money and pleasure. Now he scores them for their depraved living and thinking. He says that they "worm their way into homes." The verb is *endynō*, which means "to creep into, insinuate one's self into; to enter" (Thayer).

"Gain control over" is *aixmalōtizō* (lit., "take captive" in war), but here perhaps only "deceive" (BAG). "Weak-willed women" is one word, *gynaikaria* (only here in the NT), literally, "little women"—a contemptuous diminutive (KJV, "silly women"). These women are further described as "loaded down" or "overwhelmed," with sins—the perfect passive of the verb *sōreuō* (only here and Rom 12:20), which means "to heap on." They are also "swayed" ("led," *agomena*) "by all kinds of evil desires." Such women become an easy prey for false teachers. Verse 7 suggests that these women wanted to pose as learned people. But actually they remained in ignorance of the truth.

8,9 Jannes and Jambres are not mentioned in the OT. But there was a Jewish tradition that they were two of the Egyptian magicians who withstood Moses and Aaron. They are thus mentioned in the Targum (Aramaic paraphrase) of Jonathan on Exodus 7:11. Pliny in his *Natural History* (A.D. 77) names Jannes along with Moses. It has been suggested that the names mean "the rebel" and "the opponent" (Lock, p. 107).

Paul likens the false teachers at Ephesus to these ancient magicians. He describes them as "men of depraved minds." "Depraved" is the perfect passive participle of *kataphtheiro* (only here in the NT). It means "utterly corrupted." As far as the faith is concerned, they are "rejected" (*adokimoi*, "rejected after testing"). They cannot be trusted to teach the truth. But they will not get far. As in the case of Jannes and Jambres, their "folly" (*anoia*, only here and Luke 6:11) will be clearly seen.

Notes

6 Several lexicons discuss the verb ἐνδύνω (*endyno*) under ἐνδύω (*endyo*, "dress" or "clothe"), giving "enter" as a special meaning in this one place. But BAG lists it separately as an "epic, Ionic, poetic form beside ἐνδύω, as early as Homer" (p. 263).

VIII. Persecution and Steadfastness (3:10–17)

1. *All Christians Persecuted*

3:10–13

> 10You, however, know all about my teaching, my way of life, my purpose, faith, patience, love, endurance, 11persecutions, sufferings—what kinds of things happened to me in Antioch, Iconium and Lystra, the persecutions I endured. Yet the Lord rescued me from all of them. 12In fact, everyone who wants to live a godly life in Christ Jesus will be persecuted, 13while evil men and impostors will go from bad to worse, deceiving and being deceived.

10,11 The "you" is emphatic here, expressed by the pronoun *sy*. "Know all about" is the verb *parakoloutheo* (from *para*, "beside," and *akaloutheo*, "follow," and so "follow closely"). In the NT it occurs elsewhere only in Luke 1:3 ("investigated") and 1 Timothy 4:6 ("followed"). Thayer, A-S, and BAG all give for this passage: "follow as a rule" (standard of conduct), or "follow faithfully." NIV is in line with KJV ("fully known") and RSV ("observed"). Both of these basic ideas fit the context. NASB has the simple translation "followed," which can be taken either way. Verse 11 would seem to point toward the traditional interpretation (KJV, RSV, NIV).

In any case, Paul says that Timothy was familiar with the apostle's life and "teaching" (*didaskalia*). "Way of life" is *agoge* (only here in the NT). "Purpose" (*prothesis*) is used elsewhere by Paul only for God's purposes. *Pistis* ("faith") also means "faithfulness." It may mean here Paul's loyalty to the Christian faith. "Patience" is *makrothymia*. In KJV this is usually rendered "longsuffering"—a quality Paul had to show toward his opponents. *Agape* is the constant, steadfast "love" that God implants in our hearts. "Endurance" is *hypomone*, which Ellicott defines as "the *brave* patience with which the Christian contends against the various hindrances, persecutions, and temptations that befall him in his conflict with the inward and outward world" (comments on 1 Thess 1:3).

In v.11 Paul adds two more things that Timothy knew about: "persecutions" (*diogmois*, from *dioko*, "pursue, persecute") and "sufferings" (*pathemasin*, from *pascho*, "suffer"). These things had happened to the apostle-missionary in Pisidian Antioch, Iconium, and Lystra (Acts 13:50; 14:2, 5, 19)—cities in the Roman province of Galatia where Paul had founded churches on his first missionary journey. He was actually bombarded with stones in Lystra, and left for dead. Since Timothy was a young man in Lystra at that time and had evidently just been converted under Paul's ministry, he had poignant memories of this incident. But out of them all the Lord had delivered Paul, even reviving him from the stoning.

12,13 Paul was not alone in his sufferings. He declares that "everyone who wants [*thelontes*, 'is willing'] to live a godly life in Christ Jesus will be persecuted." Meanwhile, "evil men and imposters will go from bad to worse"—literally, "will make advance [*prokopsousin*] toward the worse." The Greek word for "impostors" is *goēs* (only here in the NT), which originally meant "a wailer, howler," and then "a juggler, enchanter"— "because incantations used to be uttered in a kind of howl"—and so finally "a deceiver, impostor" (Thayer, p. 120). BAG gives "swindler, cheat." Such men are "deceiving and being deceived." Having been deceived by false teachers, they are now deceiving others.

2. *The Adequacy of Scripture*

3:14–17

> ¹⁴But as for you, continue in what you have learned and have become convinced of, because you know those from whom you learned it, ¹⁵and how from infancy you have known the holy Scriptures, which are able to make you wise for salvation through faith in Christ Jesus. ¹⁶All Scripture is God-breathed and is useful for teaching, rebuking, correcting and training in righteousness, ¹⁷so that the man of God may be thoroughly equipped for every good work.

14,15 Timothy is not to be led astray by these impostors. Instead, he is to continue in what he had learned and had "become convinced of" (*epistōthēs*, only here in the NT), "have been firmly persuaded of," or "have been assured of." Why? "Because you know those from whom you learned it." Who were his teachers? His grandmother Lois and his mother Eunice (1:5), as the next clause shows: "and how from infancy you have known the holy Scriptures." Bernard comments, "It was the custom to teach Jewish children the law at a very early age, and to cause them to commit parts of it to memory" (p. 135). This was Timothy's heritage. "The holy Scriptures" is *ta hiera grammata* (lit., "the sacred writings"), an expression found in both Philo (*Life of Moses*, iii.39) and Josephus (*Antiq.* x.10.4) for the OT, which is what Timothy was taught as a child.

These OT Scriptures were able to make him "wise" in preparation "for salvation through faith in Christ Jesus." They disciplined him in obedience to God and also pointed forward to the coming Messiah, through whom salvation by faith would become available.

16 "All Scripture is God-breathed." That is exactly what the Greek says. The adjective *theopneustos* (only here in the NT) is compounded of *theos*, "God," and the verb *pneō*, "breathe." This is one of the greatest texts in the NT on the inspiration of the Bible. (The noun *theopneustia* does not occur in the NT.) Another outstanding passage is 2 Peter 1:21, which indicates something of how the divine inspiration took place. Here in 2 Timothy we have the fact simply and plainly stated; the process of inspiration is not dealt with.

This God-inspired Scripture is "useful" (*ōphelimos*, "profitable," only here and 1 Tim 4:8; Titus 3:8). Paul then notes some areas in which it is useful. "Teaching" (*didaskalia*) is the most general. "Rebuking" (*elegmos*, only here in the NT) is used for "conviction" of a sinner in LXX (Num 5:18ff.). "Correcting" (*epanorthōsin* only here) literally means "restoration to an upright position or a right state." *Paideia* ("training") comes from *pais*, ("child"). So it originally meant "the rearing of a child." Then it came to mean "training, learning, instruction." Christians need to be trained in "righteousness"—both inward and outward.

17 The purpose of all this is that "the man of God may be thoroughly equipped for every good work." "Thoroughly equipped" is the combination of an adjective and the perfect passive participle of a verb. The adjective is *artios* (only here in the NT). BAG defines it thus: "*complete, capable, proficient*=able to meet all demands" (p. 110). The verb is *exartizō* (only here and Acts 21:5), "equip, furnish." See F.E. Gaebelein, *The Christian Use of the Bible* (Chicago: Moody Press, 1946) for an extended treatment of 2 Timothy 3:16, 17.

Notes

16 This verse has no verb in the Gr. but "is" has to be inserted somewhere in English to make sense. ASV took θεόπνευστος (*theopneustos*, "God-breathed") as attached to γραφή (*graphē*, "Scripture"), and so reads, "Every scripture inspired of God *is* also profitable ...." Bernard (CGT) and White (EGT) both defend this translation on the twofold basis that (1) there is no evidence in the context that the inspiration of the Scriptures was being called into question and (2) the emphasis of the entire passage is on the usefulness of the Scriptures in fitting the believer for service. Bernard notes that this was the interpretation of Origen, the Vulgate and Syriac versions, Martin Luther, and also the early English translations of Wycliffe, Tyndale, Coverdale, and Cranmer (p. 137).

On the other hand, Lock (ICC) thinks it is better to take *theopneustos* as a predicate adjective: "All Scripture is inspired by God ... and therefore useful" (p. 110). Simpson presents a convincing fourfold defense of this translation, and notes that Chrysostom interpreted it this way (p. 150).

IX. Preach the Word

4:1-5

> [1]In the presence of God and of Christ Jesus, who will judge the living and the dead, and in view of his appearing and his kingdom, I give you this charge: [2]Preach the Word; be prepared in season and out of season; correct, rebuke and encourage—with great patience and careful instruction. [3]For the time will come when men will not put up with sound doctrine. Instead, to suit their own desires, they will gather around them a great number of teachers to say what their itching ears want to hear. [4]They will turn their ears away from the truth and turn aside to myths. [5]But you, keep your head in all situations, endure hardship, do the work of an evangelist, discharge all the duties of your ministry.

1 Here Paul speaks of Christ Jesus as the one who will "judge the living and the dead"—a clause found in all the early creeds of the church. The two classes mentioned here are reminiscent of 1 Thessalonians 4:16, 17.

"In view of his appearing and his kingdom" is what is called the accusative of adjuration. "I give you this charge" is one word in Greek—*diamartyromai* ("I adjure, I solemnly charge"). Simpson notes that "it has the weight of a legal affirmation" (p. 152). Timothy is to be governed in his thinking, not just by the present life but also by the coming judgment and the eternal kingdom of Christ.

2 The basic charge is: "Preach ['herald, proclaim'—*kēryxon*] the Word." The preacher is not to air his own opinions but to proclaim God's eternal, authoritative Word of truth. "Be prepared" is the verb *ephistēmi*, which means "be ready, be on hand." The minister has to be on duty constantly, ready for any emergency. "In season and out of season" is simply *eukairōs akairōs*. The first word occurs also in Mark 14:11, the second only here. In addition to preaching the Word, Timothy is to "correct" (*elenxon*, "convict, reprove"), "rebuke" (*epitimēson*, "censure, admonish"), and "encourage" (*parakaleson*, which also means "comfort" and "exhort"). But he is to do these things with great "patience" (*makrothymia*, "longsuffering") and careful "instruction" (*didachē*, the act of teaching). Bernard makes the sage observation: "Rebuke and exhortation must be accompanied with *teaching*, or they will be unprofitable" (p. 140). And it must all be done in patience and love.

3 Timothy is warned that the time will come when men will not "put up with [*anexontai*, 'endure' or 'listen to'] sound doctrine" (*hygiainousēs didaskalias*). As has already been noted (cf. 1 Tim 1:10), this is probably the key phrase of the pastoral Epistles. It occurs again in Titus 1:9; 2:1. Timothy's major responsibility in Ephesus was to defend and proclaim sound doctrine. He must do this constantly, since the time would come when people would not listen to the truth. Instead, "to suit their own desires"—*epithymias*, translated "evil desires" in 3:6—"they will gather around them" (*episōreusousi*, lit., "heap together," only here in the NT) teachers "to say what their itching ears want to hear" (*knēthomenoi tēn akoēn*, "itching in their ears"). These were ears "which were always pricking with an uneasy desire for what would gratify the taste of a carnal, self-willed heart" (Fairbairn, p. 385).

4 People like this will "turn away" (*apostrepsousin*, cf. 1:15) their ears from the truth and will "turn aside" (*ektrapēsontai*, see 1 Tim 1:6; 5:15; 6:20) to "myths" (*mythous*, see 1 Tim 1:4; 4:7). The carnal heart prefers senseless myths rather than solid truth.

5 "Keep your head" is *nēphe*. This verb literally meant "be sober, abstain from wine." But in the NT (cf. 1 Thess 5:6, 8; 1 Peter 1:13; 4:7; 5:8) it has the metaphorical sense of being self-controlled or self-possessed. Simpson thinks the meaning here is "Be wide-awake" (p. 154). But probably the idea of keeping one's self-control under all circumstances fits best in this passage. Timothy is again urged to "endure hardship" (*kakopathēson*, see 2:9). He is to do the work of an "evangelist" (*euangelistou*). This interesting word occurs only three times in the NT. It obviously comes from the familiar verb *euangelizō* ("announce the good news, preach the gospel"). In the two other passages (Acts 21:8; Eph 4:11) it may well refer to an itinerant preacher. But here it perhaps suggests that a pastor must also be an evangelist, pointing sinners to Christ.

The summary of Paul's solemn charge to Timothy is this: "Discharge all the duties of your ministry"—literally, "fulfill [or 'fill full'] your ministry" (*tēn diakonian sou plēro-*

phorēson). Timothy is to fulfill his "calling" (NEB) by packing his ministry to the full with the things Paul has been exhorting him to do in these two Epistles. Fairbairn says that the verb means "fill it up, perform it fully, or make it, as far as you can, a complete and effective service" (p. 389).

Notes

1 "Christ Jesus" is the correct reading, rather than "the Lord Jesus Christ" (KJV). Because these names for Jesus are abbreviated in the early Gr. MSS, there is much variation in the readings.
2 "Great" and "careful" both tr. the adjective πάσῃ (*pasē*, "all").

X. Paul's Final Testimony

4:6–8

> 6For I am already being poured out as a drink offering, and the time has come for my departure. 7I have fought the good fight, I have finished the race, I have kept the faith. 8Now there is in store for me the crown of righteousness, which the Lord, the righteous Judge, will award to me on that day—and not only to me, but also to all who have longed for his appearing.

6 In Philippians 2:17 Paul wrote, "But even if I am being poured out like a drink offering on the sacrifice. . . ." But here he says, "For I am already being poured out as a drink offering." In both passages "I am being poured out like a drink offering" is one word in the Greek: *spendomai* (not elsewhere in the NT). The picture is that of a drink offering poured on the lamb of sacrifice just before it was burned on the altar (Num 28:24).

There is both comparison and contrast in these unique passages. In both places Paul is talking about pouring out his life. But when he wrote to Philippi from his first Roman imprisonment he was expecting to be released soon and revisit that city (Phil 2:24). So he uses the word *if.* Probably he felt that things were fast winding up for him, but the time had not yet come for pouring out his blood "on the sacrifice and service" of his devoted ministry.

Now the case is different. He is nearing the end of his second, final imprisonment at Rome. He is conscious that his fate is sealed, for he adds, "And the time has come for my departure."

The word for "departure" is *analysis* (only here in the NT). It comes from the verb *analyō*, which literally meant "unloose." The noun was used for the "loosing" of a vessel from its moorings or of soldiers "breaking up" camp for departure. Paul was about ready to "strike tent" (leave his physical body) and forsake this earth for the presence of his Lord. This second Epistle has sometimes been called his "swan-song" or his valedictory.

7 There are two ways of interpreting this verse. One is to assume that we have here three figures of speech: the first military, the second athletic, the third religious (stewardship). Simpson insists strongly on this (p. 159).

But the three clauses of the verse may all be taken as related to athletics. The verb translated "fought" here is *agōnizomai.* It is true that in John 18:36 it clearly means "to fight" in a military way. But just as clearly it relates to athletics in 1 Corinthians 9:25, where it is translated "competes in the games." Though it may go either way in its other occurrences in the NT, it seems more natural to take it in the athletic sense in all of them—"make every effort" (Luke 13:24); "struggling" (Col 1:29); 'wrestling" (Col 4:12); "strive" (1 Tim 4:10); and "fight" (1 Tim 6:12). In the last of these (see the comments in loc.) we have the same expression as here ("agonize the good agony"). And there seems to be no question but that the popular use of the noun *agōn* here was for gatherings for games. In Hebrews 12:1 this noun is, of necessity, translated "race"—a race to be run.

If we accept the dominance of the athletic metaphor here, we can paraphrase the verse like this: "I have competed well in the athletic contest [of life], I have finished the race, I have kept the rules"—not "fouled out" and so been disqualified from winning. The word for "race" is *dromon* (only here and Acts 13:25; 20:24). It comes from the second aorist stem of *trechō* ("run"), and so clearly means a racecourse (cf. KJV).

8 One of the main reasons for preferring the athletic interpretation in v.7—which is favored by Bernard and Fairbairn, and allowed by Lock—is that it fits in perfectly with v.8. Paul says that a "crown" awaits him. This is not *diadēma* ("diadem"), the royal crown, but *stephanos*, the laurel wreath given to the winner of the Marathon race (cf. 1 Cor 9:25). The Lord, the righteous Judge (of the contest) was ready to "award" this prize to Paul at the end of the race, his victorious life. The same reward awaits all who run the Christian race successfully to the finish and long for "his appearing" (the Second Coming).

Notes

8 The genitive, τῆς δικαιοσύνης (*tēs diakaiosynēs*, "of righteousness"), is difficult to interpret. Bernard thinks it means "the crown appropriate to the righteous man, and belonging to righteousness" (p. 143). Lock defines it as "the crown which belongs to, which is won by righteousness; perhaps also the crown which consists in perfect eternal righteousness" (p. 115). This would be the genitive of apposition.

XI. Paul's Final Plea

4:9–13

9Do your best to come to me quickly, 10for Demas, because he loved this world, has deserted me and has gone to Thessalonica. Crescens has gone to Galatia, and Titus to Dalmatia. 11Only Luke is with me. Get Mark and bring him with you, because he is helpful to me in my ministry. 12I sent Tychicus to Ephesus. 13When you come, bring the cloak that I left with Carpus at Troas, and my scrolls, especially the parchments.

9 "Do your best" is *spoudason* ("make haste"). Paul had already said that he longed to see Timothy (1:4). Now he urges him to come speedily.

10 Verses 10–12 give the reasons for this. Paul was left almost alone. Demas, his trusted associate, had deserted him. During the apostle's first Roman imprisonment, he twice

mentioned Demas as one of his fellow workers (Col 4:14; Philem 24). Some have tried to put a good construction on the reference to Demas in 2 Timothy, suggesting that he had gone on a missionary errand to Thessalonica. But Paul uses the same verb *en-kataleipō* here as in v.16 ("deserted"). And we are told that Demas left "because he loved this world." He was not willing to pay the price of hardship and suffering that Paul was paying.

Crescens (mentioned only here) had gone to Galatia, and Titus to Dalmatia. The latter place was on the eastern shore of the Adriatic Sea, north of Macedonia. We are not told the reason why these two men left Paul at Rome. We would assume that they were sent by him to do missionary work, though this is not specifically stated. Incidentally, this verse also shows that Titus had completed his work in Crete (Titus 1:5) and had joined Paul at Rome.

11 "Only Luke is with me." There is pathos, "a tremulous note" (Simpson) in these words. Since Luke was alone with Paul, he was probably the one who acted as the apostle's secretary in the actual writing of this Epistle (see Introduction). Perhaps Luke's own loneliness is also reflected here.

Why did Luke stay with Paul to the end? Perhaps it was because the aged, ailing apostle needed the care of "the beloved physician" (Col 4:14, KJV) in his closing years and because Luke's deep personal devotion to Paul would lead him to stay right with him.

"Mark" had had a checkered career. We first meet him in Acts 12:12. When Peter was miraculously delivered from prison, "he went to the house of Mary the mother of John, also called Mark." Barnabas and Paul took him to Antioch (Acts 12:25) and then took him with them as "their helper" on the first missionary journey (13:5). But the young Mark "flunked out" and returned to Jerusalem (13:13). Because of this, Paul refused to take him along on the second journey (15:36–40). Later Mark matured and was with Paul in his first Roman imprisonment (Col 4:10). Now the aging apostle gives his young associate his highest accolade: "Get Mark and bring him with you, because he is helpful to me in my ministry." So John Mark is a vivid example of a young man who failed in his first assignment, but finally made good.

12 "Tychicus" was from the province of Asia and accompanied Paul on his last journey to Jerusalem (Acts 20:4). He was the bearer of the letters to the Colossians (4:7, 8) and to the Ephesians (6:21). In both places he is described as a "dear brother" and "faithful servant in the Lord." It is obvious that Paul had high regard for Tychicus.

"I sent" (*apesteila*) may well be taken as the epistolary aorist, "I am sending." If so, Tychicus was the bearer of this Epistle and was being sent by Paul to take Timothy's place as supervisor of the work at Ephesus. The apostle wanted his "dear son" (1:2) with him in the closing days of his life. We can only conjecture as to whether Timothy reached Paul before the latter's death.

13 It is evident that Timothy was not to go by ship directly to Rome from the large seaport of Ephesus, for he is requested to pick up the cloak Paul had left with Carpus at Troas. Nothing further is known about Carpus. The "cloak" was probably "a travelling cloak with long sleeves, such as would be specially desirable in cold weather" (Bernard, p. 146).

Timothy was also to bring Paul's "scrolls." The Greek is *biblia*, from which comes "Bible." *Biblion* meant "a paper, letter, written document" (A-S), and it is so used in

Matthew 19:7 and Mark 10:4. But its common use in the NT, as in the literature of that day, is for a "roll" or "scroll." These were probably made of papyrus.

Paul especially wanted his "parchments." This kind of writing material was more expensive than papyrus; *membrana* (a Latin word, only here in the NT) were scrolls or codices written on animal skins (vellum). These may have been leather scrolls of OT books. There is an interesting historical parallel to Paul's request. William Tyndale, who translated the first NT printed in English, was imprisoned in Vilvorde Castle near Brussels before his execution in 1536. In the year preceding his death he wrote to the governor, begging for warmer clothing, a woolen shirt, and above all his Hebrew Bible, grammar, and dictionary.

Notes

10 Instead of Γαλατίαν (*Galatian*, "Galatia") two old MSS (א C) have Γαλλίαν (*Gallian*, "Gaul"). But the former reading seems to be the original one. Greek writers of the first century, however, commonly used Γαλατία (*Galatia*) for Gaul (modern France), northwest of Italy. So we cannot be sure whether the reference is to Asiatic Galatia—as always elsewhere in Acts and Paul's Epistles—or to European Gaul. If it was the latter, as held by some early church fathers, the reference would show Paul's interest in the evangelization of the far west and would imply that he visited Spain between his first and second Roman imprisonments.

13 The word for "cloak" is φαιλόνης (*phailonēs*, only here in the NT). This is listed as φελόνης (*phelonēs*) in A-S, but as φαιλόνης in BAG. The latter admits, however, that φελόνης is the spelling in "the great uncials and critical editions" (p. 859).

XII. Human Opposition and Divine Support

4:14–18

¹⁴Alexander the metalworker did me a great deal of harm. The Lord will repay him for what he has done. ¹⁵You too should be on your guard against him, because he strongly opposed our message.

¹⁶At my first defense, no one came to my support, but everyone deserted me. May it not be held against them. ¹⁷But the Lord stood at my side and gave me strength, so that through me the message might be fully proclaimed and all the Gentiles might hear it. And I was delivered from the lion's mouth. ¹⁸The Lord will rescue me from every evil attack and will bring me safely to his heavenly kingdom. To him be glory for ever and ever. Amen.

14,15 We know nothing further about "Alexander." This was a common name; so there is no necessary identification with the Alexander of Acts 19:33 or 1 Timothy 1:20 (see comments there). He is called a "metalworker" (*chalkeus*, only here in the NT). Since the word comes from *chalkos*, "copper," it originally was used for a "coppersmith" (KJV), but later in a more general sense for a worker in any metal, especially iron.

We do not know when, where, or in what way Alexander did Paul "a great deal of harm." One good guess is that he had been responsible for the apostle's arrest and imprisonment.

"The Lord reward him according to his works" (KJV) sounds like an imprecatory prayer. But the oldest and best Greek text does not have *apodōē* (the optative of wishing)

415

but the future indicative *apodōsei*, "will repay." It is not an imprecation but a prophecy.

Paul warns Timothy to be on guard against this malicious enemy who "strongly opposed our message" (*logois*, "words"). This may possibly have included not only Paul's preaching but his defense before the court, mentioned in the next verse.

16 The word for "defense" is *apolgia*, from which we get "apology." But our English word has changed its meaning in common usage. Whereas now it means "I was wrong," it originally meant a speech in defense—"I was right!" (cf. Acts 22:1). This sense of the word survives in the term "apologetics" and in the transliteration "apologia," a literary term for a defense of one's position.

What is indicated by Paul's "first defense" when no one came to his support but everyone deserted him? Eusebius (4th century) held that it was in connection with Paul's first Roman imprisonment (Acts 28:30), which resulted in his release. This accords well with the end of v.17, and Lock prefers this interpretation.

But most commentators feel that the language here is too strong for that earlier event, when in accordance with Roman custom, he may have been automatically released without trial at the end of two years. Today scholars generally agree that the reference is to the *prima actio*, the first hearing in court.

Paul's magnanimous Christian love is revealed in the last sentence of this verse: "May it not be held against them." He could and did forgive his deserters for their weakness in fearing to stand by him.

17 But he did not lack support. Triumphantly and gratefully he cries, "But the Lord stood at my side and gave me strength" (*enedynamōsen me*, "infused me with strength, empowered me, made me dynamic!"). The result was that the Gentiles in Caesar's court heard the gospel, which thereby got wider publicity in Rome. When was Paul "delivered from the lion's mouth"? If we accept the reference to his first imprisonment, the answer seems simple. But was he threatened to the extent implied by this vivid figure? The only alternative would be that his first trial had seemed to go well for him, with perhaps a temporary reprieve. The "lion" would then be Nero. But if so, it was this same emperor who later, according to the unanimous tradition of the early church, condemned him and put him to death.

18 "Rescue" and "delivered" (v.17) are from the same verb in Greek, *rhyomai*. There is a striking connection between its use here and in the Lord's Prayer: "Deliver us from the evil one" (Matt 6:13). "Attack" is literally "work" (*ergon*), but the correct thought is expressed here (see Lock, p. 119). The same can be said for "bring me safely" (*sōsei*, "will save"). The exact phrase "his heavenly kingdom" (*tēn basileian autou tēn epouranion*) is not found elsewhere in the NT, but is closely paralleled by "the kingdom of heaven," found thirty-two times in Matthew. Probably the reference here, however, is to the future kingdom in the eternal realm.

Paul is fond of breaking out into spontaneous praise now and then in his Epistles. One of his many doxologies occurs here: "To him"—the Lord; that is, Christ—"be glory for ever and ever. Amen."

Notes

17 There is no definite article with λέοντος (*leontos,* "lion"). This has led some scholars to say that the reference is not to Nero or Satan, but to some imminent deadly peril. But why not allow all three applications?

XIII. Closing Greetings, Farewell

4:19–22

> ¹⁹Greet Priscilla and Aquila and the household of Onesiphorus. ²⁰Erastus stayed in Corinth, and I left Trophimus sick in Miletus. ²¹Do your best to get here before winter. Eubulus greets you, and so do Pudens, Linus, Claudia and all the brothers. ²²The Lord be with your spirit. Grace be with you.

19 Priscilla and Aquila figured prominently in Paul's life. When Paul first arrived in Corinth—evidently short of funds and disappointed at the meager results of his ministry in Athens—he found both employment and lodging with Aquila and Priscilla. Like him, they were tentmakers (Acts 18:2, 3). When Paul left Corinth, this couple sailed across the Aegean with him to Ephesus and stayed there (Acts 18:18, 19). They performed a useful function by instructing Apollos (v.26). From there they, and the church that met in their home, sent greetings to the Christians at Corinth (1 Cor 16:19). Later we apparently find them back in Rome (Rom 16:3); Paul sent greetings to them there and referred (Rom 16:4) to an occasion when they had "risked their lives" for him. But now they are once more in Ephesus. In those days prosperous Jews traveled a great deal from city to city. In four of the six places where Priscilla and Aquila are mentioned, Priscilla's name comes first. Evidently she was the stronger character of the two. It may well be that their moves were due as much to her missionary concern as to her husband's trade.

The "household of Onesiphorus" is mentioned with great appreciation in 1:16–18 (see comments there). But we know nothing further about this devoted Christian.

20 When Paul wrote to Rome from Corinth, he sent greetings from "Erastus, who is the city's director of public works" (Rom 16:23). There was also an Erastus who, along with Timothy, was Paul's helper, at Ephesus (Acts 19:22). We have no way, of course, of knowing whether these three passages refer to the same person. Lock thinks that the Erastus mentioned here was "probably" the same as the one in Romans and "perhaps" the same as the one in Acts (p. 120). At any rate, "Erastus stayed in Corinth," possibly when Paul left there for the last time.

The apostle had "left Trophimus sick in Miletus" (near Ephesus). This man is mentioned as from the province of Asia and as one of Paul's associates in carrying the offering from the Gentile churches to the poor saints at Jerusalem (Acts 20:4). There he became the cause, unintentionally, of Paul's being mobbed and arrested (Acts 21:29).

21 Paul is beginning to feel the cold and dampness in his prison cell. So now he speaks with fresh urgency: "Do your best" (*spoudason,* cf. v.9) "to get here before winter." If not, he will suffer desperately in the cold weather.

Finally, Paul sends greetings from four members of the church at Rome—Eubulus, Pudens, Linus, Claudia—"and all the brothers." Linus is mentioned by Irenaeus (*Against*

Heresies, iii.3) as the first bishop of Rome after the death of Peter and Paul. About the others, we have no certain knowledge.

Paul pronounces a personal benediction on Timothy ("your" is singular in the Greek), before concluding comprehensively: "Grace be with you all."

Notes

19 "Priscilla" is Πρίσκα (*Priska,* "Prisca") here and elsewhere in Paul's Epistles (Rom 16:3; 1 Cor 16:19). But she is better known to us as Priscilla (Πρίσκιλλα, Priskilla) in Acts 18:2, 18, 26.

TITUS

D. Edmond Hiebert

TITUS

Introduction

1. Authorship
2. Recipient
3. Occasion
4. Purpose
5. Date
6. Place of Origin
7. Theological Value
8. Text
9. Summary
10. Bibliography (See Introduction to 1 Timothy)
11. Outline

As the shortest of the pastoral Epistles, Titus has often been overshadowed by the longer Epistles to Timothy. But it is rich in doctrinal and practical values and is worthy of study in its own right.

1. Authorship

The Pauline authorship of the Epistle was not questioned in the early church. Arguments against its authenticity are of modern origin. Its claim to Pauline authorship is here accepted without reserve. (See the introduction to the pastoral Epistles.)

2. Recipient

The letter is addressed to "Titus, my true son in our common faith" (1:4). The appended identification marks a close and affectionate relation between Paul and Titus. Titus 2:6, 7 implies that he was still a comparatively young man when Paul wrote to him.

Scriptural references to Titus are surprisingly rare. Although he was closely connected with Paul, Titus's name never occurs in Acts and, aside from the letter addressed to him, his name is found in only three Pauline Epistles (2 Cor 2:13; 7:6, 13, 14; 8:6, 16, 23; 12:18; Gal. 2:1, 3; 2 Tim 4:10).

Chronologically, the first mention of Titus is in Galatians 2:1–3. When Paul went from Antioch to discuss "his" gospel with the leaders in Jerusalem, he took along Titus, an uncircumcised young Greek, as a worthy specimen of the fruits of his ministry to the Gentiles. "My true son" implies that he was Paul's convert, perhaps won during the ministry in Acts 11:25, 26. At Jerusalem Paul's position that Gentile believers are not under the Mosaic law was vindicated when Titus was not compelled to be circumcised (Gal 2:3–5). Paul's selection of Titus to test this crucial issue speaks well of the spiritual vitality of his young convert.

We hear nothing further of Titus till the time of Paul's ministry at Ephesus on the third missionary journey. Perhaps Paul took him along to Ephesus from Antioch (Acts 18:22–19:1). He was an unnamed member of the group of assistants to Paul there (Acts 19:22). Second Corinthians reveals that at this time he was an esteemed and trusted co-worker with Paul. On more than one occasion Paul sent Titus to Corinth on important missions. Most probably three separate trips to Corinth were made, but the precise number of visits and the sequence of events are uncertain from 2 Corinthians.

About a year before the writing of 2 Corinthians, Paul sent Titus to Corinth to enlist Corinthian participation in the collection for the Judean saints (1 Cor 16:1–4; 2 Cor 9:2; 12:18). Apparently shortly after writing 1 Corinthians, Paul again sent Titus to Corinth to help straighten out the tangled affairs in that church and to counter the work of opponents to Paul there. Plans called for a reunion at Troas where Paul was to engage in missionary work (2 Cor 2:12, 13). The failure of Titus to return as planned caused Paul much anxiety. Terminating the inviting work at Troas, Paul went into Macedonia, hoping in this way to meet Titus sooner. Eventually Titus appeared in Macedonia with the good news that his difficult mission to Corinth had been successful (2 Cor 7:5–7). Paul rejoiced in this success and was encouraged by the personal joy of Titus at the response of the Corinthians (2 Cor 7:6, 7, 13–15). Cheered by these developments, Paul wrote the second Epistle to the Corinthians and sent it back with Titus, instructing him also to complete the collection at Corinth (2 Cor 8:6, 7, 16–22). Paul gave Titus and the two men sent with him (8:18–22) his strong recommendation (8:23, 24), assuring any critical Corinthian that Titus could be fully trusted as one motivated by Paul's own spirit (2 Cor 12:17, 18).

When Paul came to Corinth for three months (Acts 20:2), the difficulties there had been resolved and the collection completed. Titus had successfully completed another sensitive assignment. But he was no longer at Corinth when Paul wrote to the Romans, for his name does not appear among those of Paul's co-workers who sent greetings to the Roman saints (Rom 16:21–23). Nothing further is heard of Titus till the time of the pastoral Epistles.

When Paul wrote to him, Titus was working on the island of Crete. "I left you in Crete" (1:5) indicates that Paul had been with Titus in Crete. Their joint labors there apparently were of short duration, but long enough for Paul to realize the deplorable conditions of the local churches. Apparently Titus had been working there for some time when Paul wrote. He informed Titus that as soon as a replacement arrived, he was to rejoin Paul at Nicopolis (3:12), apparently the Greek city in Epirus on the Gulf of Actium, in western Greece. The request indicates that Paul was formulating further plans for Titus.

We get a last fleeting glimpse of Titus in 2 Timothy 4:10, where Paul informed Timothy that Titus had gone to Dalmatia. This implies he had been with Paul during his second Roman imprisonment. Although the reason for the trip is not given, we may assume that he went there at the call of Christian duty.

These scanty references to Titus reveal that he was a trustworthy, efficient, and valued young co-worker. He possessed a forceful personality, was resourceful, energetic, tactful, skillful in dealing with difficult situations, and effective in conciliating people.

3. Occasion

The external occasion for the letter to Titus was the trip through Crete planned by Zenas and Apollos (3:13). They conveyed the letter to Titus. The internal occasion for writing was Paul's concern to strengthen the hand of Titus as his personal representative in Crete in carrying out a difficult assignment.

4. Purpose

One purpose of the letter was, as has just been stated, to encourage and strengthen Titus in the fulfillment of the commission from Paul. Because of conditions in Crete, Paul knew that Titus would face opposition (1:10, 11; 2:15; 3:10). He aimed to reinforce Titus's authority in working among the churches in Crete. The letter would serve as written authorization for this task, proof to them that he was working in accordance with Paul's own instructions. As the close associate of Paul, Titus must personally have been familiar with the exhortations and instructions contained in the letter, which set forth Paul's concerns for the Cretan churches.

The origin of the Cretan churches is unknown. They had evidently been in existence for some time when Paul visited Crete. Their condition was discouraging. They were inadequately organized, so Titus was directed to appoint morally and doctrinally qualified elders in the various churches (1:6–9). In view of the operation of false teachers (1:10–16), this was essential.

The prevailing moral conditons in the churches were far from what they might be. Naturally prone to be lax and indifferent, the Christians were adversely influenced by the prevailing low moral standards in Crete. Perhaps the gospel of the grace of God had been misinterpreted to mean that salvation was unrelated to daily conduct. Titus was urged to insist on the need for sound doctrine and a high level of moral and social conduct by the Christians (2:1–10; 3:1–3). Christian behavior must be grounded in the basic truths of the gospel (2:11–14; 3:4–8).

The letter also conveyed personal information for Titus. The instruction to join Paul at his winter quarters at Nicopolis after a replacement arrived (3:12) apprised Titus of the fact that Paul was formulating further plans for their joint labors.

5. Date

The date assigned the letter depends on the reconstruction accepted for Paul's journeys following his release from the first Roman imprisonment, as well as the dating for that imprisonment, commonly accepted as A.D. 61–63, though it may have been as early as 59–61. Since this letter makes no mention of the Neronian persecution, which apparently began in October 64, it seems best to date it between the time of Paul's release and the commencement of that persecution. The journeys to the east indicated in 1 Timothy and Titus were apparently made as soon as he was released. The letter to Titus may have been written during the fall of A.D. 63, not long after Paul left Crete.

6. Place of Origin

This can only be conjectured. The remark in 3:12 indicates that Paul had not yet reached Nicopolis. Any suggested place will depend on the reconstruction of Paul's movements following his release. A case can be made for Corinth as the place of origin.

7. Theological Value

The Epistle of Titus covers the same general ground as 1 Timothy but is more compact and less personal. Its greater part deals with ministerial duties and social relations, yet it contains no fewer than three summary passages that are theological gems (1:1–3; 2:11–14; 3:3–7). In 1 Timothy Paul stresses sound doctrine; in Titus he stresses worthy Christian conduct and insists that Christian conduct must be based on and regulated by Christian truth. Nowhere else does Paul more forcefully urge the essential connection between evangelical truth and the purest morality than in this brief letter. Here the basic truths of the gospel are displayed in the abiding glory of their saving and sanctifying appeal. The regenerating work of the Holy Spirit is the experiential basis for Christian conduct (3:3–7).

8. Text

Although the manuscript sources for this letter manifest the usual presence of variant readings, the text of Titus presents no unusual critical problems. The editors of the UBS text felt it desirable to include only four textual problems in their textual apparatus as significant for interpretation.

9. Summary

After the customary salutation (1:1–4), Paul deals first with the qualifications to be looked for in church officials (vv.5–9), then goes on to condemn the false teachers who were undermining the work in Crete (vv.10–16).

In chapter 2 Paul gives Titus advice on how to handle the situation there: he lays down rules for Christian behavior, with special reference to the aged (vv.1–3), younger people (vv.4–8), and slaves (vv.9, 10).

The closing verses (11–15) of that chapter reflect a more theological emphasis in the discussion that, continued into chapter 3, covers the implications of Christian living in the community (vv.1, 2). Then comes a reminder of the transformation wrought by the gospel through the appearance and work of the Savior (vv.4–7).

An admonitory word on good works (v.8; cf. v.14) and false teachers (vv.9–11) follows, and the brief Epistle concludes with personal messages and counsel, and with the benediction (vv.12–15).

10. Bibliography

(See Introduction to 1 Timothy, pp. 346–347.)

11. Outline

I. Salutation (1:1–4)
  A. The Writer (1:1–3)
  B. The Reader (1:4a)
  C. The Greeting (1:4b)
II. Concerning Elders and Errorists in Crete (1:5–16)
  A. The Appointment of Qualified Elders (1:5–9)
    1. The Duties of Titus in Crete (1:5)
    2. The Qualifications of the Elders (1:6–9)
  B. The Refutation of False Teachers (1:10–16)
    1. The picture of the false teachers (1:10–13a)
    2. The response to the situation (1:13b–14)
    3. The condemnation of the false teachers (1:15–16)
III. Concerning the Natural Groups in the Congregations (2:1–15)
  A. The Instructions for the Different Groups (2:1–10)
    1. The instructional duty of Titus (2:1)
    2. The instruction to different age groups (2:2–6)
    3. The personal example of Titus (2:7–8)
    4. The instructions to the slaves (2:9–10)
  B. The Foundation for Godly Living (2:11–14)
    1. The manifestation of God's grace (2:11)
    2. The training by God's grace (2:12)
    3. The expectation of Christ's return (2:13)
    4. The purpose of Christ's redemption (2:14)
  C. The Restatement of the Duty of Titus (2:15)
IV. Concerning Believers Among Men Generally (3:1–11)
  A. Their Obligations As Citizens (3:1–2)
  B. The Motives for Such Godly Conduct (3:3–8)
    1. The motive from our own past (3:3)
    2. The motive from our present salvation (3:4–7)
      a. Its manifestation (3:4)
      b. Its basis (3:5a)
      c. Its means (3:5b–6)
      d. Its results (3:7)
    3. The necessary connection between doctrine and conduct (3:8)
  C. The Reaction to Spiritual Error (3:9–11)
V. Conclusion (3:12–15)
  A. The Concluding Instructions (3:12–14)
  B. The Personal Greetings (3:15a)
  C. The Closing Benediction (3:15b)

Text and Exposition

I. Salutation

1:1–4

> [1]Paul, a servant of God and an apostle of Jesus Christ for the faith of God's elect and the knowledge of the truth that leads to godliness— [2]a faith and knowledge resting on the hope of eternal life, which God, who does not lie, promised before the beginning of time, [3]and at his appointed season he brought his word to light through the preaching entrusted to me by the command of God our Savior,
>
> [4]To Titus, my true son in our common faith:
>
> Grace and peace from God the Father and Christ Jesus our Savior.

The salutation is remarkably long and weight for such a brief letter. Only in the lengthy Epistle to the Romans is the salutation much longer. The paragraphing displays the usual three parts of an epistolary salutation of that day—writer, reader, greeting. Each part might be expanded according to the occasion and the writer's purpose.

A. *The Writer* (1:1–3)

1 Here, as in Romans, the length of the salutation is due to the expansion of the first part. The emphasis here on the writer and his authoritative message indicates the purpose of the letter. This solemn self-indentification of the writer was not needed by Titus as Paul's devoted co-worker; it effectively stressed the authoritative commission and message of the one for whom Titus acted in Crete. This letter was written for the preservation and furtherance of that message, which was closely linked with godliness in daily life.

To his name Paul added two credentials. "A servant of God" occurs only here in Paul; elsewhere it is "servant of Jesus Christ" (Rom 1:1; Gal 1:10; Phil 1:1). It is hard to understand why an imitator would thus vary from the uniform model. The nearest parallel is James 1:1. "Servant" (*doulos*) is the common term for "slave" and its use implies Paul's acknowledged ownership by God and complete dependence on him. It denotes his personal position. It is here best rendered "servant," since "servant of God" was used of Moses (Josh 1:2) and the prophets (Jer 7:25; Amos 3:7) to denote their use by God to accomplish his will. He is nothing less than *God's* agent. (Note the five occurrences of "God" in this salutation.) Apparently this stress was needed in Crete.

"An apostle of Jesus Christ" marks Paul's official rank among God's servants. "And" (*de*) does not equate but adds an additional fact: "and further." He is Jesus Christ's "apostle," having been called, equipped, and sent forth as his authoritative messenger. "Apostle" is here used in the narrow sense to denote the apostolic office.

"For the faith of God's elect and the knowledge of the truth" further describes his apostolic office. "For" renders the preposition *kata*, the first of four occurrences in the salutation (vv.1 [twice], 3, 4). Its local meaning is "down," and with the accusative case (so in all four occurrences), it means "down along, according to, in harmony with," and marks the standard of measurement. By usage it can mean goal or purpose, "for the purpose of, to further," thus denoting that Paul's mission was to promote Christian faith and knowledge. This is the view of the above rendering which, however, cannot be given to all four occurrences. The translation "according to" which fits all four of them in the salutation, means that his apostleship is in full accord with the faith and knowledge that God's elect have received. His apostleship is not regulated by their faith (cf. Gal

1:11–17) but is wholly in accord with it. The Cretan Christians needed to evaluate their faith by that fact.

"God's elect" are those who have responded to God's call through the gospel. The expression embodies a true balance between the divine initiative and the human response. Although surrounded with mystery, the biblical teaching on election is for believers and is intended as a practical truth. It assures faithful, struggling believers that their salvation is all of God from beginning to end.

Christian faith is linked with "knowledge of the truth," the full apprehension of "truth," the inner realization of divine reality as revealed in the gospel. Faith is a heart response to the truth of the gospel, but it must also possess the mind. God never intended his people to remain intellectually ignorant of the truth of the gospel.

Christian truth has a moral character. It "leads to godliness" (more literally, "that is according to godliness"). Conduct must be evaluated by the demands of godliness, that reverential attitude that leads to conduct well pleasing to God. Those gripped by God's truth walk in harmony with such demands. There is an intimate connection between a vital possession of truth and genuine godliness—a lesson the Cretan church needed to learn.

2 The intended connection of v.2 is not quite certain. The NIV translators have added the words "a faith and knowledge" to make clear their understanding of the connection —that the Christian life is grounded in the hope of eternal life. Others hold that the connection is with "apostle" thus giving a further description of Paul's apostleship. But this seems to narrow the thought unduly. It seems best to connect it with all that has gone before.

"Resting on" well renders the original (*epi* with the locative case). "The hope of eternal life" is the basis on which the superstructure of Christian faith and service is built. As with all of God's elect, Paul's life and service were firmly rooted in "hope," which eagerly and confidently awaits the realization of "eternal life"—life not only endless but having an eternal quality. Believers already possess eternal life (John 5:24), but its full and perfect realization awaits the return of the Prince of Life.

This hope is not a vague, pious aspiration but is sure because it is grounded in the absolute trustworthiness of God. The character of the God "who does not lie" (one word in Greek) assures the fulfillment of his promise. This characterization places God in contrast with the notorious deceptiveness of the Cretans (1:12).

God promised this eternal life "before the beginning of time" (literally, "before times eternal"), before the ages of time, begun at creation, began to roll. Some hold that the reference is to the promises made to the OT patriarchs and prophets; others say that the promise reaches back into eternity (cf. 2 Tim 1:9). William Kelly says, "It was a promise within the Godhead when neither the world nor man yet existed" (p.17). The promise is rooted in the eternal purpose of God for man.

3 The reliability of the promise, conceived in the eternal counsels of God, was demonstrated in history through the clear, public revelation it received in the preaching of the gospel. A change in the construction brings out a contrast between the promise of life before times eternal and the manifestation of "his word" at the proper time in history. "His word" is not the personal Christ, the Logos, but rather the saving message of the gospel. This message was made known "at his appointed season," the opportune seasons established by God in his eternal wisdom. All history was the preparation for that revelation. The historical appropriateness of the time is evident from the existence of the Roman peace that gave a favorable setting for the preaching of the gospel and the development of Greek as the linguistic medium of its worldwide proclamation.

The message was brought to the world "through the preaching entrusted to me." This refers, not to the act of preaching, but to the message that was heralded, the message of the gospel. There is no substitute for that message, and Paul was writing so that its purity might be preserved on the island of Crete.

That life-giving message was committed to Paul as a divine trust. He could never escape the wonder that this assignment should be given to him, unworthy as he was (1 Cor 15:9; Eph 3:8; 1 Tim 1:11–13). The personal pronoun is deliberately emphatic, "I on my part was entrusted with" this message. His call was for him a very personal, irreversible experience.

The assignment came to him "by the command of God our Savior." It is a vigorous assertion of his divine commission, underlining the authority behind this letter. "God our Savior" is not used by Paul outside the pastoral Epistles. The original order, "our Savior, God," stresses his saving activity; the One who delivers and preserves is none other than God. The pronoun "our" speaks of the believer's personal appropriation and public confession of him in this capacity. Paul's usage suggests that the reference here is to the Father. In the Pastorals the term is applied to both the Father (1 Tim 1:1; 2:3; 4:10; Titus 1:3; 2:10; 3:4) and the Son (2 Tim 1:10; Titus 1:4; 2:13; 3:6). As the ultimate source of all salvation, the designation is appropriately applied to the Father.

B. *The Reader* (1:4a)

The recipient is tersely described as "my true son in our common faith". "My true son" ("my" is not in the original) reveals the intimate relation between writer and reader. "Son" is literally "child" and expresses endearment; it implies that Titus was Paul's convert. The adjective "true" (*gnēsios*), used only in Paul's letters, means "legitimately born, or genuine" and acknowledges that Titus was running true to a parentage that was not physical but spiritual, "in our common faith." "In" (*kata*) indicates that their relationship was in accord with a "common faith," a faith mutually shared. But "common" reaches farther than writer and reader to denote a faith mutually held by God's elect. This intimate relationship assured that in Crete Titus rightly represented the position of Paul.

C. *The Greeting* (1:4b)

The greeting with "grace and peace" is characteristically Pauline. "Grace" here is the unmerited favor of God at work in the life of the believer, while "peace" is the resultant experience of harmony and well-being in the life of the reconciled. This double blessing comes "from God the Father and Christ Jesus our Savior." Paul viewed Father and Son as one source of blessing and the one object of every Christian aspiration, thus "from" is not repeated. "Our Savior," in v.3 applied to the Father, is here transferred to the Son. "Our" again signifies the common testimony of believers. This interchange is not accidental; both are involved in bestowing the same salvation. "The Son has brought to us salvation from the Father, and the Father has bestowed it through the Son" (Calvin).

Notes

4 As in 1 and 2 Timothy, TR here also reads ἔλεος (*eleos*, "mercy" between "grace" and "peace"). MS evidence, however, strongly favors its omission.

II. Concerning Elders and Errorists in Crete (1:5–16)

The first major division, designed to further the welfare of the Cretan churches, falls into two parts. Verses 5–9 give instructions concerning church officials, whereas vv.10–16 deal with the needed refutation of false teachers in Crete. The presence of the false teachers made more imperative the appointment of qualified leaders.

A. *The Appointment of Qualified Elders*

1:5–9

> ⁵The reason I left you in Crete was that you might straighten out what was left unfinished and appoint elders in every town, as I directed you. ⁶An elder must be blameless, the husband of but one wife, a man whose children believe and are not open to the charge of being wild and disobedient. ⁷Since an overseer is entrusted with God's work, he must be blameless—not overbearing, not quick-tempered, not given to much wine, not violent, not pursuing dishonest gain. ⁸Rather he must be hospitable, one who loves what is good, who is self-controlled, upright, holy and disciplined. ⁹He must hold firmly to the trustworthy message as it has been taught, so that he can encourage others by sound doctrine and refute those who oppose it.

Paul's representative in Crete must carry out his commission with the authority shown in the salutation. Verse 5 summarizes the commission given Titus, and vv.6–9 list the needed qualifications for the leaders to be appointed.

1. *The duties of Titus in Crete* (1:5)

5 "I left you in Crete" asserts their joint labors on that island; the time was probably quite brief. Paul's labors in Crete cannot be fitted into Acts 27:7–9 or before. The alternatives are to reject Pauline authorship or to accept that the reference is to a time following his Acts 28 imprisonment. The latter alternative is probable scripturally and is asserted by tradition.

"Left" (*apelipon*) implies that Titus was deliberately left behind in Crete to carry out a specific assignment. Before Paul's departure, the commission was orally delivered; now it is restated concisely in writing. Titus's task was comprehensive: to "straighten out what was left unfinished." The verb "straighten out" (*epidiorthōsē*) denotes that his task was to set things in order; the middle voice implies that he is personally involved in the process, and not merely giving orders to others. "What was left unfinished" points to several serious defects that still needed Titus's attention. The letter points to lack of organization (1:5), unchecked false teachers (1:10, 11; 3:10, 11), and the need for instruction in doctrine and conduct (2:1–10; 3:1, 2). Paul had observed and had begun to correct these matters; Titus must now complete the work. Paul was concerned that the work of grace previously begun in the church should not be left unfinished.

An initial duty was to "appoint elders in every town," in each place where there was a group of believers. Such a plural leadership in the local congregation continued Paul's own earlier practice (Acts 14:23). "Appoint" is preferable to "ordain," as it avoids modern ecclesiastical implication. The verb means "to set down, to put in charge," and does not fix the method of selection. Probably the congregation chose the elders with the encouragement of Titus who had the responsibility of formally appointing them to office.

"As I directed you" recalls that this was in accord with his previous orders. "I" (*egō*) is emphatic, stressing the apostolic authority behind the action of Titus. The middle voice of the verb implies that it would carry out Paul's ideal for these congregations.

2. The qualifications of the elders (1:6-9)

6-9 This list of qualifications corresponds closely to that given in 1 Timothy 3:1-7, yet the differences indicate that it was realistically applied to a contemporary situation. The fact that no deacons are mentioned suggests that the organization of these churches was more primitive than at Ephesus.

6 "An elder must be blameless" marks the basic qualification, demanding an irreproachable reputation in the community. The original, "if anyone is blameless," does not imply doubt but rather assumes that the fact is established. This demand is elaborated in what follows.

Two domestic qualifications are stipulated. The precise implications of "the husband of but one wife" have been debated through the centuries (See Fairbairn, *The Pastoral Epistles*, Appendix B). It has been held to prohibit a second marriage, but this seems improbable (cf. 1 Tim 5:14; Rom 7:2, 3; 1 Cor 7:39). If Paul had meant that the elder *must* be married, the reading would have been "a," not "one," wife. Most natural is the view that he must be the husband of only one living woman.

Since older men would be chosen for leadership, it is assumed that the elder would have children. The latter must "believe," share their father's Christian faith. The original (*tekna pista*) may mean "faithful children" but "believing children," is intended here, referring to those who are old enough to have made a personal decision. If they remained pagans, it would throw into question the father's ability to lead others to the faith. As professed believers, the children must personally fulfill the ethical requirements of the Christian life. They must not be chargeable as being "wild," self-indulgent and wasteful in their manner of life, like the prodigal son, nor be "disobedient," refusing to bow to parental authority. An elder's inability to train and govern his children would place in question his ability to train and govern the church.

7 The leader's true position and personal qualifications are given in vv.7, 8. The switch in v.7 to "overseer" shows that "elder" and "overseer" or "bishop" are interchangeable terms, yet with a different connotation. "Elder" (*presbyteros*) implies the maturity and dignity of the man, while "bishop" (*episkopos*) indicates his work as the "overseer" of God's flock.

The Greek is more literally, "It is necessary that the overseer be blameless as God's steward." "The" is the generic use of the article and signifies the representative of the class. The repeated "blameless" prepares for the further elaboration in vv.7-9, but now the stress is on "it is necessary" (*dei*), because of the elder's position as "God's steward." The steward was the manager of a household or estate, appointed by and accountable to the owner. The picture of the steward embodies one of Paul's favorite concepts of the ministry (1 Cor 4:1, 2; 9:17; Eph 3:2; Col 1:25). The Christian minister is not merely the servant of the church; he exercises his office under God's authority and is directly accountable to him. This high office makes high demands on the character of the man. Five negative and six positive personal qualifications are listed in vv.7, 8.

The repeated negative (*mē*) rejects any thought of the steward's being (1) "overbearing," arrogantly disregarding the interests of others in order to please himself; (2) "quick-tempered," readily yielding to anger, for pastoral work demands much patience; (3) "given to wine," literally, "alongside of wine" (*paroinon*), as addicted to its use; he must not be an alcoholic; (4) "violent," ready to assail an opponent, either with fists or by bellicose behavior; (5) "pursuing dishonest gain," using his office to profit in an underhanded and shameful way. The laborer is worthy of his hire, but he must not turn his office into a money-making business.

8 "Rather" (*alla*) introduces the contrasting positive qualifications: (1) "hospitable," literally, "lover of strangers," ready to befriend and lodge traveling or fleeing believers; (2) "one who loves what is good," an ally and zealous supporter of the good, including men as well as deeds and things; (3) "self-controlled," in control of his mind and emotions so that he can act rationally and discreetly, a virtue much needed on Crete and one stressed in the Pastorals (1 Tim 2:9, 15; 3:2; 2 Tim 1:7; Titus 2:2, 4, 5, 6, 12); (4) "upright," or just, conforming his conduct to right standards; (5) "holy" (*hosios*), denoting his personal piety, an inner attitude of conforming to what is felt to be pleasing to God and consistent with religious practices; and (6) "disciplined," having the inner strength that enables him to control his bodily appetites and passions, a virtue listed in Galatians 5:23 as one quality of the fruit of the Spirit. These last three characteristics may be viewed as looking manward, Godward, and selfward, respectively.

9 Doctrinal fitness is also necessary. The overseer must be known to "hold firmly to the trustworthy message," clinging to it despite the winds of false teaching and open opposition. "Trustworthy" underlines that the Christian gospel is perfectly reliable and completely worthy of his confidence. He must adhere to the Word "as it has been taught" and be in accord with the teaching given by the apostles. Unfaithfulness to the biblical revelation disqualifies a man for leadership in God's church. Doctrinal fidelity will give him a standing ability to perform a twofold task: First, he is to "encourage others by sound doctrine," appealing to them to adhere to and advance in their Christian faith. This can be done by proclaiming "sound doctrine," teaching that is not only correct but healthful, promoting spiritual health, in contrast to the unhealthy false teaching. Secondly, his work also demands that he "refute those who oppose" the true gospel and speak against it as the advocates of error. He must "refute" them be exposing their error and trying to convince them that they are wrong. Christian truth needs not only defense against attacks, but also clear exposition. Effective presentation of the truth is a powerful antidote to error.

B. *The Refutation of False Teachers*

1:10–16

> [10]For there are many rebellious people, mere talkers and deceivers, especially those of the circumcision group. [11]They must be silenced, because they are ruining whole households by teaching things they ought not to teach—and that for the sake of dishonest gain. [12]Even one of their own prophets has said, "Cretans are always liars, evil brutes, lazy gluttons." [13]This testimony is true. Therefore, rebuke

them sharply, so that they will be sound in the faith ¹⁴and will pay no attention to Jewish myths or to the commands of those who reject the truth. ¹⁵To the pure, all things are pure, but to those who are corrupted and do not believe, nothing is pure. In fact, both their minds and consciences are corrupted. ¹⁶They claim to know God, but by their actions they deny him. They are detestable, disobedient and unfit for doing anything good.

"For" introduces the justification for the requirement that elders must be able to expound and defend the truth (v.9). This is essential because of the false teachers described in vv.10–13a. Verses 13b, 14 state the necessary action, while vv.15, 16 present the evidence condemning these errorists.

1. The picture of the false teachers (1:10–13a)

10 "There are many rebellious people" is a general statement of the external danger facing the Cretan churches. The worst offenders were Jewish, but they were not the only ones. These false teachers, apparently Cretans by birth, are not easily identified with any specific heresy. Apparently they were gnosticizing Judaists who as professed Christians sought to infiltrate the churches with their misguided teaching. They seemingly sought to fasten onto Christianity various aspects of Judaism and to present the hybrid as a teaching containing higher philosophical insights. The view of Gealy (IB, 11:529, 530) that they were Gentile Christians who were attracted to Jewish practices and sought to retain them as obligatory, seems improbable.

Three terms describe these "many" false teachers: They are (1) "rebellious," refusing to subordinate themselves to any authority, rejecting the demands of the gospel on them; (2) "mere talkers," men fluent and impressive in speech that accomplishes nothing constructive; (3) "deceivers," men whose glib tongues exercise a fascination over the minds of their dupes and lead them astray. "Those of the circumcision group" were the most active offenders.

11 Paul demanded that these men "be silenced." "Must" (*dei*) presents this as a moral necessity for the welfare of the churches. "Silenced" translates a rare verb meaning "to close the mouth by means of a muzzle or gag." The offenders must be refused opportunity to spread their teachings in the churches; the term also includes silencing them by a logical refutation of their views, making further dissemination impossible.

Their suppression was necessary because of their seductive work. They belonged to that class of people who were "ruining whole households," disturbing and turning upside down the faith of entire families. They achieved these disastrous results "by teaching things they ought not to teach," things that simply "must not" (*mē dei*) be presented as Christian truth. Committed to God's revelation in Christ, the church may not offer "the freedom of *misleading* speech."

"For the sake of dishonest gain" unveils their materialistic motives (contrast v.7), the desire to enrich themselves at the expense of the spiritual welfare of their victims. In v.7 "dishonest gain" is one compound word in Greek, but here it is written as two words to stress the literal fact.

12 These Cretan false teachers were all the more dangerous because of the known nature of the people on whom they preyed. As evidence, Paul quoted a line from Epimenides (6th–5th century B.C.), who was held in honor on Crete as a poet, prophet, and religious reformer. The NIV rendering, "one of their own prophets," implies that Crete boasted a number of such prophets, a point not raised by Paul. The original, "A

certain one of them, their own prophet," stresses that the quoted verdict came from one who had intimate knowledge of his own people and was esteemed by them as a "prophet." Paul was willing to accept this evaluation in order to underline the authority of his own judgment. The quotation establishes the picture without exposing Paul to the charge of being anti-Cretan. It put the Cretans on the horns of a dilemma. They must either admit the truthfulness of his verdict concerning them or deny the charge and brand their own prophet a liar.

The triple charge—"Cretans are always liars, evil brutes, lazy gluttons"—is supported by other extrabiblical witnesses. The pagan moralists classified Cretans with Cilicians and Cappadocians as preeminent in wickedness. So notorious was the Cretan reputation for falsehood that the Greek word *krētizō* ("to Crete-ize") meant "to lie." "Evil brutes" stigmatizes them as having sunk to the level of beasts, unrestrained in their brutality, always on a prowl for prey. "Lazy gluttons" underlines their greed as idle sensualists who desired to be filled without exerting personal effort to earn an honest living.

13a Paul's own observations confirmed the adverse judgment. Probably he had some unpleasant experiences on the island that verified the verdict.

2. The response to the situation (1:13b–14)

13b "Therefore," or "for which cause," introduces the action demanded by this situation. Titus must continue to "rebuke them sharply," dealing pungently and incisively with the danger, like a surgeon cutting away cancerous tissue. "Rebuke," the verb rendered "refute" in v.9 above, may here be rendered "convict," effectively showing the error of the teaching that is being opposed. Generally, "them" is taken as a direct reference to the false teachers. They would obviously be dealt with whenever they sought to gain a hearing in the church, but it seems clear that the action demanded would also include those church members who were known to be receptive to the claims of the false teachers. Primary reference to the endangered church members seems clear from the contemplated results of the action commanded.

The positive result aimed at is "that they will be sound in the faith." The verb *sound* means "to be in good health, be healthy," while the present tense indicates that the apostolic concern is their continued spiritual health. "The faith" denotes the truth embodied in the gospel they have personally accepted. Their personal spiritual health will be impaired if they feed on unhealthy doctrine.

14 The realization of this positive aim will involve a twofold negative achievement. They must be led to a position where they "will pay no attention to Jewish myths." Apparently the error is the same as the one mentioned in 1 Timothy 1:4, but here stamped explicitly as Jewish. These myths seemingly were speculative and fanciful inventions drawn from the OT records such as are found in the apocryphal and pseudepigraphical writings of Judaism. The rejected teaching is further characterized as "the commands of those who reject the truth." These commands were evidently Jewish-Gnostic ritual observances that the false teachers sought to make binding on Christians (cf. 1 Tim 4:3–6). They are to be spurned because they are merely the unauthorized "commands of men" (Gr.), men characterized as "those who reject the truth," habitually turning themselves away from the truth embodied in the gospel. The commands are to be rejected because of the character of their advocates. There is a close connection between false doctrine and evil character.

3. *The condemnation of the false teachers* (1:15–16)

These teachers stand condemned by the test of character (v.15) as well as conduct (v.16).

15 The test of character is stated in the form of a double maxim. "To the pure, all things are pure" embodies a principle enunciated by Jesus himself in dealing with Jewish food laws (Matt 15:10, 11; Mark 7:14–19; Luke 11:37–41) and forcefully impressed on Peter in his vision at Joppa (Acts 10:9–15, 28). These Cretan teachers apparently were engrossed in perpetuating ceremonial distinctions between the pure and the impure. They tended to lay emphasis on outward appearance and judged others on the basis of their own external criteria. Paul teaches that true purity lies not in adherence to nonmoral external rites and regulations but in the inner purity of the regenerated heart. Material things receive their moral character from the inner attitude of the user. Paul's maxim does not mean that nothing is impure unless thinking makes it so. It does not invalidate the revelation that certain things are morally wrong.

The converse of the principle carries the attack into enemy territory. Their attribution of impurity to nonmoral things reveals their character, their inner state of corruption or defilement, as well as their unbelief. White, noting the order of the two elements, comments, "Their moral obliquity is more characteristic of them than their intellectual perversion" (EGT, 4:190). Fellowship with God acts to clarify moral perception, but indulgence in evil stultifies the powers of moral discrimination.

A moral perversion has taken place in their whole being. Their "minds," their rational nature enabling them to think and reflect on things moral and spiritual, have become polluted, and their conscience has lost its ability to make correct moral judgments, leaving them unable to make true distinctions between good and evil.

16 The false teachers also stand condemned by the test of conduct. They publicly confess that they "know God," are fully informed about him, and stand in intimate relations with him. ("God" is emphatic by position.) The claim may be pride in assumed Jewish religious privilege or an expression of the Gnostic claim to an esoteric knowledge of God. Perhaps both elements are involved. But their vaunted claim is belied by their evil conduct. Moral quality of life is the determinative test of religious profession (1 John 2:4) and by it true character is exposed. Three terms describe the corrupt and unbelieving. They are (1) "detestable," loathsome, causing horror and disgust because of their hypocrisy; (2) "disobedient," insubordinate to God's truth because of their willful adherence to their man-made rules and regulations; (3) "unfit for doing anything good," disqualifed by their impurity from performing any morally good deed. They are like coins found, upon testing, to be spurious, utterly to be rejected as worthless.

Notes

10 The editors of UBS add καὶ (*kai*, "and") as the fourth word in this verse, making it read, "For there are many *and* rebellious people," but put it into brackets to mark the uncertainty. In favor of it is the unusualness of the rhetorical expression. However, the weight of the oldest MSS is against its insertion and it is best omitted (so WH and Nestle).

III. Concerning the Natural Groups in the Congregations (2:1–15)

Chapter two, concerned with the pastoral care of the Cretan Christians, is the second main division. Verses 1–10 give ethical instructions for the different groups in the congregations; vv.11–14 unfold the grace of God as the motivating power for Christian living; and v.15 summarizes the duty of Titus on Crete.

A. *The Instructions for the Different Groups*

(2:1–10)

> ¹You must teach what is in accord with sound doctrine. ²Teach the older men to be temperate, worthy of respect, self-controlled, and sound in faith, in love and in endurance. ³Likewise, teach the older women to be reverent in the way they live, not to be slanderers or addicted to much wine, but to teach what is good. ⁴Then they can train the younger women to love their husbands and children, ⁵to be self-controlled and pure, to be busy at home, to be kind, and to be subject to their husbands, so that no one will malign the word of God.
> ⁶Similarly, encourage the young men to be self-controlled. ⁷In everything set them an example by doing what is good. In your teaching show integrity, seriousness ⁸and soundness of speech that cannot be condemned, so that those who oppose you may be ashamed because they have nothing bad to say about us.
> ⁹Teach slaves to be subject to their masters in everything, to try to please them, not to talk back to them, ¹⁰and not to steal from them, but to show that they can be fully trusted, so that in every way they will make the teaching about God our Savior attractive.

Paul here stresses the importance of building up the inner life of believers as the best antidote against error. Sound doctrine must lead to ethical conduct in the lives of all the groups in the congregations. Emphasis falls on the family groups; the false teachers there had apparently done their greatest damage (1:11).

The paragraph may be divided into four parts. Paul opens with the instructional duty of Titus (v.1); describes the desired character and conduct of various groups (vv.2–6); reminds Titus of the importance of his personal example (vv.7, 8); and adds instructions for the slaves (vv.9, 10).

1. *The instructional duty of Titus* (2:1)

1 The opening "you" (*su*) is emphatic, contrasting Titus with the false teachers. He must show the difference by continuing to "teach," orally communicate, "what is in accord with sound doctrine." "What is according to" is more literally "what is fitting, proper to." "Sound doctrine," teaching that promotes spiritual health, requires conduct consistent with the teaching professed. Correct doctrine must result in good behavior.

2. *The instruction to different age groups* (2:2–6)

These verses lay down some of the Christian attributes to be commended to different groups, divided according to age and sex. In the original there is no finite verb until v.6. "Teach" in v.2 is supplied from v.1.

2 The term "older men" (not the word rendered, "elder" in 1:5) denotes age, not office. The "senior" male members are named first as natural leaders. The value of their example will depend on their moral character. Four qualifications are insisted on; the elders must be (1) "temperate," an adjective basically meaning "abstaining from wine," but having a wider meaning, "clear-headed," manifesting self-possession under all circumstances; (2) "worthy of respect," revealing a personal dignity and seriousness of purpose that invite honor and respect; (3) "self-controlled," possessing self-mastery in thought and judgment (cf. 1:8); and (4) "sound in faith, in love and in endurance," revealing a Christian healthiness of heart and mind. In v.1 "sound" is applied to doctrine, here to character. The definite article with each of the three nouns in the Greek makes them definite and distinct, apparently carrying a possessive force, "their faith, their love, their endurance." "Faith" may be objective, as the doctrinal content of the faith professed, but the following two items suggest that here it is subjective—their personal faith in the Lord. They must be mature in their exercise of genuine love, not bitter and vindictive, and they must display active "endurance," that steadfast persistence that bravely bears the trials and afflictions of life. Endurance is a much-needed virtue, especially in old age, as revealing personal maturity and strength of character.

3 "Likewise" indicates that the same kind of deportment is expected of the "older women," although the demands on them are related to their own station in life. The basic demand is that they "be reverent in the way they live." "The way they live" translates a noun denoting manner of life as expressive of inner character, while the adjective "reverent" basically means "suitable to a sacred person" and conveys the image of a good priestess carrying out the duties of her office. The conduct of the older women must reveal that they regard life as sacred in all of its aspects.

Their reverential behavior requires that they "not be slanderers or addicted to much wine." As mature Christians, they must not be given to gossip, repeating vicious and unfounded charges against others, and must not overindulge in wine. The union of the two negatives suggests the close connection between a loose tongue and intoxicating drink.

The older women must fulfill a positive role; they must "teach what is good." By personal word and example, they must teach what is morally good, noble, and attractive. The reference is not to public instruction, but to their teaching function in the home.

4 The training of the younger women is the duty, not of Titus, but the older women, qualified to do so by position and character. "Train" means to school in the lessons of sobriety and self-control (cf. vv.2, 5). "Younger" is a positive adjective literally meaning "new" or "fresh" and probably suggests a reference to the newly married.

Paul lists seven characteristics that must be commended to such (vv.4, 5a). "To love their husbands and children" renders two separate adjectives, "devoted to husbands, devoted to children." Such domestic affection stands at the very heart of any Christian home.

5 "To be self-controlled and pure" forms another pair. Self-control is a standing duty for all Christians (cf. 1:8; 2:2, 6). "Pure" denotes not only chastity in their sex life but also purity of heart and mind in all their conduct.

"To be busy at home, to be kind" designates a third pair. The first describes the many domestic activities of the housewife that she must willingly accept as part of her position as queen of the home. The KJV rendering "keepers at home" (*oikourous*) is based on a slightly different text and has less textual support than the rare term (*oikourgous*) behind the rendering above. The latter is the more stimulating concept and agrees with Paul's condemnation of idleness in 1 Timothy 5:13, 14. The devoted wife and mother finds her absorbing interest in the innumerable duties of the home. These demand unsparing self-giving and may subject her to the temptation to be irritable and harsh in her demands on members of her household. She must therefore cultivate the virtue of being "kind," i.e., benevolent, heartily doing what is good and beneficial to others, especially those of her household.

The concluding item, "to be subject to their husbands," stresses her acceptance of the established relationship between husband and wife as her Christian duty. "To be subject to" may be in the middle voice, "subjecting themselves to," as expressing their voluntary acceptance of the headship of the husband (cf. Eph 5:22–24). The requirement to love her husband does not eliminate her duty to yield to his headship. In declaring the spiritual equality of the woman before God (Gal 3:28), Christianity immeasurably elevated her status but did not thereby abolish her functional position as the complement and support of her husband as the head of the home.

The concluding purpose clause apparently relates to all seven items. It is the first expression of Paul's strong sense of a religious purpose behind these ethical demands. If Christian wives ignored these demands and flouted the role their culture demanded of good wives, the gospel would be maligned, criticized, and discredited by non-Christians. Christianity would be judged especially by the impact that it had on the women. It therefore was the duty of the women to protect God's revelation from profanation by living discreet and wholesome lives. For Christians, no life style is justified that hinders "the word of God," the message of God's salvation in Christ.

6 The requirement for the young men is brief but comprehensive: "Similarly, encourage the young men to be self-controlled." As a young man, Titus must fittingly convey his instructions for the young women indirectly, but his age was an advantage in dealing directly with the young men. "Encourage" (*parakalei*) is the first imperative verb in vv.2–6 and is stronger than "teach" in v.1. It may be rendered "urge" or "admonish" and is an appeal to their sense of personal moral responsibility. "Similarly" implies the same acceptance of responsibility as in the previous instructions. Since young men are inclined to be somewhat impetuous and unrestrained in conduct, their basic need is to be "self-controlled," cultivating balance and self-restraint in daily practice. It was a quality of which Paul found it necessary to remind the Cretan believers (1:8; 2:2, 4, 5).

3. The personal example of Titus (2:7–8)

7 In concluding instructions to the different age groups, Paul reminded Titus that his own conduct must confirm his teaching. "Set them an example" is literally "holding yourself alongside as an example,"—a meaning made clear through the use of the reflexive pronoun (*seauton*) with the middle voice of the participle. There is no word for "them" in the original and the example is not to be restricted to the young men. "In everything" underlines the comprehensiveness of the duty. Some would connect this phrase with the self-control demanded of the young men (v.6), but a connection with v.7 gives proper emphasis to "yourself." It is expanded in what follows. "Doing what is good," being an example "of good works," places the initial stress on his conduct, reflecting his noble deeds. Personal example must precede effective teaching, but his "teaching" in its manner and content must be of the highest quality. Two qualities, "integrity" and "seriousness," must characterize his work of teaching. The former stresses his purity of motive, revealing that he himself is uninfected by the evil conduct and erroneous views of the false teachers. "Seriousness" points to his outward dignity, reflecting the high moral tone and serious manner appropriate to his sacred task.

8 Titus must also demonstrate "soundness of speech that cannot be condemned." The content of his "speech," his personal word spoken while teaching or in ordinary conversation, must have two characteristics. In the first place, it must be "sound," conforming to healthful doctrine (2:1), a demand made on elders (1:9) as well as members (1:13; 2:2). Such soundness will insure the second characteristic—that is, "cannot be condemned." No critic will be able to point out anything in it justly open to censure or rebuke. The original suggests the picture of a courtroom where the judge can find no basis for the accusation of the plaintiff. Every faithful teacher must at times declare doctrine to which some rebellious hearer may object, but such objection must prove unjustified upon faithful examination.

Paul concluded his personal remarks to Titus with another purpose clause. The expression "those who oppose you" is apparently left intentionally vague to leave room for all types of critics. (The original is singular: "the opponent, one of the opposition.") When the objections are examined, the anticipated result is that the critic "may be ashamed," either feeling personally ashamed of his own conduct or made to look foolish because he is shown to have no case. The latter view seems more probable. He will "have nothing bad to say about us." An accusation of something "bad," morally bad or worthless, "about us," including Paul and Christians generally, will be found to be groundless. If justified, such attacks would bring discredit on Christ's servants and his cause.

4. The instructions to the slaves (2:9–10)

Paul's ethical instructions are now addressed to a distinct social group that overlaps groups divided by age and sex. Slaves formed a significant element in the apostolic churches and the welfare of the faith demanded that they too accept their spiritual responsibility as believers. Paul here makes no distinction between slaves who had Christian masters and those who did not (cf. 1 Tim 6:1, 2).

9 The original has no finite verb in v.9; perhaps it would be better here to use the verb of v.6 and render "encourage" or "exhort the slaves." Their fundamental duty is "to be subject to their masters in everything," voluntarily accepting subjection to their masters as a matter of principle. "Masters" (our English word *despot*) denotes that as owners they had complete authority over their slaves. While "in everything" may be taken with what follows, the parallel in Colossians 3:22 favors a connection with the demanded subjection. It stresses the comprehensiveness of this duty. But patristic commentators were careful to point out the necessary limitation on this demand, for a Christian slave could not submit when his pagan master demanded things contrary to Christian conscience.

The character of their subjection is indicated in the appositional infinitive, "to try to please them." Instead of having a sullen disposition, let them aim to be well pleasing (*euarestous*), giving full satisfaction to their masters. Elsewhere this adjective is always used of men's relation to God. It is the distinctive contribution of Christianity that slaves should govern their relations to their masters by this high principle. Three participial clauses, two negative and one positive, further describe their relationship to their masters.

The first negative requirement is "not to talk back to them," not to dispute their commands and by deliberate resistance seek to thwart their will.

10 The second negative demand is "not to steal from them," not underhandedly to divert to themselves part of anything their masters had not intended for them. Petty theft was common among slaves in Roman households. Employment in various trades and occupations offered slaves ample opportunity to resort to the various tricks of the trade for their own advantage.

Their positive duty is "to show that they can be fully trusted," demonstrating "good faith" in their whole relationship to their masters. They must not only be Christians but actively show this by proving themselves dependable in everything "good" or beneficial to their masters. "Good" naturally excluded any wrongdoing in which their master might order participation.

Such ethical conduct Paul again undergirds with a profound spiritual motive, "so that in every way they will make the teaching about God our Savior attractive." For a Christian there can be no higher motive. A slave's acceptance of the teaching about "God our Savior" must find expression in his transformed conduct. The very difficulty of his position would make such conduct a powerful recommendation of the gospel, proving to the master the power of the gospel. "In every way" (*en pasin*) in the original stands emphatically at the end. Adornment of faith by conduct must extend to every aspect of their lives. Less probable is the view that the meaning is "among all men" as denoting that the testimony of their conduct will permeate all areas of society.

B. *The Foundation for Godly Living*

2:11–14

> [11]For the grace of God that brings salvation has appeared to all men. [12]It teaches us to say "No" to ungodliness and worldly passions, and to live self-controlled, upright and godly lives in this present age, [13]while we wait for the blessed hope—the glorious appearing of our great God and Savior, Jesus Christ, [14]who gave himself for us to redeem us from all wickedness and to purify for himself a people that are his very own, eager to do what is good.

"For" marks Paul's masterly epitome of Christian doctrine as the proper foundation for the ethical demands just made on the various groups. Christian conduct must be grounded in and motivated by Christian truth. The vitality of doctrinal profession must be demonstrated by transformed Christian conduct.

Verses 11–14 unfold the meaning of "God our Savior" in v.10. Paul could not think of Christian truth and conduct apart from God's grace. He speaks of the manifestation of God's grace (v.11), the Christian's present training by grace (v.12), the expectation of Christ's return (v.13), and the aim of Christ's redemptive work (v.14).

1. *The manifestation of God's grace* (2:11)

11 The entire program of redemption is rooted in "the grace of God," his free favor and spontaneous action toward needy sinners to deliver and transform them. In the Greek, "has appeared" stands emphatically at the beginning, stressing the manifestation of grace as a historical reality. The reference is to Christ's entire earthly life—his birth, life, death, and resurrection. The verb *epephanē*, from which we derive our word "epiphany," means "to become visible, make an appearance," and conveys the image of grace suddenly breaking in on our moral darkness, like the rising sun. (It is used of the sun in Acts 27:20.) Men could never have formed an adequate conception of that grace apart from its personal manifestation in Christ, in his incarnation and atonement.

The effect of the manifestation was redemptive, not destructive. The adjective rendered "that brings salvation" (*sōtērios*) asserts its saving efficacy. The dative "to all men" may equally be rendered "for all men," thus stressing the universality of the salvation provided. Salvation is available to all, but its saving effect is dependent on the personal response of faith. Its universal scope justifies the application of its ethical demands to all classes of its professed recipients.

2. *The training by God's grace* (2:12)

12 "It teaches us" declares that grace also operates in the lives of the saved. Grounded in God's nature, grace makes ethical demands of Christians consistent with his nature. "Teaches" pictures grace, practically personified, as instructing the believer in the things "in accord with sound doctrine" (2:1). The verb basically means "to train a child," hence "to instruct, train, educate." It comprehends the entire training process—teaching, encouragement, correction, discipline.

The negative pedagogical purpose of grace is to train us "to say 'No' to ungodliness and worldly passions." The aorist participle indicates that grace aims to lead the believer to the place where as a definite act he will voluntarily make a double renunciation of the past. He must repudiate and abandon "ungodliness," the impiety and irreverence that characterized his unsaved life, as well as "worldly passions," those cravings characteristic of the world in its estrangement from God. Such an act of renunciation, standing at the beginning of a life of Christian victory, must be maintained in daily self-denial.

This negative work clears the field for its positive aim for believers: "to live self-controlled, upright and godly lives." "Live" (aorist tense) may mean "come to live" but more probably means that our entire course of life should be consistently characterized by three qualities (state as adverbs). In the original these adverbs stand emphatically before the verb. They look in three directions, though sharp distinctions need not be pressed: (1) *inward*, "self-controlled" ("soberly"), already stipulated for different groups (1:8; 2:2, 5) and now demanded of every believer; (2) *outward*, "upright" ("righteously"), faithfully fulfilling all the demands of truth and justice in our relations with others; (3) *upward*, "godly" ("reverently"), fully devoted to God in reverence and loving obedience.

Such a life is a possibility and duty "in this present age." This present evil age (Gal 1:4) holds dangers for the believer (Rom 12:2; 2 Tim 4:10) and stands in contrast to the anticipated future.

3. *The expectation of Christ's return* (2:13)

13 Those now being trained by God's grace eagerly anticipate the eschatological future. Having renounced their sinful past, they live disciplined lives in the present and look eagerly to the future (cf. 1 Thess 1:9, 10). "Wait for" depicts their eager expectancy as they look "for the blessed hope," the personal return of Christ who will consummate our bliss in eternal glory. The present tense marks this waiting as the characteristic attitude of believers, ever ready to welcome the returning Lord.

In the Greek "the glorious appearing" has no definite article. The use of the dash in NIV assumes that "the glorious appearing of our great God and Savior" is virtually in apposition with "the blessed hope" as a further definition of that hope. The Greek connects "the blessed hope and glorious appearing" under one article, suggesting that the reference is to one event viewed from two aspects. For believers, it is indeed the blessed hope and the longed-for consummation of that hope. For Christ himself, this awaited "glorious appearing" will vindicate his character as the Lord of glory. "Glorious appearing" is more literally "appearing of the glory" and points to his present glorification in heaven. Now unrecognized and disregarded by the world, his glory at his return will be manifested in all its splendor. Verse 11 spoke of his past epiphany in grace; v.13, of his future epiphany in glory.

The NIV rendering, "the glorious appearing of our great God and Savior, Jesus Christ" (cf. also RSV; NEB; NASB; BV), relates the glory to be revealed to Christ alone. The KJV rendering, "the glorious appearing of the great God and our Saviour Jesus Christ" (cf. ASV; Mof), relates it to both the Father and Christ. Either is grammatically possible. In favor of the latter rendering are the facts that in the pastoral Epistles God and Christ are regularly named side by side, that the double glory at the Parousia is mentioned elsewhere (Luke 9:26), and that the term *God* is rarely applied to Christ in Scripture. It is also the view of most of the ancient versions. But there are stronger arguments for referring the entire expression to Christ alone: (1) Grammatically this is the most natural view since both nouns are connected by one article as referring to one person. (2) The combination "god and savior" was familiar to the Hellenistic religions. (3) The added clause in v.14 refers to Christ alone and it is most natural to take the entire preceding expression as its antecedent. (4) In the Pastorals the coming epiphany is referred to Christ alone. (5) The adjective "great" of God is rather pointless but highly significant if applied to Christ. (6) This view is in full harmony with other passages such as John 20:28; Rom 9:5; Heb 1:8; and 2 Peter 1:1. (7) It is the view of the majority of the church fathers. This view takes the statement as an explicit assertion of the deity of Christ. Under the other view his deity is assumed, for the intimate association of his glory with that of God would be blasphemous for a monotheist like Paul if he did not accept Christ's deity.

4. The purpose of Christ's redemption (2:14)

14 From the eschatological future, Paul reverts to the historical work of Christ as Savior as the foundation for present sanctification. "Who gave himself for us" summarizes that work as voluntary, exhaustive, and substitutionary. His giving of himself was the grandest of all gifts. Because of our sinfulness, his atoning work had a dual aspect.

Its negative aspect was "to redeem us from all wickedness" or "lawlessness," that assertion of self-will in defiance of God's standard that is the essence of sin (1 John 3:4). The expression stresses not our guilt as rebels but rather our deliverance from bondage to lawlessness through Christ's ransom. "From" (*apo*) indicates effective removal from that sphere and our deliverance from "all" aspects of its domination.

This negative work is the necessary prelude to the positive work of sanctification, "to purify for himself a people that are his very own." "Purify" points to the moral defilement that man's rebellion produced. Sin makes us not only guilty but also unclean before a holy God. The blood-wrought cleansing (1 John 1:7) enables men to be restored to fellowship with God as "a people that are his very own." Since they have been redeemed by his blood (1 Peter 1:18–21), Christ yearns that they voluntarily yield themselves wholly to him. Such a surrender is man's only reasonable response to divine mercy (Rom 12:1, 2).

"Eager to do what is good" delineates what this relationship involves. "Eager" in the Greek is a noun (*zēlōtēs*) meaning "a zealot, an enthusiast." For those who have been redeemed from the doom of sin and death and brought into a unique relationship with God, the true voluntary response is to be enthusiastic "to do what is good." It is the true badge of his divine ownership. He who eagerly awaits the return of the Savior will be eager also to further his cause by good works until he comes. It is another instance of the union between creed and conduct insisted upon in the pastoral Epistles.

C. The Restatement of the Duty of Titus

2:15

15These, then, are the things you should teach. Encourage and rebuke with all authority. Do not let anyone despise you.

15 "These ... things ... teach" looks back to 2:1. The same imperative is used. Titus must continually present the practical instructions to the various groups in their proper doctrinal setting. The NIV rendering regards "teach" as Titus' central duty and views the following imperatives as the two major functions of that work. In the Greek the three imperatives are closely connected: "These things teach and encourage and rebuke." All are present imperatives, Paul urging Titus to continue what he has been doing. The three form a climax. He must clearly proclaim the message, "encourage" or exhort the hearers to appropriate and practice it, and "rebuke" or convict those who are slack or fail to respond. He must perform these duties "with all authority," for the message is apostolic and authentic and its authority must be stressed. The gospel must not be presented as an optional opinion to be accepted or rejected as its hearers may please. The minister's authority rests in the nature of his message; he is not raised above the truth but the truth above him.

As the apostolic representative in Crete, Titus must "not let anyone despise" him, look down on him, or belittle his message and authority. He must not permit the message and work to be slighted or disdainfully rejected. Since this letter would be read in the churches, the remark was apparently intended as much for the Cretans as for Titus himself.

IV. Concerning Believers Among Men Generally (3:1–11)

Having dealt with church leaders (ch. 1) and the conduct of believers as members of the Christian community (ch. 2). in this final section Paul insists that believers also have duties to the government and the non-Christian world. The section is in three parts: the duties of believers as citizens (vv.1, 2), the motives for godly living (vv.3–8), and the necessary reaction to spiritual error (vv.9–11).

A. Their Obligations As Citizens

3:1–2

Remind the people to be subject to rulers and authorities, to be obedient, to be ready to do whatever is good, 2to slander no one, to be peaceable and consider- ate, and to show true humility toward all men.

1 Christians have a duty to government. "The people," literally "them," refers to the members of the churches, not to all Cretans in general. "Remind" indicates that the duties now insisted on are not new to them; the present imperative demands that Titus must repeatedly press these duties upon their consciences. Early Christian preaching was not limited to the way of salvation but included instructions concerning the practical implications of that salvation for daily living. Paul ever desired that the lives of believers should produce a favorable impression on the non-Christian world.

The duty of believers is "to be subject to rulers and authorities." "To be subject" is best taken as a middle-voice infinitive, implying their voluntary acceptance of this position of submission. "Rulers and authorities," two abstract nouns, signifies not the individual rulers but the various forms of human government. This demand for obedience to government is found in other NT letters (Rom 13:1-7; 1 Peter 2:13-17), but the known turbulence of the Cretans made it particularly appropriate here.

"To be obedient" states the result and visible demonstration of their attitude of submission. The compound infinitive (*peitharchein*) denotes practical obedience to particular authoritative orders. The context implies obedience to the particular demands of government, but the practice of obedience is not to be limited to these areas. It is assumed that the obedience·demanded does not contradict explicit Christian duties.

As good citizens, believers must also "be ready to do whatever is good"—prepared and willing to participate in activities that promote the welfare of the community. They must not stand coldly aloof from praiseworthy enterprises of government but show good public spirit, thus proving that Christianity is a constructive force in society.

2 Believers also have obligations to pagan neighbors. Negatively, they must "slander no one," abstain from the common practice of hurling curses and vicious epithets at those offending or injuring them. The demand required inner grace but was appropriate for followers of the Christ who did not revile when he was reviled (1 Peter 2:23). In the Greek, "to be peaceable" is another negative demand, "to be nonfighting" (*amachous*), refusing to engage in quarrels and conflicts. The Christian must not adopt the arts of the agitator.

Positively, he must be "considerate," gentle or yielding, not stubbornly insisting on his own rights but acting in courtesy and forbearance. A further positive duty is "to show true humility," an attitude of mind the opposite of self-assertiveness and harshness. "True" is literally "all" and stresses not its genuineness but the greatest possible manifestation of this grace. The present participle rendered "to show" suggests a continuing demonstration of humility as an essential trait of Christian character. It is not to be exhibited only in dealing with fellow believers but must be shown "toward all men," including those who are hostile and morally perverse. It is a difficult test of Christian character but one that effectively proves the genuineness of Christian profession.

B. *The Motives for Such Godly Conduct*

3:3-8

> ³At one time we too were foolish, disobedient, deceived and enslaved by all kinds of passions and pleasures. We lived in malice and envy, being hated and hating one another. ⁴But when the kindness and love of God our Savior appeared, ⁵he saved us, not because of righteous things we had done, but because of his mercy. He saved us through the washing of rebirth and renewal by the Holy Spirit, ⁶whom he poured out on us generously through Jesus Christ our Savior, ⁷so that, having been justified by his grace, we might become heirs having the hope of eternal life. ⁸This is a trustworthy saying. And I want you to stress these things, so that those who have trusted in God may be careful to devote themselves to doing what is good. These things are excellent and profitable for everyone.

Paul's opening "for" in the original (*gar,* not represented in the NIV rendering) again indicates that the required conduct is being undergirded by weighty reasons. His masterly summary of evangelical teaching encourages his readers with the reminder that such conduct is necessary and possible in view of God's transforming work in their own lives. He advances three supporting motives: their own pre-Christian past (v.3), the saving work of God in believers (vv.4–8a), and the necessary connection between Christian truth and conduct (v.8b).

1. *The motive from our own past* (3:3)

3 The remembrance of our own past should be a powerful motive for gentleness and consideration toward the unsaved. "We were," standing emphatically at the opening of the sentence, implies that what was once true of us is still true of the unsaved neighbor. The added "we too" (*kai hēmeis*) stresses that the condition described in retrospect applied to Paul and Titus as well as to the Cretan Christians; it is, in fact, true of all believers everywhere. It is salutary to remember our own past moral condition when dealing with the unsaved in their degradation.

The picture of our past is vividly and concisely drawn. We were "foolish," without spiritual understanding, lacking discernment of spiritual realities because of the darkening effect of sin on the intellect (Eph 4:18). As outward evidence of our alienated condition, we were "disobedient," wilfully disregarding authority, refusing obedience to God's law and fretting under human authority. "Deceived" pictures active straying from the true course by following false guides. Allowing our conduct to be dictated by a wide variety of personal "passions and pleasures," the inevitable result was our enslavement to them. Never finding true personal satisfaction in their pursuit, we lived our lives in the grip of the antisocial forces of "malice and envy," harboring an attitude of ill-will toward others and enviously begrudging others their good fortune. "Being hated" (*stugētoi*, only here in the NT, but see the compound form in Rom 12:9) denotes being odious, repulsive, and disgusting to others, It pictures that stage of degradation "when vice becomes odious to the vicious, stands a self-confessed failure to produce happiness" (White, EGT, 4:198). "Hating one another" marks the climax in the active operation of mutual antagonisms that hasten the disolution of the bonds of human society.

2. *The motive from our present salvation* (3:4–7)

"But" introduces the familiar Pauline contrast between what we once were and now are (Rom 6:17–23; 1 Cor 6:9–11; Eph 2:2–13; 5:7–12; Col 1:21, 22; 3:7–10). The marvelous salvation that we now know must motivate our dealings with the unsaved. This beautiful summary of the whole gospel mentions the manifestation (v.4), the basis (v.5a), the means (vv.5b, 6), and the results (v.7) of our salvation.

4 a. *Its manifestation.* Our salvation roots in a definite historical event, "when the kindness and love of God our Savior appeared." "Appeared" (the precise form in 2:11) looks back to the salvation manifested in the incarnate Christ. The salvation embodied in him manifested two aspects of the nature of "God our Savior": (1) his "kindness" or "benignity," his pitying kindness that prompts him to bestow forgiveness and blessings; (2) his "love" (*philanthrōpia*), his affection for men seen in his display of love for us in our sin and degradation. (It would have been better to retain the rendering "love toward man" to mark the unique term, used only here in the NT, and bring out the connection with John 3:16; Rom 5:8; and similar verses). Each noun has the definite article, thus

making the two concepts distinct, yet the singular verb views them as so closely connected as to form one whole. Through his action in Christ, God is now revealed as "our Savior." "Our" is strongly confessional. The plural associates Paul with all those who have appropriated this Savior as their own (cf. Gal 2:20).

5a b. *Its basis.* "He saved us" simply records the historic fact of his saving work in all who have accepted salvation in Christ. The aorist tense records the past saving act; we now possess his salvation, although it is still incomplete, awaiting its consummation at Christ's return.

The original order stresses the basis of this experienced salvation, "not because of righteous things we had done, but because of his mercy, he saved us." The order eliminates any thought of salvation due to personal merit and magnifies God's sovereign grace.

The negative clause repeats Paul's well-known denial of salvation by works (Rom 4:4, 5; Gal 2:16, 17; Eph 2:8, 9). Our salvation did not arise out of "righteous things we had done," more literally, "out of works that we ourselves had performed in righteousness." As sinners, we did no such works, nor were we able to perform them. The gospel emphatically denies the possibility of attaining salvation by human effort or merit.

Positively, God saved us "because of his mercy." In our wretchedness he graciously withheld deserved punishment and freely saved us. "Because of " is literally "according to" (*kata*) and points to his mercy as the yardstick for measuring the vastness of his saving grace. The pronouns "we" and "his" stand in intentional and emphatic contrast.

5b–6 c. *Its means.* God's salvation was mediated to us "through the washing of rebirth and renewal by the Holy Spirit." "Washing" speaks of our cleansing from the defilement of sin in regeneration. The noun (*loutron*) may mean the receptacle for washing, the "laver," or the act of washing itself. In Ephesians 5:26, the only other NT occurrence of the term, the natural meaning is "washing." Simpson remarks that "*laver* lacks corroboration, except in patristic treatises, coloured by the dogma of baptismal regeneration, and the LXX term thus translated is *loutēr*, which undoubtedly signifies a bathing-tub" (p. 114). "Washing" is thus best understood as denoting the act rather than the place of washing. (The use of *dia* with the genitive clearly asserts the washing as the means of the rebirth). Most commentators take the washing as a reference to water baptism. But if water baptism is the means that produces the spiritual rebirth, we then have the questionable teaching of a material agency as the indispensable means for producing a spiritual result (but cf. Matt 15:1–20; Rom 2:25–29; Gal 5:6). We accept the washing as a divine inner act, although the experience is symbolically pictured in Christian baptism. In the NT the inner experience is viewed as openly confessed before men in baptism, but the rite does not produce the inner experience of spiritual "rebirth," a new state of life in consequence of a new birth. The word *rebirth* (*palingenesia*) occurs elsewhere in the NT only in Matthew 19:28, where it refers to the external material rebirth of creation at Christ's return. Here it denotes the inner spiritual regeneration of the individual believer.

The expression "through the washing of rebirth and renewal by the Holy Spirit" is open to two interpretations grammatically. Both "rebirth" and "renewal" may be regarded as dependent on "washing" to form one concept. Then the washing of rebirth is further described as a renewal wrought by the Spirit. The other view holds that the preposition "through" is in thought also repeated with "renewal." This view sees two separate aspects of salvation. The fact that the preposition is not repeated is in favor of the first view, but the resultant thought favors the second view. Then the washing is viewed as producing an instantaneous change that ended the old life and began the new, while the work of renewal by the Spirit, beginning with the impartation of the new life, is a lifelong activity in the experience of the believer. In Romans 12:2 this renewal is viewed as a continuing process. In Ephesians 5:26, 27 the act of cleansing of the church is followed by the work of sanctification till no spot or wrinkle remains. The spiritual rebirth, taking place at a particular moment, is the prerequisite for the subsequent process of "renewal" (*anakainōseōs*), "a making new," the development of an entirely new nature as contrasted with the old. This process of renewal in the believer is the work of the Holy Spirit. He alone can produce a new nature that finds active expression in an entirely new manner of life.

"Whom he poured out on us generously," or "richly," stresses that God has made ample provision for the development of this renewed life. "Poured out" (aorist tense) had its primary fulfillment at Pentecost, but "on us" marks the pouring out as individually experienced at conversion (Rom 5:5). The Spirit's work in each believer as a member of the Body is a continuation of the Pentecostal outpouring. Every faulty or inadequate experience of renewal is always due to some human impediment, never to God's inadequate provision. "Through Jesus Christ our Savior" states the channel through which the Spirit's renewing presence was bestowed. That bestowal was based on the finished work of Christ as Savior (John 7:38, 39; 15:26; Acts 2:33). The "our" is again confessional. Our acceptance of Christ as Savior is the human condition for the bestowal of the Spirit. Note the Trinity in vv.5b, 6: "the Holy Spirit," "he" (the Father), "Jesus Christ." Each member of the divine Trinity has his own special function in the work of human redemption.

7 d. *Its results.* "So that" (*hina*) here denotes more than mere purpose; the aim has been accomplished. "Having been justified by his grace" relates the result of salvation to our past. Sin had brought guilt and condemnation, but when we received Christ as our Savior, we were "justified," "declared righteous," and given a standing of acceptance before him. "Justified," in reference to man, is always in the passive; it is always the act of God, motivated "by his grace." "His" (*ekeinou*), "of that one," indicates that the reference is to the grace of the Father, his free unmerited favor bestowed on the basis of Christ's perfect work. The condensed comment assumes knowledge of Paul's doctrine of justification.

The second stated result comprehends our present standing in relation to the future. "Might become heirs" denotes not just a future prospect but a present reality. As members of God's family, we now are heirs, but entrance upon our inheritance belongs to the future. Our standing as heirs is "according to" (*kata*), in full harmony with, "the hope of eternal life" (1:2). Our present experience of salvation can give us only a tantalizing foretaste of the nature of our future inheritance.

3. *The necessary connection between doctrine and conduct* (3:8)

8a "This is a trustworthy saying" clearly looks back to the doctrinal statement in vv.4–7 as a unified whole and stamps it as worthy of full approval. Confined to the pastoral Epistles (1 Tim 1:15; 3:1; 4:9; 2 Tim 2:11), here is the sole occurrence of this formula in Titus. Clearly the application in this case is not restricted to a single pithy utterance. Scholars generally accept the view that the writer is citing a hymn or confessional statement, but there is no agreement about the extent or exact contents of the assumed quotation (see Hinson, Broadman Commentary, 11:273). Whether it is a quotation or

Paul's own composition, no nobler doctrinal statement is found in any Pauline Epistle.

8b It is Paul's definite intention that Titus, as his personal representative in Crete, continue insistently "to stress these things." "These things" apparently looks back to vv.4–7 and views those doctrinal truths in their varied aspects. Their trustworthy character demands that Titus "stress," stoutly and confidently affirm, them. The orthodox preacher must proclaim his message with confidence and ringing certainty.

Such insistent preaching must aim at a definite result in the lives of believers. "Those who have trusted in God" (a perfect active participle, standing emphatically at the end of the sentence) pictures not only their initial acceptance of these truths but also their present personal faith relationship to God. Because of this present relationship, they are obligated to "be careful to devote themselves to doing what is good." The gospel message of free forgiveness for sinners on the sole basis of faith must find expression in a life characterized as taking a lead in the performance of excellent deeds. The practice of good works is the logical outcome of a true apprehension of the grace of God. The original statement can be taken to mean "that they engage in honourable occupations" (NEB), but this rendering is less probable as not strictly relevant to the theme of the passage and not in accord with the usual meaning of the statement in the NT.

Paul's summary evaluation of the instructions just given is that they are "excellent and profitable for everyone." "These things" may refer to his final demand that believers combine faith and practice, but more probably the reference is to the true teachings that Titus must insist on in his work in Crete. By their very nature they are "excellent," good, attractive, and praiseworthy. They are also "profitable for everyone," having a beneficial impact on mankind. The beneficial effects of Christian ethical standards are not limited to believers only. A vital Christianity unites the beautiful and the profitable.

C. *The Reaction to Spiritual Error*

3:9–11

> ⁹But avoid foolish controversies and genealogies and arguments and quarrels about the law, because these are unprofitable and useless. ¹⁰Warn a divisive person once, and then warn him a second time. After that, have nothing to do with him. ¹¹You may be sure that such a man is warped and sinful; he is self-condemned.

"But" introduces the necessary reaction of Titus to matters contrary to the teaching insisted on in v.8. They are described as "foolish controversies and genealogies and arguments and quarrels about the law." The picture looks back to 1:10–16; "about the law" marks the Jewish coloring. All four nouns are without the article and this stresses the quality of these things. The same sort of problems also existed at Ephesus (cf. 1 Tim 1:3–7). They comprise various "foolish" or senseless inquiries, involving speculations about the OT genealogies, and resulted in sharp dissensions and open quarrels.

All such matters Titus must "avoid," deliberately shun and stand aloof from, "because they are unprofitable and useless." They produce no spiritual benefits and lead to no constructive results.

10 Paul now passes from these reprehensible opinions to their perverted advocates. The adjective "divisive" (*hairetikon*), found only here in the NT, essentially characterizes what is a self-chosen opinion or viewpoint; because of their insistence on their opinions, devoid of a true scriptural basis, the dissidents stir up divisions. Simpson characterizes such a man as an "opinionative propagandist who promotes dissension by his pertinacity" (p. 117). When persisted in, this results in the formation of heretical parties.

Such a man Titus must "warn" or "admonish" by faithfully and lovingly pointing out his error. If a second effort to deal with him proves ineffective, let Titus "have nothing to do with him," refusing further to bother with him. Further efforts would not be a good stewardship of his time and energies and would give the offender an undeserved sense of importance.

11 His stubborn refusal of admonition would assure Titus that the man is "warped," the perfect tense marking him as being in a state of perversion, twisted and turned out, wholly out of touch with truth. The passive voice seems to point to the satanic agency behind his condition.

"Sinful" represents a present-tense verb: "he is sinning," deliberately missing the divine standard by his persistent refusal to receive correction. It reveals an inner moral condition of being "self-condemned." He knows that in his deliberate refusal to abandon his self-chosen views he is wrong and stands condemned by his own better judgment.

V. Conclusion

3:12–15

> ¹²As soon as I send Artemas or Tychicus to you, do your best to come to me at Nicopolis, because I have decided to winter there. ¹³Do everything you can to help Zenas the lawyer and Apollos on their way and see that they have everything they need. ¹⁴Our people must learn to devote themselves to doing what is good, in order that they may provide for daily necessities and not live unproductive lives. ¹⁵Everyone with me sends you greetings. Greet those who love us in the faith. Grace be with you all.

The conclusion to the Epistle, comparable in length to the opening salutation, consists of three directives from Paul (vv.12–14), mutual greetings (v.15a), and the closing benediction (v.15b).

A. *The Concluding Instructions* (3:12–14).

Verse 12 announces Paul's plans for the future as they concern Titus himself. Another worker would be sent to replace Titus in Crete. Since his assignment to Crete was not permanent, Titus obviously was not the "first bishop of the Cretans" as the scribal subscription has it. When Paul wrote, neither the time nor the final selection of the replacement had been determined. Nothing further is known of Artemas. Tychicus was a trusted co-worker who on several occasions appears as traveling with or for Paul (Acts 20:4; Eph 6:21, 22; Col 4:7, 8; 2 Tim 4:12). When a replacement arrived, not before, Titus was urged to proceed as quickly as possible to Nicopolis (lit., "victory-town"), apparently the city in Epirus on the west coast of Greece. Paul planned to spend the winter there, presumably making it a base of operation for work in Dalmatia. "There" shows that Paul was not yet there when he wrote. The place of writing is unknown, but it may have been Corinth.

13 Zenas and Apollos are almost certainly the bearers of this letter. "Zenas the lawyer" appears only here. His name is Greek, but he may have been a convert from Judaism. If he was of Jewish origin, "lawyer" means that he had been an expert in the Mosaic law;

if a Gentile, it means he had been a Roman jurist. Apollos is the well-known Alexandrian Jew who, having been fully instructed at Ephesus, effectively worked in the Corinthian church (Acts 18:24–28; 19:1; 1 Cor 1:12; 3:4–6; 4:6; 16:12). Their journey took Zenas and Apollos through Crete, and Titus must diligently assist them by seeing that their further needs are supplied. Such generous material assistance for Christian workers on their journeys characterized the early church (Acts 15:3; Rom 15:24; 1 Cor 16:6; 2 Cor 1:16; 3 John 5–8).

14 Titus need not carry the burden alone. By appealing to the churches for further funds, he had an opportunity to train them in the practice of "doing what is good" (cf. 3:8). It would further the gospel and develop their own Christian lives. This situation gave Paul a final opportunity to stress the theme that Christians must be characterized by the practice of noble deeds, thus assuring that their lives would not be "unproductive." Noble deeds are the fruit of the tree of salvation.

B. *The Personal Greetings* (3:15a)

15a All the workers with Paul joined in sending their greetings. They are left unnamed, since Zenas and Apollos would orally identify them. Titus is to pass on these greetings to "those who love us in the faith," the believers in Crete who are filled with affection for Paul and his assistants "in the faith." "Faith," without an article, may mean the sphere where their affection was operative, or it may simply mean "in faith," that is, loyally. The former view seems preferable.

C. *The Closing Benediction* (3:15b)

15b The "you" is plural, including all those to whom Titus was to convey Paul's greetings. It suggests that Paul expected the letter to be read in the various churches.

Notes

15 The closing ἀμήν (*amēn*, "amen"), found in numerous MSS, is very probably a scribal addition. It is absent from many early and diverse textual witnesses. The scribes would be more likely to add this liturgical conclusion than omit it.

PHILEMON

Arthur A. Rupprecht

PHILEMON

Introduction

1. Authorship
2. Date and Place of Origin
3. Destination
4. Occasion and Purpose
5. Literary Form
6. Theological Values
7. Bibliography
8. Outline

Philemon is a letter written by the apostle Paul to a Christian slave owner who lived in the Lycus Valley of Asia Minor. In it the apostle asks that the converted runaway slave, Onesimus, be received back into the household without punishment. There is also a hint that he should be loaned to Paul or granted his freedom so that he could help the apostle.

1. Authorship

Few, if any, dispute that Philemon is a letter written by the apostle Paul. It appeared early, in the Muratorian Fragment and in Marcion's canon. Only the Tübingen School of the nineteenth century questioned its authenticity. F.C. Baur claimed that the letter was written in the second century to instruct the church in handling the slavery question.

On the basis of the similarity of the final greetings in Philemon and Colossians, as well as on certain literary and theological considerations, some modern commentators have concluded that Colossians is "deutero-Pauline."[1] However, this is an unwarranted conclusion.

2. Date and Place of Origin

Those who hold that Colossians and Philemon were written at the same time, while Paul was in prison at Rome, date it c. A.D. 58–60. If it was written from Ephesus, as Duncan has suggested, a date c. A.D. 56 would be likely.[2] Duncan's argument that the appeal for lodging (v.22) demands an imprisonment in a place closer than Rome has real validity. Dodd answered him on the assumption that Onesimus would seek anonymity

---

[1]Eduard Lohse, *Colossians and Philemon*, p. 187.
[2]G.S. Duncan, *St. Paul's Ephesian Ministry* (London: Hodder and Staughton, 1929), pp. 72 ff.

at Rome.[3] The evidence suggests, however, that runaway slaves were apt to seek asylum almost anywhere. Until further evidence is found the question of the date will remain open to dispute.

3. Destination

The traditional view is that the letter was written to Philemon, a resident of the Lycus Valley in Asia Minor. As an alternative to this, Goodspeed suggested that Philemon is the lost letter to the Laodiceans (Col 4:16) on the ground that a letter referred to in this way would not have been lost. He identifies Onesimus with the bishop of Ephesus of the same name who put together the Pauline corpus. Goodspeed argued further that there is little likelihood that there would have been a third letter written at the same time as Colossians and Philemon.[4] To support his claim, however, it must be shown that Philemon was really a letter to the church and not to an individual. Knox follows Goodspeed, but claims that Archippus, who lived at Colosse, was the owner of the slave and the recipient of the letter.[5]

The letter is addressed to Philemon of Laodicea, who was to pass it along to Colosse and exert influence on Archippus to "complete the work" (Col 4:17), which may be Paul's request in behalf of Onesimus. The only questions have to do with which of the two cities in the Lycus Valley, Colosse or Laodicea, the letter was sent to and which of the two individuals Philemon or Archippus, the request was intended for. The evidence favors Philemon of Colosse as the recipient.

4. Occasion and Purpose

Paul wrote the letter to Philemon in typical epistolary form. He wanted to intercede in behalf of the latter's runaway slave, Onesimus. The apostle's suggestions for the handling of the matter are difficult to determine because of his obscure and deferential words. At a minimum he asked that Onesimus be reconciled to the household without harsh punishment. He also strongly hinted that the slave would be useful to him in the work of evangelism. Nowhere does Paul openly state that Philemon should set Onesimus free. Nor is it necessary to assume that Onesimus would be freed if he were to join Paul in his missionary work.

Brief and intensely personal, the letter is addressed to one person, Philemon,[6] but other interested parties are mentioned in the salutation. Apphia, his wife, would have had daily responsibility over the slaves of the household. Archippus, perhaps Philemon's son and possibly also a local pastor ("fellow soldier"), would look after the interests of the church, which is also mentioned in the salutation. No doubt the church at Colosse would find very significant the reconciliation of a runaway slave on the intercession of no less a person than the apostle Paul.

---

[3]C.H. Dodd, "The Mind of Paul: Change and Development," in *Bulletin of the John Rylands Library* 18 (1934); 69–80.

[4]E.J. Goodspeed, *The Key to Ephesians* (Chicago: University of Chicago Press, 1956), pp. xiv–xvi.

[5]John Knox, *Philemon among the Letters of Paul* (New York: Abingdon, 1959), pp. 91–108.

[6]In the phrase "the church that meets in your home" (v.2), "your" is singular and refers to Philemon as the recipient of the letter. C.F.D. Moule (*The Epistles to the Colossians and to Philemon* [Cambridge: Cambridge University Press, 1957], pp. 16, 17) argues that this reference has to be to Philemon whose name is first in the list. This fact is "fatal to the theory [Knox's] that Archippus is primarily the one addressed."

Some of the events that led to the writing of the letter can be stated without qualification. On the other hand, many of the tantalizing details are lost to us. Onesimus came in contact with Paul while the latter was in prison somewhere in the Roman world—most probably in Rome, though Caesarea and Ephesus are also possibilities (cf. Introduction to Colossians)—and was converted. Paul intimates that he had robbed his master in some way, but oddly he does not mention the details, possibly because of his sensitivity and tact. It is not likely that Paul did not know the details. Nor do we know whether or not Onesimus was a prisoner with Paul. It is most likely, however, that he was not, since the return of a fugitive slave was a complicated, technical procedure in Roman law by this time. Certainly a prisoner could not directly send back a runaway slave and fellow-prisoner. The best assumption is that the authorities were unaware of Onesimus's status and that Paul made unofficial arrangements for his return.

The traditional interpretation has been that Paul sent him back with Tychicus at the time of the writing of the Epistle to the Colossians. "If there is one thing certain, it is that Colossians and Philemon were written at the same time and place," said C.H. Dodd.[7]

A better explanation of the circumstances of the writing of Philemon may be that it was composed at a time prior to Colossians. The evidence for this is striking. According to Colossians 4, Tychicus and Onesimus were returning to Colosse together and would "tell all that is happening here" (v.9). It is usually assumed that this is the return of the runaway Onesimus. But if so, why is he described as a "faithful ... brother" (v.9). Paul usually reserved the word *pistos* ("faithful") for fellow workers who showed great determination and endurance in the work of the gospel. It is a frequent word in inscriptions for a "trusted agent" or "commissioned one."[8]

Yet the description of one who had doubtless stolen from his master upon his illegal departure as a "faithful and dear brother" is not so serious as it seems. While in prison, Paul had undoubtedly led Onesimus to Christ, as the words "my son Onesimus, who became my son while I was in chains" (v.10) show. We do not know how long Onesimus, following his conversion, spent with Paul before going back to Colosse. Evidently it was long enough for him to become helpful to Paul (v.11) and to serve him in such a way as to lead to the affectionate expressions in vv.12, 13.

There are two other considerations that suggest that Colossians and Philemon were separated in time. Philemon 22 states clearly that Paul expects to be in Colosse soon. It is difficult to understand how "prepare a guest room for me, because I hope to be restored to you," can be interpreted as a figure of speech. On the other hand, in writing Colossians the apostle is greatly distressed at the direction in which the church has gone. Yet he only says, "Pray for us also, that God may open us a door for the word." If he had expected to be released from imprisonment soon, he would probably have mentioned this to the Colossians also.

As for the traditional view that Colossians and Philemon were written at the same time, two considerations support it—the geography and the final greetings. The geogra-

---

[7] *New Testament Studies* (Manchester: Manchester University Press, 1953), p. 90. Also, Moule, *Colossians and Philemon,* p. 22 *et passim.*

[8] See BAG, p. 670; TDNT, p. 204. Onesimus was a common slave name. Calvin could not bring himself to the conclusion that Onesimus of Colossians was the same as the runaway slave of Philemon. "For it is scarcely credible that this is the slave of Philemon, for the name of a thief and a fugitive would have been liable to reproach." (*Calvin's Commentaries: the Epistles to the Galatians, Ephesians, Philippians and Colossians,* trans. Parker [Edinburgh, 1965], p. 359.)

phy of both letters is the same. They are sent to a city or cities of the Lycus Valley. The names in the greetings at the end of both Epistles are very similar. Epaphras, Mark, Demas, and Luke appear in both. This coincidence has prompted a number of scholars to conclude that a Paulinist of the first century borrowed heavily from the setting of the Epistle to Philemon to give authenticity to his letter that we know as Colossians.

A final similarity in both Epistles is that Onesimus comes back. Note carefully, however, that he accompanies Tychicus in Colossians, but Tychicus is nowhere mentioned in Philemon. That Tychicus accompanied Onesimus when the latter returned as a runaway is only an assumption.

John Knox, following Goodspeed's suggestion that Philemon is the lost letter to the Laodiceans, interprets the events very differently. He sees Archippus as the intended recipient of the letter and Onesimus as his slave. Philemon is, therefore, the lost letter to the Laodiceans mentioned in Colossians 4:16, and the work Archippus was expected to complete (v.17) was the release of Onesimus for Paul's sake. Philemon, then, was a prominent member of the church at Laodicea who was expected to intercede with Archippus upon receipt of the letter. Knox based his hypothesis on Onesimus's becoming the bishop of Ephesus mentioned by Ignatius (*Eph* 1:3; 2:1; 6:2) and later being responsible for the collection of the Pauline Epistles. For this reason, Knox contends, Ephesians is at the beginning of the Pauline corpus and Philemon was uniquely preserved because of its importance to the bishop.[9] It must be said, however, that this theory can neither be proved nor disproved. There is no clear evidence that the bishop of Ephesus was, in fact, Onesimus, the runaway slave. Nor does the exegetical evidence actually support the contention that Archippus and not Philemon was the master of Onesimus.

5. Literary Form

The letter is unique in the Pauline corpus because it is a personal letter of commendation and recommendation. There are innumerable examples of similar letters, both pagan and Christian, from the Graeco-Roman world. Among these, Philemon belongs to the kind of letter written to intercede for a delinquent slave. A well-known parallel is the beautiful letter the younger Pliny wrote to Sabinianus on behalf of a slave of the latter (quoted by Lightfoot, *in loc.*). But even more beautiful is this page from Paul's personal correspondence—a true little masterpiece of tact and sensitivity.

It begins with a salutation, followed by expressions of thanks and petition, the principal subject matter, a conclusion, and greetings. Most of the Pauline Epistles follow this format, even when they are more in the nature of theological treatises.

6. Theological Values

Paul, Philemon, and Onesimus are *dramatis personae* in a real-life drama of profound social significance. Each has heard the claims of Christianity from totally different backgrounds. Paul was once a rigorous Jew of the Dispersion who advanced in Judaism beyond all his contemporaries. Philemon was a wealthy Asiatic Gentile. Onesimus was the most despicable of all creatures, a runaway slave. They find themselves united in the

---

[9] *Philemon among the Letters of Paul.*

gospel of Christ. Here is a living example of Paul's statement that "there is neither Jew nor Greek, slave nor free, male nor female, for you are all one in Christ Jesus" (Gal 3:28). It was in this oneness that Paul sought a solution to the problem presented by the relationship of Onesimus to Philemon.

Neither Paul nor the other authors of the NT ever call for the abolition of slavery. For a new religion to do so would have been suicidal in the ancient world. Instead, he makes repeated appeals for Christian love. Philemon is not to act out of obligation to the apostle. He is to be motivated by the love of Christ within himself. Out of that, Paul suggests, should come more than mere reconciliation, "knowing that you will do even more than I ask" (v.21). Freedom of slaves, like all freedom, must come from the heart of Christ-inspired men. Under this compulsion, slavery must ultimately wilt and die. That it took so long for it to do so, that slavery was practiced by many Christians in America until the Civil War ended it, that it is still, in one form or another, in the world today—these humbling facts show the tenacity of socially entrenched sin and the failure of Christendom to deal with it. While all ethical behavior for Christians should arise out of love, rather than regulation or constraint, yet it takes fully committed disciples to put it into practice.

7. Bibliography

Calvin, John. *The Second Epistle of Paul the Apostle to the Corinthians and the Epistles to Timothy, Titus, and Philemon.* Translated by T.A. Smail. Edited by D.W. Torrance and T.F. Torrance. Grand Rapids: Eerdmans, 1964.

Harrison, P.N. "Onesimus and Philemon." In *Anglican Theological Review* 32 (1950): 268–294.

Knox, John. *Philemon Among the Letters of Paul.* New York: Abingdon, 1959.

Lightfoot, J.B. *St. Paul's Epistles to the Colossians and Philemon.* 1879. Reprint. Grand Rapids: Zondervan, 1957.

Lohse, Eduard. *Colossians and Philemon* in *Hermeneia.* Translated by Poehlmann and Karris. Philadelphia: Fortress Press, 1971.

Luther, Martin. "Preface to the Epistle of Saint Paul to Philemon, 1546 (1522)," in *Luther's Works,* American edition, vol. 35, ed. E. Theodore Bachmann. Philadelphia: Fortress, 1960.

Moule, C.F.D. *The Epistles of Paul the Apostle to the Colossians and to Philemon* in the Cambridge Greek Commentary. Cambridge: Cambridge University Press, 1957.

Müller, J.J. *The Epistles of Paul to the Philippians and to Philemon* in NIC. Grand Rapids: Eerdmans, 1955.

8. Outline

I. Salutation (1–3)

II. Thanksgiving and Prayer (4–7)

III. Plea for Onesimus (8–22)

IV. Greetings and Benediction (23–25)

Text and Exposition

I. Salutation

1–3

> ¹Paul, a prisoner of Christ Jesus, and Timothy our brother,
>
> To Philemon our dear friend and fellow worker, ²to Apphia our sister, to Archippus our fellow soldier, and to the church that meets in your home:
>
> ³Grace to you and peace from God our Father and the Lord Jesus Christ.

The salutation is significant for its departures from Paul's other salutations. The Epistle is in the form of an ancient letter of commendation, and Paul's opening words are calculated to suggest that his appeal for Onesimus should be favorably received.

Paul is a prisoner of Jesus Christ and therefore suffers for the sake of the gospel. His suffering is a mark of his apostleship, which in turn lends weight to any suggestion he might make. Furthermore, Timothy, a well-recognized young steward of the gospel, joins him in the appeal. Finally, Paul not only greets Philemon, the owner of Onesimus, but also his wife Apphia. She is as much a party to the decision as her husband, because according to the custom of the time, she had day-to-day responsibility for the slaves.

As for Archippus and the church, Paul includes them in the salutation with good reason. Archippus, one of the leading figures in the community (perhaps a pastor), and the church will bring appropriate pressure to bear on Philemon should he fail to fulfill the great apostle's request. Philemon would have had to have been a very strong-minded individual to resist the plea of Paul and his protege Timothy.

Notes

2 In the phrase κατ᾽ οἶκόν σου (kat' oikon sou, "in your home"), σου (sou, "your") is singular. A few have taken these words as a reference to Archippus's home, but the most logical understanding would be that this is a reference to the home of Philemon, since he is the first-mentioned in the greeting. This is not the only time Paul mentions a church in a private home; in Romans 16:5 he refers to the church in the house of Priscilla and Aquila and in Colossians 4:15 to the church in the house of Nympha. The early Christian Churches often met in homes. Not until about the third century do we have records of separate church buildings.

"Our fellow soldier" (τῷ συστρατιώτῃ ἡμων, tō sustratiōtē hēmōn) means nothing more than "fellow worker" in Pauline usage (cf. Phil 2:25).

Lohse (in loc.) cites examples of ancient letters in which additional names are listed alongside that of the recipient.

II. Thanksgiving and Prayer

4–7

> ⁴I always thank my God as I remember you in my prayers, ⁵because I hear about your love and faith in the Lord Jesus and your love for all the saints. ⁶I pray that you may be active in sharing your faith, so that you will have a full understanding of every good thing we have in Christ. ⁷Your love has given me great joy and encouragement, because you, brother, have refreshed the hearts of the saints.

4,5 In both pagan and Christian letters of the first centuries of the Christian era, the salutation was followed by an expression of thanksgiving and a prayer. Paul uses the fuller form of his thanksgiving. He tells when he gives thanks—"always ... in my prayers"—and also tells why he does so—"because I hear about your love and faith." Cf. Romans 1:8–10; 1 Thessalonians 1:2–5; Philippians 1:3–11; Colossians 1:3–8.

"I remember you" (v.4). The singular "you" (*sou*) here and again in v.6 supports the conclusion that the recipient of the letter is Philemon.

6 At this point, the prayer begins though the verb "I pray" is understood from the context. The prayer is in Greek that is unusually difficult to understand. With equal certainty one might suggest that 1) Paul prays that Philemon's participation in the faith will be made effective because of his full understanding of God's goodness to both of them; or, 2) he prays that Philemon will be active in the faith so that he will develop a full understanding of God's goodness to both of them. The former interpretation is more attractive than the latter one because of Paul's repeated suggestion that knowledge precedes good works (cf. Col 1:9, 10).

7 Paul has been repeatedly impressed by the expressions of Philemon's love. They have brought him much joy and comfort. Verse 7 is intended to justify Paul's expansive use of the phrases "full understanding" and "every good thing" in v.6. According to this interpretation, he is praying for great Christian maturity in his brother. The implication is that this maturity will find expression in Philemon's treatment of Onesimus.

Notes

4 "In my prayers." Ἐπί (*epi,* "in") with the genitive frequently had the meaning of "at the time of." It suggests that Paul still observed the formal times of prayer honored by Jews.
6 In other Epistles ὅπως (*hopōs,* "that") follows a verb of praying. Hence such a verb is understood here.

"We have" (NIV) is literally "in us" or "among us" (*en hēmin*) in Gr. "In you" (*en hymin*) has slightly better MS support than "in us," but the editors almost universally favor "in us." See B.M. Metzger, *A Textual Commentary on the Greek New Testament* (New York: United Bible Societies), p. 657, for the argument. Some MSS read παντός ἔργου ἀγαθοῦ (*pantos ergou agathou,* "of every good work"). The difficulty of the verse was felt early in the MS tradition.
7 Σπλάγχνα (*splanchna,* "hearts") literally means "bowels." To some Greeks, the emotions came from this part of the body. Paul's use of the word in v.12 and again in v.20 reveals the depths of his feelings in this situation. He does not argue rationally or theologically for Onesimus. He does so from the heart.

III. Plea for Onesimus

8–22

⁸Therefore, although in Christ I could be bold and order you to do what you ought to do, ⁹yet I appeal to you on the basis of love. I then, as Paul—an old man and now also a prisoner of Christ Jesus— ¹⁰I appeal to you for my son Onesimus, who

became my son while I was in chains. [11]Formerly he was useless to you, but now he has become useful both to you and to me.

[12]I am sending him—who is my very heart—back to you. [13]I would have liked to keep him with me so that he could take your place in helping me while I am in chains for the gospel. [14]But I did not want to do anything without your consent, so that any favor you do will be spontaneous and not forced. [15]Perhaps the reason he was separated from you for a little while was that you might have him back for good— [16]no longer as a slave, but better than a slave, as a dear brother. He is very dear to me but even dearer to you, both as a man and as a brother in the Lord.

[17]So if you consider me a partner, welcome him as you would welcome me. [18]If he has done you any wrong or owes you anything, charge it to me. [19]I, Paul, am writing this with my own hand. I will pay it back—not to mention that you owe me your very self. [20]I do wish, brother, that I may have some benefit from you in the Lord; refresh my heart in Christ. [21]Confident of your obedience, I write to you, knowing that you will do even more than I ask.

[22]And one thing more: Prepare a guest room for me, because I hope to be restored to you in answer to your prayers.

The situation of both Paul and Onesimus is all-important to the understanding of this section of the Epistle. Paul's circumstances are just as significant as those of Onesimus—a fact often overlooked by commentators. Because he is in prison, he cannot do the things a free man might do to help the slave. He can do little more than write a letter asking for clemency for his new-found brother and he can suggest that he hopes to visit the Lycus Valley soon to put additional pressure on Philemon. Under more usual circumstances, a free man could have assumed custody of a runaway slave after he had given guarantees of his return to the public officials, and he could have suggested that the slave be formally assigned to him for a time. This was not uncommon. A slave teacher of T. Pomponius Atticus attended M. Tullius Cicero and his family as much as he did his owner and patron. When he was manumitted, he received Cicero's praenomen (the first of the usual three names of a Roman) and Atticus's nomen (the second of the three names). He became M. Pomponius Dionysius (A.A. Rupprecht, *Slavery in the Late Roman Republic.* [diss. Ann Arbor: University of Michigan Press, 1960], pp. 91–94).

Onesimus's status was the lowest that one could reach in the ancient world. Because he was a runaway slave, he was protected by no laws and he was subject to all manner of abuse. Fugitive slaves usually went to large cities, remote parts of the Roman state, or into unsettled areas. At this time, their capture and return was largely an informal arrangement between the owner and a provincial administrator. They were frequently beaten unmercifully or put to tasks in which their life expectancy was very short.

Cicero mentions three runaway slaves in his works. He remarks of one, Licinius, a slave of the tragic actor Aesop, that he was being held in a public prison or in a *pistrinum*, a grain mill. Cicero was unsure. If the latter, Licinius would have been blindfolded and forced to walk in a circle all day long to turn the millstone—a task usually assigned to horses or mules. Cicero asks his brother, Quintus, to bring this slave back to Rome (*Q. Fr.* 1.2.14).

Paul must have put Philemon in a precarious position indeed. In pleading for forgiveness and restitution for Onesimus without a punishment that was obvious to all, he was confronting the social and economic order head on. While he does not ask for manumission, even his request for clemency for Onesimus and hint of his assignment to Paul defied Roman tradition. By this plea Paul is also giving new dignity to the slave class.

8 Paul first reminds Philemon of his apostolic authority. *Parrēsia* usually has the idea of

"freedom" or "boldness." Here it means "right" or "authority"—hence, "I could be bold and order you." The suggestion of authority was probably enough, coupled as it was with the appeals to love, old age, and imprisonment in v.9.

9 *Presbytēs* means "old age" but usually carries with it the connotation of authority. Thus, in ancient Sparta the ruling body was called a *gerousia* (from *gerōn* "old man"). Parallel to this was the Roman *senatus* (from *senex*). In antiquity, wisdom and authority were assumed to go with old age. Here, however, the stress is on the apostle's aged and feeble condition by the use of *toioutos hōs* ("such as I am").

10 "I plead with you for my son, Onesimus, who became my son while I was in chains." The imagery is very strong. The figure of the father and child was often used in Judaism and in the mystery religions as an illustration of the relationship of teacher and student or of leader and convert (see Lohse, p. 200).

"For my son." *Peri* usually means "concerning," but in this place, as elsewhere in his letters, Paul uses it in the sense of *hyper* ("in behalf of ").

11 There is a double play on words here. *Onesimus* was a common slave name. It meant "useful" or "profitable." This is also the meaning of *chrēstos*, which appears as *achrestos* ("useless") and *euchrēstos* ("useful") in this verse. *Chrēstos* in turn sounded so much like *Christos* that the Roman historian Suetonius (*Claud.* 25) takes this to be Jesus' name. An ancient reader would have thought this play on words much more clever and humorous than we would. That Paul uses it at the beginning of his plea for Onesimus shows us something of his exquisite sensitivity and tact. It is as if, realizing the radical nature (in view of the custom of the times) of what he was about to ask of Philemon, Paul deliberately introduces this bit of humor.

12 Again we see Onesimus as very dear to Paul. He is not simply the one "I am sending back." Paul adds, "him—who is my very heart."

13 The culmination of the appeal. Onesimus serves in place of (*hyper sou*) Philemon, already described as a man of great spiritual advancement (vv.6, 7).

14 The apostle has been speaking as an urbane, deferential, educated man of the classical world. But now, after he has cited a number of reasons for allowing Onesimus to remain with him, he goes further and urges Philemon to make his decision out of Christian love rather than obligation.

13,14 If Onesimus was so dear to Paul the prisoner that he wanted the comfort of his help, how could Philemon refuse Paul's plea for him? And observe Paul's sensitive regard for Philemon's personality (v.14).

15 The contrast between "for a time" and "forever" shows Paul's conviction that the hand of God was at work in the whole situation. It also shows his tact: instead of bluntly referring to Onesimus as a runaway, he speaks of his temporary separation from Philemon as a prelude to permanent reunion with him.

16 In similar fashion he contrasts "slave"—a temporal and demeaning condition—with "brother"—an eternal relationship in the Lord. The innate problem of the slavery of human beings always troubled the ancients. Onesimus was a slave, but in many of the ancient religions and in Greek and Roman law where religion was concerned, he would have been treated as an equal. Christianity was not unique in its claims of the enabling power of the love of Christ to break the economic and social barriers between people. In the ancient pagan religious experience men feared and appeased the gods. They did not, however, claim that they loved them or were loved by them as the motive for men to love one another. Paul loves Onesimus very much. Philemon will love him all the more because of long-standing human ties as well as their common faith.

Here, where Paul so sensitively suggests that Philemon take Onesimus back "no longer as a slave, but better than a slave," etc. (cf. also v.17), it almost seems as if emancipation is implied between the lines.

17 Now Paul uses a term from accountancy. "Partner" (*koinonos*), which is related to the common NT word *koinonia* ("fellowship"), here has the sense of "business partner" —a common meaning of the term in the papyri. No doubt Paul meant for the word to imply "fellowship" in the work of the risen Christ. Philemon is to receive Onesimus as he would receive Paul himself.

18 This wonderfully gracious offer to assume the financial obligation of Onesimus is an altogether astonishing statement. We can only speculate how Paul came to have such warm feelings toward him. Yet we cannot be certain the slave had robbed his master, though this was a common act of runaway slaves. It may be that Onesimus had confessed this to Paul. Or the loss may have been the result of the departure of a highly skilled slave from whose activities Philemon derived great income. In fact, slave prices in the Greco-Roman world were directly proportional to the skill and economic value of the slave. A common drudge brought only 500 *denarii* (a *denarius* was a laborer's ordinary daily wage), but skilled teachers, physicians, and actors were purchased for a hundred times as much.

Paul uses another accountant's word (*elloga*, "charge") to maintain the imagery. Observe Paul's tact in not saying that Onesimus had stolen, but he leaves that possibility open by his use of *adikeo* ("do wrong") and *opheilo* ("owe").

19 The subject is still the indebtedness of Onesimus. Now Paul says that he wrote these words himself. As in our own society, handwritten statements of obligation carried great weight and legal validity. So in v.19 Paul gives Philemon what amounts to a promissory note. Then in v.19b he shifts abruptly to another thought—viz., "not to mention that you owe me your very self." Preceding the "that" (*hina*) should be understood some phrase like "I am silent" (*sigo*), "so as not to mention," etc. In Paul's view, Philemon's spiritual indebtedness to him should easily cover all of Onesimus's wrongdoing. Again Paul's hint can hardly be missed: "I will repay it. Charge it to the bank of heaven."

What Paul did for Onesimus reflects the infinitely greater intercession and redemptive act of Christ for us, who because of our sin are all indebted to God in a way we cannot ouselves repay. As Luther said, "Here we see how Paul layeth himself out for poor Onesimus, and with all his means pleadeth his cause with his master, and so setteth himself as if he were Onesimus, and had himself done wrong to Philemon. Even as Christ did for us with God the Father, thus also doth Paul for Onesimus with Philemon. We are all his Onesimi, to my thinking" (*The New Century Bible*).

20 *Onaimēn* ("I do wish," "I would like") is the optative for expressing a wish and is the most common survival of the secondary mood of nonassertion. It was a regular element of ancient epistolary style. Its use here may be another play on words, since the name Onesimus comes from the same root.

Paul now returns to the vocabulary of v.7, where he told Philemon that he had refeshed the hearts of many. How, then, can he do less than that for the apostle to the Gentiles? In its relationship to v.7 this sentence is an excellent example of literary reenforcement.

21 Paul has avoided giving any commands to Philemon (cf. v.8), but he nonetheless expects "obedience." To what? The love of Christ? *Hyper ha legō*, ("beyond what I suggest") may be an intimation that Paul would like Onesimus set free from enslavement. He hints that Onesimus be loaned to him. Only emancipation could be beyond that. Paul never directly assaults the social and economic institutions of his day. Yet he clearly perceives in Christianity an ethic that reaches beyond human social institutions. Paul nowhere states that slaves should be set free, but he pleads for fair and gracious treatment of slaves on the basis of the love of Christ in the hearts of their owners.

22 Here the suggestion of an imminent visit lends more weight to Paul's hints and requests. The hope expressed in these words seems to imply that the apostle is nearby. He expects to be released soon and to see the outcome of his letter at first hand. Imprisonment at Ephesus, and perhaps, Caesarea, would best explain his circumstances. A trip from Rome would take weeks or even months in the best weather and would be all but impossible during periods of unsettled weather.

Notes

---

14 The meaning of "consent" for γνώμη (*gnōmē*) is frequently attested in the papyri. (See BAG, p. 162.)

16 Μάλιστα (*malista*, "especially") is an old superlative form. Here it intensifies ἀγαπητός (*a-gapētos*, "dear"). Πόσῳ μᾶλλον (*posō mallon*) is dative of degree of difference, lit., "more by much." "Very dear" and "even dearer" tr. well Paul's emphatic words.

17 Προσλαβοῦ (*proslabou*, "welcome") is the middle of προσλαμβάνω (*proslambano*, "receive kindly"). It always has a positive meaning: "to welcome into a circle of friends," or "take as a helper."

18 Cicero (*Q. Rosc.* 28) remarks that a talented slave purchased for 3,000 *denarii* had increased in value 35 times because of the training given him by the comedian Roscius. Seneca (*Ep.* 27.5) and Martial (1.58.1) both mention 50,000 d. as the price of an accomplished slave.

Ἐλλόγα (*elloga*) means "charge [to my account]." The form of the verb appears to be from *ellogao* instead of *ellogeo* (the actual root form); cf. Rom 5:13. Lohse (p. 204) gives parallel instances of this meaning from later Gr.

22 Ξενία (*xenia*) means "guest room." It also often means "hospitality," one of the highest of Classical and early Christian virtues. It would be wrong to try to separate the two meanings in this verse.

IV. Greetings and Benediction

23–25

> 23Epaphras, my fellow prisoner for Christ Jesus, sends you greetings. 24And so do Mark, Aristarchus, Demas and Luke, my fellow workers.
> 25The grace of the Lord Jesus Christ be with your spirit.

23,24 The five co-workers who send greetings to Philemon are also mentioned in Colossians 4:10–14. A sixth co-worker, Jesus Justus, is mentioned only in Colossians. Many conjecture that we should read here, "Epaphras my fellow prisoner in Christ, Jesus, Mark ... send greetings." The question remains as to why the same greetings were given in two letters that were sent at the same time. Some see the unity of the greetings as evidence that Colossians is not Pauline (see Lohse, p. 176–183). Others see it as evidence that the letters were written at the same time to the same place, while Paul was in the company of the same co-workers. One should not discount the possibility that Philemon preceded Colossians (see Introduction).

25 With his apostolic "grace," Paul ends this brief but unusually beautiful letter in which he reveals so much of himself.